HAESE MATHEMATICS

Advanced Mathematics

for AS and A Level

1

Michael Haese   *Mark Humphries*   *Chris Sangwin*   *Ngoc Vo*

ADVANCED MATHEMATICS 1 FOR AS AND A LEVEL

Michael Haese   B.Sc.(Hons.), Ph.D.
Mark Humphries   B.Sc.(Hons.)
Chris Sangwin   M.A., M.Sc., Ph.D.
Ngoc Vo   B.Ma.Sc.

Published by Haese Mathematics
152 Richmond Road, Marleston, SA 5033, AUSTRALIA
Telephone: +61 8 8210 4666, Fax: +61 8 8354 1238
Email: info@haesemathematics.com.au
Web: www.haesemathematics.com.au

National Library of Australia Card Number & ISBN 978-1-925489-30-9

© Haese & Harris Publications 2017

First Edition   2017

Cartoon artwork by John Martin and Rebecca Huang.

Cover design by Michael Haese.

Artwork by Brian Houston and Gregory Olesinski.

Computer software by Tim Lee, Nicole Szymanczyk, Brett Laishley, Ashvin Narayanan, Huda Kharrufa, Joshua Douglass-Molloy, and Linden May.

Production work by Sandra Haese, Bradley Steventon, and Rebecca Huang.

Typeset in Australia by Deanne Gallasch and Charlotte Frost. Typeset in Times Roman $10\frac{1}{2}$.

Printed in China by Prolong Press Limited.

Acknowledgements: We would like to thank Yale University for the photo of Professor Anscombe.

While every attempt has been made to trace and acknowledge copyright, the authors and publishers apologise for any accidental infringement where copyright has proved untraceable. They would be pleased to come to a suitable agreement with the rightful owner.

Disclaimer: All the internet addresses (URLs) given in this book were valid at the time of printing. While the authors and publisher regret any inconvenience that changes of address may cause readers, no responsibility for any such changes can be accepted by either the authors or the publisher.

FOREWORD

This book is written for the revised GCE Advanced level (A level) Mathematics specifications for first teaching in 2017.

The book is designed both as a complete AS Mathematics course, and as the first year of the full A level Mathematics.

Since the content for A level Mathematics is now prescribed in the syllabus, this book is suitable for any of the awarding organisations.

To reflect the principles on which the course is based, we have attempted to produce a book that embraces understanding and problem solving in order to give students different learning experiences.

The textbook and interactive online features provide an engaging and structured package, allowing students to explore and develop their confidence in mathematics. The material is presented in a clear, easy-to-follow style, free from unnecessary distractions, while effort has been made to contextualise questions so that students can relate concepts to everyday use.

Each chapter begins with an Opening Problem, offering an insight into the application of the mathematics that will be studied in the chapter. Important information and key notes are highlighted, while worked examples provide step-by-step instructions with concise and relevant explanations. Discussions, Activities, Investigations, Puzzles, and Research exercises are used throughout the chapters to develop understanding, problem solving, and reasoning, within an interactive environment.

The interactive online features include our SELF TUTOR software (see p. 5), links to graphing software, statistics software, demonstrations, calculator instructions, and a range of printable worksheets, tables, and diagrams, allowing teachers to demonstrate concepts and students to experiment for themselves.

A chapter summary for teachers is available on our website.

We welcome your feedback.   Email: info@haesemathematics.com.au
                            Web: www.haesemathematics.com.au

PMH, MAH, CS, NV

ABOUT THE AUTHORS

Michael Haese completed a BSc at the University of Adelaide, majoring in Infection and Immunity, and Applied Mathematics. He completed Honours in Applied Mathematics, and a PhD in high speed fluid flows. Michael has a keen interest in education and a desire to see mathematics come alive in the classroom through its history and relationship with other subject areas. He is passionate about girls' education and ensuring they have the same access and opportunities that boys do. His other interests are wide-ranging, including show jumping, cycling, and agriculture. He has been the principal editor for Haese Mathematics since 2008.

Mark Humphries completed a degree in Mathematical and Computer Science, and an Economics degree at the University of Adelaide. He then completed an Honours degree in Pure Mathematics. His mathematical interests include public key cryptography, elliptic curves, and number theory. Mark enjoys the challenge of piquing students' curiosity in mathematics, and encouraging students to think about mathematics in different ways. He has been working at Haese Mathematics since 2006, and is currently the writing manager.

Chris Sangwin completed a BA in Mathematics at the University of Oxford, and an MSc and PhD in Mathematics at the University of Bath. He spent thirteen years in the Mathematics Department at the University of Birmingham, and from 2000 - 2011 was seconded half time to the UK Higher Education Academy "Maths Stats and OR Network" to promote learning and teaching of university mathematics. He was awarded a National Teaching Fellowship in 2006, and is now Professor of Technology Enhanced Science Education at the University of Edinburgh.

His research interests focus on technology and mathematics education and include automatic assessment of mathematics using computer algebra, and problem solving using the Moore method and similar student-centred approaches.

Ngoc Vo completed a BMaSc at the University of Adelaide, majoring in Statistics and Applied Mathematics. Her Mathematical interests include regression analysis, Bayesian statistics, and statistical computing. Ngoc has been working at Haese Mathematics as a proof reader and writer since 2016.

ONLINE FEATURES

With the purchase of a new textbook, you will gain 15 months subscription to our online product. This subscription can be renewed annually for a small fee.

Access is granted through **SNOWFLAKE**, our book viewing software that can be used in your web browser or may be installed to your tablet or computer.

Students can revisit concepts taught in class and undertake their own revision and practice online.

COMPATIBILITY

For iPads, tablets, and other mobile devices, some of the interactive features may not work. However, the digital version of the textbook can be viewed online using any of these devices.

REGISTERING

You will need to register to access the online features of this textbook.

Visit www.haesemathematics.com.au/register and follow the instructions. Once registered, you can:
- activate your digital textbook
- use your account to make additional purchases.

To activate your digital textbook, contact Haese Mathematics. On providing proof of purchase, your digital textbook will be activated. **It is important that you keep your receipt as proof of purchase.**

For general queries about registering and subscriptions:
- Visit our **SNOWFLAKE** help page: http://snowflake.haesemathematics.com.au/help
- Contact Haese Mathematics: info@haesemathematics.com.au

ONLINE VERSION OF THE TEXTBOOK

The entire text of the book can be viewed online, allowing you to leave your textbook at school.

SELF TUTOR

Self tutor is an exciting feature of this book.

The ◀) **Self Tutor** icon on each worked example denotes an active online link.

> Simply 'click' on the ◀) **Self Tutor** (or anywhere in the example box) to access the worked example, with a teacher's voice explaining each step necessary to reach the answer.
>
> Play any line as often as you like. See how the basic processes come alive using movement and colour on the screen.

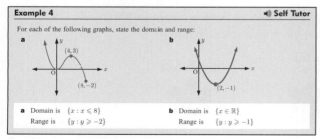

See **Chapter 4, Relations and functions**, p. 93

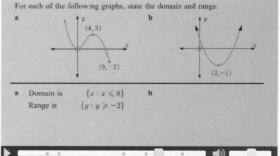

INTERACTIVE LINKS

Throughout your digital textbook, you will find interactive links to:

- Graphing software
- Statistics software
- Games
- Demonstrations
- Printable pages

CLICK ON THESE ICONS ONLINE

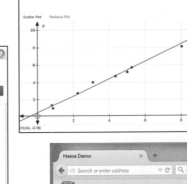

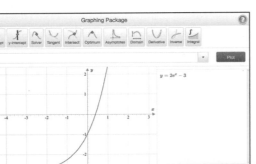

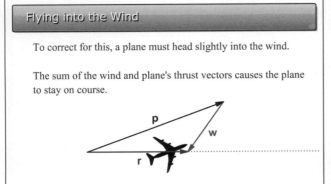

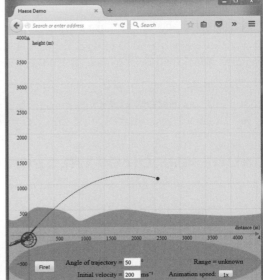

Flying into the Wind

To correct for this, a plane must head slightly into the wind.

The sum of the wind and plane's thrust vectors causes the plane to stay on course.

GRAPHICS CALCULATOR INSTRUCTIONS

Printable graphics calculator instruction booklets are available for the **Casio fx-9860G PLUS**, **Casio fx-CG20**, and the **TI-84 Plus CE**. Click on the relevant icon below.

CASIO fx-9860G PLUS

CASIO fx-CG20

TI-84 Plus CE

When additional calculator help may be needed, specific instructions can be printed from icons within the text.

GRAPHICS CALCULATOR INSTRUCTIONS

TABLE OF CONTENTS

SYMBOLS AND NOTATION USED IN THIS BOOK

$\in$	is an element of
$\notin$	is not an element of
$\varnothing$	the empty set
$\mathcal{E}$	the universal set
$\mathbb{N}$	the set of natural numbers, $\{1, 2, 3, ...\}$
$\mathbb{Z}$	the set of integers, $\{0, \pm 1, \pm 2, \pm 3, ...\}$
$\mathbb{Z}^+$	the set of positive integers, $\{1, 2, 3, ...\}$
$\mathbb{Z}_0^+$	the set of non-negative integers, $\{0, 1, 2, 3, ...\}$
$\mathbb{R}$	the set of real numbers
$\mathbb{Q}$	the set of rational numbers, $\{\frac{p}{q}: \ p \in \mathbb{Z}, \ q \in \mathbb{Z}^+\}$
$[a, b]$	the closed interval $\{x \in \mathbb{R}: \ a \leqslant x \leqslant b\}$
$[a, b)$	the interval $\{x \in \mathbb{R}: \ a \leqslant x < b\}$
$(a, b]$	the interval $\{x \in \mathbb{R}: \ a < x \leqslant b\}$
(a, b)	the open interval $\{x \in \mathbb{R}: \ a < x < b\}$
$\approx$	is approximately equal to
∞	infinity
$\propto$	is proportional to
$\therefore$	therefore
$<$	is less than
$\leqslant, \leq$	is less than or equal to, is not greater than
$>$	is greater than
$\geqslant, \geq$	is greater than or equal to, is not less than
$p \Rightarrow q$	p implies q (if p then q)
$p \Leftrightarrow q$	p implies and is implied by q (p is equivalent to q)
$\sum\limits_{i=1}^{n} a_i$	$a_1 + a_2 + ... + a_n$
$\sqrt{a}$	the non-negative square root of a
$|a|$	the modulus of a
$n!$	n factorial: $n! = n \times (n-1) \times .... \times 2 \times 1, \ n \in \mathbb{N}; \ 0! = 1$
$\binom{n}{r}$	the binomial coefficient $\dfrac{n!}{r!(n-r)!}$ for $n, r \in \mathbb{Z}_0^+, \ r \leqslant n$
	or $\dfrac{n(n-1)....(n-r+1)}{r!}$ for $n \in \mathbb{Q}, \ r \in \mathbb{Z}_0^+$
$f(x)$	the value of the function f at x
$f : x \mapsto y$	the function f maps the element x to the element y
$\lim\limits_{x \to a} f(x)$	the limit of $f(x)$ as x tends to a
$\Delta x, \ \delta x$	an increment of x
$\dfrac{dy}{dx}, \ \dfrac{d^2y}{dx^2}, \ ...., \ \dfrac{d^ny}{dx^n}$	the first, second, ..., nth derivatives of y with respect to x
$f'(x), \ f''(x), \ ...., \ f^{(n)}(x)$	the first, second, ..., nth derivatives of $f(x)$ with respect to x

$\int y \, dx$	the indefinite integral of y with respect to x
$\int_a^b y \, dx$	the definite integral of y with respect to x between $x = a$ and $x = b$
e	base of natural logarithms
e^x, $\exp x$	exponential function of x
$\log_a x$	logarithm to the base a of x
$\ln x$, $\log_e x$	natural logarithm of x
sin, cos, tan, cosec, sec, cot	the trigonometric functions
a	the vector **a**
$\overrightarrow{AB}$	the vector represented by the directed line segment AB
i, j	unit vectors in the directions of the Cartesian coordinate axes
$\lvert \mathbf{a} \rvert$	the magnitude of **a**
$\lvert \overrightarrow{AB} \rvert$, AB	the magnitude of $\overrightarrow{AB}$
$\binom{a}{b}$, $a\mathbf{i} + b\mathbf{j}$	column vector and corresponding unit vector notation
$A \cup B$	union of the events A and B
$A \cap B$	intersection of the events A and B
$\mathrm{P}(A)$	probability of the event A
A'	complement of the event A
X, Y, R, etc.	random variables
x, y, r, etc.	values of the random variables X, Y, R, etc.
$x_1, x_2, \ldots$	values of observations
$f_1, f_2, \ldots$	frequencies with which the observations $x_1, x_2, \ldots$ occur
$p(x)$, $\mathrm{P}(X = x)$	probability function of the discrete random variable X
$p_1, p_2, \ldots$	probabilities of the values $x_1, x_2, \ldots$ of the discrete random variable X
$\sim$	has the distribution
$\mathrm{B}(n, p)$	binomial distribution with parameters n and p, where n is the number of trials and p is the probability of success in a trial
μ	population mean
σ^2	population variance
σ	population standard deviation
$\overline{x}$	sample mean
s^2	sample variance
s	sample standard deviation
H_0	Null hypothesis
H_1	Alternative hypothesis
r	product moment correlation coefficient
t	time
s	displacement
u	initial velocity
v	velocity or final velocity
a	acceleration
g	acceleration due to gravity

LARGE DATA SETS

AS and A Level Mathematics specifications require students to become familiar with one or more specified large data sets.

It is important that students explore the data set(s) during the course of their study, so that they are aware of the terminology and contexts relating to the data.

In the final examination, students will be required to answer questions based on selected data or summary statistics from the large data set(s). Students who are familiar with the context and structure of the large data set(s) will be more able to engage in realistic interpretation in an examination setting.

Sample questions associated with each examination board's large data sets are provided in the icons below.

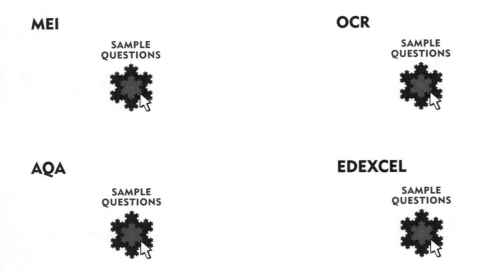

MEI

SAMPLE
QUESTIONS

OCR

SAMPLE
QUESTIONS

AQA

SAMPLE
QUESTIONS

EDEXCEL

SAMPLE
QUESTIONS

1

Lines

Contents:

Opening problem

The cycle department of a toy store sells bicycles and tricycles.

Greg observes that there are 13 cycles in total. His brother Jeff counts 31 wheels in total.

Things to think about:

a Can you write an *equation* which summarises:

   i Greg's observation   **ii** Jeff's observation?

b Is it possible to determine the numbers of bicycles and tricycles using only:

   i Greg's observation   **ii** Jeff's observation?

c What combination(s) of bicycles and tricycles satisfy:

   i Greg's observation   **ii** Jeff's observation   **iii** both boys' observations?

d How can we solve problems like this without listing all of the possible combinations?

A   LINEAR EQUATIONS

An **equation** is a formal statement that one mathematical expression is equal to another. The expressions are connected by an *equal* sign $=$ which is used to replace the words "is equal to".

We use equations:

- to assign a value to a variable, for example $x = 3$
- to describe the relationship between unknown quantities, for example $3x - y = 7$.

A **solution** of an equation is a value of the variable which makes the equation true.

For example, in the equation $3x + 4 = 19$, if we let $x = 5$ then
LHS $= 3 \times 5 + 4 = 19 =$ RHS.

$\therefore$ $x = 5$ is a solution of the equation.

LHS means left hand side.
RHS means right hand side.

Linear equations are equations in which the variable is raised only to the power 1.

All linear equations can be written in the form $ax + b = 0$ where $a, b \in \mathbb{R}$, $a \neq 0$, and x is the variable.

For example:

- $2x - 7 = 3$, $\frac{1}{2}x + 4 = 0$, $\dfrac{1 - 3x}{2} = 5$ are linear equations

- $x^2 - 3 = 5x$, $\dfrac{3}{x} = 2x$, $\sqrt{x} = 7$ are not linear equations.

We use the following steps to solve linear equations algebraically:

> *Step 1*:   Determine how the expression containing the unknown has been '**built up**'.
>
> *Step 2*:   Perform **inverse operations** on **both sides** of the equation to 'undo' how the expression was 'built up'. In this way we **isolate** the unknown.
>
> *Step 3*:   Check your solution by substitution.

> The inverse operations are performed on both sides so we maintain the balance.

Example 1

◄)) Self Tutor

Solve for x:

a $4x - 3 = 21$ **b** $\dfrac{x + 2}{5} = 3$

---

a
$$4x - 3 = 21$$
$$\therefore \ 4x - 3 + 3 = 21 + 3 \quad \text{\{adding 3 to both sides\}}$$
$$\therefore \ 4x = 24$$
$$\therefore \ \frac{4x}{4} = \frac{24}{4} \quad \text{\{dividing both sides by 4\}}$$
$$\therefore \ x = 6$$

Check: $4 \times 6 - 3 = 24 - 3 = 21$ ✓

b
$$\frac{x + 2}{5} = 3$$
$$\therefore \ 5 \times \frac{x + 2}{5} = 5 \times 3 \quad \text{\{multiplying both sides by 5\}}$$
$$\therefore \ x + 2 = 15$$
$$\therefore \ x + 2 - 2 = 15 - 2 \quad \text{\{subtracting 2 from both sides\}}$$
$$\therefore \ x = 13$$

Check: $\dfrac{13 + 2}{5} = \dfrac{15}{5} = 3$ ✓

EXERCISE 1A

1 Solve for x:

  a $3x + 5 = 14$ **b** $3 - 2x = 17$ **c** $-3x + 1 = -11$

  d $3 + \dfrac{x}{2} = 6$ **e** $8x + 7 = 103$ **f** $5 - \dfrac{2}{3}x = 1$

2 Solve for x:

  a $\dfrac{x + 3}{2} = 6$ **b** $\dfrac{1 - x}{5} = -1$ **c** $\dfrac{2x - 1}{4} = -\dfrac{3}{2}$

Example 2
◀》 **Self Tutor**

Solve for x: $3(x - 2) = 5 + 2x$

$3(x - 2) = 5 + 2x$

$\therefore \quad 3x - 6 = 5 + 2x$ {expanding the brackets}

$\therefore \quad 3x - 6 - 2x = 5 + 2x - 2x$ {subtracting $2x$ from both sides}

$\therefore \quad x - 6 = 5$

$\therefore \quad x - 6 + 6 = 5 + 6$ {adding 6 to both sides}

$\therefore \quad x = 11$

Check: LHS $= 3(11 - 2) = 3 \times 9 = 27$

         RHS $= 5 + 2(11) = 5 + 22 = 27$ ✓

> If the unknown appears more than once, we **expand brackets**, **collect like terms**, and make sure the unknown is only on one side of the equation.

3 Solve for x:

   a $3x + 5 - 2x = 7$
       b $3 - x = 7 + 2x$
       c $2(x - 1) + 3x = 6$

   d $5(x - 2) - x = 14$
       e $-3(1 + x) = 4 - x$
       f $2(1 + 3x) = 3(6 + x)$

4 Comment on the existence of solutions to:

   a $3 - 2x = -2(5 + x)$
       b $5 - 2x = -2(x - \frac{5}{2})$
       c $2(x - 3) = 5x - 3(x + 2)$

5 Solve for x:

   a $\dfrac{x - 2}{4} = \dfrac{x}{5}$
       b $\dfrac{2x + 1}{3} = \dfrac{3x}{5}$
       c $\dfrac{1 - 4x}{2} = \dfrac{7x + 8}{-3}$

6 Prove that the linear equation $ax = b$ has a rational solution for all $a, b \in \mathbb{Q}$, $a \neq 0$.

Example 3
◀》 **Self Tutor**

A school has three basketball squads: A, B, and C. Squad A has two fewer members than both squads B and C. In total, 43 students play basketball. How many students are in squad A?

Let x be the number of students in squad A.

$\therefore$ there are $x + 2$ students in both squads B and C.

Since 43 students play basketball in total, $x + 2(x + 2) = 43$

$\therefore \quad x + 2x + 4 = 43$

$\therefore \quad 3x = 39$

$\therefore \quad x = 13$

There are 13 students in squad A.

7 Jane bought a dress costing £35. This was £3 more than twice what she spent on a shirt. Find the cost of the shirt.

8 There are three Year 11 classes at my school, with 79 students in total. There are 26 students in the first class, and there are 5 fewer students in the third class than in the second. Find the number of students in the third class.

9 A profit of €2518.56 is split between shareholders in the ratio $3 : 4 : 5$. Find the largest share.

B EQUATIONS OF STRAIGHT LINES

> The **equation of a line** is an equation which connects the x and y values for every point on the line.

In previous years we have seen that:

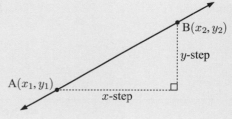

The **gradient** of a line passing through $A(x_1, y_1)$ and $B(x_2, y_2)$ is

$$\frac{y\text{-step}}{x\text{-step}} = \frac{y_2 - y_1}{x_2 - x_1}.$$

Using this formula, the position of a general point (x, y) on a line with gradient m passing through (x_1, y_1), is given by $\frac{y - y_1}{x - x_1} = m$.

Rearranging, we find the **equation of the line** is

$$y - y_1 = m(x - x_1) \quad \text{or} \quad y = y_1 + m(x - x_1)$$

We call this **gradient-point** form.

For a line with gradient m and y-intercept c we substitute $x_1 = 0$, $y_1 = c$, and rearrange to obtain the **gradient-intercept form**

$$y = mx + c$$

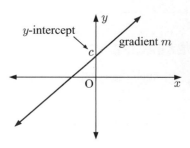

We can also rearrange the equation into the **general form**

$$Ax + By + C = 0$$

for some $A, B, C \in \mathbb{R}$.

The general form allows us to write the equations of vertical lines, for which the gradient is undefined.

For the line $x = 1$ we let $A = 1$, $B = 0$, and $C = -1$.

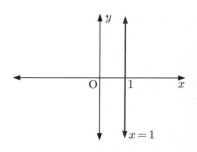

GRADIENTS OF PARALLEL AND PERPENDICULAR LINES

- Two lines are **parallel** if and only if their gradients are **equal**.

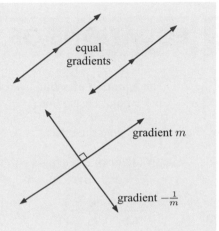

- If two lines are **perpendicular**, then their gradients are **negative reciprocals**.
  If the gradient of one line is m, then the gradient of the other line is $-\dfrac{1}{m}$.

Example 4   ◀》 **Self Tutor**

Find, in gradient-intercept form, the equation of the line with gradient -3 that passes through $(4, -5)$.

> The equation of the line is $y - (-5) = -3(x - 4)$
>
> $\therefore\ \ y + 5 = -3x + 12$
>
> $\therefore\ \ y = -3x + 7$

We are given the gradient and a point which lies on the line.

EXERCISE 1B

1 State the gradient and y-intercept of the line with equation:

   a $y = 3x + 7$ **b** $y = -2x - 5$ **c** $y = \frac{2}{3}x - \frac{1}{3}$

   d $y = 11 - 4x$ **e** $y = -6 - x$ **f** $y = \frac{9}{5} - \frac{6}{5}x$

   g $y = \dfrac{7x + 2}{9}$ **h** $y = \dfrac{2x - 3}{6}$ **i** $y = \dfrac{3 - 5x}{8}$

2 Find, in gradient-intercept form, the equation of the line which has:

   a gradient 3 and passes through $(4, 1)$

   b gradient -2 and passes through $(-3, 5)$

   c gradient $\frac{1}{4}$ and passes through $(4, -3)$

   d gradient $-\frac{2}{3}$ and passes through $(-2, -7)$

   e gradient 2 and y-intercept -9

   f gradient $-\frac{3}{4}$ and y-intercept 4.

Example 5   ◆)) Self Tutor

Find, in general form, the equation of the line with gradient $\frac{2}{3}$ that passes through $(-2, -1)$.

The equation of the line is $y - (-1) = \frac{2}{3}(x - (-2))$

$$\therefore \ y + 1 = \frac{2}{3}(x + 2)$$
$$\therefore \ 3(y + 1) = 2(x + 2)$$
$$\therefore \ 3y + 3 = 2x + 4$$
$$\therefore \ 2x - 3y + 1 = 0$$

3 Find, in general form, the equation of the line which has:

   a gradient -4 and passes through $(1, 2)$

   b gradient $\frac{1}{2}$ and passes through $(3, -5)$

   c gradient $-\frac{5}{3}$ and passes through $(-2, 6)$

   d gradient $\frac{7}{6}$ and passes through $(-1, -4)$.

Example 6   ◆)) Self Tutor

Write the equation:

   a $y = -\frac{2}{3}x + 2$ in general form

   b $3x - 4y + 2 = 0$ in gradient-intercept form.

a
$$y = -\frac{2}{3}x + 2$$
$$\therefore \ 3y = -2x + 6 \quad \text{\{multiplying both sides by 3\}}$$
$$\therefore \ 2x + 3y = 6 \quad \text{\{adding } 2x \text{ to both sides\}}$$
$$\therefore \ 2x + 3y - 6 = 0 \quad \text{\{subtracting 6 from both sides\}}$$

b $3x - 4y + 2 = 0$
$$\therefore \ -4y = -3x - 2 \quad \text{\{subtracting } 3x + 2 \text{ from both sides\}}$$
$$\therefore \ y = \frac{3}{4}x + \frac{1}{2} \quad \text{\{dividing both sides by } -4\}$$

4 Write in general form:

   a $y = -4x + 6$ **b** $y = 5x - 3$ **c** $y = -\frac{3}{4}x + \frac{5}{4}$

   d $y = -\frac{2}{9}x + \frac{8}{9}$ **e** $y = \frac{3}{5}x - \frac{1}{5}$ **f** $y = \frac{5}{6}x + 3$

5 Write in gradient-intercept form:

   a $5x + y - 2 = 0$ **b** $3x + 7y - 2 = 0$ **c** $4x + 3y + 1 = 0$

   d $2x - y - 6 = 0$ **e** $3x - 13y + 4 = 0$ **f** $10x - 3y - 7 = 0$

6 Explain why the gradient of the line with general form $Ax + By + C = 0$ is $-\dfrac{A}{B}$.

7 Match pairs of lines which are parallel:

    A $\;y = -x + 3$ **B** $\;y + 2 = 3(x - 1)$ **C** $\;3x - y + 2 = 0$ **D** $\;x + y - 4 = 0$

8 Match pairs of lines which are perpendicular:

    A $\;x + 2y - 1 = 0$ **B** $\;2x + y + 3 = 0$ **C** $\;y - 7 = 2(x + 4)$ **D** $\;y = 2x - 7$

Example 7   ◆ঠ) **Self Tutor**

Find, in gradient-intercept form, the equation of the line which passes through A(3, 2) and B(5, −1).

The line has gradient $= \dfrac{-1 - 2}{5 - 3} = \dfrac{-3}{2} = -\dfrac{3}{2}$,

and passes through the point A(3, 2).

We could use *either* A or B as the point which lies on the line.

∴ the equation of the line is

$$y - 2 = -\tfrac{3}{2}(x - 3)$$
$$\therefore \;\; y - 2 = -\tfrac{3}{2}x + \tfrac{9}{2}$$
$$\therefore \;\; y = -\tfrac{3}{2}x + \tfrac{13}{2}$$

---

9 Find, in gradient-intercept form, the equation of the line which passes through:

    a   A(−2, 1) and B(3, 11)   **b**   A(7, 2) and B(4, 5)

    c   A(−5, 13) and B(1, −17)   **d**   P(6, −4) and Q(−3, −10)

    e   M(−2, −5) and N(3, 2)   **f**   R(5, −1) and S(−7, 9).

10 Find, in general form, the equation of each line:

    a   **b**   **c**

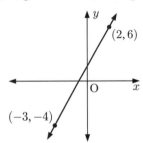 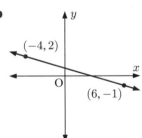 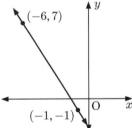

11 **a** Find, in gradient-intercept form, the equation of *line 2*.

     b Hence, find the y-intercept of *line 2*.

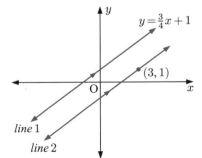

12   **a**   Find, in general form, the equation of *line 2*.

   b   Hence, find the x-intercept of *line 2*.

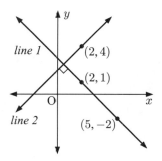

13   Find the equation of the line which is:

   a   parallel to $y = 3x - 2$ and passes through $(1, 4)$

   b   parallel to $2x - y + 3 = 0$ and passes through $(3, -1)$

   c   perpendicular to $y = -2x + 1$ and passes through $(-1, 5)$

   d   perpendicular to $x + 2y - 6 = 0$ and passes through $(-2, -1)$.

C   POINTS ON LINES

A point lies on a line if its coordinates satisfy the equation of the line.

Example 8   ◀⫯⫯ Self Tutor

Determine whether:

   a $(2, -2)$ lies on the line with equation $y = -x + 1$

   b $(3, -1)$ lies on the line with equation $3x - 2y - 11 = 0$

   c $(-1, 3)$ lies on the line with equation $y + 3 = 2(x + 4)$.

---

a   When $x = 2$, we have

$$y = -(2) + 1$$
$$= -1 \; \textbf{✗}$$

So, $(2, -2)$ does *not* lie on the line.

b   Substituting $x = 3$ and $y = -1$
into the LHS gives $3(3) - 2(-1) - 11$
$$= 9 + 2 - 11$$
$$= 0 \; ✓$$

So, $(3, -1)$ does lie on the line.

c   Substituting $x = -1$ and $y = 3$ gives   LHS $= 3 + 3 = 6$
RHS $= 2(-1 + 4) = 6$ ✓

So, $(-1, 3)$ does lie on the line.

EXERCISE 1C

1   Determine whether:

   a $(3, 11)$ lies on the line with equation $y = 4x - 1$

   b $(-6, -2)$ lies on the line with equation $y = \frac{2}{3}x - 6$.

2 Determine whether:

   a $(-4, -8)$ lies on the line with equation $7x - 3y + 4 = 0$

   b $(-\frac{1}{2}, 2)$ lies on the line with equation $6x + 10y - 17 = 0$.

3 Determine whether:

   a $(3, 4)$ lies on the line with equation $y - 13 = -5(x - 2)$

   b $(-\frac{1}{2}, -\frac{3}{2})$ lies on the line with equation $y - 9 = 7(x - 1)$.

Example 9 ◀)) **Self Tutor**

   a Find m given that $(-2, 3)$ lies on the line with equation $y = mx + 7$.

   b Find k given that $(3, k)$ lies on the line with equation $x + 4y + 9 = 0$.

   a Substituting $x = -2$ and $y = 3$ into the equation gives

$$3 = m(-2) + 7$$
$$\therefore \quad 2m = 4$$
$$\therefore \quad m = 2$$

   b Substituting $x = 3$ and $y = k$ into the equation gives

$$3 + 4k + 9 = 0$$
$$\therefore \quad 4k = -12$$
$$\therefore \quad k = -3$$

---

4   **a** Find c given that $(2, 15)$ lies on the line with equation $y = 4x + c$.

   b Find m given that $(\frac{1}{2}, 3)$ lies on the line with equation $y = mx - \frac{5}{2}$.

   c Find t given that $(t, 4)$ lies on the line with equation $y = \frac{2}{3}x - \frac{4}{3}$.

5 Find k given that:

   a $(6, -3)$ lies on the line with equation $2x + 5y - k = 0$

   b $(-8, -5)$ lies on the line with equation $7x - y - k = 0$

   c $(k, 0)$ lies on the line with equation $3x - 4y + 36 = 0$.

6   **a** Find m given that $(\frac{3}{2}, \frac{7}{2})$ lies on the line with equation $y - 3 = m(x - 5)$.

   b Find t given that $(t, 6)$ lies on the line with equation $y + 2 = 4(x - 3)$.

D   GRAPHING LINES

To draw the graph of $y = mx + c$ we:

- Use the y-intercept c to plot the point $(0, c)$.
- Use x and y-steps from the gradient m to locate another point on the line.
- Join the two points and extend the line in either direction.

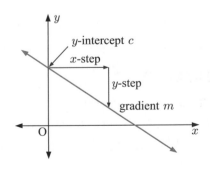

To draw the graph of $y - y_1 = m(x - x_1)$, we start with the point (x_1, y_1) then follow the remainder of the procedure on the previous page.

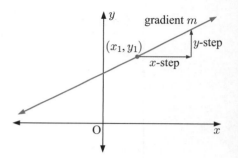

Example 10 ◀) Self Tutor

Draw the graph of:

a $y = \frac{3}{2}x - 4$ **b** $y + 3 = -1(x - 4)$

a For $y = \frac{3}{2}x - 4$:

* the y-intercept is $c = -4$
* the gradient is $m = \frac{3}{2} \leftarrow y\text{-step}$
  $\leftarrow x\text{-step}$

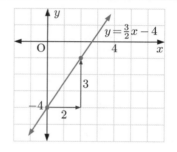

b For $y + 3 = -1(x - 4)$:

* a point is $(4, -3)$
* the gradient is

  $m = -1 = \frac{-1}{1} \leftarrow y\text{-step}$
  $ \leftarrow x\text{-step}$

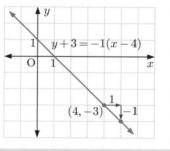

Choose a positive x-step.

GRAPHING LINES IN GENERAL FORM

We draw the graph of $Ax + By + C = 0$ as follows:

* If $C \neq 0$ then:
  ▸ Find the y-intercept by letting $x = 0$.
  ▸ Find the x-intercept by letting $y = 0$.
  ▸ Join the points where the line cuts the axes and extend the line in either direction.

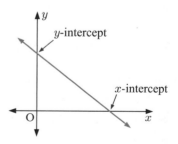

* If $C = 0$ then $(0, 0)$ lies on the line and we plot $y = -\dfrac{A}{B}x$ using its gradient.

Example 11
◀) **Self Tutor**

Draw the graph of $3x + 5y - 15 = 0$.

When $x = 0$, $5y - 15 = 0$

$\therefore \; 5y = 15$

$\therefore \;\; y = 3$

So, the y-intercept is 3.

When $y = 0$, $3x - 15 = 0$

$\therefore \; 3x = 15$

$\therefore \;\; x = 5$

So, the x-intercept is 5.

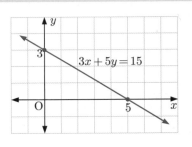

EXERCISE 1D

1 Draw the graph of:

  a $y = 3x + 2$
     b $y = 2x - 4$
     c $y = \frac{3}{5}x$

  d $y = \frac{3}{2}x - 1$
     e $y = -2x + 1$
     f $y = -x - 5$

  g $y = -\frac{2}{3}x + 2$
     h $y = -\frac{5}{4}x - 3$

2 Draw the graph of:

  a $y - 1 = 3(x + 2)$
     b $y + 1 = \frac{1}{2}(x + 3)$
     c $y - 3 = -2(x + 5)$

  d $y + 3 = -\frac{1}{3}(x - 6)$
     e $y - 4 = \frac{2}{3}(x - 1)$
     f $y + \frac{1}{2} = -\frac{3}{2}(x - \frac{5}{2})$

3 Draw the graph of:

  a $2x + y - 6 = 0$
     b $x - 4y - 8 = 0$
     c $3x + 4y - 24 = 0$

  d $x + y - 7 = 0$
     e $2x - 5y - 5 = 0$
     f $x - y + 4 = 0$

  g $4x - 5y - 60 = 0$
     h $3x + 4y - 30 = 0$

4 Consider the line with equation $y = -\frac{3}{4}x + 2$.

  a Find the: **i** gradient   **ii** y-intercept of the line.

  b Determine whether the following points lie on the line:

    i $(8, -4)$
      ii $(1, 3)$
      iii $(-2, \frac{7}{2})$

  c Draw the graph of the line, showing your results from **a** and **b**.

5 Consider the line with equation $2x - 3y - 18 = 0$.

  a Find the: **i** x-intercept   **ii** y-intercept of the line.

  b Determine whether: **i** $(3, -4)$ **ii** $(7, -2)$ lies on the line.

  c Find c such that $(-3, c)$ lies on the line.

  d Draw the graph of the line, showing your results from **a**, **b**, and **c**.

E ▌ LINEAR RELATIONSHIPS

In general, when we consider the relationship between two variables, the value of one of the variables is *dependent* on the value of the other *independent* variable. We place the independent variable on the horizontal axis, and the dependent variable on the vertical axis.

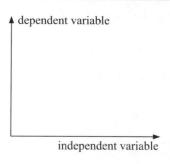

> Two variables are **linearly related** if the graph connecting them is a straight line.

Ted the taxi driver charges passengers an initial fee of £4, and then £2 for each kilometre travelled.

To study the relationship between the *distance travelled* (d km) and the *cost* (C pounds), we construct a table of values and draw a graph. The *cost* is dependent on the *distance travelled*, so we place d on the horizontal axis, and C on the vertical axis.

Distance travelled (d km)	0	1	2	3	4
Cost (£C)	4	6	8	10	12

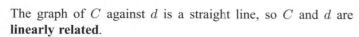
$+2 \quad +2 \quad +2 \quad +2$

The graph of C against d is a straight line, so C and d are **linearly related**.

Notice in the graph that:

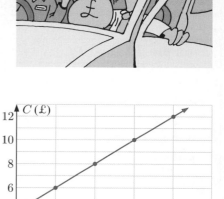

- The C-intercept of the graph is 4. This is the initial fee, in pounds, of the taxi ride.
- The gradient of the graph is 2. This is the cost, in pounds, of each additional kilometre travelled.
- The variables are related by the equation $C = 2d + 4$.

DIRECT PROPORTION

For some linear relationships, the graph passes through the origin. In this case we say the variables are in *direct proportion*.

> *∝ reads "is directly proportional to".*

> Two variables are **directly proportional** if multiplying one of them by a number results in the other one being multiplied by the same number.
>
> If two quantities x and y are **directly proportional**, we write $y \propto x$.
>
> In this case the variables are related by the equation $y = mx$, where m is the gradient of the graph and is called the **proportionality constant**.

Discussion

1 In the case of Ted's taxi fares, the variables C and d are linearly related, but they are *not* directly proportional.

How could Ted change his fare structure so the variables C and d are directly proportional?

2 Which of the following situations correspond to variables in direct proportion? What is it that gives you a clue?

- A loan value V starts at £10 000 and the bank charges simple interest of £600 per year for t years.
- Children in a family attending a football game are charged €10 entry for the first child, and then €5 entry for each additional child.
- To convert lengths from miles M to kilometres k, we multiply by approximately 1.61.
- To convert temperatures from degrees Celsius C to degrees Fahrenheit F, we multiply by $\frac{9}{5}$ then add 32.

Example 12   ◀》 **Self Tutor**

Belinda the baker uses 3 eggs in each cake she makes.

a Show that x, the number of cakes made, is directly proportional to y, the total number of eggs used.

b Find the proportionality constant.

c Find the equation connecting x and y.

a

x	0	1	2	3	4
y	0	3	6	9	12

The points lie in a straight line passing through the origin, so $y \propto x$.

b The gradient of the line $= \dfrac{3-0}{1-0} = 3$, so the proportionality constant $m = 3$.

c The equation connecting x and y is $y = 3x$.

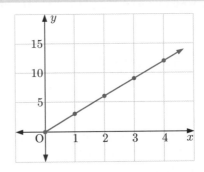

EXERCISE 1E

1 For each table of values:

    i Draw a graph connecting the variables.

    ii Explain why the variables are linearly related.

    iii State whether the variables are in direct proportion.

    iv Find the equation connecting the variables.

a

x	0	1	2	3	4
y	1	4	7	10	13

b

P	0	1	2	3	4
t	0	5	10	15	20

c

M	0	1	2	3	4
n	3	5	7	9	11

2 A plumber charges customers a £50 call-out fee, and then £80 for each hour he spends on the job.

    a Copy and complete this table of values:

Time (t hours)	0	1	2	3	4
Cost (£C)					

    b Draw the graph of C against t.

    c Are C and t linearly related? If so, are they in direct proportion?

    d Find the C-intercept and gradient of the graph.

    e Hence write an equation which connects the variables.

3 A shop sells bottles of juice for £2.50 each.

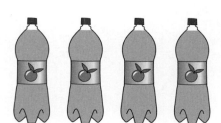

    a Show that x, the number of bottles bought, is directly proportional to y, the total cost of the bottles.

    b Find the proportionality constant.

    c Find the equation connecting x and y.

4 Deb receives a water bill every 3 months. She is charged a flat £100 service fee, plus £3 for every kilolitre of water she uses.

    a Copy and complete this table of values:

Water used (w kL)	0	10	20	30	40
Cost (£C)					

    b Draw the graph of C against w.

    c Are C and w linearly related? If so, are they in direct proportion? Explain your answer.

    d Find the C-intercept and gradient of the graph. Comment on your answers.

5 Suppose y is directly proportional to x. Describe what happens to:

    a y when x is trebled

    b y when x is halved

    c x when y is multiplied by 7

    d x when y is increased by 40%

    e y when x is decreased by 10%

    f x when 5 is added to y.

6   Lachlan uses 2 cm by 4 cm dominoes to create rectangles, as shown below.

1 domino   2 dominoes   3 dominoes

Suppose a collection of n dominoes creates a rectangle of perimeter P cm and area A cm^2.

a   **i** Are n and P directly proportional? If so, state the proportionality constant.

    ii Find the equation connecting n and P.

b   **i** Are n and A directly proportional? If so, state the proportionality constant.

    ii Find the equation connecting n and A.

7   Suppose x and y are directly proportional, and y and z are directly proportional. Are x and z directly proportional? Explain your answer.

8   The *number of trees* N which Raymond can plant is directly proportional to the *time* t he spends planting them.
In 50 minutes, Raymond can plant 6 trees.

a   Find an equation connecting the variables.

b   How many trees can Raymond plant in 125 minutes?

c   How long will it take Raymond to plant 20 trees?

9

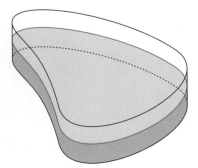

The *amount of water* V in a pool is directly proportional to the *depth of the water* d.
When filled to a depth of 1.25 metres, the pool contains 73 kL of water.

a   Find an equation connecting the variables.

b   Find the depth of the water if the pool contains 40 kL.

c   How much water is needed to fill the pool to a depth of 1.8 metres?

F   SIMULTANEOUS LINEAR EQUATIONS

In the **Opening Problem** on page **14**, we can summarise Greg and Jeff's observations using two linear equations.

We suppose there are x bicycles and y tricycles.

From Greg's observation that there are 13 cycles in total, $x + y = 13$.

From Jeff's observation that there are 31 wheels in total, $2x + 3y = 31$.

We need to find the values for x and y which satisfy both equations *at the same time*. Systems of equations like these are therefore called **simultaneous equations**.

In this Section we consider three methods of solution for simultaneous linear equations:

- graphical solutions
- algebraic substitution
- algebraic elimination.

GRAPHICAL SOLUTION

One of the simplest methods for solving simultaneous linear equations is to graph the lines on the same set of axes. The point of intersection gives us the solution to the simultaneous equations.

Example 13   ◀⑴ Self Tutor

Solve the following simultaneous equations graphically: $\begin{cases} y = 3x - 1 \\ x + y = 3 \end{cases}$

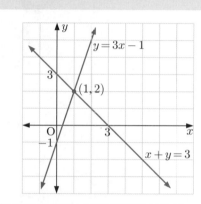

We draw the graphs of $y = 3x - 1$ and $x + y = 3$ on the same set of axes.

The graphs meet at the point $(1, 2)$.

$\therefore$ the solution is $x = 1$, $y = 2$.

Check:

Substituting these values into:

- $y = 3x - 1$ gives $2 = 3(1) - 1$ ✓
- $x + y = 3$ gives $1 + 2 = 3$ ✓

EXERCISE 1F.1

1 Solve the following simultaneous equations graphically:

a $\begin{cases} y = 3x + 2 \\ y = x - 2 \end{cases}$

b $\begin{cases} y = -4x + 1 \\ y = 3x - 6 \end{cases}$

c $\begin{cases} y = 2x - 5 \\ y = \frac{1}{2}x + 4 \end{cases}$

2 Solve the following simultaneous equations graphically:

a $\begin{cases} y = x - 1 \\ 2x + 3y = 12 \end{cases}$

b $\begin{cases} x + 3y = 9 \\ x - 2y = 4 \end{cases}$

c $\begin{cases} 3x - 2y = 30 \\ 4x + y = -4 \end{cases}$

3 Try to solve the following simultaneous equations graphically. State the number of solutions in each case.

a $\begin{cases} y = -2x + 5 \\ y = -2x - 1 \end{cases}$

b $\begin{cases} x - \frac{1}{4}y = -2 \\ y = 4x + 8 \end{cases}$

c $\begin{cases} 3x + 4y = -24 \\ 3x + 4y = -12 \end{cases}$

SOLUTION BY SUBSTITUTION

The method of **solution by substitution** is used most easily when at least one equation is given with either x or y as the **subject** of the formula. We **substitute** an expression for this variable into the other equation.

Example 14

◀)) **Self Tutor**

Solve simultaneously by substitution: $\begin{cases} y = x - 3 \\ 2x + 3y = 16 \end{cases}$

$y = x - 3$ .... (1)
$2x + 3y = 16$ .... (2)

Substituting (1) into (2) gives $2x + 3(x - 3) = 16$
$$\therefore \quad 2x + 3x - 9 = 16$$
$$\therefore \quad 5x = 25$$
$$\therefore \quad x = 5$$

Substituting $x = 5$ into (1) gives $y = 5 - 3$
$$\therefore \quad y = 2$$

The solution is $x = 5$, $y = 2$.

Check: Substituting into (2), $2(5) + 3(2) = 10 + 6 = 16$ ✓

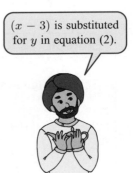

$(x - 3)$ is substituted for y in equation (2).

EXERCISE 1F.2

1 Solve the following sets of simultaneous equations:

a $\begin{cases} y = x + 2 \\ 2x + 3y = 21 \end{cases}$

b $\begin{cases} y = 2x - 3 \\ 4x - 3y = 7 \end{cases}$

c $\begin{cases} 5x + 3y = 19 \\ y = 6 - 2x \end{cases}$

d $\begin{cases} y = 3x + 1 \\ y = 7x - 1 \end{cases}$

e $\begin{cases} y = 6x - 8 \\ 3x + 2y = -6 \end{cases}$

f $\begin{cases} 4x - 7y = 1 \\ y = 11 - 3x \end{cases}$

2 Solve the following sets of simultaneous equations:

a $\begin{cases} x = y - 3 \\ 5x - 2y = 9 \end{cases}$

b $\begin{cases} 2x - 3y = -8 \\ x = 3y - 1 \end{cases}$

c $\begin{cases} x = 4y + 3 \\ x = 9 + 7y \end{cases}$

d $\begin{cases} y = 5x - 3 \\ x = 2y + 3 \end{cases}$

e $\begin{cases} 3x + 4y = -13 \\ x = 8y - 2 \end{cases}$

f $\begin{cases} x = -5y - 2 \\ 7x + 4y = -10 \end{cases}$

3 Solve the following sets of simultaneous equations:

a $\begin{cases} y = \frac{1}{2}x + 5 \\ 3x + 4y = 5 \end{cases}$

b $\begin{cases} x = -\frac{3}{4}y \\ 4x - 5y = -24 \end{cases}$

c $\begin{cases} x + 6y = -6 \\ y = \frac{1}{3}x - 5 \end{cases}$

d $\begin{cases} y = -\frac{1}{2}x + 3 \\ 5x + 4y = 14 \end{cases}$

e $\begin{cases} 3x + 7y = 6 \\ x = \frac{5}{3}y - 1 \end{cases}$

f $\begin{cases} 3x + 4y = 10 \\ y = \frac{3}{4}x + 2 \end{cases}$

SOLUTION BY ELIMINATION

If both equations are presented in the form $Ax + By = C$, then solution by substitution is tedious. We instead use the method of **elimination**.

In this method, we make the coefficients of x (or y) the **same size** but **opposite in sign**, and then **add** the equations. This has the effect of **eliminating** one of the variables.

Example 15

◄)) **Self Tutor**

Solve by elimination: $\begin{cases} 5x - 2y = 7 \\ 3x + 2y = 17 \end{cases}$

The coefficients of y are the same size but opposite in sign.

We *add* the LHSs and the RHSs to get an equation which contains x only.

$$5x - 2y = 7 \quad \text{.... (1)}$$
$$\underline{3x + 2y = 17 \quad \text{.... (2)}}$$

Adding, $\quad 8x \quad = 24$

$\quad \therefore \quad x = 3$

By adding the equations, we **eliminate** the y variable.

Substituting $x = 3$ into (1) gives $\quad 5(3) - 2y = 7$

$$\therefore \quad 15 - 2y = 7$$
$$\therefore \quad -2y = -8$$
$$\therefore \quad y = 4$$

The solution is $x = 3$, $y = 4$.

Check: In (2): $3(3) + 2(4) = 9 + 8 = 17$ ✓

In problems where the coefficients of x (or y) are **not** the **same size** or **opposite in sign**, we must first **multiply** one or both equations by a constant.

Example 16

◄)) **Self Tutor**

Solve by elimination: $\begin{cases} 3x + 4y = 2 \\ 2x - 3y = 7 \end{cases}$

$3x + 4y = 2 \quad \text{.... (1)}$
$2x - 3y = 7 \quad \text{.... (2)}$

To make the coefficients of y the same size but opposite in sign, we multiply (1) by 3 and (2) by 4.

$$\therefore \quad 9x + 12y = 6 \quad \{(1) \times 3\}$$
$$\underline{8x - 12y = 28 \quad \{(2) \times 4\}}$$

Adding, $\quad 17x \quad\quad = 34$

$\quad \therefore \quad x = 2$

We can choose to eliminate either x or y.

Substituting $x = 2$ into (1) gives $\quad 3(2) + 4y = 2$

$$\therefore \quad 6 + 4y = 2$$
$$\therefore \quad 4y = -4$$
$$\therefore \quad y = -1$$

The solution is $x = 2$, $y = -1$.

Check: In (2): $2(2) - 3(-1) = 4 + 3 = 7$ ✓

EXERCISE 1F.3

1 Solve using the method of elimination:

a $\begin{cases} 3x - y = 5 \\ 4x + y = 9 \end{cases}$

b $\begin{cases} 5x - 2y = 17 \\ 3x + 2y = 7 \end{cases}$

c $\begin{cases} -4x + 3y = 31 \\ 4x - y = -21 \end{cases}$

d $\begin{cases} 6x + 5y = 9 \\ -6x + 7y = -45 \end{cases}$

e $\begin{cases} 2x - 3y = 18 \\ 5x + 3y = 24 \end{cases}$

f $\begin{cases} -4x + 6y = -21 \\ 4x - 2y = 11 \end{cases}$

2 Solve using the method of elimination:

a $\begin{cases} 3x + y = 16 \\ 7x - 2y = 7 \end{cases}$

b $\begin{cases} 4x + 3y = -14 \\ -x + 5y = 15 \end{cases}$

c $\begin{cases} 5x - 2y = 7 \\ 2x - y = 4 \end{cases}$

d $\begin{cases} 3x - 7y = -27 \\ -6x + 5y = 18 \end{cases}$

e $\begin{cases} 9x + 2y = -24 \\ -7x + 4y = 27 \end{cases}$

f $\begin{cases} 3x - 7y = -8 \\ 9x + 11y = 16 \end{cases}$

3 Solve using the method of elimination:

a $\begin{cases} 4x + 3y = 14 \\ 3x - 4y = 23 \end{cases}$

b $\begin{cases} 2x - 3y = 6 \\ 5x - 4y = 1 \end{cases}$

c $\begin{cases} 5x + 6y = 17 \\ 3x - 7y = 42 \end{cases}$

d $\begin{cases} 2x + 10y = -5 \\ 3x - 7y = 9 \end{cases}$

e $\begin{cases} 4x + 2y = -23 \\ 5x - 7y = -5 \end{cases}$

f $\begin{cases} 4x - 7y = 9 \\ 5x - 8y = -2 \end{cases}$

Activity

What to do:

1 Consider the simultaneous equations $\begin{cases} y = 4x + 7 \\ 2y - 8x = 1 \end{cases}$.

   a Graph each line on the same set of axes. What do you notice?

   b Try to solve the simultaneous equations using:

      i substitution   **ii** elimination.

   c How many solutions does this set of simultaneous equations have?

2 Consider the simultaneous equations $\begin{cases} y = -2x + 5 \\ 4x + 2y = 10 \end{cases}$.

   a Graph each line on the same set of axes. What do you notice?

   b Try to solve the simultaneous equations using:

      i substitution   **ii** elimination.

   c How many solutions does this set of simultaneous equations have?

PROBLEM SOLVING WITH SIMULTANEOUS EQUATIONS

Many problems can be described using a pair of linear equations. You should follow these steps:

Step 1:   Decide on the two unknowns, for example x and y. Do not forget the units.

Step 2:   Write down **two** equations connecting x and y.

Step 3:   Solve the equations simultaneously.

Step 4:   Check your solutions with the original data given.

Step 5:   Write your answer in sentence form.

Example 17

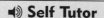 **Self Tutor**

Two adults' tickets and three children's tickets to a cricket match cost £45. Three adults' and four children's tickets cost £64. Find the cost of each type of ticket.

Let £x be the cost of an adult's ticket and £y be the cost of a child's ticket.

$\therefore$ $2x + 3y = 45$ .... (1)

   $3x + 4y = 64$ .... (2)

$\therefore$ $6x + 9y = 135$ $\{3 \times (1)\}$

   $\underline{-6x - 8y = -128}$ $\{-2 \times (2)\}$

Adding, $y = 7$

Substituting $y = 7$ into (1) gives $2x + 3(7) = 45$

$\therefore$ $2x + 21 = 45$

$\therefore$ $2x = 24$

$\therefore$ $x = 12$

So, an adult's ticket costs £12 and a child's ticket costs £7.

Check: In (2): $3(12) + 4(7) = 36 + 28 = 64$ $\checkmark$

EXERCISE 1F.4

1 Five plates and two bowls cost £53. Three plates and eight bowls cost £93. Find the cost of each item.

2 A violinist is learning a waltz and a sonatina. One day she practises for 33 minutes by playing the waltz 4 times and the sonatina 3 times. The next day she plays the waltz 6 times and the sonatina only once, for a total of 25 minutes. Determine the length of each piece.

3 A shop sells two lengths of extension cable. Tomasz buys 2 short cables and 5 long cables with total length 26 m. Alicja buys 3 short cables and 4 long cables with total length 24.3 m. Find the two different lengths of the extension cables.

4 In an archery competition, competitors fire 8 arrows at a target. They are awarded points based on which region of the target is hit. The results for two of the competitors are shown opposite.

How many points are awarded for hitting the:

    a red   **b** blue region?

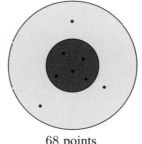 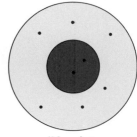

 68 points   56 points

5 A hardware store sells 3 litre cans of paint for £15 and 5 litre cans of paint for £20. In one day the store sells 71 litres of paint worth a total of £320. How many cans of paint did the store sell?

6 Lidia is paid at a standard rate per hour before 5 pm, and then at a higher rate per hour after 5 pm. On Monday she worked from 2 pm to 7 pm, and earned £110. On Tuesday she worked from 11 am to 8 pm, and earned £195.

On Wednesday Lidia worked from noon to 6 pm. How much did she earn on Wednesday?

7 Kristen can run at 9 km h^{-1} and walk at 3 km h^{-1}. She completed a 42 km marathon in 6 hours. What distance did Kristen run during the marathon?

MARATHON
DRINK
STATION

Review set 1A

1 Solve for x:

    a $4x + 7 = 39$ **b** $5 - \frac{1}{2}x = 3$ **c** $\dfrac{3x - 1}{2} = 7$

2 Solve for x:

    a $7x + 8 - 5x = -11$ **b** $-5(2 + x) = 7 - 2x$ **c** $\dfrac{x + 5}{3} = \dfrac{x - 13}{5}$

3 Martin bought a microwave oven and a toaster from a department store. He spent a total of £85, and the toaster was £35 cheaper than the microwave oven. Find the cost of the microwave oven.

4 **a** Find, in gradient-intercept form, the equation of the line which has gradient $-\frac{1}{3}$ and passes through $(6, 2)$.

    b Write the equation of the line in general form.

5 **a** Find, in general form, the equation of *line 2*.

    b Hence find the x-intercept of *line 2*.

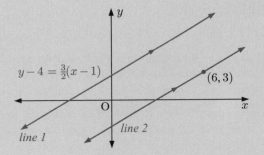

$y - 4 = \frac{3}{2}(x - 1)$

$(6, 3)$

line 1

line 2

6 Determine whether:

    a $(5, -2)$ lies on the line with equation $y = -x + 3$

    b $(-3, \frac{1}{2})$ lies on the line with equation $3x + 8y + 5 = 0$

    c $(\frac{2}{3}, -1)$ lies on the line with equation $y - 4 = 6(x - 2)$.

7 Draw the graph of:

    a $y = \frac{2}{3}x + 1$ **b** $y - 2 = \frac{1}{4}(x + 3)$ **c** $2x + 5y - 20 = 0$

8 For each table of values:

    i Draw a graph connecting the variables.

    ii Explain why the variables are linearly related.

    iii State whether the variables are in direct proportion.

    iv Find the equation connecting the variables.

a

x	1	2	3	4	5
y	4	8	12	16	20

b

P	0	1	2	3	4
n	2	7	12	17	22

9 Consider the line with equation $y = -\frac{1}{2}x + 4$.

  a Write down the gradient and y-intercept of the line.

  b Determine whether $(6,\ 1)$ lies on the line.

  c Find k such that $(k,\ 5)$ lies on the line.

  d Draw the graph of the line, showing your results from **a**, **b**, and **c**.

10 A bowl initially contains 200 mL of water. Water is poured into the bowl at a rate of 50 mL per minute.

  a Copy and complete this table of values:

Time (t minutes)	0	1	2	3	4
Amount of water (A mL)					

  b Graph A against t.

  c Are A and t linearly related? If so, are they directly proportional?

  d Find an equation connecting the variables.

11 Solve the following simultaneous equations:

  a $\begin{cases} y = 3x + 4 \\ 2x - y = -5 \end{cases}$

  b $\begin{cases} x = 2y - 5 \\ 3x + 4y = 5 \end{cases}$

  c $\begin{cases} 3x + 2y = 7 \\ 5x - 2y = 17 \end{cases}$

  d $\begin{cases} 2x + 7y = 13 \\ -4x + 3y = 25 \end{cases}$

  e $\begin{cases} y = x - 3 \\ 2x - 5y = 3 \end{cases}$

  f $\begin{cases} 3x - 5y = 19 \\ 9x - 2y = -8 \end{cases}$

12 A furniture store sells tables and chairs. Two possible arrangements and their costs are shown alongside.

Find the cost of:

  a each table   **b** each chair.

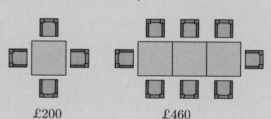

£200   £460

Review set 1B

1 Solve for x:

  a $4 - 3x = 2$

  b $7 + \dfrac{x}{4} = -3$

  c $\dfrac{6 - x}{3} = -2$

2 Solve for x:

  a $3(x - 2) + 4x = 1$

  b $2(6 - x) = 5(3x + 2)$

  c $\dfrac{1 - x}{5} = \dfrac{x + 2}{4}$

3 A 750 mL drink is shared between three children in the ratio $2 : 3 : 5$. Find the smallest share.

4 Find, in general form, the equation of the line which has:

  a gradient 5 and passes through $(2,\ -1)$ **b** gradient $-\frac{1}{4}$ and passes through $(-3,\ -4)$.

5 Find the equation of the line which is:

  a parallel to $y = 3x - 8$ and passes through $(2,\ 7)$

  b perpendicular to $2x + 5y - 7 = 0$ and passes through $(-1,\ -1)$.

6 Find k given that:

   a $(2, k)$ lies on the line with equation $y = 5x - 3$

   b $(k, -1)$ lies on the line with equation $y - 4 = \frac{1}{2}(x + 3)$

   c $(\frac{1}{2}, -\frac{3}{2})$ lies on the line with equation $5x + 9y - k = 0$.

7 Draw the graph of:

   a $y = -2x + 5$ **b** $y + 1 = \frac{1}{3}(x - 2)$ **c** $3x + 2y - 18 = 0$

8 Consider the line with equation $y + 2 = \frac{2}{3}(x - 1)$.

   a Find the gradient of the line.

   b Determine whether: **i** $(-2, -4)$ **ii** $(4, 5)$ lie on the line.

   c Draw the graph of the line, showing your results from **a** and **b**.

9 Suppose y is directly proportional to x. Describe what happens to y when x is decreased by 15%.

10 A service station sells petrol for £1.25 per litre.

   a Show that x, the number of litres bought, is directly proportional to y, the total cost of the petrol in pounds.

   b Find the proportionality constant.

   c Find the equation connecting x and y.

11 A phone company offers two different pricing plans:

   Plan A: £0.50 connection fee, £1 per minute

   Plan B: No connection fee, £1.25 per minute

   a For each plan, copy and complete a table of values like the one below:

Length of call (t minutes)	0	1	2	3	4
Cost of call (£C)					

   b Graph C against t for each plan on the same set of axes.

   c Discuss whether each plan represents a linear relationship.

   d Discuss whether each plan represents a direct proportion.

   e Find an equation connecting the variables for each plan.

12 Solve the following simultaneous equations:

   a $\begin{cases} y = 6x + 2 \\ 3x - 2y = -7 \end{cases}$ **b** $\begin{cases} y = \frac{1}{2}x + 5 \\ 4x + 3y = 4 \end{cases}$ **c** $\begin{cases} 3x + 2y = 8 \\ 5x - 4y = 17 \end{cases}$

   d $\begin{cases} 4x + 6y = -15 \\ 3x - 5y = 22 \end{cases}$ **e** $\begin{cases} x + 4y = -23 \\ 3x - 5y = 16 \end{cases}$ **f** $\begin{cases} x = 2y + 3 \\ 4x + 7y = -8 \end{cases}$

13 There are 500 tickets for sale in a raffle. Tickets cost £3 each, or £20 for a book of 10. All 500 tickets were sold, and £1350 was raised. How many books of 10 tickets were sold?

2

Reciprocal relationships

Contents:

Opening problem

In a 40 minute craft lesson, children are making greeting cards.

The *number of cards* a child can make depends on the *time taken* to make each card.

Things to think about:

a Tiffany takes 8 minutes to make a card. How many cards can she make in the lesson?

b As the *time taken* to make each card increases, will the *number of cards* made increase or decrease?

c If the *time taken* to make each card doubles, what happens to the *number of cards* made?

d Can you write an equation connecting the variables?

e What would the graph connecting these variables look like?

A ▌ INVERSE PROPORTION

We have seen that two variables are directly proportional if multiplying one of them by a number results in the other being multiplied by the same number.

By contrast:

> Two variables are **inversely proportional** if multiplying one of them by a number results in the other being *divided* by the same number.

In this case, one variable is directly proportional to the **reciprocal** of the other. The reciprocal is the *inverse* of multiplication.

> If two quantities x and y are **inversely proportional**, we write $y \propto \dfrac{1}{x}$.
>
> The variables are related by the equation $y = \dfrac{k}{x}$, where k is a constant.

Since $y = \dfrac{k}{x}$, we find that $xy = k$, a constant, for every point on the graph of the relationship.

Discussion

- What will the graph of a relationship which is an inverse proportion look like?
- In what real-world situations would an inverse proportion be observed?

Hugh is mowing the lawn on the school oval. If he works by himself, he will take 60 minutes to complete the job.

Now suppose a second groundsperson Chika helps with the task, so there are two mowers in operation. The job will now only take half as long, so it will take 30 minutes to complete the job.

By doubling the *number of mowers*, we halve the *time taken*. The variables are **inversely proportional**.

Some other combinations are shown in the table below, and are graphed alongside.

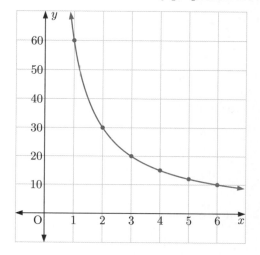

Number of mowers (x)	1	2	3	4	5	6
Time taken (y minutes)	60	30	20	15	12	10

The shape of the graph is part of a **hyperbola**.

Notice that $xy = 60$ for each point on the graph.

Discussion

As the number of mowers is increased, the time taken decreases.

The graph therefore gets closer and closer to the x-axis.

Could the graph ever actually reach the x-axis? What explanation can be given for your answer?

Example 1   ◀) **Self Tutor**

Su, Jenna, and Kate must each type a 1000 word assignment.

The table alongside shows the typing speed of each student, as well as the time it will take them to complete the task.

	Su	Jenna	Kate
Typing speed (x words per minute)	50	25	100
Time taken (y minutes)	20	40	10

a Draw the graph of y against x.

b Show that x and y are inversely proportional, and find the equation connecting the variables.

a

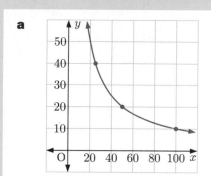

If x and y are inversely proportional, then xy is constant for every data pair (x, y).

b For each of the data pairs $(50, 20)$, $(25, 40)$, and $(100, 10)$, we find that $xy = 1000$.

∴ x and y are inversely proportional, and the equation connecting the variables is $y = \dfrac{1000}{x}$.

EXERCISE 2A

1 For each table of values:

  i Draw a graph connecting the variables.

  ii Decide whether the variables are in inverse proportion. If they are, find the equation connecting the variables.

a

x	2	5	8	20
y	40	16	10	4

b

x	1	3	5	6
y	30	10	8	5

c

C	2	5	10	15
t	25	10	6	4

d

P	1	4	6	8
t	24	6	4	3

2 **a** Copy and complete this table:

x	1	2	3	4	6
$\dfrac{1}{x}$	1	$\frac{1}{2}$			
y	12	6	4	3	2

  b Draw the graph of y against x.

  c Show that x and y are inversely proportional.

  d Draw the graph of y against $\dfrac{1}{x}$.

  e Show that $\dfrac{1}{x}$ and y are directly proportional.

3 For a school project, students must use 900 cm^2 of material to design a rectangular school flag. The dimensions of some of the students' flags are shown below.

Length (l cm)	36	30	40	50	45
Width (w cm)	25	30	22	18	20

  a Are all of the students' values correct? If not, find the correct value of w for the given value of l.

  b Draw the graph of l against w.

  c Show that l and w are inversely proportional, and find the equation connecting the variables.

4 For a moving object, the *speed*, *distance travelled*, and *time taken* are related by the equation
$$\text{speed} = \frac{\text{distance}}{\text{time}}.$$

  a For an object travelling a fixed *distance*, what is the relationship between *speed* and *time*?

  b For objects moving at the same *speed*, what is the relationship between *distance* and *time*?

  c For journeys which take the same amount of *time*, what is the relationship between *distance* and *speed*?

5 Suppose 20 litres of water are poured into a container with a square base. The *depth of water* depends on the *base length* of the container.

This table shows the water depth for various sizes of containers.

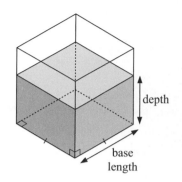

Base length (x cm)	10	20	25	40	50
Depth of water (y cm)	200	50	32	12.5	8

  a Draw the graph connecting the variables.

  b Are the *base length* and *depth of water* inversely proportional? Explain your answer.

6 Suppose y is inversely proportional to x. Describe what happens to:

  a y when x is doubled

  c x when y is multiplied by 10

  e x when y is increased by 20%

  b y when x is divided by 6

  d y when x is divided by 3.5

  f y when x is decreased by 7%.

7 Justine has bought some food for her fish. The *length of time* the food will last is inversely proportional to the *number of fish* she has.

Justine currently has 25 fish, and expects the food to last for 28 days. However, her brother goes away on a holiday, leaving Justine 10 extra fish to look after. How long will the food last now?

B   RECIPROCAL FUNCTIONS

In the graph alongside, y is inversely proportional to x. The variables are connected by the equation $y = \dfrac{20}{x}$.

However, this is not the complete graph of $y = \dfrac{20}{x}$, because we have only considered positive values of x and y.

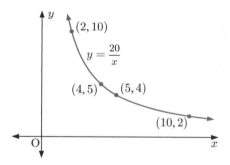

By extending the graph to include negative values of x and y, we can draw the complete graph of $y = \dfrac{20}{x}$.

$y = \dfrac{20}{x}$ is an example of a **reciprocal function**.

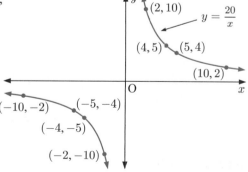

The graph of the **reciprocal function** $y = \dfrac{k}{x}$, $k \neq 0$, is called a **rectangular hyperbola**.

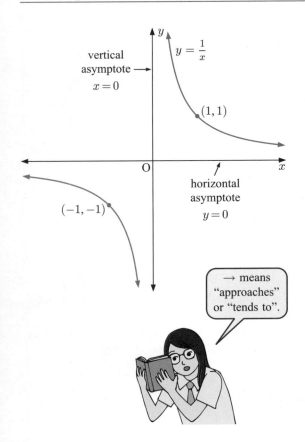

The graph of $y = \dfrac{1}{x}$ is shown alongside.

Notice that:

- The graph has two branches.

- $y = \dfrac{1}{x}$ is undefined when $x = 0$

- The graph exists in the first and third quadrants only.

- The graph gets closer and closer to the horizontal line $y = 0$, but never reaches it. We say that $y = 0$ is a **horizontal asymptote**.

  We write: as $x \to \infty$, $\dfrac{1}{x} \to 0^+$

  as $x \to -\infty$, $\dfrac{1}{x} \to 0^-$

- The graph gets closer and closer to the vertical line $x = 0$, but never reaches it. We say that $x = 0$ is a **vertical asymptote**.

  We write: as $x \to 0^-$, $\dfrac{1}{x} \to -\infty$

  as $x \to 0^+$, $\dfrac{1}{x} \to \infty$

$\to$ means "approaches" or "tends to".

When sketching the graph of a reciprocal function, it is useful to determine some points which lie on the graph.

The reciprocal function $y = \dfrac{k}{x}$ passes through the points $(1,\, k)$, $(k,\, 1)$, $(-1,\, -k)$, and $(-k,\, -1)$.

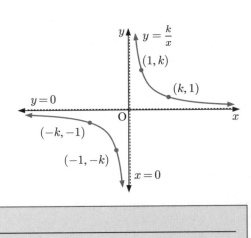

Discussion

- Can you explain why the graph of $y = \dfrac{k}{x}$ never cuts:
  - the y-axis
  - the x-axis?
- How close does the graph get to these axes?

EXERCISE 2B.1

1 **a** Sketch the graphs of $y = \dfrac{1}{x}$, $y = \dfrac{2}{x}$, and $y = \dfrac{4}{x}$ on the same set of axes.

b Describe the effect of varying k on the graph of $y = \dfrac{k}{x}$.

DEMO

2 a Sketch the graphs of $y = -\dfrac{1}{x}$, $y = -\dfrac{2}{x}$, and $y = -\dfrac{4}{x}$ on the same set of axes.

   b Comment on the shape of the graph of $y = \dfrac{k}{x}$ when $k < 0$.

3 Determine the equation of each reciprocal function:

a

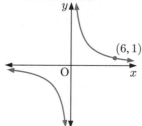

$(6, 1)$

b

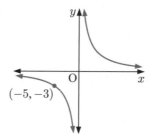

$(-5, -3)$

c

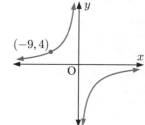

$(-9, 4)$

4 Answer the **Opening Problem** on page **38**. Let n be the *number of cards* made and t be the *time taken*.

THE RECIPROCAL OF x^2

The cylinder shown has height y cm, radius x cm, and volume 500 cm^3.

$$\therefore\ \ \pi x^2 y = 500$$
$$\therefore\ \ y = \frac{500}{\pi x^2}$$

In this case $y = \dfrac{k}{x^2}$ where $k = \dfrac{500}{\pi}$ is a constant.

So, y is inversely proportional to x^2.

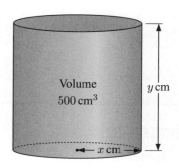

Volume 500 cm^3

y cm

x cm

EXERCISE 2B.2

1 a Copy and complete this table of values for $y = \dfrac{1}{x^2}$.

x	-3	-2	-1	-0.5	-0.2	0	0.2	0.5	1	2	3
y											

   b Hence sketch the graph of $y = \dfrac{1}{x^2}$.

   c What quadrants does the graph appear in?

   d State the vertical asymptote of $y = \dfrac{1}{x^2}$.

   e State the horizontal asymptote of $y = \dfrac{1}{x^2}$.

2 a Sketch the graphs of $y = \dfrac{1}{x}$ and $y = \dfrac{1}{x^2}$ on the same set of axes.

   b Comment on the similarities and differences.

3 a Sketch the graphs of $y = \dfrac{1}{x^2}$, $y = \dfrac{2}{x^2}$, and $y = \dfrac{4}{x^2}$ on the same set of axes.

   b Describe the effect of varying k on the graph of $y = \dfrac{k}{x^2}$.

GRAPHING PACKAGE

C | EQUATIONS INVOLVING RECIPROCALS

Example 2   ◄) **Self Tutor**

Greg can varnish a wooden floor in 72 minutes. If Erica helps, they can do the job together in 40 minutes. How long would it take Erica to varnish the floor by herself?

Suppose it would take Erica x minutes to varnish the floor by herself.

Erica varnishes $\frac{1}{x}$ of the floor in 1 minute. Greg varnishes $\frac{1}{72}$ of the floor in 1 minute.

It would take 40 minutes for the two of them to varnish the whole floor, so

$$40\left(\frac{1}{x} + \frac{1}{72}\right) = 1$$

$$\therefore \quad \frac{1}{x} + \frac{1}{72} = \frac{1}{40}$$

$$\therefore \quad \frac{1}{x} = \frac{1}{90}$$

$$\therefore \quad x = 90$$

It would take Erica 90 minutes to varnish the floor by herself.

EXERCISE 2C

1 Solve for x:

   a $\dfrac{1}{x} = \dfrac{1}{12}$ **b** $\dfrac{3}{x} = 21$ **c** $\dfrac{5}{x} = \dfrac{4}{3}$

   d $\dfrac{1}{x} - \dfrac{1}{5} = \dfrac{1}{3}$ **e** $\dfrac{2}{x} + \dfrac{1}{4} = \dfrac{1}{3}$ **f** $\dfrac{25}{x^2} = \dfrac{9}{4}$

2 It would take Tim 4.5 hours to paint his fence. With the help of his friend James, it could be done in 2.5 hours. How long would it take James to paint the fence by himself?

3 It takes Sally 18 minutes to saw a log into 3 pieces.

   a How long would it take Sally to make a single saw cut through a similar log?

   b It takes Ethan 25 minutes to saw a log into n pieces. Write an expression for the time t it takes Ethan to make a single saw cut through a similar log.

4 Joe and Ken are painting a wall. Joe could paint the wall in 5 days by himself, and Ken could paint the wall in 4 days by himself. How long will they take to paint the wall together?

Review set 2A

1 Genevieve wants to buy £12 worth of kiwifruit. The *number of kiwifruit* she can buy depends on the *price* of each kiwifruit.

Some possible combinations of purchases are shown below.

Price (p pence)	40	50	60	80
Number of kiwifruit (N)	30	24	20	15

   a Draw the graph of N against p.

   b Show that N and p are inversely proportional, and find the equation connecting the variables.

2 Suppose x and y are inversely proportional, and y and z are inversely proportional. Are x and z inversely proportional? Explain your answer.

3 Jethro is playing a video game. In the game, the *strength level s* of a weapon is directly proportional to the *damage d* it inflicts.

Jethro currently has a level 5 weapon which inflicts 60 units of damage.

   a Find an equation connecting the variables.

   b Suppose Jethro finds a level 8 weapon. How many units of damage can it inflict?

   c To defeat the final enemy in the game, Jethro needs a weapon which can inflict 180 units of damage. What level of weapon will he need?

4 Draw the graph of:

   a $y = \dfrac{10}{x}$ **b** $y = -\dfrac{9}{x}$ **c** $y = \dfrac{3}{x^2}$

5 It takes Donna 108 minutes to set the tables in her restaurant. If Peter helps her, the task can be done in 60 minutes. How long would it take Peter to do the job by himself?

Review set 2B

1 Suppose M is inversely proportional to n. Describe what happens to n when M is multiplied by 2.5 .

2 For each table of values:

   i Draw a graph connecting the variables.

   ii Decide whether the variables are in inverse proportion. If they are, find the equation connecting the variables.

   a

x	2	5	7	10
y	15	6	4	3

   b

W	3	6	9	18
t	12	6	4	2

3 A building company is constructing a house. The *time* it will take is inversely proportional to the *number of workers*.

5 workers would take 96 days to construct the house. How long would it take 8 workers to complete the building?

4 Determine the equation of each reciprocal function:

a

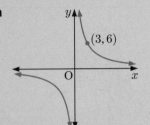

$(3, 6)$

b

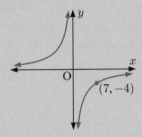

$(7, -4)$

c

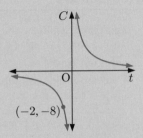

$(-2, -8)$

5 Draw the graph of $y = -\dfrac{1}{x^2}$ and describe its key features.

6 A rectangle has length l cm, width w cm, and area 36 cm^2.

   a Are l and w inversely proportional? Explain your answer.

   b Sketch a graph of l against w.

3

Quadratics

Contents:

Opening problem

Abiola and Badrani are standing 40 metres apart, throwing a ball between them. When Abiola throws the ball, it travels in a smooth arc. At the time when the ball has travelled x metres horizontally towards Badrani, its height is y metres.

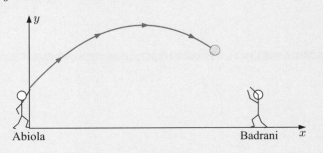

SIMULATION

x (m)	0	5	10	15	20	25	30
y (m)	1.25	10	16.25	20	21.25	20	16.25

Things to think about:

a Use technology to plot these points.

b What *shape* is the graph of y against x?

c What is the maximum height reached by the ball?

d What *formula* gives the height of the ball when it has travelled x metres horizontally towards Badrani?

e Will the ball reach Badrani before it bounces?

Historical note

Galileo Galilei (1564 - 1642) was born in Pisa, Tuscany. He was a philosopher who played a significant role in the scientific revolution of that time.

Within his research he conducted a series of experiments on the paths of projectiles, attempting to find a mathematical description of falling bodies.

Two of Galileo's experiments consisted of rolling a ball down a grooved ramp that was placed at a fixed height above the floor and inclined at a fixed angle to the horizontal. In one experiment the ball left the end of the ramp and descended to the floor. In the second, a horizontal shelf was placed at the end of the ramp, and the ball travelled along this shelf before descending to the floor.

In each experiment Galileo altered the release height h of the ball and measured the distance d the ball travelled before landing. The units of measurement were called 'punti' (points).

Galileo

In both experiments Galileo found that once the ball left the ramp or shelf, its path was *parabolic* and could therefore be modelled by a *quadratic* function.

QUADRATICS

A **quadratic equation** is an equation of the form $ax^2 + bx + c = 0$ where a, b, and c are constants, $a \neq 0$.

A **quadratic function** is a function of the form $y = ax^2 + bx + c$, $a \neq 0$.

Quadratic functions are members of the family of **polynomials**. The first few members of this family are shown in the table.

Polynomial function	Type
$y = ax + b$, $a \neq 0$	linear
$y = ax^2 + bx + c$, $a \neq 0$	quadratic
$y = ax^3 + bx^2 + cx + d$, $a \neq 0$	cubic
$y = ax^4 + bx^3 + cx^2 + dx + e$, $a \neq 0$	quartic

A   QUADRATIC EQUATIONS

The **roots** or **solutions** of $ax^2 + bx + c = 0$ are the values of x which satisfy the equation, or make it true.

For example: Consider $x^2 - 3x + 2 = 0$.

When $x = 2$, $x^2 - 3x + 2 = (2)^2 - 3(2) + 2$
$$= 4 - 6 + 2$$
$$= 0 \quad \checkmark$$

So, $x = 2$ is a root of the equation $x^2 - 3x + 2 = 0$.

METHODS FOR SOLVING QUADRATIC EQUATIONS

To solve quadratic equations we have the following methods to choose from:

- rewrite the quadratic in **factored form** and use the **Null Factor law**:

  If $ab = 0$ then $a = 0$ or $b = 0$.

- rewrite the quadratic in **completed square form** $a(x - h)^2 + k$, then rearrange $a(x - h)^2 + k = 0$ to isolate x
- use the **quadratic formula**
- use **technology**.

SOLVING BY FACTORISATION

Step 1:   If necessary, rearrange the equation so one side is zero.

Step 2:   Fully factorise the other side.

Step 3:   Use the Null Factor law: If $ab = 0$ then $a = 0$ or $b = 0$.

Step 4:   Solve the resulting linear equations.

Example 1
🔊 **Self Tutor**

Solve for x: **a** $3x^2 + 5x = 0$ **b** $x^2 = 5x + 6$

a $\qquad 3x^2 + 5x = 0$	**b** $\qquad x^2 = 5x + 6$
$\therefore \quad x(3x + 5) = 0$	$\therefore \quad x^2 - 5x - 6 = 0$
$\therefore \quad x = 0 \ \text{ or } \ 3x + 5 = 0$	$\therefore \quad (x - 6)(x + 1) = 0$
$\therefore \quad x = 0 \ \text{ or } \ x = -\frac{5}{3}$	$\therefore \quad x = 6 \ \text{ or } \ -1$

Example 2
🔊 **Self Tutor**

Solve for x: **a** $4x^2 + 1 = 4x$ **b** $6x^2 = 11x + 10$

a $\qquad 4x^2 + 1 = 4x$	**b** $\qquad 6x^2 = 11x + 10$
$\therefore \quad 4x^2 - 4x + 1 = 0$	$\therefore \quad 6x^2 - 11x - 10 = 0$
$\therefore \quad (2x - 1)^2 = 0$	$\therefore \quad (2x - 5)(3x + 2) = 0$
$\therefore \quad x = \frac{1}{2}$	$\therefore \quad x = \frac{5}{2} \ \text{ or } \ -\frac{2}{3}$

Caution:

- Do not be tempted to divide both sides by an expression involving x. If you do this then you may lose one of the solutions.

  For example, consider $x^2 = 5x$.

By dividing both sides by x, we lose the solution $x = 0$.

Correct solution	*Incorrect solution*
$x^2 = 5x$	$x^2 = 5x$
$\therefore \quad x^2 - 5x = 0$	$\therefore \quad \dfrac{x^2}{x} = \dfrac{5x}{x}$
$\therefore \quad x(x - 5) = 0$	
$\therefore \quad x = 0 \text{ or } 5$	$\therefore \quad x = 5$

- Be careful when taking square roots of both sides of an equation. If you do this then you may lose one of the solutions.

  For example, consider $(2x - 7)^2 = (x + 1)^2$.

Correct solution	*Incorrect solution*
$(2x - 7)^2 = (x + 1)^2$	$(2x - 7)^2 = (x + 1)^2$
$\therefore \quad (2x - 7)^2 - (x + 1)^2 = 0$	$\therefore \quad 2x - 7 = x + 1$
$\therefore \quad (2x - 7 + x + 1)(2x - 7 - x - 1) = 0$	$\therefore \quad x = 8$
$\therefore \quad (3x - 6)(x - 8) = 0$	
$\therefore \quad x = 2 \text{ or } 8$	

EXERCISE 3A.1

1 Solve for x:

    a $4x^2 + 7x = 0$ **b** $6x^2 + 2x = 0$ **c** $3x^2 - 7x = 0$

    d $2x^2 - 11x = 0$ **e** $3x^2 = 8x$ **f** $9x = 6x^2$

    g $x^2 - 5x + 6 = 0$ **h** $x^2 = 2x + 8$ **i** $x^2 + 21 = 10x$

    j $9 + x^2 = 6x$ **k** $x^2 + x = 12$ **l** $x^2 + 8x = 33$

2 Solve for x:

a $9x^2 - 12x + 4 = 0$ **b** $2x^2 - 13x - 7 = 0$ **c** $3x^2 = 16x + 12$

d $3x^2 + 5x = 2$ **e** $2x^2 + 3 = 5x$ **f** $3x^2 + 8x + 4 = 0$

g $3x^2 = 10x + 8$ **h** $4x^2 + 4x = 3$ **i** $4x^2 = 11x + 3$

j $12x^2 = 11x + 15$ **k** $7x^2 + 6x = 1$ **l** $15x^2 + 2x = 56$

Example 3 🔊 **Self Tutor**

RHS is short for Right Hand Side.

Solve for x: $\quad 3x + \dfrac{2}{x} = -7$

$$3x + \frac{2}{x} = -7$$

$\therefore \quad 3x^2 + 2 = -7x \qquad$ {multiplying both sides by x}

$\therefore \quad 3x^2 + 7x + 2 = 0 \qquad$ {making the RHS 0}

$\therefore \quad (x + 2)(3x + 1) = 0 \qquad$ {factorising}

$\therefore \quad x = -2$ or $-\frac{1}{3}$

---

3 Solve for x:

a $(x + 1)^2 = 2x^2 - 5x + 11$

b $(x + 2)(1 - x) = -4$

c $5 - 4x^2 = 3(2x + 1) + 2$

d $x + \dfrac{2}{x} = 3$

e $2x - \dfrac{1}{x} = -1$

f $\dfrac{x + 3}{1 - x} = -\dfrac{9}{x}$

g $(x + 3)(2 - x) = 4$

h $(x - 4)(x + 2) = 16$

i $(x - 5)(x + 3) = 20$

j $(4x - 5)(4x - 3) = 143$

SOLVING BY "COMPLETING THE SQUARE"

As you would be aware by now, not all quadratics factorise easily.

For example, $x^2 + 4x + 1$ cannot be factorised by easily identifying factors. In particular, we cannot write $x^2 + 4x + 1$ in the form $(x - a)(x - b)$ where a and b are rational numbers.

An alternative method is to rewrite the quadratic in **completed square form** $a(x - h)^2 + k$. We refer to this process as "completing the square".

> Start with the quadratic equation in the form $ax^2 + bx + c = 0$.
>
> *Step 1:* If $a \neq 1$, divide both sides by a.
>
> *Step 2:* Rearrange the equation so that only the constant coefficient is on the RHS.
>
> *Step 3:* Add to both sides $\left(\dfrac{\text{coefficient of } x}{2}\right)^2$.
>
> *Step 4:* Factorise the LHS.
>
> *Step 5:* Use the rule: If $X^2 = a$ then $X = \pm\sqrt{a}$.

Example 4
🔊 **Self Tutor**

Solve exactly for x: $x^2 + 4x + 1 = 0$

$x^2 + 4x + 1 = 0$
$\therefore \ x^2 + 4x = -1$ {writing the constant on the RHS}
$\therefore \ x^2 + 4x + 2^2 = -1 + 2^2$ {completing the square}
$\therefore \ (x + 2)^2 = 3$ {factorising the LHS}
$\therefore \ x + 2 = \pm\sqrt{3}$
$\therefore \ x = -2 \pm \sqrt{3}$

The squared number we add to both sides is $\left(\dfrac{\text{coefficient of } x}{2}\right)^2$

Example 5
🔊 **Self Tutor**

Solve exactly for x: $-3x^2 + 12x + 5 = 0$

$-3x^2 + 12x + 5 = 0$
$\therefore \ x^2 - 4x - \frac{5}{3} = 0$ {dividing both sides by -3}
$\therefore \ x^2 - 4x = \frac{5}{3}$ {writing the constant on the RHS}
$\therefore \ x^2 - 4x + (-2)^2 = \frac{5}{3} + (-2)^2$ {completing the square}
$\therefore \ (x - 2)^2 = \frac{17}{3}$ {factorising the LHS}
$\therefore \ x - 2 = \pm\sqrt{\frac{17}{3}}$
$\therefore \ x = 2 \pm \sqrt{\frac{17}{3}}$

If the coefficient of x^2 is not 1, we first divide throughout to make it 1.

EXERCISE 3A.2

1 Solve exactly for x:

  a $(x + 5)^2 = 2$ **b** $(x + 6)^2 = -11$ **c** $(x - 4)^2 = 8$

  d $(x - 8)^2 = 7$ **e** $2(x + 3)^2 = 10$ **f** $3(x - 2)^2 = 18$

  g $(x + 1)^2 + 1 = 11$ **h** $(2x + 1)^2 = 3$ **i** $(1 - 3x)^2 - 7 = 0$

2 Solve exactly by completing the square:

  a $x^2 - 4x + 1 = 0$ **b** $x^2 + 6x + 2 = 0$ **c** $x^2 - 14x + 46 = 0$

  d $x^2 = 4x + 3$ **e** $x^2 + 6x + 7 = 0$ **f** $x^2 = 2x + 6$

  g $x^2 + 6x = 2$ **h** $x^2 + 10 = 8x$ **i** $x^2 + 6x = -11$

3 Solve exactly by completing the square:

  a $2x^2 + 4x + 1 = 0$ **b** $2x^2 - 10x + 3 = 0$ **c** $3x^2 + 12x + 5 = 0$

  d $3x^2 = 6x + 4$ **e** $5x^2 - 15x + 2 = 0$ **f** $4x^2 + 4x = 5$

4 Solve for x:

  a $3x - \dfrac{2}{x} = 4$ **b** $1 - \dfrac{1}{x} = -5x$ **c** $3 + \dfrac{1}{x^2} = -\dfrac{5}{x}$

5 Suppose $ax^2 + bx + c = 0$ where a, b, and c are constants, $a \neq 0$.
  Solve for x by completing the square.

Investigation 1   "Completing the square" and factorisation

You are already familiar with the difference of two squares identity $(x - a)(x + a) = x^2 - a^2$.

This identity is particularly useful because the LHS is factored, and the RHS is in completed square form (with $h = 0$ and $k = -a^2$).

We can use this identity to transform a quadratic into factored form without working through all the different combinations of factor pairs. To do this we:

- complete the square
- write the constant term as a square and use the difference of two squares identity.

For example:

$$
\begin{aligned}
& x^2 + 6x + 5 \\
&= x^2 + 6x + 9 - 9 + 5 && \text{\{completing the square\}} \\
&= (x + 3)^2 - 4 && \text{\{completed square form\}} \\
&= (x + 3)^2 - 2^2 \\
&= (x + 3 - 2)(x + 3 + 2) && \text{\{difference of two squares\}} \\
&= (x + 1)(x + 5)
\end{aligned}
$$

What to do:

1 The figure alongside shows a rectangle with side lengths $x + a$ and $x - a$, and a square with side length a.

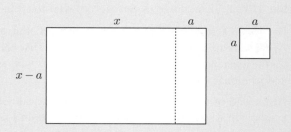

   a Rearrange the pieces to form a square with side length x.

   b Hence explain the difference of two squares identity.

2 Complete the square and use the difference of two squares to write the following quadratics in factored form:

   a $x^2 - 6x + 5$ **b** $x^2 + 2x - 8$ **c** $x^2 - 2x - 15$

THE QUADRATIC FORMULA

Historical note   The quadratic formula

Thousands of years ago, people knew how to calculate the area of a rectangular shape given its side lengths. When they wanted to find the side lengths necessary to give a certain area, however, they ended up with a quadratic equation which they needed to solve.

The first known solution of a quadratic equation is written on the Berlin Papyrus from the Middle Kingdom (2160 - 1700 BC) in Egypt. By 400 BC, the Babylonians were using the method of 'completing the square'.

Pythagoras and **Euclid** both used geometric methods to explore the problem. Pythagoras noted that the square root was not always an integer, but he refused to accept that irrational solutions existed. Euclid also discovered that the square root was not always rational, but concluded that irrational numbers *did* exist.

A major jump forward was made in India around 700 AD, when Hindu mathematician **Brahmagupta** devised a general (but incomplete) solution for the quadratic equation $ax^2 + bx = c$ which was equivalent to $x = \dfrac{\sqrt{4ac + b^2} - b}{2a}$. Taking into account the sign of c, this is one of the two solutions we know today.

Brahmagupta also added *zero* to our number system!

The final, complete solution as we know it today first came around 1100 AD, by another Hindu mathematician called **Bhaskhara**. He was the first to recognise that any positive number has two square roots, which could be negative or irrational. In fact, the quadratic formula is known in some countries today as 'Bhaskhara's Formula'.

While the Indians had knowledge of the quadratic formula even at this early stage, it took somewhat longer for the quadratic formula to arrive in Europe.

Around 820 AD, the Islamic mathematician **Muhammad bin Musa Al-Khwarizmi**, who was familiar with the work of Brahmagupta, recognised that for a quadratic equation to have real solutions, the value $b^2 - 4ac$ could not be negative.

Al-Khwarizmi's work was brought to Europe by the Jewish mathematician and astronomer **Abraham bar Hiyya** (also known as Savasorda) who lived in Barcelona around 1100 AD.

By 1545, **Girolamo Cardano** had blended the algebra of Al-Khwarizmi with the Euclidean geometry. His work allowed for the existence of roots which are not real, as well as negative and irrational roots.

From the name Al-Khwarizmi we get the word 'algorithm'.

At the end of the 16th Century the mathematical notation and symbolism was introduced by **François Viète** in France.

In 1637, when **René Descartes** published *La Géométrie*, the quadratic formula adopted the form we see today.

In many cases, factorising a quadratic or completing the square can be long or difficult. We can instead use the **quadratic formula**:

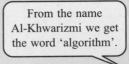

If $ax^2 + bx + c = 0$, $a \neq 0$, then $x = \dfrac{-b \pm \sqrt{b^2 - 4ac}}{2a}$.

Proof:

$$\text{If} \quad ax^2 + bx + c = 0, \quad a \neq 0$$

$$\text{then} \quad x^2 + \frac{b}{a}x + \frac{c}{a} = 0 \qquad \{\text{dividing each term by } a, \text{ as } a \neq 0\}$$

$$\therefore \quad x^2 + \frac{b}{a}x = -\frac{c}{a}$$

$$\therefore \quad x^2 + \frac{b}{a}x + \left(\frac{b}{2a}\right)^2 = -\frac{c}{a} + \left(\frac{b}{2a}\right)^2 \qquad \{\text{completing the square}\}$$

$$\therefore \quad \left(x + \frac{b}{2a}\right)^2 = \frac{b^2 - 4ac}{4a^2} \qquad \{\text{factorising}\}$$

$$\therefore \quad x + \frac{b}{2a} = \pm\sqrt{\frac{b^2 - 4ac}{4a^2}}$$

$$\therefore \quad x = \frac{-b \pm \sqrt{b^2 - 4ac}}{2a}$$

Example 6

◆)) **Self Tutor**

Solve for x: **a** $x^2 - 2x - 6 = 0$ **b** $2x^2 + 3x - 6 = 0$

a $x^2 - 2x - 6 = 0$ has
     $a = 1$, $b = -2$, $c = -6$

$$\therefore \; x = \frac{-(-2) \pm \sqrt{(-2)^2 - 4(1)(-6)}}{2(1)}$$

$$\therefore \; x = \frac{2 \pm \sqrt{28}}{2}$$

$$\therefore \; x = \frac{2 \pm 2\sqrt{7}}{2} = 1 \pm \sqrt{7}$$

b $2x^2 + 3x - 6 = 0$ has
     $a = 2$, $b = 3$, $c = -6$

$$\therefore \; x = \frac{-3 \pm \sqrt{3^2 - 4(2)(-6)}}{2(2)}$$

$$\therefore \; x = \frac{-3 \pm \sqrt{57}}{4}$$

EXERCISE 3A.3

1   Use the quadratic formula to solve exactly for x:

   a $x^2 - 4x - 3 = 0$ **b** $x^2 + 6x + 7 = 0$ **c** $x^2 + 1 = 4x$

   d $x^2 + 4x = 1$ **e** $x^2 - 4x + 2 = 0$ **f** $2x^2 - 2x - 3 = 0$

   g $3x^2 - 5x - 1 = 0$ **h** $-x^2 + 4x + 6 = 0$ **i** $-2x^2 + 7x - 2 = 0$

2   Rearrange the following equations so they are written in the form $ax^2 + bx + c = 0$, then use the quadratic formula to solve exactly for x.

   a $(x + 2)(x - 1) = 2 - 3x$ **b** $(2x + 1)^2 = 3 - x$ **c** $(x - 2)^2 = 1 + x$

   d $(3x + 1)^2 = -2x$ **e** $(x + 3)(2x + 1) = 9$ **f** $(2x + 3)(2x - 3) = x$

   g $\dfrac{x - 1}{2 - x} = 2x + 1$ **h** $x - \dfrac{1}{x} = 1$ **i** $2x - \dfrac{1}{x} = 3$

SOLVING USING TECHNOLOGY

You can use your graphics calculator to solve quadratic equations.

If the right hand side is zero, you can graph the expression on the left hand side. The x-intercepts of the graph are the solutions to the quadratic equation.

GRAPHICS
CALCULATOR
INSTRUCTIONS

If the right hand side is non-zero, you can either:

- rearrange the equation so the right hand side is zero, then graph the expression and find the x-intercepts, or
- graph the expressions on the left and right hand sides on the same set of axes, then find the x-coordinates of the point where they meet.

Use technology to check your answers to **Exercise 3A.3**.

B   THE DISCRIMINANT OF A QUADRATIC

We can determine how many real solutions a quadratic equation has, without actually solving the equation. In the quadratic formula, the quantity $b^2 - 4ac$ under the square root sign is called the **discriminant**.

The symbol **delta** Δ is used to represent the discriminant, so $\Delta = b^2 - 4ac$.

The quadratic formula becomes $x = \dfrac{-b \pm \sqrt{\Delta}}{2a}$ where Δ replaces $b^2 - 4ac$.

- If $\Delta > 0$, $\sqrt{\Delta}$ is a positive real number, so there are **two distinct real roots**

$$x = \frac{-b + \sqrt{\Delta}}{2a} \quad \text{and} \quad x = \frac{-b - \sqrt{\Delta}}{2a}.$$

- If $\Delta = 0$, $x = \frac{-b}{2a}$ is the **only solution**, which we call a **repeated** or **double root**.

- If $\Delta < 0$, $\sqrt{\Delta}$ is not a real number and so there are **no real roots**.

- If a, b, and c are rational and Δ is a **square** then the equation has two rational roots which can be found by factorisation.

Example 7
◀) **Self Tutor**

Use the discriminant to determine the nature of the roots of:

a $2x^2 - 2x + 3 = 0$

b $3x^2 - 4x - 2 = 0$

a $\Delta = b^2 - 4ac$
$\quad = (-2)^2 - 4(2)(3)$
$\quad = -20$

Since $\Delta < 0$, there are no real roots.

b $\Delta = b^2 - 4ac$
$\quad = (-4)^2 - 4(3)(-2)$
$\quad = 40$

Since $\Delta > 0$, but 40 is not a square, there are 2 distinct irrational roots.

EXERCISE 3B

1 Consider the quadratic equation $x^2 - 7x + 9 = 0$.
   a Find the discriminant.   **b** Hence, state the nature of the roots of the equation.
   c Check your answer to **b** by solving the equation.

2 Consider the quadratic equation $4x^2 - 4x + 1 = 0$.
   a Find the discriminant.   **b** Hence, state the nature of the roots of the equation.
   c Check your answer to **b** by solving the equation.

3 **a** Without using the discriminant, explain why the equation $x^2 + 5 = 0$ has no real roots.
   b Check that $\Delta < 0$ for this equation.

4 Using the discriminant only, state the nature of the solutions of:
   a $x^2 + 7x - 3 = 0$ **b** $x^2 - 3x + 2 = 0$ **c** $3x^2 + 2x - 1 = 0$
   d $5x^2 + 4x - 3 = 0$ **e** $x^2 + x + 5 = 0$ **f** $16x^2 - 8x + 1 = 0$

5 Using the discriminant only, determine which of the following quadratic equations have rational roots which can be found by factorisation.
   a $6x^2 - 5x - 6 = 0$ **b** $2x^2 - 7x - 5 = 0$ **c** $3x^2 + 4x + 1 = 0$
   d $6x^2 - 47x - 8 = 0$ **e** $4x^2 - 3x + 2 = 0$ **f** $8x^2 + 2x - 3 = 0$

Example 8
◀) **Self Tutor**

Consider $x^2 - 2x + m = 0$.   Find the discriminant Δ, and hence find the values of m for which the equation has:

a a repeated root   **b** two distinct real roots   **c** no real roots.

$x^2 - 2x + m = 0$ has $a = 1$, $b = -2$, and $c = m$

$\therefore \quad \Delta = b^2 - 4ac$

$\qquad = (-2)^2 - 4(1)(m)$

$\qquad = 4 - 4m$

a For a repeated root

$\Delta = 0$

$\therefore \quad 4 - 4m = 0$

$\therefore \quad 4 = 4m$

$\therefore \quad m = 1$

b For two distinct real roots

$\Delta > 0$

$\therefore \quad 4 - 4m > 0$

$\therefore \quad -4m > -4$

$\therefore \quad m < 1$

c For no real roots

$\Delta < 0$

$\therefore \quad 4 - 4m < 0$

$\therefore \quad -4m < -4$

$\therefore \quad m > 1$

6 For each of the following quadratic equations, find the discriminant Δ in simplest form. Hence find the values of m for which the equation has:

   i a repeated root   **ii** two distinct real roots   **iii** no real roots.

  a $x^2 + 4x + m = 0$ **b** $mx^2 + 3x + 2 = 0$ **c** $mx^2 - 3x + 1 = 0$

C   THE SUM AND PRODUCT OF THE ROOTS

If $ax^2 + bx + c = 0$ has roots α and β, then $\alpha + \beta = -\dfrac{b}{a}$ and $\alpha\beta = \dfrac{c}{a}$.

For example: If α and β are the roots of $2x^2 - 2x - 1 = 0$ then $\alpha + \beta = -\dfrac{-2}{2} = 1$ and $\alpha\beta = -\dfrac{1}{2}$.

Proof:

If α and β are the roots of $ax^2 + bx + c = 0$,

then $ax^2 + bx + c = a(x - \alpha)(x - \beta)$

$\qquad\qquad\qquad\quad = a(x^2 - [\alpha + \beta]x + \alpha\beta)$

$\therefore \quad x^2 + \dfrac{b}{a}x + \dfrac{c}{a} = x^2 - [\alpha + \beta]x + \alpha\beta$

Equating coefficients, $\alpha + \beta = -\dfrac{b}{a}$ and $\alpha\beta = \dfrac{c}{a}$.

Example 9   ◀) Self Tutor

Find the sum and product of the roots of $25x^2 - 20x + 1 = 0$.
Check your answer by solving the quadratic.

If α and β are the roots then $\alpha + \beta = -\dfrac{b}{a} = \dfrac{20}{25} = \dfrac{4}{5}$ and $\alpha\beta = \dfrac{c}{a} = \dfrac{1}{25}$

Check: $25x^2 - 20x + 1 = 0$ has roots

$$\frac{20 \pm \sqrt{400 - 4(25)(1)}}{50} = \frac{20 \pm \sqrt{300}}{50} = \frac{20 \pm 10\sqrt{3}}{50} = \frac{2 \pm \sqrt{3}}{5}$$

These have sum $= \dfrac{2 + \sqrt{3}}{5} + \dfrac{2 - \sqrt{3}}{5} = \dfrac{4}{5}$ ✓

and product $= \left(\dfrac{2 + \sqrt{3}}{5}\right)\left(\dfrac{2 - \sqrt{3}}{5}\right) = \dfrac{4 - 3}{25} = \dfrac{1}{25}$ ✓

EXERCISE 3C

1 For each of the following quadratic equations:

    i Find the sum and product of the roots.

    ii Check your answer by solving the quadratic.

  a $x^2 + 4x - 21 = 0$ **b** $4x^2 - 12x + 5 = 0$ **c** $3x^2 - 4x - 2 = 0$

2 **a** Show that the sum of the roots of $x^2 - 5x + 5 = 0$ is equal to the product of the roots.

  b Check this by solving the quadratic.

3 For the equation $kx^2 - (1 + k)x + (3k + 2) = 0$, the sum of the roots is twice their product. Find k and the two roots.

4 The quadratic equation $ax^2 - 6x + a - 2 = 0$, $a \neq 0$, has one root which is double the other.

  a Let the roots be α and 2α. Hence find two equations involving α.

  b Find a and the two roots of the quadratic equation.

5 The quadratic equation $kx^2 + (k - 8)x + (1 - k) = 0$, $k \neq 0$, has one root which is two more than the other. Find k and the two roots.

Example 10   ◀) **Self Tutor**

The roots of the equation $4x^2 + 5x - 1 = 0$ are α and β.

Find a quadratic equation with roots 3α and 3β.

If α and β are the roots of $4x^2 + 5x - 1 = 0$, then $\alpha + \beta = -\frac{5}{4}$ and $\alpha\beta = -\frac{1}{4}$.

For the quadratic equation with roots 3α and 3β,

the sum of the roots $= 3\alpha + 3\beta$ and   the product of the roots $= (3\alpha)(3\beta)$

$$= 3(\alpha + \beta) \qquad\qquad\qquad\qquad = 9\alpha\beta$$

$$= 3\left(-\frac{5}{4}\right) \qquad\qquad\qquad\qquad = 9\left(-\frac{1}{4}\right)$$

$$= -\frac{15}{4} \qquad\qquad\qquad\qquad\qquad = -\frac{9}{4}$$

So, we have $-\dfrac{b}{a} = -\dfrac{15}{4}$ and $\dfrac{c}{a} = -\dfrac{9}{4}$.

The simplest solution is $a = 4$, $b = 15$, $c = -9$

$\therefore$ the quadratic equation is $4x^2 + 15x - 9 = 0$.

---

6 The roots of the equation $3x^2 + 2x - 4 = 0$ are α and β.

  Find a quadratic equation with roots: **a** $-\alpha$ and $-\beta$ **b** 2α and 2β.

7 The roots of the equation $x^2 - 6x + 7 = 0$ are α and β.

  Find a quadratic equation with roots $\alpha + \dfrac{1}{\beta}$ and $\beta + \dfrac{1}{\alpha}$.

8 The roots of $2x^2 - 3x - 5 = 0$ are p and q.

  Find *all* quadratic equations with roots $p^2 + q$ and $q^2 + p$.

D   QUADRATIC FUNCTIONS

A **quadratic function** has the form $y = ax^2 + bx + c$ where $a \neq 0$.

The simplest quadratic function is $y = x^2$.   Its graph can be drawn from a table of values.

x	-3	-2	-1	0	1	2	3
y	9	4	1	0	1	4	9

The graph of a quadratic function is called a **parabola**.

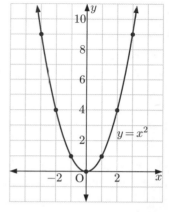

There are many examples of parabolas in everyday life, including water fountains, bridges, and radio telescopes.

TERMINOLOGY

The graph of a quadratic function $y = ax^2 + bx + c,\ a \neq 0$ is called a **parabola**.

The point where the graph 'turns' is called the **vertex**.

If the graph opens upwards, the vertex is the **minimum** or **minimum turning point**, and the graph is **concave upwards**.

If the graph opens downwards, the vertex is the **maximum** or **maximum turning point**, and the graph is **concave downwards**.

The vertical line that passes through the vertex is called the **axis of symmetry**. Every parabola is symmetrical about its axis of symmetry.

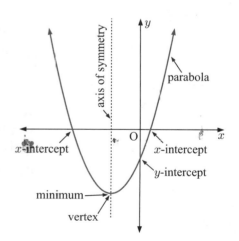

The value of y where the graph crosses the y-axis is the **y-intercept**.

The values of x (if they exist) where the graph crosses the x-axis are called the **x-intercepts**. They correspond to the **roots** of the equation $y = 0$.

Investigation 2   Graphing $y = a(x - p)(x - q)$

In this Investigation we consider the properties of the graph of a quadratic stated in factored form. It is best done using a **graphing package** or **graphics calculator**.

What to do:

GRAPHING
PACKAGE

1 a Use technology to help you to sketch:

$y = (x - 1)(x - 3)$, $y = 2(x - 1)(x - 3)$, $y = -(x - 1)(x - 3)$,

$y = -3(x - 1)(x - 3)$,   and $y = -\frac{1}{2}(x - 1)(x - 3)$

   b Find the x-intercepts for each function in **a**.

   c What is the geometrical significance of a in $y = a(x - 1)(x - 3)$?

2 a Use technology to help you to sketch:

$y = 2(x - 1)(x - 4)$, $y = 2(x - 3)(x - 5)$, $y = 2(x + 1)(x - 2)$,

$y = 2x(x + 5)$,   and $y = 2(x + 2)(x + 4)$

   b Find the x-intercepts for each function in **a**.

   c What is the geometrical significance of p and q in $y = 2(x - p)(x - q)$?

3 a Use technology to help you to sketch:

$y = 2(x - 1)^2$, $y = 2(x - 3)^2$, $y = 2(x + 2)^2$, $y = 2x^2$

   b Find the x-intercepts for each function in **a**.

   c What is the geometrical significance of p in $y = 2(x - p)^2$?

4 Copy and complete:

   • If a quadratic has the form $y = a(x - p)(x - q)$ then it ...... the x-axis at ......

   • If a quadratic has the form $y = a(x - p)^2$ then it ...... the x-axis at ......

Investigation 3   Graphing $y = a(x - h)^2 + k$

In this Investigation we consider the properties of the graph of a quadratic stated in completed square form. It is best done using a **graphing package** or **graphics calculator**.

What to do:

GRAPHING
PACKAGE

1 a Use technology to help you to sketch:

$y = (x - 3)^2 + 2$, $y = 2(x - 3)^2 + 2$, $y = -2(x - 3)^2 + 2$,

$y = -(x - 3)^2 + 2$,   and $y = -\frac{1}{3}(x - 3)^2 + 2$

   b Find the coordinates of the vertex for each function in **a**.

   c What is the geometrical significance of a in $y = a(x - 3)^2 + 2$?

2 a Use technology to help you to sketch:

$y = 2(x - 1)^2 + 3$, $y = 2(x - 2)^2 + 4$, $y = 2(x - 3)^2 + 1$,

$y = 2(x + 1)^2 + 4$, $y = 2(x + 2)^2 - 5$,   and $y = 2(x + 3)^2 - 2$

   b Find the coordinates of the vertex for each function in **a**.

   c What is the geometrical significance of h and k in $y = 2(x - h)^2 + k$?

3 Copy and complete:

If a quadratic has the form $y = a(x - h)^2 + k$ then its vertex has coordinates ......

Quadratic form, $a \neq 0$	Graph	Facts
• $y = a(x - p)(x - q)$ where $p, q \in \mathbb{R}$		x-intercepts are p and q axis of symmetry is $x = \dfrac{p + q}{2}$ vertex has x-coordinate $\dfrac{p + q}{2}$
• $y = a(x - h)^2$ where $h \in \mathbb{R}$		touches x-axis at h axis of symmetry is $x = h$ vertex is $(h, 0)$
• $y = a(x - h)^2 + k$ where $h, k \in \mathbb{R}$		axis of symmetry is $x = h$ vertex is (h, k)

You should have found that a, the coefficient of x^2, controls the width of the graph and whether it opens upwards or downwards.

For a quadratic function $y = ax^2 + bx + c$, $a \neq 0$:

- $a > 0$ produces the shape $\smile$ called concave up.

  $a < 0$ produces the shape $\frown$ called concave down.

- If $-1 < a < 1$, $a \neq 0$ the graph is wider than $y = x^2$.
  If $a < -1$ or $a > 1$ the graph is narrower than $y = x^2$.

Example 11

◀)) **Self Tutor**

Using axes intercepts only, sketch the graphs of:

a $y = 2(x+3)(x-1)$ **b** $y = -2(x-1)(x-2)$ **c** $y = \frac{1}{2}(x+2)^2$

a $y = 2(x+3)(x-1)$
has x-intercepts -3, 1
When $x = 0$,
$$y = 2(3)(-1)$$
$$= -6$$
$\therefore$ y-intercept is -6

b $y = -2(x-1)(x-2)$
has x-intercepts 1, 2
When $x = 0$,
$$y = -2(-1)(-2)$$
$$= -4$$
$\therefore$ y-intercept is -4

c $y = \frac{1}{2}(x+2)^2$
touches x-axis at -2
When $x = 0$,
$$y = \frac{1}{2}(2)^2$$
$$= 2$$
$\therefore$ y-intercept is 2

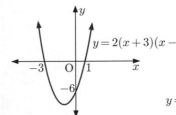

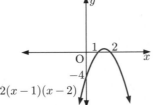

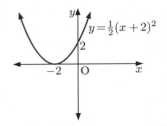

EXERCISE 3D.1

1 Using axes intercepts only, sketch the graph of:

a $y = (x-4)(x+2)$ **b** $y = -(x-4)(x+2)$

c $y = 2(x+3)(x+5)$ **d** $y = -3(x+1)(x+5)$

e $y = 2(x+3)^2$ **f** $y = -\frac{1}{4}(x+2)^2$

2 State the equation of the axis of symmetry for each graph in question **1**.

> The axis of symmetry is midway between the x-intercepts.

3 Match each quadratic function with its corresponding graph.

a $y = 2(x-1)(x-4)$ **b** $y = -(x+1)(x-4)$ **c** $y = (x-1)(x-4)$

d $y = (x+1)(x-4)$ **e** $y = 2(x+4)(x-1)$ **f** $y = -3(x+4)(x-1)$

g $y = 2(x+1)(x+4)$ **h** $y = -(x-1)(x-4)$ **i** $y = -3(x-1)(x-4)$

A

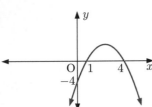

B

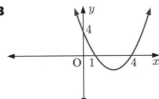

C

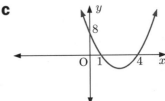

D
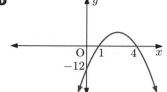

E
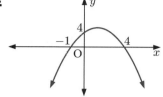

F
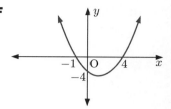

G
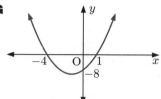

H
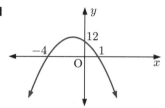

I
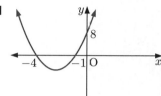

Example 12 ◀) Self Tutor

Use the vertex, axis of symmetry, and y-intercept to graph
$y = -2(x + 1)^2 + 4$.

The axis of symmetry is $x = -1$.

The vertex is $(-1, 4)$.

When $x = 0$, $y = -2(1)^2 + 4$
$\qquad\qquad\quad = 2$

$a < 0$ so the shape is

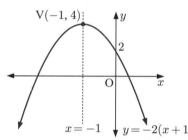

> This quadratic is given in completed square form.

4 Use the vertex, axis of symmetry, and y-intercept to graph:

  a $\ y = (x - 1)^2 + 3$ **b** $\ y = 2(x + 2)^2 + 1$ **c** $\ y = -2(x - 1)^2 - 3$

  d $\ y = \frac{1}{2}(x - 3)^2 + 2$ **e** $\ y = -\frac{1}{3}(x - 1)^2 + 4$ **f** $\ y = -\frac{1}{10}(x + 2)^2 - 3$

5 Match each quadratic function with its corresponding graph:

  a $\ y = -(x + 1)^2 + 3$ **b** $\ y = -2(x - 3)^2 + 2$ **c** $\ y = x^2 + 2$

  d $\ y = -(x - 1)^2 + 1$ **e** $\ y = (x - 2)^2 - 2$ **f** $\ y = \frac{1}{3}(x + 3)^2 - 3$

  g $\ y = -x^2$ **h** $\ y = -\frac{1}{2}(x - 1)^2 + 1$ **i** $\ y = 2(x + 2)^2 - 1$

A
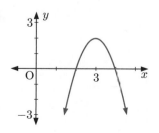

B
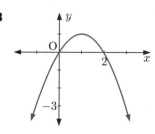

C
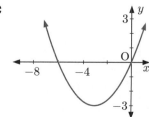

D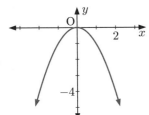

E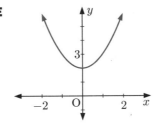

F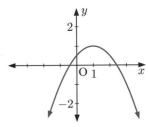

G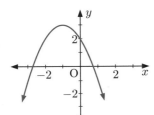

H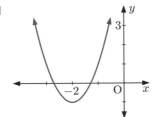

I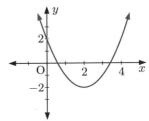

SKETCHING GRAPHS BY "COMPLETING THE SQUARE"

If we wish to graph a quadratic given in general form $y = ax^2 + bx + c$, one approach is to use **"completing the square"** to convert it to the completed square form $y = a(x - h)^2 + k$. We can then read off the coordinates of the vertex (h, k).

Consider the simple case $y = x^2 - 6x + 7$, for which $a = 1$.

$$y = x^2 - 6x + 7$$
$$\therefore \quad y = \underbrace{x^2 - 6x + 3^2}\ \underbrace{+7 - 3^2}$$
$$\therefore \quad y = \quad (x-3)^2 \quad\ \ -2$$

So, the axis of symmetry is $x = 3$ and the vertex is $(3, -2)$.

When $x = 0$, $y = 7$, so the y-intercept is 7.

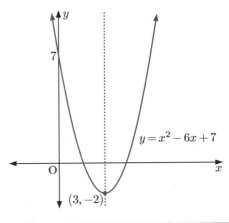

$y = x^2 - 6x + 7$

$(3, -2)$

Example 13   ◀⁙ Self Tutor

Write $y = x^2 + 4x + 3$ in the form $y = (x - h)^2 + k$ by "completing the square".
Hence sketch $y = x^2 + 4x + 3$, stating the coordinates of the vertex.

$$y = x^2 + 4x + 3$$
$$\therefore \quad y = x^2 + 4x + 2^2 + 3 - 2^2$$
$$\therefore \quad y = (x + 2)^2 - 1$$

So, the axis of symmetry is $x = -2$ and the vertex is $(-2, -1)$.

When $x = 0$, $y = 3$

$\therefore$ the y-intercept is 3.

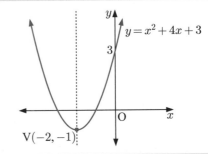

$y = x^2 + 4x + 3$

$V(-2, -1)$

Example 14

◀ࣿ **Self Tutor**

a Convert $y = 3x^2 - 4x + 1$ to the completed square form $y = a(x - h)^2 + k$.

b Hence write down the coordinates of the vertex, and sketch the quadratic.

a $y = 3x^2 - 4x + 1$

$\quad = 3[x^2 - \frac{4}{3}x + \frac{1}{3}]$ {taking out a factor of 3}

$\quad = 3[x^2 - 2(\frac{2}{3})x + (\frac{2}{3})^2 + \frac{1}{3} - (\frac{2}{3})^2]$ {completing the square}

$\quad = 3[(x - \frac{2}{3})^2 + \frac{3}{9} - \frac{4}{9}]$ {writing as a perfect square}

$\quad = 3[(x - \frac{2}{3})^2 - \frac{1}{9}]$

$\quad = 3(x - \frac{2}{3})^2 - \frac{1}{3}$

b The vertex is $(\frac{2}{3}, -\frac{1}{3})$
and the y-intercept is 1.

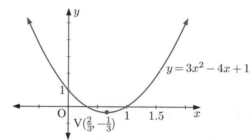

EXERCISE 3D.2

1 Write the following quadratics in the form $y = (x - h)^2 + k$ by "completing the square". Hence sketch each function, stating the coordinates of the vertex.

  a $y = x^2 - 2x + 3$ **b** $y = x^2 + 4x - 2$ **c** $y = x^2 - 4x$

  d $y = x^2 + 3x$ **e** $y = x^2 + 5x - 2$ **f** $y = x^2 - 3x + 2$

  g $y = x^2 - 6x + 5$ **h** $y = x^2 + 8x - 2$ **i** $y = x^2 - 5x + 1$

2 For each of the following quadratics:

  i Write the quadratic in the completed square form
$y = a(x - h)^2 + k$.

  ii State the coordinates of the vertex.

  iii Find the y-intercept.

  iv Sketch the graph of the quadratic.

a is always the factor to be "taken out".

  a $y = 2x^2 + 4x + 5$ **b** $y = 2x^2 - 8x + 3$

  c $y = 2x^2 - 6x + 1$ **d** $y = 3x^2 - 6x + 5$

  e $y = -x^2 + 4x + 2$ **f** $y = -2x^2 - 5x + 3$

QUADRATICS OF THE FORM $y = ax^2 + bx + c$

We now consider a method of graphing quadratics of the form $y = ax^2 + bx + c$ directly, without having to first convert them to a different form.

We know that the quadratic equation $ax^2 + bx + c = 0$ has solutions $\dfrac{-b - \sqrt{\Delta}}{2a}$ and $\dfrac{-b + \sqrt{\Delta}}{2a}$ where $\Delta = b^2 - 4ac$.

If $\Delta \geqslant 0$, these are the x-intercepts of the graph of the quadratic function $y = ax^2 + bx + c$.

The average of the values is $\dfrac{-b}{2a}$, so we conclude that:

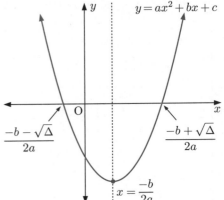

- the axis of symmetry is $x = \dfrac{-b}{2a}$
- the vertex of the quadratic has x-coordinate $\dfrac{-b}{2a}$.

To graph a quadratic of the form $y = ax^2 + bx + c$, we:
- Find the axis of symmetry $x = \dfrac{-b}{2a}$.
- Substitute this value to find the y-coordinate of the vertex.
- State the y-intercept c.
- Find the x-intercepts by solving $ax^2 + bx + c = 0$, either by factorisation or using the quadratic formula.

Example 15   ◀)) **Self Tutor**

Consider the quadratic $y = 2x^2 + 8x - 10$.

  a Find the axis of symmetry.   **b** Find the coordinates of the vertex.

  c Find the axes intercepts.   **d** Hence, sketch the quadratic.

$y = 2x^2 + 8x - 10$ has $a = 2$, $b = 8$, and $c = -10$. Since $a > 0$, the shape is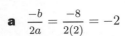

a $\dfrac{-b}{2a} = \dfrac{-8}{2(2)} = -2$

    The axis of symmetry is $x = -2$.

b When $x = -2$,

    $y = 2(-2)^2 + 8(-2) - 10$

    $ = -18$

    The vertex is $(-2, -18)$.

c The y-intercept is -10.

    When $y = 0$, $2x^2 + 8x - 10 = 0$

    $\therefore \quad 2(x^2 + 4x - 5) = 0$

    $\therefore \quad 2(x + 5)(x - 1) = 0$

    $\therefore \quad x = -5 \text{ or } 1$

$\therefore$ the x-intercepts are -5 and 1.

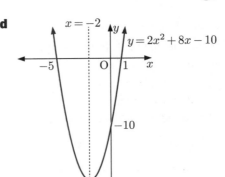

EXERCISE 3D.3

1 Locate the turning point or vertex for each of the following quadratics:

The vertex lies on the axis of symmetry.

a $y = x^2 - 4x + 2$

b $y = x^2 + 2x - 3$

c $y = 2x^2 + 4$

d $y = -3x^2 + 1$

e $y = 2x^2 + 8x - 7$

f $y = -x^2 - 4x - 9$

g $y = 2x^2 + 6x - 1$

h $y = 2x^2 - 10x + 3$

i $y = -\frac{1}{2}x^2 + x - 5$

j $y = \frac{1}{4}x^2 - 7x + 6$

2 For each of the following quadratics:

   i State the axis of symmetry.
   ii Find the coordinates of the vertex.
   iii Find the axes intercepts.
   iv Hence, sketch the quadratic.

a $y = x^2 - 8x + 7$

b $y = -x^2 - 6x - 8$

c $y = 6x - x^2$

d $y = -x^2 + 3x - 2$

e $y = 2x^2 + 4x - 24$

f $y = -3x^2 + 4x - 1$

g $y = 2x^2 - 5x + 2$

h $y = 4x^2 - 8x - 5$

i $y = -\frac{1}{4}x^2 + 2x - 3$

Activity

Click on the icon to run a card game for quadratics.

CARD GAME

THE DISCRIMINANT AND THE GRAPH OF A QUADRATIC

The discriminant of the quadratic equation $ax^2 + bx + c = 0$ is $\Delta = b^2 - 4ac$.

We have used Δ to determine the number of real roots of the equation. If they exist, these roots correspond to zeros of the quadratic $y = ax^2 + bx + c$. Δ therefore tells us about the relationship between the graph of a quadratic function and the x-axis.

The graphs of $y = x^2 - 2x - 3$, $y = x^2 - 2x + 1$, and $y = x^2 - 2x + 3$ all have the same axis of symmetry, $x = 1$.

$y = x^2 - 2x - 3$	$y = x^2 - 2x + 1$	$y = x^2 - 2x + 3$
(graph cutting x-axis at −1 and 3, y-intercept −3, x = 1)	*(graph touching x-axis, y-intercept 1, x = 1)*	*(graph above x-axis, vertex at 3, x = 1)*
$\Delta = b^2 - 4ac$ $= (-2)^2 - 4(1)(-3)$ $= 16$	$\Delta = b^2 - 4ac$ $= (-2)^2 - 4(1)(1)$ $= 0$	$\Delta = b^2 - 4ac$ $= (-2)^2 - 4(1)(3)$ $= -8$
$\Delta > 0$	$\Delta = 0$	$\Delta < 0$
cuts the x-axis twice	touches the x-axis	does not cut the x-axis

For a quadratic function $y = ax^2 + bx + c$, we consider the discriminant $\Delta = b^2 - 4ac$.

If $\Delta > 0$, the graph cuts the x-axis twice.

If $\Delta = 0$, the graph *touches* the x-axis.

If $\Delta < 0$, the graph does not cut the x-axis.

POSITIVE DEFINITE AND NEGATIVE DEFINITE QUADRATICS

Positive definite quadratics are quadratics which are positive for all values of x. So, $ax^2 + bx + c > 0$ for all $x \in \mathbb{R}$.

A quadratic is **positive definite** if and only if $a > 0$ and $\Delta < 0$.

Negative definite quadratics are quadratics which are negative for all values of x. So, $ax^2 + bx + c < 0$ for all $x \in \mathbb{R}$.

A quadratic is **negative definite** if and only if $a < 0$ and $\Delta < 0$.

Example 16   ◀) **Self Tutor**

Use the discriminant to determine the relationship between the graph of each function and the x-axis:

a $y = x^2 + 3x + 4$

b $y = -2x^2 + 5x + 1$

a $a = 1$, $b = 3$, $c = 4$

$\therefore \ \Delta = b^2 - 4ac$

$\quad = 9 - 4(1)(4)$

$\quad = -7$

Since $\Delta < 0$, the graph does not cut the x-axis.

Since $a > 0$, the graph is concave up.

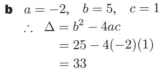

The graph is positive definite, which means that it lies entirely above the x-axis.

b $a = -2$, $b = 5$, $c = 1$

$\therefore \ \Delta = b^2 - 4ac$

$\quad = 25 - 4(-2)(1)$

$\quad = 33$

Since $\Delta > 0$, the graph cuts the x-axis twice.

Since $a < 0$, the graph is concave down.

EXERCISE 3D.4

1   Use the discriminant to determine the relationship between the graph of each function and the x-axis:

a $y = x^2 + x - 2$

b $y = x^2 - 4x + 1$

c $y = -x^2 - 3$

d $y = x^2 + 7x - 2$

e $y = x^2 + 8x + 16$

f $y = -2x^2 + 3x + 1$

g $y = 6x^2 + 5x - 4$

h $y = -x^2 + x + 6$

i $y = 9x^2 + 6x + 1$

2 Consider the graph of $y = 2x^2 - 5x + 1$.

    a Describe the shape of the graph.

    b Use the discriminant to show that the graph cuts the x-axis twice.

    c Find the x-intercepts, rounding your answers to 2 decimal places.

    d State the y-intercept.

    e Hence, sketch the function.

3 Consider the graph of $y = -x^2 + 4x - 7$.

    a Use the discriminant to show that the graph does not cut the x-axis.

    b Is the graph positive definite or negative definite?

    c Find the vertex and y-intercept.

    d Hence, sketch the function.

4 Show that:

    a $2x^2 - 4x + 7$ is positive definite   **b** $-2x^2 + 3x - 4$ is negative definite

    c $x^2 - 3x + 6 > 0$ for all x **d** $4x - x^2 - 6 < 0$ for all x.

5 Explain why $3x^2 + kx - 1$ is never positive definite for any value of k.

6 Under what conditions is $2x^2 + kx + 2$ positive definite?

E | FINDING A QUADRATIC FROM ITS GRAPH

If we are given sufficient information on or about a graph, we can determine the quadratic in whatever form is required.

Example 17   ◀⑴ Self Tutor

Find the equation of the quadratic with graph:

a

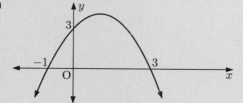

b

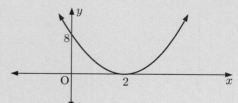

---

    a Since the x-intercepts are -1 and 3,
        $y = a(x + 1)(x - 3)$.

    The graph is concave down, so $a < 0$.

    When $x = 0$, $y = 3$

        $\therefore \ 3 = a(1)(-3)$

        $\therefore \ a = -1$

    The quadratic is $y = -(x + 1)(x - 3)$.

    b The graph touches the x-axis at $x = 2$,
        so $y = a(x - 2)^2$.

    The graph is concave up, so $a > 0$.

    When $x = 0$, $y = 8$

        $\therefore \ 8 = a(-2)^2$

        $\therefore \ a = 2$

    The quadratic is $y = 2(x - 2)^2$.

Example 18

◀ঊ **Self Tutor**

Find the equation of the quadratic with graph:

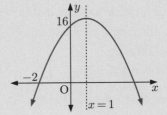

The axis of symmetry $x = 1$ lies midway between the x-intercepts.

∴ the other x-intercept is 4.

∴ the quadratic has the form
$$y = a(x + 2)(x - 4) \quad \text{where} \quad a < 0$$

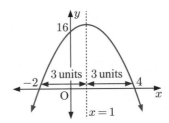

But when $x = 0$, $y = 16$

∴ $16 = a(2)(-4)$

∴ $a = -2$

The quadratic is $y = -2(x + 2)(x - 4)$.

EXERCISE 3E

1 Find the equation of the quadratic with graph:

a
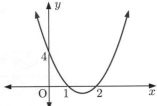

b
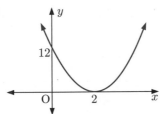

c
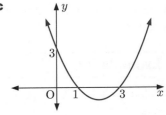

d
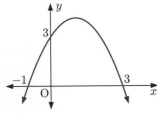

e
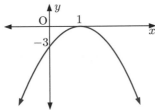

f
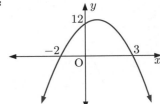

2 Find the quadratic with graph:

a
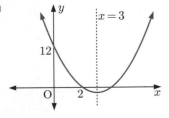

b
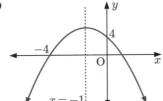

c
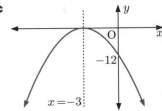

Example 19 ◀)) **Self Tutor**

Find the equation of the quadratic whose graph cuts the x-axis at 4 and -3, and which passes through the point $(2, -20)$. Give your answer in the form $y = ax^2 + bx + c$.

Since the x-intercepts are 4 and -3, the quadratic has the form $y = a(x - 4)(x + 3)$, $a \neq 0$.

When $x = 2$, $y = -20$

$\therefore \quad -20 = a(2 - 4)(2 + 3)$

$\therefore \quad -20 = a(-2)(5)$

$\therefore \quad a = 2$

The quadratic is $\quad y = 2(x - 4)(x + 3)$

$\qquad\qquad\qquad = 2(x^2 - x - 12)$

$\qquad\qquad\qquad = 2x^2 - 2x - 24$

3 Find, in the form $y = ax^2 + bx + c$, the equation of the quadratic whose graph:

   a cuts the x-axis at 5 and 1, and passes through $(2, -9)$

   b cuts the x-axis at 2 and $-\frac{1}{2}$, and passes through $(3, -14)$

   c touches the x-axis at 3 and passes through $(-2, -25)$

   d touches the x-axis at -2 and passes through $(-1, 4)$

4 Find, in the form $y = ax^2 + bx + c$, the equation of the quadratic whose graph:

   a cuts the x-axis at 3, passes through $(5, 12)$, and has axis of symmetry $x = 2$

   b cuts the x-axis at 5, passes through $(2, 5)$, and has axis of symmetry $x = 1$.

Example 20 ◀)) **Self Tutor**

Find the equation of the quadratic with graph:

a

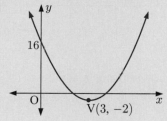

b

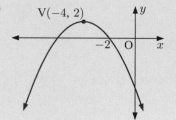

a Since the vertex is $(3, -2)$, the quadratic has the form $y = a(x - 3)^2 - 2$ where $a > 0$.

When $x = 0$, $y = 16$

$\therefore \quad 16 = a(-3)^2 - 2$

$\therefore \quad 16 = 9a - 2$

$\therefore \quad 18 = 9a$

$\therefore \quad a = 2$

The quadratic is $y = 2(x - 3)^2 - 2$.

b Since the vertex is $(-4, 2)$, the quadratic has the form $y = a(x + 4)^2 + 2$ where $a < 0$.

When $x = -2$, $y = 0$

$\therefore \quad 0 = a(2)^2 + 2$

$\therefore \quad 4a = -2$

$\therefore \quad a = -\frac{1}{2}$

The quadratic is $y = -\frac{1}{2}(x + 4)^2 + 2$.

5 If V is the vertex, find the equation of the quadratic with graph:

a
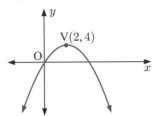

b
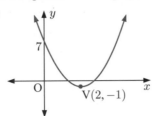

c
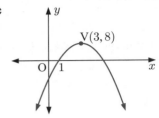

d
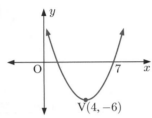

e
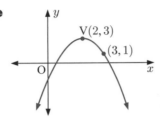

f
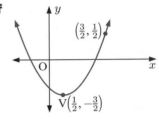

6 A quadratic has vertex $(2, -5)$, and passes through the point $(-1, 13)$. Find the value of the quadratic when $x = 4$.

Investigation 4   Finding quadratics

For the quadratic $y = 2x^2 + 3x + 7$ we can construct a table of values for $x = 0, 1, 2, 3, 4, 5$.

x	0	1	2	3	4	5
y	7	12	21	34	51	72

We turn this table into a **difference table** by adding two further rows:

- the row Δ_1 gives the differences between successive y-values

- the row Δ_2 gives the differences between successive Δ_1-values.

x	0	1	2	3	4	5
y	7	12	21	34	51	72
Δ_1		5	9	13	17	21
Δ_2			4	4	4	4

$$9 - 5 \qquad 34 - 21 \qquad 72 - 51$$

What to do:

1 Construct difference tables for $x = 0, 1, 2, 3, 4, 5$ for each of the following quadratics:

   a $y = x^2 + 4x + 3$ **b** $y = 3x^2 - 4x$ **c** $y = 5x - x^2$ **d** $y = 4x^2 - 5x + 2$

2 What do you notice about the Δ_2 row for each quadratic in **1**?

3 Consider the general quadratic $y = ax^2 + bx + c, \quad a \neq 0$.

   a Copy and complete the following difference table:

x	0	1	2	3	4	5
y	©	$a + b + c$	$4a + 2b + c$	......	......	......
Δ_1	○	......		......	......	......
Δ_2		○	......	......	......	

   b Comment on the Δ_2 row.

   c What can the circled numbers be used for?

4 Use your observations in **3** to determine, if possible, the quadratic with the following tables of values:

a

x	0	1	2	3	4
y	6	5	8	15	26

b

x	0	1	2	3	4
y	8	10	18	32	52

c

x	0	1	2	3	4
y	1	2	-1	-8	-19

d

x	0	1	2	3	4
y	5	3	-1	-7	-15

5 We wish to determine the **maximum** number of pieces into which a pizza can be cut using n cuts across it.

For example, for $n = 1$ we have which has 2 pieces

for $n = 3$ we have which has 7 pieces.

a Copy and complete:

Number of cuts, n	0	1	2	3	4	5
Maximum number of pieces, P_n						

b Complete the Δ_1 and Δ_2 rows. Hence determine a quadratic formula for P_n.

c For a huge pizza with 12 cuts across it, find the maximum number of pieces which can result.

F SIMULTANEOUS EQUATIONS

Consider the graphs of a quadratic function and a linear function on the same set of axes.

There are three possible scenarios for intersection:

cutting
(2 points of intersection)

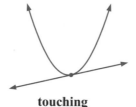

touching
(1 point of intersection)

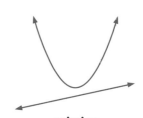

missing
(no points of intersection)

If the graphs meet, the coordinates of the point(s) of intersection of the graphs can be found by solving the two equations **simultaneously**.

Example 21

◀) **Self Tutor**

Find the coordinates of the point(s) of intersection of the graphs with equations
$y = x^2 - x - 18$ and $y = x - 3$.

$y = x^2 - x - 18$ meets $y = x - 3$ where

$$x^2 - x - 18 = x - 3$$
$$\therefore \quad x^2 - 2x - 15 = 0 \qquad \{\text{RHS} = 0\}$$
$$\therefore \quad (x - 5)(x + 3) = 0 \qquad \{\text{factorising}\}$$
$$\therefore \quad x = 5 \text{ or } -3$$

Substituting into $y = x - 3$, when $x = 5$, $y = 2$ and when $x = -3$, $y = -6$.

$\therefore$ the graphs meet at $(5, 2)$ and $(-3, -6)$.

EXERCISE 3F

1 Find the coordinates of the point(s) of intersection of:

   a $y = x^2 - 2x + 8$ and $y = x + 6$ **b** $y = -x^2 + 3x + 9$ and $y = 2x - 3$

   c $y = x^2 - 4x + 3$ and $y = 2x - 6$ **d** $y = -x^2 + 4x - 7$ and $y = 5x - 4$

Example 22

◀) **Self Tutor**

$y = 2x + k$ is a tangent to $y = 2x^2 - 3x + 4$. Find k.

$y = 2x + k$ meets $y = 2x^2 - 3x + 4$ where
$$2x^2 - 3x + 4 = 2x + k$$
$$\therefore \quad 2x^2 - 5x + (4 - k) = 0$$

Since the graphs touch, this quadratic has $\Delta = 0$
$$\therefore \quad (-5)^2 - 4(2)(4 - k) = 0$$
$$\therefore \quad 25 - 8(4 - k) = 0$$
$$\therefore \quad 25 - 32 + 8k = 0$$
$$\therefore \quad 8k = 7$$
$$\therefore \quad k = \tfrac{7}{8}$$

A line which is a *tangent* to a quadratic will *touch* the curve.

2 For which value of c is the line $y = 3x + c$ a tangent to the parabola with equation $y = x^2 - 5x + 7$?

3 Find the values of m for which the lines $y = mx - 2$ are tangents to the curve with equation $y = x^2 - 4x + 2$.

4 Find the gradients of the lines with y-intercept 1 that are tangents to the curve $y = 3x^2 + 5x + 4$.

5 **a** For what values of c do the lines $y = x + c$ never meet the parabola with equation $y = 2x^2 - 3x - 7$?

   b Choose one of the values of c found in part **a** above. Illustrate with a sketch that these graphs never meet.

6 Consider the curve $y = x^2 + 4x - 1$ and the line $y = 2x + c$. Find the values of c for which the line:

  a meets the curve twice

  b is a tangent to the curve

  c does not meet the curve.

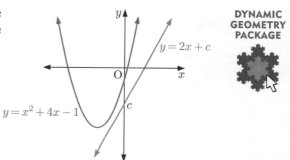

DYNAMIC GEOMETRY PACKAGE

7 Consider the curve $y = -x^2 + 3x - 6$ and the line $y = mx - 2$. Find the values of m for which the line:

  a meets the curve twice

  b is a tangent to the curve

  c does not meet the curve.

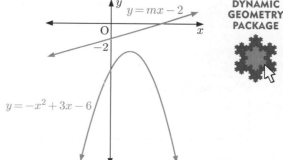

DYNAMIC GEOMETRY PACKAGE

8

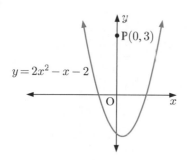

Show that any linear function passing through $P(0, 3)$ will meet the curve $y = 2x^2 - x - 2$ twice.

G   PROBLEM SOLVING WITH QUADRATICS

Some real world problems can be solved using a quadratic equation. We are generally only interested in any **real solutions** which result.

Any answer we obtain must be checked to see if it is reasonable. For example:

- if we are finding a length then it must be positive and we reject any negative solutions
- if we are finding 'how many people are present' then the answer must be a positive integer.

We employ the following general problem solving method:

Step 1: If the information is given in words, translate it into algebra using a variable such as x. Be sure to define what x represents, and include units if appropriate. Write down the resulting equation.

Step 2: Solve the equation by a suitable method.

Step 3: Examine the solutions carefully to see if they are acceptable.

Step 4: Give your answer in a sentence, making sure you answer the question.

Example 23   ◄ᴅ) **Self Tutor**

A rectangle has length 3 cm longer than its width, and its area is 42 cm². Find the width of the rectangle.

If the width is x cm then the length is $(x + 3)$ cm.

$\therefore \quad x(x + 3) = 42 \quad$ {equating areas}

$\therefore \quad x^2 + 3x - 42 = 0$

$\therefore \quad x = \dfrac{-3 \pm \sqrt{3^2 - 4(1)(-42)}}{2}$

$\therefore \quad x = \dfrac{-3 \pm \sqrt{177}}{2}$

$\therefore \quad x \approx -8.15 \quad \text{or} \quad 5.15$

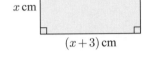

We reject the negative solution as lengths are positive.

The width is about 5.15 cm.

EXERCISE 3G

1 Two integers differ by 12, and the sum of their squares is 74. Find the integers.

2 The sum of a number and its reciprocal is $\frac{26}{5}$. Find the number.

3 The product of two consecutive even numbers is 360. Find the numbers.

4 The number of diagonals of an n-sided polygon is given by the formula $D = \dfrac{n}{2}(n - 3)$.
    A polygon has 90 diagonals. How many sides does it have?

5 The length of a rectangle is 4 cm longer than its width. The rectangle has area 26 cm². Find its width.

6 A rectangular box has a square base. Its height is 1 cm longer than its base side length. The total surface area of the box is 240 cm².
    Suppose the sides of the base are x cm long.

   a Show that the total surface area is given by $A = 6x^2 + 4x$ cm².

   b Find the dimensions of the box.

7

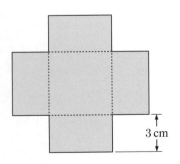

An open box can hold 80 cm³. It is made from a square piece of tinplate with 3 cm squares cut from each of its 4 corners. Find the dimensions of the original piece of tinplate.

Example 24

◀⬤ **Self Tutor**

Is it possible to bend a 12 cm length of wire to form the perpendicular sides of a right angled triangle with area 20 cm^2?

Suppose the wire is bent x cm from one end.

The area $A = \frac{1}{2}x(12 - x)$

$\therefore \quad \frac{1}{2}x(12 - x) = 20$

$\therefore \quad x(12 - x) = 40$

$\therefore \quad 12x - x^2 - 40 = 0$

$\therefore \quad x^2 - 12x + 40 = 0$

becomes

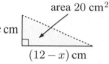

Now $\Delta = (-12)^2 - 4(1)(40)$

$\qquad = -16$ which is < 0

There are no real solutions, indicating this situation is **impossible**.

8 Is it possible to bend a 20 cm length of wire into a rectangle with area 30 cm^2?

9 The rectangle ABCD is divided into a square and a smaller rectangle by [XY] which is parallel to its shorter sides.

The smaller rectangle BCXY is *similar* to the original rectangle, so rectangle ABCD is a **golden rectangle**.

The ratio $\dfrac{AB}{AD}$ is called the **golden ratio**.

Show that the golden ratio is $\dfrac{1 + \sqrt{5}}{2}$.

Hint: Let   AB $= x$ units   and   AD $= 1$ unit.

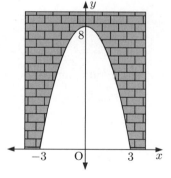

10 A truck carrying a wide load needs to pass through the parabolic tunnel shown. The units are metres.

The truck is 5 m high and 4 m wide.

a Find the quadratic function which describes the shape of the tunnel.

b Determine whether the truck will fit.

11 A stone is thrown into the air from the top of a cliff 60 m above sea level. The stone reaches a maximum height of 80 m above sea level after 2 seconds.

a Find the quadratic function which describes the stone's height above sea level.

b Find the stone's height above sea level after 3 seconds.

c How long will it take for the stone to hit the water?

12 Answer the **Opening Problem** on page **48**.

H   QUADRATIC OPTIMISATION

The process of finding a maximum or minimum value is called **optimisation**.

For the quadratic $y = ax^2 + bx + c$, we have seen that the vertex has x-coordinate $-\dfrac{b}{2a}$.

- If $a > 0$, the **minimum** value of y occurs at $x = -\dfrac{b}{2a}$.

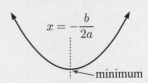

- If $a < 0$, the **maximum** value of y occurs at $x = -\dfrac{b}{2a}$.

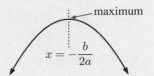

Example 25   ◀) Self Tutor

Find the maximum or minimum value of the following quadratics, and the corresponding value of x:

a $y = x^2 + x - 3$ **b** $y = 3 + 3x - 2x^2$

a $y = x^2 + x - 3$ has
$a = 1$, $b = 1$, and $c = -3$.

Since $a > 0$, the shape is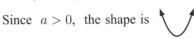

The minimum value occurs

when $x = \dfrac{-b}{2a} = -\dfrac{1}{2}$

and $y = (-\dfrac{1}{2})^2 + (-\dfrac{1}{2}) - 3 = -3\dfrac{1}{4}$

So, the minimum value of y is $-3\dfrac{1}{4}$,

occurring when $x = -\dfrac{1}{2}$.

b $y = -2x^2 + 3x + 3$ has
$a = -2$, $b = 3$, and $c = 3$.

Since $a < 0$, the shape is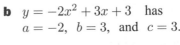

The maximum value occurs

when $x = \dfrac{-b}{2a} = \dfrac{-3}{-4} = \dfrac{3}{4}$

and $y = -2(\dfrac{3}{4})^2 + 3(\dfrac{3}{4}) + 3 = 4\dfrac{1}{8}$

So, the maximum value of y is $4\dfrac{1}{8}$,

occurring when $x = \dfrac{3}{4}$.

EXERCISE 3H

1 Find the maximum or minimum value for each quadratic, and the corresponding value of x:

  a $y = x^2 - 2x$ **b** $y = 7 - 2x - x^2$ **c** $y = 8 + 2x - 3x^2$

  d $y = 2x^2 + x - 1$ **e** $y = 4x^2 - x + 5$ **f** $y = 7x - 2x^2$

2 The profit in manufacturing x refrigerators per day, is given by $P = -3x^2 + 240x - 800$ pounds.

  a How many refrigerators should be made each day to maximise the total profit?

  b What is the maximum profit?

Example 26
🔊 **Self Tutor**

A gardener has 40 m of fencing to enclose a rectangular garden plot, where one side is an existing brick wall. Suppose the two new equal sides are x m long.

a Show that the area enclosed is given by $A = x(40 - 2x)$ m^2.

b Find the dimensions of the garden of maximum area.

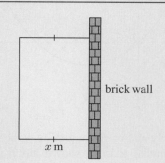

brick wall

x m

a Side [XY] has length $(40 - 2x)$ m.

Now, area $=$ length $\times$ width

$\therefore$ $A = x(40 - 2x)$ m^2

b $A = 0$ when $x = 0$ or 20.

The vertex of the function lies midway between these values, so $x = 10$.

Since $a < 0$, the shape is

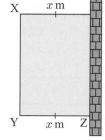

$\therefore$ the area is maximised when $YZ = 10$ m and $XY = 20$ m.

---

3 A rectangular plot is enclosed by 200 m of fencing and has an area of A square metres. Show that:

a $A = 100x - x^2$ where x m is the length of one of its sides

b the area is maximised if the rectangle is a square.

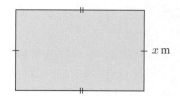

x m

4 Three sides of a rectangular paddock are to be fenced, the fourth side being an existing straight water drain. If 1000 m of fencing is available, what dimensions should be used for the paddock to maximise its area?

5 1800 m of fencing is available to fence six identical pens as shown in the diagram.

a Explain why $9x + 8y = 1800$.

b Show that the area of each pen is given by $A = -\frac{9}{8}x^2 + 225x$ m^2.

c If the area enclosed is to be maximised, what are the dimensions of each pen?

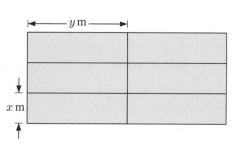

y m

x m

6 500 m of fencing is available to make 4 rectangular pens of identical shape. Find the dimensions that maximise the area of each pen if the plan is:

a

b

7

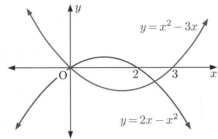

The graphs of $y = x^2 - 3x$ and $y = 2x - x^2$ are illustrated.

a Show that the graphs meet where $x = 0$ and $x = 2\frac{1}{2}$.

b Find the maximum vertical separation between the curves for $0 \leqslant x \leqslant 2\frac{1}{2}$.

8 Infinitely many rectangles may be inscribed within the right angled triangle shown alongside. One of them is illustrated.

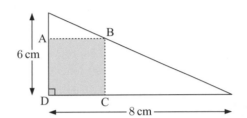

a Let $AB = x$ cm and $BC = y$ cm. Use similar triangles to find y in terms of x.

b Find the dimensions of rectangle ABCD of maximum area.

Review set 3A

1 Consider the quadratic $y = -2(x + 2)(x - 1)$.

  a State the x-intercepts.   **b** State the equation of the axis of symmetry.

  c Find the y-intercept.   **d** Find the coordinates of the vertex.

  e Sketch the function.

2 Solve the following equations, giving exact answers:

  a $3x^2 - 12x = 0$ **b** $3x^2 - x - 10 = 0$ **c** $x^2 - 11x = 60$

3 Solve using the quadratic formula:

  a $x^2 + 5x + 3 = 0$ **b** $3x^2 + 11x - 2 = 0$

4 Find the sum and product of the roots of:

  a $x^2 + 8x - 11 = 0$ **b** $5x^2 - 15x + 7 = 0$

5 Use the vertex, axis of symmetry, and y-intercept to graph:

  a $y = (x - 2)^2 - 4$ **b** $y = -\frac{1}{2}(x + 4)^2 + 6$

6 Find, in the form $y = ax^2 + bx + c$, the equation of the quadratic whose graph:

  a touches the x-axis at 4 and passes through $(2, 12)$

  b has vertex $(-4, 1)$ and passes through $(1, 11)$.

7 Find the maximum or minimum value of $y = -2x^2 + 4x + 3$, and the value of x at which this occurs.

8 Find the points of intersection of $y = x^2 - 3x$ and $y = 3x^2 - 5x - 24$.

9 For what values of k does the graph of $y = -2x^2 + 5x + k$ not cut the x-axis?

10 Find the values of m for which $2x^2 - 3x + m = 0$ has:

  a a repeated root   **b** two distinct real roots   **c** no real roots.

11 The sum of a number and its reciprocal is $2\frac{1}{30}$. Find the number.

12 Show that no line with a y-intercept of 10 will ever be tangential to the curve with equation $y = 3x^2 + 7x - 2$.

13 **a** Write the quadratic $y = 2x^2 + 4x - 3$ in the form $y = a(x - h)^2 + k$.
   b Hence, sketch the graph of the quadratic.

14 Find the equation of the quadratic with graph:

a
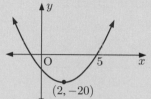

b
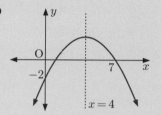

c
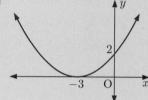

15 When Annie hits a softball, the height of the ball above the ground after t seconds is given by $h = -4.9t^2 + 19.6t + 1.4$ metres. Find the maximum height reached by the ball.

Review set 3B

1 Consider the quadratic $y = \frac{1}{2}(x - 2)^2 - 4$.
   a State the equation of the axis of symmetry.   **b** Find the coordinates of the vertex.
   c Find the y-intercept.   **d** Sketch the function.

2 Solve the following equations:
   a $x^2 - 5x - 3 = 0$ **b** $2x^2 - 7x - 3 = 0$

3 By using the discriminant only, state the nature of the solutions of:
   a $x^2 - 8x + 16 = 0$ **b** $2x^2 - x - 5 = 0$ **c** $3x^2 + 5x + 3 = 0$

4 The roots of $3x^2 - x + 7 = 0$ are α and β. Find the simplest quadratic equation with roots $\frac{1}{\alpha}$ and $\frac{1}{\beta}$.

5 Consider the quadratic $y = -3x^2 + 8x + 7$. Find the equation of the axis of symmetry, and the coordinates of the vertex.

6 Use the discriminant only to find the relationship between the graph and the x-axis for:
   a $y = 2x^2 + 3x - 7$ **b** $y = -3x^2 - 7x + 4$

7 Determine whether each quadratic is positive definite, negative definite, or neither:
   a $y = -2x^2 + 3x + 2$ **b** $y = 3x^2 + x + 11$

8 Find the equation of the quadratic with vertex $(2, 25)$ and y-intercept 1.

9 Consider the quadratic $y = 2x^2 + 4x - 1$.

   a State the axis of symmetry.   **b** Find the coordinates of the vertex.

   c Find the axes intercepts.   **d** Hence sketch the function.

10 **a** For what values of c do the lines with equations $y = 3x + c$ intersect the parabola $y = x^2 + x - 5$ in two distinct points?

   b Choose one such value of c and find the points of intersection in this case.

11 **a** Find the equation of the quadratic illustrated.

   b Hence find its vertex and axis of symmetry.

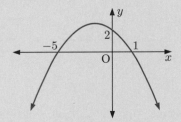

12 Find the maximum or minimum value of each quadratic, and the corresponding value of x:

   a $y = 3x^2 + 4x + 7$ **b** $y = -2x^2 - 5x + 2$

13

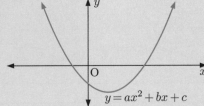

Consider the graph of $y = ax^2 + bx + c$ alongside. Determine the sign of:

   a a **b** b **c** c **d** Δ

Give reasons for your answers.

14 For each of the following quadratics:

   i Write the quadratic in completed square form.

   ii Write the quadratic in factored form.

   iii Sketch the graph of the quadratic, identifying its axes intercepts, vertex, and axis of symmetry.

   a $y = x^2 + 4x + 3$ **b** $y = x^2 + 2x - 3$

   c $y = 2x^2 - 8x - 10$ **d** $y = -x^2 + 6x + 7$

15 600 m of fencing is used to construct 6 rectangular animal pens as shown.

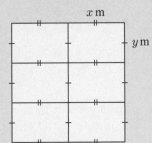

   a Show that the area A of each pen is $A = x\left(\dfrac{600 - 8x}{9}\right)$ m^2.

   b Find the dimensions of each pen so that it has the maximum possible area.

   c What is the area of each pen in this case?

4

Relations and functions

Contents:

Opening problem

The charges for parking a car in a short-term car park at an airport are shown in the table and graph below. The total charge is *dependent* on the length of time t the car is parked.

Car park charges	
Time t (hours)	*Charge*
$0 < t \leqslant 1$	£5.00
$1 < t \leqslant 2$	£9.00
$2 < t \leqslant 3$	£11.00
$3 < t \leqslant 6$	£13.00
$6 < t \leqslant 9$	£18.00
$9 < t \leqslant 12$	£22.00
$12 < t \leqslant 24$	£28.00

Things to think about:

a What values of *time* are illustrated in the graph?

b What are the possible charges?

c What feature of the graph ensures that there is only one charge for any given time?

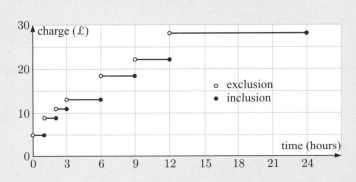

In the **Opening Problem**, we have a relationship between two variables *time* and *charge*. The schedule of charges is an example of a **relation**.

In this Chapter we will study relations and also **functions**, which are a special type of relation.

A   RELATIONS AND FUNCTIONS

A **relation** is any set of points which connect two variables.

A relation is often expressed in the form of an **equation** connecting the **variables** x and y.

For example, $y = x + 3$ and $x = y^2$ are the equations of two relations. Each equation generates a set of ordered pairs, which we can graph:

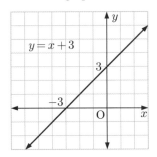

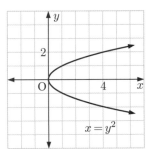

However, a relation may not be able to be defined by an equation. Below are two examples which show this:

(1)

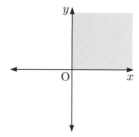

The set of all points in the first quadrant is the relation $x > 0$, $y > 0$.

(2)

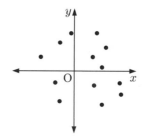

These 13 points form a relation.

FUNCTIONS

A **function** is a relation in which no two different ordered pairs have the same x-coordinate or first component.

We can see from this definition that a function is a special type of relation.

Every function is a relation, but not every relation is a function.

ALGEBRAIC TEST FOR FUNCTIONS

Suppose a relation is given as an equation. If the substitution of any value for x results in at most one value of y, then the relation is a function.

For example:

• $y = 3x - 1$ is a function, since for any value of x there is only one corresponding value of y

• $x = y^2$ is not a function, since if $x = 4$ then $y = \pm 2$.

GEOMETRIC TEST OR VERTICAL LINE TEST FOR FUNCTIONS

Suppose we draw all possible vertical lines on the graph of a relation.

• If each line cuts the graph at most once, then the relation is a function.

• If at least one line cuts the graph more than once, then the relation is not a function.

Example 1

◀) **Self Tutor**

Which of the following relations are functions?

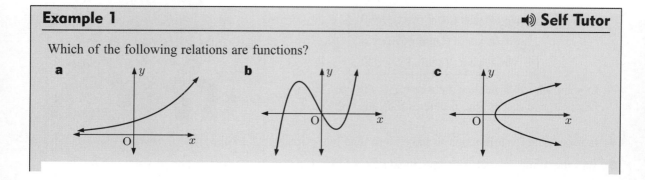

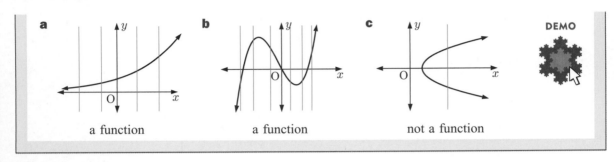

a a function   **b** a function   **c** not a function

GRAPHICAL NOTE

- If a graph contains a small **open circle** such as ———∘——— , this point is **not included**.
- If a graph contains a small **filled-in circle** such as ———• , this point is **included**.
- If a graph contains an **arrowhead** at an end such as ———▶ , then the graph continues indefinitely in that general direction, or the shape may repeat as it has done previously.

EXERCISE 4A

1 Use algebraic methods to decide whether these relations are functions. Explain your answer.

    a $y = x^2 - 9$ **b** $x + y = 9$ **c** $x^2 + y^2 = 9$

2 Use the vertical line test to determine which of the following relations are functions:

a 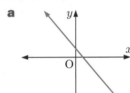   **b** 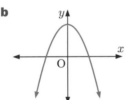   **c** 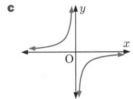   **d**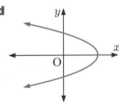

e 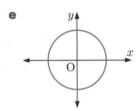   **f** 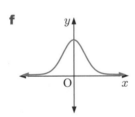   **g** 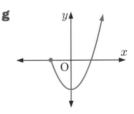   **h**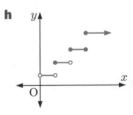

3 The managers of a new amusement park are discussing the schedule of ticket prices. Maurice suggests the following schedule:

Age	Cost
0 - 2 years (infants)	£0
2 - 16 years (children)	£20
16+ years (adults)	£30

Explain why this relation between *age* and *cost* is not a function, and discuss the problems that this will cause.

4 Is it possible for a function to have more than one y-intercept? Explain your answer.

5 Will the graph of a straight line always be a function? Give evidence to support your answer.

6 Consider the relation $y^2 = x$.

a Copy and complete the following table of values for the relation:

GRAPHING PACKAGE

x							
y	-3	-2	-1	0	1	2	3

b Hence sketch the curve $y^2 = x$.

c Discuss the similarities and differences between the curves $y^2 = x$ and $y = x^2$. You should include whether each curve is a function, and the vertex and axis of symmetry of each. You may consider what transformation maps one curve onto the other.

d Using $y^2 = x$, we can write $y = \pm\sqrt{x}$.

   i What part of the graph of $y^2 = x$ corresponds to $y = \sqrt{x}$?

   ii Is $y = \sqrt{x}$ a function? Explain your answer.

Discussion

- Is the relation describing the car park charges in the **Opening Problem** a function?
- If we know the *time* somebody parked for, can we determine the exact *cost* of parking?
- If we know the amount somebody pays, can we determine the exact time they have parked for?

B ┃ FUNCTION NOTATION

Function machines are sometimes used to illustrate how functions behave.

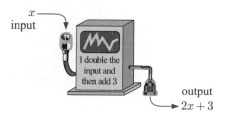

If 4 is the input fed into the machine, the output is $2(4) + 3 = 11$.

The above 'machine' has been programmed to perform a particular function. If we use f to represent that particular function, we can write:

f is the function that will convert x into $2x + 3$.

So, f would convert $\quad 2$ into $\quad 2(2) + 3 = 7 \quad$ and
$\qquad\qquad\qquad -4$ into $\quad 2(-4) + 3 = -5$.

This function can be written as:

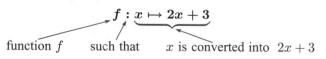

$$f : x \mapsto 2x + 3$$

function f such that x is converted into $2x + 3$

$f(x)$ is read as "f of x".

Two other equivalent forms we use are $\quad f(x) = 2x + 3 \quad$ and $\quad y = 2x + 3$.

$f(x)$ is the value of y for a given value of x, so $\quad y = f(x)$.

f is the function which converts x into $f(x)$, so we write
$f : x \mapsto f(x)$.

$y = f(x)$ is sometimes called the **function value** or **image** of x.

For $f(x) = 2x + 3$:

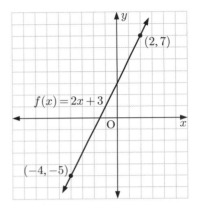

- $f(2) = 2(2) + 3 = 7$

  $\therefore$ the point $(2, 7)$ lies on the graph of the function.

- $f(-4) = 2(-4) + 3 = -5$

  $\therefore$ the point $(-4, -5)$ also lies on the graph.

Example 2   ◀ᴗ **Self Tutor**

If $f : x \mapsto 2x^2 - 3x$, find the value of:

  a $f(5)$ **b** $f(-4)$

$f(x) = 2x^2 - 3x$

  a $f(5) = 2(5)^2 - 3(5)$ {replacing x with (5)}

          $= 2 \times 25 - 15$

          $= 35$

  b $f(-4) = 2(-4)^2 - 3(-4)$ {replacing x with (-4)}

            $= 2(16) + 12$

            $= 44$

We use brackets to help avoid confusion with minus and negative signs.

EXERCISE 4B

1 If $f(x) = 3x - x^2 + 2$, find the value of:

  a $f(0)$ **b** $f(3)$ **c** $f(-3)$ **d** $f(-7)$ **e** $f(\frac{3}{2})$

2 If $g : x \mapsto x - \dfrac{4}{x}$, find the value of:

  a $g(1)$ **b** $g(4)$ **c** $g(-1)$ **d** $g(-4)$ **e** $g(-\frac{1}{2})$

3 The graph of $y = f(x)$ is shown alongside.

  a Find:

    i $f(2)$ **ii** $f(3)$

  b Find the value of x such that $f(x) = 4$.

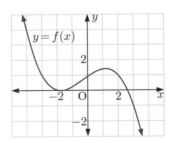

4 Suppose $G(x) = \dfrac{2x + 3}{x - 4}$.

  a Evaluate: **i** $G(2)$ **ii** $G(0)$ **iii** $G(-\frac{1}{2})$

  b Find a value of x such that $G(x)$ does not exist.

  c Find x such that $G(x) = -3$.

Example 3
🔊 **Self Tutor**

If $f(x) = 5 - x - x^2$,   find in simplest form:

  a $f(-x)$ **b** $f(x + 2)$

  a $f(-x) = 5 - (-x) - (-x)^2$ {replacing x with $(-x)$}

             $= 5 + x - x^2$

  b $f(x + 2) = 5 - (x + 2) - (x + 2)^2$ {replacing x with $(x + 2)$}

                     $= 5 - x - 2 - [x^2 + 4x + 4]$

                     $= 3 - x - x^2 - 4x - 4$

                     $= -x^2 - 5x - 1$

5 If $f(x) = 7 - 3x$,   find in simplest form:

  a $f(a)$ **b** $f(-a)$ **c** $f(a + 3)$

  d $f(2a)$ **e** $f(x + 2)$ **f** $f(x + h)$

6 If $F(x) = 2x^2 + 3x - 1$,   find in simplest form:

  a $F(x + 4)$ **b** $F(2 - x)$ **c** $F(-x)$

  d $F(x^2)$ **e** $F(3x)$ **f** $F(x + h)$

7 f represents a function. Explain the difference in meaning between f and $f(x)$.

8 On the same set of axes, draw the graphs of three different functions $f(x)$ such that $f(2) = 1$ and $f(5) = 3$.

9 Find a linear function $f(x) = ax + b$ for which $f(2) = 1$ and $f(-3) = 11$.

10 Samantha is filling her car with petrol. The amount of petrol in the tank after t minutes is given by $P(t) = 5 + 10t$ litres.

  a Find $P(3)$, and interpret your answer.

  b Find t when $P(t) = 50$, and explain what this represents.

  c How many litres of petrol were in the tank when Samantha started to fill it?

11 For a hot air balloon ride, the function $H(t)$ gives the height of the balloon after t minutes. Its graph is shown alongside.

  a Find $H(30)$, and explain what your answer means.

  b Find the values of t such that $H(t) = 600$. Interpret your answer.

  c For what values of t was the height of the balloon recorded?

  d What range of heights was recorded for the balloon?

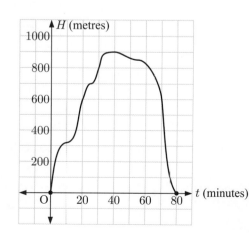

12 The value of a photocopier t years after purchase is given by
$V(t) = 9000 - 900t$ pounds.

  a Find $V(4)$, and state what $V(4)$ means.

  b Find t when $V(t) = 3600$, and explain what this means.

  c Find the original purchase price of the photocopier.

  d For what values of t is it reasonable to use this function?

C | DOMAIN AND RANGE

We have seen that a relation is a set of points which connects two
variables.

> The **domain** of a relation is the set of values which the variable
> on the horizontal axis can take. This variable is usually x.
>
> The **range** of a relation is the set of values which the variable
> on the vertical axis can take. This variable is usually y.

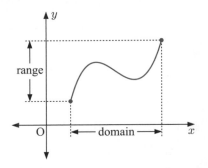

The domain and range of a relation can be described using **set notation**, **interval notation**, or a **number
line graph**.

SET AND INTERVAL NOTATION

> An **interval** is a connected subset of the number line $\mathbb{R}$.
>
> An interval is **closed** if *both* of its endpoints are included.
>
> An interval is **open** if *both* of its endpoints are *not* included.

For $x \in \mathbb{R}$, we commonly use the following notation to concisely write intervals:

$[a, b]$ represents the closed interval $\{x : a \leqslant x \leqslant b\}$

$[a, b)$ represents the interval $\{x : a \leqslant x < b\}$

$(a, b]$ represents the interval $\{x : a < x \leqslant b\}$

(a, b) represents the open interval $\{x : a < x < b\}$

An interval which extends to infinity has no defined endpoint. So, for $\{x : x \geqslant a\}$ we write $[a, \infty)$.

You might notice that $a \leqslant x \leqslant b$ means both $x \geqslant a$ *and* $x \leqslant b$. It is therefore a short way of writing
$x \geqslant a \cap x \leqslant b$.

We use the "or" symbol $\cup$ more frequently, since it helps us describe numbers *outside* a particular interval.

 $x \in (-\infty, a) \cup (b, \infty)$

The following table gives examples of set and interval notation and its use:

Set notation	Interval notation	Number line graph	Meaning
$\{x : x \geqslant 3\}$	$x \in [3, \infty)$		the set of all x such that x is greater than or equal to 3
$\{x : x < 2\}$	$x \in (-\infty, 2)$		the set of all x such that x is less than 2
$\{x : -2 < x \leqslant 1\}$	$x \in (-2, 1]$		the set of all x such that x is between -2 and 1, including 1
$\{x : x \leqslant 0 \ \cup \ x > 4\}$	$x \in (-\infty, 0] \cup (4, \infty)$		the set of all x such that x is less than or equal to 0, or greater than 4

EXERCISE 4C.1

1 Copy and complete:

Set notation	Interval notation	Number line graph	Meaning
$\{x : x < 4\}$			
	$x \in (-\infty, 9)$		
			the set of all x such that x is between $\frac{2}{5}$ and $\frac{8}{5}$ inclusive
$\{x : x \geqslant 17\}$			
	$x \in (0, 4) \cup (6, \infty)$		
			the set of all x such that x is less than 5 or greater than or equal to 11

2 Describe using interval notation:

a

b

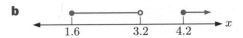

DOMAIN AND RANGE OF FUNCTIONS

To find the domain and range of a function, we can observe its graph.

For example:

(1) Consider again the car park charges in the **Opening Problem**.

The function is defined for all times t such that $0 < t \leqslant 24$.

$\therefore$ the domain is $\{t : 0 < t \leqslant 24\}$.

The possible charges are £5, £9, £11, £13, £18, £22, and £28.

$\therefore$ the range is
$\{5, 9, 11, 13, 18, 22, 28\}$.

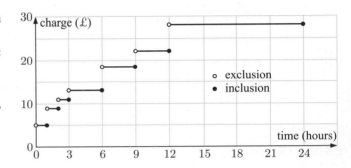

(2)

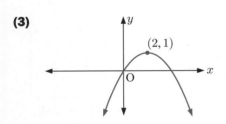

All values of $x \geqslant -1$ are included,
so the domain is $\{x : x \geqslant -1\}$ or $x \in [-1, \infty)$.

All values of $y \geqslant -3$ are included,
so the range is $\{y : y \geqslant -3\}$ or $y \in [-3, \infty)$.

(3)

x can take any value,
so the domain is
  $\{x \in \mathbb{R}\}$ or $x \in \mathbb{R}$.

y cannot be > 1,
so the range is
  $\{y : y \leqslant 1\}$ or $y \in (-\infty, 1]$.

$x \in \mathbb{R}$ means
"x can be any
real number".

(4)

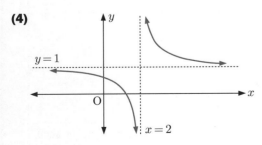

x can take all values except 2,
so the domain is $\{x : x \neq 2\}$ or $x \neq 2$.

y can take all values except 1,
so the range is $\{y : y \neq 1\}$ or $y \neq 1$.

> To fully describe a function, we need both a rule *and* a domain.

For example, we can specify $f(x) = x^2$ where $x \geqslant 0$.

If a domain is not specified, we use the **natural domain**, which is the largest part of $\mathbb{R}$ for which $f(x)$ is defined.

Some examples of natural domains are shown in the table opposite.

DOMAIN
AND RANGE

$f(x)$	Natural domain
x^2	$x \in \mathbb{R}$
$\sqrt{x}$	$x \geqslant 0$
$\dfrac{1}{x}$	$x \neq 0$
$\dfrac{1}{\sqrt{x}}$	$x > 0$

Click on the icon to obtain software for finding the natural domain and range of different functions.

Example 4
◀) **Self Tutor**

For each of the following graphs, state the domain and range:

a

b

a Domain is $\{x : x \leqslant 8\}$

Range is $\{y : y \geqslant -2\}$

b Domain is $\{x \in \mathbb{R}\}$

Range is $\{y : y \geqslant -1\}$

EXERCISE 4C.2

1 A driver who exceeds the speed limit receives demerit points as shown in the table.

  a Draw a graph to display this information.

  b Find the domain and range of the relation.

Amount over speed limit (x km h^{-1})	Demerit points (y)
$0 < x < 10$	2
$10 \leqslant x < 20$	3
$20 \leqslant x < 30$	5
$30 \leqslant x < 45$	7
$x \geqslant 45$	9

2 This graph shows the temperature in Barcelona over a 30 minute period as the wind shifts.

  a Explain why a temperature graph like this must be a function.

  b Find the domain and range of the function.

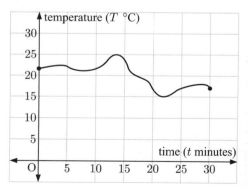

3 For each of the following graphs, find the domain and range:

a
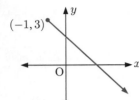

b
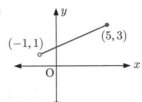

c
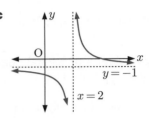

d
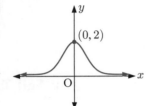

e
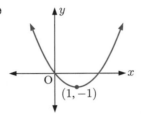

f
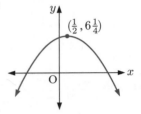

g
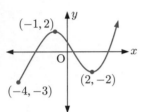

h
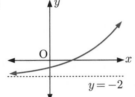

i
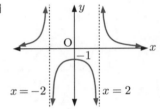

4 Consider the graph of $y = f(x)$ alongside.
Decide whether each statement is true or false:

  a -5 is in the domain of f.

  b 2 is in the range of f.

  c 9 is in the range of f.

  d $\sqrt{2}$ is in the domain of f.

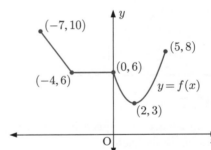

5 Graph each of the following quadratic functions, and hence find their domain and range:

  a $y = x^2 - 7x + 10$ **b** $f : x \mapsto 5x - 3x^2$

Example 5   ◀ೃ **Self Tutor**

State the domain and range of each of the following functions:

  a $f(x) = \sqrt{x - 5}$ **b** $f(x) = \dfrac{1}{x - 5}$ **c** $f(x) = \dfrac{1}{\sqrt{x - 5}}$

a $\sqrt{x - 5}$ is defined when $x - 5 \geqslant 0$
                       $\therefore \ x \geqslant 5$

$\therefore$ the domain is $\{x : x \geqslant 5\}$.
A square root cannot be negative.

$\therefore$ the range is $\{y : y \geqslant 0\}$.

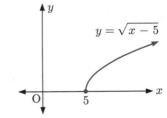

b $\dfrac{1}{x-5}$ is defined when $x - 5 \neq 0$

$$\therefore \quad x \neq 5$$

$\therefore$ the domain is $\{x : x \neq 5\}$.

No matter how large or small x is,
$y = f(x)$ is never zero.

$\therefore$ the range is $\{y : y \neq 0\}$.

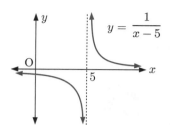

c $\dfrac{1}{\sqrt{x-5}}$ is defined when $x - 5 > 0$

$$\therefore \quad x > 5$$

$\therefore$ the domain is $\{x : x > 5\}$.

$y = f(x)$ is always positive and never zero.

$\therefore$ the range is $\{y : y > 0\}$.

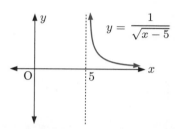

6 State the values of x for which $f(x)$ is defined, and hence state the domain of the function.

a $f(x) = \sqrt{x + 6}$ **b** $f : x \mapsto \dfrac{1}{x^2}$ **c** $f(x) = \dfrac{-7}{\sqrt{3 - 2x}}$

7 Consider the function $f(x) = \sqrt{x}$.

a State the values of x for which $f(x)$ is defined.

b Find: **i** $f(0)$ **ii** $f(1)$ **iii** $f(4)$

c Sketch the graph of the function.

d Find the domain and range of the function.

DOMAIN AND RANGE

8 Use technology to help sketch graphs of the following functions. Find the domain and range of each.

a $f(x) = \sqrt{x - 2}$ **b** $f : x \mapsto \dfrac{1}{x^2}$ **c** $f : x \mapsto \sqrt{4 - x}$

d $f(x) = \sqrt{x^2 + 4}$ **e** $f(x) = \sqrt{x^2 - 4}$ **f** $f : x \mapsto x + \dfrac{1}{x}$

g $y = \dfrac{x + 4}{x - 2}$ **h** $y = x^3 - 3x^2 - 9x + 10$ **i** $f : x \mapsto \dfrac{3x - 9}{x^2 - x - 2}$

j $y = x^2 + x^{-2}$ **k** $y = x^3 + \dfrac{1}{x^3}$ **l** $f : x \mapsto x^4 + 4x^3 - 16x + 3$

Investigation 1   Fluid filling functions

When water is added at a **constant rate** to a cylindrical container, the depth of water in the container is a linear function of time. This is because the volume of water added is directly proportional to the time taken to add it. If the water was *not* added at a constant rate, depth of water over time would *not* be a linear function.

The linear depth-time graph for a cylindrical container is shown alongside.

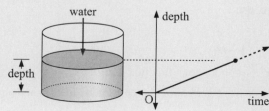

In this Investigation we explore the changes in the graph for different shaped containers such as a conical vase.

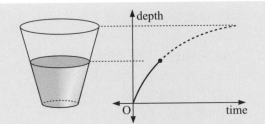

DEMO

What to do:

1 By examining the shape of each container, predict the depth-time graph when water is added at a constant rate.

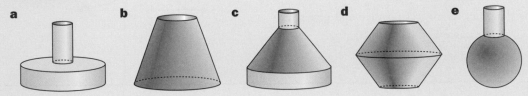

2 Use the water filling demonstration to check your answers to question **1**.

3 Write a brief report on the connection between the shape of a vessel and the corresponding shape of its depth-time graph. First examine cylindrical containers, then conical, then other shapes.

4 Suggest containers which would have the following depth-time graphs:

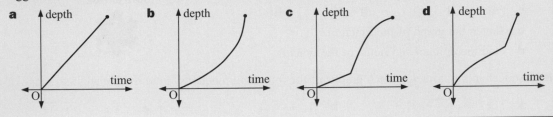

D | TRANSFORMATIONS

Different parts of a function's equation affect the properties of its graph. If we understand what part of the function controls a particular feature, we can learn how to **transform** the function.

The transformations we will study in this course are **translations** and **dilations**.

TRANSLATIONS $y = f(x) + a$ AND $y = f(x - b)$

Investigation 2   **Translations**

What to do:

GRAPHING PACKAGE

1 **a** If $f(x) = x^3$, write down:

   i $f(x) + 2$ **ii** $f(x) - 3$ **iii** $f(x) + 6$

   b Graph all four functions on the same set of axes.

   c What effect does the constant a have when $y = f(x)$ is transformed to $y = f(x) + a$?

2   **a**   For $f(x) = x^2$, find in simplest form:

   i $f(x - 2)$ **ii** $f(x + 1)$ **iii** $f(x - 5)$

   b   Graph all four functions on the same set of axes.

   c   What effect does the constant b have when $y = f(x)$ is transformed to $y = f(x - b)$?

- For $y = f(x) + a$, the effect of a is to **translate** the graph **vertically** through a units.
  ‣ If $a > 0$ it moves **upwards**.   ‣ If $a < 0$ it moves **downwards**.
- For $y = f(x - b)$, the effect of b is to **translate** the graph **horizontally** through b units.
  ‣ If $b > 0$ it moves to the **right**.   ‣ If $b < 0$ it moves to the **left**.
- For $y = f(x - b) + a$, the graph is translated horizontally b units and vertically a units.

  We say it is **translated by the vector** $\begin{pmatrix} b \\ a \end{pmatrix}$.

Example 6   ◀ͻ **Self Tutor**

Consider the graph of $y = f(x)$ alongside.

On separate axes, draw the graphs of:

a $y = f(x) + 2$ **b** $y = f(x + 4)$

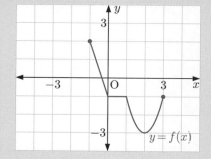

a   The graph of $y = f(x) + 2$ is found by translating $y = f(x)$ 2 units upwards.

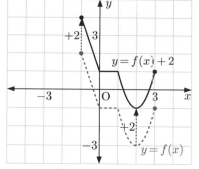

b   The graph of $y = f(x + 4)$ is found by translating $y = f(x)$ 4 units to the left.

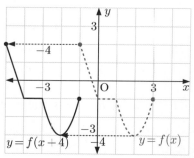

EXERCISE 4D.1

1 Consider the graph of $y = f(x)$ alongside.

On separate axes, draw the graphs of:

    a $f(x) + 5$ **b** $f(x - 3)$

    c $f(x - 3) + 5$

**PRINTABLE
DIAGRAM**

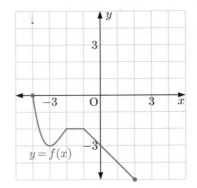

2

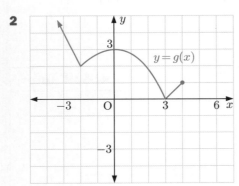

Consider the graph of $y = g(x)$ alongside.

On separate axes, draw the graphs of:

    a $g(x) - 3$ **b** $g(x + 1)$

    c $g(x + 1) - 3$ **d** $g(x - 2) - 1$

3 Write $g(x)$ in terms of $f(x)$:

    a

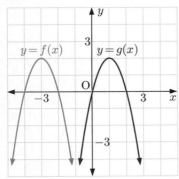

    b

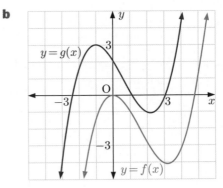

4 Find the equation of the resulting graph $g(x)$ when:

    a $f(x) = 2x + 3$ is translated 4 units downwards

    b $f(x) = 3x - 4$ is translated 2 units to the left

    c $f(x) = -x^2 + 5x - 7$ is translated 3 units upwards

    d $f(x) = x^2 + 4x - 1$ is translated 5 units to the right.

5 Find the equation of the resulting graph when $f(x) = x^2$ is translated through $\begin{pmatrix} h \\ k \end{pmatrix}$.

Discuss how the equation you have found provides the coordinates of the vertex of the translated quadratic.

6 The point $(-2, -5)$ lies on the graph of $y = f(x)$. Find the coordinates of the corresponding point on the graph of $g(x) = f(x - 3) - 4$.

7 Suppose the graph of $y = f(x)$ has x-intercepts -3 and 4, and y-intercept 2. What can you say about the axes intercepts of:

    a $g(x) = f(x) - 3$ **b** $h(x) = f(x - 1)$ **c** $j(x) = f(x + 2) - 4$?

DILATIONS $y = cf(x)$ AND $y = f(kx)$

Investigation 3   Dilations

What to do:

GRAPHING PACKAGE

1   **a** For $f(x) = x + 2$, find in simplest form:

      i $3f(x)$ **ii** $\frac{1}{2}f(x)$ **iii** $5f(x)$

  b Graph all four functions on the same set of axes.

  c What effect does the constant c have when $y = f(x)$ is transformed to $y = cf(x)$, $c > 0$?

2   **a** For $f(x) = x^2$, find in simplest form:

      i $f(2x)$ **ii** $f(3x)$ **iii** $f\left(\frac{x}{4}\right)$

  b Graph all four functions on the same set of axes.

  c What effect does the constant k have when $y = f(x)$ is transformed to $y = f(kx)$, $k > 0$?

For $y = cf(x)$, $c > 0$, the effect of c is to **vertically dilate** the graph by the **scale factor** c.

- If $c > 1$ it moves points of $y = f(x)$ **further away** from the x-axis.
- If $0 < c < 1$ it moves points of $y = f(x)$ **closer** to the x-axis.

For $y = cf(x)$, each point becomes c times its previous distance from the x-axis.

For $y = f(kx)$, $k > 0$, the effect of k is to **horizontally dilate** the graph by the **scale factor** $\frac{1}{k}$.

- If $k > 1$ it moves points of $y = f(x)$ **closer** to the y-axis.
- If $0 < k < 1$ it moves points of $y = f(x)$ **further away** from the y-axis.

For $y = f(kx)$, each point becomes $\frac{1}{k}$ times its previous distance from the y-axis.

Example 7

◆》 **Self Tutor**

Consider the graph of $y = f(x)$ alongside.

On separate axes, draw the graphs of:

a $3f(x)$ b $f(2x)$

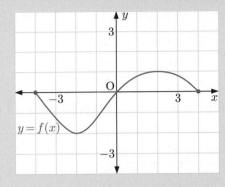

a The graph of $y = 3f(x)$ is found by vertically dilating $y = f(x)$ with scale factor 3.

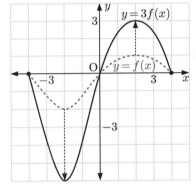

b The graph of $y = f(2x)$ is found by horizontally dilating $y = f(x)$ with scale factor $\frac{1}{2}$.

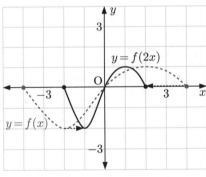

EXERCISE 4D.2

1 Consider the graph of $y = f(x)$ alongside.
On separate axes, draw the graphs of:

a $y = 2f(x)$ b $f(3x)$

PRINTABLE GRIDS

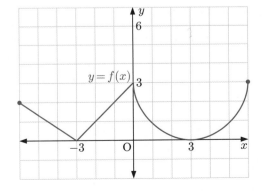

2

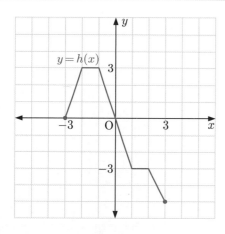

Consider the graph of $y = h(x)$ alongside.

On separate axes, draw the graphs of:

    a $y = \frac{1}{3}h(x)$ **b** $y = h\left(\dfrac{x}{2}\right)$

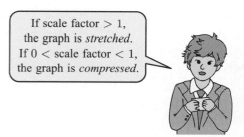

If scale factor > 1, the graph is *stretched*. If $0 <$ scale factor < 1, the graph is *compressed*.

3   Write $g(x)$ in terms of $f(x)$:

    a

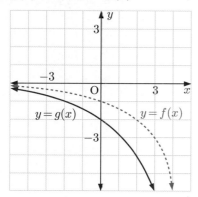

    b

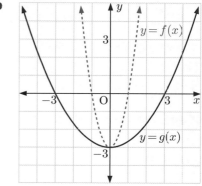

4   A linear function with gradient m is vertically dilated with scale factor c. Find the gradient of the resulting line.

5   Suppose f and g are functions such that $g(x) = f(5x)$.

    a   Given that $(10, 25)$ lies on $y = f(x)$, find the coordinates of the corresponding point on $y = g(x)$.

    b   Given that $(-5, -15)$ lies on $y = g(x)$, find the coordinates of the corresponding point on $y = f(x)$.

6   Find the equation of the resulting graph $g(x)$ when:

    a $f(x) = x^2 + 2$ is vertically dilated with scale factor 2

    b $f(x) = 5 - 3x$ is horizontally dilated with scale factor 3

    c $f(x) = x^3 + 8x^2 - 2$ is vertically dilated with scale factor $\frac{1}{4}$

    d $f(x) = 2x^2 + x - 3$ is horizontally dilated with scale factor $\frac{1}{2}$.

7   Graph on the same set of axes $y = x^2$, $y = 3x^2$, and $y = 3(x + 1)^2 - 2$.

    Describe the combination of transformations which transform $y = x^2$ to $y = 3(x + 1)^2 - 2$.

8   Graph on the same set of axes $y = x^2$, $y = \frac{1}{2}x^2$, and $y = \frac{1}{2}(x + 1)^2 + 3$.

    Describe the combination of transformations which transform $y = x^2$ to $y = \frac{1}{2}(x + 1)^2 + 3$.

9 Graph on the same set of axes $y = x^2$, $y = \frac{1}{4}x^2$, and $y = \frac{1}{4}(x-2)^2 - 1$.

Describe the combination of transformations which transform $y = x^2$ to $y = \frac{1}{4}(x-2)^2 - 1$.

10 Graph on the same set of axes $y = x^2$, $y = 2x^2$, and $y = 2(x - \frac{3}{2})^2 + 1$.

Describe the combination of transformations which transform $y = x^2$ to $y = 2(x - \frac{3}{2})^2 + 1$.

Discussion

For a vertical dilation with scale factor c, each point on the function is moved vertically so it is c times as far from the x-axis.

1 Using this definition of a vertical dilation, does it make sense to talk about negative values of c?

2 If a function is transformed from $f(x)$ to $-f(x)$, what transformation has actually occurred?

3 What *combinations* of transformations would transform $f(x)$ to $-2f(x)$?

4 What can we say about $y = f(kx)$ for:

   a $k = -1$ **b** $k < 0$, $k \neq -1$?

REFLECTIONS IN THE AXES

Investigation 4   Reflections

In this Investigation we consider **reflections** with the forms $y = -f(x)$ and $y = f(-x)$.

What to do:

GRAPHING
PACKAGE

1 Consider $f(x) = 2x + 3$.

   a Find in simplest form:

      i $-f(x)$ **ii** $f(-x)$

   b Graph $y = f(x)$, $y = -f(x)$, and $y = f(-x)$ on the same set of axes.

2 Consider $f(x) = x^3 + 1$.

   a Find in simplest form:

      i $-f(x)$ **ii** $f(-x)$

   b Graph $y = f(x)$, $y = -f(x)$, and $y = f(-x)$ on the same set of axes.

3 What transformation moves:

   a $y = f(x)$ to $y = -f(x)$ **b** $y = f(x)$ to $y = f(-x)$?

From the **Investigation** you should have discovered that:

- For $y = -f(x)$, we **reflect** $y = f(x)$ in the **x-axis**.
- For $y = f(-x)$, we **reflect** $y = f(x)$ in the **y-axis**.

Example 8

Consider the graph of $y = f(x)$ alongside.
On separate axes, draw the graphs of:

a $-f(x)$ **b** $f(-x)$

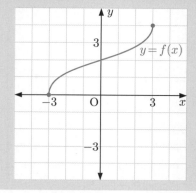

a The graph of $y = -f(x)$ is found by reflecting $y = f(x)$ in the x-axis.

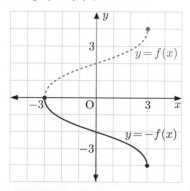

b The graph of $y = f(-x)$ is found by reflecting $y = f(x)$ in the y-axis.

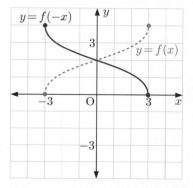

EXERCISE 4D.3

1 Consider the graph of $y = f(x)$ alongside.
On separate axes, draw the graphs of:

a $y = -f(x)$ **b** $y = f(-x)$

PRINTABLE
GRIDS

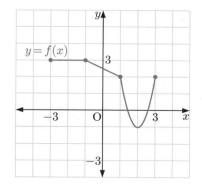

2 Copy the following graphs for $y = f(x)$ and sketch the graphs of $y = -f(x)$ on the same axes.

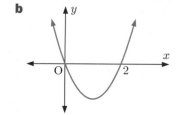
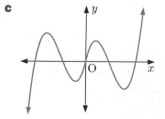

3 Copy the following graphs of $y = f(x)$ and sketch the graphs of $y = f(-x)$ on the same axes.

a
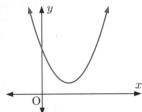

b
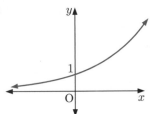

c
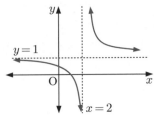

4 The function $y = f(x)$ is transformed to $g(x) = -f(x)$.

a Find the point on $y = g(x)$ corresponding to the point $(3, 0)$ on $y = f(x)$.

b Find the point on $y = f(x)$ that has been transformed to the point $(7, -1)$ on $y = g(x)$.

5 The function $y = f(x)$ is transformed to $h(x) = f(-x)$.

a Find the image point on $y = h(x)$ for the point $(2, -1)$ on $y = f(x)$.

b Find the point on $y = f(x)$ corresponding to the point $(5, -4)$ on $y = h(x)$.

6 Let $f(x) = x + 2$.

a Describe the transformation which transforms $y = f(x)$ to $y = -f(x)$.

b Describe the transformation which transforms $y = -f(x)$ to $y = -3f(x)$.

c Hence draw the graphs of $y = f(x)$, $y = -f(x)$, and $y = -3f(x)$ on the same set of axes.

7 Let $f(x) = (x - 1)^2 - 4$.

a Describe the transformation which transforms $y = f(x)$ to $y = f(-x)$.

b Describe the transformation which transforms $y = f(-x)$ to $y = f(-\frac{1}{2}x)$.

c Hence draw the graphs of $y = f(x)$, $y = f(-x)$, and $y = f(-\frac{1}{2}x)$ on the same set of axes.

MISCELLANEOUS TRANSFORMATIONS

A summary of all the transformations is given in the printable concept map.

CONCEPT MAP

Example 9 ◀) **Self Tutor**

Consider $f(x) = \frac{1}{2}x + 1$. On separate sets of axes graph:

a $y = f(x)$ and $y = f(x + 2)$

b $y = f(x)$ and $y = f(x) + 2$

c $y = f(x)$ and $y = 2f(x)$

d $y = f(x)$ and $y = -f(x)$

a
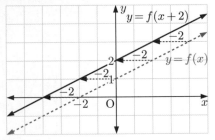

b
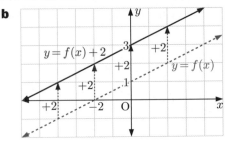

c 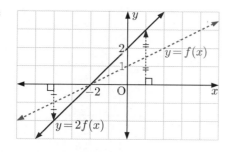   **d**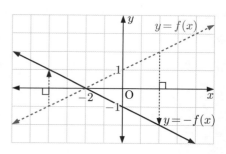

EXERCISE 4D.4

1 Consider $f(x) = x^2 - 1$.

   a Graph $y = f(x)$ and state its axes intercepts.

   b Graph each function and describe the transformation which has occurred:

     i $y = f(x) + 3$ **ii** $y = f(x - 1)$ **iii** $y = 2f(x)$ **iv** $y = -f(x)$

2 In each graph, $f(x)$ is transformed to $g(x)$ using a single transformation.

     i Describe the transformation.   **ii** Write $g(x)$ in terms of $f(x)$.

a 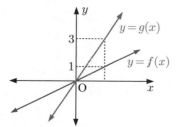   **b**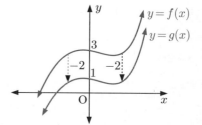

c 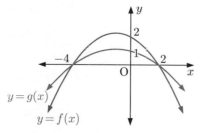   **d**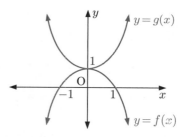

3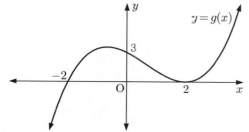

For the graph of $y = g(x)$ given, sketch the graph of:

   a $y = g(x) + 2$ **b** $y = -g(x)$

   c $y = g(-x)$ **d** $y = g(x + 1)$

4 For the graph of $y = h(x)$ given, sketch the graph of:

a $y = h(x) + 1$

b $y = \frac{1}{2}h(x)$

c $y = h(-x)$

d $y = h\left(\frac{x}{2}\right)$

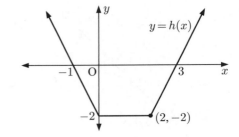

Example 10   ◀)) **Self Tutor**

Consider a function $f(x)$.

a What function results if $y = f(x)$ is reflected in the x-axis, then translated through $\begin{pmatrix} 3 \\ -1 \end{pmatrix}$, then dilated vertically with scale factor 2?

b Fully describe the transformations which map $y = f(x)$ onto $y = -2 + 3f(2x - 1)$.

a $f(x) \xrightarrow[\text{in } x\text{-axis}]{\text{reflection}} -f(x) \xrightarrow[\text{through } \begin{pmatrix} 3 \\ -1 \end{pmatrix}]{\text{translation}} -f(x - 3) - 1 \xrightarrow[\text{scale factor 2}]{\text{vertical dilation with}} 2(-f(x - 3) - 1)$

The resulting function is $-2f(x - 3) - 2$.

b $y = -2 + 3f(2x - 1)$
$\quad = 3f(2(x - \frac{1}{2})) - 2$

$f(x) \xrightarrow[\text{with scale factor } \frac{1}{2}]{\text{horizontal dilation}} f(2x) \xrightarrow[\text{with scale factor 3}]{\text{vertical dilation}} 3f(2x) \xrightarrow[\text{through } \begin{pmatrix} \frac{1}{2} \\ -2 \end{pmatrix}]{\text{translation}} 3f(2(x - \frac{1}{2})) - 2$
$\qquad\qquad\qquad\qquad\qquad\qquad\qquad\qquad\qquad\qquad\qquad\qquad\qquad\qquad = -2 + 3f(2x - 1)$

---

5 Consider a function $f(x)$. Find the function which results if $y = f(x)$ is:

a translated through $\begin{pmatrix} 4 \\ -1 \end{pmatrix}$ then reflected in the y-axis

b reflected in the y-axis then translated through $\begin{pmatrix} 4 \\ -1 \end{pmatrix}$

c translated through $\begin{pmatrix} -2 \\ 1 \end{pmatrix}$ then dilated vertically with scale factor $\frac{1}{2}$

d dilated vertically with scale factor $\frac{1}{2}$ then translated through $\begin{pmatrix} -2 \\ 1 \end{pmatrix}$.

6 Fully describe the transformations which map $y = f(x)$ onto:

a $y = -f(x + 1) + 3$

b $y = f(\frac{1}{2}x) - 7$

c $y = f(3x - 1)$

d $y = -1 + 2f(\frac{1}{4}x - 1)$

e $y = 5 + 2f(-x + 1)$

Discussion

For which combinations of two transformations on $y = f(x)$ is the order in which the transformations are performed:

- important
- not important?

E | RATIONAL FUNCTIONS

In **Chapter 2** we introduced the reciprocal functions $y = \dfrac{1}{x}$ and $y = \dfrac{1}{x^2}$. We saw that these functions are characterised by the presence of both a **horizontal asymptote** and a **vertical asymptote**.

In this Section we consider transformations of these reciprocal functions. The results form part of a broader set of functions called **rational functions**.

A **polynomial** is a function in which the variable is only raised to non-negative integer powers. For example, the linear and quadratic functions we have already studied are polynomials.

A **rational function** is an algebraic fraction formed by the division of two polynomials.

We will study polynomials more thoroughly in **Chapter 8**.

Example 11
◀) **Self Tutor**

The function $g(x)$ results when $y = \dfrac{1}{x}$ is transformed by a vertical dilation with scale factor 2, followed by a translation of $\begin{pmatrix} 3 \\ -2 \end{pmatrix}$.

a Write an expression for $g(x)$ in the form $g(x) = \dfrac{ax + b}{cx + d}$.

b Find the asymptotes of $y = g(x)$. **c** Sketch $y = g(x)$.

a Under a vertical dilation with scale factor 2, $f(x)$ becomes $2f(x)$.

$$\therefore \quad \frac{1}{x} \text{ becomes } 2\left(\frac{1}{x}\right) = \frac{2}{x}.$$

Under a translation of $\begin{pmatrix} 3 \\ -2 \end{pmatrix}$, $f(x)$ becomes $f(x - 3) - 2$.

$$\therefore \quad \frac{2}{x} \text{ becomes } \frac{2}{x - 3} - 2.$$

So, $y = \dfrac{1}{x}$ becomes $\quad g(x) = \dfrac{2}{x - 3} - 2$

$$= \frac{2 - 2(x - 3)}{x - 3}$$

$$= \frac{-2x + 8}{x - 3}$$

$g(x)$ is a rational function which is $\dfrac{\text{linear}}{\text{linear}}$.

b The asymptotes of $y = \dfrac{1}{x}$ are $x = 0$ and $y = 0$.

These are unchanged by the dilation, and shifted $\begin{pmatrix} 3 \\ -2 \end{pmatrix}$ by the translation.

$\therefore$ the vertical asymptote is $x = 3$ and the horizontal asymptote is $y = -2$.

c

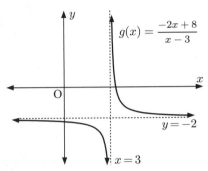

Example 12   ◀)) **Self Tutor**

Consider the function $f(x) = \dfrac{2x - 6}{x + 1}$.

a Find the asymptotes of $y = f(x)$.

b Discuss the behaviour of the graph near these asymptotes.

c Find the axes intercepts of $y = f(x)$.

d Sketch the graph of the function.

e Describe the transformations which transform $y = \dfrac{1}{x}$ into $y = f(x)$.

f Describe the transformations which transform $y = f(x)$ into $y = \dfrac{1}{x}$.

a $f(x) = \dfrac{2x - 6}{x + 1}$

$\qquad = \dfrac{2(x + 1) - 8}{x + 1}$

$\qquad = \dfrac{-8}{x + 1} + 2$

$y = f(x)$ is a translation of $y = \dfrac{-8}{x}$ through $\begin{pmatrix} -1 \\ 2 \end{pmatrix}$.

Now $y = \dfrac{-8}{x}$ has asymptotes $x = 0$ and $y = 0$.

$\therefore$ $y = f(x)$ has vertical asymptote $x = -1$ and horizontal asymptote $y = 2$.

b As $x \to -1^-$, $y \to \infty$.

As $x \to -1^+$, $y \to -\infty$.

As $x \to -\infty$, $y \to 2^+$.

As $x \to \infty$, $y \to 2^-$.

c When $x = 0$, $y = \dfrac{-8}{1} + 2 = -6$.

$\therefore$ the y-intercept is -6.

When $y = 0$, $2x - 6 = 0$

$\qquad\qquad\therefore$ $x = 3$

$\therefore$ the x-intercept is 3.

d

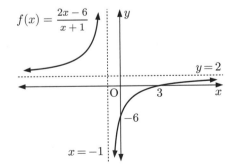

e $\dfrac{1}{x}$ becomes $\dfrac{8}{x}$ under a vertical dilation with scale factor 8.

$\dfrac{8}{x}$ becomes $\dfrac{-8}{x}$ under a reflection in the y-axis.

$\dfrac{-8}{x}$ becomes $\dfrac{-8}{x+1} + 2$ under a translation through $\begin{pmatrix} -1 \\ 2 \end{pmatrix}$.

So, $y = \dfrac{1}{x}$ is transformed to $y = f(x)$ under a vertical dilation with scale factor 8, followed by a reflection in the y-axis, followed by a translation through $\begin{pmatrix} -1 \\ 2 \end{pmatrix}$.

f   To transform $y = f(x)$ into $y = \dfrac{1}{x}$,   we need to reverse the process in **e**.

We need a translation through $\begin{pmatrix} 1 \\ -2 \end{pmatrix}$,   followed by a reflection in the y-axis, followed by a vertical dilation with scale factor $\frac{1}{8}$.

EXERCISE 4E

1   Write, in the form $y = \dfrac{ax+b}{cx+d}$,   the function that results when $y = \dfrac{1}{x}$ is transformed by:

    a   a vertical dilation with scale factor $\frac{1}{2}$ **b**   a horizontal dilation with scale factor 3

    c   a horizontal translation of -3 **d**   a vertical translation of 4.

2   The function $g(x)$ results when $y = \dfrac{1}{x}$ is transformed by a vertical dilation with scale factor 3, followed by a translation of $\begin{pmatrix} 1 \\ -1 \end{pmatrix}$.

    a   Write an expression for $g(x)$ in the form $g(x) = \dfrac{ax+b}{cx+d}$.

    b   Find the asymptotes of $y = g(x)$.

    c   State the domain and range of $g(x)$.

    d   Sketch $y = g(x)$.

3   For each of the following functions f, find:

    i   the asymptotes   **ii**   how to transform $y = \dfrac{1}{x}$ into $y = f(x)$.

    a $f : x \mapsto \dfrac{2x+4}{x-1}$ **b** $f : x \mapsto \dfrac{3x-2}{x+1}$ **c** $f : x \mapsto \dfrac{2x+1}{2-x}$

4   For each of the following functions $f(x)$:

    i   Find the asymptotes of $y = f(x)$.

    ii   Discuss the behaviour of the graph near these asymptotes.

    iii   Find the axes intercepts of $y = f(x)$.

    iv   Sketch the graph of $y = f(x)$.

    v   Describe the transformations which transform $y = \dfrac{1}{x}$ into $y = f(x)$.

    vi   Describe the transformations which transform $y = f(x)$ into $y = \dfrac{1}{x}$.

    a $y = \dfrac{2x+3}{x+1}$ **b** $y = \dfrac{3}{x-2}$ **c** $y = \dfrac{2x-1}{3-x}$ **d** $y = \dfrac{5x-1}{2x+1}$

5 In order to remove noxious weeds from her property, Helga sprays with a weedicide. The chemical is slow to act, and the average number of weeds remaining after t days is modelled by $N = 20 + \dfrac{100}{t+2}$ weeds per hectare.

a How many weeds per hectare were alive before the spraying?

b How many weeds will be alive after 8 days?

c How long will it take for the average number of weeds still alive to be 40 per hectare?

d Sketch the graph of N against t.

e According to the model, is the spraying going to eradicate all weeds?

6 Find the function which results when $y = \dfrac{1}{x^2}$ is:

a horizontally dilated with scale factor 2

b reflected in the y-axis

c translated through $\begin{pmatrix} 3 \\ -1 \end{pmatrix}$.

7 Suppose $y = \dfrac{1}{x^2}$ is translated through $\begin{pmatrix} -1 \\ 2 \end{pmatrix}$ and then vertically dilated with scale factor 3.

a Write an expression for the function.

b Sketch the graph of the function.

8 **a** Use transformations of $y = \dfrac{1}{x}$ to graph $y = \dfrac{1}{x-1} + 3$ and $y = \dfrac{3}{x+1}$ on the same set of axes.

b Hence explain why $\dfrac{1}{x-1} + 3 = \dfrac{3}{x+1}$ has no solutions.

9 **a** Use transformations of $y = \dfrac{1}{x}$ to graph $y = \dfrac{3+x}{x-2}$ and $y = \dfrac{2x-1}{x+1}$ on the same set of axes.

b Hence estimate the solutions to $\dfrac{3+x}{x-2} = \dfrac{2x-1}{x+1}$.

c Solve $\dfrac{3+x}{x-2} = \dfrac{2x-1}{x+1}$ exactly using the quadratic formula.

Review set 4A

1 For each graph, state:

    i the domain   **ii** the range   **iii** whether the graph shows a function.

a
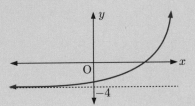

b
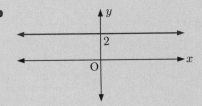

c

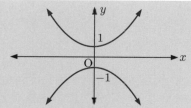

d

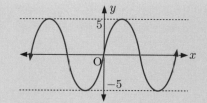

2 If $f(x) = 2x - x^2$, find:

    a $f(2)$ **b** $f(-3)$ **c** $f(-\frac{1}{2})$

3 The graph of $y = f(x)$ is shown alongside.

    a Find:

        i $f(-3)$ **ii** $f(2)$

    b Find the value of x such that $f(x) = 4$.

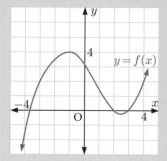

4 Describe using interval notation:

    a

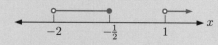

    b

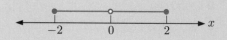

5 This graph shows the noise level at a stadium during a football match.

Find the domain and range of the function.

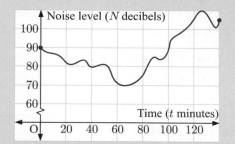

6 Consider $f(x) = \dfrac{-2}{x^2}$.

    a For what value of x is $f(x)$ undefined, or not a real number?

    b Sketch the function using technology.

    c State the domain and range of the function.

7 Consider $f(x) = x^2$ and $g(x) = 1 - 6x$.

    a Show that $f(-3) = g(-\frac{4}{3})$.

    b Find x such that $g(x) = f(5)$.

8 Graph $y = x^2 - 7x + 12$. Hence find its domain and range.

9 The function $f(x)$ has domain $\{x : -2 \leqslant x \leqslant 3\}$ and range $\{y : -1 \leqslant y \leqslant 7\}$.

Find the domain and range of $g(x) = f(x + 3) - 4$. Explain your answers.

10 Consider the graph of $y = f(x)$ alongside.

On separate axes, draw the graphs of:

a $f(x - 1)$ **b** $f(2x)$

c $f(x) + 3$ **d** $2f(x)$

e $f(-x)$ **f** $-f(x)$

PRINTABLE
GRIDS

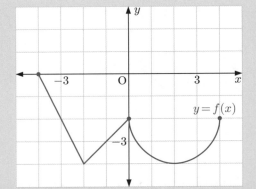

11 Find the equation of the resulting graph $g(x)$ when:

a $f(x) = x^2 - 3x$ is reflected in the x-axis

b $f(x) = 14 - x$ is translated 2 units upwards

c $f(x) = \frac{1}{3}x + 2$ is horizontally dilated with scale factor 4.

12 The function $g(x)$ results when $y = \dfrac{1}{x}$ is transformed by a translation through $\begin{pmatrix} -1 \\ 2 \end{pmatrix}$ followed by a reflection in the y-axis.

a Write an expression for $g(x)$ in the form $g(x) = \dfrac{ax + b}{cx + d}$.

b Find the asymptotes of $y = g(x)$.

c State the domain and range of $g(x)$.

d Sketch $y = g(x)$.

13 Suppose $y = \dfrac{1}{x^2}$ is horizontally dilated with scale factor $\frac{1}{2}$ and then translated through $\begin{pmatrix} 3 \\ 2 \end{pmatrix}$.

a Write an expression for the function.

b Sketch the graph of the function.

Review set 4B

1 If $g(x) = x^2 - 3x$, find in simplest form:

a $g(x + 1)$ **b** $g(4x)$

2 For each of the following graphs, determine:

  i the domain and range   **ii** the x and y-intercepts   **iii** whether it is a function.

a   **b**

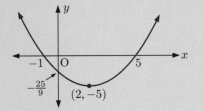   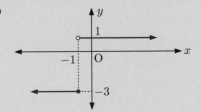

3 Use algebraic methods to determine whether these relations are functions:

a $x + 2y = 10$ **b** $x + y^2 = 10$

4 Suppose $f(x) = \dfrac{3x - 1}{x + 2}$.

   a Evaluate: **i** $f(-1)$ **ii** $f(0)$ **iii** $f(5)$

   b Find a value of x such that $f(x)$ does not exist.

   c Find $f(x - 1)$ in simplest form.

   d Find x if $f(x) = 4$.

5 Copy and complete:

Set notation	Interval notation	Number line graph	Meaning
			the set of all x such that x is more than 4 and less than 9
$\{x : -3 < x \leqslant 7\}$			
	$x \in (-\infty, 2) \cup (3, 4]$		

6 **a** Use technology to help sketch the graph of the relation $y = \sqrt{9 - x}$.

   b Determine whether the relation is a function.

   c Find the domain and range of the relation.

7 Find the equation of the resulting graph $g(x)$ when:

   a $f(x) = 4x - 7$ is translated 3 units downwards

   b $f(x) = x^2 + 6$ is vertically dilated with scale factor 5

   c $f(x) = 7 - 3x$ is translated 4 units to the left

   d $f(x) = 2x^2 - x + 4$ is horizontally dilated with scale factor 3

   e $f(x) = x^3$ is reflected in the y-axis.

8 Consider a function $f(x)$. Find the function which results if $y = f(x)$ is:

   a reflected in the x-axis then translated through $\begin{pmatrix} -2 \\ 3 \end{pmatrix}$

   b translated through $\begin{pmatrix} 4 \\ -1 \end{pmatrix}$ then vertically dilated with scale factor 2.

9 Suppose the graph of $y = f(x)$ has x-intercepts -5 and 1, and y-intercept -3. What can you say about the axes intercepts of:

   a $y = f(x + 4)$ **b** $y = 3f(x)$ **c** $y = f\left(\dfrac{x}{2}\right)$ **d** $y = -f(x)$?

10 The point $(-1, 6)$ lies on the graph of $y = f(x)$. Find the corresponding point on the graph of $y = \frac{1}{2}f(x - 2) + 3$.

11 Fully describe the transformations which map $y = f(x)$ onto:

   a $y = 2f(x + 1) + 3$ **b** $y = -f(\frac{2}{3}x) - 6$ **c** $y = \frac{1}{3}f(-x + 2)$

12 For the function $f(x) = \dfrac{4x - 1}{x + 3}$:

    a Find the asymptotes of $y = f(x)$.

    b Discuss the behaviour of the graph near these asymptotes.

    c Find the axes intercepts of $y = f(x)$.

    d Sketch the graph of $y = f(x)$.

    e Describe the transformations which transform $y = \dfrac{1}{x}$ into $y = f(x)$.

    f Describe the transformations which transform $y = f(x)$ into $y = \dfrac{1}{x}$.

13 **a** Use transformations of $y = \dfrac{1}{x}$ to graph $y = \dfrac{x + 2}{x - 6}$ and $y = \dfrac{2x - 3}{x + 1}$ on the same set of axes.

    b Hence estimate the solution(s) to $\dfrac{x + 2}{x - 6} = \dfrac{2x - 3}{x + 1}$.

    c Solve $\dfrac{x + 2}{x - 6} = \dfrac{2x - 3}{x + 1}$ exactly.

5

Inequalities

Contents:

Opening problem

Jon observed that if $x^2 < k^2$ then $-k < x < k$.

To solve $x^2 - 3x + 2 < 0$, he used the following method:

$$x^2 - 3x + 2 < 0$$
$$\therefore \ x^2 - 3x < -2$$
$$\therefore \ x^2 - 3x + \left(\tfrac{3}{2}\right)^2 < -2 + \left(\tfrac{3}{2}\right)^2 \qquad \text{\{completing the square\}}$$
$$\therefore \ \left(x - \tfrac{3}{2}\right)^2 < \tfrac{1}{4}$$
$$\therefore \ \left(x - \tfrac{3}{2}\right)^2 < \left(\tfrac{1}{2}\right)^2$$
$$\therefore \ -\tfrac{1}{2} < x - \tfrac{3}{2} < \tfrac{1}{2} \qquad \text{\{using observed property\}}$$
$$\therefore \ 1 < x < 2$$

Things to think about:

a By drawing the graph of $y = x^2 - 3x + 2$, can you explain why Jon is correct?

b By factorising $x^2 - 3x + 2 = (x - 1)(x - 2)$, is there an easier way to solve the inequality?

An **algebraic inequality** is a statement comparing the sizes of two expressions.
It must involve one of the symbols $>$, $\geqslant$, $<$, or $\leqslant$.

$$2x + 3 > 11 - x \quad \text{and} \quad \frac{2x - 1}{x} \leqslant \frac{x + 3}{5} \quad \text{are examples of inequalities.}$$

When we have solved equations previously, we have performed the same operation on both sides of the equation to maintain the balance. When dealing with inequalities we need to be more careful to ensure the sign of the inequality is always correct.

For example:

$$3 < 5 \qquad\qquad\qquad\qquad 3 < 5$$
$$\therefore \ 3 \times 2 < 5 \times 2 \qquad\qquad \therefore \ 3 \times -2 < 5 \times -2$$
$$\therefore \ 6 < 10 \ \text{ is correct.} \qquad\qquad \therefore \ -6 < -10 \ \text{ is incorrect!}$$

We therefore need a set of rules to make sure we handle inequalities correctly. The rules we use are based on the following **number properties**:

(1) If $a > b$ and $c \in \mathbb{R}$, then $a + c > b + c$.

(2) If $a > b$ and $c > 0$, then $ac > bc$.

(3) If $a > b$ and $c < 0$, then $ac < bc$.

(4) If $a > b > 0$, then $a^2 > b^2$.

(5) If $a < b < 0$, then $a^2 > b^2$.

RULES FOR SOLVING INEQUALITIES

- If we **swap** the LHS and RHS, we **reverse** the inequality sign.
- If we **add to** or **subtract from** both sides of an inequality, the sign is maintained.
- If we **multiply** or **divide** both sides by:
  - a **positive** number we **keep** the inequality sign
  - a **negative** number we **reverse** the inequality sign.

For example:

$$3 < 5$$
$$\therefore \quad 3 \times 2 < 5 \times 2$$
$$\therefore \quad 6 < 10$$

$$3 < 5$$
$$\therefore \quad 3 \times -2 > 5 \times -2$$
$$\therefore \quad -6 > -10$$

A | LINEAR INEQUALITIES

An inequality is **linear** if it can be written in the form $ax + b \geqslant 0$ or $ax + b > 0$ where $a \neq 0$.

For example, $5x - 2 > 7$ is a **linear inequality** which indicates that the value of the expression $5x - 2$ is greater than 7.

Example 1
◀) **Self Tutor**

Solve the following inequalities, and plot the solutions on separate number lines:

a $a - 4 > 5$ **b** $3b \leqslant 9$ **c** $4 - 2x > 0$

a $a - 4 > 5$
$\therefore \quad a - 4 + 4 > 5 + 4$
$\therefore \quad a > 9$

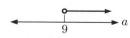

Check: We choose a value of a which satisfies $a > 9$, say $a = 10$.
If $a = 10$, we have $10 - 4 > 5$
$\therefore \quad 6 > 5$ which is true. ✓

b $3b \leqslant 9$
$\therefore \quad \dfrac{3b}{3} \leqslant \dfrac{9}{3}$
$\therefore \quad b \leqslant 3$

Check: If $b = 2$, we have $3 \times 2 \leqslant 9$
$\therefore \quad 6 \leqslant 9$ which is true. ✓

c $4 - 2x > 0$
$\therefore \quad 4 - 4 - 2x > 0 - 4$
$\therefore \quad -2x > -4$
$\therefore \quad \dfrac{-2x}{-2} < \dfrac{-4}{-2}$ {reversing the sign}
$\therefore \quad x < 2$

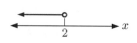

Check: If $x = 0$, we have $4 - 2 \times 0 > 0$
$\therefore \quad 4 > 0$ which is true. ✓

EXERCISE 5A.1

1 Write a mathematical sentence for:

a the speed S if the speed limit is 40 km h^{-1}

b the age A if the minimum age is 18

c a is greater than 3

d b is less than or equal to -3

e d is less than 5

f -20 is greater than or equal to x

g 4 is less than y

h z is greater than or equal to 0.

2 Rewrite the following inequalities with the variable on the LHS:

It is customary to write the variable on the LHS of an inequality.

   a $2 < x$ **b** $5 > b$ **c** $2\frac{1}{2} \leqslant c$

   d $-7 \geqslant d$ **e** $-19 > a$ **f** $-3 < p$

3 Solve the following inequalities, and show their solutions on separate number lines:

   a $a + 4 > 6$ **b** $3b \leqslant -9$ **c** $s - 4 < 2$

   d $\dfrac{c}{5} < 2$ **e** $x - 8 \geqslant -3$ **f** $-4b > 16$

   g $5 + t > 0$ **h** $5k < -30$ **i** $-\dfrac{m}{5} \geqslant 12$

4 Solve the following inequalities, and show their solutions on separate number lines:

   a $2x + 5 > 11$ **b** $5m - 3 \leqslant 17$ **c** $3a - 2 \geqslant 8$ **d** $4a + 9 < 1$

   e $7 - 2b < -3$ **f** $16 + 7s > 2$ **g** $2a - 4 \leqslant 0$ **h** $12 - 5b > -3$

   i $3b - 1 \geqslant 0$ **j** $5n + 7 < -3$ **k** $18 - x > 5$ **l** $11 - 4b \leqslant 4$

Example 2   ◀) **Self Tutor**

Solve $\dfrac{x}{4} - 2 \geqslant 3$, and show its solution on a number line.

$$\dfrac{x}{4} - 2 \geqslant 3$$

$$\therefore \quad \dfrac{x}{4} - 2 + 2 \geqslant 3 + 2 \qquad \text{\{adding 2 to both sides\}}$$

$$\therefore \quad \dfrac{x}{4} \geqslant 5$$

$$\therefore \quad \dfrac{x}{4} \times 4 \geqslant 5 \times 4 \qquad \text{\{multiplying both sides by 4\}}$$

$$\therefore \quad x \geqslant 20$$

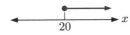

Check: If $x = 32$, we have $\dfrac{32}{4} - 2 \geqslant 3$

$$\therefore \quad 6 \geqslant 3 \quad \text{which is true.} \quad \checkmark$$

---

5 Solve the following inequalities, and show their solutions on separate number lines:

   a $\dfrac{x}{3} + 1 > 4$ **b** $\dfrac{b}{5} - 2 \leqslant -3$ **c** $\dfrac{c}{4} + 4 \geqslant 8$

   d $\dfrac{2x}{3} - 2 < 4$ **e** $\dfrac{3x}{2} + 5 \geqslant -2$ **f** $1 - \dfrac{x}{2} < 4$

   g $2 - \dfrac{x}{4} \geqslant -3$ **h** $3 - \dfrac{2x}{5} < 2$ **i** $5 - \dfrac{3x}{4} > -2$

6 Solve the following inequalities, and show their solutions on separate number lines:

   a $\dfrac{a - 3}{2} < 6$ **b** $\dfrac{b + 5}{4} \geqslant 1$ **c** $\dfrac{4c + 3}{5} \leqslant -1$

   d $\dfrac{4 - a}{2} > 5$ **e** $\dfrac{5 - 3x}{2} \leqslant -6$ **f** $\dfrac{3 - 2x}{3} \geqslant -1$

7   Solve the following inequalities by first expanding the brackets:

   a $3(c+1) > 8$ **b** $5(1+3a) \leqslant -4$ **c** $3(1-2a) \geqslant -5$

   d $2(2a+1) - 3 \leqslant -5$ **e** $4(2a+5) - 12 > 9$ **f** $2(3-4a) + 3 < 7$

8   Solve the following inequalities by first interchanging the LHS and RHS:

   a $5 > 4 + x$ **b** $2 \leqslant 6c + 14$ **c** $-4 > 2b$

   d $7 \leqslant \dfrac{a}{3}$ **e** $3 < \dfrac{d-2}{4}$ **f** $6 \geqslant 3(p+2) - 11$

9   Solve for x, and show the solution on a number line:

   a $5x - 3 > 3x + 1$ **b** $2x + 1 \geqslant 4x + 7$ **c** $8x + 6 < 3x + 1$

   d $2x + 7 > 7x + 3$ **e** $6x + 2 \leqslant 3x - 7$ **f** $x - 11 \leqslant 6x - 1$

   g $\dfrac{3x+1}{3} > \dfrac{x-1}{2}$ **h** $\dfrac{2x-5}{3} \leqslant \dfrac{1-2x}{4}$ **i** $\dfrac{3-x}{2} \geqslant \dfrac{5x+1}{3}$

Example 3   ◄ϡ **Self Tutor**

Jamie is driving 516 miles from London to Fort William. He will complete the journey over two days. He wants to drive no more than 250 miles on the second day. How far must he travel on the first day?

Suppose Jamie travels x miles on the first day.

$\therefore$ he will need to travel $(516 - x)$ miles on the second day.

Jamie wants to travel *no more than* 250 miles on the second day, so

$$516 - x \leqslant 250$$
$$\therefore \quad -x \leqslant -266 \qquad \text{\{subtracting 516 from both sides\}}$$
$$\therefore \quad x \geqslant 266 \qquad \text{\{dividing both sides by } -1 \text{, reversing the sign\}}$$

So, Jamie must travel *at least* 266 miles on the first day.

---

10   Patricia's mathematics class is given 4 tests during a term, each out of 20 marks. Patricia must score an average of at least 17 marks per test to achieve an 'A'. She scored 18.5, 16.5, and 19 in the first 3 tests. What scores could she obtain in the last test to achieve an 'A' for the term?

11   As part of a special promotion, a furniture store is offering customers the choice of either:

        A   £30 off the purchase price

  or   **B**   15% off the purchase price.

Determine the purchase prices for which customers would be better off choosing option **B**.

12   The cost of sending a parcel depends on its weight. The fees charged by two delivery services are:

    Swift Delivery: £8 flat fee plus £1.30 per kg

    Lightning Pace: £6 flat fee plus £1.50 per kg

Determine the weights for which it is cheaper to use *Lightning Pace*.

GRAPHING REGIONS USING LINEAR INEQUALITIES

We can use linear inequalities to define **regions** of the Cartesian plane.

All points satisfying $ax + by < d$ lie on one side of the line $ax + by = d$, and all points satisfying $ax + by > d$ lie on the other side.

For example, consider the regions either side of the line with equation $2x - 3y = 6$.

The regions are defined by the inequalities $2x - 3y < 6$ and $2x - 3y > 6$.

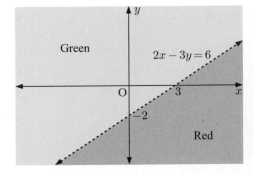

We can identify which region is which by substituting the coordinates of a point to establish a true statement.

For example, substituting the origin $(0, 0)$, we see that $2(0) - 3(0) = 0 < 6$

$\therefore$ the green region is defined by $2x - 3y < 6$
and the red region is defined by $2x - 3y > 6$.

To include the line itself, the inequality symbol is changed to include the equality case also.

For example:

- $2x - 3y \leqslant 6$ defines the green region *including* the line
- $2x - 3y \geqslant 6$ defines the red region *including* the line.

If the line is included then we draw it solid rather than dashed.

Example 4   ◀) Self Tutor

Sketch the region defined by $3x + y \leqslant 9$.

The boundary line $3x + y = 9$ is included in the region.

When $x = 0$, $y = 9$

When $y = 0$, $3x = 9$

$\therefore\ x = 3$

So, $(0, 9)$ and $(3, 0)$ lie on the boundary.

If we substitute $(0, 0)$ into $3x + y \leqslant 9$ we obtain $0 \leqslant 9$ which is true.

$\therefore$ $(0, 0)$ lies in the region.

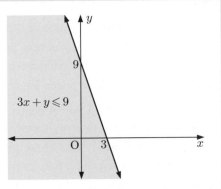

EXERCISE 5A.2

1 Sketch the region defined by:

  a $x < 0$ **b** $y \geqslant 2$ **c** $x \geqslant -1$ **d** $y \leqslant -3$

2 On the same set of axes, sketch the region described by each set of inequalities:

  a $x \geqslant 6$ and $y \geqslant 5$

  b $x \geqslant 6$ and $0 \leqslant y \leqslant 5$

  c $0 \leqslant x \leqslant 6$ and $0 \leqslant y \leqslant 5$

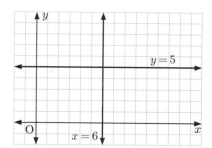

3 Sketch the region described by:

  a $0 \leqslant x \leqslant 4$ **b** $0 \leqslant y \leqslant 7$ **c** $x \geqslant 2$ and $y \geqslant 3$

4 Sketch the region defined by:

  a $x + 3y \leqslant 6$ **b** $x + y \geqslant 4$ **c** $x - 2y < -2$

  d $2x + 3y > 15$ **e** $5x + 4y \leqslant 60$ **f** $-2x + 4y > 1$

  g $4x + 3y \leqslant 48$ **h** $8x + 15y > 120$ **i** $3x - 5y < 30$

Check your answers using the **region plotter** or your **graphics calculator**.

REGION PLOTTER

GRAPHICS CALCULATOR INSTRUCTIONS

5 Sketch the region described by:

  a $x \geqslant 0$, $y \geqslant 0$, $2x + 3y \leqslant 12$ **b** $x \geqslant 5$, $y \geqslant 0$, $5x + 3y \leqslant 60$

6 At the supermarket I will buy x loaves of bread at £2 per loaf, and y blocks of cheese at £5 each. I need at least three of each item, and can spend at most £40.

  a Find the inequalities for the variables x and y.

  b Graph the region described by the inequalities.

7 Sarah will buy x watches and y clocks for her shop. The watches cost £25 each, and the clocks cost £40 each. She needs at least four watches and five clocks, and can spend at most £1000 on the purchase.

  a Find the inequalities for the variables x and y.

  b Graph the region described by the inequalities.

8 Cedric bought x hammers and y screwdrivers. The hammers cost £8 each, and the screwdrivers cost £5 each. Cedric needed at least three hammers, and could spend at most £120.

  a Find the inequalities for the variables x and y.

  b Graph the region described by the inequalities.

Example 5

◄)) **Self Tutor**

Graph the region defined by: $x \geqslant 0, \ y \geqslant 0, \ x + y \leqslant 8, \ x + 2y \leqslant 12$

The boundary lines are: $x = 0, \ y = 0, \ x + y = 8, \ x + 2y = 12$

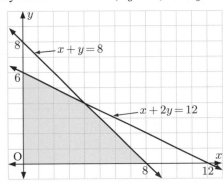

The points in the region must satisfy *all* of the inequalities.

9 Graph the region defined by:

   a $x + 4y \leqslant 12, \ x + y \leqslant 6, \ x \geqslant 0, \ y \geqslant 0$

   b $x + 2y \leqslant 12, \ 3x + 2y \leqslant 24, \ x \geqslant 0, \ y \geqslant 0$

   c $2x + y \leqslant 10, \ x + y \leqslant 6, \ x \geqslant 0, \ y \geqslant 0$

   d $x + 2y \leqslant 22, \ x + y \leqslant 12, \ y \geqslant 2x, \ x \geqslant 0, \ y \geqslant 0.$

Check your answers using technology.

REGION PLOTTER

10 Consider the shaded region within the boundary lines $-x + y = 3, \ x + y = 3, \ x = 3, \ y = 1,$ and $y = 5.$

   a Determine the inequalities which define the region.

   b Determine the coordinates of the vertices of the region.

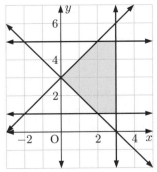

B   SIGN DIAGRAMS

Sometimes we do not wish to draw a time-consuming graph of a function, but wish only to know when the function is positive, negative, zero, or undefined. A **sign diagram** allows us to do this.

For the function $f(x)$, the sign diagram consists of:

- a **horizontal line** which represents the x-axis
- **positive** $(+)$ and **negative** $(-)$ signs indicating where the graph is **above** and **below** the x-axis respectively
- the **zeros** of the function, which are the x-intercepts of the graph of $y = f(x)$, and the **roots** of the equation $f(x) = 0$
- values of x where the graph is undefined.

Consider the three functions below:

Function	$y = (x + 2)(x - 1)$	$y = -2(x - 1)^2$	$y = \dfrac{4}{x}$
Graph	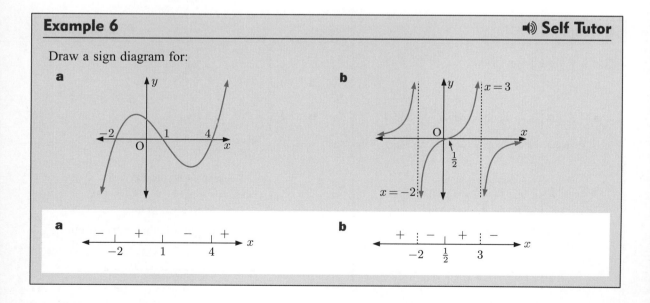		
Sign diagram			

You should notice that:

- A sign change occurs about a zero of the function for single linear factors such as $(x + 2)$ and $(x - 1)$. This indicates **cutting** of the x-axis.

- No sign change occurs about a zero of the function for squared linear factors such as $(x - 1)^2$. This indicates **touching** of the x-axis.

- ⎯⎯⎯⎮⎯⎯⎯ indicates that a function is **undefined** at $x = 0$.
     0

> In general:
> - when a linear factor has an **odd power** there is a change of sign about that zero
> - when a linear factor has an **even power** there is no sign change about that zero.

Example 6   ◀ﹻ Self Tutor

Draw a sign diagram for:

a

b

EXERCISE 5B

1 Draw a sign diagram for each graph:

a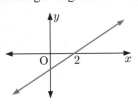

b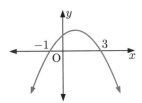

c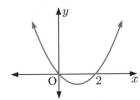

d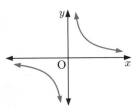

e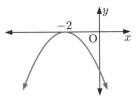

f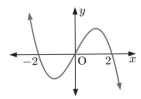

g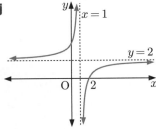

h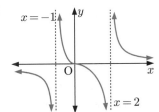

i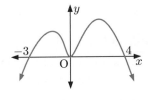

j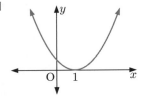

k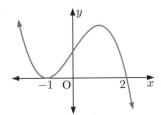

l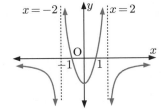

Example 7   ◀》 **Self Tutor**

Draw a sign diagram for:

a $(x+3)(x-1)$

b $-4(x-3)^2$

a $(x+3)(x-1)$ has zeros -3 and 1.

We substitute any number > 1.
When $x = 2$ we have $(5)(1) > 0$,
so we put a $+$ sign here.

As the factors are single, the signs alternate.

b $-4(x-3)^2$ has zero 3.

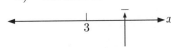

We substitute any number > 3.
When $x = 4$ we have $-4(1)^2 < 0$,
so we put a $-$ sign here.

As the factor is squared, the signs do not change.

2 Draw a sign diagram for:

    a $(x+4)(x-2)$ **b** $(x+1)(x-5)$ **c** $x(x-3)$ **d** $x(x+2)$

    e $(2x+1)(x-4)$ **f** $-(x+1)(x-3)$ **g** $-(3x-2)(x+1)$ **h** $(2x-1)(3-x)$

    i $(5-x)(1-2x)$ **j** $2(x-3)^2$ **k** $-3(x+4)^2$ **l** $-\frac{1}{2}(2x+5)^2$

Example 8   ◀⑨ **Self Tutor**

Draw a sign diagram for $\dfrac{x-1}{2x+1}$.

$\dfrac{x-1}{2x+1}$ is zero when $x=1$ and undefined when $x=-\frac{1}{2}$.

When $x=10$, $\dfrac{x-1}{2x+1}=\dfrac{9}{21}>0$

Since $(x-1)$ and $(2x+1)$ are single factors, the signs alternate.

---

3 Draw a sign diagram for:

    a $\dfrac{x+2}{x-1}$ **b** $\dfrac{x}{x+3}$ **c** $\dfrac{x+1}{x+5}$ **d** $\dfrac{x-2}{2x+1}$

    e $\dfrac{2x+3}{4-x}$ **f** $\dfrac{4x-1}{2-x}$ **g** $\dfrac{3x}{x-2}$ **h** $\dfrac{-8x}{3-x}$

    i $\dfrac{(x-1)^2}{x}$ **j** $\dfrac{4x}{(x+1)^2}$ **k** $\dfrac{(x+2)(x-1)}{3-x}$ **l** $\dfrac{x(x-1)}{2-x}$

    m $\dfrac{(x+2)(x-2)}{-x}$ **n** $\dfrac{3-x}{(2x+3)(x-2)}$ **o** $\dfrac{(x+5)(x-1)}{(x+2)^2}$ **p** $\dfrac{(2x-1)(x+3)}{(x-4)^2}$

C   QUADRATIC INEQUALITIES

An inequality is **quadratic** if it can be written in the form
$ax^2+bx+c\geqslant 0$ or $ax^2+bx+c>0$ where $a\neq 0$.

To solve quadratic inequalities we use the following procedure:

- Make the RHS zero by shifting all terms to the LHS.
- Fully factorise the LHS.
- Draw a sign diagram for the LHS.
- Determine the values required from the sign diagram.

Example 9
🔊 **Self Tutor**

Solve for x:

a $3x^2 + 5x \geqslant 2$ **b** $x^2 + 9 < 6x$

a $3x^2 + 5x \geqslant 2$
  $\therefore \ 3x^2 + 5x - 2 \geqslant 0$ {making RHS zero}
  $\therefore \ (3x - 1)(x + 2) \geqslant 0$ {fully factorising LHS}

Sign diagram of LHS is

  $\therefore \ \ x \in (-\infty, \ -2]$ or $x \in [\frac{1}{3}, \ \infty)$.

b $x^2 + 9 < 6x$
  $\therefore \ x^2 - 6x + 9 < 0$ {making RHS zero}
  $\therefore \ (x - 3)^2 < 0$ {fully factorising LHS}

Sign diagram of LHS is

So, the inequality is not true for any real x.

EXERCISE 5C.1

1 Solve for x:

a $(2 - x)(x + 3) \geqslant 0$ **b** $(x - 1)^2 < 0$ **c** $(2x + 1)(3 - x) > 0$

d $x^2 \geqslant x$ **e** $x^2 \geqslant 3x$ **f** $3x^2 + 2x < 0$

g $x^2 < 4$ **h** $2x^2 \geqslant 4$ **i** $x^2 + 4x + 4 > 0$

j $2x^2 \geqslant x + 3$ **k** $4x^2 - 4x + 1 < 0$ **l** $6x^2 + 7x < 3$

m $3x^2 > 8(x + 2)$ **n** $2x^2 - 4x + 2 > 0$ **o** $6x^2 + 1 \leqslant 5x$

p $1 + 5x < 6x^2$ **q** $12x^2 \geqslant 5x + 2$ **r** $2x^2 + 9 > 9x$

2 **a** For what real numbers is it true that three times the number is less than its square?

   b Three times the square of a number is at least equal to four more than the number quadrupled. What are the possible values of the number?

3 Consider the quadratic inequality $ax^2 + bx + c \leqslant 0$ where $\Delta = b^2 - 4ac$ and $a > 0$. For what values of Δ does the inequality have:

   a no real solution   **b** a unique real solution   **c** infinitely many solutions?

GRAPHING REGIONS USING QUADRATIC INEQUALITIES

Suppose $y = f(x)$ where $f(x)$ is a quadratic function.

   $y > f(x)$ defines the region above the function.

   $y \geqslant f(x)$ defines the region on or above the function.

   $y < f(x)$ defines the region below the function.

   $y \leqslant f(x)$ defines the region on or below the function.

EXERCISE 5C.2

1 Sketch $y = x^2 - 5x + 4$. Shade in red the region $y > x^2 - 5x + 4$, and in blue the region $y < x^2 - 5x + 4$.

2 Sketch $y = x^2 - 5x - 6$. Shade in red the region $y > x^2 - 5x - 6$, and in blue the region $y < x^2 - 5x - 6$.

3 Sketch $y = x^2 - 3x + 1$. Shade in red the region $y > x^2 - 3x + 1$, and in blue the region $y < x^2 - 3x + 1$.

4 Sketch:

   a $y \leqslant x^2 + 3x + 2$ **b** $y \geqslant x^2 - x - 6$ **c** $y \geqslant -x^2 - 5$ **d** $y \leqslant -x^2 + 3x - 2$

5 **a** Sketch $y = -x^2 - x + 9$ and $y = 2x - 5$ on the same set of axes.

   b On copies of your graph, sketch the region for which:

      i $y > -x^2 - x + 9$ *and* $y \leqslant 2x - 5$

      ii $y \geqslant -x^2 - x + 9$ *or* $y < 2x - 5$

      iii $y < -x^2 - x + 9$ *and* $y > 2x - 5$

      iv $y \leqslant -x^2 - x + 9$ *or* $y \geqslant 2x - 5$

D | RATIONAL INEQUALITIES (EXTENSION)

When solving **rational inequalities**, we need to take care with asymptotes.

Example 10
◀⑴ **Self Tutor**

Solve for x:

a $\dfrac{1}{x} \leqslant 10$ **b** $\dfrac{3x + 2}{x - 4} \leqslant 1$

a
$$\frac{1}{x} \leqslant 10$$

$$\therefore \quad \frac{1}{x} - 10 \leqslant 0$$

$$\therefore \quad \frac{1}{x} - 10 \times \frac{x}{x} \leqslant 0$$

$$\therefore \quad \frac{1 - 10x}{x} \leqslant 0$$

$$\xleftarrow[\quad 0 \qquad \frac{1}{10} \quad]{\; - \; \vdots \; + \; \mid \; - \;} x$$

$$\therefore \quad x < 0 \text{ or } x \geqslant \tfrac{1}{10}$$

b
$$\frac{3x + 2}{x - 4} \leqslant 1$$

$$\therefore \quad \frac{3x + 2}{x - 4} - 1 \leqslant 0$$

$$\therefore \quad \frac{3x + 2}{x - 4} - \frac{x - 4}{x - 4} \leqslant 0$$

$$\therefore \quad \frac{3x + 2 - (x - 4)}{x - 4} \leqslant 0$$

$$\therefore \quad \frac{2x + 6}{x - 4} \leqslant 0$$

$$\therefore \quad \frac{2(x + 3)}{x - 4} \leqslant 0$$

$$\xleftarrow[\quad -3 \qquad 4 \quad]{\; + \; \mid \; - \; \vdots \; + \;} x$$

$$\therefore \quad -3 \leqslant x < 4$$

We cannot include a value where the function is undefined.

EXERCISE 5D

1 Solve for x:

   a $\dfrac{x+4}{2x-1} > 0$ **b** $\dfrac{x+1}{4-x} < 0$ **c** $\dfrac{x+3}{2x+3} \geqslant 0$

   d $\dfrac{2x}{x-3} \geqslant 1$ **e** $\dfrac{x+2}{x-1} \geqslant -3$ **f** $\dfrac{x+2}{2x-1} < \dfrac{1}{2}$

   g $\dfrac{1}{x} > 100$ **h** $\dfrac{x}{2x-1} \geqslant 5$ **i** $\dfrac{1-x}{1+x} < 4$

2 Answer the **Opening Problem** on page **116**.

3 Solve for x:

   a $\dfrac{2}{2x-5} < \dfrac{1}{x+7}$ **b** $\dfrac{x^2-2x}{x+3} > 0$ **c** $\dfrac{x^2+5x}{x^2-4} \leqslant 0$

   d $\dfrac{x}{x+2} > \dfrac{1}{x}$ **e** $x > \dfrac{4}{x}$ **f** $\dfrac{1}{x} \leqslant x$

Review set 5A

1 Solve the following inequalities, and show their solutions on separate number lines:

   a $3 - 2x \geqslant -4$ **b** $\dfrac{2x+3}{2} < -3$ **c** $3(x+2) - 1 \geqslant 1 - 4x$

2 Roger was told to think of a number, add 20, then divide the result by 3. The answer was lower than Roger's original number.

   Determine the range of possible numbers Roger may have originally chosen.

3 **a** Solve the inequality $\dfrac{x}{5} - 3 > -5$ and display the solution on a number line.

   b Solve the inequality $8 - 3(x+2) \geqslant 1$ and display the solution on a number line.

   c Find the values of x which satisfy *both* inequalities.

4 Sketch the region defined by:

   a $x \leqslant 3$ and $y \geqslant 2$ **b** $x - y \leqslant 5$

5 Sketch the region defined by:

   a $3x + 2y \leqslant 32, \quad x \geqslant 0, \quad y \geqslant 0$

   b $x + 4y \geqslant 32, \quad 2x + 3y \leqslant 48, \quad x \geqslant 0, \quad y \geqslant 0$

6 Draw a sign diagram for each graph:

   a 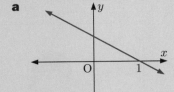   **b**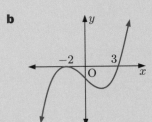

7 Draw a sign diagram for:

   a $(x+2)(x-5)$ **b** $-(x+3)^2$

8 Solve for x:

  a $(3-x)(x+2) < 0$ **b** $x^2 - 5 \leqslant 4x$ **c** $2x^2 + x > 10$

9 Sketch $y = -x^2 + 4x + 3$. Shade in red the region $y > -x^2 + 4x + 3$, and in blue the region $y < -x^2 + 4x + 3$.

10 Sketch the region for which $y > x^2 - 5x + 4$ and $y \leqslant 0$.

11 Solve for x:

  a $\dfrac{x^2 - 3x - 4}{x + 2} > 0$ **b** $\dfrac{3}{x - 1} > \dfrac{5}{2x + 1}$

Review set 5B

1 **a** Solve the inequality $\dfrac{11 - 3x}{2} < -1$ and display the solution on a number line.

  b How many solutions does the inequality have?

  c Use your number line to determine whether the following values satisfy the inequality:

   i $x = 5$ **ii** $x = 2\frac{1}{2}$ **iii** $x = 4\frac{1}{3}$ **iv** $x = 4\frac{1}{2}$

2 Solve the following inequalities:

  a $3 - 2x \geqslant 0$ **b** $\dfrac{x}{5} - 3 < -1$ **c** $6(2x + 1) \geqslant 6 - 13x$

3 Alona and Bethany have different phone plans for international calls:

   Alona: £0.20 flat fee plus £1.10 per minute
   Bethany: £0.60 flat fee plus £1.05 per minute

  For what call times is it cheaper to use Bethany's phone?

4 Sketch the region defined by:

  a $2x + 5y > 30$ **b** $-x + 3y < 18$

5 Nick is buying x cups and y bowls. The cups cost £3 each, and the bowls cost £5 each. He needs at least 4 cups and 2 bowls, and can spend up to £60.

  a Find the inequalities for the variables x and y.

  b Graph the region described by the inequalities.

6 Draw a sign diagram for:

  a $(3x + 2)(4 - x)$ **b** $\dfrac{2x - 5}{x - 4}$ **c** $\dfrac{x - 3}{(x + 2)^2}$

7 Solve for x:

  a $4x^2 < 3x$ **b** $2x^2 \geqslant 3x + 5$ **c** $\frac{11}{3}x \leqslant 2x^2 + 1$

8 Sketch:

  a $y \geqslant 3x^2 + 1 - 4x$ **b** $y \leqslant -x^2 + 4x$

9 Henry used the following method to solve the inequality $\frac{3}{5} < \frac{2}{x}$:

$$\frac{3}{5} < \frac{2}{x}$$

$$\therefore \quad \frac{3 \times x}{5 \times x} < \frac{2 \times 5}{x \times 5} \qquad \{\text{to achieve a common denominator}\}$$

$$\therefore \quad 3x < 10 \qquad \{\text{equating numerators}\}$$

$$\therefore \quad x < 3\tfrac{1}{3} \qquad \{\text{dividing both sides by 3}\}$$

    a By checking the case when $x = -2$, show that Henry's solution is incorrect.

    b Why is Henry's solution incorrect?

10   **a** Draw a sign diagram for $\dfrac{(x+2)(x-3)}{x-1}$.

      b Hence solve $\dfrac{x^2 - x - 6}{x - 1} < 0.$

11 Solve for x:

    a $\dfrac{x-3}{x+4} \geqslant 0$ **b** $\dfrac{x-2}{3-x} \leqslant \dfrac{1}{2}$ **c** $\dfrac{x^2 + 3x}{x + 2} < 0$

6

Surds, indices, and exponentials

Contents:

Opening problem

At an antiques fair, Bernard purchases a clock for £500 and a vase for £400. The clock increases in value by 5% each year, and the vase increases in value by 7% each year.

Things to think about:

a What is the value of each item 1 year after purchase?

b Can you write a formula for the value of each item t years after purchase?

c Which item is more valuable 15 years after purchase?

d How can we determine when the items are equal in value?

We often deal with numbers that are repeatedly multiplied together. Mathematicians use **indices**, also called **powers** or **exponents**, to represent them.

Indices have many applications in finance, engineering, physics, electronics, biology, and computer science. They are most important in situations where there is **exponential growth** or **decay**.

A   SURDS

A **radical** is any number which is written with the **radical sign** $\sqrt{}$.

A **surd** is a real, irrational radical such as $\sqrt{2}$, $\sqrt{3}$, $\sqrt{5}$, or $\sqrt{6}$.

For example, $\sqrt{4}$ is a radical, but it is not a surd because it simplifies to 2.

$$\sqrt{a} \text{ is the non-negative number such that } \sqrt{a} \times \sqrt{a} = a.$$

Important properties of surds are:

- $\sqrt{a}$ is never negative, so $\sqrt{a} \geqslant 0$.
- $\sqrt{a}$ is only real if $a \geqslant 0$.
- $\sqrt{ab} = \sqrt{a} \times \sqrt{b}$ for $a \geqslant 0$ and $b \geqslant 0$.
- $\sqrt{\dfrac{a}{b}} = \dfrac{\sqrt{a}}{\sqrt{b}}$ for $a \geqslant 0$ and $b > 0$.

Example 1
◀⦚ **Self Tutor**

Write as a single surd: **a** $\sqrt{2} \times \sqrt{3}$ **b** $\dfrac{\sqrt{18}}{\sqrt{6}}$

a $\quad \sqrt{2} \times \sqrt{3}$
$\quad = \sqrt{2 \times 3}$
$\quad = \sqrt{6}$

b $\quad \dfrac{\sqrt{18}}{\sqrt{6}}$
$\quad = \sqrt{\dfrac{18}{6}}$
$\quad = \sqrt{3}$

EXERCISE 6A.1

1 Write as a single surd or rational number:

    a $\sqrt{11} \times \sqrt{11}$
    b $\sqrt{3} \times \sqrt{5}$
    c $(\sqrt{3})^2$
    d $\sqrt{5} \times \sqrt{6}$

    e $2\sqrt{2} \times \sqrt{2}$
    f $3\sqrt{2} \times 2\sqrt{2}$
    g $3\sqrt{7} \times 2\sqrt{7}$
    h $(3\sqrt{5})^2$

    i $\dfrac{\sqrt{12}}{\sqrt{2}}$
    j $\dfrac{\sqrt{18}}{\sqrt{3}}$
    k $\dfrac{\sqrt{20}}{\sqrt{5}}$
    l $\dfrac{\sqrt{6} \times \sqrt{10}}{\sqrt{12}}$

Example 2
🔊 **Self Tutor**

Write $\sqrt{18}$ in the form $a\sqrt{b}$ where a and b are integers and a is as large as possible.

$$\sqrt{18}$$
$$= \sqrt{9 \times 2} \qquad \text{\{9 is the largest perfect square factor of 18\}}$$
$$= \sqrt{9} \times \sqrt{2}$$
$$= 3\sqrt{2}$$

---

2 Write in the form $a\sqrt{b}$ where a and b are integers and a is as large as possible:

    a $\sqrt{8}$
    b $\sqrt{12}$
    c $\sqrt{20}$
    d $\sqrt{32}$

    e $\sqrt{27}$
    f $\sqrt{45}$
    g $\sqrt{48}$
    h $\sqrt{54}$

    i $\sqrt{50}$
    j $\sqrt{80}$
    k $\sqrt{96}$
    l $\sqrt{108}$

OPERATING WITH SURDS

The rules for adding, subtracting, and multiplying by surds are the same as those for ordinary algebra.

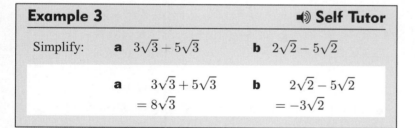

Example 3
🔊 **Self Tutor**

Simplify: **a** $3\sqrt{3} - 5\sqrt{3}$ **b** $2\sqrt{2} - 5\sqrt{2}$

    a $3\sqrt{3} + 5\sqrt{3}$
        $= 8\sqrt{3}$

    b $2\sqrt{2} - 5\sqrt{2}$
        $= -3\sqrt{2}$

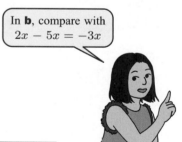

In **b**, compare with
$2x - 5x = -3x$

Example 4
🔊 **Self Tutor**

Expand and simplify:

    a $\sqrt{5}(6 - \sqrt{5})$
    b $(6 + \sqrt{3})(1 + 2\sqrt{3})$

    a $\sqrt{5}(6 - \sqrt{5})$
        $= \sqrt{5} \times 6 + \sqrt{5} \times (-\sqrt{5})$
        $= 6\sqrt{5} - 5$

    b $(6 + \sqrt{3})(1 + 2\sqrt{3})$
        $= 6 + 6(2\sqrt{3}) + \sqrt{3}(1) + \sqrt{3}(2\sqrt{3})$
        $= 6 + 12\sqrt{3} + \sqrt{3} + 6$
        $= 12 + 13\sqrt{3}$

EXERCISE 6A.2

1 Simplify:

a $2\sqrt{2} + 3\sqrt{2}$ **b** $2\sqrt{2} - 3\sqrt{2}$ **c** $5\sqrt{5} - 3\sqrt{5}$ **d** $5\sqrt{5} + 3\sqrt{5}$

e $3\sqrt{5} - 5\sqrt{5}$ **f** $7\sqrt{3} + 2\sqrt{3}$ **g** $9\sqrt{6} - 12\sqrt{6}$ **h** $\sqrt{2} + \sqrt{2} + \sqrt{2}$

2 Simplify:

a $\sqrt{2}(3 - \sqrt{2})$ **b** $\sqrt{5}(\sqrt{5} + 1)$ **c** $\sqrt{10}(3 + 2\sqrt{10})$ **d** $\sqrt{7}(3\sqrt{7} - 4)$

e $-\sqrt{3}(5 + \sqrt{3})$ **f** $2\sqrt{6}(\sqrt{6} - 7)$ **g** $-\sqrt{8}(\sqrt{8} - 5)$ **h** $-3\sqrt{2}(4 - 6\sqrt{2})$

3 Simplify:

a $(5 + \sqrt{2})(4 + \sqrt{2})$ **b** $(7 + 2\sqrt{3})(4 + \sqrt{3})$ **c** $(9 - \sqrt{7})(4 + 2\sqrt{7})$

d $(\sqrt{3} + 1)(2 - 3\sqrt{3})$ **e** $(\sqrt{8} - 6)(2\sqrt{8} - 3)$ **f** $(2\sqrt{5} - 7)(1 - 4\sqrt{5})$

Example 5   ◄⑴ **Self Tutor**

Simplify:

a $(5 - \sqrt{2})^2$ **b** $(7 + 2\sqrt{5})(7 - 2\sqrt{5})$

a $(5 - \sqrt{2})^2$ **b** $(7 + 2\sqrt{5})(7 - 2\sqrt{5})$
      $= 5^2 + 2(5)(-\sqrt{2}) + (\sqrt{2})^2$ $= 7^2 - (2\sqrt{5})^2$
      $= 25 - 10\sqrt{2} + 2$ $= 49 - (4 \times 5)$
      $= 27 - 10\sqrt{2}$ $= 29$

---

4 Simplify:

a $(3 + \sqrt{2})^2$ **b** $(6 - \sqrt{3})^2$ **c** $(\sqrt{5} + 1)^2$ **d** $(\sqrt{8} - 3)^2$

e $(4 + 2\sqrt{3})^2$ **f** $(3\sqrt{5} + 1)^2$ **g** $(7 - 2\sqrt{10})^2$ **h** $(5\sqrt{6} - 4)^2$

5 Simplify:

a $(3 + \sqrt{7})(3 - \sqrt{7})$ **b** $(\sqrt{2} + 5)(\sqrt{2} - 5)$ **c** $(4 - \sqrt{3})(4 + \sqrt{3})$

d $(2\sqrt{2} + 1)(2\sqrt{2} - 1)$ **e** $(4 + 3\sqrt{8})(4 - 3\sqrt{8})$ **f** $(9\sqrt{3} - 5)(9\sqrt{3} + 5)$

DIVISION BY SURDS

Numbers like $\dfrac{6}{\sqrt{2}}$ and $\dfrac{9}{5 + \sqrt{2}}$ involve dividing by a surd.

It is customary to "simplify" these numbers by rewriting them without the surd in the denominator.

For any fraction of the form $\dfrac{b}{\sqrt{a}}$, we can remove the surd from the denominator by multiplying by $\dfrac{\sqrt{a}}{\sqrt{a}}$.

Since $\dfrac{\sqrt{a}}{\sqrt{a}} = 1$, this does not change the value of the number.

Example 6 ◀)) **Self Tutor**

Write with an integer denominator:

a $\dfrac{6}{\sqrt{5}}$ **b** $\dfrac{35}{\sqrt{7}}$

a $\dfrac{6}{\sqrt{5}}$

$= \dfrac{6}{\sqrt{5}} \times \dfrac{\sqrt{5}}{\sqrt{5}}$

$= \dfrac{6\sqrt{5}}{5}$

b $\dfrac{35}{\sqrt{7}}$

$= \dfrac{35}{\sqrt{7}} \times \dfrac{\sqrt{7}}{\sqrt{7}}$

$= \dfrac{^5\cancel{35}\sqrt{7}}{1\cancel{7}}$

$= 5\sqrt{7}$

Multiplying the original number by $\dfrac{\sqrt{5}}{\sqrt{5}}$ or $\dfrac{\sqrt{7}}{\sqrt{7}}$ does not change its value.

For any fraction of the form $\dfrac{c}{a + \sqrt{b}}$, we can remove the surd from the denominator by multiplying by $\dfrac{a - \sqrt{b}}{a - \sqrt{b}}$.

Expressions such as $a + \sqrt{b}$ and $a - \sqrt{b}$ are known as **radical conjugates**. They are identical except for the sign in front of the radical.

Example 7 ◀)) **Self Tutor**

Write $\dfrac{5}{3 - \sqrt{2}}$ with an integer denominator.

$\dfrac{5}{3 - \sqrt{2}} = \left(\dfrac{5}{3 - \sqrt{2}}\right)\left(\dfrac{3 + \sqrt{2}}{3 + \sqrt{2}}\right)$

$= \dfrac{5(3 + \sqrt{2})}{3^2 - (\sqrt{2})^2}$ {using the difference of two squares}

$= \dfrac{15 + 5\sqrt{2}}{7}$

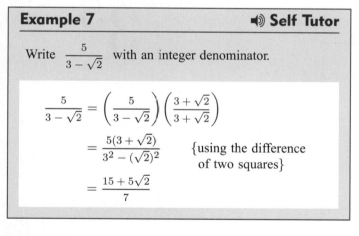

The radical conjugate of $3 - \sqrt{2}$ is $3 + \sqrt{2}$.

EXERCISE 6A.3

1 Write with an integer denominator:

a $\dfrac{1}{\sqrt{3}}$ **b** $\dfrac{3}{\sqrt{3}}$ **c** $\dfrac{9}{\sqrt{3}}$ **d** $\dfrac{11}{\sqrt{3}}$ **e** $\dfrac{\sqrt{2}}{3\sqrt{3}}$

f $\dfrac{2}{\sqrt{2}}$ **g** $\dfrac{6}{\sqrt{2}}$ **h** $\dfrac{12}{\sqrt{2}}$ **i** $\dfrac{\sqrt{3}}{\sqrt{2}}$ **j** $\dfrac{1}{4\sqrt{2}}$

k $\dfrac{5}{\sqrt{5}}$ **l** $\dfrac{15}{\sqrt{5}}$ **m** $\dfrac{-3}{\sqrt{5}}$ **n** $\dfrac{200}{\sqrt{5}}$ **o** $\dfrac{1}{3\sqrt{5}}$

p $\dfrac{7}{\sqrt{7}}$ **q** $\dfrac{21}{\sqrt{7}}$ **r** $\dfrac{2}{\sqrt{11}}$ **s** $\dfrac{26}{\sqrt{13}}$ **t** $\dfrac{1}{(\sqrt{3})^3}$

2 Write with integer denominator:

a $\dfrac{1}{3+\sqrt{2}}$ **b** $\dfrac{2}{3-\sqrt{2}}$ **c** $\dfrac{1}{2+\sqrt{5}}$ **d** $\dfrac{\sqrt{2}}{2-\sqrt{2}}$

e $\dfrac{10}{\sqrt{6}-1}$ **f** $\dfrac{\sqrt{3}}{\sqrt{7}+2}$ **g** $\dfrac{1+\sqrt{2}}{1-\sqrt{2}}$ **h** $\dfrac{\sqrt{3}}{4-\sqrt{3}}$

i $\dfrac{-2\sqrt{2}}{1-\sqrt{2}}$ **j** $\dfrac{1+\sqrt{5}}{2-\sqrt{5}}$ **k** $\dfrac{\sqrt{3}+2}{\sqrt{3}-1}$ **l** $\dfrac{\sqrt{10}-7}{\sqrt{10}+4}$

m $\dfrac{3+\sqrt{5}}{4+\sqrt{5}}$ **n** $\dfrac{6-\sqrt{2}}{5-\sqrt{2}}$ **o** $\dfrac{\sqrt{7}+5}{\sqrt{7}-2}$ **p** $\dfrac{\sqrt{11}-3}{4-\sqrt{11}}$

3 Write in the form $a+b\sqrt{2}$:

a $(\sqrt{2}-1)^2$ **b** $(3+\sqrt{2})^2$ **c** $\dfrac{\sqrt{2}-1}{\sqrt{2}+1}$ **d** $\dfrac{5-\sqrt{2}}{6-\sqrt{2}}$

e $\dfrac{1}{(\sqrt{2}+1)^2}$ **f** $\dfrac{1}{(3-\sqrt{2})^2}$ **g** $\dfrac{1}{3+2\sqrt{2}}$ **h** $\dfrac{1}{2\sqrt{2}-7}$

B   INDICES

Rather than writing $3\times3\times3\times3\times3$, we can write this product as 3^5.

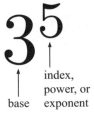

If n is a positive integer, then a^n is the product of n factors of a.

$$a^n = \underbrace{a\times a\times a\times a\times\ ....\ \times a}_{n\ \text{factors}}$$

We say that a is the **base**, and n is the **index** or **exponent**.

index,
power, or
base   exponent

NEGATIVE BASES

$(-1)^1 = -1$ $(-2)^1 = -2$

$(-1)^2 = (-1)\times(-1) = 1$ $(-2)^2 = (-2)\times(-2) = 4$

$(-1)^3 = (-1)\times(-1)\times(-1) = -1$ $(-2)^3 = (-2)\times(-2)\times(-2) = -8$

$(-1)^4 = (-1)\times(-1)\times(-1)\times(-1) = 1$ $(-2)^4 = (-2)\times(-2)\times(-2)\times(-2) = 16$

From the patterns above we can see that:

A **negative** base raised to an **odd** power is **negative**.
A **negative** base raised to an **even** power is **positive**.

CALCULATOR USE

Although different calculators vary in the appearance of keys, they all perform operations of raising to powers in a similar manner. Click on the icon for instructions for calculating indices.

**GRAPHICS
CALCULATOR
INSTRUCTIONS**

Example 8

◀ᴼ Self Tutor

Find, using your calculator: **a** 6^5 **b** $(-5)^4$ **c** -7^4

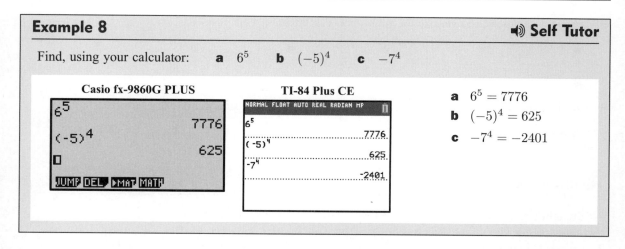

a $6^5 = 7776$

b $(-5)^4 = 625$

c $-7^4 = -2401$

Example 9

◀ᴼ Self Tutor

Find using your calculator: **a** 5^{-2} **b** $\dfrac{1}{5^2}$.   Comment on your results.

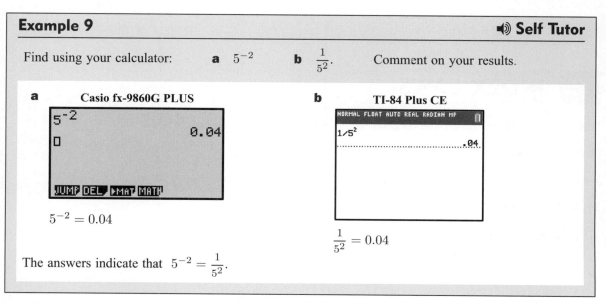

a $5^{-2} = 0.04$

b $\dfrac{1}{5^2} = 0.04$

The answers indicate that $5^{-2} = \dfrac{1}{5^2}$.

EXERCISE 6B

1 List the first six powers of: **a** 2   **b** 3   **c** 4

2 Copy and complete the values of these common powers:

    a $5^1 = \ldots\ldots$, $5^2 = \ldots\ldots$, $5^3 = \ldots\ldots$, $5^4 = \ldots\ldots$

    b $6^1 = \ldots\ldots$, $6^2 = \ldots\ldots$, $6^3 = \ldots\ldots$, $6^4 = \ldots\ldots$

    c $7^1 = \ldots\ldots$, $7^2 = \ldots\ldots$, $7^3 = \ldots\ldots$, $7^4 = \ldots\ldots$

3 Simplify, then use a calculator to check your answer:

    a $(-1)^5$ **b** $(-1)^6$ **c** $(-1)^{14}$ **d** $(-1)^{19}$ **e** $(-1)^8$ **f** -1^8

    g $-(-1)^8$ **h** $(-2)^5$ **i** -2^5 **j** $-(-2)^6$ **k** $(-5)^4$ **l** $-(-5)^4$

4 Use your calculator to find the value of the following, recording the entire display:

    a 4^7 **b** 7^4 **c** -5^5 **d** $(-5)^5$ **e** 8^6 **f** $(-8)^6$

    g -8^6 **h** 2.13^9 **i** -2.13^9 **j** $(-2.13)^9$

5 Use your calculator to evaluate the following. Comment on your results.

a 9^{-1} **b** $\dfrac{1}{9^1}$ **c** 6^{-2} **d** $\dfrac{1}{6^2}$ **e** 3^{-4} **f** $\dfrac{1}{3^4}$

g 17^0 **h** $(0.366)^0$

6 Consider $3^1, 3^2, 3^3, 3^4, 3^5, ...$ Look for a pattern and hence find the last digit of 3^{101}.

7 What is the last digit of 7^{217}?

Historical note

Nicomachus discovered an interesting number pattern involving cubes and the sums of odd numbers. Nicomachus was born in Roman Syria (now Jerash, Jordan) around 100 AD. He wrote in Greek and was a Pythagorean.

$$1 = 1^3$$
$$3 + 5 = 8 = 2^3$$
$$7 + 9 + 11 = 27 = 3^3$$
$$\vdots$$

C   INDEX LAWS

When n is a positive integer, the notation a^n means a multiplied together n times.

From this definition, $a^m a^n = a^{m+n}$ and $(a^m)^n = a^{m \times n}$.

We observe that to transform a^n to a^{n+1}, we need to multiply by a.

So, to transform a^n to a^{n-1} we need to divide by a.

$\therefore$ we define $a^0 = \dfrac{a^n}{a^n} = 1$ to be consistent with the existing rules.

Dividing further by a enough times, we find $a^{-n} = \dfrac{1}{a^n}$.

Using arguments like this, we arrive at the **index laws** for $m, n \in \mathbb{Z}$:

$a^m \times a^n = a^{m+n}$	To **multiply** numbers with the **same base**, keep the base and **add** the indices.
$\dfrac{a^m}{a^n} = a^{m-n}, \quad a \neq 0$	To **divide** numbers with the same base, keep the base and **subtract** the indices.
$(a^m)^n = a^{m \times n}$	When **raising** a **power** to a **power**, keep the base and **multiply** the indices.
$(ab)^n = a^n b^n$	The power of a product is the product of the powers.
$\left(\dfrac{a}{b}\right)^n = \dfrac{a^n}{b^n}, \quad b \neq 0$	The power of a quotient is the quotient of the powers.
$a^0 = 1, \quad a \neq 0$	Any non-zero number raised to the power zero is 1.
$a^{-n} = \dfrac{1}{a^n}$ and $\dfrac{1}{a^{-n}} = a^n$ and in particular $a^{-1} = \dfrac{1}{a}, \quad a \neq 0.$	

Example 10

◀) **Self Tutor**

Simplify using the index laws: **a** $3^5 \times 3^4$ **b** $\dfrac{5^3}{5^5}$ **c** $(m^4)^3$

a $3^5 \times 3^4$
$= 3^{5+4}$
$= 3^9$

b $\dfrac{5^3}{5^5}$
$= 5^{3-5}$
$= 5^{-2}$
$= \frac{1}{25}$

c $(m^4)^3$
$= m^{4 \times 3}$
$= m^{12}$

Example 11

◀) **Self Tutor**

Write as powers of 2:

a 16   **b** $\frac{1}{16}$ **c** 1   **d** 4×2^n **e** $\dfrac{2^m}{8}$

a   16
$= 2 \times 2 \times 2 \times 2$
$= 2^4$

b $\dfrac{1}{16}$
$= \dfrac{1}{2^4}$
$= 2^{-4}$

c   1
$= 2^0$

d 4×2^n
$= 2^2 \times 2^n$
$= 2^{2+n}$

e $\dfrac{2^m}{8}$
$= \dfrac{2^m}{2^3}$
$= 2^{m-3}$

EXERCISE 6C

1 Simplify using the index laws:

a $5^4 \times 5^7$ **b** $d^2 \times d^6$ **c** $\dfrac{k^8}{k^3}$ **d** $\dfrac{7^5}{7^6}$ **e** $(x^2)^5$ **f** $(3^4)^4$

g $\dfrac{p^3}{p^7}$ **h** $n^3 \times n^9$ **i** $(5^t)^3$ **j** $7^x \times 7^2$ **k** $\dfrac{10^3}{10^q}$ **l** $(c^4)^m$

2 Write as powers of 2:

a 4   **b** $\frac{1}{4}$ **c** 8   **d** $\frac{1}{8}$ **e** 32   **f** $\frac{1}{32}$

g 2   **h** $\frac{1}{2}$ **i** 64   **j** $\frac{1}{64}$ **k** 128   **l** $\frac{1}{128}$

3 Write as powers of 3:

a 9   **b** $\frac{1}{9}$ **c** 27   **d** $\frac{1}{27}$ **e** 3   **f** $\frac{1}{3}$

g 81   **h** $\frac{1}{81}$ **i** 1   **j** 243   **k** $\frac{1}{243}$

4 Write as a single power of 2:

a 2×2^a **b** 4×2^b **c** 8×2^t **d** $(2^{x+1})^2$ **e** $(2^{1-n})^{-1}$

f $\dfrac{2^c}{4}$ **g** $\dfrac{2^m}{2^{-m}}$ **h** $\dfrac{4}{2^{1-n}}$ **i** $\dfrac{2^{x+1}}{2^x}$ **j** $\dfrac{4^x}{2^{1-x}}$

5 Write as a single power of 3:

a 9×3^p **b** 27^a **c** 3×9^n **d** 27×3^d **e** 9×27^t

f $\dfrac{3^y}{3}$ **g** $\dfrac{3}{3^y}$ **h** $\dfrac{9}{27^t}$ **i** $\dfrac{9^a}{3^{1-a}}$ **j** $\dfrac{9^{n+1}}{3^{2n-1}}$

Example 12
◀ﾞ) **Self Tutor**

Write in simplest form, without brackets:

a $(-3a^2)^4$ **b** $\left(-\dfrac{2a^2}{b}\right)^3$

a $\quad (-3a^2)^4$

$= (-3)^4 \times (a^2)^4$

$= 81 \times a^{2 \times 4}$

$= 81a^8$

b $\quad \left(-\dfrac{2a^2}{b}\right)^3$

$= \dfrac{(-2)^3 \times (a^2)^3}{b^3}$

$= \dfrac{-8a^6}{b^3}$

6 Write without brackets:

a $(2a)^2$ **b** $(3b)^3$ **c** $(ab)^4$ **d** $(pq)^3$ **e** $\left(\dfrac{m}{n}\right)^2$

f $\left(\dfrac{a}{3}\right)^3$ **g** $\left(\dfrac{b}{c}\right)^4$ **h** $\left(\dfrac{2a}{b}\right)^0$ **i** $\left(\dfrac{m}{3n}\right)^4$ **j** $\left(\dfrac{xy}{2}\right)^3$

7 Write in simplest form, without brackets:

a $(-2a)^2$ **b** $(-6b^2)^2$ **c** $(-2a)^3$ **d** $(-3m^2n^2)^3$

e $(-2ab^4)^4$ **f** $\left(\dfrac{-2a^2}{b^2}\right)^3$ **g** $\left(\dfrac{-4a^3}{b}\right)^2$ **h** $\left(\dfrac{-3p^2}{q^3}\right)^2$

Example 13
◀ﾞ) **Self Tutor**

Write without negative indices: $\dfrac{a^{-3}b^2}{c^{-1}}$

$a^{-3} = \dfrac{1}{a^3}$ and $\dfrac{1}{c^{-1}} = c^1$

$\therefore \quad \dfrac{a^{-3}b^2}{c^{-1}} = \dfrac{b^2c}{a^3}$

8 Write without negative indices:

a ab^{-2} **b** $(ab)^{-2}$ **c** $(2ab^{-1})^2$ **d** $(3a^{-2}b)^2$ **e** $\dfrac{a^2b^{-1}}{c^2}$

f $\dfrac{a^2b^{-1}}{c^{-2}}$ **g** $\dfrac{1}{a^{-3}}$ **h** $\dfrac{a^{-2}}{b^{-3}}$ **i** $\dfrac{2a^{-1}}{d^2}$ **j** $\dfrac{12a}{m^{-3}}$

Example 14
◀ﾞ) **Self Tutor**

Write $\dfrac{1}{2^{1-n}}$ in non-fractional form.

$\dfrac{1}{2^{1-n}} = 2^{-(1-n)}$

$= 2^{-1+n}$

$= 2^{n-1}$

9 Write in non-fractional form:

a $\dfrac{1}{a^n}$ **b** $\dfrac{5}{a^m}$ **c** $\dfrac{1}{b^{-n}}$ **d** $\dfrac{1}{2^{n-3}}$

e $\dfrac{1}{3^{2-n}}$ **f** $\dfrac{3}{a^{4-m}}$ **g** $\dfrac{a^n}{b^{-m}}$ **h** $\dfrac{a^{-n}}{a^{2+n}}$

10 Write in non-fractional form:

a $\dfrac{1}{x^2}$ **b** $\dfrac{2}{x}$ **c** $x + \dfrac{1}{x}$ **d** $x^2 - \dfrac{2}{x^3}$

e $\dfrac{1}{x} + \dfrac{3}{x^2}$ **f** $\dfrac{4}{x} - \dfrac{5}{x^3}$ **g** $7x - \dfrac{4}{x} + \dfrac{5}{x^2}$ **h** $\dfrac{3}{x} - \dfrac{2}{x^2} + \dfrac{5}{x^4}$

11 Simplify, giving your answers in simplest rational form:

a $\left(\dfrac{5}{3}\right)^0$ **b** $\left(\dfrac{7}{4}\right)^{-1}$ **c** $\left(\dfrac{1}{6}\right)^{-1}$ **d** $\dfrac{3^3}{3^0}$

e $\left(\dfrac{4}{3}\right)^{-2}$ **f** $2^1 + 2^{-1}$ **g** $\left(1\dfrac{2}{3}\right)^{-3}$ **h** $5^2 + 5^1 + 5^{-1}$

12 Write as powers of 2, 3, and/or 5:

a $\dfrac{1}{9}$ **b** $\dfrac{1}{16}$ **c** $\dfrac{1}{125}$ **d** $\dfrac{3}{5}$

e $\dfrac{4}{27}$ **f** $\dfrac{2^c}{8 \times 9}$ **g** $\dfrac{9^k}{10}$ **h** $\dfrac{6^p}{75}$

13 Read about Nicomachus' pattern on page **138** and find the series of odd numbers for:

a 5^3 **b** 7^3 **c** 12^3

D   RATIONAL INDICES

The index laws used previously can also be applied to **rational indices**, or indices which are written as a fraction.

For $a > 0$, notice that $\quad a^{\frac{1}{2}} \times a^{\frac{1}{2}} = a^{\frac{1}{2}+\frac{1}{2}} = a^1 = a \quad$ {index laws}

$\qquad\qquad\qquad$ and $\quad \sqrt{a} \times \sqrt{a} = a \quad$ also.

$\qquad$ So, $\qquad a^{\frac{1}{2}} = \sqrt{a} \qquad\qquad$ {by direct comparison}

Likewise $\quad a^{\frac{1}{3}} \times a^{\frac{1}{3}} \times a^{\frac{1}{3}} = a^1 = a$

$\qquad$ and $\quad \sqrt[3]{a} \times \sqrt[3]{a} \times \sqrt[3]{a} = a$

$\qquad$ suggests $\qquad a^{\frac{1}{3}} = \sqrt[3]{a}$

$\qquad$ In general, $\qquad a^{\frac{1}{n}} = \sqrt[n]{a} \qquad$ where $\sqrt[n]{a}$ reads "the nth root of a" for $n \in \mathbb{Z}^+$.

We can now determine that $\quad \sqrt[n]{a^m} = (a^m)^{\frac{1}{n}}$

$\qquad\qquad\qquad\qquad\qquad\qquad = a^{\frac{m}{n}}$

$\therefore \quad a^{\frac{m}{n}} = \sqrt[n]{a^m} \quad$ for $a > 0$, $n \in \mathbb{Z}^+$, $m \in \mathbb{Z}$

Example 15

◀》 **Self Tutor**

Write as a single power of 2:

a $\sqrt[3]{2}$
b $\dfrac{1}{\sqrt{2}}$
c $\sqrt[5]{4}$

a $\sqrt[3]{2}$

    $= 2^{\frac{1}{3}}$

b $\dfrac{1}{\sqrt{2}}$

    $= \dfrac{1}{2^{\frac{1}{2}}}$

    $= 2^{-\frac{1}{2}}$

c $\sqrt[5]{4}$

    $= (2^2)^{\frac{1}{5}}$

    $= 2^{2 \times \frac{1}{5}}$

    $= 2^{\frac{2}{5}}$

EXERCISE 6D

1 Write as a single power of 2:

a $\sqrt[5]{2}$
b $\dfrac{1}{\sqrt[5]{2}}$
c $2\sqrt{2}$
d $4\sqrt{2}$
e $\dfrac{1}{\sqrt[3]{2}}$

f $2 \times \sqrt[3]{2}$
g $\dfrac{4}{\sqrt{2}}$
h $(\sqrt{2})^3$
i $\dfrac{1}{\sqrt[3]{16}}$
j $\dfrac{1}{\sqrt{8}}$

2 Write as a single power of 3:

a $\sqrt[3]{3}$
b $\dfrac{1}{\sqrt[3]{3}}$
c $\sqrt[4]{3}$
d $3\sqrt{3}$
e $\dfrac{1}{9\sqrt{3}}$

3 Write in the form a^k, where a is a prime number and k is rational:

a $\sqrt[3]{7}$
b $\sqrt[4]{27}$
c $\sqrt[5]{16}$
d $\sqrt[3]{32}$
e $\sqrt[7]{49}$

f $\dfrac{1}{\sqrt[3]{7}}$
g $\dfrac{1}{\sqrt[4]{27}}$
h $\dfrac{1}{\sqrt[5]{16}}$
i $\dfrac{1}{\sqrt[3]{32}}$
j $\dfrac{1}{\sqrt[7]{49}}$

4 Write in the form x^k, where k is rational:

a $\sqrt{x}$
b $x\sqrt{x}$
c $\dfrac{1}{\sqrt{x}}$
d $x^2\sqrt{x}$
e $\dfrac{1}{x\sqrt{x}}$

Example 16

◀》 **Self Tutor**

Use your calculator to evaluate, correct to 6 decimal places:

a $2^{\frac{7}{5}}$
b $\dfrac{1}{\sqrt[3]{4}}$

a   **Casio fx-9860G PLUS**

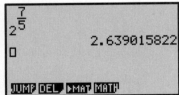

$2^{\frac{7}{5}} \approx 2.639\,016$

b   **TI-84 Plus CE**

$\dfrac{1}{\sqrt[3]{4}} = 4^{-\frac{1}{3}} \approx 0.629\,961$

Example 17
◀)) **Self Tutor**

Without using a calculator, write in simplest rational form:

a $8^{\frac{4}{3}}$　　　　　　　　　　　　　　　　　**b** $27^{-\frac{2}{3}}$

a　$8^{\frac{4}{3}}$

$= (2^3)^{\frac{4}{3}}$

$= 2^{3 \times \frac{4}{3}}$　　$\{(a^m)^n = a^{mn}\}$

$= 2^4$

$= 16$

b　$27^{-\frac{2}{3}}$

$= (3^3)^{-\frac{2}{3}}$

$= 3^{3 \times -\frac{2}{3}}$

$= 3^{-2}$

$= \frac{1}{9}$

---

5 Use your calculator to find, correct to 3 significant figures:

a $3^{\frac{3}{4}}$　　　　　**b** $4^{-\frac{3}{5}}$　　　　　**c** $\sqrt[4]{8}$　　　　　**d** $\sqrt[5]{27}$　　　　　**e** $\dfrac{1}{\sqrt[3]{7}}$

6 Without using a calculator, write in simplest rational form:

a $4^{\frac{3}{2}}$　　　　　**b** $8^{\frac{5}{3}}$　　　　　**c** $16^{\frac{3}{4}}$　　　　　**d** $25^{\frac{3}{2}}$　　　　　**e** $32^{\frac{2}{5}}$

f $4^{-\frac{1}{2}}$　　　　　**g** $9^{-\frac{3}{2}}$　　　　　**h** $8^{-\frac{4}{3}}$　　　　　**i** $27^{-\frac{4}{3}}$　　　　　**j** $125^{-\frac{2}{3}}$

E   ALGEBRAIC EXPANSION AND FACTORISATION

EXPANSION

We can use the usual expansion laws to simplify expressions containing indices:

$$a(b + c) = ab + ac$$
$$(a + b)(c + d) = ac + ad + bc + bd$$
$$(a + b)(a - b) = a^2 - b^2$$
$$(a + b)^2 = a^2 + 2ab + b^2$$
$$(a - b)^2 = a^2 - 2ab + b^2$$

Example 18
◀)) **Self Tutor**

Expand and simplify:　$x^{-\frac{1}{2}}(x^{\frac{3}{2}} + 2x^{\frac{1}{2}} - 3x^{-\frac{1}{2}})$

$x^{-\frac{1}{2}}(x^{\frac{3}{2}} + 2x^{\frac{1}{2}} - 3x^{-\frac{1}{2}})$

$= x^{-\frac{1}{2}} \times x^{\frac{3}{2}} + x^{-\frac{1}{2}} \times 2x^{\frac{1}{2}} - x^{-\frac{1}{2}} \times 3x^{-\frac{1}{2}}$　　$\{$each term is multiplied by $x^{-\frac{1}{2}}\}$

$= x^1 + 2x^0 - 3x^{-1}$　　　　　　$\{$adding indices$\}$

$= x + 2 - \dfrac{3}{x}$

Example 19
◄)) **Self Tutor**

Expand and simplify:

a $(2^x + 3)(2^x + 1)$

b $(7^x + 7^{-x})^2$

a $(2^x + 3)(2^x + 1)$
$= 2^x \times 2^x + 2^x + 3 \times 2^x + 3$
$= 2^{2x} + 4 \times 2^x + 3$

b $(7^x + 7^{-x})^2$
$= (7^x)^2 + 2 \times 7^x \times 7^{-x} + (7^{-x})^2$
$= 7^{2x} + 2 \times 7^0 + 7^{-2x}$
$= 7^{2x} + 2 + 7^{-2x}$

EXERCISE 6E.1

1 Expand and simplify:

a $x^2(x^3 + 2x^2 + 1)$

b $2^x(2^x + 1)$

c $x^{\frac{1}{2}}(x^{\frac{1}{2}} + x^{-\frac{1}{2}})$

d $7^x(7^x + 2)$

e $3^x(2 - 3^{-x})$

f $x^{\frac{1}{2}}(x^{\frac{3}{2}} + 2x^{\frac{1}{2}} + 3x^{-\frac{1}{2}})$

g $2^{-x}(2^x + 5)$

h $5^{-x}(5^{2x} + 5^x)$

i $x^{-\frac{1}{2}}(x^2 + x + x^{\frac{1}{2}})$

j $3^x(3^x + 5 + 3^{-x})$

k $x^{-\frac{1}{2}}(2x^2 - x + 5x^{\frac{1}{2}})$

l $2^{2x}(2^x - 3 - 2^{-2x})$

2 Expand and simplify:

a $(2^x - 1)(2^x + 3)$

b $(3^x + 2)(3^x + 5)$

c $(5^x - 2)(5^x - 4)$

d $(2^x + 3)^2$

e $(3^x - 1)^2$

f $(4^x + 7)^2$

g $(x^{\frac{1}{2}} + 2)(x^{\frac{1}{2}} - 2)$

h $(2^x + 3)(2^x - 3)$

i $(x^{\frac{1}{2}} + x^{-\frac{1}{2}})(x^{\frac{1}{2}} - x^{-\frac{1}{2}})$

j $(x + \frac{2}{x})^2$

k $(7^x - 7^{-x})^2$

l $(5 - 2^{-x})^2$

FACTORISATION

Example 20
◄)) **Self Tutor**

Factorise:

a $2^{n+3} + 2^n$

b $2^{n+3} + 8$

c $2^{3n} + 2^{2n}$

a $2^{n+3} + 2^n$
$= 2^n 2^3 + 2^n$
$= 2^n(2^3 + 1)$
$= 2^n \times 9$

b $2^{n+3} + 8$
$= 2^n 2^3 + 8$
$= 8(2^n) + 8$
$= 8(2^n + 1)$

c $2^{3n} + 2^{2n}$
$= 2^{2n} 2^n + 2^{2n}$
$= 2^{2n}(2^n + 1)$

Example 21

◀ঈ Self Tutor

Factorise: **a** $4^x - 9$ **b** $9^x + 4(3^x) + 4$

a $4^x - 9$
   $= (2^x)^2 - 3^2$ {compare $a^2 - b^2 = (a+b)(a-b)$}
   $= (2^x + 3)(2^x - 3)$

b $9^x + 4(3^x) + 4$
   $= (3^x)^2 + 4(3^x) + 4$ {compare $a^2 + 4a + 4$}
   $= (3^x + 2)^2$ {as $a^2 + 4a + 4 = (a+2)^2$}

EXERCISE 6E.2

1 Factorise:

  a $5^{2x} + 5^x$ **b** $3^{n+2} + 3^n$ **c** $7^n + 7^{3n}$

  d $5^{n+1} - 5$ **e** $6^{n+2} - 6$ **f** $4^{n+2} - 16$

2 Factorise:

  a $9^x - 4$ **b** $4^x - 25$ **c** $16 - 9^x$

  d $25 - 4^x$ **e** $9^x - 4^x$ **f** $4^x + 6(2^x) + 9$

  g $9^x + 10(3^x) + 25$ **h** $4^x - 14(2^x) + 49$ **i** $25^x - 4(5^x) + 4$

3 Factorise:

  a $4^x + 9(2^x) + 18$ **b** $4^x - 2^x - 20$ **c** $9^x + 9(3^x) + 14$

  d $9^x + 4(3^x) - 5$ **e** $25^x + 5^x - 2$ **f** $49^x - 7^{x+1} + 12$

F   EXPONENTIAL EQUATIONS

An **exponential equation** is an equation in which the unknown occurs as part of the index or exponent.

For example: $2^x = 8$ and $30 \times 3^x = 7$ are both exponential equations.

There are a number of methods we can use to solve exponential equations. These include graphing, using technology, and by using **logarithms**, which we will study in **Chapter 7**. However, in some cases we can solve the equation algebraically.

If both sides of an exponential equation are written as powers with the same base numbers, we can **equate indices**.

So, if $a^x = a^k$ then $x = k$.

For example, if $2^x = 8$ then $2^x = 2^3$. Thus $x = 3$, and this is the only solution.

Example 22   🔊 **Self Tutor**

Solve for x:

  a $2^x = 16$

  b $3^{x+2} = \frac{1}{27}$

  a $2^x = 16$
  $\therefore\ 2^x = 2^4$
  $\therefore\ \ x = 4$

  b $3^{x+2} = \frac{1}{27}$
  $\therefore\ 3^{x+2} = 3^{-3}$
  $\therefore\ \ x + 2 = -3$
  $\therefore\ \ \ x = -5$

Once we have the same base we then equate the indices.

Example 23   🔊 **Self Tutor**

Solve for x:

  a $4^x = 8$

  b $9^{x-2} = \frac{1}{3}$

  a $4^x = 8$
  $\therefore\ (2^2)^x = 2^3$
  $\therefore\ \ 2^{2x} = 2^3$
  $\therefore\ \ \ 2x = 3$
  $\therefore\ \ \ \ x = \frac{3}{2}$

  b $9^{x-2} = \frac{1}{3}$
  $\therefore\ (3^2)^{x-2} = 3^{-1}$
  $\therefore\ \ 3^{2(x-2)} = 3^{-1}$
  $\therefore\ \ 2(x - 2) = -1$
  $\therefore\ \ 2x - 4 = -1$
  $\therefore\ \ \ \ 2x = 3$
  $\therefore\ \ \ \ \ x = \frac{3}{2}$

EXERCISE 6F

1 Solve for x:

  a $2^x = 32$
  b $5^x = 25$
  c $3^x = 81$
  d $7^x = 1$

2 Solve for x:

  a $3^x = \frac{1}{3}$
  b $2^x = \sqrt{2}$
  c $5^x = \frac{1}{125}$
  d $4^{x+1} = 64$

  e $2^{x-2} = \frac{1}{32}$
  f $3^{x+1} = \frac{1}{27}$
  g $7^{x+1} = 343$
  h $5^{1-2x} = \frac{1}{5}$

3 Solve for x:

  a $8^x = 32$
  b $4^x = \frac{1}{8}$
  c $9^x = \frac{1}{27}$
  d $25^x = \frac{1}{5}$

  e $27^x = \frac{1}{9}$
  f $16^x = \frac{1}{32}$
  g $4^{x+2} = 128$
  h $25^{1-x} = \frac{1}{125}$

  i $4^{4x-1} = \frac{1}{2}$
  j $9^{x-3} = 27$
  k $\left(\frac{1}{2}\right)^{x+1} = 8$
  l $\left(\frac{1}{3}\right)^{x+2} = 9$

  m $81^x = 27^{-x}$
  n $\left(\frac{1}{4}\right)^{1-x} = 32$
  o $\left(\frac{1}{7}\right)^x = 49$
  p $\left(\frac{1}{3}\right)^{x+1} = 243$

4 Solve for x, if possible:

  a $4^{2x+1} = 8^{1-x}$
  b $9^{2-x} = \left(\frac{1}{3}\right)^{2x+1}$
  c $2^x \times 8^{1-x} = \frac{1}{4}$

5 Solve for x:

  a $3 \times 2^x = 24$
  b $7 \times 2^x = 28$
  c $4 \times 3^{x+2} = 12$

  d $12 \times 3^{-x} = \frac{4}{3}$
  e $4 \times \left(\frac{1}{3}\right)^x = 36$
  f $5 \times \left(\frac{1}{2}\right)^x = 20$

Example 24

 **Self Tutor**

Solve for x: $4^x + 2^x - 20 = 0$

$$4^x + 2^x - 20 = 0$$
$$\therefore \ (2^x)^2 + 2^x - 20 = 0 \qquad \{\text{compare} \ \ a^2 + a - 20 = 0\}$$
$$\therefore \ (2^x - 4)(2^x + 5) = 0 \qquad \{a^2 + a - 20 = (a-4)(a+5)\}$$
$$\therefore \ 2^x = 4 \ \text{ or } \ 2^x = -5$$
$$\therefore \ 2^x = 2^2 \qquad \{2^x \text{ cannot be negative}\}$$
$$\therefore \ x = 2$$

6 Solve for x:

    a $4^x - 6(2^x) + 8 = 0$ **b** $4^x - 2^x - 2 = 0$ **c** $9^x - 12(3^x) + 27 = 0$

    d $9^x = 3^x + 6$ **e** $25^x - 23(5^x) - 50 = 0$ **f** $49^x + 1 = 2(7^x)$

Check your answers using technology. You can get instructions for doing this by clicking on the icon.

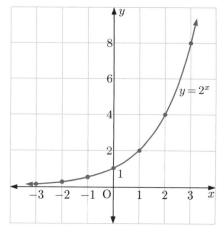

GRAPHICS CALCULATOR INSTRUCTIONS

G   EXPONENTIAL FUNCTIONS

We have already seen how to evaluate a^n when $n \in \mathbb{Q}$, or in other words when n is a rational number.

But how do we evaluate a^n when $n \in \mathbb{R}$, so n is real but not necessarily rational?

To answer this question, we can study the graphs of exponential functions.

> The most simple **exponential function** has the form $y = a^x$ where $a > 0$, $a \neq 1$.

For example, $y = 2^x$ is an exponential function.

We construct a table of values from which we graph the function:

x	-3	-2	-1	0	1	2	3
y	$\frac{1}{8}$	$\frac{1}{4}$	$\frac{1}{2}$	1	2	4	8

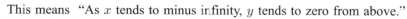

When $x = -10$, $y = 2^{-10} \approx 0.001$.

When $x = -50$, $y = 2^{-50} \approx 8.88 \times 10^{-16}$.

As x becomes large and negative, the graph of $y = 2^x$ approaches the x-axis from above. However, it never touches the x-axis, since 2^x becomes very small but never zero.

We write: as $x \to -\infty$, $y \to 0^+$.

This means "As x tends to minus infinity, y tends to zero from above."

We say that $y = 2^x$ is "**asymptotic** to the x-axis" or "$y = 0$ is a **horizontal asymptote**".

Plotting $y = a^n$ for $n \in \mathbb{Q}$ suggests a smooth, continuous curve. This allows us to complete the curve $y = a^n$ for all $n \in \mathbb{R}$.

Investigation 1   Graphs of exponential functions

In this Investigation we examine the graphs of various families of exponential functions.

DYNAMIC GRAPHING PACKAGE

Click on the icon to run the **dynamic graphing package**, or use your **graphics calculator**.

What to do:

1 Explore the family of curves of the form $y = a^x$ where $a > 0$.
For example, consider $y = 2^x$, $y = 10^x$, $y = (0.8)^x$, and $y = (0.5)^x$.

   a What effect does a have on the shape of the graph?

   b What is the y-intercept of each graph?

   c What is the horizontal asymptote of each graph?

2 Explore the family of curves of the form $y = 2^x + b$ where $b \in \mathbb{R}$.
For example, consider $y = 2^x$, $y = 2^x + 1$, and $y = 2^x - 2$.

   a What effect does b have on the position of the graph?

   b What effect does b have on the shape of the graph?

   c What is the horizontal asymptote of each graph?

   d What is the horizontal asymptote of $y = 2^x + b$?

   e What transformation is used to graph $y = 2^x + b$ from $y = 2^x$?

3 Explore the family of curves of the form $y = 2^{x-c}$ where $c \in \mathbb{R}$.
For example, consider $y = 2^x$, $y = 2^{x-1}$, $y = 2^{x+2}$, and $y = 2^{x-3}$.

   a What effect does c have on the position of the graph?

   b What effect does c have on the shape of the graph?

   c What is the horizontal asymptote of each graph?

   d What transformation is used to graph $y = 2^{x-c}$ from $y = 2^x$?

4 Explore the relationship between $y = a^x$ and $y = a^{-x}$ where $a > 0$.
For example, consider $y = 2^x$ and $y = 2^{-x}$.

   a What is the y-intercept of each graph?

   b What is the horizontal asymptote of each graph?

   c What transformation moves $y = 2^x$ to $y = 2^{-x}$?

5 Explore the family of curves of the form $y = k \times 2^x$ where k is a constant.

   a Consider functions where $k > 0$, such as $y = 2^x$, $y = 3 \times 2^x$, and $y = \frac{1}{2} \times 2^x$. Comment on the effect on the graph.

   b Consider functions where $k < 0$, such as $y = -2^x$, $y = -3 \times 2^x$, and $y = -\frac{1}{2} \times 2^x$. Comment on the effect on the graph.

   c What is the horizontal asymptote of each graph? Explain your answer.

From your **Investigation** you should have discovered that:

For the general exponential function $y = k \times a^{x-c} + b$ where $a > 0$, $a \neq 1$, $k \neq 0$:

- a controls how steeply the graph increases or decreases
- c controls horizontal translation
- b controls vertical translation
- the equation of the horizontal asymptote is $y = b$

- if $k > 0$, $a > 1$
  the function is
  increasing

- if $k > 0$, $0 < a < 1$
  the function is
  decreasing

- if $k < 0$, $a > 1$
  the function is
  decreasing

- if $k < 0$, $0 < a < 1$
  the function is
  increasing.

We can sketch the graphs of exponential functions using:

- the horizontal asymptote
- the y-intercept
- two other points, for example, when
  $x = 2$, $x = -2$.

All exponential graphs are
similar in shape and have a
horizontal asymptote.

Example 25

◀)) **Self Tutor**

Sketch the graph of $y = 2^{-x} - 3$.
Hence state the domain and range of $f(x) = 2^{-x} - 3$.

For $y = 2^{-x} - 3$,
the horizontal asymptote is $y = -3$.

When $x = 0$, $y = 2^0 - 3$
$\qquad = 1 - 3$
$\qquad = -2$

∴ the y-intercept is -2.

When $x = 2$, $y = 2^{-2} - 3$
$\qquad = \frac{1}{4} - 3$
$\qquad = -2\frac{3}{4}$

When $x = -2$, $y = 2^2 - 3 = 1$

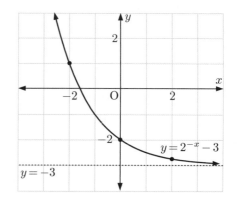

The domain is $\{x : x \in \mathbb{R}\}$. The range is $\{y : y > -3\}$.

Consider the graph of $y = 2^x$ alongside.
We can use the graph to estimate:

- the value of 2^x for a given value of x.
  For example, $2^{1.8} \approx 3.5$ {point A}

- the solutions of the exponential equation
  $2^x = b$.
  For example, if $2^x = 5$ then $x \approx 2.3$
  {point B}.

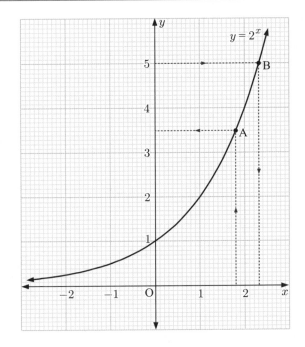

> Graphical methods can be used
> to solve equations like $2^x = 5$
> where we cannot equate indices.

EXERCISE 6G

1 Use the graph above to estimate the value of:

   a $2^{\frac{1}{2}}$ or $\sqrt{2}$ **b** $2^{0.8}$ **c** $2^{1.5}$ **d** $2^{-\sqrt{2}}$

2 Use the graph above to estimate the solution to:

   a $2^x = 3$ **b** $2^x = 0.6$

3 Use the graph of $y = 2^x$ to explain why $2^x = 0$ has no solutions.

4 Draw freehand sketches of the following pairs of graphs using your observations from the previous **Investigation**:

GRAPHING PACKAGE

   a $y = 2^x$ and $y = 2^x - 2$ **b** $y = 2^x$ and $y = 2^{-x}$

   c $y = 2^x$ and $y = 2^{x-2}$ **d** $y = 2^x$ and $y = 2(2^x)$

5 Draw freehand sketches of the following pairs of graphs:

   a $y = 3^x$ and $y = 3^{-x}$ **b** $y = 3^x$ and $y = 3^x + 1$

   c $y = 3^x$ and $y = -3^x$ **d** $y = 3^x$ and $y = 3^{x-1}$

6 Consider the exponential function $f(x) = 3^x - 2$.

   a Find: **i** $f(0)$ **ii** $f(2)$ **iii** $f(-2)$

   b State the equation of the horizontal asymptote.

   c Sketch the graph of the function.

   d State the domain and range of the function.

7 For each of the functions below:

   i Sketch the graph of the function.   **ii** State the domain and range.

   iii Use your calculator to find the value of y when $x = \sqrt{2}$.

   iv Discuss the behaviour of y as $x \to \pm\infty$.   **v** Determine the horizontal asymptote.

   a $y = 2^x + 1$ **b** $y = 2 - 2^x$ **c** $y = 2^{-x} + 3$ **d** $y = 3 - 2^{-x}$

Example 26   ◀》 **Self Tutor**

Use technology to solve the equation $3^x = 7$.

We graph $Y_1 = 3^X$ and $Y_2 = 7$ on the same set of axes, and find their point of intersection.

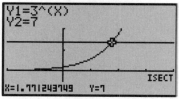

Casio fx-9860G PLUS   Casio fx-CG20   TI-84 Plus CE

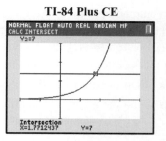

The solution is $x \approx 1.77$.

8 Use technology to solve:

   a $2^x = 11$ **b** $3^x = 15$ **c** $4^x + 5 = 10$

   d $3^{x+2} = 4$ **e** $5 \times 2^x = 18$ **f** $3^{-x} = 0.9$

Discussion

For the exponential function $y = a^x$, why do we choose to specify $a > 0$?

What would the graph of $y = (-2)^x$ look like? What is its domain and range?

H ▍ GROWTH AND DECAY

In this Section we will examine situations where quantities are either increasing or decreasing exponentially. These situations are known as **growth** and **decay** modelling, and occur frequently in the world around us.

Populations of animals, people, and bacteria usually *grow* in an exponential way.

Radioactive substances, cooling, and items that depreciate in value, usually *decay* exponentially.

GROWTH

Consider a population of 100 mice which under favourable conditions is increasing by 20% each week.

To increase a quantity by 20%, we multiply it by 1.2.

If P_n is the population after n weeks, then:

$P_0 = 100$ {the *original* population}
$P_1 = P_0 \times 1.2 = 100 \times 1.2$
$P_2 = P_1 \times 1.2 = 100 \times (1.2)^2$
$P_3 = P_2 \times 1.2 = 100 \times (1.2)^3$, and so on.

From this pattern we see that $P_n = 100 \times (1.2)^n$, $n \in \mathbb{Z}$, which is a geometric sequence.

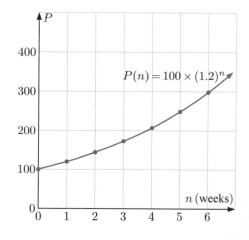

However, while the population of mice must always be an integer, we expect that the population will grow continuously throughout the year, rather than in big, discrete jumps. We therefore expect it will be well approximated by the corresponding exponential function $P(n) = 100 \times (1.2)^n$, $n \in \mathbb{R}$.

Example 27

◀)) **Self Tutor**

An entomologist monitoring a grasshopper plague notices that the area affected by the grasshoppers is given by $A(n) = 1000 \times (1.15)^n$ hectares, where n is the number of weeks after the initial observation.

a Find the original affected area.

b Find the affected area after:
   i 5 weeks   **ii** 10 weeks.

c Draw the graph of the affected area over time.

d Use your graph or technology to find how long it will take for the affected area to reach 8000 hectares.

a $A(0) = 1000 \times 1.15^0$
$= 1000 \times 1$
$= 1000$

∴   the original affected area was 1000 hectares.

b   **i** $A(5) = 1000 \times 1.15^5$
≈ 2010

The affected area is about 2010 hectares.

ii $A(10) = 1000 \times 1.15^{10}$
≈ 4050

The affected area is about 4050 hectares.

c
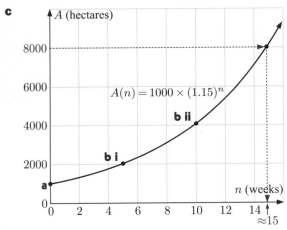

d   From the graph in **c**, it appears that it would take about 15 weeks for the affected area to reach 8000 hectares.

or   Using technology, the solution is ≈ 14.9 weeks.

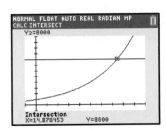

EXERCISE 6H.1

1 The weight W of bacteria in a culture t hours after establishment is given by $W(t) = 100 \times (1.07)^t$ grams.

$a > 1$ indicates growth.

  a Find the initial weight.
  b Find the weight after:
    i 4 hours   **ii** 10 hours   **iii** 24 hours.
  c Sketch the graph of the bacteria weight over time using the results of **a** and **b** only.
  d Use technology to graph $Y_1 = 100 \times (1.07)^X$ and check your answers to **a**, **b**, and **c**.

GRAPHING PACKAGE

2 A breeding program to ensure the survival of pygmy possums is established with an initial population of 50 (25 pairs). From a previous program, the expected population P in n years' time is given by $P(n) = P_0 \times (1.23)^n$.
  a What is the value of P_0?
  b What is the expected population after:
    i 2 years   **ii** 5 years   **iii** 10 years?
  c Sketch the graph of the population over time using **a** and **b** only.
  d Use technology to graph $Y_1 = 50 \times (1.23)^X$ and check your answers to **b**.
  e How long will it take for the population to reach 500?

3 A species of bear is introduced to a large island off Alaska where previously there were no bears. 6 pairs of bears were introduced in 1998. It is expected that the population will increase according to $B(t) = B_0 \times (1.13)^t$ where t is the time, in years, since the introduction.

  a Find B_0.
  b Find the expected bear population in 2018.
  c Find the expected percentage increase in population from 2008 to 2018.
  d How long will it take for the population to reach 200?

4 The speed V of a chemical reaction is given by $V(t) = V_0 \times 2^{0.05t}$ where t is the temperature in °C.
  a Find the reaction speed at:
    i 0°C   **ii** 20°C.
  b Find the percentage increase in reaction speed at 20°C compared with 0°C.
  c Find $\left(\dfrac{V(50) - V(20)}{V(20)} \right) \times 100\%$ and explain what this calculation means.

5 Kayla deposited £5000 into an account. The amount in the account increases by 10% each year.
  a Write a formula for the amount $A(t)$ in the account after t years.
  b Find the amount in the account after:
    i 2 years   **ii** 5 years.
  c Sketch the graph of $A(t)$.

DECAY

Consider a radioactive substance with original weight 20 grams. It *decays* or reduces by 5% each year. The multiplier for this is 95% or 0.95.

If W_n is the weight after n years, then:

$$W_0 = 20 \text{ grams}$$
$$W_1 = W_0 \times 0.95 = 20 \times 0.95 \text{ grams}$$
$$W_2 = W_1 \times 0.95 = 20 \times (0.95)^2 \text{ grams}$$
$$W_3 = W_2 \times 0.95 = 20 \times (0.95)^3 \text{ grams}$$
$$\vdots$$
$$W_{20} = 20 \times (0.95)^{20} \approx 7.2 \text{ grams}$$
$$\vdots$$
$$W_{100} = 20 \times (0.95)^{100} \approx 0.1 \text{ grams}.$$

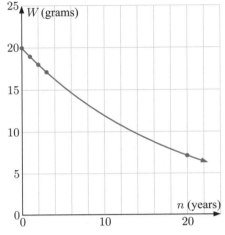

From this pattern we see that $W_n = 20 \times (0.95)^n$, $n \in \mathbb{Z}$, which is again a geometric sequence.

However, we know that radioactive decay is a continuous process, so the weight remaining will actually be given by the smooth exponential curve $W(n) = 20 \times (0.95)^n$, $n \in \mathbb{R}$:

Example 28   ◀》 Self Tutor

When a diesel-electric generator is switched off, the current dies away according to the formula $I(t) = 24 \times (0.25)^t$ amps, where t is the time in seconds after the power is cut.

a Find $I(t)$ when $t = 0$, 1, 2, and 3.

b What current flowed in the generator at the instant it was switched off?

c Plot the graph of $I(t)$ for $t \geqslant 0$ using the information above.

d Use your graph or technology to find how long it takes for the current to reach 4 amps.

a $I(t) = 24 \times (0.25)^t$ amps

$I(0)$	$I(1)$	$I(2)$	$I(3)$
$= 24 \times (0.25)^0$	$= 24 \times (0.25)^1$	$= 24 \times (0.25)^2$	$= 24 \times (0.25)^3$
$= 24$ amps	$= 6$ amps	$= 1.5$ amps	$= 0.375$ amps

b $I(0) = 24$

When the generator was switched off, 24 amps of current flowed in the circuit.

c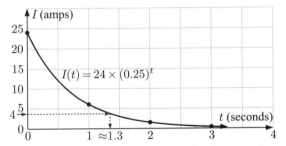

d From the graph above, the time to reach 4 amps is about 1.3 seconds.

or Using technology, the solution is ≈ 1.29 seconds.

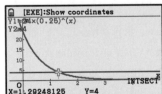

EXERCISE 6H.2

1 The weight of a radioactive substance t years after being set aside is given by $W(t) = 250 \times (0.998)^t$ grams.

> $0 < a < 1$
> indicates decay.

a How much radioactive substance was initially set aside?

b Determine the weight of the substance after:

    i 400 years   **ii** 800 years   **iii** 1200 years.

c Sketch the graph of $W(t)$ for $t \geqslant 0$ using **a** and **b** only.

d Use your graph or graphics calculator to find how long it takes for the substance to decay to 125 grams.

2 The temperature T of a liquid which has been placed in a refrigerator is given by $T(t) = 100 \times (0.986)^t$ °C where t is the time in minutes.

a Find the initial temperature of the liquid.

b Find the temperature after:

    i 15 minutes   **ii** 20 minutes   **iii** 78 minutes.

c Sketch the graph of $T(t)$ for $t \geqslant 0$ using **a** and **b** only.

3 The weight W of radioactive substance remaining after t years is given by $W(t) = 1000 \times (0.979)^t$ grams.

a Find the initial weight of the radioactive substance.

b Find the weight remaining after:

    i 10 years   **ii** 100 years   **iii** 1000 years.

c Graph the weight remaining over time using **a** and **b** only.

d Use your graph or graphics calculator to find the time when 10 grams of the substance remains.

e Write an expression for the amount of substance that has decayed after t years.

4 An initial count of orangutans in a forest found that the forest contained 400 orangutans. Since then, the destruction of their habitat has caused the population to fall by 8% each year.

a Write a formula for the population P of orangutans t years after the initial count.

b Find the population of orangutans after:

    i 1 year   **ii** 5 years.

c Sketch the graph of the population over time.

d How long will it take for the population to fall to 200?

5 The interior of a freezer has temperature -10°C. When a packet of peas is placed in the freezer, its temperature after t minutes is given by $T(t) = -10 + 32 \times 2^{-0.2t}$ °C.

a What was the temperature of the packet of peas:

    i when it was first placed in the freezer   **ii** after 5 minutes

    iii after 10 minutes?

b Sketch the graph of $T(t)$.

c How long does it take for the temperature of the packet of peas to fall to 0°C?

d Will the temperature of the packet of peas ever reach -10°C? Explain your answer.

I   THE NATURAL EXPONENTIAL e^x

We have seen that the simplest exponential functions have the form $f(x) = a^x$ where $a > 0$, $a \neq 1$.

Graphs of some of these functions are shown alongside.

We can see that for all positive values of the base a, the graph is always positive.

Hence $\qquad$ $a^x > 0$ for all $a > 0$.

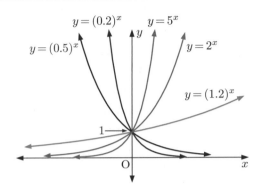

There are an infinite number of possible choices for the base number.

However, where exponential data is examined in science, engineering, and finance, the base $e \approx 2.7183$ is commonly used.

e is a special number in mathematics. It is irrational like π, and just as π is the ratio of a circle's circumference to its diameter, e also has a physical meaning. We explore this meaning in the following **Investigation**.

Investigation 2 $\qquad$ Continuous compound interest

A discrete formula for calculating the amount to which an investment grows under compound interest is $u_n = u_0(1 + i)^n$ where:

u_n is the final amount, $\qquad$ u_0 is the initial amount,

i is the interest rate per compounding period,

n is the number of periods, or times the interest is compounded.

We will investigate the final value of an investment for various values of n, and allow n to become extremely large.

What to do:

1 Suppose £1000 is invested for one year at a fixed rate of 6% per annum. Use your calculator to find the final amount or *maturing value* if the interest is paid:

   a annually $(n = 1, \ i = 6\% = 0.06)$

   b quarterly $(n = 4, \ i = \frac{6\%}{4} = 0.015)$

   c monthly

   d daily

   e by the second

   f by the millisecond.

2 Comment on your answers from 1.

3 If r is the percentage rate per year, t is the number of years, and N is the number of interest payments per year, then $i = \dfrac{r}{N}$ and $n = Nt$.

   If we let $a = \dfrac{N}{r}$, show that the growth formula becomes $u_n = u_0\left[\left(1 + \dfrac{1}{a}\right)^a\right]^{rt}$.

4 For continuous compound growth, the number of interest payments per year N gets very large.

a	$\left(1 + \dfrac{1}{a}\right)^a$
10	
100	
1000	
10 000	
100 000	
1 000 000	
10 000 000	

a Explain why a gets very large as N gets very large.

b Copy and complete the table, giving your answers as accurately as technology permits.

5 You should have found that for very large values of a,

$$\left(1 + \frac{1}{a}\right)^a \approx 2.718\,281\,828\,459....$$

Use the $\boxed{e^x}$ key of your calculator to find the value of e^1. What do you notice?

6 For continuous growth, $u_n = u_0 e^{rt}$ where u_0 is the initial amount, r is the annual percentage rate, and t is the number of years.

Use this formula to find the final amount if £1000 is invested for 4 years at a fixed rate of 6% per annum, where the interest is paid continuously.

From **Investigation 2** we observe that:

If interest is paid *continuously* or *instantaneously* then the formula for calculating a compounding amount $u_n = u_0(1 + i)^n$ can be replaced by $u_n = u_0 e^{rt}$, where r is the percentage rate per annum and t is the number of years.

Historical note

The natural exponential e was first described in 1683 by Swiss mathematician **Jacob Bernoulli**. He discovered the number while studying compound interest, just as we did in **Investigation 2**.

The natural exponential was first called e by Swiss mathematician and physicist **Leonhard Euler** in a letter to the German mathematician **Christian Goldbach** in 1731. The number was then published with this notation in 1736.

In 1748, Euler evaluated e correct to 18 decimal places.

Leonhard Euler

Euler also discovered some patterns in **continued fraction** expansions of e. He wrote that

$$\frac{e-1}{2} = \cfrac{1}{1 + \cfrac{1}{6 + \cfrac{1}{10 + \cfrac{1}{14 + \cfrac{1}{18 + ...}}}}}$$

and $\quad e - 1 = 1 + \cfrac{1}{1 + \cfrac{1}{2 + \cfrac{1}{1 + \cfrac{1}{4 + \cfrac{1}{1 + \frac{1}{1 + ...}}}}}}$

One may think that e was chosen because it was the first letter of Euler's name or for the word exponential, but it is likely that it was just the next vowel available since he had already used a in his work.

EXERCISE 6I

1 Sketch, on the same set of axes, the graphs of $y = 2^x$, $y = e^x$, and $y = 3^x$.
Comment on any observations.

2 Sketch, on the same set of axes, the graphs of $y = e^x$ and $y = e^{-x}$.
What is the geometric connection between these two graphs?

3 For the general exponential function $y = ae^{kx}$, what is the y-intercept?

4 Consider $y = 2e^x$.

   a Explain why y can never be negative.

   b Find y if:

      i $x = -20$ **ii** $x = 20$.

5 Find, to 3 significant figures, the value of:

   a e^2 **b** e^3 **c** $e^{0.7}$ **d** $\sqrt{e}$ **e** e^{-1}

6 Write the following as powers of e:

   a $\sqrt{e}$ **b** $\dfrac{1}{\sqrt{e}}$ **c** $\dfrac{1}{e^2}$ **d** $e\sqrt{e}$

7 Expand and simplify:

   a $(e^x + 1)^2$ **b** $(1 + e^x)(1 - e^x)$ **c** $e^x(e^{-x} - 3)$

8 Factorise:

   a $e^{2x} + e^x$ **b** $e^{2x} - 16$ **c** $e^{2x} - 8e^x + 12$

9   **a** On the same set of axes, sketch and clearly label the graphs of:

      $f : x \mapsto e^x$, $g : x \mapsto e^{x-2}$, $h : x \mapsto e^x + 3$

   b State the domain and range of each function.

10   **a** On the same set of axes, sketch and clearly label the graphs of:

      $f : x \mapsto e^x$, $g : x \mapsto -e^x$, $h : x \mapsto 10 - e^x$

   b State the domain and range of each function.

   c Describe the behaviour of each function as $x \to \pm\infty$.

11 The weight of bacteria in a culture is given by $W(t) = 2e^{\frac{t}{2}}$ grams where t is the time in hours after
the culture was set to grow.

   a Find the weight of the culture:

      i initially

      ii after 30 minutes

      iii after $1\frac{1}{2}$ hours

      iv after 6 hours.

   b Hence sketch the graph of $W(t) = 2e^{\frac{t}{2}}$.

12 Solve for x: **a** $e^x = \sqrt{e}$ **b** $e^{\frac{1}{2}x} = \dfrac{1}{e^2}$

13 The current flowing in an electrical circuit t seconds after it is switched off is given by $I(t) = 75e^{-0.15t}$ amps.

a What current is still flowing in the circuit after:

   i 1 second   **ii** 10 seconds?

b Use your graphics calculator to help sketch the graph of $I(t) = 75e^{-0.15t}$.

c How long will it take for the current to fall to 1 amp?

Activity

Click on the icon to run a card game for exponential functions.

CARD GAME

Research

Researching e

What to do:

1 The "bell curve" of the normal distribution is shown alongside. Research the equation of this curve.

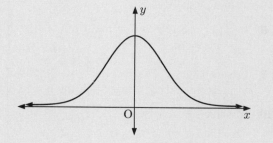

2 The function $f(x) = 1 + x + \frac{1}{2}x^2 + \frac{1}{2\times3}x^3 + \frac{1}{2\times3\times4}x^4 + ...$ is an infinite series.

It can be shown that $f(x) = e^x$.

Check this statement by finding an approximation for $f(1)$ using its first 20 terms.

Review set 6A

1 Simplify:

   a $5\sqrt{3}(4 - \sqrt{3})$ **b** $(6 - 5\sqrt{2})^2$ **c** $(3 + \sqrt{5})(3 - \sqrt{5})$

2 Simplify:

   a $-(-1)^{10}$ **b** $-(-3)^3$ **c** $3^0 - 3^{-1}$

3 Simplify using the index laws:

   a $a^4b^5 \times a^2b^2$ **b** $6xy^5 \div 9x^2y^5$ **c** $\dfrac{5(x^2y)^2}{(5x^2)^2}$

4 Evaluate:

    a $8^{\frac{2}{3}}$

    b $27^{-\frac{2}{3}}$

5 Solve for x:

    a $2^{x-3} = \frac{1}{32}$

    b $9^x = 27^{2-2x}$

    c $e^{2x} = \frac{1}{\sqrt{e}}$

6 Expand and simplify:

    a $e^x(e^{-x} + e^x)$

    b $(2^x + 5)^2$

    c $(x^{\frac{1}{2}} - 7)(x^{\frac{1}{2}} + 7)$

7 Consider the graph of $y = 3^x$ alongside.

    a Use the graph to estimate the value of:

        i $3^{0.7}$ **ii** $3^{-0.5}$

    b Use the graph to estimate the solution to:

        i $3^x = 5$ **ii** $3^x = \frac{1}{2}$

        iii $6 \times 3^x = 20$

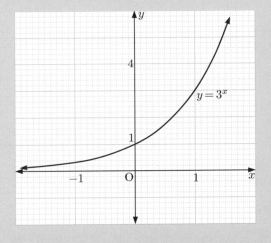

8 If $f(x) = 3 \times 2^x$, find the value of:

    a $f(0)$

    b $f(3)$

    c $f(-2)$

9 On the same set of axes, draw the graphs of $y = 2^x$ and $y = 2^x - 4$. Include on your graph the y-intercept and the equation of the horizontal asymptote of each function.

10 Consider $y = 3^x - 5$.

    a Find y when $x = 0, \pm 1, \pm 2$.

    b Discuss y as $x \to \pm\infty$.

    c Sketch the graph of $y = 3^x - 5$.

    d State the equation of any asymptote.

11 The temperature of a dish t minutes after it is removed from the microwave, is given by $T(t) = 80 \times (0.913)^t$ °C.

    a Find the initial temperature of the dish.

    b Find the temperature after:

        i 12 minutes   **ii** 24 minutes   **iii** 36 minutes.

    c Draw the graph of T against t for $t \geqslant 0$, using the above or technology.

    d Hence, find the time taken for the temperature of the dish to fall to 25°C.

12 **a** On the same set of axes, sketch and clearly label the graphs of:

        $f : x \mapsto e^x, \quad g : x \mapsto e^{x-1}, \quad h : x \mapsto 3 - e^x$

    b State the domain and range of each function in **a**.

    c Describe the behaviour of each function as $x \to \pm\infty$.

Review set 6B

1 Simplify:

   a $(7 + 2\sqrt{3})(5 - 3\sqrt{3})$ **b** $(6 + 2\sqrt{2})(6 - 2\sqrt{2})$

2 Write with integer denominator:

   a $\dfrac{2}{\sqrt{3}}$ **b** $\dfrac{\sqrt{7}}{\sqrt{5}}$ **c** $\dfrac{1}{4 + \sqrt{7}}$

3 Write without brackets or negative exponents:

   a $x^{-2} \times x^{-3}$ **b** $2(ab)^{-2}$ **c** $2ab^{-2}$

4 Write as a single power of 3:

   a $\dfrac{27}{9^a}$ **b** $(\sqrt{3})^{1-x} \times 9^{1-2x}$

5 Evaluate, correct to 3 significant figures:

   a $3^{\frac{3}{4}}$ **b** $27^{-\frac{1}{5}}$ **c** $\sqrt[4]{100}$

6 Factorise:

   a $3^{x+2} - 3^x$ **b** $4^x - 2^x - 12$ **c** $e^{2x} + 2e^x - 15$

7 Solve for x:

   a $2^{x+1} = 32$ **b** $4 \times \left(\frac{1}{3}\right)^x = 324$ **c** $9^x - 10(9^x) + 9 = 0$

8 Consider the graph of $y = 4^x$ alongside.

   a Use the graph to estimate the value of:

      i $4^{0.6}$ **ii** $4^{-1.1}$

   b Use the graph to estimate the solution to $4^x = 3$.

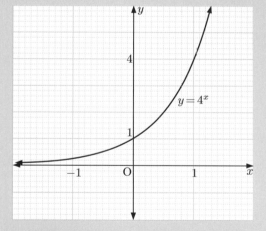

9 Suppose $f(x) = 2^{-x} + 1$.

   a Find $f\left(\frac{1}{2}\right)$.   **b** Find a such that $f(a) = 3$.

10 Consider $y = 2e^{-x} + 1$.

   a Find y when $x = 0, \pm 1, \pm 2$.   **b** Discuss y as $x \to \pm\infty$.

   c Sketch the graph of $y = 2e^{-x} + 1$.   **d** State the equation of any asymptote.

11 Answer the **Opening Problem** on page **132**.

12 Match each equation to its corresponding graph:

a $y = -e^x$ **b** $y = 3 \times 2^x$ **c** $y = e^x + 1$ **d** $y = 3^{-x}$ **e** $y = -e^{-x}$

A
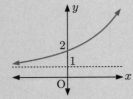

B
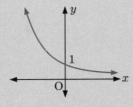

C
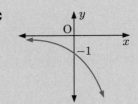

D
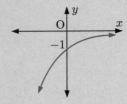

E
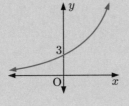

7

Logarithms

Contents:

Opening problem

In a plentiful springtime, a population of 1000 mice will double every week.

The population after t weeks is given by the exponential function $P(t) = 1000 \times 2^t$ mice.

Things to think about:

a What does the graph of the population over time look like?

b How long will it take for the population to reach 20 000 mice?

c Can we write a function for t in terms of P, which determines the time at which the population P is reached?

In **Chapter 6**, we used graphical methods to find approximate solutions to exponential equations.

In this Chapter we will use **logarithms** to find exact solutions to these equations.

A   LOGARITHMS IN BASE 10

Consider the graph of $y = 10^x$ shown.

Notice that the range of the function is $\{y : y > 0\}$. This means that every positive integer y can be written in the form 10^x. For example:

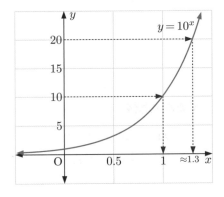

- When $y = 10$, $x = 1$, so $10 = 10^1$.

- When $y = 20$, $x \approx 1.3$, so $20 \approx 10^{1.3}$.

When we write a positive number y in the form 10^x, we say that x is the **logarithm in base 10** of y.

> The **logarithm in base 10** of a positive number is the power that 10 must be raised to in order to obtain that number.

For example:

- The logarithm in base 10 of 1000 is 3, since $1000 = 10^3$.
  We write $\log_{10} 1000 = 3$ or simply $\log 1000 = 3$.

- $\log(0.01) = -2$ since $0.01 = 10^{-2}$.

> If no base is indicated we assume it means base 10. $\log a$ means $\log_{10} a$.

By observing that $\log 1000 = \log(10^3) = 3$ and $\log(0.01) = \log(10^{-2}) = -2$, we conclude

that $\boldsymbol{\log 10^x = x}$ for any $x \in \mathbb{R}$.

Example 1   ◀) Self Tutor

Find: **a** $\log 100$ **b** $\log \sqrt[4]{10}$

       a $\log 100 = \log(10^2)$ **b** $\log \sqrt[4]{10} = \log(10^{\frac{1}{4}})$

               $= 2$ $= \frac{1}{4}$

The logarithms in **Example 1** can be found by hand because it is easy to write 100 and $\sqrt[4]{10}$ as powers of 10. The logarithms of most values, however, can only be found using a calculator.

For example, $\log 34 \approx 1.53$

        so $34 \approx 10^{1.53}$

Logarithms allow us to write any number as
a power of 10. In particular:

 **GRAPHICS CALCULATOR INSTRUCTIONS**

$$x = 10^{\log x} \quad \text{for any} \quad x > 0.$$

Example 2   ◀) Self Tutor

Use your calculator to write the following in the form 10^x where x is correct to 4 decimal places:

a 8   **b** 800   **c** 0.08

a $8 = 10^{\log 8}$ **b** $800 = 10^{\log 800}$ **c** $0.08 = 10^{\log 0.08}$

    $\approx 10^{0.9031}$ $\approx 10^{2.9031}$ $\approx 10^{-1.0969}$

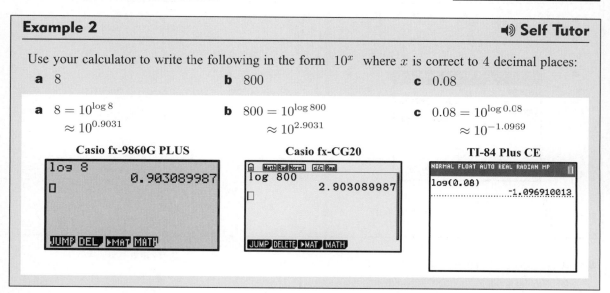

Casio fx-9860G PLUS   Casio fx-CG20   TI-84 Plus CE

EXERCISE 7A

1 Without using a calculator, find:

    a $\log 10\,000$ **b** $\log 0.001$ **c** $\log 10$ **d** $\log 1$

    e $\log \sqrt{10}$ **f** $\log \sqrt[3]{10}$ **g** $\log\left(\dfrac{1}{\sqrt[4]{10}}\right)$ **h** $\log\left(10\sqrt{10}\right)$

    i $\log \sqrt[3]{100}$ **j** $\log\left(\dfrac{100}{\sqrt{10}}\right)$ **k** $\log\left(10 \times \sqrt[3]{10}\right)$ **l** $\log\left(1000\sqrt{10}\right)$

    Check your answers using your calculator.

2 Simplify:

    a $\log(10^n)$ **b** $\log(10^a \times 100)$ **c** $\log\left(\dfrac{10}{10^m}\right)$ **d** $\log\left(\dfrac{10^a}{10^b}\right)$

3 **a** Explain why $\log 237$ must lie between 2 and 3.

    b Use your calculator to evaluate $\log 237$ correct to 2 decimal places.

4 **a** Between which two consecutive whole numbers does $\log(0.6)$ lie?

    b Check your answer by evaluating $\log(0.6)$ correct to 2 decimal places.

5 Use your calculator to evaluate, correct to 2 decimal places:

    a $\log 76$ **b** $\log 114$ **c** $\log 3$ **d** $\log 831$

    e $\log(0.4)$ **f** $\log 3247$ **g** $\log(0.008)$ **h** $\log(-7)$

6 For what values of x is $\log x$:

    a positive   **b** zero   **c** negative   **d** undefined?

7 Use your calculator to write the following in the form 10^x where x is correct to 4 decimal places:

    a 6   **b** 60   **c** 6000   **d** 0.6   **e** 0.006

    f 15   **g** 1500   **h** 1.5   **i** 0.15   **j** 0.000 15

Example 3   ◀) **Self Tutor**

  a Use your calculator to find: **i** $\log 2$ **ii** $\log 20$

  b Explain why $\log 20 = \log 2 + 1$.

a
```
NORMAL FLOAT AUTO REAL RADIAN MP
log(2)
                    .3010299957
log(20)
                    1.301029996
```

    i $\log 2 \approx 0.3010$

    ii $\log 20 \approx 1.3010$

b $\log 20 = \log(2 \times 10)$

          $= \log(10^{\log 2} \times 10^1)$ $\{x = 10^{\log x}\}$

          $= \log(10^{\log 2 + 1})$ $\{\text{adding indices}\}$

          $= \log 2 + 1$

---

8 **a** Use your calculator to find: **i** $\log 3$ **ii** $\log 300$

    b Explain why $\log 300 = \log 3 + 2$.

9 **a** Use your calculator to find: **i** $\log 5$ **ii** $\log(0.05)$

    b Explain why $\log(0.05) = \log 5 - 2$.

Example 4   ◀) **Self Tutor**

Find x such that:

  a $\log x = 3$ **b** $\log x \approx -0.271$

  a $\log x = 3$

      $\therefore \ 10^{\log x} = 10^3$

         $\therefore \ x = 1000$

  b $\log x \approx -0.271$

      $\therefore \ 10^{\log x} \approx 10^{-0.271}$

         $\therefore \ x \approx 0.536$

Remember that $10^{\log x} = x$.

10 Find x such that:

   a $\log x = 2$

   b $\log x = 1$

   c $\log x = 0$

   d $\log x = -1$

   e $\log x = \frac{1}{2}$

   f $\log x = -\frac{1}{2}$

   g $\log x = 4$

   h $\log x = -5$

   i $\log x \approx 0.8351$

   j $\log x \approx 2.1457$

   k $\log x \approx -1.378$

   l $\log x \approx -3.1997$

B   LOGARITHMS IN BASE a

In the previous Section we defined the logarithm in base 10 of a number as the power that 10 must be raised to in order to obtain that number.

We can use the same principle to define logarithms in other bases:

> The **logarithm in base a of b** is the power that a must be raised to in order to obtain b.

> The logarithm in base a of b is written $\log_a b$.

For example, to find $\log_2 8$, we ask "What power must 2 be raised to in order to obtain 8?". We know that $2^3 = 8$, so $\log_2 8 = 3$.

$a^x = b$ and $x = \log_a b$ are *equivalent* statements.

We write: $a^x = b \;\Leftrightarrow\; x = \log_a b$

Example 5   ◀) Self Tutor

   a Write an equivalent exponential statement for $\log_{10} 1000 = 3$.

   b Write an equivalent logarithmic statement for $3^4 = 81$.

   a From $\log_{10} 1000 = 3$ we deduce that $10^3 = 1000$.

   b From $3^4 = 81$ we deduce that $\log_3 81 = 4$.

EXERCISE 7B

1 Write an equivalent exponential statement for:

   a $\log_{10} 100 = 2$

   b $\log_{10} 10\,000 = 4$

   c $\log_{10}(0.1) = -1$

   d $\log_{10} \sqrt{10} = \frac{1}{2}$

   e $\log_2 8 = 3$

   f $\log_3 9 = 2$

   g $\log_2 \left(\frac{1}{4}\right) = -2$

   h $\log_3 \sqrt{27} = 1.5$

   i $\log_5 \left(\frac{1}{\sqrt{5}}\right) = -\frac{1}{2}$

2 Write an equivalent logarithmic statement for:

   a $2^2 = 4$

   b $4^3 = 64$

   c $5^2 = 25$

   d $7^2 = 49$

   e $2^6 = 64$

   f $2^{-3} = \frac{1}{8}$

   g $10^{-2} = 0.01$

   h $2^{-1} = \frac{1}{2}$

   i $3^{-3} = \frac{1}{27}$

Example 6
◀)) **Self Tutor**

Find:

a $\log_2 16$ **b** $\log_5(0.2)$ **c** $\log_{10} \sqrt[5]{100}$ **d** $\log_2\left(\frac{1}{\sqrt{2}}\right)$

a $\log_2 16$
$= \log_2(2^4)$
$= 4$

b $\log_5(0.2)$
$= \log_5\left(\frac{1}{5}\right)$
$= \log_5(5^{-1})$
$= -1$

c $\log_{10} \sqrt[5]{100}$
$= \log_{10}((10^2)^{\frac{1}{5}})$
$= \log_{10}(10^{\frac{2}{5}})$
$= \frac{2}{5}$

d $\log_2\left(\frac{1}{\sqrt{2}}\right)$
$= \log_2(2^{-\frac{1}{2}})$
$= -\frac{1}{2}$

3 Find:

    a $\log_{10} 100\,000$ **b** $\log_{10}(0.01)$ **c** $\log_3 \sqrt{3}$

    d $\log_2 4$ **e** $\log_2 64$ **f** $\log_2 128$

    g $\log_5 25$ **h** $\log_5 125$ **i** $\log_2(0.125)$

    j $\log_9 3$ **k** $\log_4 16$ **l** $\log_{36} 6$

    m $\log_3 243$ **n** $\log_2 \sqrt[3]{2}$ **o** $\log_8 2$

    p $\log_6\left(6\sqrt{6}\right)$ **q** $\log_4 1$ **r** $\log_9 9$

    s $\log_3\left(\frac{1}{3}\right)$ **t** $\log_{10} \sqrt[4]{1000}$ **u** $\log_7\left(\frac{1}{\sqrt{7}}\right)$

    v $\log_5\left(25\sqrt{5}\right)$ **w** $\log_3\left(\frac{1}{\sqrt{27}}\right)$ **x** $\log_4\left(\frac{1}{2\sqrt{2}}\right)$

> To find $\log_a b$ write b as a power of a.

4 Simplify:

    a $\log_x(x^2)$ **b** $\log_t\left(\frac{1}{t}\right)$ **c** $\log_x \sqrt{x}$ **d** $\log_m(m^3)$

    e $\log_x(x\sqrt{x})$ **f** $\log_a\left(\frac{1}{a^2}\right)$ **g** $\log_a\left(\frac{1}{\sqrt{a}}\right)$ **h** $\log_m \sqrt{m^5}$

Example 7
◀)) **Self Tutor**

Solve for x: $\log_3 x = 5$

$\log_3 x = 5$
$\therefore \ x = 3^5$
$\therefore \ x = 243$

5 Solve for x:

    a $\log_2 x = 3$ **b** $\log_4 x = \frac{1}{2}$ **c** $\log_x 81 = 4$ **d** $\log_2(x - 6) = 3$

6 Suppose $\log_a b = x$. Find, in terms of x, the value of $\log_b a$.

C LAWS OF LOGARITHMS

Investigation 1   **Discovering the laws of logarithms**

What to do:

1 **a** Use your calculator to find:

      i $\log 2 + \log 3$ **ii** $\log 3 + \log 7$ **iii** $\log 4 + \log 20$

      iv $\log 6$ **v** $\log 21$ **vi** $\log 80$

  b From your answers, suggest a possible simplification for $\log m + \log n$.

2 **a** Use your calculator to find:

      i $\log 6 - \log 2$ **ii** $\log 12 - \log 3$ **iii** $\log 3 - \log 5$

      iv $\log 3$ **v** $\log 4$ **vi** $\log(0.6)$

  b From your answers, suggest a possible simplification for $\log m - \log n$.

3 **a** Use your calculator to find:

      i $3\log 2$ **ii** $2\log 5$ **iii** $-4\log 3$

      iv $\log(2^3)$ **v** $\log(5^2)$ **vi** $\log(3^{-4})$

  b From your answers, suggest a possible simplification for $m\log b$.

From the **Investigation**, you should have discovered the three important **laws of logarithms**:

- $\log m + \log n = \log(mn)$ for $m, n > 0$
- $\log m - \log n = \log\left(\dfrac{m}{n}\right)$ for $m, n > 0$
- $m\log b = \log(b^m)$ for $b > 0$

More generally, in any base a where $a \neq 1$, $a > 0$, we have these **laws of logarithms**:

- $\log_a m + \log_a n = \log_a(mn)$ for $m, n > 0$
- $\log_a m - \log_a n = \log_a\left(\dfrac{m}{n}\right)$ for $m, n > 0$
- $m\log_a b = \log_a(b^m)$ for $b > 0$

Proof:

-   $\log_a(mn)$

    $= \log_a\left(a^{\log_a m} \times a^{\log_a n}\right)$

    $= \log_a\left(a^{\log_a m + \log_a n}\right)$

    $= \log_a m + \log_a n$

-   $\log_a\left(\dfrac{m}{n}\right)$

    $= \log_a\left(\dfrac{a^{\log_a m}}{a^{\log_a n}}\right)$

    $= \log_a\left(a^{\log_a m - \log_a n}\right)$

    $= \log_a m - \log_a n$

-   $\log_a(b^m)$

    $= \log_a\left(\left(a^{\log_a b}\right)^m\right)$

    $= \log_a\left(a^{m\log_a b}\right)$

    $= m\log_a b$

Example 8   ◀) **Self Tutor**

Use the laws of logarithms to write as a single logarithm or as an integer:

  a $\log 5 + \log 3$ **b** $\log_3 24 - \log_3 8$ **c** $\log_2 5 - 1$

a $\log 5 + \log 3$ **b** $\log_3 24 - \log_3 8$ **c** $\log_2 5 - 1$

$= \log(5 \times 3)$ $= \log_3\left(\frac{24}{8}\right)$ $= \log_2 5 - \log_2(2^1)$

$= \log 15$ $= \log_3 3$ $= \log_2\left(\frac{5}{2}\right)$

                       $= 1$

Example 9   ◀) **Self Tutor**

Simplify by writing as a single logarithm or as a rational number:

  a $2\log 7 - 3\log 2$ **b** $2\log 3 + 3$ **c** $\dfrac{\log 8}{\log 4}$

a $2\log 7 - 3\log 2$ **b** $2\log 3 + 3$ **c** $\dfrac{\log 8}{\log 4} = \dfrac{\log(2^3)}{\log(2^2)}$

$= \log(7^2) - \log(2^3)$ $= \log(3^2) + \log(10^3)$ $= \dfrac{3\log 2}{2\log 2}$

$= \log 49 - \log 8$ $= \log 9 + \log 1000$

$= \log\left(\frac{49}{8}\right)$ $= \log(9000)$ $= \frac{3}{2}$

EXERCISE 7C

1 Write as a single logarithm or as an integer:

  a $\log 8 + \log 2$ **b** $\log 4 + \log 5$ **c** $\log 40 - \log 5$

  d $\log p - \log m$ **e** $\log_4 8 - \log_4 2$ **f** $\log 5 + \log(0.4)$

  g $\log 250 + \log 4$ **h** $\log_5 100 - \log_5 4$ **i** $\log 2 + \log 3 + \log 4$

  j $\log 5 + \log 4 - \log 2$ **k** $\log_3 6 - \log_3 2 - \log_3 3$ **l** $\log\left(\frac{4}{3}\right) + \log 3 + \log 7$

2 Write as a single logarithm:

  a $\log 7 + 2$ **b** $\log 4 - 1$ **c** $1 + \log_2 3$

  d $\log_3 5 - 2$ **e** $2 + \log 2$ **f** $\log 50 - 4$

  g $t + \log w$ **h** $\log_m 40 - 2$ **i** $3 - \log_5 50$

3 Write as a single logarithm or integer:

  a $5\log 2 + \log 3$ **b** $2\log 3 + 3\log 2$ **c** $3\log 4 - \log 8$

  d $2\log_3 5 - 3\log_3 2$ **e** $\frac{1}{2}\log_6 4 + \log_6 3$ **f** $\frac{1}{3}\log\left(\frac{1}{8}\right)$

  g $3 - \log 2 - 2\log 5$ **h** $1 - 3\log 2 + \log 20$ **i** $2 - \frac{1}{2}\log_n 4 - \log_n 5$

4 Simplify without using a calculator:

  a $\dfrac{\log 4}{\log 2}$ **b** $\dfrac{\log_5 27}{\log_5 9}$ **c** $\dfrac{\log 8}{\log 2}$ **d** $\dfrac{\log 3}{\log 9}$ **e** $\dfrac{\log_3 25}{\log_3(0.2)}$ **f** $\dfrac{\log_4 8}{\log_4(0.25)}$

Example 10

🔊 Self Tutor

Show that:

a $\log\left(\frac{1}{9}\right) = -2\log 3$

b $\log 500 = 3 - \log 2$

a $\log\left(\frac{1}{9}\right)$
$= \log(3^{-2})$
$= -2\log 3$

b $\log 500$
$= \log\left(\frac{1000}{2}\right)$
$= \log 1000 - \log 2$
$= \log(10^3) - \log 2$
$= 3 - \log 2$

5 Show that:

a $\log 9 = 2\log 3$

b $\log\sqrt{2} = \frac{1}{2}\log 2$

c $\log\left(\frac{1}{8}\right) = -3\log 2$

d $\log\left(\frac{1}{5}\right) = -\log 5$

e $\log 5 = 1 - \log 2$

f $\log 5000 = 4 - \log 2$

6 Suppose $p = \log_b 2$, $q = \log_b 3$, and $r = \log_b 5$. Write in terms of p, q, and r:

a $\log_b 6$

b $\log_b 45$

c $\log_b 108$

d $\log_b\left(\frac{5\sqrt{3}}{2}\right)$

e $\log_b\left(\frac{5}{32}\right)$

f $\log_b(0.\overline{2})$

$0.\overline{2}$ means
$0.222\,222\,....$

7 Suppose $\log_2 P = x$, $\log_2 Q = y$, and $\log_2 R = z$. Write in terms of x, y, and z:

a $\log_2(PR)$

b $\log_2(RQ^2)$

c $\log_2\left(\frac{PR}{Q}\right)$

d $\log_2\left(P^2\sqrt{Q}\right)$

e $\log_2\left(\frac{Q^3}{\sqrt{R}}\right)$

f $\log_2\left(\frac{R^2\sqrt{Q}}{P^3}\right)$

8 If $\log_t M = 1.29$ and $\log_t N^2 = 1.72$, find:

a $\log_t N$

b $\log_t(MN)$

c $\log_t\left(\frac{N^2}{\sqrt{M}}\right)$

9 Write $\log(8!) - \log(7!) + \log(6!) - \log(5!) + \log(4!) - \log(3!) + \log(2!) - \log(1!)$ as a single logarithm.

10 Write $\log_2(6!)$ in the form $a + \log_2 b$, where $a, b \in \mathbb{Z}$ and b is as small as possible.

D | NATURAL LOGARITHMS

In **Chapter 6** we came across the **natural exponential** $e \approx 2.718\,28$.

The logarithm in base e is called the **natural logarithm**.

We use $\ln x$ to represent $\log_e x$, and call $\ln x$ the natural logarithm of x.

$$\ln e^x = x \quad \text{and} \quad e^{\ln x} = x.$$

Example 11

◀⅁ Self Tutor

Find:　**a** $\ln e^3$　　**b** $\ln \sqrt{e}$　　**c** $e^{2\ln 5}$

a　$\ln e^3$ $= 3$	**b**　$\ln \sqrt{e}$ $= \ln(e^{\frac{1}{2}})$ $= \frac{1}{2}$	**c**　$e^{2\ln 5}$ $= (e^{\ln 5})^2$ $= 5^2$ $= 25$

As with base 10 logarithms, we can use our calculator to find natural logarithms.

For example, $\ln 30 \approx 3.40$, which means that $30 \approx e^{3.40}$.

GRAPHICS CALCULATOR INSTRUCTIONS

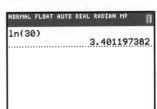

NORMAL FLOAT AUTO REAL RADIAN MP

ln(30)

3.401197382

Example 12

◀⅁ Self Tutor

Use your calculator to write the following in the form e^k where k is correct to 4 decimal places:

a 50　　　　　　　　　　**b** 0.005

a　50 $= e^{\ln 50}$　$\{x = e^{\ln x}\}$ $\approx e^{3.9120}$	**b**　0.005 $= e^{\ln 0.005}$ $\approx e^{-5.2983}$

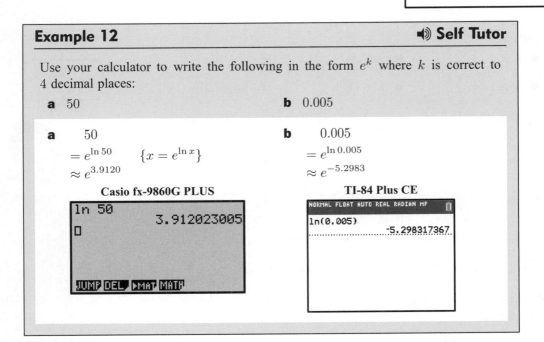

Casio fx-9860G PLUS

ln 50
　　　　　3.912023005
□

JUMP DEL ▶MAT MATH

TI-84 Plus CE

NORMAL FLOAT AUTO REAL RADIAN MP

ln(0.005)
　　　　　-5.298317367

EXERCISE 7D.1

1 Without using a calculator find:

　a $\ln(e^2)$　　　**b** $\ln(e^4)$　　　**c** $\ln\big((\sqrt{e})^3\big)$　　　**d** $\ln 1$

　e $\ln\left(\dfrac{1}{e}\right)$　　**f** $\ln \sqrt[3]{e}$　　**g** $\ln\left(\dfrac{1}{e^2}\right)$　　**h** $\ln\left(\dfrac{1}{\sqrt{e}}\right)$

　Check your answers using a calculator.

2 Simplify:

　a $e^{\ln 3}$　　　**b** $e^{2\ln 3}$　　　**c** $e^{-\ln 5}$　　　**d** $e^{-2\ln 2}$

　e $\ln e^a$　　　**f** $\ln(e \times e^a)$　　**g** $\ln(e^a \times e^b)$　　**h** $\ln\big((e^a)^b\big)$

3 Use your calculator to find, correct to 3 decimal places:

    a $\ln 12$ **b** $\ln 68$ **c** $\ln(1.4)$ **d** $\ln(0.7)$ **e** $\ln 500$

4 Explain why $\ln(-2)$ and $\ln 0$ cannot be found.

5 Use your calculator to write the following in the form e^k where k is correct to 4 decimal places:

    a 6   **b** 60   **c** 6000   **d** 0.6   **e** 0.006

    f 15   **g** 1500   **h** 1.5   **i** 0.15   **j** 0.000 15

Example 13 ◀)) Self Tutor

Find x if:

    a $\ln x = 2.17$ **b** $\ln x = -0.384$

If $\ln x = a$ then $x = e^a$.

    a $\quad \ln x = 2.17$
        $\therefore \; x = e^{2.17}$
        $\therefore \; x \approx 8.76$

    b $\quad \ln x = -0.384$
        $\therefore \; x = e^{-0.384}$
        $\therefore \; x \approx 0.681$

---

6 Find x if:

    a $\ln x = 3$ **b** $\ln x = 1$ **c** $\ln x = 0$ **d** $\ln x = -1$

    e $\ln x = -5$ **f** $\ln x \approx 0.835$ **g** $\ln x \approx 2.145$ **h** $\ln x \approx -3.2971$

7 **a** Write in simplest form: **i** $\ln(e^x)$ **ii** $e^{\ln x}$

    b What does this tell us about the functions $y = e^x$ and $y = \ln x$?

LAWS OF NATURAL LOGARITHMS

The laws for natural logarithms are the laws for logarithms written in base e:

- $\ln m + \ln n = \ln(mn)$ for $m, n > 0$
- $\ln m - \ln n = \ln\left(\dfrac{m}{n}\right)$ for $m, n > 0$
- $m \ln b = \ln(b^m)$ for $b > 0$

Example 14 ◀)) Self Tutor

Use the laws of logarithms to write as a single logarithm:

    a $\ln 5 + \ln 3$ **b** $\ln 24 - \ln 8$ **c** $\ln 5 - 1$

    a $\quad \ln 5 + \ln 3$
        $= \ln(5 \times 3)$
        $= \ln 15$

    b $\quad \ln 24 - \ln 8$
        $= \ln\left(\frac{24}{8}\right)$
        $= \ln 3$

    c $\quad \ln 5 - 1$
        $= \ln 5 - \ln(e^1)$
        $= \ln\left(\frac{5}{e}\right)$

Example 15
🔊 Self Tutor

Use the laws of logarithms to simplify:

a $2\ln 7 - 3\ln 2$ **b** $2\ln 3 + 3$

a $2\ln 7 - 3\ln 2$
 $= \ln(7^2) - \ln(2^3)$
 $= \ln 49 - \ln 8$
 $= \ln\left(\frac{49}{8}\right)$

b $2\ln 3 + 3$
 $= \ln(3^2) + \ln(e^3)$
 $= \ln 9 + \ln(e^3)$
 $= \ln(9e^3)$

EXERCISE 7D.2

1 Write as a single logarithm or integer:

a $\ln 15 + \ln 3$
b $\ln 15 - \ln 3$
c $\ln 20 - \ln 5$

d $\ln 4 + \ln 6$
e $\ln 5 + \ln(0.2)$
f $\ln 2 + \ln 3 + \ln 5$

g $1 + \ln 4$
h $\ln 6 - 1$
i $\ln 5 + \ln 8 - \ln 2$

j $2 + \ln 4$
k $\ln 20 - 2$
l $\ln 12 - \ln 4 - \ln 3$

2 Write in the form $\ln a, \ a \in \mathbb{Q}$:

a $5\ln 3 + \ln 4$
b $3\ln 2 + 2\ln 5$
c $3\ln 2 - \ln 8$

d $3\ln 4 - 2\ln 2$
e $\frac{1}{3}\ln 8 + \ln 3$
f $\frac{1}{3}\ln\left(\frac{1}{27}\right)$

g $-\ln 2$
h $-\ln\left(\frac{1}{2}\right)$
i $-2\ln\left(\frac{1}{4}\right)$

3 Show that:

a $\ln 27 = 3\ln 3$
b $\ln\sqrt{3} = \frac{1}{2}\ln 3$
c $\ln\left(\frac{1}{16}\right) = -4\ln 2$

d $\ln\left(\frac{1}{6}\right) = -\ln 6$
e $\ln\left(\frac{1}{\sqrt{2}}\right) = -\frac{1}{2}\ln 2$
f $\ln\left(\frac{e}{5}\right) = 1 - \ln 5$

Historical note   The invention of logarithms

It is easy to take modern technology, such as the electronic calculator, for granted. Until electronic computers became affordable in the 1980s, a "calculator" was a *profession*, literally someone who would spend their time performing calculations by hand. They used mechanical calculators and techniques such as logarithms. They often worked in banks, but sometimes for astronomers and other scientists.

The logarithm was invented by **John Napier** (1550 - 1617) and first published in 1614 in a Latin book which translates as a *Description of the Wonderful Canon of Logarithms*. John Napier was the 8th Lord of Merchiston, which is now part of Edinburgh, Scotland. Napier wrote a number of other books on many subjects including religion and mathematics. One of his other inventions was a device for performing long multiplication which is now called "Napier's Bones". Other calculators, such as slide rules, used logarithms as part of their design. He also popularised the use of the decimal point in mathematical notation.

John Napier

Logarithms were an extremely important development, and they had an immediate effect on the seventeenth century scientific community. **Johannes Kepler** used logarithms to assist with his calculations. This helped him develop his laws of planetary motion. Without logarithms these calculations would have taken many years. Kepler published a letter congratulating and acknowledging Napier. Kepler's laws gave **Sir Isaac Newton** important evidence to support his theory of universal gravitation. 200 years later, **Laplace** said that logarithms "by shortening the labours, doubled the life of the astronomer".

Johannes Kepler

E | SOLVING EXPONENTIAL EQUATIONS USING LOGARITHMS

In **Chapter 6** we found solutions to simple exponential equations where we could make equal bases and then equate exponents. However, it is not always easy to make the bases the same. In these situations we use **logarithms** to find the exact solution.

Example 16
◀ﬂ **Self Tutor**

a Solve the equation $2^x = 30$ exactly.

b Use your calculator to find the approximate solution. Give your answer correct to 2 decimal places.

a
$$2^x = 30$$
$$\therefore \ \log(2^x) = \log 30 \qquad \{\text{taking the logarithm of each side}\}$$
$$\therefore \ x \log 2 = \log 30 \qquad \{\log(b^m) = m \log b\}$$
$$\therefore \ x = \frac{\log 30}{\log 2}$$

b $\dfrac{\log 30}{\log 2} \approx 4.91$, so the solution is $x \approx 4.91$.

EXERCISE 7E

1 Consider the equation $2^x = 20$.

a Explain why the solution to this equation lies between $x = 4$ and $x = 5$.

b Find the solution exactly.

c Use your calculator to find the approximate solution. Give your answer correct to 2 decimal places.

2 Consider the equation $3^x = 40$.

    a Between which two consecutive whole numbers does the solution lie?

    b Find the solution exactly.

    c Use your calculator to find the approximate solution. Give your answer correct to 2 decimal places.

3 Solve for x: **i** exactly   **ii** correct to 2 decimal places.

    a $2^x = 10$ **b** $3^x = 20$ **c** $4^x = 50$

    d $\left(\frac{1}{2}\right)^x = 0.0625$ **e** $\left(\frac{3}{4}\right)^x = 0.1$ **f** $10^x = 0.000\,015$

Example 17   ◀ᴾ Self Tutor

Find x exactly:

    a $e^x = 30$ **b** $3e^{\frac{x}{2}} = 21$

    a $e^x = 30$ **b** $3e^{\frac{x}{2}} = 21$

       $\therefore \ x = \ln 30$ $\therefore \ e^{\frac{x}{2}} = 7$

                                     $\therefore \ \frac{x}{2} = \ln 7$

                                     $\therefore \ x = 2\ln 7$

---

4 Solve for x, giving an exact answer:

    a $e^x = 10$ **b** $e^x = 1000$ **c** $2e^x = 0.3$

    d $e^{\frac{x}{2}} = 5$ **e** $e^{2x} = 18$ **f** $e^{-\frac{x}{2}} = 1$

5 Solve for x, giving an exact answer:

    a $3 \times 2^x = 75$ **b** $7 \times (1.5)^x = 20$ **c** $5 \times (0.8)^x = 3$

    d $4 \times 2^{-x} = 0.12$ **e** $300 \times 5^{0.1x} = 1000$ **f** $32 \times e^{-0.25x} = 4$

6 Solve for x exactly:

    a $25^x - 3 \times 5^x = 0$ **b** $8 \times 9^x - 3^x = 0$ **c** $2^x - 2 \times 4^x = 0$

7 **a** Suppose a, b, $c > 0$ and that b, $c \neq 1$. By letting $\log_b a = x$ and showing that $x = \dfrac{\log_c a}{\log_c b}$,

     prove the **change of base** rule $\log_b a = \dfrac{\log_c a}{\log_c b}$.

    b Solve for x:

      i $\log_4(x^3) + \log_2 \sqrt{x} = 8$ **ii** $\log_{16}(x^5) = \log_{64} 125 - \log_4 \sqrt{x}$

     iii $4^x \times 5^{4x+3} = 10^{2x+3}$

    c Without using technology, show that $2^{\frac{4}{\log_5 4} + \frac{3}{\log_7 8}} = 175$.

F   GROWTH AND DECAY

In **Chapter 6** we showed how exponential functions can be used to model growth and decay situations such as the growth of populations and the decay of radioactive substances. In this Section we revisit growth and decay problems, focusing particularly on how logarithms can be used in their solution.

Example 18

A farmer monitoring an insect plague finds that the area affected by the insects is given by $A(n) = 1000 \times 2^{0.7n}$ hectares, where n is the number of weeks after the initial observation.

a Use technology to help sketch the graph of $A(n)$. Hence estimate the time taken for the affected area to reach 5000 hectares.

b Check your answer to **a** using logarithms.

a From the graph, it appears that it will take about 3.3 weeks for the affected area to reach 5000 hectares.

b When $A(n) = 5000$,

$1000 \times 2^{0.7n} = 5000$

$\therefore \quad 2^{0.7n} = 5$

$\therefore \quad \log(2^{0.7n}) = \log 5$

$\therefore \quad 0.7n \log 2 = \log 5$

$\therefore \quad n = \dfrac{\log 5}{0.7 \times \log 2}$

$\therefore \quad n \approx 3.32$

$\therefore$ it will take about 3 weeks and 2 days.

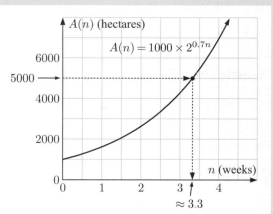

EXERCISE 7F

1 The population of turtles in an isolated colony is $P(t) = 852 \times (1.07)^t$, where t is the time in years after the colony was first recorded. How long will it take for the population to reach:

   a 1000 turtles   **b** 1500 turtles?

2 The weight of bacteria in a culture t hours after establishment is given by $W(t) = 20 \times 2^{0.15t}$ grams. Find, using logarithms, the time for the weight of the culture to reach:

   a 30 grams   **b** 100 grams.

3 A biologist is modelling an infestation of fire ants. He determines that the area affected by the ants is given by $A(n) = 2000 \times e^{0.57n}$ hectares, where n is the number of weeks after the initial observation.

   a Use technology to help sketch the graph of $A(n)$.

   b Use your graph to estimate the time taken for the infested area to reach 10 000 hectares.

   c Check your answer to **b** using logarithms.

4 A house is expected to increase in value at an average rate of 7.5% p.a. If the house is worth £360 000 now, when would you expect it to be worth £550 000?

5 Answer the **Opening Problem** on page **164**.

6 A sky diver jumps from an aeroplane. His speed of descent is given by $V(t) = 50(1 - e^{-0.2t})$ m s^{-1}, where t is the time in seconds. Show that it will take $5\ln 5$ seconds for the sky diver's speed to reach 40 m s^{-1}.

7 A meteor hurtling through the atmosphere has speed of descent given by

$$V(t) = 650(4 + 2 \times e^{-0.1t}) \text{ m s}^{-1}$$

where t is the time in seconds after the meteor is sighted.

a Is the meteor's speed increasing or decreasing?

b Find the speed of the meteor:

   i when it was first sighted

   ii after 2 minutes.

c How long will it take for the meteor's speed to reach 3000 m s^{-1}?

Investigation 2   **The "rule of 72"**

The "rule of 72" is used to estimate the time a quantity takes to double in value, given the rate at which the quantity grows.

The "rule of 72" states that:

> If a quantity increases by $r\%$ each year, then the quantity will take approximately $\dfrac{72}{r}$ years to double in value.

For example, if a population increases by 6% each year, then the population will double in approximately $\frac{72}{6} = 12$ years.

What to do:

1 Use the "rule of 72" to estimate the doubling time for a population which is growing at:

   a 2% per year   **b** 8% per year   **c** 12% per year.

2 **a** Use logarithms to find, correct to 3 decimal places, the actual doubling time for the growth rates in **1**.

   b How close were your estimates using the "rule of 72"?

3 **a** Use logarithms to find an exact formula for the doubling time T of a population with growth rate $r\%$ per year.

   b Use technology to graph the formula and the "rule of 72" formula $T = \dfrac{72}{r}$ on the same set of axes.

                                                      GRAPHING PACKAGE

   c For which growth rates is the "rule of 72" estimate:

      i most accurate   **ii** least accurate?

G LOGARITHMIC FUNCTIONS

We have seen that $\log_a a^x = a^{\log_a x} = x$.

So, writing $f(x) = \log_a x$ and $g(x) = a^x$, we have $fg = gf = x$.

We therefore say that the logarithmic function $\log_a x$ is the **inverse** of the exponential function a^x.

Algebraically, this has the effect that the logarithmic and exponential functions "undo" one another.

Geometrically, it means that the graph of $y = \log_a x$, $a > 0$, $a \neq 1$ is the *reflection* of the graph of $y = a^x$ in the line $y = x$.

We have seen previously the shape of the exponential function $y = a^x$ where $a > 0$, $a \neq 1$.

For $0 < a < 1$:

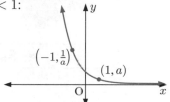

For $a > 1$:

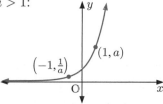

The horizontal asymptote for all of these functions is the x-axis $y = 0$.

By reflecting these graphs in the line $y = x$, we obtain the graphs for $y = \log_a x$.

For $0 < a < 1$:

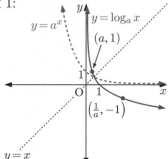

For $a > 1$:

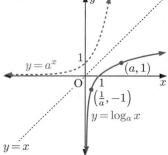

The **vertical asymptote** of $y = \log_a x$ is the y-axis $x = 0$.

For $0 < a < 1$:   as $x \to \infty$, $y \to -\infty$

as $x \to 0^+$, $y \to \infty$

For $a > 1$:   as $x \to \infty$, $y \to \infty$

as $x \to 0^+$, $y \to -\infty$

$\to$ means "tends to" or "approaches".

PROPERTIES OF $y = \log_a x$

Since we can only find logarithms of positive numbers, the domain of $y = \log_a x$ is $\{x : x > 0\}$.

We can compare the functions $y = a^x$ and $y = \log_a x$ as follows:

Function	$y = a^x$	$y = \log_a x$
Domain	$\{x : x \in \mathbb{R}\}$	$\{x : x > 0\}$
Range	$\{y : y > 0\}$	$\{y : y \in \mathbb{R}\}$
Asymptote	horizontal $y = 0$	vertical $x = 0$

TRANSFORMATIONS OF $y = \log_a x$

Click on the icon to explore the graphs of functions of the form
$y = k\ln(b(x - c))$, where k, b, c are constants.

LOGARITHMIC GRAPHS

Example 19   ◀) **Self Tutor**

Consider the function $f(x) = \log_2(x - 1) + 1$.

a Find the domain and range of f.

b Find any asymptotes and axes intercepts.

c Sketch the graph of $y = f(x)$ showing all important features.

a $x - 1 > 0$ when $x > 1$

So, the domain is $\{x : x > 1\}$ and the range is $\{y : y \in \mathbb{R}\}$.

b As $x \to 1$ from the right, $y \to -\infty$, so the vertical asymptote is $x = 1$.

As $x \to \infty$, $y \to \infty$, so there is no horizontal asymptote.

When $x = 0$, y is undefined, so there is no y-intercept.

When $y = 0$, $\log_2(x - 1) = -1$

$$\therefore \quad x - 1 = 2^{-1}$$

$$\therefore \quad x = \tfrac{3}{2}$$

So, the x-intercept is $\tfrac{3}{2}$.

c When $x = 2$, $y = \log_2(2 - 1) + 1$

$\qquad\qquad\qquad = 1$

When $x = 5$, $y = \log_2(5 - 1) + 1$

$\qquad\qquad\qquad = \log_2 4 + 1$

$\qquad\qquad\qquad = 2 + 1$

$\qquad\qquad\qquad = 3$

GRAPHICS CALCULATOR INSTRUCTIONS

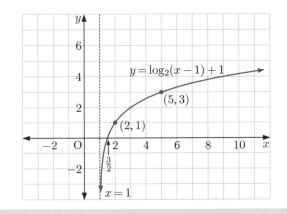

EXERCISE 7G

1 For each of the following functions f:

   i Find the domain and range.

  ii Find any asymptotes and axes intercepts.

 iii Sketch the graph of $y = f(x)$, showing all important features.

 iv Solve $f(x) = -1$ algebraically and check the solution on your graph.

a $f : x \mapsto \log_2 x - 2$ **b** $f : x \mapsto \log_3(x + 1)$ **c** $f : x \mapsto 1 - \log_3(x + 1)$

d $f : x \mapsto \log_5(x - 2) - 2$ **e** $f : x \mapsto 1 - \log_5(x - 2)$ **f** $f : x \mapsto 1 - 2\log_2 x$

2 For each of the functions f:

    i   State the domain and range.

    ii Find any asymptotes and intercepts.

    iii Sketch the graph of $y = f(x)$, showing all important features.

    a $f(x) = \ln x - 4$ **b** $f(x) = \ln(x - 1) + 2$

3 Consider the curves A and B. One of them is the graph of
$y = \ln x$ and the other is the graph of $y = \ln(x - 2)$.

    a Identify which curve is which, giving evidence for
your answer.

    b Copy the graphs onto a new set of axes, and then
draw the graph of $y = \ln(x + 2)$.

    c Find the equation of the vertical asymptote for each
graph.

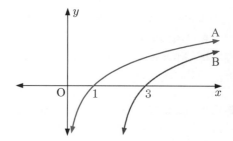

4 Kelly said that in order to graph $y = \ln(x^2)$, $x > 0$, you
could first graph $y = \ln x$ and then double the distance
of each point on the graph from the x-axis.

Is Kelly correct? Explain your answer.

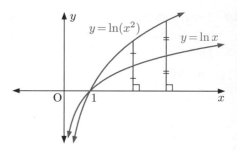

5 Draw, on the same set of axes, the graphs of:

    a $y = \ln x$ and $y = \ln(x^3)$ **b** $y = \ln x$ and $y = \ln\left(\dfrac{1}{x}\right)$

    c $y = \ln x$ and $y = \ln(x + e)$ **d** $y = \ln x$ and $y = \ln(x - 2) - 3$

    e $y = 2\ln x$ and $y = \ln(x^2) + 2$

6 The mass M_t of bacteria in a culture t hours after establishment is given by $M_t = 25 \times e^{0.1t}$ grams.
Show that the time required for the mass of the culture to reach 50 grams is $10\ln 2$ hours.

Example 20   ◀ⁱ⁾ **Self Tutor**

Iryna has £5000 to invest in an account that pays 5.2% p.a. interest compounded annually.
Use logarithms to find how long it will take for her investment to reach £20 000.

$$t_{n+1} = 20\,000 \quad \text{after } n \text{ years}$$
$$t_1 = 5000$$
$$r = 105.2\% = 1.052$$

Now $t_{n+1} = t_1 \times r^n$

$\therefore$ $20\,000 = 5000 \times (1.052)^n$

$\therefore$ $(1.052)^n = 4$

$\therefore$ $\log\big((1.052)^n\big) = \log 4$

$\therefore$ $n \times \log(1.052) = \log 4$

$\therefore$ $n = \dfrac{\log 4}{\log(1.052)} \approx 27.3$ years

The investment must be made for a whole number of time periods, so it will take 28 years for the
investment to reach £20 000.

7 Thabo has £10 000 to invest in an account that pays 4.8% p.a. compounded annually. How long will it take for his investment to grow to £15 000?

8 Dien invests £15 000 at 8.4% p.a. compounded *monthly*. He will withdraw his money when it reaches £25 000, at which time he plans to travel around the world. The formula $t_{n+1} = t_1 \times r^n$ can be used to model the investment, where n is the time in months.

   a Explain why $r = 1.007$.

   b After how many months will Dien withdraw his money?

9 The mass M_t of radioactive substance remaining after t years is given by $M_t = 1000 \times e^{-0.04t}$ grams. Find the time taken for the mass to:

   a halve   **b** reach 25 grams   **c** reach 1% of its original value.

10 The temperature of a liquid t minutes after it is placed in a refrigerator, is given by $T = 4 + 96 \times e^{-0.03t}$ °C.

Find the time required for the temperature to reach:

   a 25°C   **b** 5°C.

11 The weight of radioactive substance remaining after t years is given by $W = 1000 \times 2^{-0.04t}$ grams.

   a Sketch the graph of W against t.

   b Write t as a function of W.

   c Hence find the time required for the weight to reach:

       i 20 grams   **ii** 0.001 grams.

12 The weight of radioactive uranium remaining after t years is given by $W(t) = W_0 \times 2^{-0.0002t}$ grams, $t \geqslant 0$. Find the time required for the weight to fall to:

   a 25% of its original value   **b** 0.1% of its original value.

13 The current I flowing in a transistor radio t seconds after it is switched off is given by $I = I_0 \times 2^{-0.02t}$ amps.

Show that it will take $\dfrac{50}{\log 2}$ seconds for the current to drop to 10% of its original value.

14 A parachutist jumps from the basket of a stationary hot air balloon. His speed of descent is given by $V = 60(1 - 2^{-0.2t})$ m s^{-1} where t is the time in seconds. Write an expression for the time taken for his speed to reach v m s^{-1}.

Activity

Click on the icon to obtain a card game for logarithmic functions.

CARD GAME

Investigation 3   Logarithmic scales

In a **logarithmic scale**, equally spaced major tick marks correspond to integer *powers* of a base number. We often call these **orders of magnitude**.

For example, in the logarithmic scale alongside, each major tick mark represents a power of 10.

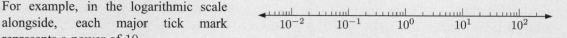

The minor tick marks correspond to integer *multiples* of each power of 10. So the minor tick marks between 10^1 and 10^2 represent 20, 30, 40, ..., and so on.

Logarithmic scales are useful when we want to represent both very large and very small numbers on the same number line. They allow us to compare real world quantities or events which are many orders of magnitude apart.

In this Investigation, we will explore the use of logarithmic scales in a variety of contexts.

What to do:

1 **a** For the logarithmic scale alongside, state the values of the points A, B, and C.

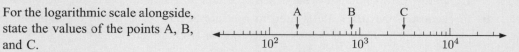

    b Explain why the minor tick marks in a logarithmic scale are not equally spaced.

    c Where is the value 0 on a logarithmic scale? Explain your answer.

2 Musical notes are named according to the frequency of their sound waves. They are labelled with letters of the alphabet.

A note which has *twice* the frequency of another is said to be one **octave** higher than it. So, one C is an octave below the next C.

    a How many orders of magnitude apart are the frequencies of two notes separated by 3 octaves?

    b Write an expression for the frequency of a musical note f, in terms of the number of octaves n *above* middle C.

    c There are 12 different notes in an octave. They are equally spaced on the logarithmic scale. Find the ratio of frequencies between two adjacent notes.

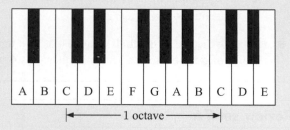

"Middle C" has the frequency $f_C = 261.6$ Hz.

3 In some situations, the logarithm is already applied to values placed on the number line. In these cases, the major tick marks represent the *exponents* rather than the numbers themselves.

For example, suppose the scale alongside is logarithmic with base 10. The major tick mark "2" represents the value 10^2, the major tick mark "3" represents the value 10^3, and so on.

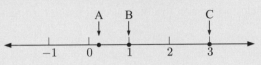

a How many times larger is the value at C than the value at B?

b Estimate the position on the scale representing the value:

   i 10 times smaller than A
   ii twice as large as B.

4 Earthquakes can range from microscopic tremors to huge natural disasters. The magnitude of earthquakes is measured on the **Richter scale** which relates to the energy released by the earthquake.

For this logarithmic scale, the logarithm is part of the formula. It is calculated as $M = \log\left(\dfrac{I}{I_0}\right)$, where I is the earthquake intensity and I_0 is a reference intensity level.

a What does it mean for a tremor to have magnitude: **i** 0   **ii** 1?

b Explain why an earthquake of magnitude 6 is *not* twice as intense as a magnitude 3 earthquake.

c Find the magnitude of an earthquake which has half the intensity of a magnitude 4 earthquake.

5 The *acidity* of a solution is determined by the concentration of hydronium ions (H_3O^+).
The higher the concentration of H_3O^+, the more acidic it is. The opposite of acidic is *alkaline*.

a In extremely acidic solutions, the concentration of H_3O^+ is typically more than 10^{-3} units. In very alkaline solutions, it is usually less than 10^{-12} units.
Explain why a logarithmic scale would be useful in describing the acidity of a solution.

b In chemistry, the **pH** scale is used to measure acidity. The pH of a solution is given by $pH = -\log C$, where C is the concentration of H_3O^+. Find:

   i the pH of a solution with H_3O^+ concentration $0.000\,234$ units
   ii the H_3O^+ concentration in a solution with pH 7.

c Is it possible for a solution to have a negative pH? Explain what this means in terms of the concentration of H_3O^+.

6 Research the use of **decibels** in acoustics as a unit of measurement for loudness of sound. Compare the use of decibels to the scales in questions **4** and **5**.

Review set 7A

1 Find:

   a $\log \sqrt{10}$
   b $\log\left(\dfrac{1}{\sqrt[3]{10}}\right)$
   c $\log(10^a \times 10^{b+1})$

2 Find:

   a $\log_4 64$
   b $\log_2 256$
   c $\log_2(0.25)$
   d $\log_{25} 5$

   e $\log_8 1$
   f $\log_{81} 3$
   g $\log_9(0.\overline{1})$
   h $\log_k \sqrt{k}$

3 Use your calculator to evaluate, correct to 3 decimal places:

   a $\log 27$
   b $\log(0.58)$
   c $\log 400$
   d $\ln 40$

4 Simplify:

a $4\ln 2 + 2\ln 3$ **b** $\frac{1}{2}\ln 9 - \ln 2$ **c** $2\ln 5 - 1$ **d** $\frac{1}{4}\ln 81$

5 Write as a single logarithm:

a $\log 16 + 2\log 3$ **b** $\log_2 16 - 2\log_2 3$ **c** $2 + \log_4 5$

6 Suppose $A = \log_5 2$ and $B = \log_5 3$. Write in terms of A and B:

a $\log_5 36$ **b** $\log_5 54$ **c** $\log_5\left(8\sqrt{3}\right)$

d $\log_5\left(\sqrt{6}\right)$ **e** $\log_5(20.25)$ **f** $\log_5(0.\overline{8})$

7 Find x if:

a $\log_2 x = -3$ **b** $\log_5 x \approx 2.743$ **c** $\log_3 x \approx -3.145$

8 Solve for x: **i** exactly   **ii** rounded to 2 decimal places.

a $2^x = 50$ **b** $7^x = 4$ **c** $(0.6)^x = 0.01$

9 Suppose $\log_a b = x$. Find, in terms of x, the value of $\log_a\left(\frac{1}{b}\right)$.

10 A population of seals is given by $P(t) = 80 \times (1.15)^t$ where t is the time in years, $t \geqslant 0$.

a Find the time required for the population to double in size.

b Find the percentage increase in population during the first 4 years.

11 For each of the following functions:

     i State the domain and range.

     ii Find any asymptotes and axes intercepts.

     iii Sketch the graph of the function, showing all important features.

a $f(x) = \log_2(x + 4) - 1$ **b** $f(x) = \ln x + 2$

12 Draw, on the same set of axes, the graphs of:

a $y = \ln x$ and $y = \ln(x - 3)$ **b** $y = \ln x$ and $y = \frac{1}{2}\ln x$

13 The temperature of a mug of water t minutes after it has been poured from a kettle is given by $T = 60e^{-0.1t} + 20$ °C.

Show that it will take $10\ln 3$ seconds for the temperature of the water to fall to 40°C.

Review set 7B

1 Without using a calculator, find the base 10 logarithms of:

   a $\sqrt{1000}$ **b** $\dfrac{10}{\sqrt[3]{10}}$ **c** $\dfrac{10^a}{10^{-b}}$

2 Find:

   a $\log_2 128$ **b** $\log_3\left(\frac{1}{27}\right)$ **c** $\log_5\left(\frac{1}{\sqrt{5}}\right)$

3 Write in the form 10^x, giving x correct to 4 decimal places:

   a 32 **b** 0.0013 **c** 8.963×10^{-5}

4 Find:

   a $\ln(e\sqrt{e})$ **b** $\ln\left(\frac{1}{e^3}\right)$ **c** $\ln(e^{2x})$ **d** $\ln\left(\frac{e}{e^x}\right)$

5 Simplify:

   a $\dfrac{\log_2 25}{\log_2 125}$ **b** $\dfrac{\log 64}{\log 32}$ **c** $\dfrac{\log_5 81}{\log_5 \sqrt{3}}$

6 Solve for x: **i** exactly   **ii** rounded to 2 decimal places.

   a $5^x = 7$ **b** $2^x = 0.1$

7 Write as a single logarithm:

   a $\ln 60 - \ln 20$ **b** $\ln 4 + \ln 1$ **c** $\ln 200 - \ln 8 + \ln 5$

8 Solve for x, giving exact answers:

   a $e^{2x} = 70$ **b** $3 \times (1.3)^x = 11$ **c** $5 \times 2^{0.3x} = 16$

9 What is the only value of x for which $\log x = \ln x$?

10 The weight of a radioactive isotope after t years is given by $W(t) = 2500 \times 3^{-\frac{t}{3000}}$ grams.

   a Find the initial weight of the isotope.

   b Find the time taken for the isotope to reduce to 30% of its original weight.

11 Solve for x, giving an exact answer:

   a $5^{\frac{x}{2}} = 9$ **b** $e^x = 30$ **c** $e^{1-3x} = 2$

12 Draw, on the same set of axes, the graphs of:

   a $y = \ln x$ and $y = \ln(x + 2)$ **b** $y = \ln x$ and $y = \ln(ex)$

13 *Hick's law* models the time taken for a person to make a selection from a number of possible options.

For a particular person, Hick's law determines that the time taken to choose between n equally probable choices is $T = 2\ln(n + 1)$ seconds.

   a Sketch the graph of T against n for $0 \leqslant n \leqslant 50$.

   b How long will it take this person to choose between:

      i 5 possible choices   **ii** 15 possible choices?

   c If the number of possible choices increases from 20 to 40, how much longer will the person take to make a selection?

8

Real polynomials

Contents:

Opening problem

For his Technical Studies project, Marcus is using a 40 cm by 30 cm sheet of tinplate to make a container.

Squares are cut from the corners of the sheet, and the metal is then folded upwards along the dashed lines.

The edges are welded together to form the open rectangular container.

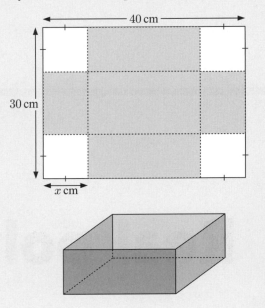

The volume of the container will depend on the size of the squares cut from the corners. When considering what this size should be, Marcus supposes that squares with side length x cm are cut from the corners.

Things to think about:

  a Can you explain why the volume of the container is given by the function
       $V = x(40 - 2x)(30 - 2x)$ cm^3 ?

  b What type of function is this?

  c For what values of x is it reasonable to use this function?

  d What does the graph of this function look like?

  e What size squares should be cut from the corners to make a container with volume 2000 cm^3 ?

To model the world around us, we need to be able to select and apply appropriate mathematical functions. Usually, we will be fitting a curve to a set of data points, and in this case we use functions whose values are always real numbers.

In the past we have studied linear, quadratic, exponential, and trigonometric functions. We now consider a more general class of functions which includes linear and quadratic. These are the **polynomials**.

A   POLYNOMIALS

A **polynomial** is a function which can be written in the form

$P(x) = a_n x^n + a_{n-1} x^{n-1} + ... + a_2 x^2 + a_1 x + a_0$ where $a_0, a_1, ..., a_n$ are constants, $a_n \neq 0$.

We say that: x is the **variable**
              a_0 is the **constant term**
              a_n is the **leading coefficient**
              a_r is the **coefficient of x^r** for $r = 0, 1, 2, ..., n$
              n is the **degree** of the polynomial, being the highest power of the variable.

In **summation notation** we write $P(x) = \sum_{r=0}^{n} a_r x^r$,

which reads: "the sum from $r = 0$ to n, of $a_r x^r$ ".

A **real polynomial** $P(x)$ is a polynomial for which $a_r \in \mathbb{R}$, $r = 0, 1, 2, ..., n$.

The low degree members of the polynomial family have special names, some of which you are already familiar with. For these polynomials, we commonly write their coefficients as a, b, c, ...

Polynomial function	Degree	Name
$ax + b$, $a \neq 0$	1	linear
$ax^2 + bx + c$, $a \neq 0$	2	quadratic
$ax^3 + bx^2 + cx + d$, $a \neq 0$	3	cubic
$ax^4 + bx^3 + cx^2 + dx + e$, $a \neq 0$	4	quartic

EXERCISE 8A

1 For each of the following polynomials, state the:

    i degree   **ii** leading coefficient   **iii** constant term.

  a $P(x) = 2x^3 + x^2 - 2x + 5$ **b** $f(x) = x^4 - 5x^2 + 3x - 2$

  c $Q(x) = -3x^5 - x^3 + 4x^2 + 1$ **d** $g(x) = 5x^3 - 3x^2 + 4x$

  e $P(x) = 8 - x^4$ **f** $h(x) = 2x^2 - 4x^3 + 7 - 3x$

2 State the:

  a coefficient of x^2 in $P(x) = 4x^3 + 7x^2 - 5x + 2$

  b coefficient of x in $f(x) = x^4 + 2x^3 - 4x + 1$

  c coefficient of x^3 in $Q(x) = x^5 - 3x^4 + 2x^2 - 7$

  d coefficient of x^2 in $g(x) = 2x^3 + x^2 - x + 6$

  e leading coefficient in $P(x) = 7 + 5x - x^4$.

B   OPERATIONS WITH POLYNOMIALS

ADDITION AND SUBTRACTION

> To **add** or **subtract** two polynomials, we collect "like" terms.

Example 1   ◀ঈ) Self Tutor

If $P(x) = x^3 - 2x^2 + 3x - 5$ and $Q(x) = 2x^3 + x^2 - 11$, find:

 a $P(x) + Q(x)$ **b** $P(x) - Q(x)$

  a $P(x) + Q(x)$
      $= \quad x^3 - 2x^2 + 3x - 5$
         $+ 2x^3 + \quad x^2 \qquad\quad - 11$
      $= \quad 3x^3 - \quad x^2 + 3x - 16$

Collecting "like" terms is made easier by writing them one above the other.

b $\quad P(x) - Q(x)$

$\begin{aligned} &= x^3 - 2x^2 + 3x - 5 - (2x^3 + x^2 - 11) \\ &= \quad x^3 - 2x^2 + 3x - 5 \\ &\quad \underline{-2x^3 - \;\; x^2 \qquad\quad + 11} \\ &= \;\; -x^3 - 3x^2 + 3x + 6 \end{aligned}$

> The brackets around $Q(x)$ help us get the signs correct in the next line.

SCALAR MULTIPLICATION

To **multiply** a polynomial by a **scalar** (constant) we multiply each term by the scalar.

Example 2

🔊 **Self Tutor**

If $P(x) = x^4 - 2x^3 + 4x + 7$, find:

a $\quad 3P(x)$

b $\quad -2P(x)$

a $\quad 3P(x)$
$\quad = 3(x^4 - 2x^3 + 4x + 7)$
$\quad = 3x^4 - 6x^3 + 12x + 21$

b $\quad -2P(x)$
$\quad = -2(x^4 - 2x^3 + 4x + 7)$
$\quad = -2x^4 + 4x^3 - 8x - 14$

POLYNOMIAL MULTIPLICATION

To **multiply** two polynomials, we multiply each term of the first polynomial by each term of the second polynomial, and then collect like terms.

Example 3

🔊 **Self Tutor**

If $P(x) = x^3 - 2x + 4$ and $Q(x) = 2x^2 + 3x - 5$, find $P(x)Q(x)$.

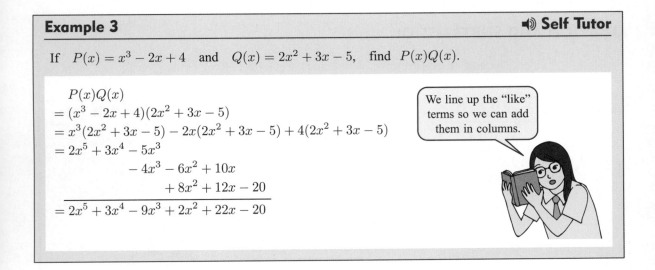

$P(x)Q(x)$
$= (x^3 - 2x + 4)(2x^2 + 3x - 5)$
$= x^3(2x^2 + 3x - 5) - 2x(2x^2 + 3x - 5) + 4(2x^2 + 3x - 5)$
$= 2x^5 + 3x^4 - 5x^3$
$\qquad\qquad - 4x^3 - 6x^2 + 10x$
$\qquad\qquad\qquad\quad + 8x^2 + 12x - 20$
$= 2x^5 + 3x^4 - 9x^3 + 2x^2 + 22x - 20$

> We line up the "like" terms so we can add them in columns.

We can also perform polynomial multiplication using:

- **synthetic multiplication** where we just use the coefficients

$$
\begin{array}{rrrrr}
1 & 0 & -2 & 4 & \longleftarrow \text{ coefficients of } x^3 - 2x + 4 \\
\times & 2 & 3 & -5 & \longleftarrow \text{ coefficients of } 2x^2 + 3x - 5 \\
\hline
-5 & 0 & 10 & -20 \\
3 & 0 & -6 & 12 \\
2 \quad 0 & -4 & 8 \\
\hline
2 \quad 3 & -9 & 2 & 22 & -20 \\
\end{array}
$$

$$x^5 \quad x^4 \quad x^3 \quad x^2 \quad x \quad \text{constant term}$$

Unlike long multiplication with numbers, we do not "carry" tens, and we can have negative coefficients.

$$\therefore \quad (x^3 - 2x + 4)(2x^2 + 3x - 5)$$
$$= 2x^5 + 3x^4 - 9x^3 + 2x^2 + 22x - 20$$

- a **grid** where we can add "like" terms along diagonals.

GRID METHOD

EXERCISE 8B

1 If $P(x) = x^2 + 2x + 3$ and $Q(x) = 4x^2 + 5x + 6$, find in simplest form:

   a $3P(x)$ **b** $P(x) + Q(x)$ **c** $P(x) - 2Q(x)$ **d** $P(x)Q(x)$

2 If $f(x) = x^2 - x + 2$ and $g(x) = x^3 - 3x + 5$, find in simplest form:

   a $f(x) + g(x)$ **b** $g(x) - f(x)$ **c** $2f(x) + 3g(x)$

   d $g(x) + xf(x)$ **e** $f(x)\,g(x)$ **f** $[f(x)]^2$

3 Expand and simplify:

   a $(x^2 - 2x + 3)(2x + 1)$ **b** $(x - 1)^2(x^2 + 3x - 2)$ **c** $(x + 2)^3$

   d $(2x^2 - x + 3)^2$ **e** $(2x - 1)^4$ **f** $(3x - 2)^2(2x + 1)(x - 4)$

4 Find the following products:

   a $(2x^2 - 3x + 5)(3x - 1)$ **b** $(4x^2 - x + 2)(2x + 5)$

   c $(2x^2 + 3x + 2)(5 - x)$ **d** $(x - 2)^2(2x + 1)$

   e $(x^2 - 3x + 2)(2x^2 + 4x - 1)$ **f** $(3x^2 - x + 2)(5x^2 + 2x - 3)$

   g $(x^2 - x + 3)^2$ **h** $(2x^2 + x - 4)^2$

   i $(2x + 5)^3$ **j** $(x^3 + x^2 - 2)^2$

5 Suppose the polynomial $P(x)$ has degree 3. Find the degree of $Q(x) = (x - 1)P(x)$. Explain your answer.

6 Suppose $P(x) = (x^2 - 3x + 4)Q(x)$ has degree 5. Find the degree of $Q(x)$.

7 $P(x)$ has degree 2, leading coefficient 3, and constant term 5. $Q(x)$ has degree 4, leading coefficient -5, and constant term -2. Find the degree, leading coefficient, and constant term of $P(x)Q(x)$.

8 If $P(x)$ and $Q(x)$ are polynomials with degrees p and q respectively, state possibilities for the degree of:

   a $P(x) + Q(x)$, $P(x) \neq -Q(x)$ **b** $kP(x)$, $k \neq 0$ **c** $P(x)Q(x)$ **d** $(P(x))^2$

Explain each answer.

Activity 1   Polynomials in powers of $x \pm k$

We sometimes wish to write a polynomial in powers of a simple linear expression of the form $x + k$ or $x - k$.

For example, we may wish to write

$x^3 + 2x^2 - 3x + 7$ in the form $a(x + 1)^3 + b(x + 1)^2 + c(x + 1) + d$, or

$x^4 + 2x^2 - x + 6$ in the form $a(x - 2)^4 + b(x - 2)^3 + c(x - 2)^2 + d(x - 2) + e$.

Forms like this are useful when we look at:

- transformations of functions
- cubic splines
- calculus, especially in Taylor series expansions.

An efficient method used to write a polynomial in this form is a process of **shift-expand-shift**.

> Suppose we wish to write the polynomial $P(x)$ as a polynomial in powers of $x + k$.
>
> *Step 1:*   Let $Q(x) = P(x - k)$.
>
> *Step 2:*   Expand the brackets in $Q(x)$ and collect like terms.
>
> *Step 3:*   Evaluate $Q(x + k) = P(x)$.

For example, consider writing $P(x) = x^3 + 2x^2 - 3x + 7$ in the form
$a(x + 1)^3 + b(x + 1)^2 + c(x + 1) + d$.

$$\begin{aligned}
\text{Let}\quad Q(x) &= P(x - 1) \\
&= (x - 1)^3 + 2(x - 1)^2 - 3(x - 1) + 7 \\
&= x^3 - 3x^2 + 3x - 1 \\
&\quad\ + 2x^2 - 4x + 2 \\
&\qquad\qquad - 3x + 3 \\
&\qquad\qquad\qquad + 7 \\
&= x^3 - x^2 - 4x + 11
\end{aligned}$$

$$\begin{aligned}
\therefore\quad P(x) &= Q(x + 1) \\
&= (x + 1)^3 - (x + 1)^2 - 4(x + 1) + 11
\end{aligned}$$

What to do:

1 Express:

   a $x^3 - 2x^2 + 3x + 5$ in the form $a(x - 2)^3 + b(x - 2)^2 + c(x - 2) + d$

   b $x^4 + 2x^2 - 6$ in the form $a(x + 1)^4 + b(x + 1)^3 + c(x + 1)^2 + d(x + 1) + e$

   c z^4 as a polynomial in powers of $z - 1$

   d $z^4 + z^2$ as a polynomial in powers of $z + 3$.

2 Show that:

   a $z^3 - 8z^2 + 28z - 20 > 0$ for all $z > 3$

   b $x^4 - 4x^3 + 8x^2 - 5x + 3 > 0$ for all $x > 1$

   c $x^3 + 8x^2 + 24x + 25 > 0$ for all $x > -2$.

C ZEROS, ROOTS, AND FACTORS

A **zero** of a polynomial is a value of the variable which makes the polynomial equal to zero.

⇔ means "if and only if".

α is a **zero** of polynomial $P(x)$ ⇔ $P(\alpha) = 0$.

The **roots** of a polynomial **equation** are the solutions to the equation.

α is a **root** (or **solution**) of $P(x) = 0$ ⇔ $P(\alpha) = 0$.

The **roots** of $P(x) = 0$ are the **zeros** of $P(x)$ and the x-intercepts of the graph of $y = P(x)$.

Consider
$$P(x) = x^3 - 2x^2 + x - 12$$
$$\therefore \quad P(3) = 3^3 - 2(3)^2 + 3 - 12$$
$$= 27 - 18 + 3 - 12$$
$$= 0$$

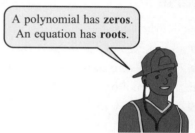

A polynomial has **zeros**. An equation has **roots**.

This tells us:

• 3 is a zero of $x^3 - 2x^2 + x - 12$
• 3 is a root of $x^3 - 2x^2 + x - 12 = 0$
• the graph of $y = x^3 - 2x^2 + x - 12$ has the x-intercept 3.

FACTORISATION AND EXPANSION

Polynomials can be written in **factorised form** or **expanded form**.

For example, the **expansion** of
$$(x + 1)(x - 2)(x - 4)$$
$$= (x^2 - x - 2)(x - 4)$$
$$= x^3 - 5x^2 + 2x + 8$$

In reverse, the process of writing $x^3 - 5x^2 + 2x + 8$ as $(x + 1)(x - 2)(x - 4)$ is called **factorisation**.

expansion

$(x + 1)(x - 2)(x - 4)$ $x^3 - 5x^2 + 2x + 8$

factorised form   factorisation   expanded form

If $P(x) = (2x + 1)(x - 3)(x - 1)$, then $(2x + 1)$, $(x - 3)$, and $(x - 1)$ are its **linear factors**.

Likewise $P(x) = (x + 2)^2(x - 1)$ has been factorised into 3 linear factors, one of which is repeated.

$(x - \alpha)$ is a **linear factor** of the polynomial $P(x)$ ⇔ there exists a polynomial $Q(x)$ such that $P(x) = (x - \alpha)Q(x)$.

If $\alpha \in \mathbb{R}$ then $(x - \alpha)$ is a **real linear factor**.

Example 4

◀) **Self Tutor**

Fully factorise: $x^3 + 6x^2 + 8x$.

$$x^3 + 6x^2 + 8x = x(x^2 + 6x + 8) \qquad \{x \text{ is a factor}\}$$
$$= x(x + 4)(x + 2) \qquad \{\text{factorising the quadratic}\}$$

Some polynomials have quadratic factors which cannot be written as the product of real linear factors.

For example, $P(x) = (x - 2)(x^2 + x + 1)$ has only one real linear factor since the quadratic factor $(x^2 + x + 1)$ has $\Delta < 0$. In this case 2 is the only real zero of $P(x)$.

EXERCISE 8C

1 Decide whether:

   a 3 is a zero of $x^2 - 5x + 6$

   b -1 is a zero of $x^3 + 2x^2 - 4x + 3$

   c 2 is a root of $3x^2 - 5x - 4 = 0$

   d -2 is a root of $x^3 + 3x^2 + 5x + 6 = 0$.

2 Find the zeros of:

   a $(x + 3)(x - 7)$ **b** $2x^2 - 5x - 12$ **c** $x^2 + 6x - 1$

3 Find the roots of:

   a $3x^2 - 13x + 4 = 0$ **b** $x^2 + 8x - 3 = 0$ **c** $x(x - 3)(x + 5) = 0$

4 Use expansion to verify that:

   a $(x - 4)(x - 2)(x + 3)$ is the factorised form of $x^3 - 3x^2 - 10x + 24$

   b $(3x + 1)(x + 3)(x - 4)$ is the factorised form of $3x^3 - 2x^2 - 37x - 12$

   c $(2x + 1)(2x - 3)(x + 2)$ is the factorised form of $4x^3 + 4x^2 - 11x - 6$.

5 Fully factorise:

   a $x^3 - 4x$ **b** $x^3 + 2x^2 - 3x$ **c** $x^3 - 4x^2 - 21x$

   d $x^3 - 9x^2 + 20x$ **e** $x^3 + 11x^2 + 24x$ **f** $2x^3 - 3x^2 - 2x$

   g $3x^3 + 10x^2 - 8x$ **h** $5x^3 - 9x^2 - 2x$ **i** $6x^3 - 7x^2 - 20x$

6 Find the real linear factors and corresponding zeros of:

   a $x^2 - 6x - 16$ **b** $2x^2 - 7x - 15$ **c** $x^2 + 3x + 4$

   d $x^3 + 2x^2 - 4x$ **e** $x^3 - 7x$ **f** $6z^3 - z^2 - 2z$

   g $z^4 - 6z^2 + 5$ **h** $z^4 + 3z^2 - 18$ **i** $(x + 5)(x^2 - 2x + 2)$

7 If $P(x) = a(x - \alpha)(x - \beta)(x - \gamma)$ then α, β, and γ are its zeros.

   Verify this statement by finding $P(\alpha)$, $P(\beta)$, and $P(\gamma)$.

8 The graph of the polynomial $P(x)$ has three x-intercepts, α, β, and γ.

   a State the values of $P(\alpha)$, $P(\beta)$, and $P(\gamma)$.

   b Explain why $P(x)$ cannot have a factor $(x - a)$ such that $a \neq \alpha$, β, or γ.

Example 5
◄) **Self Tutor**

Find *all* quartic polynomials with zeros 2, $-\frac{1}{3}$, and $-1 \pm \sqrt{5}$.

The zeros $-1 \pm \sqrt{5}$ have $\quad$ sum $= -1 + \sqrt{5} - 1 - \sqrt{5} = -2$

$\quad\quad\quad\quad$ and $\quad$ product $= (-1 + \sqrt{5})(-1 - \sqrt{5}) = -4$

$\therefore$ they come from the quadratic factor $x^2 + 2x - 4$.

The zeros 2 and $-\frac{1}{3}$ come from the linear factors $(x - 2)$ and $(3x + 1)$.

$\therefore \quad P(x) = a(x - 2)(3x + 1)(x^2 + 2x - 4), \quad a \neq 0.$

9 Find *all* cubic polynomials with zeros:

  a $-3, 4, 5$ **b** $\pm 2, 3$ **c** $3, 1 \pm \sqrt{5}$ **d** $-1, -2 \pm \sqrt{2}$

10 Find *all* quartic polynomials with zeros:

  a $\pm 2, \pm \sqrt{3}$ **b** $\frac{1}{2}, -1, \pm \sqrt{5}$ **c** $2 \pm \sqrt{2}, 4, 0$ **d** $\pm \sqrt{3}, -1 \pm \sqrt{2}$

Example 6
◄) **Self Tutor**

Consider the equation $kx^2 + (k + 3)x = 1$. Using a sign diagram for the discriminant Δ, find the values of k for which the equation has:

  a two distinct real roots   **b** two real roots   **c** a repeated root   **d** no real roots.

$kx^2 + (k + 3)x - 1 = 0$ $\quad$ has $\quad a = k$, $\quad b = (k + 3)$, and $\quad c = -1$

$\therefore \quad \Delta = b^2 - 4ac$

$\quad\quad = (k + 3)^2 - 4(k)(-1)$

$\quad\quad = k^2 + 6k + 9 + 4k$

$\quad\quad = k^2 + 10k + 9$

$\quad\quad = (k + 9)(k + 1)$ $\quad\quad$ So, Δ has sign diagram:

  a For two distinct real roots, $\quad \Delta > 0 \quad \therefore \quad k < -9$ or $k > -1$, $k \neq 0$.

  b For two real roots, $\quad\quad\quad\quad \Delta \geqslant 0 \quad \therefore \quad k \leqslant -9$ or $k \geqslant -1$, $k \neq 0$.

  c For a repeated root, $\quad\quad\quad \Delta = 0 \quad \therefore \quad k = -9$ or $k = -1$.

  d For no real roots, $\quad\quad\quad\quad \Delta < 0 \quad \therefore \quad -9 < k < -1$.

11 For each of the following quadratic equations, find the discriminant Δ and hence draw its sign diagram. Find all values of k for which the equation has:

    i two distinct real roots   **ii** two real roots   **iii** a repeated root   **iv** no real roots.

  a $2x^2 + kx - k = 0$ **b** $kx^2 - 2x + k = 0$

  c $x^2 + (k + 2)x + 4 = 0$ **d** $2x^2 + (k - 2)x + 2 = 0$

  e $x^2 + (3k - 1)x + (2k + 10) = 0$ **f** $(k + 1)x^2 + kx + k = 0$

12 $kx^2 + (k + 2)x - 3 = 0$ $\quad$ has roots which are real and positive.

  Find the possible values that k may have.

D   POLYNOMIAL EQUALITY

Two polynomials are **equal** if and only if they have the **same degree** (order) and corresponding terms have equal coefficients.

If we know two polynomials are **equal**, we can **equate coefficients** to find unknown coefficients.

For example, if $x^3 - 2x^2 + 3x + 7 = ax^3 + bx^2 + cx + d,$ where $a, b, c, d \in \mathbb{R},$ then
$a = 1, b = -2, c = 3,$ and $d = 7.$

Example 7   ◀)) Self Tutor

Find constants a, b, and c given that: $4x^3 + 10x^2 - x + 15 = (x + 3)(ax^2 + bx + c)$ for all x.

$$
\begin{aligned}
4x^3 + 10x^2 - x + 15 &= (x + 3)(ax^2 + bx + c) \\
&= ax^3 + bx^2 + cx + 3ax^2 + 3bx + 3c \\
&= ax^3 + (3a + b)x^2 + (3b + c)x + 3c
\end{aligned}
$$

Since this is true for all x, we equate coefficients:

$\therefore$ $\underbrace{a = 4}_{x^3 \text{ s}}$ $\underbrace{3a + b = 10}_{x^2 \text{ s}}$ $\underbrace{3b + c = -1}_{x \text{ s}}$ and $\underbrace{3c = 15}_{\text{constant terms}}$

$\therefore$ $a = 4$ and $c = 5$

$12 + b = 10$ and $3b + 5 = -1$ $\Rightarrow$ $b = -2$ in both equations.

So, $a = 4$, $b = -2$, and $c = 5$.

Example 8   ◀)) Self Tutor

Find constants a and b if $z^4 + 9 = (z^2 + az + 3)(z^2 + bz + 3)$ for all z.

$$
\begin{aligned}
z^4 + 9 &= (z^2 + az + 3)(z^2 + bz + 3)   \text{ for all } z \\
&= z^4 + bz^3 + 3z^2 \\
&\quad + az^3 + abz^2 + 3az \\
&\quad + 3z^2 + 3bz + 9 \\
&= z^4 + (a + b)z^3 + (ab + 6)z^2 + (3a + 3b)z + 9   \text{ for all } z
\end{aligned}
$$

Equating coefficients gives $\begin{cases} a + b = 0 & \text{.... (1)} \quad \{z^3 \text{ s}\} \\ ab + 6 = 0 & \text{.... (2)} \quad \{z^2 \text{ s}\} \\ 3a + 3b = 0 & \text{.... (3)} \quad \{z \text{ s}\} \end{cases}$

From (1) and (3), $b = -a$

$\therefore$ in (2), $a(-a) + 6 = 0$ $\therefore$ $a^2 = 6$

$\therefore$ $a = \pm\sqrt{6}$ and so $b = \mp\sqrt{6}$

$\therefore$ $a = \sqrt{6}, b = -\sqrt{6}$ or $a = -\sqrt{6}, b = \sqrt{6}$

> When simultaneously solving more equations than there are unknowns, we must check that any solutions fit **all** equations. If they do not, there are **no solutions**.

EXERCISE 8D

1 Find constants a, b, and c given that:

   a $2x^2 + 4x + 5 = ax^2 + (2b - 6)x + c$ for all x

   b $x^3 + 2x^2 - 3x + 4 = (x - 2)(x^2 + ax + b) + c$ for all x

   c $2x^3 - x^2 + 6 = (x - 1)^2(2x + a) + bx + c$ for all x.

2 Find constants a and b if:

   a $z^4 + 4 = (z^2 + az + 2)(z^2 + bz + 2)$ for all z

   b $z^4 + z^3 + z^2 - 9z - 10 = (z^2 + az + 5)(z^2 + bz - 2)$ for all z

   c $2z^4 + 5z^3 + 4z^2 + 7z + 6 = (z^2 + az + 2)(2z^2 + bz + 3)$ for all z.

3 Show that $z^4 + 64$ can be factorised into two real quadratic factors of the form $z^2 + az + 8$ and $z^2 + bz + 8$, but cannot be factorised into two real quadratic factors of the form $z^2 + az + 16$ and $z^2 + bz + 4$.

4 Find real numbers a and b such that $x^4 - 4x^2 + 8x - 4 = (x^2 + ax + 2)(x^2 + bx - 2)$.
Hence find $x \in \mathbb{R}$ such that $x^4 + 8x = 4x^2 + 4$.

5 Find real numbers c and d such that $x^4 - 10x^2 + 1 = (x^2 + cx + 1)(x^2 + dx + 1)$.
Hence find $x \in \mathbb{R}$ such that $x^4 + 1 = 10x^2$.

Example 9

◀）**Self Tutor**

$(x + 3)$ is a factor of $P(x) = x^3 + ax^2 - 7x + 6$.   Find $a \in \mathbb{R}$ and the other factors.

The coefficient of x^3 is $1 \times 1 = 1$

This must be 2 so the constant term is $3 \times 2 = 6$

$$x^3 + ax^2 - 7x + 6 = (x + 3)(x^2 + bx + 2) \quad \text{for some constant } b$$
$$= x^3 + bx^2 + 2x + 3x^2 + 3bx + 6$$
$$= x^3 + (b + 3)x^2 + (3b + 2)x + 6$$

Equating coefficients gives $3b + 2 = -7$ and $a = b + 3$

$\therefore \quad b = -3$ and $a = 0$

$\therefore \quad P(x) = x^3 - 7x + 6$
$$= (x + 3)(x^2 - 3x + 2)$$
$$= (x + 3)(x - 1)(x - 2)$$

The other factors are $(x - 1)$ and $(x - 2)$.

---

6 **a** $(2z - 3)$ is a factor of $2z^3 + az^2 - 17z + 12$. Find $a \in \mathbb{R}$ and all zeros of the cubic.

     b $(3z + 2)$ is a factor of $3z^3 - z^2 + (a - 4)z + a$. Find $a \in \mathbb{R}$ and all the zeros of the cubic.

Example 10

◀) **Self Tutor**

$(2x + 3)$ and $(x - 1)$ are factors of $2x^4 + ax^3 - 3x^2 + bx + 3$.

Find constants a and b and all zeros of the polynomial.

Since $(2x + 3)$ and $(x - 1)$ are factors,

The coefficient of x^4 is $2 \times 1 \times 1 = 2$

This must be -1 so the constant term is $3 \times -1 \times -1 = 3$

$$\begin{aligned}
2x^4 + ax^3 - 3x^2 + bx + 3 &= (2x + 3)(x - 1)(x^2 + cx - 1) \quad \text{for some } c \\
&= (2x^2 + x - 3)(x^2 + cx - 1) \\
&= 2x^4 + 2cx^3 - 2x^2 \\
&\quad + x^3 + cx^2 - x \\
&\quad - 3x^2 - 3cx + 3 \\
&= 2x^4 + (2c + 1)x^3 + (c - 5)x^2 + (-1 - 3c)x + 3
\end{aligned}$$

Equating coefficients gives $2c + 1 = a$, $c - 5 = -3$, and $-1 - 3c = b$

$$\therefore \quad c = 2$$

$$\therefore \quad a = 5 \text{ and } b = -7$$

$$\begin{aligned}
\therefore \quad P(x) &= 2x^4 + 5x^3 - 3x^2 - 7x + 3 \\
&= (2x + 3)(x - 1)(x^2 + 2x - 1)
\end{aligned}$$

Now $x^2 + 2x - 1$ has zeros $\dfrac{-2 \pm \sqrt{4 - 4(1)(-1)}}{2} = \dfrac{-2 \pm 2\sqrt{2}}{2} = -1 \pm \sqrt{2}$

$\therefore \quad P(x)$ has zeros $-\frac{3}{2}$, 1, and $-1 \pm \sqrt{2}$.

---

7 **a** $(2x + 1)$ and $(x - 2)$ are factors of $P(x) = 2x^4 + ax^3 + bx^2 + 18x + 8$.
    Find constants a and b, and all zeros of $P(x)$.

  b $(x + 3)$ and $(2x - 1)$ are factors of $2x^4 + ax^3 + bx^2 + ax + 3$.
    Find constants a and b, and hence determine all zeros of the quartic.

8 Find k given that $4x^4 - 4x^3 + kx^2 - 6x + 9$ is a perfect square.

9 Write $x^4 - 2x^3 - 3x^2 + 4x + 3$ in the form $a(x^2 - x)^2 + b(x^2 - x) + c$ where a, b, c are constants.
  Hence find all zeros of the polynomial.

10 **a** $x^3 + x^2 - 16x + k$, $k \in \mathbb{R}$, has two identical linear factors. Find k, and hence factorise the cubic into linear factors.

  b $x^3 + 3x^2 - 9x + c$, $c \in \mathbb{R}$, has two identical linear factors. Prove that c is either 5 or -27, and factorise the cubic into linear factors in each case.

  c $3x^3 + 4x^2 - x + m$, $m \in \mathbb{R}$, has two identical linear factors. Find the possible values of m, and find the zeros of the polynomial in each case.

E   POLYNOMIAL DIVISION

We have seen that a **rational function** is the division of two polynomials.

We can use a division process to find the result of polynomial division. This is usually only useful if the degree of the denominator is less than or equal to the degree of the numerator.

In this course we only consider division by linear functions.

DIVISION BY LINEARS

Consider $(2x^2 + 3x + 4)(x + 2) + 7$.

If we expand this expression we obtain $(2x^2 + 3x + 4)(x + 2) + 7 = 2x^3 + 7x^2 + 10x + 15$.

Dividing both sides by $(x + 2)$, we obtain

$$\frac{2x^3 + 7x^2 + 10x + 15}{x + 2} = \frac{(2x^2 + 3x + 4)(x + 2) + 7}{x + 2}$$

$$= \frac{(2x^2 + 3x + 4)(x + 2)}{x + 2} + \frac{7}{x + 2}$$

$$= 2x^2 + 3x + 4 + \frac{7}{x + 2} \quad \text{where} \quad x + 2 \quad \text{is the divisor,}$$
$$2x^2 + 3x + 4 \quad \text{is the quotient,}$$
$$\text{and} \quad 7 \quad \text{is the remainder.}$$

> If $P(x)$ is divided by $ax + b$ until a constant remainder R is obtained, then
>
> $$\frac{P(x)}{ax + b} = Q(x) + \frac{R}{ax + b} \quad \text{where} \quad ax + b \quad \text{is the **divisor**, } D(x),$$
> $$Q(x) \quad \text{is the **quotient**,}$$
> $$\text{and} \quad R \quad \text{is the **remainder**.}$$
>
> Notice that $P(x) = Q(x) \times (ax + b) + R$.

DIVISION ALGORITHM

We can divide a polynomial by another polynomial using an algorithm similar to that used for division of whole numbers:

Step 1:   What do we multiply x by to get $2x^3$?
The answer is $2x^2$, so we expand
$2x^2(x + 2) = 2x^3 + 4x^2$ and write
it underneath.

Step 2:   We then subtract $2x^3 + 4x^2$ from
$2x^3 + 7x^2$. The answer is $3x^2$.

Step 3:   Bring down the $10x$ to obtain $3x^2 + 10x$.

Return to *Step 1* with the question:

What must we multiply x by to get $3x^2$?
The answer is $3x$, and $3x(x + 2) = 3x^2 + 6x$.

We continue the process until we are left with a constant.

$$\begin{array}{r}
2x^2 + 3x + 4 \\
x + 2 \enclose{longdiv}{2x^3 + 7x^2 + 10x + 15} \\
-(2x^3 + 4x^2) \quad\quad\quad\quad \\
\overline{}3x^2 + 10x \quad\quad \\
-(3x^2 + 6x) \quad\quad \\
\overline{}4x + 15 \\
-(4x + 8) \\
\overline{}7
\end{array}$$

We find that $\dfrac{2x^3 + 7x^2 + 10x + 15}{x + 2} = 2x^2 + 3x + 4 + \dfrac{7}{x + 2}$.

The division algorithm can also be performed by leaving out the variable, as shown alongside.

$$
\begin{array}{r}
2\quad 3\quad 4 \\
1\ 2\,\big|\ \ 2\quad 7\quad 10\quad 15 \\
-(2\quad 4)\ \downarrow \\
\hline
3\quad 10 \\
-(3\quad 6)\ \downarrow \\
\hline
4\quad 15 \\
-(4\quad 8) \\
\hline
7
\end{array}
$$

Example 11   ◀ᵈ⟩ **Self Tutor**

Perform the division $\dfrac{x^4 + 2x^2 - 1}{x + 3}$. Hence write $x^4 + 2x^2 - 1$ in the form $Q(x) \times (x+3) + R$.

$$
\begin{array}{r}
x^3 - 3x^2 + 11x - 33 \\
x+3\,\big|\ \ x^4 + 0x^3 + 2x^2 + 0x - 1 \\
-(x^4 + 3x^3)\ \downarrow \\
\hline
-3x^3 + 2x^2 \\
-(-3x^3 - 9x^2)\ \downarrow \\
\hline
11x^2 + 0x \\
-(11x^2 + 33x)\ \downarrow \\
\hline
-33x - 1 \\
-(-33x - 99) \\
\hline
98
\end{array}
$$

Notice the insertion of $0x^3$ and $0x$ to keep "like" terms in columns.

$\therefore\ \dfrac{x^4 + 2x^2 - 1}{x + 3} = x^3 - 3x^2 + 11x - 33 + \dfrac{98}{x + 3}$

$\therefore\ x^4 + 2x^2 - 1 = (x^3 - 3x^2 + 11x - 33)(x + 3) + 98$

EXERCISE 8E

1 Find the quotient and remainder for the following, and hence write the division in the form $P(x) = Q(x)\,D(x) + R$, where $D(x)$ is the divisor.

a $\dfrac{x^2 + 2x - 3}{x + 2}$ **b** $\dfrac{x^2 - 5x + 1}{x - 1}$ **c** $\dfrac{2x^3 + 6x^2 - 4x + 3}{x - 2}$

2 Perform the following divisions, and hence write the division in the form $P(x) = Q(x)\,D(x) + R$.

a $\dfrac{x^2 - 3x + 6}{x - 4}$ **b** $\dfrac{x^2 + 4x - 11}{x + 3}$ **c** $\dfrac{2x^2 - 7x + 2}{x - 2}$

d $\dfrac{2x^3 + 3x^2 - 3x - 2}{2x + 1}$ **e** $\dfrac{3x^3 + 11x^2 + 8x + 7}{3x - 1}$ **f** $\dfrac{2x^4 - x^3 - x^2 + 7x + 4}{2x + 3}$

3 Perform the divisions:

a $\dfrac{x^2 + 5}{x - 2}$ **b** $\dfrac{2x^2 + 3x}{x + 1}$ **c** $\dfrac{3x^2 + 2x - 5}{x + 2}$

d $\dfrac{x^3 + 2x^2 - 5x + 2}{x - 1}$ **e** $\dfrac{2x^3 - x}{x + 4}$ **f** $\dfrac{x^3 + x^2 - 5}{x - 2}$

Example 12

◆)) **Self Tutor**

Carry out the division, and hence factorise the numerator into linear factors:

$$\frac{2x^3 - x^2 - 13x - 6}{x - 3}$$

$$
\begin{array}{r}
2x^2 + 5x + 2 \\
x - 3 \overline{\smash{\big)}\ 2x^3 - x^2 - 13x - 6} \\
-\,(2x^3 - 6x^2) \\
\hline
5x^2 - 13x \\
-\,(5x^2 - 15x) \\
\hline
2x - 6 \\
-\,(2x - 6) \\
\hline
0
\end{array}
$$

$$\therefore \quad \frac{2x^3 - x^2 - 13x - 6}{x - 3} = 2x^2 + 5x + 2 \qquad \text{\{the remainder is 0\}}$$

$$\therefore \quad 2x^3 - x^2 - 13x - 6 = (x - 3)(2x^2 + 5x + 2)$$
$$= (x - 3)(2x + 1)(x + 2)$$

---

4 Carry out the division, and hence factorise the numerator into linear factors:

a $\dfrac{3x^3 - 5x^2 - 4x + 4}{x + 1}$
b $\dfrac{2x^3 + 7x^2 - 10x - 24}{x - 2}$
c $\dfrac{4x^3 + 21x^2 + 2x - 15}{x + 5}$

5 **a** Use the division process to divide $\dfrac{x^3 + a^3}{x + a}$.

Check your answer by expanding and simplifying $(x^2 - ax + a^2)(x + a)$.

b Hence, factorise into two factors:

i $x^3 + 1$ **ii** $x^3 + 8$ **iii** $x^3 + 125$

6 **a** Carry out the following divisions:

i $\dfrac{x^2 - a^2}{x - a}$ **ii** $\dfrac{x^3 - a^3}{x - a}$ **iii** $\dfrac{x^4 - a^4}{x - a}$ **iv** $\dfrac{x^5 - a^5}{x - a}$

b Hence, deduce the factorisation of $x^n - a^n$ into two factors, one of which is linear.

c Write as a product of two factors, one of which is linear:

i $x^3 - 8$ **ii** $x^4 - 1$ **iii** $x^4 - 16$ **iv** $x^5 - 243$

Activity 2   **Synthetic division**

Click on the icon to learn an alternative procedure for performing division of a polynomial by a linear factor.

SYNTHETIC DIVISION

F THE REMAINDER THEOREM

Consider the real cubic polynomial $P(x) = x^3 + 5x^2 - 11x + 3$.

If we divide $P(x)$ by $x - 2$, we find that

A real polynomial is a polynomial with real *coefficients*.

$$\frac{x^3 + 5x^2 - 11x + 3}{x - 2} = x^2 + 7x + 3 + \frac{9}{x - 2} \longleftarrow \text{remainder}$$

So, when $P(x)$ is divided by $x - 2$, the remainder is 9.

Notice that $P(2) = 8 + 20 - 22 + 3$
$= 9$,   which is the remainder.

By considering other examples like the one above, we formulate
the **Remainder theorem**:

> When a polynomial $P(x)$ is divided by $x - k$ until a constant remainder R
> is obtained, then $R = P(k)$.

Proof: By the division algorithm, $P(x) = Q(x)(x - k) + R$
Letting $x = k$, $P(k) = Q(k) \times 0 + R$
$\therefore \quad P(k) = R$

When using the Remainder theorem, it is important to realise that the following statements are equivalent:

- $P(x) = (x - k)Q(x) + R$
- $P(k) = R$
- $P(x)$ divided by $x - k$ leaves a remainder of R.

Example 13   ◀) **Self Tutor**

Use the Remainder theorem to find the remainder when $x^4 - 3x^3 + x - 4$ is divided by $x + 2$.

If $P(x) = x^4 - 3x^3 + x - 4$,   then
$P(-2) = (-2)^4 - 3(-2)^3 + (-2) - 4$
$= 16 + 24 - 2 - 4$
$= 34$
$\therefore$ when $x^4 - 3x^3 + x - 4$ is divided by $x + 2$, the remainder is 34.   {Remainder theorem}

EXERCISE 8F

1 For $P(x)$ a real polynomial, write two equivalent statements for each of:

   a If $P(2) = 7$, then ......

   b If $P(x) = Q(x)(x + 3) - 8$, then ......

   c If $P(x)$ divided by $x - 5$ has a remainder of 11 then ......

2 Without performing division, find the remainder when:

   a $x^3 + 2x^2 - 7x + 5$ is divided by $x - 1$

   b $2x^3 - 8x + 11$ is divided by $x + 3$

   c $x^4 - 2x^2 + 3x - 1$ is divided by $x + 2$.

3 Find $a \in \mathbb{R}$ given that:

   a when $x^3 - 2x + a$ is divided by $x - 2$, the remainder is 7

   b when $2x^3 + x^2 + ax - 5$ is divided by $x + 1$, the remainder is -8.

Example 14   ◄) **Self Tutor**

When $x^3 + 4x^2 + ax + b$ is divided by $x - 2$ the remainder is 20, and when divided by $x + 5$ the remainder is 6. Find a and b.

Let $P(x) = x^3 + 4x^2 + ax + b$

$\therefore P(2) = 20$ and $P(-5) = 6$ {Remainder theorem}

So, $(2)^3 + 4(2)^2 + a(2) + b = 20$

$\therefore 8 + 16 + 2a + b = 20$

$\therefore 2a + b = -4$ .... (1)

and $(-5)^3 + 4(-5)^2 + a(-5) + b = 6$

$\therefore -125 + 100 - 5a + b = 6$

$\therefore -5a + b = 31$ .... (2)

Solving simultaneously: $2a + b = -4$ {(1)}

                       $5a - b = -31$ $\{-(2)\}$

         Adding, $7a = -35$

$\therefore a = -5$

Substituting $a = -5$ into (1), $2(-5) + b = -4$

$\therefore b = 6$

---

4 When $x^3 + 2x^2 + ax + b$ is divided by $x - 1$ the remainder is 4, and when divided by $x + 2$ the remainder is 16. Find constants a and b.

5 $2x^n + ax^2 - 6$ leaves a remainder of -7 when divided by $x - 1$, and 129 when divided by $x + 3$. Find a and n given that $n \in \mathbb{Z}^+$.

6 Consider $f(x) = 2x^3 + ax^2 - 3x + b$. When $f(x)$ is divided by $x + 1$, the remainder is 7. When $f(x)$ is divided by $x - 2$, the remainder is 28. Find the remainder when $f(x)$ is divided by $x + 3$.

7 **a** Suppose a polynomial $P(x)$ is divided by $2x - 1$ until a constant remainder R is obtained. Show that $R = P(\frac{1}{2})$.

    Hint: $P(x) = Q(x)(2x - 1) + R$.

  b Hence find the remainder when:

    i $4x^2 - 10x + 1$ is divided by $2x - 1$ **ii** $2x^3 - 5x^2 + 8$ is divided by $2x - 1$.

8 Find the remainder when $4x^3 + 7x - 3$ is divided by $2x + 1$.

9 When $2x^3 + ax^2 + bx + 4$ is divided by $x + 1$ the remainder is -5, and when divided by $2x - 1$ the remainder is 10. Find a and b.

G   THE FACTOR THEOREM

For any polynomial $P(x)$, k is a zero of $P(x)$ $\Leftrightarrow$ $(x - k)$ is a factor of $P(x)$.

Proof: k is a zero of $P(x) \Leftrightarrow P(k) = 0$ {definition of a zero}

$\Leftrightarrow R = 0$ {Remainder theorem}

$\Leftrightarrow P(x) = Q(x)(x - k)$ {division algorithm}

$\Leftrightarrow (x - k)$ is a factor of $P(x)$ {definition of a factor}

The **Factor theorem** says that if 2 is a zero of $P(x)$ then $(x - 2)$ is a factor of $P(x)$, and vice versa.

Example 15   ◀) Self Tutor

Find k given that $(x - 2)$ is a factor of $x^3 + kx^2 - 3x + 6$.
Hence, fully factorise $x^3 + kx^2 - 3x + 6$.

Let $P(x) = x^3 + kx^2 - 3x + 6$

Since $(x - 2)$ is a factor, $P(2) = 0$ {Factor theorem}

$\therefore \ (2)^3 + k(2)^2 - 3(2) + 6 = 0$

$\therefore \ 8 + 4k = 0$

$\therefore \ k = -2$

We now use division to find the other factors of $P(x)$:

$$
\begin{array}{r}
x^2 \qquad\quad - 3 \\
x - 2 \overline{\smash{\big)}\ x^3 - 2x^2 - 3x + 6} \\
\underline{- (x^3 - 2x^2)} \quad\downarrow\ \ \ \downarrow \\
0 \ - 3x + 6 \\
\underline{- (-3x + 6)} \\
0
\end{array}
$$

$\therefore \ P(x) = (x - 2)(x^2 - 3)$

$= (x - 2)(x + \sqrt{3})(x - \sqrt{3})$

EXERCISE 8G

1 Use the Factor theorem to determine whether:

a $(x - 2)$ is a factor of $x^3 - 3x^2 + 3x - 2$

b $(x + 1)$ is a factor of $x^4 - 2x^3 + 3x^2 - 4$

c $(x + 3)$ is a factor of $2x^3 + 5x^2 + x + 12$.

2 Find a given that:

    a $(x - 1)$ is a factor of $2x^3 - 3x^2 + ax - 4$

    b $(x + 2)$ is a factor of $3x^5 + ax^3 - 7x + 3$.

3 Find the constant k and hence factorise the polynomial if:

    a $2x^3 + x^2 + kx - 4$ has the factor $(x + 2)$

    b $x^4 - 3x^3 - kx^2 + 6x$ has the factor $(x - 3)$.

4 $(x - 4)$ is a factor of $P(x) = 3x^3 - 17x^2 + kx + 8$.

    a Find k.

    b Write $P(x)$ in the form $P(x) = (x - 4)(ax^2 + bx + c)$.

    c Hence find the roots of $P(x) = 0$.

5 Find constants a and b given that $2x^3 + ax^2 + bx + 5$ has factors $(x - 1)$ and $(x + 5)$.

6 Suppose 3 is a zero of $P(z) = z^3 - z^2 + (k - 5)z + (k^2 - 1)$.

    Find the possible values of $k \in \mathbb{R}$ and all the corresponding zeros of $P(z)$.

7 Show that $(z - 2)$ is a factor of $P(z) = z^3 + mz^2 + (3m - 2)z - 10m - 4$ for all values of $m \in \mathbb{R}$. For what value of m is $(z - 2)^2$ a factor of $P(z)$?

8 $(x + 3)$ is a factor of $P(x) = 2x^3 + 9x^2 + ax + b$. When $P(x)$ is divided by $x + 4$, the remainder is -18.

    a Find a and b.

    b Find the remainder when $P(x)$ is divided by $x - 2$.

    c Write $P(x)$ in the form $P(x) = (x + 3)(px^2 + qx + r)$.

    d Find the zeros of $P(x)$.

9 $(2x - 1)$ is a factor of $P(x) = 2x^3 + ax^2 - 8x + b$. When $P(x)$ is divided by $x - 1$, the remainder is 3.

    a Find a and b.

    b Find the irrational roots of $P(x) = 0$, giving your answer in the form $x = p \pm \sqrt{q}$ where $p, q \in \mathbb{Z}$.

10 Prove that $(x + 1)$ is a factor of $x^n + 1$, $n \in \mathbb{Z}$ $\Leftrightarrow$ n is odd.

11 Find the real number a such that $(x - 1 - a)$ is a factor of $P(x) = x^3 - 3ax - 9$.

H   SUM AND PRODUCT OF ROOTS THEOREM

We have seen that for the quadratic equation $ax^2 + bx + c = 0$, $a \neq 0$, the sum of the roots is $-\dfrac{b}{a}$ and the product of the roots is $\dfrac{c}{a}$.

> For the polynomial equation $\displaystyle\sum_{r=0}^{n} a_r x^r = 0$, $a_n \neq 0$
>
> the sum of the roots is $\dfrac{-a_{n-1}}{a_n}$, and the product of the roots is $\dfrac{(-1)^n a_0}{a_n}$.

We can explain this result as follows:

Consider the polynomial equation $a_n(x - \alpha_1)(x - \alpha_2)(x - \alpha_3)....(x - \alpha_n) = 0$
with roots $\alpha_1, \alpha_2, \alpha_3, ..., \alpha_n$.

Expanding the LHS we have

$$a_n(x - \alpha_1)(x - \alpha_2)(x - \alpha_3)(x - \alpha_4)....(x - \alpha_n)$$
$$= a_n(x^2 - [\alpha_1 + \alpha_2]x + (-1)^2\alpha_1\alpha_2)(x - \alpha_3)(x - \alpha_4)....(x - \alpha_n)$$
$$= a_n(x^3 - [\alpha_1 + \alpha_2 + \alpha_3]x^2 + ... + (-1)^3\alpha_1\alpha_2\alpha_3)(x - \alpha_4)....(x - \alpha_n)$$

{the term of order x is no longer important as it will not contribute to
either the x^{n-1} term or the constant term}

$$\vdots$$

$$= a_n(x^n - [\alpha_1 + \alpha_2 + \alpha_3 + ... + \alpha_n]x^{n-1} + ... + (-1)^n\alpha_1\alpha_2\alpha_3.... \alpha_n)$$
$$= a_nx^n - a_n[\alpha_1 + \alpha_2 + \alpha_3 + ... + \alpha_n]x^{n-1} + ... + (-1)^n\alpha_1\alpha_2\alpha_3.... \alpha_n a_n$$

Equating coefficients,

$$a_{n-1} = -a_n[\alpha_1 + \alpha_2 + \alpha_3 + ... + \alpha_n] \quad \text{and} \quad a_0 = (-1)^n\alpha_1\alpha_2\alpha_3.... \alpha_n a_n$$

$$\therefore \quad -\frac{a_{n-1}}{a_n} = \alpha_1 + \alpha_2 + \alpha_3 + ... + \alpha_n \quad \text{and} \quad \frac{(-1)^n a_0}{a_n} = \alpha_1\alpha_2\alpha_3.... \alpha_n$$

Example 16   ◀) Self Tutor

Find the sum and product of the roots of $2x^3 - 7x^2 + 8x - 1 = 0$.

The sum of the roots $= -\dfrac{(-7)}{2}$

$$= \tfrac{7}{2}$$

The polynomial equation has degree 3.

$\therefore$ the product of the roots $= \dfrac{(-1)^3(-1)}{2}$

$$= \tfrac{1}{2}$$

EXERCISE 8H

1 Find the sum and product of the roots of:

a $2x^2 - 3x + 4 = 0$

b $3x^3 - 4x^2 + 8x - 5 = 0$

c $x^4 - x^3 + 2x^2 + 3x - 4 = 0$

d $2x^5 - 3x^4 + x^2 - 8 = 0$

e $x^7 - x^5 + 2x - 9 = 0$

f $x^6 - 1 = 0$

2 A real cubic polynomial $P(x)$ has zeros $3 \pm \sqrt{2}$ and $\tfrac{2}{3}$, and its leading coefficient is 6. Find:

a the sum and product of its zeros

b the coefficient of x^2

c the constant term.

3 A real polynomial of degree 4 has leading coefficient -1. Its zeros are -2, 3, and $\sqrt{k} \pm 1$, and its graph has y-intercept 18. Find:

    a k **b** the coefficient of x^3.

4 A real quartic polynomial has leading coefficient 1 and constant term -2. Its zeros have the form $2 \pm a$ and $1 \pm a$, where $a \in \mathbb{R}$. Find the possible values that a may take.

5 $x^3 - px^2 + qx - r = 0$ has non-zero roots p, q, and r, where $p, q, r \in \mathbb{R}$.

    a Show that $q = -r$ and $p = -\dfrac{1}{r}$.

    b Hence find p, q, and r.

GRAPHING CUBIC FUNCTIONS

The most basic cubic function is $y = x^3$. Its graph is shown alongside.

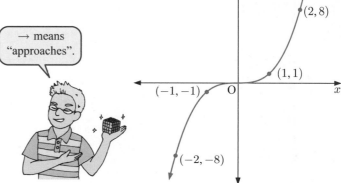

Notice that:

- The graph is horizontal at $(0, 0)$.
- As x gets very large and positive, y also gets very large and positive. We write:

  As $x \to \infty$, $y \to \infty$.

  > $\to$ means "approaches".

- As x gets very large and negative, y also gets very large and negative. We write:

  As $x \to -\infty$, $y \to -\infty$.

Investigation 1   Families of cubics

In this Investigation we will graph some different types of cubic functions, and observe the geometrical significance of each type.

What to do:

1 **a** Use technology to help you sketch the graphs of:

      i $y = x^3$, $y = 2x^3$, $y = \frac{1}{2}x^3$,   and $y = \frac{1}{3}x^3$

      ii $y = x^3$ and $y = -x^3$

      iii $y = -x^3$, $y = -2x^3$, $y = -\frac{1}{2}x^3$,   and $y = -\frac{1}{10}x^3$

                                       GRAPHING PACKAGE

    b For the curve $y = ax^3$, what is the geometrical significance of a? You should comment on both the sign and the size of a.

2 **a** Use technology to help you sketch the graphs of:

      i $y = x^3$ and $y = (x - 2)^3 + 3$

      ii $y = 2x^3$ and $y = 2(x + 1)^3 - 4$

      iii $y = -\frac{1}{2}x^3$ and $y = -\frac{1}{2}(x - 3)^3 + 2$

    b Describe how the graph of $y = a(x - b)^3 + c$ is obtained from the graph of $y = ax^3$.

From **Investigation 1**, you should have found that:

- The graph of $y = ax^3$ has shape:

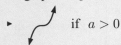 if $a > 0$ 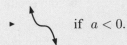 if $a < 0$.

- As the size of a increases, the graph of $y = ax^3$ becomes steeper.
- The graph of $y = a(x - b)^3 + c$ is obtained by translating the graph of $y = ax^3$ by the vector $\begin{pmatrix} b \\ c \end{pmatrix}$.

Example 17   ◀⁾ **Self Tutor**

On the same set of axes, sketch the graph of $y = x^3$ and $y = (x - 2)^3 - 1$.

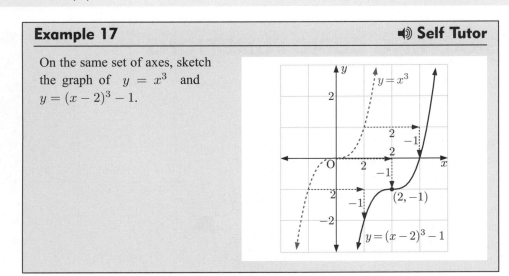

CUBICS IN FACTORISED FORM

The factorised form of a cubic tells us the number and nature of the x-intercepts of its graph.

Investigation 2   **Graphs of cubic polynomials**

Every real cubic polynomial can be categorised into one of four types. In each case $a \in \mathbb{R}$, $a \neq 0$, and the constants α, β, and γ correspond to zeros.

Type 1:   Three real, distinct zeros: $P(x) = a(x - \alpha)(x - \beta)(x - \gamma)$

Type 2:   Two real zeros, one repeated: $P(x) = a(x - \alpha)^2(x - \beta)$

Type 3:   One real zero repeated three times: $P(x) = a(x - \alpha)^3$

Type 4:   One real zero: $P(x) = (x - \alpha)(ax^2 + bx + c)$, $\Delta = b^2 - 4ac < 0$.

What to do:

1 Experiment with the graphs of *Type 1* cubics. State the effect of changing both the size and sign of a. What is the geometrical significance of α, β, and γ?

GRAPHING PACKAGE

2 Experiment with the graphs of *Type 2* cubics. What is the geometrical significance of the squared factor?

3 Experiment with the graphs of *Type 3* cubics. What is the geometrical significance of α?

4 Experiment with the graphs of *Type 4* cubics. What is the geometrical significance of α? What is the significance of the quadratic factor which has no real zeros?

From **Investigation 2** you should have discovered that:

- If $a > 0$, the graph has shape 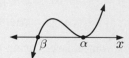 or . If $a < 0$ it is or .

- Every cubic polynomial must cut the x-axis at least once, and so has at least one real zero.

- For a cubic of the form $P(x) = a(x - \alpha)(x - \beta)(x - \gamma)$ where $\alpha,\ \beta,\ \gamma \in \mathbb{R},$ the graph has three distinct x-intercepts corresponding to the three distinct zeros $\alpha,\ \beta,$ and $\gamma.$ The graph crosses over or **cuts** the x-axis at these points.

- For a cubic of the form $P(x) = a(x - \alpha)^2(x - \beta)$ where $\alpha,\ \beta \in \mathbb{R},$ the graph **touches** the x-axis at α and **cuts** it at $\beta.$

- For a cubic of the form $P(x) = a(x - \alpha)^3,\ x \in \mathbb{R},$ the graph has only one x-intercept, $\alpha.$ The graph is horizontal at this point.

- For a cubic of the form $P(x) = (x - \alpha)(ax^2 + bx + c)$ where $\Delta < 0,$ there is only one x-intercept, $\alpha.$ The graph cuts the x-axis at this point.

Example 18

◀) **Self Tutor**

Use the axes intercepts to sketch the graph of:

a $y = 2(x + 3)(x - 1)(x - 3)$

b $y = -(x - 2)^2(2x + 1)$

a The graph cuts the x-axis at $-3,$ $1,$ and $3.$
When $x = 0,$
$$y = 2(3)(-1)(-3) = 18$$
$\therefore$ the y-intercept is $18.$

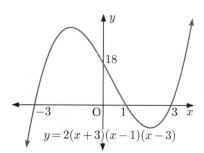

b The graph touches the x-axis at 2 and cuts the x-axis at $-\frac{1}{2}.$
When $x = 0,$
$$y = -(-2)^2(1) = -4$$
$\therefore$ the y-intercept is $-4.$

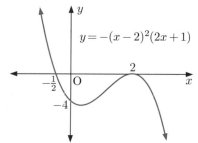

EXERCISE 8I

1 Sketch the following graphs. Use a separate set of axes for each part.

  a $y = x^3$ and $y = (x + 3)^3 + 2$ **b** $y = -x^3$ and $y = -(x - 1)^3 - 4$

  c $y = 3x^3$ and $y = 3(x - 2)^3 + 5$ **d** $y = -\frac{1}{2}x^3$ and $y = -\frac{1}{2}(x + 4)^3 - 3$

2 Use axes intercepts to sketch the graph of:

  a $y = (x + 4)(x + 1)(x - 2)$ **b** $y = (x - 1)^2(x + 3)$

  c $y = (x + 2)^3$ **d** $f(x) = -(x + 2)^2(2x - 3)$

  e $y = 3x(x + 4)(x - 2)$ **f** $f(x) = -2(x - 4)^3$

  g $y = \frac{1}{2}(x + 4)^2(3x - 2)$ **h** $f(x) = \frac{1}{3}(2x - 1)(x + 3)(x - 2)$

  i $f(x) = -4(2x + 5)^2(3x - 1)$

GRAPHING PACKAGE

Check your answers using technology.

Example 19

◀)) **Self Tutor**

Find the equation of the cubic with graph:

a

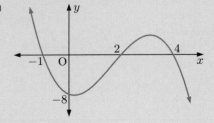

b

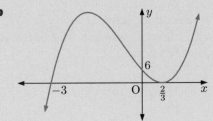

a The x-intercepts are -1, 2, 4.

   ∴ $y = a(x + 1)(x - 2)(x - 4)$

  But when $x = 0$, $y = -8$

   ∴ $a(1)(-2)(-4) = -8$

             ∴ $a = -1$

  So, $y = -(x + 1)(x - 2)(x - 4)$

b The graph touches the x-axis at $\frac{2}{3}$, indicating a squared factor $(3x - 2)^2$.

  The other x-intercept is -3,

  so $y = a(3x - 2)^2(x + 3)$.

  But when $x = 0$, $y = 6$

      ∴ $a(-2)^2(3) = 6$

           ∴ $a = \frac{1}{2}$

  So, $y = \frac{1}{2}(3x - 2)^2(x + 3)$

---

3 Find the equation of the cubic with graph:

a

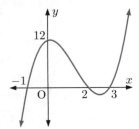

b

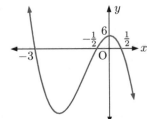

c

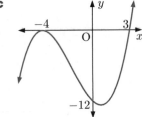

d 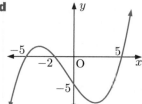 **e** 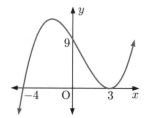 **f**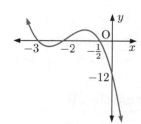

4 **a** Show that -2 is an x-intercept of the graph of $f(x) = 2x^3 - 3x^2 - 11x + 6$.

    b Fully factorise $2x^3 - 3x^2 - 11x + 6$.

    c Hence, sketch the graph of $f(x) = 2x^3 - 3x^2 - 11x + 6$.

    d State the domain and range of the function.

    e Describe the behaviour of the graph as $x \to \infty$ and $x \to -\infty$.

5 Find the equation of the cubic whose graph:

    a cuts the x-axis at 3, 1, and -2, and passes through $(2, -4)$

    b cuts the x-axis at -2, 0, and $\frac{1}{2}$, and passes through $(-1, 9)$

    c touches the x-axis at 1, cuts the x-axis at -2, and passes through $(4, 54)$

    d touches the x-axis at $-\frac{2}{3}$, cuts the x-axis at 4, and passes through $(1, 25)$.

6 Match each cubic function with its graph:

    a $y = 2(x - 1)(x + 2)(x + 4)$ **b** $y = 2(x - 3)^3$ **c** $y = (x - 3)(x^2 - 4x + 5)$

    d $y = (x - 3)^2(x + 1)$ **e** $y = (x - 3)(x^2 + 2x + 3)$ **f** $y = -2(x - 3)^3$

    g $y = 2(x - 1)(x - 2)(x + 4)$ **h** $y = (x + 1)^2(x - 3)$ **i** $y = (x - 3)(x^2 + 2x - 3)$

A 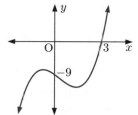 **B** 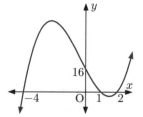 **C**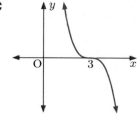

D 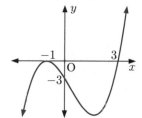 **E** 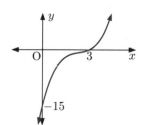 **F**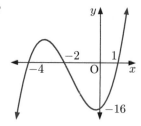

G 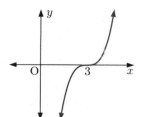 **H** 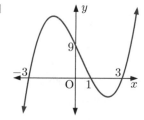 **I**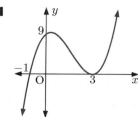

7 **a** Given that 1 is a zero of $-2x^3 - 2x^2 + 10x - 6$, fully factorise the polynomial.

b Hence, sketch the graph of $y = -2x^3 - 2x^2 + 10x - 6$.

c Describe the behaviour of the graph as $x \to \infty$ and $x \to -\infty$.

Example 20 🔊 **Self Tutor**

Find the equation of the cubic which cuts the x-axis at 2 and -3, cuts the y-axis at -48, and which passes through the point $(1, -40)$.

The zeros are 2 and -3, so $y = (x - 2)(x + 3)(ax + b)$, $a \neq 0$.

When $x = 0$, $y = -48$ When $x = 1$, $y = -40$
$\therefore \ (-2)(3)b = -48$ $\therefore \ (-1)(4)(a + 8) = -40$
$\therefore \ b = 8$ $\therefore \ a + 8 = 10$
          $\therefore \ a = 2$

So, the equation is $y = (x - 2)(x + 3)(2x + 8)$
which we can write as $y = 2(x - 2)(x + 3)(x + 4)$

The third zero is unknown, so we use the factor $(ax + b)$.

---

8 Find the equation of a real cubic polynomial which:

a cuts the x-axis at $\frac{1}{2}$ and -3, cuts the y-axis at 30, and passes through $(1, -20)$

b touches the x-axis at -2, cuts the y-axis at 8, and passes through $(-1, 4)$

c cuts the x-axis at 2, cuts the y-axis at -4, and passes through $(1, -1)$ and $(-1, -21)$.

If two zeros are unknown, use the factor $(ax^2 + bx + c)$.

9 A scientist is trying to design a crash test barrier with the characteristics shown in the graph below. The independent variable t is the time after impact, measured in milliseconds with $0 \leqslant t \leqslant 700$. The dependent variable is the distance the barrier is depressed during the impact, measured in millimetres.

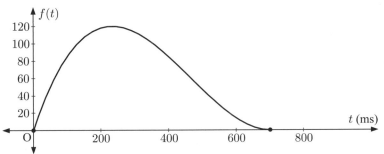

a The equation for this graph has the form $f(t) = kt(t - a)^2$, $0 \leqslant t \leqslant 700$.
Use the graph to find a. Discuss the significance of this value.

b The ideal crash barrier is depressed by 85 mm after 100 milliseconds. Find the value of k which gives this result, and hence find the equation of the graph given.

10 Consider the **Opening Problem** on page **188**.

    a Explain why the volume of the container is $V = x(40 - 2x)(30 - 2x)$ cm^3.

    b For what values of x is it reasonable to use this function?

    c Use technology to help sketch the function.

    d What size squares should be cut from the corners to make a container with volume 2000 cm^3 ?

J   GRAPHING QUARTIC FUNCTIONS

A **quartic function** is a function of the form $y = ax^4 + bx^3 + cx^2 + dx + e$ where a, b, c, d, and e are constants, $a \neq 0$.

The simplest quartic function is $y = x^4$.

Notice that:

- the graph opens upwards
- the graph is 'flat' at $(0, 0)$
- as $x \to \infty$, $y \to \infty$
- as $x \to -\infty$, $y \to \infty$.

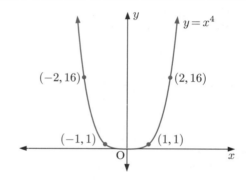

As with quadratic and cubic functions, quartic functions may be written in **expanded form** such as $y = x^4 - 4x^3 - x^2 + 16x - 12$, or in **factorised form** such as $y = (x + 2)(x - 1)(x - 2)(x - 3)$. The factorised form of a quartic function gives us the most information about the function's graph.

Investigation 3   Graphs of quartic functions

What to do:

1 Experiment with the graphs of quartics which have:

    a four distinct real linear factors

    b a squared real linear factor and two distinct real linear factors

    c two squared real linear factors

    d a cubed real linear factor and one distinct real linear factor

    e a real linear factor raised to the fourth power

    f one real quadratic factor with $\Delta < 0$ and two real linear factors

    g two real quadratic factors each with $\Delta < 0$.

GRAPHING PACKAGE

2 Summarise your observations.

From **Investigation 3** you should have discovered that:

- For a quartic polynomial in which a is the coefficient of x^4:
  ▸ If $a > 0$ the graph opens upwards.
  ▸ If $a < 0$ the graph opens downwards.

- If a quartic with $a > 0$ is fully factorised into real linear factors, then:
  ▸ for a **single factor** $(x - \alpha)$, the graph **cuts** the x-axis at α

  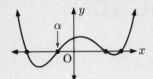

  ▸ for a **square factor** $(x - \alpha)^2$, the graph **touches** the x-axis at α

  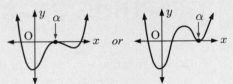

  ▸ for a **cubed factor** $(x - \alpha)^3$, the graph **cuts** the x-axis at α and is 'flat' at α

  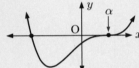

  ▸ for a **quadruple factor** $(x - \alpha)^4$, the graph **touches** the x-axis and is 'flat' at that point.

  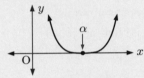

  ▸ If a quartic with $a > 0$ has one real quadratic factor with $\Delta < 0$ we could have:

  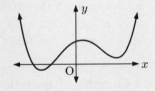

  ▸ If a quartic with $a > 0$ has two real quadratic factors both with $\Delta < 0$, the graph does not meet the x-axis at all.

  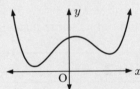

Example 21   ◀)) **Self Tutor**

Sketch the graph of:

a $y = (3x - 2)(x + 3)(x + 1)^2$

b $y = -(x - 3)^2(x + 2)^2$

a $a > 0$, so the graph opens upwards.

The graph cuts the x-axis at $\frac{2}{3}$ and -3, and touches the x-axis at -1.

When $x = 0$,
$$y = (-2)(3)(1)^2 = -6$$
∴ the y-intercept is -6.

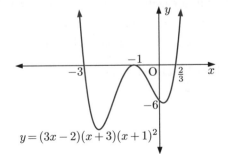

$y = (3x - 2)(x + 3)(x + 1)^2$

b $a < 0$, so the graph opens downwards.

The graph touches the x-axis at 3 and -2.

When $x = 0$,

$$y = -(-3)^2(2)^2 = -36$$

$\therefore$ the y-intercept is -36.

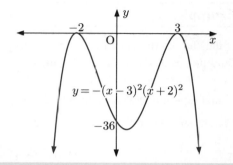

$y = -(x-3)^2(x+2)^2$

EXERCISE 8J

1 Sketch the graph of:

   a $y = x^2(x-1)(2x+3)$ **b** $y = 3x^2(x-2)^2$

   c $f(x) = 2(x+3)(x+1)(x-1)(x-2)$ **d** $y = -2x(x-1)^2(x+3)$

   e $f(x) = -(x-1)(x+1)^3$ **f** $f(x) = -2(x+2)^2(2x-1)^2$

2 **a** Fully factorise $x^4 - x^3 - 2x^2$.

   b Hence, sketch the graph of $f(x) = x^4 - x^3 - 2x^2$.

Example 22   ◀)) **Self Tutor**

Find the equation of the quartic with graph:

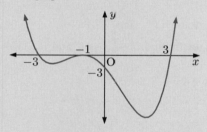

The graph touches the x-axis at -1 and cuts it at -3 and 3.

$\therefore \quad y = a(x+1)^2(x+3)(x-3), \quad a \neq 0$

But when $x = 0$, $y = -3$

$\therefore \quad -3 = a(1)^2(3)(-3)$

$\therefore \quad -3 = -9a$

$\therefore \quad a = \frac{1}{3}$

$\therefore \quad y = \frac{1}{3}(x+1)^2(x+3)(x-3)$

---

3 Find the equation of the quartic with graph:

   a   **b**   **c**

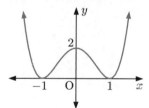 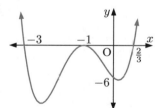 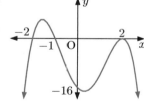

   d   **e**   **f**

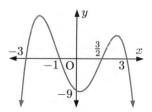 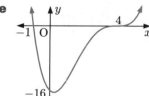 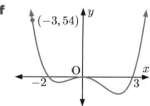

Example 23

◀) **Self Tutor**

Find the quartic function $P(x)$ which touches the x-axis at 2, cuts the x-axis at -3, and passes through $(1, -12)$ and $(3, 6)$.

The graph *touches* the x-axis at 2, so $(x - 2)^2$ is a factor.

The graph *cuts* the x-axis at -3, so $(x + 3)$ is a factor.

$\therefore \quad P(x) = (x - 2)^2(x + 3)(ax + b)$ where a and b are constants, $a \neq 0$.

Now $\qquad\qquad\qquad P(1) = -12$

$\therefore \quad (-1)^2(4)(a + b) = -12$

$\therefore \quad a + b = -3$ .... (1)

and $\qquad\qquad\qquad P(3) = 6$

$\therefore \quad (1)^2(6)(3a + b) = 6$

$\therefore \quad 3a + b = 1$ .... (2)

Solving (1) and (2) simultaneously gives $a = 2$, $b = -5$.

$\therefore \quad P(x) = (x - 2)^2(x + 3)(2x - 5)$

4 Find the equation of the quartic whose graph:

a cuts the x-axis at -4 and $\frac{1}{2}$, touches it at 2, and passes through the point $(1, 5)$

b touches the x-axis at $\frac{2}{3}$ and -3, and passes through the point $(-4, 49)$

c cuts the x-axis at $\pm\frac{1}{2}$ and ± 2, and passes through the point $(1, -18)$

d touches the x-axis at 1, cuts the y-axis at -1, and passes through $(-1, -4)$ and $(2, 15)$.

5 Match the given graphs to the corresponding quartic functions:

a $y = (x - 1)^2(x + 1)(x + 3)$ **b** $y = -2(x - 1)^2(x + 1)(x + 3)$

c $y = (x - 1)(x + 1)^2(x + 3)$ **d** $y = (x - 1)(x + 1)^2(x - 3)$

e $y = -\frac{1}{3}(x - 1)(x + 1)(x + 3)^2$ **f** $y = -(x - 1)(x + 1)(x - 3)^2$

A

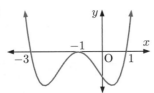

B

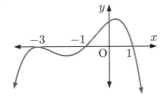

C

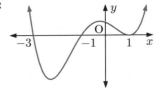

D

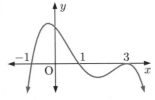

E

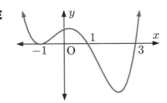

F

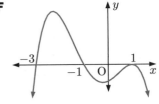

6 Find the equation of the quartic graphed alongside. Give your answer in expanded form.

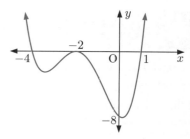

7 The graph of $f(x) = x^4 - x^3 - 5x^2 + 12$ touches the x-axis at 2.

a By fully factorising $x^4 - x^3 - 5x^2 + 12$, show that the graph does not meet the x-axis anywhere else.

b Use technology to help sketch the graph of $y = f(x)$.

8 **a** Given that $x^2 + x + 1$ is a factor of $x^4 - 4x^3 + 3x^2 + 2x + 7$, write $x^4 - 4x^3 + 3x^2 + 2x + 7$ as a product of two quadratic factors.

b Hence, show that the graph of $f(x) = x^4 - 4x^3 + 3x^2 + 2x + 7$ does not meet the x-axis at all.

c Use technology to help sketch the graph of $f(x) = x^4 - 4x^3 + 3x^2 + 2x + 7$.

9 The heat radiated from a person is given by the quartic function $H(t) \approx (9.5 \times 10^{-8})t^4$ joules per second, where t is the person's body temperature in Kelvins (K).

Find the heat radiated by:

a a person with a normal body temperature of $37°C$ or 310 K

b a person who has a fever, with body temperature $39°C$ or 312 K.

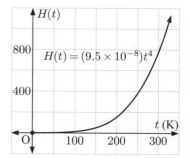

10 The graph alongside shows the height (h metres) of a roller coaster above the ground against the horizontal distance travelled (x metres), for $0 \leqslant x \leqslant 200$.

The equation for this graph has the form

$$h(x) = \frac{-x(x-a)^2(x-b)}{k}, \quad 0 \leqslant x \leqslant 200.$$

a Use the graph to find a and b.

b Given that the roller coaster is 4 m above the ground after travelling 100 m, find the value of k.

c Find the height of the roller coaster above the ground, after it has travelled 150 m.

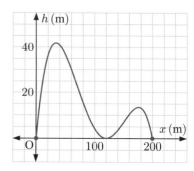

Discussion   **General polynomials**

Consider the general polynomial $P(x) = a_n x^n + a_{n-1}x^{n-1} + \ldots + a_1 x + a_0$, $a_n \neq 0$.

- Discuss the behaviour of the graph as $x \to -\infty$ and $x \to \infty$ depending on
  - the sign of a_n
  - whether n is odd or even.
- Under what circumstances is $P(x)$ guaranteed to have at least one real zero?

K | POLYNOMIAL EQUATIONS

We have already seen that every real cubic polynomial must cut the x-axis at least once, and so has at least one real zero.

If the exact value of the zero is difficult to find, we can use technology to help us. We can then factorise the cubic as a linear factor times a quadratic, and if necessary use the quadratic formula to find the other zeros.

This method is useful if we have one rational zero and two irrational zeros that are radical conjugates.

Example 24   🔊 **Self Tutor**

Find the real zeros of $P(x) = 3x^3 - 14x^2 + 5x + 2$.

Using technology $x \approx 0.666\,667 = \frac{2}{3}$ is a zero.

$\therefore$ $(3x - 2)$ is a factor.

$\therefore$ $3x^3 - 14x^2 + 5x + 2 = (3x - 2)(x^2 + ax - 1)$ for some a.

Equating coefficients of x^2: $3a - 2 = -14$

$\therefore$ $3a = -12$

$\therefore$ $a = -4$

Equating coefficients of x: $-3 - 2a = 5$ ✓

$\therefore$ $P(x) = (3x - 2)(x^2 - 4x - 1)$ which has zeros $\frac{2}{3}$ and $2 \pm \sqrt{5}$ {quadratic formula}

GRAPHING PACKAGE

[EXE]:Show coordinates
Y1=3x^(3)−14x²+5x+2

ROOT
X=0.6666666667 Y=0

Example 25   🔊 **Self Tutor**

Find the real roots of $6x^3 + 13x^2 + 20x + 3 = 0$.

Using technology, $x \approx -0.166\,666\,67 = -\frac{1}{6}$ is a root, so $(6x + 1)$ is a factor of the cubic.

$\therefore$ $6x^3 + 13x^2 + 20x + 3 = (6x + 1)(x^2 + ax + 3)$ for some a.

Equating coefficients of x^2: $1 + 6a = 13$

$\therefore$ $6a = 12$

$\therefore$ $a = 2$

Equating coefficients of x: $a + 18 = 20$ ✓

$\therefore$ $(6x + 1)(x^2 + 2x + 3) = 0$

Since $x^2 + 2x + 3$ has $\Delta = 4 - 12 = -8 < 0$, $x = -\frac{1}{6}$ is the only real root.

[EXE]:Show coordinates
Y1=6x^(3)+13x²+20x+3

ROOT
X=-0.1666666667 Y=0

For a quartic polynomial $P(x)$ we first need to establish if there are any x-intercepts at all. If there are not then the polynomial has no real zeros. If there *are* x-intercepts then we can identify linear or quadratic factors.

EXERCISE 8K

1 Find all real zeros of:

    a $x^3 - 3x^2 - 3x + 1$ **b** $x^3 - 3x^2 + 4x - 2$ **c** $2x^3 - 3x^2 - 4x - 35$

    d $2x^3 - x^2 + 20x - 10$ **e** $4x^4 - 4x^3 - 25x^2 + x + 6$ **f** $x^4 - 6x^3 + 22x^2 - 48x + 40$

2 Find all real roots of:

a $x^3 + 2x^2 + 3x + 6 = 0$

b $2x^3 + 3x^2 - 3x - 2 = 0$

c $x^3 - 6x^2 + 12x - 8 = 0$

d $2x^3 + 18 = 5x^2 + 9x$

e $x^4 - x^3 - 9x^2 + 11x + 6 = 0$

f $2x^4 - 13x^3 + 27x^2 = 13x + 15$

3 Solve for $x \in \mathbb{R}$:

a $x^3 - 3x^2 + 4x - 4 = 0$

b $x^3 + 3x^2 + 4x + 12 = 0$

c $2x^3 - 9x^2 + 6x - 1 = 0$

d $x^3 - 4x^2 + 9x - 10 = 0$

e $4x^3 - 8x^2 + x + 3 = 0$

f $3x^4 + 4x^3 + 5x^2 + 12x - 12 = 0$

g $2x^4 - 3x^3 + 5x^2 + 6x - 4 = 0$

h $2x^3 + 5x^2 + 8x + 20 = 0$

4 The following cubics will not factorise neatly. Solve for x using only technology:

a $x^3 + 2x^2 - 6x - 6 = 0$

b $x^3 + x^2 - 7x - 8 = 0$

5 Last year, the volume of water in a particular reservoir could be described by the model
$V(t) = -t^3 + 30t^2 - 131t + 250$ ML, where t is the time in months.

The local government rules state that if the volume falls below 100 ML, irrigation is prohibited. During which months, if any, was irrigation prohibited in the last twelve months? Include in your answer a neat sketch of any graphs you may have used.

6 A ladder of length 10 metres is leaning against a wall so that it is just touching a cube of edge length one metre.

What height up the wall does the ladder reach?

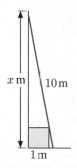

Review set 8A

1 Let $P(z) = 2z^3 - z^2 + 4z$ and $Q(z) = 3 - z$. Find, in simplest form:

a $P(z) + 2Q(z)$

b $P(z)\,Q(z)$

c $\dfrac{P(z)}{Q(z)}$

2 Expand and simplify:

a $(3x^3 + 2x - 5)(4x - 3)$

b $(2x^2 - x + 3)^2$

3 Carry out the divisions:

a $\dfrac{x^3}{x + 2}$

b $\dfrac{2x^3 - 3x + 4}{x - 1}$

4 Decide whether:

a 4 is a zero of $x^3 - 3x^2 - 5x + 4$

b -3 is a root of $2x^3 + 5x^2 - x - 6 = 0$.

5 Find constants a and b given that:

a $4x^2 - 7x + 5 = 4x^2 + ax + (a + b)$ for all x

b $6x^3 + 11x^2 - 9x - 4 = (2x^2 + 3x - 4)(ax + b)$ for all x.

6 Find the zeros of $(x + 2)(x + 4)(x - 3)$.

7 Fully factorise:

    a $x^3 - 2x^2 - 8x$ **b** $3x^3 + x^2 - 10x$

8 Find *all* quartic polynomials with zeros $2 \pm \sqrt{3}$, $1 \pm \sqrt{2}$.

9 $x = -5$ is a solution of $x^3 + 9x^2 + 18x - 10 = 0$. Find the remaining solutions.

10 $(2x - 3)$ is a factor of $2x^3 + 3x^2 - 29x + 30$. Fully factorise the polynomial.

11 $(3x + 2)$ and $(x - 2)$ are factors of $6x^3 + ax^2 - 4ax + b$. Find a and b.

12 $P(x) = 2x^3 + 7x^2 + kx - k$ is the product of 3 linear factors, 2 of which are identical.

    a Show that k can take 3 distinct values.

    b Write $P(x)$ as the product of its linear factors with the largest value of k.

13 $2x^3 + 15x^2 + 24x + k$ has 3 linear factors, two of which are identical. Find k, and hence factorise the cubic.

14 State and prove the Remainder theorem.

15 Find the remainder when $2x^{17} + 5x^{10} - 7x^3 + 6$ is divided by $x - 2$.

16 $P(x) = x^m + 6x^2 + 50$ leaves a remainder of -54 when divided by $x + 2$. Find m.

17 Find constants a and b given $x^3 + x^2 + ax + b$ has factors $(x + 2)$ and $(x - 4)$.

18 If α and β are two of the roots of $x^3 - x + 1 = 0$, show that $\alpha\beta$ is a root of $x^3 + x^2 - 1 = 0$.
    Hint: Let $x^3 - x + 1 = (x - \alpha)(x - \beta)(x - \gamma)$.

19 Find the sum and product of the zeros of:

    a $3x^4 - 4x^3 + 3x^2 + 8$ **b** $2x^6 + 2x^4 - x^3 + 7x - 10$

20 On the same set of axes, sketch the graphs of $y = \frac{1}{2}x^3$ and $y = \frac{1}{2}(x + 2)^3 - 3$.

21 Find the equation of the cubic with graph:

    a

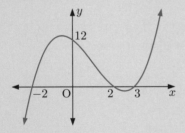

    b

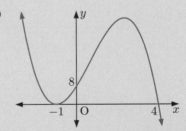

22 Sketch the graph of:

    a $y = x(x + 2)(x - 1)(x - 4)$ **b** $y = -2(x + 3)^2(x - 2)(x + 1)$

    c $y = (3x - 1)^2(x + 2)^2$

23 A quartic polynomial $P(x)$ has graph $y = P(x)$ which touches the x-axis at $(-2, 0)$, cuts the x-axis at $(1, 0)$, cuts the y-axis at $(0, 12)$, and passes through $(2, 80)$.

    Find an expression for $P(x)$ in factored form, and hence sketch the graph of $y = P(x)$.

24 $(2x - 1)$ is a factor of $P(x) = 2x^4 + 7x^3 + 4x^2 - 4x$.

    a Fully factorise $P(x)$.   **b** Hence sketch the graph of $y = P(x)$.

    c For what values of x is $P(x) \geqslant 0$?

25 Find all real roots of:

   a $6x^3 + 17x^2 = 5x + 6$ **b** $3x^4 + x^3 + 18x^2 - 54x - 20 = 0$

Review set 8B

1 Let $f(x) = x^4 - 5x^3 + 2x - 1$ and $g(x) = -2x^3 + 3x^2 + 7$.

   a Find $f(x) - g(x)$, giving your answer in simplest form.

   b For the product $f(x)\,g(x)$, state the:

      i degree   **ii** leading coefficient   **iii** constant term.

2 Expand and simplify:

   a $(3x^2 - 2x + 1)(x^3 + 5x^2 - 2)$ **b** $(x^3 - 2x^2 + 1)^2$

3 Find the real linear factors and corresponding zeros of:

   a $3x^2 - 11x + 6$ **b** $x^4 - 7x^2 + 12$

4 Use expansion to verify that $(3x - 2)(x + 2)(x - 3)$ is the factorisation of $3x^3 - 5x^2 - 16x + 12$.

5 Find *all* cubic polynomials with zeros:

   a -4, 1, and 6   **b** $\frac{1}{3}$ and $3 \pm \sqrt{5}$.

6 Using the sign diagram of Δ, find the values of k for which $kx^2 + kx - 2 = 0$ has:

   a a repeated root   **b** two distinct real roots   **c** no real roots.

7 Find a, b, and c such that $2x^4 + 3x^3 + 11x^2 + ax + 15 = (2x^2 + bx + c)(x^2 + 2x + 5)$ for all x.

8 Carry out the divisions:

   a $\dfrac{2x^3 + 9x^2 + 5x - 1}{2x + 3}$ **b** $\dfrac{x^4 + x^2 + 2}{x - 1}$

9 $(3x - 2)$ is a factor of $6x^3 + 23x^2 - 33x + 10$. Fully factorise the polynomial.

10 Given that $(2x + 1)$ is a factor of $4x^3 - 8x^2 - 11x - 3$, find all of the solutions of $4x^3 - 8x^2 - 11x - 3 = 0$.

11 Show that $x = \frac{1}{4}$ is the only real solution of $4x^3 - 13x^2 + 15x - 3 = 0$.

12 Suppose a and k are real. For what values of k does $z^3 + az^2 + kz + ka = 0$ have:

   a one real root   **b** 3 real roots?

13 Find the remainder when $x^{47} - 3x^{26} + 5x^3 + 11$ is divided by $x + 1$.

14 When $P(x) = x^n + 3x^2 + kx + 6$ is divided by $x + 1$ the remainder is 12. When $P(x)$ is divided by $x - 1$ the remainder is 8. Find k and n given that $34 < n < 38$.

15 Find a given that $(x + 1)$ is a factor of $3x^4 - 2x^3 + ax^2 - (a - 2)x + 4$.

16 $(x - 3)$ is a factor of $P(x) = x^3 + ax^2 + bx - 15$. When $P(x)$ is divided by $x + 1$, the remainder is -48.

   a Find a and b.

   b Find the remainder when $P(x)$ is divided by $x - 4$.

   c Find the zeros of $P(x)$.

17 Find the sum and product of the roots of:

    a $2x^3 + 3x^2 - 4x + 6 = 0$ **b** $4x^4 = x^2 + 2x - 6$

18

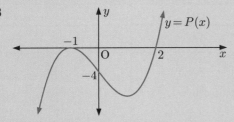

Find the cubic polynomial $P(x)$ with the graph shown.

19 Use axes intercepts to sketch the graphs of:

    a $y = (x + 5)(x + 1)(x - 3)$ **b** $y = -(x + 2)^3$

    c $f(x) = 2(x - 2)^2(2x + 3)$

20   **a** Show that -5 is an x-intercept of the graph of $f(x) = x^3 + 3x^2 - 14x - 20$.

    b Find the other x-intercepts.

    c Hence, sketch the graph of $f(x) = x^3 + 3x^2 - 14x - 20$.

    d Describe the behaviour of the graph as $x \to \infty$ and $x \to -\infty$.

21 The power generated by a wind turbine is given by $P = 20v^3$ watts, where v is the wind speed in $m\,s^{-1}$.

    a For what values of v is it reasonable to use this function?

    b Find the power generated at a wind speed of $6\ m\,s^{-1}$.

    c Use technology to help sketch the graph of the function for $v \geqslant 0$.

    d Find, rounded to 2 decimal places, the wind speed required to generate $10\,000$ watts of power.

22 The graph of the cubic $y = P(x)$ cuts the x-axis at $(-1,\ 0)$, touches it at $(2,\ 0)$, and passes through $(-2,\ 32)$. Find $P(x)$ in expanded form.

23 Find the equation of the quartic with graph:

    a

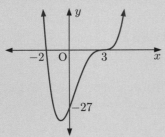

    b

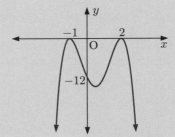

24 The graph of $f(x) = 2x^4 - 12x^3 + 15x^2 + 9x - 20$ cuts the x-axis at -1 and 4. By fully factorising $2x^4 - 12x^3 + 15x^2 + 9x - 20$, show that the graph does not meet the x-axis anywhere else. Hence sketch the graph of $y = f(x)$.

25 Find all real zeros of:

    a $2z^3 + z^2 + 10z + 5$ **b** $x^3 + 6x^2 - 9x - 14$

9

The binomial theorem

Contents:

Opening problem

We have previously seen the "perfect square" expansion $(a + b)^2 = a^2 + 2ab + b^2$. This expansion is extremely useful, and we would like a similar rule for higher powers.

Consider the expansion of $(a + b)^3$. To understand the outcome better, we label each a and b according to the factor it comes from:

$(a + b)^3$

$= (a_1 + b_1)(a_2 + b_2)(a_3 + b_3)$

$= (a_1 + b_1)(a_2 a_3 + a_2 b_3 + b_2 a_3 + b_2 b_3)$

$= a_1 a_2 a_3 + a_1 a_2 b_3 + a_1 b_2 a_3 + a_1 b_2 b_3 + b_1 a_2 a_3 + b_1 a_2 b_3 + b_1 b_2 a_3 + b_1 b_2 b_3$

$= \underbrace{a_1 a_2 a_3}_{} + \underbrace{a_1 a_2 b_3 + a_1 b_2 a_3 + b_1 a_2 a_3}_{} + \underbrace{a_1 b_2 b_3 + b_1 a_2 b_3 + b_1 b_2 a_3}_{} + \underbrace{b_1 b_2 b_3}_{}$ {rearranging}

$= \quad a^3 \quad + \quad\quad\quad 3a^2 b \quad\quad\quad + \quad\quad\quad 3ab^2 \quad\quad\quad + \quad b^3$

So, the expansion of $(a + b)^3$ yields $2^3 = 8$ terms. When we collect "like" terms, we see that:

- there is only one a^3 which is the product from choosing the a in each factor
- there are three $a^2 b$ terms which are the products of choosing two as and one b from the three factors, and there are three ways to do this
- there are three ab^2 terms which are the products of choosing one a and two bs from the three factors, and there are three ways to do this
- there is only one b^3 which is the product from choosing the b in each factor.

In order to quickly expand higher powers of $(a + b)$, we need a formula for the number of ways of choosing $(n - r)$ as and r bs from n factors. We will call this value nCr or $\binom{n}{r}$.

Things to think about:

a Fully expand $(a + b)^4$, labelling a and b according to each factor it comes from.

   i How many terms are there in total?

   ii By collecting "like" terms, can you show that $(a + b)^4 = a^4 + 4a^3 b + 6a^2 b^2 + 4ab^3 + b^4$?

b How can we write a formula for nCr, the number of ways of choosing $(n - r)$ as and r bs from n choices of a or b?

c How can we write a general expansion of $(a + b)^n$ in a concise way?

The sum **$a + b$** is called a **binomial** as it contains two terms.

Any expression of the form **$(a + b)^n$** is called a **power of a binomial**.

In this Chapter we derive a concise formula for the **binomial expansion** of $(a + b)^n$. However, before we can achieve this, we need some notation associated with **combinations**.

A   FACTORIAL NOTATION

For $n \geqslant 1$, $n!$ is the product of the first n positive integers.

$$n! = n(n - 1)(n - 2) \dots 3 \times 2 \times 1$$

$n!$ is read "n factorial".

For example, $5 \times 4 \times 3 \times 2 \times 1 = 5!$

An alternative definition of factorial numbers is that $n! = n \times (n-1)!$ for $n \geqslant 1$.

For example, $6! = 6 \times 5!$

Under this rule we notice that $1! = 1 \times 0!$

We therefore define $0! = 1$

Example 1 ◀》 Self Tutor

Express in factorial form:

a $9 \times 8 \times 7$

b $\dfrac{11 \times 10 \times 9 \times 8}{4 \times 3 \times 2 \times 1}$

a $9 \times 8 \times 7 = \dfrac{9 \times 8 \times 7 \times 6 \times 5 \times 4 \times 3 \times 2 \times 1}{6 \times 5 \times 4 \times 3 \times 2 \times 1} = \dfrac{9!}{6!}$

b $\dfrac{11 \times 10 \times 9 \times 8}{4 \times 3 \times 2 \times 1} = \dfrac{11 \times 10 \times 9 \times 8 \times 7 \times 6 \times 5 \times 4 \times 3 \times 2 \times 1}{4 \times 3 \times 2 \times 1 \times 7 \times 6 \times 5 \times 4 \times 3 \times 2 \times 1} = \dfrac{11!}{4!7!}$

EXERCISE 9A

1 Evaluate:

  a $3!$ **b** $5!$ **c** $6!$ **d** $10!$

2 Express in factorial form:

  a $4 \times 3 \times 2 \times 1$ **b** $7 \times 6 \times 5 \times 4 \times 3 \times 2 \times 1$ **c** $8 \times 7 \times 6$

  d $15 \times 14 \times 13 \times 12$ **e** $\dfrac{9 \times 8 \times 7}{3 \times 2 \times 1}$ **f** $\dfrac{13 \times 12 \times 11 \times 10}{4 \times 3 \times 2 \times 1}$

3 Simplify without using a calculator:

  a $\dfrac{7!}{6!}$ **b** $\dfrac{8!}{6!}$ **c** $\dfrac{12!}{10!}$ **d** $\dfrac{120!}{119!}$ **e** $\dfrac{10!}{8! \times 2!}$ **f** $\dfrac{100!}{98! \times 2!}$

4 Simplify:

  a $\dfrac{n!}{(n-1)!}$ **b** $\dfrac{(n+2)!}{n!}$ **c** $\dfrac{(n+1)!}{(n-1)!}$

Example 2 ◀》 Self Tutor

Write as a product by factorising:

  a $8! + 6!$ **b** $10! - 9! + 8!$

a $8! + 6!$
$= 8 \times 7 \times 6! + 6!$
$= 6!(8 \times 7 + 1)$
$= 6! \times 57$

b $10! - 9! + 8!$
$= 10 \times 9 \times 8! - 9 \times 8! + 8!$
$= 8!(90 - 9 + 1)$
$= 8! \times 82$

---

5 Write as a product by factorising:

  a $5! + 4!$ **b** $11! - 10!$ **c** $6! + 8!$ **d** $12! - 10!$

  e $9! + 8! + 7!$ **f** $7! - 6! + 8!$ **g** $12! - 2 \times 11!$ **h** $3 \times 9! + 5 \times 8!$

Example 3

◄)) **Self Tutor**

Simplify $\dfrac{7! - 6!}{6}$ by factorising.

$$\dfrac{7! - 6!}{6}$$

$$= \dfrac{7 \times 6! - 6!}{6}$$

$$= \dfrac{6!(7 - 1)^{1}}{\cancel{6}_{1}}$$

$$= 6!$$

6 Simplify by factorising:

a $\dfrac{12! - 11!}{11}$

b $\dfrac{10! + 9!}{11}$

c $\dfrac{10! - 8!}{89}$

d $\dfrac{10! - 9!}{9!}$

e $\dfrac{6! + 5! - 4!}{4!}$

f $\dfrac{n! + (n-1)!}{(n-1)!}$

g $\dfrac{n! - (n-1)!}{n-1}$

h $\dfrac{(n+2)! + (n+1)!}{n+3}$

B   COUNTING

The mathematical principle of **counting** is not formally part of this course. However, we need to be able to count the number of ways of choosing $(n - r)$ as and r bs from n choices of a or b. We therefore introduce **permutations** and **combinations**.

PERMUTATIONS

> A **permutation** of a group of symbols is *any arrangement* of those symbols in a *definite order*.

For example, consider the three symbols A, B, and C.

There are six different permutations on the symbols A, B, and C.
They are: ABC, ACB, BAC, BCA, CAB, and CBA.

When we have lots of symbols, counting permutations by listing all of them becomes very difficult. For example, we would not want to list and then count all of the permutations on the alphabet letters A to Z. We therefore need an alternative method for counting permutations.

Consider again writing the symbols A, B, and C in order.

We see that there are 3 positions to fill:

1st	2nd	3rd

In the 1st position we can put any of the 3 original symbols.

3		
1st	2nd	3rd

In the 2nd position we can put either of the 2 remaining symbols.

3	2	
1st	2nd	3rd

Finally, the 1 remaining symbol must go in the 3rd position.

3	2	1
1st	2nd	3rd

The total number of different permutations is $3 \times 2 \times 1 = 3! = 6$.

Discussion

Why do we *multiply* the numbers of choices in each box to get the total number of different permutations?

Now suppose we have five symbols A, B, C, D, and E. These symbols represent children in a race. We can count the number of ways the first three children can finish as follows:

There are 3 positions to fill:

In the 1st position we could have any of the 5 children.

In the 2nd position we could have any of the remaining 4 children.

In the 3rd position we could have any of the remaining 3 children.

The total number of orderings is $5 \times 4 \times 3 = \dfrac{5!}{2!} = 60$.

Notice that the positions of the last two children are not important. This means that the total number of permutations for ordering the children, 5!, is divided by the number of permutations for ordering the last two children, 2!, to give our result.

COMBINATIONS

A **combination** is a selection of objects *without* regard to order.

Suppose we have five children A, B, C, D, and E. We want to select a team of three children from the five. In this case the order of the children *not* selected is not important, and neither is the order of children who *are* selected.

So, the number of possible combinations $= \dfrac{5!}{3! \times 2!} = 10$.

number of ways to order 5 children

order of those in the team is not important

order of those not in the team is not important

The 10 possible teams are:
ABC   ABD   ABE   ACD   ACE   ADE
BCD   BCE   BDE
CDE

Using a similar argument, we conclude that:

The number of **combinations** on n distinct symbols taken r at a time is

$$nCr = \binom{n}{r} = \frac{n!}{r!(n-r)!} \quad \text{for } n, r \in \mathbb{Z}_0^+, \; r \leqslant n.$$

Example 4

◄) **Self Tutor**

Use the formula $\binom{n}{r} = \dfrac{n!}{r!(n-r)!}$ to evaluate: **a** $\binom{5}{2}$ **b** $\binom{11}{7}$

a $\binom{5}{2} = \dfrac{5!}{2!(5-2)!}$

$= \dfrac{5!}{2! \times 3!}$

$= \dfrac{5 \times 4 \times 3 \times 2 \times 1}{2 \times 1 \times 3 \times 2 \times 1}$

$= 10$

b $\binom{11}{7} = \dfrac{11!}{7!(11-7)!}$

$= \dfrac{11!}{7! \times 4!}$

$= \dfrac{11 \times 10 \times 9 \times 8 \times 7 \times 6 \times 5 \times 4 \times 3 \times 2 \times 1}{7 \times 6 \times 5 \times 4 \times 3 \times 2 \times 1 \times 4 \times 3 \times 2 \times 1}$

$= \dfrac{7920}{24}$

$= 330$

We can use a graphics calculator to find values of $\binom{n}{r}$. Click on the icon for instructions.

GRAPHICS CALCULATOR INSTRUCTIONS

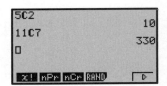

EXERCISE 9B

1 Evaluate:

   a $\binom{3}{2}$ **b** $\binom{6}{4}$ **c** $\binom{5}{1}$ **d** $\binom{7}{2}$

   Use your calculator to check your answers.

2 **a** List the different teams of 2 that can be chosen from a squad of 5 players named P, Q, R, S, and T.

   b Check that $\binom{5}{2}$ gives the total number of teams.

3 **a** List the different teams of 4 that can be chosen from a squad of 6 players named A, B, C, D, E, and F.

   b Check that $\binom{6}{4}$ gives the total number of teams.

4 **a** Evaluate: **i** $\binom{4}{1}$ **ii** $\binom{7}{1}$ **iii** $\binom{10}{1}$

   b Use combinations to explain why $\binom{n}{1} = n$ for any $n \in \mathbb{N}$.

5 **a** Evaluate: **i** $\binom{5}{0}$ **ii** $\binom{5}{5}$ **iii** $\binom{9}{0}$ **iv** $\binom{9}{9}$

   b Use combinations to explain why, for any $n \in \mathbb{N}$:

     i $\binom{n}{0} = 1$ **ii** $\binom{n}{n} = 1$

6 **a** Evaluate: **i** $\binom{7}{2}$ and $\binom{7}{5}$ **ii** $\binom{10}{3}$ and $\binom{10}{7}$

   b Use the formula $\binom{n}{r} = \dfrac{n!}{r!(n-r)!}$ to show that $\binom{n}{k} = \binom{n}{n-k}$ for any $n, k \in \mathbb{N}$, $0 \leqslant k \leqslant n$.

   c Use combinations to explain why this is true.

C ┃ BINOMIAL EXPANSIONS

Consider the cube alongside, which has sides of length $(a + b)$ cm.

The cube has been subdivided into 8 blocks by making 3 cuts parallel to the cube's surfaces as shown.

We know that the total volume of the cube is $(a + b)^3$ cm³. However, we can also find an expression for the cube's volume by adding the volumes of the 8 individual blocks.

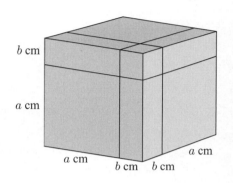

ANIMATION

We have: 1 block $a \times a \times a$
           3 blocks $a \times a \times b$
           3 blocks $a \times b \times b$
           1 block $b \times b \times b$

$\therefore$ the cube's volume $= a^3 + 3a^2b + 3ab^2 + b^3$
    $\therefore$ $(a + b)^3 = a^3 + 3a^2b + 3ab^2 + b^3$

This matches the algebraic expansion we saw in the **Opening Problem**:

$$\begin{aligned}(a + b)^3 &= (a + b)(a + b)^2 \\ &= (a + b)(a^2 + 2ab + b^2) \\ &= a^3 + 2a^2b + ab^2 + a^2b + 2ab^2 + b^3 \\ &= a^3 + 3a^2b + 3ab^2 + b^3\end{aligned}$$

> The **binomial expansion** of $(a + b)^2$ is $a^2 + 2ab + b^2$.
> The **binomial expansion** of $(a + b)^3$ is $a^3 + 3a^2b + 3ab^2 + b^3$.

Investigation   The binomial expansion

What to do:

1 Expand $(a + b)^4$ in the same way as for $(a + b)^3$ above.
   Hence expand $(a + b)^5$ and $(a + b)^6$.

2 The cubic expansion $(a + b)^3 = a^3 + 3a^2b + 3ab^2 + b^3$ contains 4 terms. They are written in order so that the powers of a decrease. We observe that their coefficients are: 1   3   3   1

   a With the terms written in this order, what happens to the powers of b?

   b Does the pattern in **a** continue for the expansions of $(a + b)^4$, $(a + b)^5$, and $(a + b)^6$?

   c Use your results to continue this pattern of coefficients up to the case $n = 6$.

$n = 1$			1	1	
$n = 2$		1	2	1	
$n = 3$	1	3	3	1	⟵ row 3
⋮					

3 Construct this triangle of numbers:

$$\binom{1}{0} \quad \binom{1}{1}$$
$$\binom{2}{0} \quad \binom{2}{1} \quad \binom{2}{2}$$
$$\binom{3}{0} \quad \binom{3}{1} \quad \binom{3}{2} \quad \binom{3}{3}$$
$$\binom{4}{0} \quad \binom{4}{1} \quad \binom{4}{2} \quad \binom{4}{3} \quad \binom{4}{4}$$
$$\binom{5}{0} \quad \binom{5}{1} \quad \binom{5}{2} \quad \binom{5}{3} \quad \binom{5}{4} \quad \binom{5}{5}$$
$$\binom{6}{0} \quad \binom{6}{1} \quad \binom{6}{2} \quad \binom{6}{3} \quad \binom{6}{4} \quad \binom{6}{5} \quad \binom{6}{6}$$

How does it compare with the triangle of coefficients you found in **2 c**?

4 The triangle of numbers we are considering is called **Pascal's triangle**.

   a How can each row of Pascal's triangle be predicted from the previous one?

   b Write a formula for the sum of the numbers in the nth row of Pascal's triangle.

   c Hence predict the elements of the 7th row of Pascal's triangle.

   d Hence write down the binomial expansion of $(a+b)^7$.

   e Check your result algebraically by using $(a+b)^7 = (a+b)(a+b)^6$ and your results from **1**.

From the **Investigation**, you should have observed:

- For the expansion of $(a+b)^n$ where $n \in \mathbb{N}$, suppose we write the terms in order so that as we look from left to right across the expansion, the powers of a *decrease* by 1, while the powers of b *increase* by 1. Then:
  - ▸ the sum of the powers of a and b in each term of the expansion is n
  - ▸ the number of terms in the expansion is $n+1$
  - ▸ the coefficients of the terms are row n of Pascal's triangle.

- The rth number in the nth row of Pascal's triangle is $\binom{n}{r}$ where $n, r \in \mathbb{Z}_0^+$, $r \leqslant n$.

- In Pascal's triangle, the values on the end of each row are always 1. Each of the remaining values is found by adding the two values diagonally above it. This gives us **Pascal's Rule** or **Van der Monde's Rule** $\binom{n}{r} + \binom{n}{r+1} = \binom{n+1}{r+1}$.

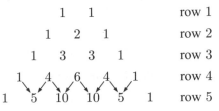

1	1			row 1
1	2	1		row 2
1	3	3	1	row 3
1	4	6	4	1	row 4
1	5	10	10	5	1	row 5

- $(a+b)^4 = a^4 + 4a^3b + 6a^2b^2 + 4ab^3 + b^4$
- $(a+b)^5 = a^5 + 5a^4b + 10a^3b^2 + 10a^2b^3 + 5ab^4 + b^5$

Example 5

◀) **Self Tutor**

Use $(a+b)^3 = a^3 + 3a^2b + 3ab^2 + b^3$ to find the binomial expansion of:

  a $(2x+3)^3$ **b** $(x-5)^3$

a In the expansion of $(a+b)^3$ we substitute $a = (2x)$ and $b = (3)$.

$\therefore\ (2x+3)^3 = (2x)^3 + 3(2x)^2(3) + 3(2x)^1(3)^2 + (3)^3$
$\qquad\qquad\quad = 8x^3 + 36x^2 + 54x + 27$

b We substitute $a = (x)$ and $b = (-5)$

$\therefore\ (x-5)^3 = (x)^3 + 3(x)^2(-5) + 3(x)(-5)^2 + (-5)^3$
$\qquad\qquad\quad = x^3 - 15x^2 + 75x - 125$

Brackets are essential!

EXERCISE 9C

1 Use $(a+b)^3 = a^3 + 3a^2b + 3ab^2 + b^3$ to expand and simplify:

    a $(p+q)^3$ **b** $(x+1)^3$ **c** $(x-3)^3$

    d $(2+x)^3$ **e** $(3x-1)^3$ **f** $(2x+5)^3$

    g $(2a-b)^3$ **h** $\left(3x - \dfrac{1}{3}\right)^3$ **i** $\left(2x + \dfrac{1}{x}\right)^3$

2 Use $(a+b)^4 = a^4 + 4a^3b + 6a^2b^2 + 4ab^3 + b^4$ to expand and simplify:

    a $(1+x)^4$ **b** $(p-q)^4$ **c** $(x-2)^4$

    d $(3-x)^4$ **e** $(1+2x)^4$ **f** $(2x-3)^4$

    g $(2x+b)^4$ **h** $\left(x + \dfrac{1}{x}\right)^4$ **i** $\left(2x - \dfrac{1}{x}\right)^4$

3 Use $(a+b)^5 = a^5 + 5a^4b + 10a^3b^2 + 10a^2b^3 + 5ab^4 + b^5$ to expand and simplify:

    a $(x+2)^5$ **b** $(x-2y)^5$ **c** $(1+2x)^5$ **d** $\left(x - \dfrac{1}{x}\right)^5$

4 Expand and simplify:

    a $\left(1+\sqrt{2}\right)^3$ **b** $\left(\sqrt{5}+2\right)^4$ **c** $\left(2-\sqrt{2}\right)^5$

5 **a** Expand $(2+x)^5$.   **b** Hence find the value of $(2.01)^5$.

6 Expand and simplify $(2x+3)(x+1)^4$.

7 Find the coefficient of:

    a a^3b^2 in the expansion of $(3a+b)^5$ **b** a^3b^3 in the expansion of $(2a+3b)^6$.

D | THE BINOMIAL THEOREM

In the binomial expansion of $(a+b)^n$ there is a total of 2^n terms. Each term corresponds to a possible *permutation* of choosing a or b from each factor to multiply together.

When we collect the "like" terms, we group the *combinations* which have the same numbers of as and bs. They are combinations because which factors the as and bs come from is not important.

Given there are n factors $(a+b)$, suppose we choose $(n-r)$ as and r bs. There are $\binom{n}{r}$ combinations for doing this, so the coefficient of $a^{n-r}b^r$ is $\binom{n}{r}$. We call this the **binomial coefficient**.

The **binomial theorem** states that

$$(a+b)^n = a^n + \binom{n}{1}a^{n-1}b + \ldots + \binom{n}{r}a^{n-r}b^r + \ldots + b^n$$

where $\binom{n}{r}$ is the **binomial coefficient** of $a^{n-r}b^r$ and $r = 0, 1, 2, 3, \ldots, n$.

The binomial theorem allows us to perform a binomial expansion or find a particular term in a binomial expansion, without having to draw Pascal's triangle each time.

> The **general term** or $(r+1)$th term in the binomial expansion $(a+b)^n$ is
> $$T_{r+1} = \binom{n}{r} a^{n-r} b^r.$$
>
> Using **summation notation** we write $(a+b)^n = \displaystyle\sum_{r=0}^{n} \binom{n}{r} a^{n-r} b^r$
>
> where $\displaystyle\sum_{r=0}^{n}$ reads "the sum from r equals zero to n of".

Example 6   ◄⧘ **Self Tutor**

Write down the first three and last two terms of the expansion of $\left(2x + \dfrac{1}{x}\right)^{12}$.
Do not simplify your answer.

$$\left(2x + \frac{1}{x}\right)^{12} = \sum_{r=0}^{12} \binom{12}{r}(2x)^{n-r}\left(\frac{1}{x}\right)^r$$

$$= (2x)^{12} + \binom{12}{1}(2x)^{11}\left(\frac{1}{x}\right)^1 + \binom{12}{2}(2x)^{10}\left(\frac{1}{x}\right)^2 + \dots.$$

$$\dots. + \binom{12}{11}(2x)^1\left(\frac{1}{x}\right)^{11} + \left(\frac{1}{x}\right)^{12}$$

Example 7   ◄⧘ **Self Tutor**

Find the 7th term of $\left(3x - \dfrac{4}{x^2}\right)^{14}$.   Do not simplify your answer.

$a = (3x)$, $b = \left(\dfrac{-4}{x^2}\right)$, and $n = 14$

Given the general term $T_{r+1} = \binom{n}{r} a^{n-r} b^r$,   we let $r = 6$

$$\therefore \ T_7 = \binom{14}{6}(3x)^8 \left(\frac{-4}{x^2}\right)^6$$

EXERCISE 9D

1 Write down the first three and last two terms of the following binomial expansions. Do not simplify your answers.

    a $(1 + 2x)^{11}$
    b $\left(3x + \dfrac{2}{x}\right)^{15}$
    c $\left(2x - \dfrac{3}{x}\right)^{20}$

2 Without simplifying, write down:

    a the 6th term of $(2x + 5)^{15}$
    b the 4th term of $\left(x^2 + y\right)^9$

    c the 10th term of $\left(x - \dfrac{2}{x}\right)^{17}$
    d the 9th term of $\left(2x^2 - \dfrac{1}{x}\right)^{21}$.

Example 8

🔊 **Self Tutor**

In the expansion of $\left(x^2 + \dfrac{4}{x}\right)^{12}$, find:

a the coefficient of x^6 **b** the constant term.

$a = (x^2)$, $b = \left(\dfrac{4}{x}\right)$, and $n = 12$

$\therefore$ the general term $T_{r+1} = \binom{12}{r}(x^2)^{12-r}\left(\dfrac{4}{x}\right)^r$

$\qquad\qquad\qquad\quad = \binom{12}{r}x^{24-2r} \times \dfrac{4^r}{x^r}$

$\qquad\qquad\qquad\quad = \binom{12}{r}4^r x^{24-3r}$

a If $24 - 3r = 6$

then $3r = 18$

$\therefore r = 6$

$\therefore T_7 = \binom{12}{6}4^6 x^6$

$\therefore$ the coefficient of x^6 is

$\binom{12}{6}4^6$ or $3\,784\,704$.

b If $24 - 3r = 0$

then $3r = 24$

$\therefore r = 8$

$\therefore T_9 = \binom{12}{8}4^8 x^0$

$\therefore$ the constant term is

$\binom{12}{8}4^8$ or $32\,440\,320$.

3 Consider the expansion of $(x+2)^8$.

  a Write down the general term of the expansion.

  b Find the coefficient of x^5.

4 Consider the expansion of $(x+b)^7$.

  a Write down the general term of the expansion.

  b Find b given that the coefficient of x^4 is -280.

5 Find the constant term in the expansion of:

  a $\left(x + \dfrac{2}{x^2}\right)^{15}$ **b** $\left(x - \dfrac{3}{x^2}\right)^{9}$

6 Find the coefficient of:

  a x^{10} in the expansion of $(3 + 2x^2)^{10}$ **b** x^3 in the expansion of $\left(2x^2 - \dfrac{3}{x}\right)^6$

  c $x^6 y^3$ in the expansion of $\left(2x^2 - 3y\right)^6$ **d** x^{12} in the expansion of $\left(2x^2 - \dfrac{1}{x}\right)^{12}$.

7 Consider the expression $\left(x^2 y - 2y^2\right)^6$. Find the term in which x and y are raised to the same power.

8 The third term of $(1+x)^n$ is $36x^2$. Find n, and hence find the fourth term.

9 Find a if the coefficient of x^{11} in the expansion of $\left(x^2 + \dfrac{1}{ax}\right)^{10}$ is 15.

Example 9   ◀)) **Self Tutor**

Find the coefficient of x^5 in the expansion of $(x+3)(2x-1)^6$.

$(x+3)(2x-1)^6$
$= (x+3)[(2x)^6 + \binom{6}{1}(2x)^5(-1) + \binom{6}{2}(2x)^4(-1)^2 + ...]$
$= (x+3)(2^6 x^6 - \binom{6}{1}2^5 x^5 + \binom{6}{2}2^4 x^4 - ....)$

So, the terms containing x^5 are $\binom{6}{2}2^4 x^5$ from (1)

and $-3\binom{6}{1}2^5 x^5$ from (2)

∴   the coefficient of x^5 is $\binom{6}{2}2^4 - 3\binom{6}{1}2^5 = -336$

10 Find:

   a   the coefficient of x^4 in the expansion of $(x+4)(x-3)^6$

   b   the coefficient of x^5 in the expansion of $(x+2)(x^2+1)^8$

   c   the term containing x^6 in the expansion of $(2-x)(3x+1)^9$.

11 Consider the expression $\left(x^2 y - 2y^2\right)^6$. Find the term in which x and y are raised to the same power.

12 If $(1+kx)^n = 1 - 12x + 60x^2 - ....$, $n \in \mathbb{Z}^+$, find the values of k and n.

13 **a**   Write down the first 5 rows of Pascal's triangle.

   b   Find the sum of the numbers in:

     i   row 1   **ii**   row 2   **iii**   row 3   **iv**   row 4   **v**   row 5.

   c   Copy and complete: "The sum of the numbers in row n of Pascal's triangle is ......"

   d   Show that $(1+x)^n = \binom{n}{0} + \binom{n}{1}x + \binom{n}{2}x^2 + ... + \binom{n}{n-1}x^{n-1} + \binom{n}{n}x^n$.

   e   Hence deduce that:

     i $\binom{n}{0} + \binom{n}{1} + \binom{n}{2} + ... + \binom{n}{n-1} + \binom{n}{n} = 2^n$

     ii $\binom{n}{0} - \binom{n}{1} + \binom{n}{2} - \binom{n}{3} + ... + (-1)^n \binom{n}{n} = 0$

     iii $\binom{2n+1}{0} + \binom{2n+1}{1} + \binom{2n+1}{2} + ... + \binom{2n+1}{n} = 4^n$

   f   By considering the binomial expansion of $(1+x)^n$, find $\displaystyle\sum_{r=0}^{n} 2^r \binom{n}{r}$.

14 **a**   Write down the first four and last two terms of the binomial expansion $(3+x)^n$.

   b   Hence simplify $3^n + \binom{n}{1}3^{n-1} + \binom{n}{2}3^{n-2} + \binom{n}{3}3^{n-3} + ... + 3n + 1$.

15 By considering $(1+x)^n(1+x)^n = (1+x)^{2n}$, show that

$\binom{n}{0}^2 + \binom{n}{1}^2 + \binom{n}{2}^2 + \binom{n}{3}^2 + ... + \binom{n}{n}^2 = \binom{2n}{n}$.

16 **a** Prove that $r \binom{n}{r} = n \binom{n-1}{r-1}$.

b Hence show that $\binom{n}{1} + 2 \binom{n}{2} + 3 \binom{n}{3} + 4 \binom{n}{4} + \dots + n \binom{n}{n} = n2^{n-1}$.

c Suppose the set of numbers $\{P_r\}$ are defined by
$$P_r = \binom{n}{r} p^r (1-p)^{n-r} \quad \text{for} \quad r = 0, 1, 2, 3, \dots, n.$$

Prove that: **i** $\displaystyle\sum_{r=0}^{n} P_r = 1$ **ii** $\displaystyle\sum_{r=1}^{n} rP_r = np$

Historical note   The binomial theorem

The binomial theorem is one of the most important results in mathematics.

The process of multiplying out binomial terms dates back to the beginning of algebra. Mathematicians had noticed relationships between the coefficients for many centuries, and Pascal's triangle was certainly widely used long before Pascal.

Sir Isaac Newton discovered the binomial theorem in 1665, but he did not publish his results until much later. Newton was the first person to give a formula for the binomial coefficients. He did this because he wanted to go further. Newton's ground-breaking result included a generalisation of the binomial theorem to the case of $(a+b)^n$ where n is a rational number, such as $\frac{1}{2}$. In doing this, Newton was the first person to confidently use the exponential notation that we recognise today for both negative and fractional powers.

Sir Isaac Newton

Review set 9A

1 Express in factorial form:

a $8 \times 7 \times 6 \times 5 \times 4 \times 3 \times 2 \times 1$ **b** $10 \times 9 \times 8$

2 Simplify: **a** $\dfrac{n!}{(n-2)!}$ **b** $\dfrac{n! + (n+1)!}{n!}$

3 Use the binomial expansion to expand and simplify: **a** $(x+3)^3$ **b** $(x-2)^5$

4 Without simplifying, write down:

a the 5th term of $(2x+3)^9$ **b** the 8th term of $\left(3x - \dfrac{1}{x}\right)^{12}$.

5 Expand and simplify:

a $\left(5 + \sqrt{3}\right)^3$ **b** $(x+3)(x-1)^4$

6 Use the expansion of $(4+x)^3$ to find the exact value of $(4.02)^3$.

7 Use Pascal's triangle to expand $(a+b)^6$.

Hence, find the binomial expansion of: **a** $(x-3)^6$ **b** $\left(1 + \dfrac{1}{x}\right)^6$

8 Find the coefficient of x^{-6} in the expansion of $\left(2x - \dfrac{3}{x^2}\right)^{12}$.

9 Find the coefficient of x^5 in the expansion of $(2x + 3)(x - 2)^6$.

10 Find c given that the expansion $(1 + cx)(1 + x)^4$ includes the term $22x^3$.

11 **a** Write down the first four and last two terms of the binomial expansion $(2 + x)^n$.

   b Hence simplify $2^n + \binom{n}{1} 2^{n-1} + \binom{n}{2} 2^{n-2} + \binom{n}{3} 2^{n-3} + \ldots + 2n + 1$.

12 Find the possible values of a if the coefficient of x^3 in $\left(2x + \dfrac{1}{ax^2}\right)^9$ is 288.

Review set 9B

1 Simplify: **a** $\dfrac{9!}{7!}$ **b** $\dfrac{8!}{3!5!}$

2 Evaluate:

   a $\binom{4}{2}$ **b** $\binom{6}{5}$ **c** $\binom{9}{2}$

3 Use the binomial expansion to find:

   a $(x - 2y)^3$ **b** $(3x + 2)^4$

4 Find the coefficient of x^3 in the expansion of $(2x + 5)^6$.

5 Find the constant term in the expansion of $\left(2x^2 - \dfrac{1}{x}\right)^6$.

6 Expand and simplify:

   a $\left(2 - \sqrt{2}\right)^6$ **b** $(x + 3)(2x + 1)^3$

7 Write down the first three and last two terms of the following binomial expansions. Do not simplify your answers.

   a $(2x - 7)^{10}$ **b** $\left(3x + \dfrac{4}{x}\right)^{13}$

8 In the expansion of $\left(3x^2 + \dfrac{1}{x}\right)^9$, find:

   a the coefficient of x^{12} **b** the constant term.

9 The first three terms in the expansion of $(1 + kx)^n$, $n \in \mathbb{Z}^+$, are $1 - 4x + \dfrac{15}{2}x^2$. Find k and n.

10 Find k in the expansion $(m - 2n)^{10} = m^{10} - 20m^9 n + km^8 n^2 - \ldots + 1024n^{10}$.

11 Find the possible values of q if the constant terms in the expansions of $\left(x^3 + \dfrac{q}{x^3}\right)^8$ and $\left(x^3 + \dfrac{q}{x^3}\right)^4$ are equal.

10

Circles

Contents:

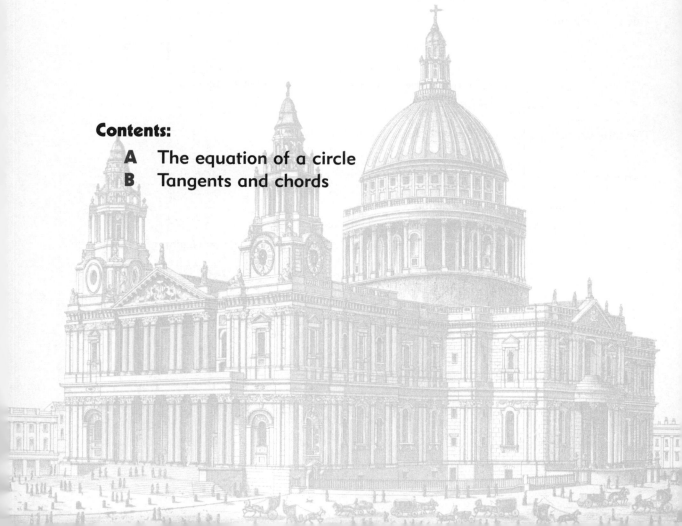

A   THE EQUATION OF A CIRCLE

A **circle** is a set of points which are equidistant from a fixed point. The fixed point is called the **centre** of the circle, and the distance from the centre to the circle is the **radius**.

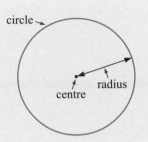

If we know the centre and radius of a circle on a Cartesian plane, we can find the **equation** of the circle.

Consider a circle with centre $C(2, 5)$ and radius 3 units.
For any point $P(x, y)$ on the circle,

$$CP = 3$$

$$\therefore \ \sqrt{(x-2)^2 + (y-5)^2} = 3 \qquad \{\text{distance formula}\}$$

$$\therefore \ (x-2)^2 + (y-5)^2 = 3^2 \qquad \{\text{squaring both sides}\}$$

This is the equation of the circle.

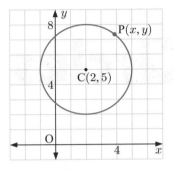

The equation of a circle with centre (a, b) and radius r units is
$(x - a)^2 + (y - b)^2 = r^2$.

This form of the equation of a circle is called **centre-radius form**.

Discussion

- Is the equation of a circle a relation?
- Can the equation of a circle be written as a function?
- Can you explain how the equation $(x - a)^2 + (y - b)^2 = r^2$ is the translation of a circle with radius r centred at the origin?

Example 1   ◀) Self Tutor

Write down the equation of the circle with:

a   centre $(4, -1)$ and radius 5 units

b   centre $(-2, 3)$ and radius $\sqrt{7}$ units.

a   The circle has equation $(x - 4)^2 + (y - (-1))^2 = 5^2$
$$\therefore \ (x - 4)^2 + (y + 1)^2 = 25$$

b   The circle has equation $(x - (-2))^2 + (y - 3)^2 = (\sqrt{7})^2$
$$\therefore \ (x + 2)^2 + (y - 3)^2 = 7$$

EXERCISE 10A.1

1 Write down the equation of the circle with:

  a centre $(5, 1)$ and radius 2 units

  b centre $(-3, 4)$ and radius 6 units

  c centre $(-6, 2)$ and radius $\sqrt{3}$ units

  d centre $(0, 0)$ and radius 1 unit

  e centre $(-4, 0)$ and radius $\sqrt{17}$ units

  f centre $(-3, -7)$ and radius 9 units.

2 For each circle:

  i Find the centre and radius.

  ii Write down the equation of the circle.

a
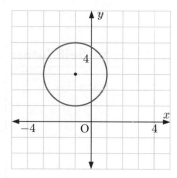

b
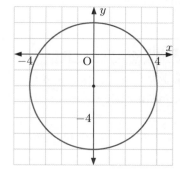

c
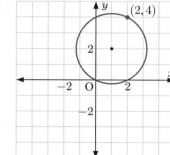

d
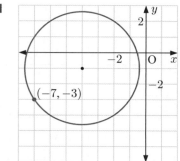

3 Find the centre and radius of the circle with equation:

  a $(x - 2)^2 + (y - 3)^2 = 4$
    b $x^2 + (y + 3)^2 = 9$
    c $(x - 2)^2 + y^2 = 7$

4 Draw the circle with equation:

GRAPHING PACKAGE

  a $(x - 1)^2 + (y - 3)^2 = 16$
    b $(x + 2)^2 + (y - 2)^2 = 1$

  c $x^2 + y^2 = 25$
    d $(x - 3)^2 + y^2 = 36$

Use technology to check your answers.

5 Find, in centre-radius form, the equation of the circle with the properties:

  a centre $(3, -2)$ and touching the x-axis

  b centre $(-4, 3)$ and touching the y-axis

  c centre $(5, 3)$ and passing through $(4, -1)$

  d $(-2, 3)$ and $(6, 1)$ are end-points of a diameter

  e radius $\sqrt{7}$ and concentric with $(x + 3)^2 + (y - 2)^2 = 5$.

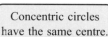

Concentric circles have the same centre.

6   Describe what the following equations represent on the Cartesian plane:

   a $(x+2)^2 + (y-7)^2 = 5$ **b** $(x+2)^2 + (y-7)^2 = 0$

7   **a**   On the same set of axes, draw the circles $(x-3)^2 + (y+1)^2 = 9$ and $(x+2)^2 + (y-3)^2 = 16$.

   b   Hence, find the only point with integer coordinates which lies inside *both* circles.

8   **a**   Draw the circle with equation $(x+2)^2 + (y-1)^2 = 9$.

   b   Is the circle a function? Explain your answer.

   c   Find the domain and range.

Example 2   ◀) **Self Tutor**

The point $(m, 2)$ lies on the circle with equation $(x-2)^2 + (y-5)^2 = 25$. Find the possible values of m.

Since $(m, 2)$ lies on the circle, $(m-2)^2 + (2-5)^2 = 25$
$$\therefore \; (m-2)^2 + 9 = 25$$
$$\therefore \; (m-2)^2 = 16$$
$$\therefore \; m - 2 = \pm 4$$
$$\therefore \; m = 6 \text{ or } -2$$

---

9   Find m given that:

   a $(3, m)$ lies on the circle with equation $(x+1)^2 + (y-2)^2 = 25$

   b $(m, -2)$ lies on the circle with equation $(x+2)^2 + (y-3)^2 = 36$

   c $(3, -1)$ lies on the circle with equation $(x+4)^2 + (y+m)^2 = 53$.

10   Consider the shaded region inside the circle with centre (a, b) and radius r units. Let $P(x, y)$ be any point inside the circle.

   a   Show that $(x-a)^2 + (y-b)^2 < r^2$.

   b   What region is defined by the inequality $(x-a)^2 + (y-b)^2 > r^2$?

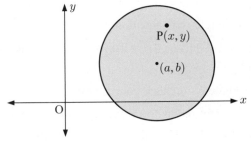

   c   Without sketching the circle with equation $(x+2)^2 + (y-3)^2 = 25$, determine whether the following points lie on the circle, inside the circle, or outside the circle:

   i   A(2, 0)   **ii**   B(1, 1)   **iii**   C(3, 0)   **iv**   D(4, 1)

11 T is a mobile telephone tower in a remote country town, and its region of reception is defined by the inequality $(x - 3)^2 + (y - 2)^2 \leqslant 40$. David's car has broken down on the highway at grid reference D(9, 5). Each grid unit represents 5 km.

    a Write down the grid reference of the mobile telephone tower.

    b Find the radius of the region of reception for this tower.

    c If there are no other mobile telephone towers in the near vicinity, will David be able to use his telephone to ring for roadside assistance? If not, how far will he have to walk in order to receive a signal?

12 Consider a circle with centre (c, b) and radius r. Let $A(x_A, y_A)$ be one end of a diameter [AB], and let $C(x_C, y_C)$ be any other point on the circle.

    a If B has coordinates (x_B, y_B), write expressions for x_B and y_B.

    b Write an expression for the gradient of:

      i [AC]   **ii** [BC]

    c Hence prove the angle in a semi-circle theorem.

13 Consider a circle with centre (a, b) and radius r. Let $A(x_A, y_A)$ and $B(x_B, y_B)$ be any two points on the circle such that AB is *not* a diameter.

    a Write an expression for the gradient of [AB].

    b Hence write down the equation of the line through the centre of the circle which is perpendicular to [AB].

    c Prove that this line bisects [AB].

THE EXPANDED FORM $x^2 + y^2 + Ax + By + C = 0$

Consider again the circle with centre $(2, 5)$ and radius 3 units.

In centre-radius form, its equation is $(x - 2)^2 + (y - 5)^2 = 9$

        Expanding this gives $x^2 - 4x + 4 + y^2 - 10y + 25 = 9$

                    $\therefore \ x^2 + y^2 - 4x - 10y + 20 = 0$

This form of the equation of a circle is called the **expanded form**.

> The **expanded form** of the equation of a circle is $x^2 + y^2 + Ax + By + C = 0$.

Example 3   ◀⑳ Self Tutor

Find, in expanded form, the equation of the circle with centre $(4, -1)$ and radius 2 units.

The circle has equation $(x - 4)^2 + (y + 1)^2 = 4$

          $\therefore \ x^2 - 8x + 16 + y^2 + 2y + 1 = 4$

            $\therefore \ x^2 + y^2 - 8x + 2y + 13 = 0$

If we are given a circle's equation in expanded form, we can convert the equation into centre-radius form by **completing the square** on the x and y terms. We can hence find the circle's centre and radius.

To complete the square on the x term, we add $\left(\dfrac{\text{coefficient of } x}{2}\right)^2$ to both sides of the equation. Similarly, to complete the square on the y term, we add $\left(\dfrac{\text{coefficient of } y}{2}\right)^2$ to both sides of the equation.

Example 4 — Self Tutor

Find the centre and radius of the circle with equation $x^2 + y^2 + 8x - 6y - 11 = 0$.

$$x^2 + y^2 + 8x - 6y - 11 = 0$$
$$\therefore \ x^2 + 8x \quad + y^2 - 6y \quad = 11 \qquad \{\text{rearranging}\}$$
$$\therefore \ x^2 + 8x + 4^2 + y^2 - 6y + (-3)^2 = 11 + 4^2 + (-3)^2 \qquad \{\text{completing the squares}\}$$
$$\therefore \ (x+4)^2 + (y-3)^2 = 36$$

$\therefore$ the circle has centre $(-4, 3)$ and radius 6 units.

EXERCISE 10A.2

1 Find, in expanded form, the equation of the circle with:

a centre $(2, 3)$ and radius 1 unit

b centre $(5, -1)$ and radius 3 units

c centre $(-4, 0)$ and radius $\sqrt{10}$ units

d centre $(-6, -9)$ and radius $\sqrt{73}$ units.

2 Find, in expanded form, the equation of each circle:

a

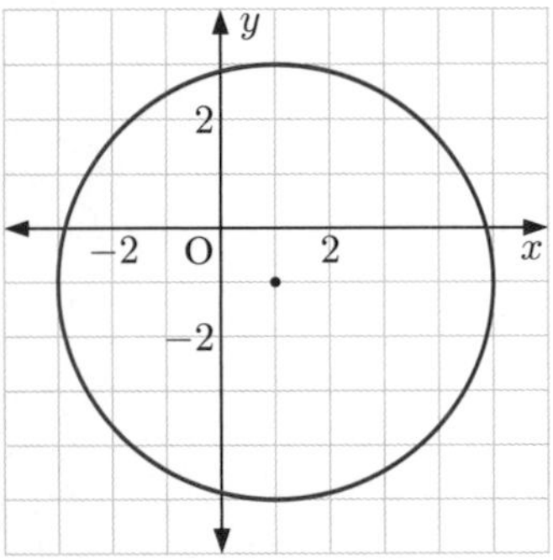

b

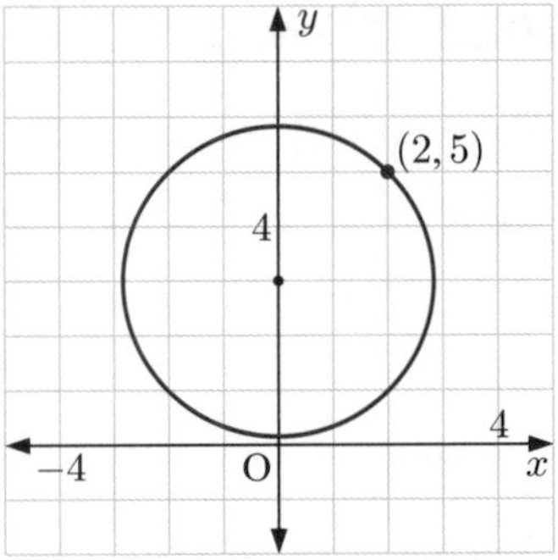

3 Find the centre and radius of the circle with equation:

a $x^2 + y^2 + 6x - 2y - 3 = 0$

b $x^2 + y^2 - 6x - 2 = 0$

c $x^2 + y^2 + 4y - 1 = 0$

d $x^2 + y^2 + 4x - 8y + 3 = 0$

e $x^2 + y^2 - 4x - 6y - 3 = 0$

f $x^2 + y^2 - 8x = 0$

4 Draw the circle with equation:

a $x^2 + y^2 - 6x + 4y + 9 = 0$

b $x^2 + y^2 + 2x + 8y + 8 = 0$

5 Explain why $x^2 + y^2 - 4x + 2y + 14 = 0$ is not the equation of a circle.

6 Find k given that:

    a $x^2 + y^2 - 12x + 8y + k = 0$ is a circle with radius 4 units

    b $x^2 + y^2 + 6x - 4y = k$ is a circle with radius $\sqrt{11}$ units

    c $x^2 + y^2 + 4x - 2y + k = 0$ represents a circle.

7 **a** Pete's pizza shop is located at the grid reference $(3,\ 4)$, where each grid unit equals 1 km. The shop offers free delivery to homes within 8 km.

      Write an inequality to describe the free delivery region in:

      i centre-radius form   **ii** expanded form.

    b Pamela's pizza shop has a free delivery region defined by the inequality $x^2 + y^2 + 10x + 14y + 38 \leqslant 0$.

      i Find the location of this pizza shop.

      ii Find the radius of its free delivery region.

    c Graph both regions on the same set of axes.

    d Find the only point with integer coordinates which lies in the free delivery region of *both* shops. Find, to 1 decimal place, its distance from each shop.

8 In general form, a circle has equation $x^2 + y^2 + Ax + By + C = 0$.

    a Show that its centre is $\left(-\dfrac{A}{2},\ -\dfrac{B}{2}\right)$ and its radius $r = \sqrt{\dfrac{A^2}{4} + \dfrac{B^2}{4} - C}$ where $A^2 + B^2 > 4C$.

    b Hence, find the centre and radius of the circle with equation $3x^2 + 3y^2 + 6x - 9y + 2 = 0$.

    c Comment on the locus with equation $x^2 + y^2 + Ax + By + C = 0$ in the case:

      i $A^2 + B^2 = 4C$ **ii** $A^2 + B^2 < 4C$

> A *locus* is a set of points.

9 Suppose A is $(1,\ 0)$, B is $(5,\ 0)$, and k is a constant. $P(x,\ y)$ is a point such that $\dfrac{\text{AP}}{\text{BP}} = k$ for all positions of P. Find the equation and nature of the locus of P if:

    a $k = 3$ **b** $k = \frac{1}{3}$ **c** $k = 1$

Activity 1   Spider squash

Click on the icon to play the game.

SPIDER SQUASH

B   TANGENTS AND CHORDS

For a given circle in the plane, we can describe any line as:

- **external** if it does not meet the circle
- a **tangent** if it touches the circle at one point
- a **secant** if it cuts the circle at two points.

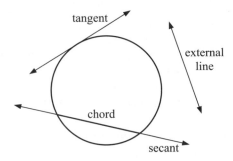

For any point A on the circle, there is a unique tangent through A called the **tangent at A**.

For any external point P there are exactly 2 tangents, called the **external tangents from P**. In the diagram, A and B are the two points of contact.

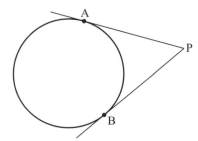

Example 5   ◀)) Self Tutor

Find the equation of the tangent to the circle with equation $x^2 + y^2 - 8x - 4 = 0$ at the point $P(8, -2)$.

$$x^2 + y^2 - 8x - 4 = 0$$
$$\therefore \quad x^2 - 8x \quad\;\; + y^2 = 4$$
$$\therefore \quad x^2 - 8x + 4^2 + y^2 = 4 + 4^2$$
$$\therefore \quad (x - 4)^2 + y^2 = 20$$

$\therefore$ the circle has centre $(4, 0)$.

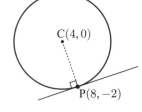

The gradient of [CP] is $\dfrac{-2 - 0}{8 - 4} = \dfrac{-2}{4} = -\dfrac{1}{2}$

$\therefore$ the gradient of the tangent is 2

$\therefore$ the equation of the tangent is $y - (-2) = 2(x - 8)$

which is $y = 2x - 18$.

EXERCISE 10B

1 Find the equation of the tangent to the circle with equation:

    a $x^2 + y^2 + 6x - 10y + 17 = 0$ at the point $P(-2, 1)$

    b $x^2 + y^2 + 6y = 16$ at the point $P(0, 2)$.

2 The boundary of a circular pond is defined by the equation
$x^2 + y^2 - 24x - 16y + 111 = 0$.

A straight path meets the edge of the lake at grid reference A(3, 4).

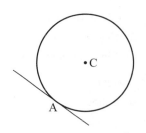

   a Given that the grid units are metres, find the diameter of the circular pond.

   b Find the equation of the straight path.

Example 6 ◀⅃ **Self Tutor**

Find the equations of the tangents from the external point P(0, −4) to the circle with equation $x^2 + y^2 - 10x - 2y + 16 = 0$.

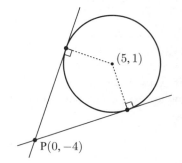

Suppose an external tangent through P has gradient m.

∴   its equation is $y = mx - 4$

The tangent meets the circle when

$$x^2 + (mx - 4)^2 - 10x - 2(mx - 4) + 16 = 0$$
$$\therefore \ x^2 + m^2x^2 - 8mx + 16 - 10x - 2mx + 8 + 16 = 0$$
$$\therefore \ (m^2 + 1)x^2 - (10 + 10m)x + 40 = 0$$

For a line to be a tangent, it must *touch* the circle.

∴   the quadratic equation in x must have a repeated solution.

$$\therefore \ \Delta = b^2 - 4ac = 0$$
$$\therefore \ (10 + 10m)^2 - 4(m^2 + 1)(40) = 0$$
$$\therefore \ 100 + 200m + 100m^2 - 160m^2 - 160 = 0$$
$$\therefore \ -60m^2 + 200m - 60 = 0$$
$$\therefore \ 3m^2 - 10m + 3 = 0$$
$$\therefore \ (m - 3)(3m - 1) = 0$$
$$\therefore \ m = 3 \ \text{ or } \ \tfrac{1}{3}$$

∴   the tangents are $y = 3x - 4$ and $y = \tfrac{1}{3}x - 4$.

---

3 A circle has centre (2, 3) and radius 4 units. P(8, 7) is external to the circle. Find the equations of the two tangents from P to the circle.

4 Find the equations of the two tangents from the origin O to the circle with centre (4, 3) and radius 2 units.

5

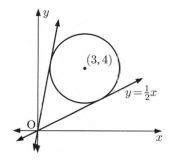

A circle has centre (3, 4). One tangent from the origin O has equation $y = \tfrac{1}{2}x$.

Find the equation of the other tangent.

6 A circle with centre $(3, -2)$ has a tangent with equation $3x - 4y + 8 = 0$.

   a Find the equation of the circle.

   b Find the tangent's point of contact with the circle.

7 Consider the circle $x^2 + y^2 - 4x + 2y = 0$. Find the value(s) of k for which $3x + 4y = k$ is:

   a a tangent   **b** a secant   **c** an external line.

8

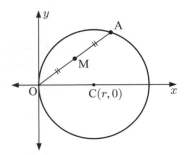

$C(r, 0)$ is the centre of a fixed circle with radius r.
A is a point which is free to move on the circle, and M is the midpoint of [OA].

   a Find the Cartesian equation of the locus of M.

   b Describe the locus of M.

Activity 2   A cat, a ladder, and a spinning wheel

In this Activity we present two famous locus problems, both relating to circles, and indeed rather surprisingly related to one another.

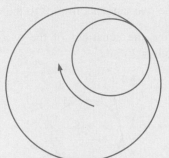

What to do:

1 A ladder is standing upright against a wall, with a cat sitting on the middle rung. The ladder slips and slides down the wall.

Use coordinate geometry to find the path followed by the cat.

2 A wheel is housed within another wheel twice its diameter. The larger wheel is fixed, while the smaller wheel spins and thereby rolls around the larger wheel. The wheels are called a **Tusi couple** after the 13th century Persian astronomer **Nasir al-Din al-Tusi**.

Use a deductive argument to find the path followed by a particular point on the smaller wheel.

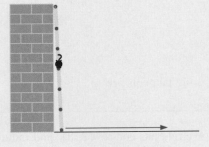

3 Explain how these problems are related.

4 Research the astrological significance of the Tusi couple.

Activity 3   Conic sections

In this course we have now studied parabolas, hyperbolae, and circles. These shapes
are all **conic sections**, which means they can be formed by cutting a cone with a plane.

Click on the icon to explore the coordinate geometry of these curves in greater detail.

CONIC
SECTIONS

Review set 10A

1 Write down, in centre-radius form, the equation of the circle with:

   a centre $(2, -1)$ and radius 5 units   **b** centre $(-4, -6)$ and radius $\sqrt{7}$ units.

2 Find, in expanded form, the equation of each circle:

  a

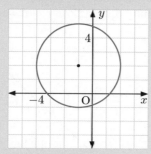

  b

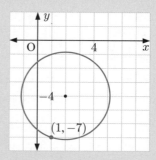

3 Draw the circle with equation:

   a $x^2 + (y - 3)^2 = 16$ **b** $x^2 + y^2 + 6x - 8y + 21 = 0$

4 Find m given that $(2, m)$ lies on the circle with equation $(x - 1)^2 + (y - 1)^2 = 36$.

5 Find the equation of the tangent to the circle with equation $x^2 + y^2 + 8x - 6y = 40$ at the point $(0, -4)$.

6 Find the equations of the tangents from the external point $P(5, 5)$ to the circle with equation $x^2 + y^2 - 4x + 5y - 10 = 0$.

7 Consider the circle $x^2 + y^2 - 6x + 4y = 0$. Find the values of k for which $2x + 3y = k$ is:

   a a tangent   **b** a secant   **c** an external line.

Review set 10B

1 Find the centre and radius of the circle with equation:

   a $(x + 1)^2 + (y - 3)^2 = 4$ **b** $(x - 4)^2 + (y - 2)^2 = 5$

2 Draw the circle with equation:

   a $(x - 3)^2 + (y + 2)^2 = 16$ **b** $x^2 + y^2 - x - 2y - 1 = 0$

3 Write down the equation of the circle with:

   a radius $\sqrt{3}$ and centre $(2, 4)$

   b a diameter that has endpoints $(-1, -3)$ and $(4, 5)$.

4 Ship A is equipped with a radar which detects objects within a certain distance of the ship. The radar's detection region is defined by the inequality $x^2 + y^2 - 8x - 4y - 5 \leqslant 0$. Each grid unit is equal to 10 km.

   a Find the location of the ship.

   b Find the radius of the ship's radar detection region.

   c Ship B is located at $(6, -2)$.

   i Will ship A be able to detect ship B?

   ii Ship B's radar has a detection region defined by $x^2 + y^2 - 12x + 4y + 24 \leqslant 0$. Will ship B be able to detect ship A?

   d Draw a graph which shows each ship's location and detection region.

5 Find k given that $x^2 + y^2 + 6x - 4y + k = 0$ is a circle with radius $\sqrt{12}$ units. Also state the centre of the circle.

6 Find the points where the secant $y = x + 2$ meets the circle $x^2 + y^2 = 20$.

7 A circle has centre $(5, 3)$. One tangent from the origin has equation $y = \frac{1}{3}x$. Find the equation of the other tangent.

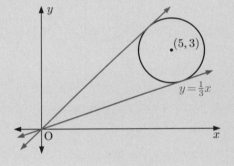

11

Trigonometry

Contents:

Opening problem

A triangular sail is to be cut from a section of cloth. Two of the sides
must have lengths 4 m and 6 m as illustrated. The total area for the sail
must be 11.6 m², the maximum allowed for the boat to race in its class.

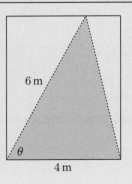

Things to think about:

a Can you find the size of the angle θ between the two sides of given
length?

b Can you find the length of the third side of the sail?

In this Chapter we will see how trigonometry can be used to solve problems involving non-right angled
triangles, for example the **Opening Problem** above.

We will also use a **unit circle** to find trigonometric ratios, and angles which have particular trigonometric
ratios.

A   THE UNIT CIRCLE

The **unit circle** is the circle with
centre $(0, 0)$ and radius 1 unit.

The equation of the unit circle is
$x^2 + y^2 = 1$.

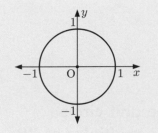

ANGLE MEASUREMENT

Suppose P lies anywhere on the unit circle, and A is $(1, 0)$.
Let θ be the angle measured from [OA] on the positive x-axis.

> θ is **positive** for anticlockwise rotations and
> **negative** for clockwise rotations.

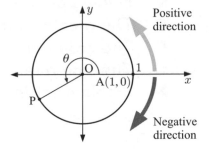

For example: $\theta = 210°$
         $\phi = -150°$

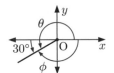

DEFINITION OF SINE AND COSINE

Consider a point $P(a, b)$ which lies on the unit circle in the first quadrant. [OP] makes an angle θ with the x-axis as shown.

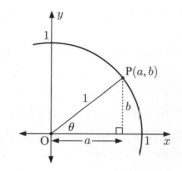

Using right angled triangle trigonometry:

$$\cos\theta = \frac{\text{ADJ}}{\text{HYP}} = \frac{a}{1} = a$$

$$\sin\theta = \frac{\text{OPP}}{\text{HYP}} = \frac{b}{1} = b$$

$$\tan\theta = \frac{\text{OPP}}{\text{ADJ}} = \frac{b}{a} = \frac{\sin\theta}{\cos\theta}$$

More generally, we define:

If P is any point on the unit circle such that [OP] makes an angle θ measured anticlockwise from the positive x-axis:

- $\cos\theta$ is the x-coordinate of P
- $\sin\theta$ is the y-coordinate of P

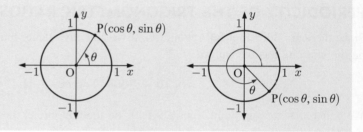

For all points on the unit circle, $-1 \leqslant x \leqslant 1$, $-1 \leqslant y \leqslant 1$, and $x^2 + y^2 = 1$. We therefore conclude:

For any angle θ:

- $-1 \leqslant \cos\theta \leqslant 1$ and $-1 \leqslant \sin\theta \leqslant 1$
- $\cos^2\theta + \sin^2\theta = 1$

DEFINITION OF TANGENT

Suppose we extend [OP] to meet the tangent from $A(1, 0)$.

We let the intersection between these lines be point Q.

Note that as P moves, so does Q.

The position of Q relative to A is defined as the **tangent function**.

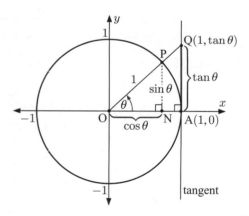

Notice that triangles ONP and OAQ are equiangular and therefore similar.

Consequently $\dfrac{\text{AQ}}{\text{OA}} = \dfrac{\text{NP}}{\text{ON}}$ and hence $\dfrac{\text{AQ}}{1} = \dfrac{\sin\theta}{\cos\theta}$.

Under the definition that $\text{AQ} = \tan\theta$, $\qquad \tan\theta = \dfrac{\sin\theta}{\cos\theta}$.

SIGNS OF THE TRIGONOMETRIC RATIOS

By considering the definitions of $\cos\theta$ and $\sin\theta$ as the coordinates of a point P on the unit circle, we establish:

- $\sin\theta$, $\cos\theta$, and $\tan\theta$ are positive in quadrant 1
- only $\sin\theta$ is positive in quadrant 2
- only $\tan\theta$ is positive in quadrant 3
- only $\cos\theta$ is positive in quadrant 4.

We can use a letter to show which trigonometric ratios are positive in each quadrant. The A stands for *all* of the ratios.

You might like to remember them using

　　　All Silly Turtles Crawl.

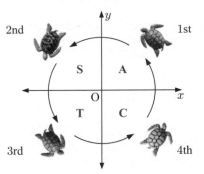

PERIODICITY OF THE TRIGONOMETRIC RATIOS

Since there are $360°$ in a full revolution, if we add any integer multiple of $360°$ to θ, then the position of P on the unit circle is unchanged.

> For any $k \in \mathbb{Z}$, $\cos(\theta + 360k°) = \cos\theta$ and $\sin(\theta + 360k°) = \sin\theta$.

We notice that for any point $(\cos\theta, \sin\theta)$ on the unit circle, the point directly opposite is $(-\cos\theta, -\sin\theta)$

$$\therefore \quad \cos(\theta + 180°) = -\cos\theta$$
$$\sin(\theta + 180°) = -\sin\theta$$
$$\text{and} \quad \tan(\theta + 180°) = \frac{-\sin\theta}{-\cos\theta} = \frac{\sin\theta}{\cos\theta} = \tan\theta$$

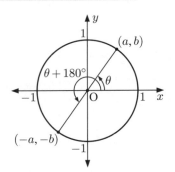

> For any $k \in \mathbb{Z}$, $\tan(\theta + 180k°) = \tan\theta$.

This **periodic** feature is an important property of the trigonometric ratios.

EXERCISE 11A

1 For each unit circle illustrated:

　i state the exact coordinates of points A, B, and C in terms of sine and cosine

　ii use your calculator to give the coordinates of A, B, and C correct to 3 significant figures.

a

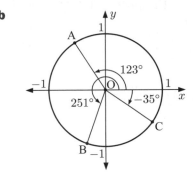

b

2 With the aid of a unit circle, complete the following table:

θ	0°	90°	180°	270°	360°	450°
$\sin\theta$						
$\cos\theta$						
$\tan\theta$						

3　**a**　Use your calculator to evaluate:

i $\sin 100°$　　**ii** $\sin 80°$　　**iii** $\sin 105°$　　**iv** $\sin 75°$　　**v** $\sin 153°$　　**vi** $\sin 27°$

b　Use the results from **a** to copy and complete:　$\sin(180° - \theta) = $ ......

c　Justify your answer using the diagram alongside:

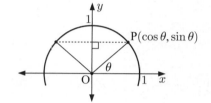

d　Find the obtuse angle with the same sine as:

i $45°$　　**ii** $51°$

4　**a**　Use your calculator to evaluate:

i $\cos 70°$　　**ii** $\cos 110°$　　**iii** $\cos 25°$　　**iv** $\cos 155°$　　**v** $\cos 80°$　　**vi** $\cos 100°$

b　Use the results from **a** to copy and complete:　$\cos(180° - \theta) = $ ......

c　Justify your answer using the diagram alongside:

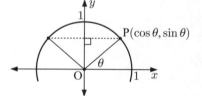

d　Find the obtuse angle which has the negative cosine of:

i $40°$　　**ii** $19°$

5 Without using your calculator, find:

a $\sin 137°$ if $\sin 43° \approx 0.6820$　　　　**b** $\sin 59°$ if $\sin 121° \approx 0.8572$

c $\cos 143°$ if $\cos 37° \approx 0.7986$　　　　**d** $\cos 24°$ if $\cos 156° \approx -0.9135$

e $\sin 115°$ if $\sin 65° \approx 0.9063$　　　　**f** $\cos 132°$ if $\cos 48° \approx 0.6691$

6　**a**　If $A\widehat{O}P = B\widehat{O}Q = \theta$, state the measure of $A\widehat{O}Q$.

b　Copy and complete:

[OQ] is a reflection of [OP] in the ......
and so Q has coordinates ......

c　What trigonometric formulae can be deduced from **a** and **b**?

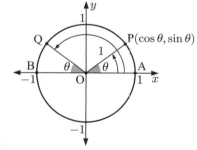

7

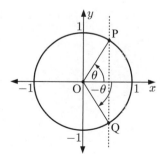

The coordinates of P are $(\cos\theta, \sin\theta)$.

a　By writing the coordinates of Q in terms of θ in *two different* ways, prove that $\cos(-\theta) = \cos\theta$ and $\sin(-\theta) = -\sin\theta$.

b　Hence write expressions for $\cos(360° - \theta)$ and $\sin(360° - \theta)$.

B   THE MULTIPLES OF 30° AND 45°

MULTIPLES OF 45°

Consider $\theta = 45°$.

Angle OPB also measures 45°, so triangle OBP is isosceles.

$\therefore$ we let   OB = BP = a

Now $a^2 + a^2 = 1^2$ {Pythagoras}

$\therefore$ $a^2 = \frac{1}{2}$

$\therefore$ $a = \frac{1}{\sqrt{2}}$ {since $a > 0$}

$\therefore$ P is $\left(\frac{1}{\sqrt{2}}, \frac{1}{\sqrt{2}}\right)$ where $\frac{1}{\sqrt{2}} \approx 0.7$.

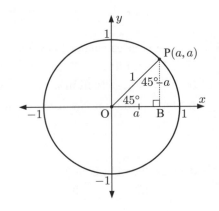

We can now find the coordinates of all points on the unit circle corresponding to multiples of 45° by using rotations and reflections.

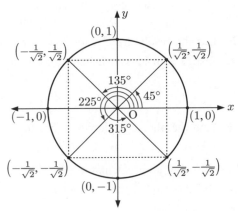

MULTIPLES OF 30°

Consider $\theta = 60°$.

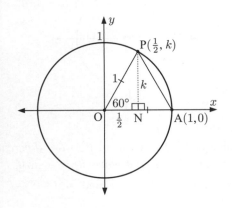

Since   OA = OP,   triangle OAP is isosceles.

Now $\widehat{AOP} = 60°$,   so the remaining angles are therefore also 60°. Triangle AOP is therefore equilateral.

The altitude [PN] bisects base [OA], so   ON $= \frac{1}{2}$.

If P is $\left(\frac{1}{2}, k\right)$,   then $\left(\frac{1}{2}\right)^2 + k^2 = 1$

$\therefore$ $k^2 = \frac{3}{4}$

$\therefore$ $k = \frac{\sqrt{3}}{2}$ {since $k > 0$}

$\therefore$ P is $\left(\frac{1}{2}, \frac{\sqrt{3}}{2}\right)$ where $\frac{\sqrt{3}}{2} \approx 0.9$.

We can now find the coordinates of all points on the unit circle corresponding to multiples of $30°$ by using rotations and reflections.

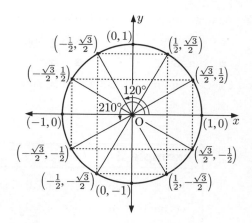

Summary:

- If θ is a **multiple of 90°**, the coordinates of the points on the unit circle involve 0 and ± 1.
- If θ is a **multiple of 45°**, but not a multiple of $90°$, the coordinates involve $\pm \frac{1}{\sqrt{2}}$.
- If θ is a **multiple of 30°**, but not a multiple of $90°$, the coordinates involve $\pm \frac{1}{2}$ and $\pm \frac{\sqrt{3}}{2}$.

For any angle θ, we can calculate the **tangent** of the angle using $\quad \boxed{\tan \theta = \dfrac{\sin \theta}{\cos \theta}}$.

Example 1 ◀ Self Tutor

Use a unit circle diagram to find $\sin \theta$, $\cos \theta$, and $\tan \theta$ for:

a $\theta = 60°$ **b** $\theta = 150°$ **c** $\theta = 225°$

a

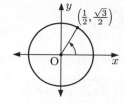

$\sin 60° = \frac{\sqrt{3}}{2}$

$\cos 60° = \frac{1}{2}$

$\tan 60° = \dfrac{\frac{\sqrt{3}}{2}}{\frac{1}{2}} = \sqrt{3}$

b

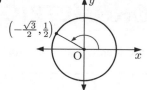

$\sin 150° = \frac{1}{2}$

$\cos 150° = -\frac{\sqrt{3}}{2}$

$\tan 150° = \dfrac{\frac{1}{2}}{-\frac{\sqrt{3}}{2}} = -\frac{1}{\sqrt{3}}$

c

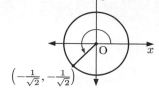

$\sin 225° = -\frac{1}{\sqrt{2}}$

$\cos 225° = -\frac{1}{\sqrt{2}}$

$\tan 225° = 1$

EXERCISE 11B

1 Use a unit circle to find $\sin \theta$, $\cos \theta$, and $\tan \theta$ for:

a $\theta = 30°$	**b** $\theta = 45°$	**c** $\theta = 0°$	**d** $\theta = 135°$
e $\theta = 90°$	**f** $\theta = 120°$	**g** $\theta = 270°$	**h** $\theta = 180°$
i $\theta = 210°$	**j** $\theta = 240°$	**k** $\theta = 330°$	**l** $\theta = 360°$
m $\theta = 300°$	**n** $\theta = 315°$	**o** $\theta = 495°$	**p** $\theta = 900°$

2 Without using a calculator, find the exact value of:

    a $\sin^2 45°$ **b** $\cos^2 60°$

    c $\tan^2 30°$ **d** $\cos^2(-30°)$

Check your answers using a calculator.

$\sin^2 45°$ means $(\sin 45°)^2$.

Example 2   ◀)) **Self Tutor**

Use a unit circle diagram to find the angle between $0°$ and $360°$ which has a cosine of $\frac{1}{2}$ and a sine of $-\frac{\sqrt{3}}{2}$.

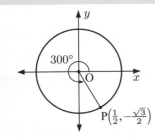

P is at $\left(\frac{1}{2}, -\frac{\sqrt{3}}{2}\right)$.

Since $\frac{1}{2}$ and $-\frac{\sqrt{3}}{2}$ are involved, the angle is a multiple of $30°$.

The angle is $300°$.

---

3 Use a unit circle diagram to find the angle between $0°$ and $360°$ which has:

    a a cosine of $-\frac{\sqrt{3}}{2}$ and a sine of $\frac{1}{2}$ **b** a cosine of $-\frac{1}{\sqrt{2}}$ and a sine of $-\frac{1}{\sqrt{2}}$

    c a cosine of $\frac{\sqrt{3}}{2}$ and a tangent of $\frac{1}{\sqrt{3}}$ **d** a sine of $-\frac{1}{\sqrt{2}}$ and a tangent of -1.

C | FINDING TRIGONOMETRIC RATIOS

In this Section we use the unit circle and the identity $\cos^2\theta + \sin^2\theta = 1$ to find trigonometric ratios.

Example 3   ◀)) **Self Tutor**

Find the possible values of $\cos\theta$ for $\sin\theta = \frac{2}{3}$. Illustrate your answers.

$$\cos^2\theta + \sin^2\theta = 1$$
$$\therefore \cos^2\theta + \left(\tfrac{2}{3}\right)^2 = 1$$
$$\therefore \cos^2\theta = \tfrac{5}{9}$$
$$\therefore \cos\theta = \pm\tfrac{\sqrt{5}}{3}$$

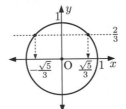

EXERCISE 11C

1 Find the possible values of $\cos\theta$ for:

    a $\sin\theta = \frac{1}{2}$ **b** $\sin\theta = -\frac{1}{3}$ **c** $\sin\theta = 0$ **d** $\sin\theta = -1$

2 Find the possible values of $\sin\theta$ for:

a $\cos\theta = \frac{4}{5}$ **b** $\cos\theta = -\frac{3}{4}$ **c** $\cos\theta = 1$ **d** $\cos\theta = 0$

Example 4   ◀) **Self Tutor**

If $\sin\theta = -\frac{3}{4}$ and $180° < \theta < 270°$, find $\cos\theta$ and $\tan\theta$. Give exact answers.

Now $\cos^2\theta + \sin^2\theta = 1$

$\therefore \cos^2\theta + \frac{9}{16} = 1$

$\therefore \cos^2\theta = \frac{7}{16}$

$\therefore \cos\theta = \pm\frac{\sqrt{7}}{4}$

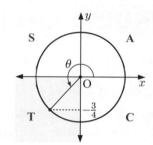

But $180° < \theta < 270°$, so θ lies in quadrant 3.

$\therefore \cos\theta$ is negative.

$\therefore \cos\theta = -\frac{\sqrt{7}}{4}$ and $\tan\theta = \dfrac{\sin\theta}{\cos\theta} = \dfrac{-\frac{3}{4}}{-\frac{\sqrt{7}}{4}} = \dfrac{3}{\sqrt{7}}$

---

3 Find the exact value of:

a $\sin\theta$ if $\cos\theta = \frac{2}{3}$ and θ is acute

b $\cos\theta$ if $\sin\theta = \frac{2}{5}$ and $90° < \theta < 180°$

c $\cos\theta$ if $\sin\theta = -\frac{3}{5}$ and $270° < \theta < 360°$

d $\sin\theta$ if $\cos\theta = -\frac{5}{13}$ and $180° < \theta < 270°$.

4 Find the exact value of $\tan\theta$ given that:

a $\sin\theta = \frac{1}{3}$ and θ is obtuse   **b** $\cos\theta = \frac{1}{5}$ and $270° < \theta < 360°$

c $\sin\theta = -\frac{1}{\sqrt{3}}$ and $180° < \theta < 270°$ **d** $\cos\theta = -\frac{3}{4}$ and $90° < \theta < 180°$.

Example 5   ◀) **Self Tutor**

If $\tan\theta = -2$ and θ is reflex, find $\sin\theta$ and $\cos\theta$. Give exact answers.

$\tan\theta = \dfrac{\sin\theta}{\cos\theta} = -2$

$\therefore \sin\theta = -2\cos\theta$

Now $\sin^2\theta + \cos^2\theta = 1$

$\therefore (-2\cos\theta)^2 + \cos^2\theta = 1$

$\therefore 4\cos^2\theta + \cos^2\theta = 1$

$\therefore 5\cos^2\theta = 1$

$\therefore \cos\theta = \pm\frac{1}{\sqrt{5}}$

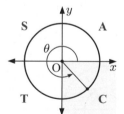

But θ is reflex and $\tan\theta < 0$, so θ lies in quadrant 4.

$\therefore \cos\theta$ is positive and $\sin\theta$ is negative.

$\therefore \cos\theta = \frac{1}{\sqrt{5}}$ and $\sin\theta = -\frac{2}{\sqrt{5}}$.

5 Find exact values for $\sin x$ and $\cos x$ given that:

   a $\tan x = \frac{2}{3}$ and x is acute

   b $\tan x = -\frac{4}{3}$ and $90° < x < 180°$

   c $\tan x = -\frac{\sqrt{5}}{3}$ and x is obtuse

   d $\tan x = -\frac{12}{5}$ and $270° < x < 360°$.

6 Suppose $\tan \theta = k$ where k is a constant and θ is obtuse. Write expressions for $\sin \theta$ and $\cos \theta$ in terms of k.

D   FINDING ANGLES

In **Exercise 11A** you should have discovered the following identities:

> For any angle θ:
> - $\sin(180° - \theta) = \sin \theta$
> - $\sin(360° - \theta) = -\sin \theta$
> - $\cos(180° - \theta) = -\cos \theta$
> - $\cos(360° - \theta) = \cos \theta$

We need results such as these, and also the periodicity of the trigonometric ratios, to find angles which have a particular sine, cosine, or tangent.

Example 6   **Self Tutor**

Find the two angles θ on the unit circle, with $0° \leqslant \theta \leqslant 360°$, such that:

  a $\cos \theta = \frac{1}{3}$ **b** $\sin \theta = \frac{3}{4}$ **c** $\tan \theta = 2$

a $\cos^{-1}\left(\frac{1}{3}\right) \approx 70.5°$

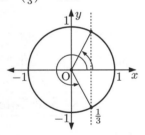

$\therefore \ \theta \approx 70.5°$ or $360° - 70.5°$
$\therefore \ \theta \approx 70.5°$ or $289.5°$

b $\sin^{-1}\left(\frac{3}{4}\right) \approx 48.6°$

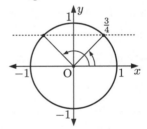

$\therefore \ \theta \approx 48.6°$ or $180° - 48.6°$
$\therefore \ \theta \approx 48.6°$ or $131.4°$

c $\tan^{-1}(2) \approx 63.4°$

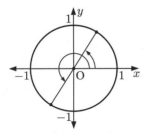

$\therefore \ \theta \approx 63.4°$ or $180° + 63.4°$
$\therefore \ \theta \approx 63.4°$ or $243.4°$

> If $\cos \theta$, $\sin \theta$, or $\tan \theta$ is positive, your calculator will give θ in the domain $0° < \theta < 90°$

EXERCISE 11D

1 Find two angles θ on the unit circle, with $0° \leqslant \theta \leqslant 360°$, such that:

a $\tan \theta = 4$ **b** $\cos \theta = 0.83$ **c** $\sin \theta = \frac{3}{5}$

d $\cos \theta = 0$ **e** $\tan \theta = 1.2$ **f** $\cos \theta = 0.7816$

g $\sin \theta = \frac{1}{11}$ **h** $\tan \theta = 20.2$ **i** $\sin \theta = \frac{39}{40}$

Example 7   ◀ᴗ Self Tutor

Find two angles θ on the unit circle, with $0° \leqslant \theta \leqslant 360°$, such that:

a $\sin \theta = -0.4$ **b** $\cos \theta = -\frac{2}{3}$ **c** $\tan \theta = -\frac{1}{3}$

a $\sin^{-1}(-0.4) \approx -23.6°$

But $0° \leqslant \theta \leqslant 360°$

$\therefore \quad \theta \approx 180° + 23.6°$ or

$\qquad 360° - 23.6°$

$\therefore \quad \theta \approx 203.6°$ or $336.4°$

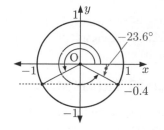

If $\sin \theta$ or $\tan \theta$ is negative, your calculator will give θ in the domain $-90° < \theta < 0°$.

b $\cos^{-1}(-\frac{2}{3}) \approx 131.8°$

But $0° \leqslant \theta \leqslant 360°$

$\therefore \quad \theta \approx 131.8°$ or

$\qquad 360° - 131.8°$

$\therefore \quad \theta \approx 131.8°$ or $228.2°$

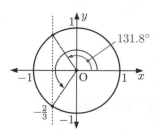

The green arrow shows the angle that your calculator gives.

c $\tan^{-1}(-\frac{1}{3}) \approx -18.4°$

But $0° \leqslant \theta \leqslant 360°$

$\therefore \quad \theta \approx 180° - 18.4°$ or

$\qquad 360° - 18.4°$

$\therefore \quad \theta \approx 161.6°$ or $341.6°$

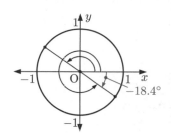

---

2 Find two angles θ on the unit circle, with $0° \leqslant \theta \leqslant 360°$, such that:

a $\cos \theta = -\frac{1}{4}$ **b** $\sin \theta = 0$ **c** $\tan \theta = -3.1$

d $\sin \theta = -0.421$ **e** $\tan \theta = -6.67$ **f** $\cos \theta = -\frac{2}{17}$

g $\tan \theta = -\sqrt{5}$ **h** $\cos \theta = -\frac{1}{\sqrt{3}}$ **i** $\sin \theta = -\frac{\sqrt{2}}{\sqrt{5}}$

E   THE AREA OF A TRIANGLE

We have seen in previous years that the area of any triangle can be calculated using:

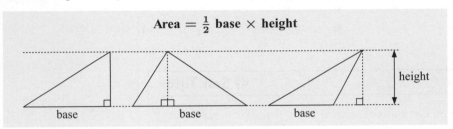

Area = $\frac{1}{2}$ base × height

However, if we do not know the perpendicular height of a triangle, we can use trigonometry to calculate the area.

To do this we need to know two sides of the triangle and the **included angle** between them. For example, in the triangle alongside the angle 49° is *included* between the sides of length 8 cm and 10 cm.

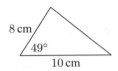

CONVENTION FOR LABELLING TRIANGLES

For triangle ABC, the angles at vertices A, B, and C are labelled A, B, and C respectively. The sides opposite these angles are labelled a, b, and c respectively.

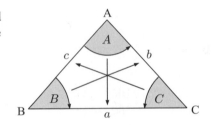

CALCULATING THE AREA OF A TRIANGLE

Any triangle that is not right angled must be either acute or obtuse. We will consider both cases:

Acute case:

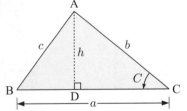

Obtuse case:

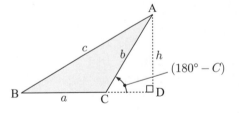

In both triangles the altitude h is constructed from A to D on [BC] (extended if necessary).

Acute case: $\sin C = \dfrac{h}{b}$

$\therefore$ $h = b \sin C$

Obtuse case: $\sin(180° - C) = \dfrac{h}{b}$

$\therefore$ $h = b \sin(180° - C)$

But $\sin(180° - C) = \sin C$

$\therefore$ $h = b \sin C$

So, since area $= \frac{1}{2}ah$, we now have   **Area $= \frac{1}{2}ab \sin C$.**

Using different altitudes we can show that the area is also $\frac{1}{2}bc \sin A$ or $\frac{1}{2}ac \sin B$.

Given the lengths of two sides of a triangle, and the size of the included angle between them, the area of the triangle is

> *half of the product of two sides and the sine of the included angle.*

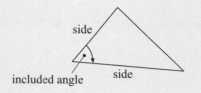

Example 8 ◀⟩ Self Tutor

Find the area of triangle ABC.

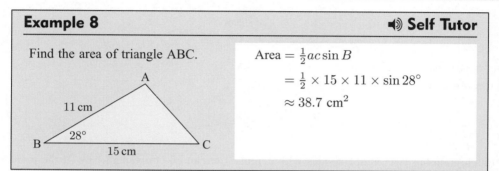

$$\text{Area} = \tfrac{1}{2}ac\sin B$$
$$= \tfrac{1}{2} \times 15 \times 11 \times \sin 28°$$
$$\approx 38.7 \text{ cm}^2$$

Example 9 ◀⟩ Self Tutor

A triangle has two sides with lengths 10 cm and 11 cm, and an area of 50 cm². Determine the possible measures of the included angle. Give your answers accurate to 1 decimal place.

If the included angle is θ, then $\quad \tfrac{1}{2} \times 10 \times 11 \times \sin\theta = 50$

$$\therefore \;\; \sin\theta = \tfrac{50}{55}$$

Now $\;\; \sin^{-1}\left(\tfrac{50}{55}\right) \approx 65.4°$

$$\therefore \;\; \theta \approx 65.4° \;\; \text{or} \;\; 180° - 65.4°$$
$$\therefore \;\; \theta \approx 65.4° \;\; \text{or} \;\; 114.6°$$

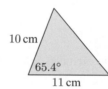
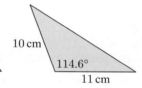

The two different possible angles are 65.4° and 114.6°.

EXERCISE 11E

1 Find the area of:

a

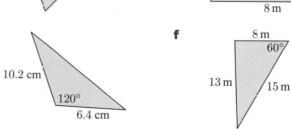

9 cm
40°
10 cm

b

31 km
82°
25 km

c

5 m
90°
8 m

d

9.7 cm
140°
6 cm

e

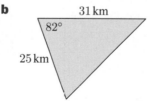

10.2 cm
120°
6.4 cm

f

8 m
60°
13 m
15 m

2 Which of these triangles is the:

    a largest   **b** smallest?

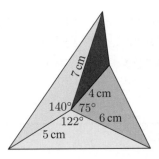

3 Triangle ABC has area 150 cm². Find the value of x.

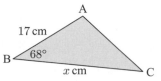

4 A parallelogram has two adjacent sides with lengths 4 cm and 6 cm respectively. If the included angle measures 52°, find the area of the parallelogram.

5 A rhombus has sides of length 12 cm and an angle of 72°. Find its area.

6 Find the area of a regular hexagon with sides of length 12 cm.

7 A rhombus has area 50 cm² and an internal angle of size 63°. Find the length of its sides.

8 A regular pentagonal garden plot has centre of symmetry O and an area of 338 m². Find the distance OA.

9 Find the possible values of the included angle of a triangle with:

    a sides of length 5 cm and 8 cm, and area 15 cm²

    b sides of length 45 km and 53 km, and area 800 km².

10 The Australian 50 cent coin has the shape of a regular dodecagon, which is a polygon with 12 sides.

  Eight of these 50 cent coins will fit exactly on an Australian $10 note as shown. What fraction of the $10 note is *not* covered?

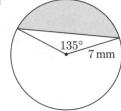

11 Find the shaded area in:

  a   **b**   **c**

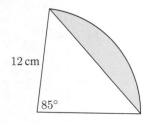

12 ADB is an arc of the circle with centre C and radius 7.3 cm. AEB is an arc of the circle with centre F and radius 8.7 cm.

Find the shaded area.

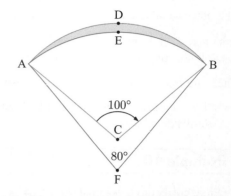

F | THE COSINE RULE

The **cosine rule** relates the three sides of a triangle and one of the angles.

In any $\triangle ABC$:

$$a^2 = b^2 + c^2 - 2bc \cos A$$
$$or \quad b^2 = a^2 + c^2 - 2ac \cos B$$
$$or \quad c^2 = a^2 + b^2 - 2ab \cos C$$

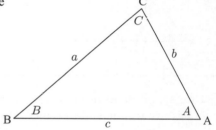

We will develop the first formula for both an acute and an obtuse triangle.

Proof:

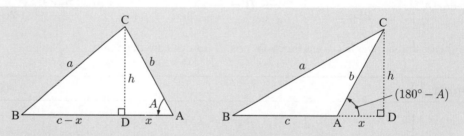

In both triangles draw the altitude from C to [AB] (extended if necessary), meeting it at D.

Let $AD = x$ and let $CD = h$.

Apply the theorem of Pythagoras in $\triangle BCD$:

$$a^2 = h^2 + (c - x)^2 \qquad\qquad a^2 = h^2 + (c + x)^2$$
$$\therefore \ a^2 = h^2 + c^2 - 2cx + x^2 \qquad \therefore \ a^2 = h^2 + c^2 + 2cx + x^2$$

In both cases, applying Pythagoras to $\triangle ADC$ gives $h^2 + x^2 = b^2$.

$\therefore \ h^2 = b^2 - x^2$, and we substitute this into the equations above.

$$\therefore \ a^2 = b^2 + c^2 - 2cx \qquad\qquad \therefore \ a^2 = b^2 + c^2 + 2cx$$

In $\triangle ADC$, $\cos A = \dfrac{x}{b}$ $\qquad\qquad \cos(180° - A) = \dfrac{x}{b}$

$$\therefore \ x = b \cos A \qquad\qquad\qquad \therefore \ -\cos A = \dfrac{x}{b}$$
$$\therefore \ a^2 = b^2 + c^2 - 2bc \cos A \qquad\qquad \therefore \ x = -b \cos A$$
$$\therefore \ a^2 = b^2 + c^2 - 2bc \cos A$$

The other variations of the cosine rule can be developed by rearranging the vertices of $\triangle ABC$.

Note that if $A = 90°$ then $\cos A = 0$, and $a^2 = b^2 + c^2 - 2bc \cos A$ reduces to $a^2 = b^2 + c^2$, which is the Pythagorean Rule.

There are two situations in which the cosine rule can be used.

- If we are given **two sides** and an **included angle**, the cosine rule can be used to find the length of the third side.

Example 10   ◀ၡ **Self Tutor**

Find, correct to 2 decimal places, the length of [BC].

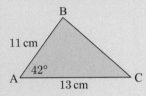

By the cosine rule:

$$BC^2 = 11^2 + 13^2 - 2 \times 11 \times 13 \times \cos 42°$$

$$\therefore \quad BC = \sqrt{(11^2 + 13^2 - 2 \times 11 \times 13 \times \cos 42°)}$$

$$\therefore \quad BC \approx 8.80$$

$\therefore$ [BC] is about 8.80 cm in length.

- If we are given **all three sides** of a triangle, the cosine rule can be used to find any of the angles. To do this, we rearrange the original cosine rule formulae:

$$\cos A = \frac{b^2 + c^2 - a^2}{2bc} \qquad \cos B = \frac{c^2 + a^2 - b^2}{2ca} \qquad \cos C = \frac{a^2 + b^2 - c^2}{2ab}$$

We then use the inverse cosine function $\cos^{-1}$ to evaluate the angle.

Example 11   ◀ၡ **Self Tutor**

In triangle ABC, $AB = 7$ cm, $BC = 5$ cm, and $CA = 8$ cm.

  a Find the measure of $B\widehat{C}A$.   **b** Find the exact area of triangle ABC.

a
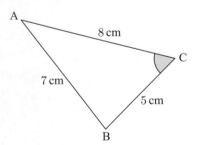

By the cosine rule:

$$\cos C = \frac{(5^2 + 8^2 - 7^2)}{(2 \times 5 \times 8)}$$

$$\therefore \quad C = \cos^{-1}\left(\frac{5^2 + 8^2 - 7^2}{2 \times 5 \times 8}\right)$$

$$\therefore \quad C = \cos^{-1}\left(\tfrac{1}{2}\right)$$

$$\therefore \quad C = 60°$$

So, $B\widehat{C}A$ measures 60°.

b   The area of $\triangle ABC = \tfrac{1}{2} \times 8 \times 5 \times \sin 60°$

$$\approx 17.3 \text{ cm}^2$$

EXERCISE 11F

1 Find the length of the remaining side in each triangle:

a

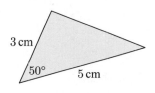

b

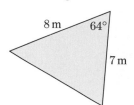

c

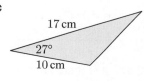

d

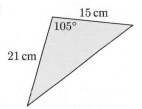

e

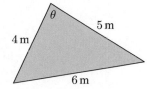

f

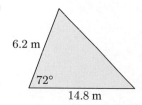

2 Find the measure of the angle marked θ:

a

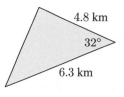

b

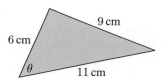

c

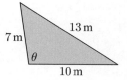

3 Find the measure of all angles of:

4 **a** Find the measure of obtuse $\widehat{PQR}$.

b Hence find the area of $\triangle PQR$.

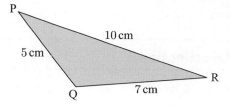

5 **a** Find the smallest angle of a triangle with sides 11 cm, 13 cm, and 17 cm.

b Find the largest angle of a triangle with sides 4 cm, 7 cm, and 9 cm.

The smallest angle is opposite the shortest side.

6 **a** Find $\cos \theta$ but not θ.

b Hence, find the value of x.

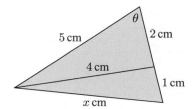

7 Solve the **Opening Problem** on page **250**.

8

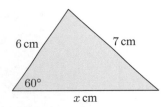

a Show that $x^2 - 6x - 13 = 0$.

b Hence, find the exact value of x.

9 Show that there are two possible values for x in this triangle:

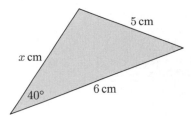

10

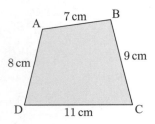

In quadrilateral ABCD, the diagonal [AC] has length 12 cm. Find the length of the other diagonal [BD].

G ┃ THE SINE RULE

The **sine rule** is a set of equations which connects the lengths of the sides of any triangle with the sines of the angles of the triangle. The triangle does not have to be right angled for the sine rule to be used.

Investigation 1   **The sine rule**

You will need: Paper, scissors, ruler, protractor

What to do:

1 Cut out a large triangle. Label the sides a, b, and c, and the opposite angles A, B, and C.

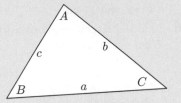

2 Use your ruler to measure the length of each side.

3 Use your protractor to measure the size of each angle.

4 Copy and complete this table:

a	b	c	A	B	C	$\dfrac{\sin A}{a}$	$\dfrac{\sin B}{b}$	$\dfrac{\sin C}{c}$

5 Comment on your results.

In any triangle ABC with sides a, b, and c units in length, and opposite angles A, B, and C respectively,

$$\frac{\sin A}{a} = \frac{\sin B}{b} = \frac{\sin C}{c} \quad or \quad \frac{a}{\sin A} = \frac{b}{\sin B} = \frac{c}{\sin C}.$$

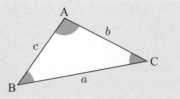

Proof: The area of any triangle ABC is given by $\frac{1}{2} bc \sin A = \frac{1}{2} ac \sin B = \frac{1}{2} ab \sin C$.

Dividing each expression by $\frac{1}{2} abc$ gives $\frac{\sin A}{a} = \frac{\sin B}{b} = \frac{\sin C}{c}$.

FINDING SIDE LENGTHS

If we are given two angles and one side of a triangle we can use the sine rule to find another side length.

Example 12 ◀)) **Self Tutor**

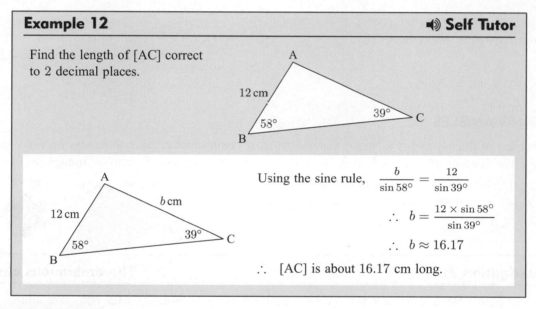

Find the length of [AC] correct to 2 decimal places.

Using the sine rule, $\dfrac{b}{\sin 58°} = \dfrac{12}{\sin 39°}$

$\therefore \ b = \dfrac{12 \times \sin 58°}{\sin 39°}$

$\therefore \ b \approx 16.17$

$\therefore$ [AC] is about 16.17 cm long.

EXERCISE 11G.1

1 Find the value of x:

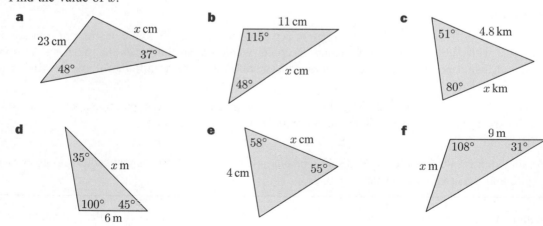

2 Find *all* unknown sides and angles of:

a
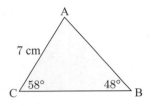

b
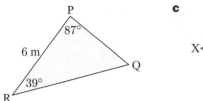

c
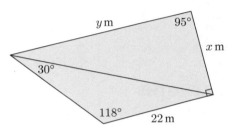

3 Find x and y in the given figure.

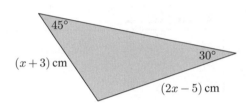

4 Find the exact value of x, giving your answer in the
form $a + b\sqrt{2}$ where $a, b \in \mathbb{Q}$.

FINDING ANGLES

The problem of finding angles using the sine rule is more complicated because there may be two possible answers. For example, if $\sin \theta = \frac{1}{2}$ then $\theta = 30°$ or $150°$. We call this situation an **ambiguous case**.

You can click on the icon to obtain an interactive demonstration of the ambiguous case, or else you can work through the following **Investigation**.

DEMO

Investigation 2   **The ambiguous case**

You will need a blank sheet of paper, a ruler, a protractor, and a compass for the tasks that follow. In each task you will be required to construct triangles from given information. You could also do this using a computer package such as "The Geometer's Sketchpad".

What to do:

1 Draw AB = 10 cm. Construct an angle of $30°$ at point A. Using B as the centre, draw an arc of a circle with radius 6 cm. Let C denote the point where the arc intersects the ray from A. How many different possible points C are there, and therefore how many different triangles ABC may be constructed?

2 Repeat the procedure from **1** three times, starting with AB = 10 cm and constructing an angle of $30°$ at point A. When you draw the arc with centre B, use the radius:

   a 5 cm   **b** 3 cm   **c** 12 cm

3 Using your results from **1** and **2**, discuss the possible number of triangles you can obtain given two sides and a non-included angle.

You should have discovered that when you are given two sides and a non-included angle, you could get two triangles, one triangle, or it may be impossible to draw any triangles at all.

Now consider the calculations involved in each of the cases in the **Investigation**.

Case 1:   Given: $c = 10$ cm, $a = 6$ cm, $A = 30°$

$$\frac{\sin C}{c} = \frac{\sin A}{a}$$

$$\therefore \quad \sin C = \frac{c \sin A}{a}$$

$$\therefore \quad \sin C = \frac{10 \times \sin 30°}{6} \approx 0.8333$$

$$\therefore \quad C \approx 56.44° \;\; or \;\; 180° - 56.44° = 123.56°$$

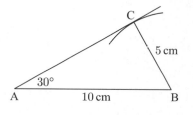

Case 2:   Given: $c = 10$ cm, $a = 5$ cm, $A = 30°$

$$\frac{\sin C}{c} = \frac{\sin A}{a}$$

$$\therefore \quad \sin C = \frac{c \sin A}{a}$$

$$\therefore \quad \sin C = \frac{10 \times \sin 30°}{5} = 1$$

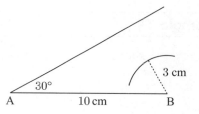

There is only one possible solution for C in the range from $0°$ to $180°$, and that is $C = 90°$. Only one triangle is therefore possible. Complete the solution of the triangle yourself.

Case 3:   Given: $c = 10$ cm, $a = 3$ cm, $A = 30°$

$$\frac{\sin C}{c} = \frac{\sin A}{a}$$

$$\therefore \quad \sin C = \frac{c \sin A}{a}$$

$$\therefore \quad \sin C = \frac{10 \times \sin 30°}{3} \approx 1.6667$$

There is no angle that has a sine value > 1, so no triangles can be drawn to match the information given.

Case 4:   Given: $c = 10$ cm, $a = 12$ cm, $A = 30°$

$$\frac{\sin C}{c} = \frac{\sin A}{a}$$

$$\therefore \quad \sin C = \frac{c \sin A}{a}$$

$$\therefore \quad \sin C = \frac{10 \times \sin 30°}{12} \approx 0.4167$$

$$\therefore \quad C \approx 24.62° \;\; or$$
$$180° - 24.62° = 155.38°$$

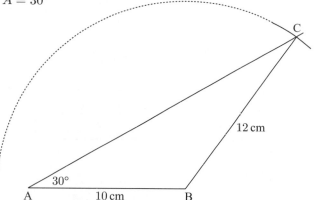

However, in this case only one of these two angles is valid. Since $A = 30°$, C cannot possibly equal $155.38°$ because $30° + 155.38° > 180°$.

Therefore, there is only one possible solution, $C \approx 24.62°$.

Conclusion: Each situation using the sine rule with two sides and a non-included angle must be examined very carefully.

Example 13

◀» **Self Tutor**

Find the measure of angle C in triangle ABC if $AC = 7$ cm, $AB = 11$ cm, and angle B measures $25°$.

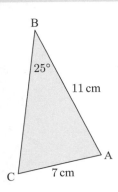

$$\frac{\sin C}{c} = \frac{\sin B}{b} \quad \text{\{sine rule\}}$$

$$\therefore \quad \frac{\sin C}{11} = \frac{\sin 25°}{7}$$

$$\therefore \quad \sin C = \frac{11 \times \sin 25°}{7}$$

$$\therefore \quad C = \sin^{-1}\left(\frac{11 \times \sin 25°}{7}\right) \quad \text{or its supplement} \\ \text{\{as } C \text{ may be obtuse\}}$$

$$\therefore \quad C \approx 41.6° \quad \text{or} \quad 180° - 41.6°$$

$$\therefore \quad C \approx 41.6° \quad \text{or} \quad 138.4°$$

$\therefore$ C measures $41.6°$ if angle C is acute, or $138.4°$ if angle C is obtuse.

In this case there is insufficient information to determine the actual shape of the triangle. There are two possible triangles.

Example 14

◀» **Self Tutor**

Find the measure of angle L in triangle KLM given that angle K measures $56°$, $LM = 16.8$ m, and $KM = 13.5$ m.

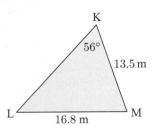

$$\frac{\sin L}{13.5} = \frac{\sin 56°}{16.8} \quad \text{\{by the sine rule\}}$$

$$\therefore \quad \sin L = \frac{13.5 \times \sin 56°}{16.8}$$

$$\therefore \quad L = \sin^{-1}\left(\frac{13.5 \times \sin 56°}{16.8}\right) \quad \text{or its supplement}$$

$$\therefore \quad L \approx 41.8° \quad \text{or} \quad 180° - 41.8°$$

$$\therefore \quad L \approx 41.8° \quad \text{or} \quad 138.2°$$

We reject $L \approx 138.2°$, since $138.2° + 56° > 180°$ which is impossible in a triangle.

$\therefore$ $L \approx 41.8°$, a unique solution in this case.

EXERCISE 11G.2

1 Triangle ABC has angle $B = 40°$, and sides $b = 8$ cm and $c = 11$ cm. Find the two possible measures of angle C.

2 Consider triangle ABC.

   a Given $a = 14.6$ cm, $b = 17.4$ cm, and $A\widehat{B}C = 65°$, find the measure of $B\widehat{A}C$.

   b Given $b = 43.8$ cm, $c = 31.4$ cm, and $A\widehat{C}B = 43°$, find the measure of $A\widehat{B}C$.

   c Given $a = 6.5$ km, $c = 4.8$ km, and $B\widehat{A}C = 71°$, find the measure of $A\widehat{C}B$.

3 Is it possible to have a triangle with the measurements shown? Explain your answer.

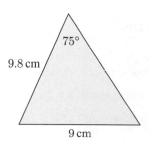

4 In triangle ABC, $A\widehat{B}C = 30°$, AC = 9 cm, and AB = 7 cm.

    a Find the measure of:

        i $A\widehat{C}B$ **ii** $B\widehat{A}C$

    b Hence, find the area of the triangle.

5 In triangle PQR, $P\widehat{R}Q = 50°$, PR = 11 m, and PQ = 9 m.

    a Show that there are two possible measures of $P\widehat{Q}R$.

    b Sketch triangle PQR for each case.

    c For each case, find:

        i the measure of $Q\widehat{P}R$

       ii the area of the triangle

      iii the perimeter of the triangle.

H   PROBLEM SOLVING

If we are given a problem involving a triangle, we must first decide which rule is best to use.

If the triangle is right angled then the trigonometric ratios or Pythagoras' theorem can be used. For some problems we can add an extra line or two to the diagram to create a right angled triangle.

However, if we do not have a right angled triangle then we usually have to choose between the sine and cosine rules. In these cases the following checklist may be helpful:

> Use the **cosine rule** when given:
>
> - three sides
> - two sides and an included angle.
>
> Use the **sine rule** when given:
>
> - one side and two angles
> - two sides and a non-included angle, but beware of an *ambiguous case* which can occur when the smaller of the two given sides is opposite the given angle.

Example 15
🔊 **Self Tutor**

The angles of elevation to the top of a mountain are measured from two beacons A and B at sea.

The measurements are shown on the diagram.

If the beacons are 1473 m apart, how high is the mountain?

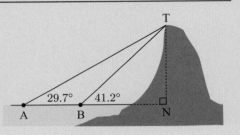

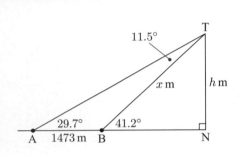

Let BT be x m and NT be h m.

$A\widehat{T}B = 41.2° − 29.7°$ {exterior angle of $\triangle$BNT}

$= 11.5°$

We find x in $\triangle$ABT using the sine rule:

$$\frac{x}{\sin 29.7°} = \frac{1473}{\sin 11.5°}$$

$$\therefore \quad x = \frac{1473}{\sin 11.5°} \times \sin 29.7°$$

$$\approx 3660.62$$

Now, in $\triangle$BNT, $\sin 41.2° = \dfrac{h}{x} \approx \dfrac{h}{3660.62}$

$$\therefore \quad h \approx \sin 41.2° \times 3660.62$$

$$\approx 2410$$

The mountain is about 2410 m high.

EXERCISE 11H

1 Rodrigo wishes to determine the height of a flagpole. He takes a sighting to the top of the flagpole from point P. He then moves 20 metres further away from the flagpole to point Q, and takes a second sighting. The information is shown in the diagram alongside. How high is the flagpole?

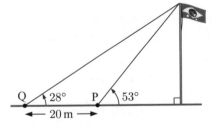

2

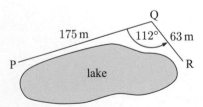

To get from P to R, a park ranger has to walk along a path to Q and then to R.

What is the distance in a straight line from P to R?

3 A golfer played his tee shot a distance of 220 m to point A. He then played a 165 m six iron to the green. If the distance from tee to green is 340 m, determine the angle the golfer was off line with his tee shot.

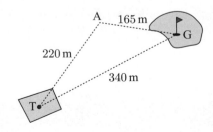

4 A football goal is 5 metres wide. When a player is 26 metres from one goal post and 23 metres from the other, he shoots for goal. What is the angle of view of the goals that the player sees?

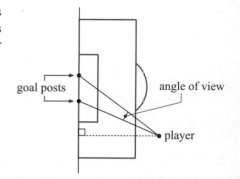

goal posts

angle of view

player

5 A tower 42 metres high stands on top of a hill. From a point some distance from the base of the hill, the angle of elevation to the top of the tower is $13.2°$, and the angle of elevation to the bottom of the tower is $8.3°$. Find the height of the hill.

6 From the foot of a building I have to look $22°$ upwards to sight the top of a tree. From the top of the building, 150 metres above ground level, I have to look down at an angle of $50°$ below the horizontal to sight the tree top.

  a How high is the tree?

  b How far from the building is this tree?

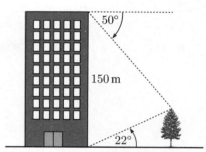

$50°$

150 m

$22°$

Example 16

◀) **Self Tutor**

Find the measure of $R\widehat{P}V$.

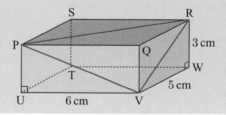

S   R

P   3 cm

Q   W

T   5 cm

U   6 cm   V

In $\triangle RVW$, $RV = \sqrt{5^2 + 3^2} = \sqrt{34}$ cm.   {Pythagoras}

In $\triangle PUV$, $PV = \sqrt{6^2 + 3^2} = \sqrt{45}$ cm.   {Pythagoras}

In $\triangle PQR$, $PR = \sqrt{6^2 + 5^2} = \sqrt{61}$ cm.   {Pythagoras}

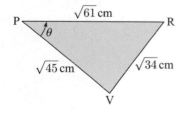

$\sqrt{61}$ cm

P θ R

$\sqrt{45}$ cm $\sqrt{34}$ cm

V

By rearrangement of the cosine rule,

$$\cos\theta = \frac{(\sqrt{61})^2 + (\sqrt{45})^2 - (\sqrt{34})^2}{2\sqrt{61}\sqrt{45}}$$

$$= \frac{61 + 45 - 34}{2\sqrt{61}\sqrt{45}}$$

$$= \frac{72}{2\sqrt{61}\sqrt{45}}$$

$$\therefore \ \theta = \cos^{-1}\left(\frac{36}{\sqrt{61}\sqrt{45}}\right) \approx 46.6°$$

$\therefore$ $R\widehat{P}V$ measures about $46.6°$.

7 Find the measure of $P\widehat{Q}R$:

a

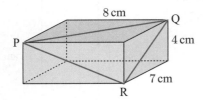

b

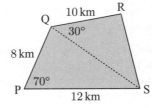

8 Two observation posts A and B are 12 km apart. A third observation post C is located 15 km from A such that $C\widehat{B}A$ is 67°. Find the measure of $C\widehat{A}B$.

9 Stan and Olga are considering buying a sheep farm. A surveyor has supplied them with the given accurate sketch. Find the area of the property, giving your answer in:

  a km^2 **b** hectares.

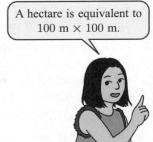

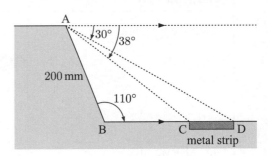

10 Thabo and Palesa start at point A. They each walk in a straight line at an angle of 120° to one another. Thabo walks at 6 km h^{-1} and Palesa walks at 8 km h^{-1}. How far apart are they after 45 minutes?

11 The cross-section design of the kerbing for a driverless-bus roadway is shown opposite. The metal strip is inlaid into the concrete and is used to control the direction and speed of the bus. Find the width of the metal strip.

12 An orienteer runs for $4\frac{1}{2}$ km, then turns through an angle of 32° and runs for another 6 km. How far is she from her starting point?

13 A helicopter A observes two ships B and C. B is 23.8 km from the helicopter and C is 31.9 km from it. The angle of view $B\widehat{A}C$ from the helicopter to B and C, is 83.6°. How far are the ships apart?

14 A surveyor has produced this diagram of a recreation park.
Find the area of the park.

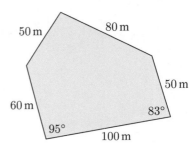

Activity 1   True bearings

We can describe a direction by comparing it with the **true north direction**. We call this a **true bearing**.

The bearing of B from A is the clockwise measure of the angle between the 'north' line through A, and [AB].

In the diagram alongside, the bearing of B from A is $63°$ from true north. We write this as $63°$T or $063°$.

Similarly, the bearing of A from B is $243°$.

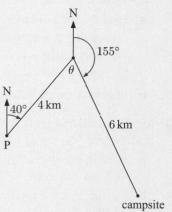

1 Hikers Ritva and Esko leave point P at the same time. Ritva walks 4 km on the bearing $040°$, then a further 6 km on the bearing $155°$.

Esko hikes directly from P to the campsite.

  a Find the value of θ.

  b How far does Esko hike?

  c In which direction does Esko hike?

  d Ritva hikes at 10 km h^{-1} and Esko hikes at 6 km h^{-1}.

    i Who will arrive at the campsite first?

    ii How long will this person need to wait before the other person arrives?

  e On what bearing should the hikers walk from the campsite to return to P?

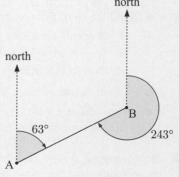

2 A boat sails 10 km on the bearing $053°$, then 15 km on the bearing $127°$, then 20 km on the bearing $250°$. The captain of the boat wants to return to his starting point, but he is completely lost. Can you advise the captain regarding the direction in which he should travel?

Activity 2   Sharing taxis

Suppose you and your friend are both in town, and need to catch a taxi home. Is it cheaper to take a separate taxi each, or to share a taxi?

The answer to this depends on the distance and direction that each of you lives from town.

For the purposes of this Activity, we will assume there is no "flagfall" taxi fee, and that the cost of the fare is directly proportional to the distance travelled. We can therefore minimise the total cost of the fare by minimising the total distance travelled.

What to do:

1 Suppose A and B live 5 km and 7 km from town respectively. They live in roughly the same direction from town. The angle between them is 40°.

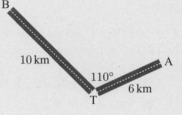

   a Find the total distance travelled if:

     i A and B each take a separate taxi home

     ii they share a taxi which travels to A's house and then to B's house.

   b Should A and B share a taxi in this case?

   c When sharing a taxi, is it always cheaper to stop first at the house which is *closest* to town? Explain your answer.

2 Now suppose A and B live 6 km and 10 km from town respectively, and the angle between them is 110°.

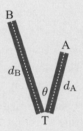

   a Find the total distance travelled if:

     i A and B each take a separate taxi home

     ii they share a taxi which travels to A's house and then to B's house.

   b Should A and B share a taxi in this case?

3 More generally, suppose A and B live d_A km and d_B km from town, where $d_A < d_B$, and the angle between them is θ.

   a Explain why A and B should share a taxi if B is closer to A than to town.

   b Devise a test involving d_A, d_B, and θ to determine whether A and B should share a taxi.

   c Use your test to determine whether A and B should share a taxi in the following situations:

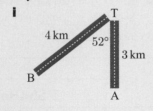 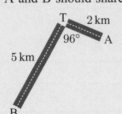 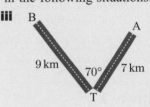

   d For what values of θ should A and B:

     i always share a taxi, regardless of the distances involved

     ii never share a taxi, regardless of the distances involved?

4 **a** What assumptions have been made in this Activity?

   b How would the introduction of a "flagfall" fee affect your calculations?

   c Suppose A and B were not as concerned with the cost, but wanted to get home as *quickly* as possible. How would this affect their strategy?

Review set 11A

1 Find the acute angles that would have the same:

   a sine as 120°   **b** sine as 165°   **c** cosine as 276°.

2 Use the unit circle to find θ such that $\cos\theta = -\sin\theta$, $0° \leqslant \theta \leqslant 360°$.

3 Find $\sin\theta$, $\cos\theta$, and $\tan\theta$ for θ equal to:

   a 360°   **b** 120°   **c** −180°   **d** 390°

4 If $\cos\theta = \frac{3}{4}$ find the possible values of $\sin\vartheta$.

5 Given $\tan x = -\frac{3}{2}$ and x is reflex, find $\cos x$ and $\sin x$.

6 Find two angles on the unit circle, with $0° \leqslant \theta \leqslant 360°$, such that:

   a $\cos\theta = -\frac{1}{6}$ **b** $\sin\theta = \frac{1}{3}$ **c** $\tan\theta = -3.2$

7 Find the area of:

   a 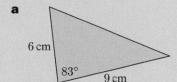   **b** 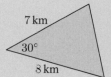   **c**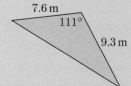

8 A rhombus has sides of length 5 cm and an angle of 65°. Find its area.

9 Find the length of the remaining side in each triangle:

   a 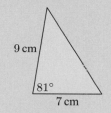   **b**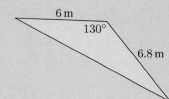

10 Find the unknown in:

   a 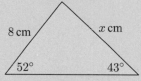   **b** 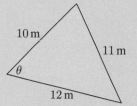   **c**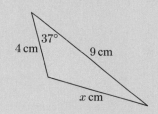

11 Find the area of quadrilateral ABCD:

12 Find the area of this triangle.

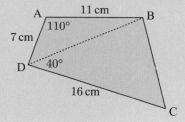

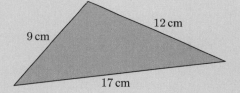

13 From point A, the angle of elevation to the top of a tall building is $20°$. On walking 80 m towards the building, the angle of elevation is now $23°$. How tall is the building?

14 Find the measure of $\widehat{EDG}$:

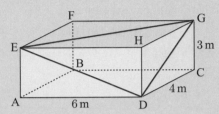

15 Find x and y in this figure.

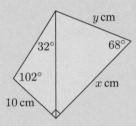

16 In triangle ABC, $\widehat{ACB} = 42°$, AB = 5 cm, and AC = 7 cm.

    a Find the two possible measures of $\widehat{ABC}$.

    b Find the area of triangle ABC in each case.

Review set 11B

1 Find:

    a $\sin 159°$ if $\sin 21° \approx 0.358$
        b $\cos 92°$ if $\cos 88° \approx 0.035$

    c $\cos 75°$ if $\cos 105° \approx -0.259$
        d $\sin(-133°)$ if $\sin 47° \approx 0.731$

2 Illustrate the regions where $\sin \theta$ and $\cos \theta$ have the same sign.

3 Suppose $m = \sin p$, where p is acute. Write an expression in terms of m for:

    a $\sin(180° - p)$
    b $\sin(p + 360°)$
    c $\cos p$
    d $\tan p$

4 Suppose $\cos \theta = \frac{\sqrt{11}}{\sqrt{17}}$ and θ is acute. Find the exact value of $\tan \theta$.

5 If $\sin \theta = -\frac{2}{5}$, $270° < \theta < 360°$ find $\cos \theta$ and $\tan \theta$.

6 Find the angle between $0°$ and $360°$ which has:

    a a cosine of $-\frac{1}{2}$ and a sine of $\frac{\sqrt{3}}{2}$
        b a sine of $-\frac{1}{2}$ and a tangent of $\frac{1}{\sqrt{3}}$.

7 Find two angles θ with $0° \leqslant \theta \leqslant 360°$, such that:

    a $\cos \theta = \frac{2}{3}$
        b $\sin \theta = -\frac{1}{4}$
        c $\tan \theta = 3$

8 Find the value of x:

    a

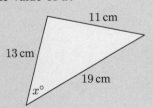

    b

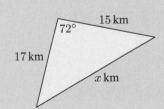

9 A triangle has two sides with lengths 11.3 cm and 19.2 cm, and an area of 80 cm². Find the possible measures of the included angle.

10 Find the measure of the angle marked θ:

a

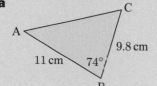

b

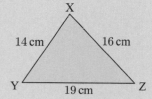

11 Find any unknown sides and angles in:

a

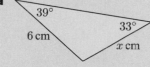

b

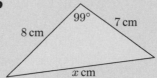

c

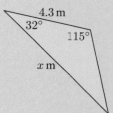

12 Find x in each triangle:

a

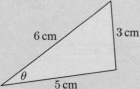

b

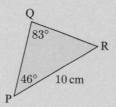

c

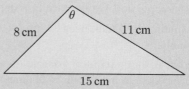

13 In quadrilateral ABCD, $\widehat{ABC} = 105°$. Find the measure of the other three angles.

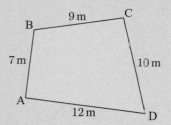

14 Find the measure of angle Q in triangle PQR given that $Q\widehat{P}R = 47°$, QR = 11 m, and PR = 9.6 m.

15 Anke and Lucas are considering buying a block of land. The land agent supplies them with the given accurate sketch. Find the area of the property, giving your answer in:

a m²   **b** hectares.

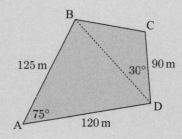

16 Soil contractor Frank was given the following dimensions over the telephone:

The triangular garden plot ABC has $\hat{CAB}$ measuring 44°, [AC] is 8 m long, and [BC] is 6 m long. Frank needs to supply soil for the plot to a depth of 10 cm.

a Explain why Frank needs extra information from his client.

b What is the maximum volume of soil that could be needed if his client is unable to supply the necessary information?

12

Trigonometric functions

Contents:

Opening problem

A steamroller has a spot of paint on its roller. As the steamroller moves, the spot rotates around the axle.

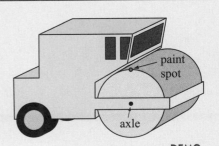

Things to think about:

a How does the *height* of the spot above ground level change over time?
What would the graph of the spot's height over time look like?

b Suppose the roller has a radius of 1 metre.
How would this be shown in the graph?

c Suppose the roller completes one full revolution every 2 seconds.
How would this be shown in the graph?

d Can we use a function involving a trigonometric ratio to determine the height of the spot over time?

A   PERIODIC BEHAVIOUR

Periodic phenomena occur all the time in the physical world. For example, in:

- seasonal variations in our climate
- variations in average maximum and minimum monthly temperatures
- the number of daylight hours at a particular location
- tidal variations in the depth of water in a harbour
- the phases of the moon
- animal populations.

These phenomena illustrate variable behaviour which is repeated over time. The repetition may be called **periodic**, **oscillatory**, or **cyclic** in different situations.

In this Chapter we will see how trigonometric functions can be used to model periodic phenomena.

OBSERVING PERIODIC BEHAVIOUR

The table below shows the mean monthly maximum temperature for Cape Town, South Africa.

Month	Jan	Feb	Mar	Apr	May	Jun	Jul	Aug	Sep	Oct	Nov	Dec
Temperature T (°C)	28	27	$25\frac{1}{2}$	22	$18\frac{1}{2}$	16	15	16	18	$21\frac{1}{2}$	24	26

On the scatter diagram alongside we plot the temperature T on the vertical axis. We assign January as $t = 1$ month, February as $t = 2$ months, and so on for the 12 months of the year.

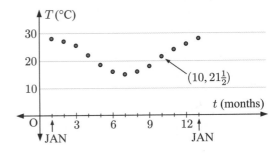

$(10, 21\frac{1}{2})$

The temperature shows a variation from an average of 28°C in January through a range of values across the months. The cycle will approximately repeat itself for each subsequent 12 month period. By the end of the Chapter we will be able to establish a **periodic function** which approximately fits this set of points.

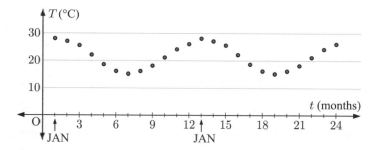

Historical note

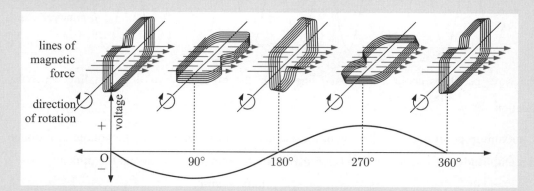

In 1831, **Michael Faraday** discovered that an electric current was generated by rotating a coil of wire through 360° in a magnetic field. The electric current produced showed a voltage which varied between positive and negative values in a periodic function called a **sine wave**.

TERMINOLOGY USED TO DESCRIBE PERIODICITY

A **periodic function** is one which repeats itself over and over in a horizontal direction, in intervals of the same length.

The **period** of a periodic function is the length of one repetition or cycle.

$f(x)$ is a periodic function with period p if $f(x + p) = f(x)$ for all x, and p is the smallest positive value for this to be true.

A **cycloid** is an example of a periodic function. It is the curve traced out by a point on a circle as the circle rolls across a flat surface in a straight line.

DEMO

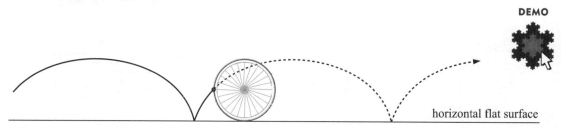

horizontal flat surface

Activity   Periodic functions

Use a **graphing package** to examine the function $f(x) = x - \lfloor x \rfloor$
where $\lfloor x \rfloor$ is "the largest integer less than or equal to x".

In the graphing package, you type $\lfloor x \rfloor$ as `floor(x)`.

Is $f(x)$ periodic?   What is its period?

GRAPHING
PACKAGE

WAVES

In this course we are mainly concerned with periodic phenomena which show a wave pattern:

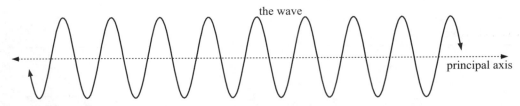

the wave

principal axis

The wave oscillates about a horizontal line called the **principal axis** or **mean line** which has
equation $y = \dfrac{\text{max} + \text{min}}{2}$.

A **maximum point** occurs at the top of a crest, and a **minimum point** at the bottom of a trough.

The **amplitude** is the distance between a maximum (or minimum) point and the principal axis.

$$\text{amplitude} = \frac{\text{max} - \text{min}}{2}$$

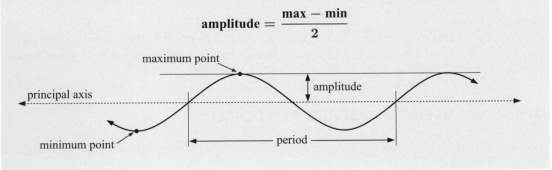

maximum point

principal axis

amplitude

minimum point

period

EXERCISE 12A

1 Which of these graphs show periodic behaviour?

a

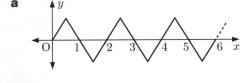

b

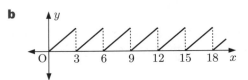

c

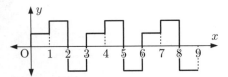

d

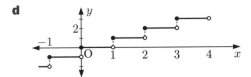

e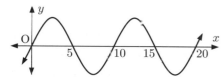

f

g

h

2 Paul spun the wheel of his bicycle. The following tabled values show the height above the ground of a point on the wheel at various times.

Time (seconds)	0	0.2	0.4	0.6	0.8	1	1.2	1.4	1.6	1.8	2
Height above ground (cm)	0	6	23	42	57	64	59	43	23	7	1

Time (seconds)	2.2	2.4	2.6	2.8	3	3.2	3.4	3.6	3.8	4
Height above ground (cm)	5	27	40	55	63	60	44	24	9	3

a Plot the graph of height against time.

b Is it reasonable to fit a curve to this data, or should we leave it as discrete points?

c Is the data periodic? If so, estimate:

   i the equation of the principal axis   **ii** the maximum value

   iii the period   **iv** the amplitude.

3 Draw a scatter diagram for each set of data below. Is there any evidence to suggest the data is periodic?

a

x	0	1	2	3	4	5	6	7	8	9	10	11	12
y	0	1	1.4	1	0	−1	−1.4	−1	0	1	1.4	1	0

b

x	0	2	3	4	5	6	7	8	9	10	12
y	0	4.7	3.4	1.7	2.1	5.2	8.9	10.9	10.2	8.4	10.4

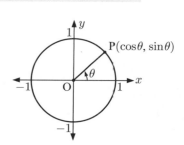

GRAPHICS CALCULATOR INSTRUCTIONS

B | THE SINE AND COSINE FUNCTIONS

A **trigonometric function** is a function which involves one of the trigonometric ratios.

Consider the point $P(\cos\theta, \sin\theta)$ on the unit circle.

As θ increases, the point P moves around the unit circle, and the values of $\cos\theta$ and $\sin\theta$ change.

We can draw the graphs of $y = \sin\theta$ and $y = \cos\theta$ by plotting the values of $\sin\theta$ and $\cos\theta$ against θ.

THE GRAPH OF $y = \sin \theta$

The diagram alongside gives the y-coordinates for all points on the unit circle at intervals of $30°$.

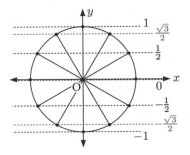

A table for $\sin \theta$ can be constructed from these values:

θ	$0°$	$30°$	$60°$	$90°$	$120°$	$150°$	$180°$	$210°$	$240°$	$270°$	$300°$	$330°$	$360°$
$\sin \theta$	0	$\frac{1}{2}$	$\frac{\sqrt{3}}{2}$	1	$\frac{\sqrt{3}}{2}$	$\frac{1}{2}$	0	$-\frac{1}{2}$	$-\frac{\sqrt{3}}{2}$	-1	$-\frac{\sqrt{3}}{2}$	$-\frac{1}{2}$	0

Plotting $\sin \theta$ against θ gives:

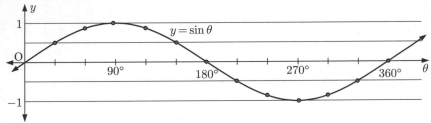

The graph of $y = \sin \theta$ shows the y-coordinate of P as P moves around the unit circle.

Once we reach $360°$, P has completed a full revolution of the unit circle, and so this pattern repeats itself.

DEMO

THE GRAPH OF $y = \cos \theta$

By considering the x-coordinates of the points on the unit circle at intervals of $30°$, we can create a table of values for $\cos \theta$:

θ	$0°$	$30°$	$60°$	$90°$	$120°$	$150°$	$180°$	$210°$	$240°$	$270°$	$300°$	$330°$	$360°$
$\cos \theta$	1	$\frac{\sqrt{3}}{2}$	$\frac{1}{2}$	0	$-\frac{1}{2}$	$-\frac{\sqrt{3}}{2}$	-1	$-\frac{\sqrt{3}}{2}$	$-\frac{1}{2}$	0	$\frac{1}{2}$	$\frac{\sqrt{3}}{2}$	1

Plotting $\cos \theta$ against θ gives:

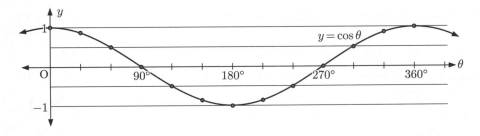

EXERCISE 12B.1

1 Below is an accurate graph of $y = \sin\theta$.

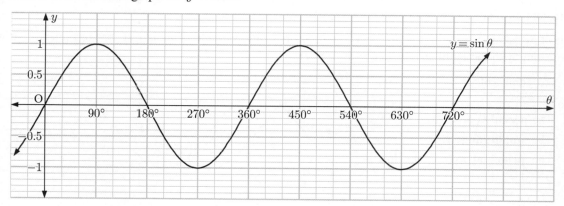

a Find the y-intercept of the graph.

b Find the values of θ on $0° \leqslant \theta \leqslant 720°$ for which:

   i $\sin\theta = 0$ **ii** $\sin\theta = -1$ **iii** $\sin\theta = \frac{1}{2}$ **iv** $\sin\theta = \frac{\sqrt{3}}{2}$

c Use the graph to estimate the values of θ on $0° \leqslant \theta \leqslant 720°$ for which $\sin\theta = 0.3$.

d Find the intervals on $0° \leqslant \theta \leqslant 720°$ where $\sin\theta$ is:

   i positive   **ii** negative.

e Find the range of the function.

2 Below is an accurate graph of $y = \cos\theta$.

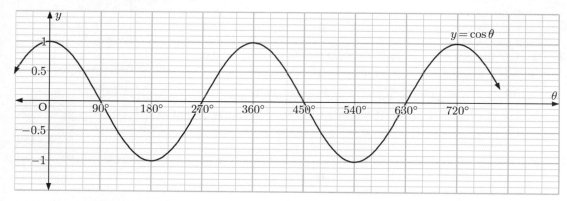

a Find the y-intercept of the graph.

b Find the values of θ on $0° \leqslant \theta \leqslant 720°$ for which:

   i $\cos\theta = 0$ **ii** $\cos\theta = 1$ **iii** $\cos\theta = -\frac{1}{2}$ **iv** $\cos\theta = -\frac{1}{\sqrt{2}}$

c Use the graph to estimate the values of θ on $0° \leqslant \theta \leqslant 720°$ for which $\cos\theta = 0.3$.

d Find the intervals on $0° \leqslant \theta \leqslant 720°$ where $\cos\theta$ is:

   i positive   **ii** negative.

e Find the range of the function.

USING TRANSFORMATIONS TO GRAPH TRIGONOMETRIC FUNCTIONS

Now we are familiar with the graphs of $y = \sin\theta$ and $y = \cos\theta$, we can use transformations to graph more complicated trigonometric functions.

Instead of using θ, we will now use x to represent the angle variable. This is just for convenience, so we are dealing with the familiar function form $y = f(x)$.

For the graphs of $y = \sin x$ and $y = \cos x$:

- The **period** is 360°.
- The **amplitude** is 1.
- The **principal axis** is the line $y = 0$.

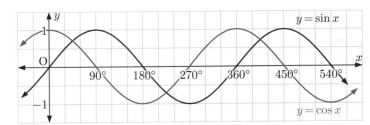

In the following **Investigation**, we will use technology to draw graphs related to $y = \sin x$.

Investigation   **Families of trigonometric functions**

What to do:

1 a Use the graphing package to graph on the same set of axes:

    i $y = \sin x$ **ii** $y = 2\sin x$ **iii** $y = \frac{1}{2}\sin x$

    iv $y = -\sin x$ **v** $y = -\frac{1}{3}\sin x$ **vi** $y = -\frac{3}{2}\sin x$

  b For graphs of the form $y = a\sin x$, comment on the significance of:

    i the sign of a **ii** the size of a, or $|a|$.

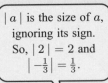

$|a|$ is the size of a, ignoring its sign. So, $|2| = 2$ and $\left|-\frac{1}{3}\right| = \frac{1}{3}$.

2 a Use the graphing package to graph on the same set of axes:

    i $y = \sin x$ **ii** $y = \sin 2x$

    iii $y = \sin\left(\frac{1}{2}x\right)$ **iv** $y = \sin 3x$

  b For graphs of the form $y = \sin bx$, $b > 0$, what is the period of the graph?

3 a Graph on the same set of axes:

    i $y = \sin x$ **ii** $y = \sin(x - 60°)$

    iii $y = \sin(x + 30°)$

  b What translation moves $y = \sin x$ to $y = \sin(x - c)$?

4 a Graph on the same set of axes:

    i $y = \sin x$ **ii** $y = \sin x + 2$ **iii** $y = \sin x - 2$

  b What translation moves $y = \sin x$ to $y = \sin x + d$?

  c What is the principal axis of $y = \sin x + d$?

5 What sequence of transformations maps $y = \sin x$ onto $y = a\sin b(x - c) + d$?

From the **Investigation** you should have observed the following properties about the **general sine function** $y = a \sin b(x - c) + d$:

- $$y = a \sin b(x - c) + d$$

affects	affects	affects	affects
amplitude	**period**	**horizontal translation**	**vertical translation**

- the amplitude is $|a|$
- the period is $\dfrac{360°}{b}$ for $b > 0$
- the principal axis is $y = d$
- $y = a \sin b(x - c) + d$ is obtained from $y = \sin x$ by a vertical dilation with scale factor a and a horizontal dilation with scale factor $\dfrac{1}{b}$, followed by a horizontal translation of c units and a vertical translation of d units.

Click on the icon to obtain a demonstration for the general sine function.

DEMO

The properties of the **general cosine function** $y = a \cos b(x - c) + d$ are the same as those of the general sine function.

Example 1

◀) **Self Tutor**

Sketch the graph of the following for $0° \leqslant x \leqslant 720°$:

a $y = \sin x + 1$ b $y = 3 \cos x$ c $y = \sin 2x$ d $y = \cos(x - 90°)$

a We translate $y = \sin x$ 1 unit upwards.

b We dilate $y = \cos x$ vertically with scale factor 3.
∴ $y = 3 \cos x$ has amplitude 3.

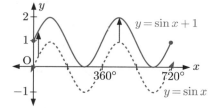

c We dilate $y = \sin x$ horizontally with scale factor $\frac{1}{2}$.
∴ $y = \sin 2x$ has period $\dfrac{360°}{2} = 180°$.

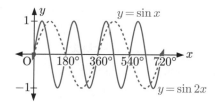

d We translate $y = \cos x$ to the right by a distance equivalent to $90°$ on the x-axis.

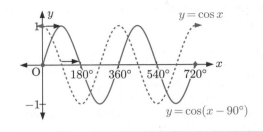

EXERCISE 12B.2

1 Find the amplitude of:

    a $y = 4\sin x$ **b** $y = -2\cos x + 1$ **c** $y = -\frac{1}{3}\sin(x - 30°)$

2 Find the period of:

    a $y = \cos 3x$ **b** $y = 5\sin 4x + 2$ **c** $y = -\cos\left(\frac{x}{2}\right)$

3 Find the principal axis of:

    a $y = \sin x - 3$ **b** $y = -2\cos x + 5$ **c** $y = \frac{1}{4}\sin(x + 60°)$

4 Sketch the graph of the following for $0° \leqslant x \leqslant 720°$:

    a $y = 3\sin x$ **b** $y = \sin x - 2$ **c** $y = -2\sin x$

    d $y = \sin 3x$ **e** $y = \sin\left(\frac{x}{2}\right)$ **f** $y = \sin(x - 60°)$

5 Sketch the graph of the following for $0° \leqslant x \leqslant 720°$:

    a $y = 2\cos x$ **b** $y = \cos x + 3$ **c** $y = -\frac{1}{3}\cos x$

    d $y = \cos 2x$ **e** $y = \cos(x + 90°)$ **f** $y = \cos\left(\frac{3x}{2}\right)$

6 Sketch the graph of the following for $0° \leqslant x \leqslant 360°$:

    a $y = 2\cos x + 1$ **b** $y = \sin 2x + 3$ **c** $y = \frac{1}{2}\cos 3x$ **d** $y = 3\sin 4x + 7$

7 **a** Sketch the graph of $y = 6\sin x + 10$ for $0° \leqslant x \leqslant 720°$.

    b Find the value of y when $x = 30°$.

    c Find the maximum value of y, and the values of x at which the maximum occurs.

    d Find the minimum value of y, and the values of x at which the minimum occurs.

C PROBLEM SOLVING WITH TRIGONOMETRIC FUNCTIONS

We have already seen how the sine and cosine functions are periodic. They can be used to describe many situations in the real world that exhibit this behaviour. We call these situations **periodic phenomena**.

Examples of periodic phenomena include:

- average daily temperatures through the seasons
- the depth of water in a harbour varying with the tide
- the number of daylight hours at a particular location.

Example 2

◄》 **Self Tutor**

The average daytime temperature for a city is given by the function $D(t) = 5\cos(30t)° + 20$ °C, where t is the time in months after January.

  a Sketch the graph of D against t for $0 \leqslant t \leqslant 24$.

  b Find the average daytime temperature during May.

  c Find the minimum average daytime temperature, and the month in which it occurs.

a For $D(t) = 5\cos(30t)° + 20$:

    • the amplitude is 5

    • the period is $\dfrac{360}{30} = 12$ months

    • the principal axis is $D = 20$.

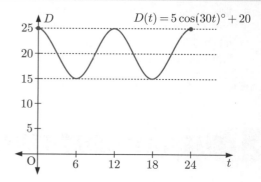

b May is 4 months after January.

    When $t = 4$, $D = 5 \times \cos 120° + 20$

                    $= 5 \times (-\tfrac{1}{2}) + 20$

                    $= 17.5$

  So, the average daytime temperature during May is 17.5°C.

c The minimum average daytime temperature is $20 - 5 = 15$°C, which occurs when $t = 6$ or 18.

  So, the minimum average daytime temperature occurs during July.

EXERCISE 12C

1 The temperature inside Vanessa's house t hours after midday is given by the function $T(t) = 6\sin(15t)° + 26$ °C.

  a Sketch the graph of T against t for $0 \leqslant t \leqslant 24$.

  b Find the temperature inside Vanessa's house at:

    i midnight   **ii** 2 pm.

  c Find the maximum temperature inside Vanessa's house, and the time at which it occurs.

2 The depth of water in a harbour t hours after midnight is $D(t) = 4\cos(30t)° + 6$ metres.

  a Sketch the graph of D against t for $0 \leqslant t \leqslant 24$.

  b Find the highest and lowest depths of the water, and the times at which they occur.

  c A boat requires a water depth of 5 metres to sail in. Will the boat be able to enter the harbour at 8 pm?

3 The tip of a clock's minute hand is $H(t) = 15\cos(6t)° + 150$ cm above ground level, where t is the time in minutes after 5 pm.

  a Sketch the graph of H against t for $0 \leqslant t \leqslant 180$.

  b Find the length of the minute hand.

  c Find, rounded to 1 decimal place, the height of the minute hand's tip at:

    i 5:08 pm   **ii** 5:37 pm   **iii** 5:51 pm   **iv** 6:23 pm

4 On a mini-golf hole, golfers must putt the ball through a castle's entrance. The entrance is protected by a gate which moves up and down.

The height of the gate above the ground t seconds after it touches the ground is $H(t) = 4\sin[45(t-2)]° + 4$ cm.

a Sketch the graph of H against t for $0 \leqslant t \leqslant 16$.

b Find the height of the gate above the ground 2 seconds after the gate touches the ground.

c Eric is using a golf ball with radius 2.14 cm. He putts the ball 1 second after the gate touches the ground, and the ball takes 5.3 seconds to reach the castle's entrance. Will the ball pass through the entrance?

5 Answer the **Opening Problem** on page **282**.

D | THE TANGENT FUNCTION

We have seen that if $P(\cos\theta, \sin\theta)$ is a point which is free to move around the unit circle, and if [OP] is extended to meet the tangent at $A(1, 0)$, the intersection between these lines occurs at $Q(1, \tan\theta)$.

This enables us to define the **tangent function**

$$\tan\theta = \frac{\sin\theta}{\cos\theta}.$$

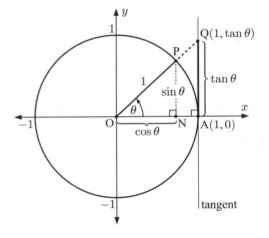

We have also seen that $\tan\theta$ is:

- positive in quadrants 1 and 3
- negative in quadrants 2 and 4
- periodic with period $180°$.

Discussion

What happens to $\tan\theta$ when P is at:

a $(1, 0)$ and $(-1, 0)$
b $(0, 1)$ and $(0, -1)$?

THE GRAPH OF $y = \tan x$

Since $\tan x = \dfrac{\sin x}{\cos x}$, $\tan x$ will be:

- zero whenever $\sin x = 0$
- undefined whenever $\cos x = 0$.

The zeros of the function $y = \cos x$ correspond to vertical asymptotes of the function $y = \tan x$.

The graph of $y = \tan x$ is

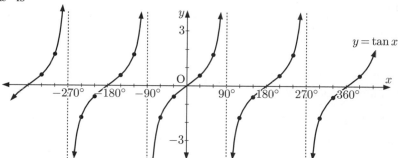

We observe that $y = \tan x$ has:

- **period** $180°$
- **range** $y \in \mathbb{R}$
- **vertical asymptotes** $x = (90 + 180k)°$ for all $k \in \mathbb{Z}$.

Click on the icon to explore how the tangent function is produced from the unit circle.

TRANSFORMATIONS OF THE TANGENT FUNCTION

As with the sine and cosine functions, we can perform transformations of the tangent function to obtain a related function.

- The graph of $y = \tan bx$, $b > 0$, is obtained by a horizontal dilation of $y = \tan x$ with scale factor $\frac{1}{b}$.

  The graph has period $\frac{180°}{b}$.

- The graph of $y = \tan(x - c)$ is obtained by a horizontal translation of $y = \tan x$ by a distance c.

To sketch these graphs, it is helpful to observe how the transformation affects the x-intercepts and vertical asymptotes of the graph.

Example 3

◀)) **Self Tutor**

Without using technology, sketch the graph of $y = \tan(x + 45°)$ for $0° \leqslant x \leqslant 540°$.

$y = \tan(x + 45°)$ is a horizontal translation of $y = \tan x$ to the left by a distance equivalent to $45°$ on the scale.

$y = \tan x$ has vertical asymptotes $x = 90°$, $x = 270°$, $x = 450°$, and its x-intercepts are $0°$, $180°$, $360°$, and $540°$.

∴ $y = \tan(x + 45°)$ has vertical asymptotes $x = 45°$, $x = 225°$, $x = 405°$, and x-intercepts $135°$, $315°$, and $495°$.

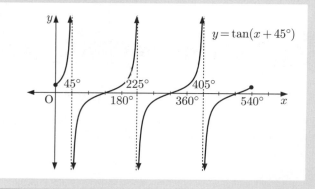

Example 4

◄⁐ **Self Tutor**

Without using technology, sketch the graph of $y = \tan 2x$ for $-180° \leqslant x \leqslant 180°$.

$y = \tan 2x$ is a horizontal dilation of $y = \tan x$ with scale factor $\frac{1}{2}$.

Since $b = 2$, the period is $90°$.

The vertical asymptotes are
$x = \pm 45°$, $x = \pm 135°$,
and the x-intercepts are at
$0°$, $\pm 90°$, $\pm 180°$.

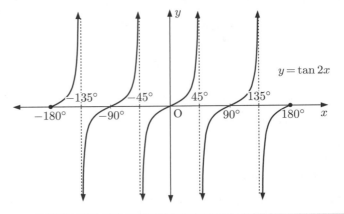

EXERCISE 12D

1   a *Sketch* the following functions for $0° \leqslant x \leqslant 540°$:

  i $y = \tan(x - 90°)$ **ii** $y = \tan(x + 60°)$

  iii $y = \tan 3x$

GRAPHING
PACKAGE

b Use technology to check your answers to **a**.
   Look in particular for asymptotes and the x-intercepts.

2 Describe the transformation(s) which move:

  a $y = \tan x$ to $y = \tan(x - 40°)$ **b** $y = \tan x$ to $y = \tan\left(\frac{x}{4}\right)$

3 State the period of:

GRAPHING
PACKAGE

  a $y = \tan x$ **b** $y = \tan 3x$ **c** $y = \tan nx$, $n > 0$

4 Draw the graphs of $y = \tan(x - 135)°$ and $y = \tan(x + 45°)$ for $0° \leqslant x \leqslant 540°$.
   Comment on your results.

E   TRIGONOMETRIC EQUATIONS

In this Section we will solve equations involving the trigonometric ratios $\sin\theta$, $\cos\theta$, and $\tan\theta$.

If you are required to solve equations over an interval larger than $0° \leqslant \theta \leqslant 360°$, you will need to add or subtract multiples of $360°$ to the solutions you read straight from the unit circle.

Example 5

⏵) **Self Tutor**

Solve $2\cos\theta - 1 = 0$ on the interval $0° \leqslant \theta \leqslant 720°$.

$2\cos\theta - 1 = 0$

$\therefore \ \cos\theta = \frac{1}{2}$

On the interval $0° \leqslant \theta \leqslant 360°$,
the solutions are $\theta = 60°$ or $300°$.

$\therefore$ on the interval $0° \leqslant \theta \leqslant 720°$,
the solutions are $\theta = 60°$, $300°$, $420°$, and $660°$.

$$\underset{60° + 360°}{\uparrow} \qquad \underset{300° + 360°}{\uparrow}$$

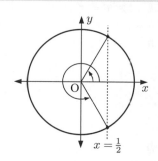

EXERCISE 12E

1 Solve for θ on the interval $0° \leqslant \theta \leqslant 360°$:

  a $\cos\theta = 0$ **b** $\tan\theta - 1 = 0$ **c** $2\sin\theta = -\sqrt{3}$

  d $\sqrt{2}\sin\theta - 1 = 0$ **e** $2\cos\theta + 3 = 1$ **f** $\sqrt{3}\tan\theta + 1 = 0$

2 Solve the following equations on the intervals given:

  a $\sqrt{2}\cos\theta = 1$, $0° \leqslant \theta \leqslant 720°$ **b** $5\sin x + 2 = 7$, $0° \leqslant x \leqslant 720°$

  c $\sqrt{3}\tan x + 3 = 0$, $0° \leqslant x \leqslant 720°$ **d** $6\sin\theta + 8 = 11$, $-360° \leqslant \theta \leqslant 360°$

  e $4\cos\theta + 2\sqrt{3} = 0$, $-360° \leqslant \theta \leqslant 360°$ **f** $\sin x + \cos x = 0$, $0° \leqslant x \leqslant 1080°$

Example 6

⏵) **Self Tutor**

Solve $2\sin 3x = 1$ on the interval $0° \leqslant x \leqslant 180°$.

$2\sin 3x = 1$

$\therefore \ \sin 3x = \frac{1}{2}$

Since $0° \leqslant x \leqslant 180°$
$\qquad\quad 0° \leqslant 3x \leqslant 540°$

$\therefore \ 3x = 30°, 150°, 390°, \text{ or } 510°$

$\therefore \ x = 10°, 50°, 130°, \text{ or } 170°$

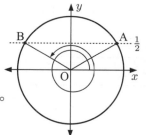

Start at angle $0°$ and
work around to $540°$,
noting down the angle
every time you reach
points A and B.

3 Solve for x on the interval $0° \leqslant x \leqslant 180°$:

  a $2\cos 2x = \sqrt{3}$ **b** $2\sin 3x = -1$ **c** $\sin 2x = -\sqrt{3}\cos 2x$

  d $3\sin 2x = 1$ **e** $\tan 3x = 8$ **f** $\frac{1}{2}\cos 3x = \frac{1}{3}$

Example 7

◀)) **Self Tutor**

Solve for θ on the interval $0° \leqslant \theta \leqslant 360°$:

a $\cos^2 \theta = \frac{3}{4}$ **b** $2 \sin^2 \theta = \sin \theta$

a $\cos^2 \theta = \frac{3}{4}$

  $\therefore \cos \theta = \pm \frac{\sqrt{3}}{2}$

  $\therefore \theta = 30°, 150°, 210°, \text{ or } 330°$

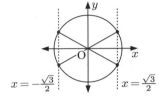

$x = -\frac{\sqrt{3}}{2}$ $x = \frac{\sqrt{3}}{2}$

b $2 \sin^2 \theta = \sin \theta$

  $\therefore 2 \sin^2 \theta - \sin \theta = 0$

  $\therefore \sin \theta (2 \sin \theta - 1) = 0$

    $\therefore \sin \theta = 0 \text{ or } \frac{1}{2}$

      $\therefore \theta = 0°, 30°, 150°, 180°, \text{ or } 360°$

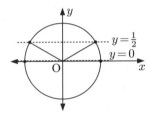

$y = \frac{1}{2}$
$y = 0$

---

4 Solve for θ on the interval $0° \leqslant \theta \leqslant 360°$:

a $\sin^2 \theta = \frac{1}{2}$ **b** $\tan^2 \theta = 3$ **c** $\cos^2 \theta + \cos \theta = 0$

d $2 \sin^2 \theta - \sqrt{3} \sin \theta = 0$ **e** $2 \cos^2 \theta - \cos \theta - 1 = 0$ **f** $\sin^2 \theta - \cos^2 \theta = 0$

5 The population of ants on a hill during 2011 is given by $P(t) = 50 \sin t + 300$, where t is the number of days after January 1st, $0 \leqslant t \leqslant 365$.

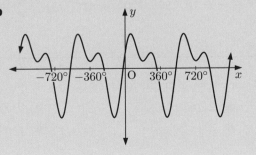

a Find the ant population on:

   i January 1st   **ii** January 31st.

b Find the maximum population of ants, and the date on which it occurs.

c On what dates are there 275 ants on the hill?

d Sketch the graph of P against t for $0 \leqslant t \leqslant 365$. Include all of the information found above.

Review set 12A

1 Which of the following graphs display periodic behaviour?

a
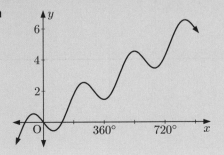

b

2

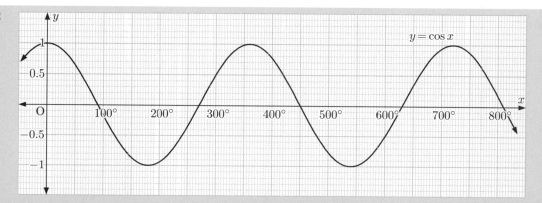

Use the graph of $y = \cos x$ to find the solutions of:

  a $\cos x = -0.4$, $0 \leqslant x \leqslant 800°$ **b** $\cos x = 0.9$, $0 \leqslant x \leqslant 600°$

3 Find the amplitude of: **a** $y = 5\cos 2x + 3$ **b** $y = -\frac{1}{4}\sin(x - 60°)$

4 Sketch the graph of the following for $0° \leqslant x \leqslant 720°$:

  a $y = \frac{1}{4}\sin x$ **b** $y = 2\cos x - 3$ **c** $y = \tan\left(\frac{1}{3}x\right)$

  d $y = \sin\left(\frac{2}{3}x\right) + 1$ **e** $y = -\cos(x - 45°)$ **f** $y = \tan(x - 30°)$

5 The fraction of the Moon which is illuminated each night is given by the function $M(t) = \frac{1}{2}\cos 12t + \frac{1}{2}$, where t is the time in days after January 1st.

  a Sketch the graph of M against t for $0 \leqslant t \leqslant 60$.

  b Find the fraction of the Moon which is illuminated on the night of:

    i January 6th   **ii** January 21st

    iii January 27th   **iv** February 19th.

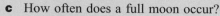

  c How often does a full moon occur?

  d On what dates during January and February is the Moon not illuminated at all?

6 Solve for θ on the interval $0° \leqslant \theta \leqslant 720°$:

  a $2\cos\theta = -1$ **b** $\sqrt{3}\sin\theta - \cos\theta = 0$ **c** $\dfrac{\sqrt{3}}{\sin\theta} = 2$

7 Solve for x on the interval $0° \leqslant x \leqslant 180°$:

  a $6\cos 2x = -3$ **b** $\sqrt{2}\sin 3x = -1$ **c** $\cos 2x = -2\sin 2x$

8 Consider the function $y = 5\sin 2x + 4$.

  a Find the amplitude of the function.   **b** Find the principal axis of the function.

  c Find the period of the function.   **d** Hence, sketch the function for $0 \leqslant x \leqslant 360°$.

  e Find the value of y when $x = 45°$.

9 **a** Sketch the graph of $y = -2\sin x + 7$ for $0° \leqslant x \leqslant 720°$.

  b Find the value of y when $x = 150°$.

  c Find the maximum value of y, and the values of x for which the maximum occurs.

  d Find the minimum value of y, and the values of x for which the minimum occurs.

Review set 12B

1 Consider the graph alongside.

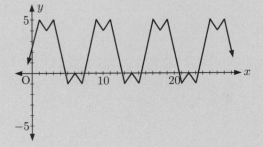

   a Explain why this graph shows periodic behaviour.

   b State:

     i the period

     ii the maximum value

     iii the minimum value.

2 Find the period of:

   a $y = 2\sin 3x$

   b $y = -4\cos\left(\frac{x}{2}\right) - 1$

3 Find the principal axis of:

   a $y = -\frac{1}{3}\sin(x - 45°) + 5$

   b $y = 2\cos\left(\frac{x}{3}\right) - 4$

4 Sketch the graph of the following for $0° \leqslant x \leqslant 720°$:

   a $y = \cos x - 3$

   b $y = \sin(x - 90°)$

   c $y = \tan(x - 135°)$

5 Sketch the graph of the following for $0° \leqslant x \leqslant 360°$:

   a $y = \frac{3}{2}\sin 3x$

   b $y = 2\cos 3x - 1$

   c $y = \tan 4x$

6 Solve for θ on the interval $0° \leqslant \theta \leqslant 720°$:

   a $2\sin\theta + 2 = 0$

   b $6\cos\theta - 3\sqrt{3} = 0$

7 Solve for x on the interval $0° \leqslant x \leqslant 360°$:

   a $3\tan^2 x = 1$

   b $4\cos^2 x - 2\cos x = 0$

8 Consider the equation $\sqrt{2}\cos^2\theta + \cos\theta = 0$.

   a By substituting $\theta = 120°$ and $\theta = 135°$, determine which of these values is a solution to the equation.

   b Find the other solutions to the equation on the interval $0° \leqslant \theta \leqslant 360°$.

   c Find the solutions to the equation on the interval $-360° \leqslant \theta \leqslant 720°$.

9 As the tip of a windmill's blade rotates, its height above ground is given by $H(t) = 10\cos(30t)° + 20$ metres, where t is the time in seconds.

   a Sketch the graph of H against t for $0 \leqslant t \leqslant 36$.

   b Find the height of the blade's tip after 9 seconds.

   c Find the minimum height of the blade's tip.

   d How long does the blade take to complete a full revolution?

13

Reasoning and proof

Contents:

Opening problem

A group of people are involved in a business meeting. Alice looks at Bob and Bob looks at Clare. Alice is married but Clare is not.

Things to think about:

a Do we know whether Bob is married?

b Can we *prove* that a married person looks at an unmarried person?

c What is necessary for a mathematical argument to be convincing and complete?

In the courses you have already done, you will have had a lot of practice in carefully writing mathematical arguments. In this Chapter we bring together some important advice on mathematical reasoning, and identify valuable techniques for proving mathematical statements.

WHAT IS PROOF?

Science relies on experimental evidence. Mathematics relies on logic and reasoning.

> A **mathematical proof** is a correct argument which establishes the truth of a mathematical statement.
>
> A mathematical proof:
>
> - starts with assumptions called **hypotheses**
> - is a sequence of correct mathematical steps
> - ends in a **conclusion**.

A mathematical proof can include logic, calculation, or a combination of the two. We will discuss both of these during the Chapter.

In the **Opening Problem**, we do not know whether or not Bob is married, so we need to consider both cases. We could write the following proof:

Proof:

Bob is either married or he is not married.

- If Bob is married, then when Bob looks at Clare, a married person looks at an unmarried person.
- If Bob is *not* married, then when Alice looks at Bob, a married person looks at an unmarried person.

In both cases, a married person looks at an unmarried person.

Therefore, a married person always looks at an unmarried person.

In this proof, notice that:

- "Alice is married" is a *hypothesis*.
- The *conclusion* is that a married person looks at an unmarried person.
- This *style* of proof is called *proof by exhaustion*, because we have considered all possible cases: Bob is married, and Bob is not married.
- This proof contains logic only. There is no calculation.

THE PURPOSES OF PROOF

Mathematical proof is important:

- **to convince**

  Proofs help you decide if and why a statement is true or false. This is important when the result seems strange.
- **to understand**

  Proofs help you understand how and why all the different assumptions play a part in the result.
- **to communicate**

  Mathematicians use proofs to communicate and debate ideas with each other.
- **to organize**

  Proofs help you organize your thoughts.
- **to discover new mathematics**

  By carefully examining each step of a proof, mathematicians discover new mathematics.

ADVICE ON WRITING PROOFS

- State what you are proving. Make it clear when you have reached your conclusion.
- Include enough detail to make your proof easy to check.
- Your proof should be written in good English, including simple, complete, correct sentences.
- Present your calculations on the page in a manner which makes them easy to follow. Use your layout to clearly separate the parts or different cases considered in your proof.
- Use diagrams when appropriate to give a visual representation of the situation.
- It is often useful to use examples when exploring a problem. However, a single example is usually not sufficient to complete a proof.
- Check to see where you have used each hypothesis. If you have not used a particular hypothesis then either:
  - ▸ you did not need it, or
  - ▸ your proof should have made use of it, and is incorrect!
- Do not expect to write a complete proof the first time. Expect to use rough working first, and then write a neat version.

A   LOGICAL CONNECTIVES

Mathematical language uses **logical connectives** to link mathematical statements together:

Connective	Symbol	Formal name
and	$\wedge$	conjunction
or	$\vee$	disjunction
not	$\neg$	negation
if .... then	$\Rightarrow$	implication
if, and only if	$\Leftrightarrow$	equivalence

We can illustrate the use of these connectives using *variables* such as A, B, C, ...

For example, $(A \wedge B) \Rightarrow C$ means "A and B implies C". The two arguments $(A \wedge B)$ and C are connected by the connective $\Rightarrow$. The argument $(A \wedge B)$ is itself made up of arguments A and B, connected by the connective $\wedge$. It is therefore helpful to think of statements as mathematical trees, connected by the logical connectives.

NEGATION

The negation of a variable A is its opposite. If A is true then $\neg A$ is false, and vice versa.

For example:

- the negation of "Today is Wednesday" is "Today is not Wednesday"
- if we know $x \in \mathbb{Z}$, the negation of "x is an even integer" is "x is an odd integer"
- if we know $x \in \mathbb{R}$, the negation of "x is an even integer" is "x is not an even integer", since x might be an odd integer, or it might also be a non-integer.

IMPLICATIONS

Implications commonly arise when we deduce one thing from another.

For the implication $A \Rightarrow B$, we start with the statement A, and from it we deduce the statement B. The statement A is called the **hypothesis**, and B is called the **conclusion**.

In English there are many words we can use to show an implication.

For example:

$$A \left\{ \begin{array}{c} \text{implies} \\ \text{so} \\ \text{hence} \\ \text{thus} \\ \text{therefore} \end{array} \right\} B.$$

We use $\therefore$ to mean "therefore".

The **converse** of the implication $A \Rightarrow B$ is the statement $B \Rightarrow A$.

It is important to recognise that while the implication $A \Rightarrow B$ may be true, its converse may not be true.

For example, the statement "If $x = 2$ then $x^2 = 4$" is true. However, its converse "If $x^2 = 4$ then $x = 2$" is false, since x may be -2.

EQUIVALENCE

Two statements A and B are **equivalent** if both $A \Rightarrow B$ *and* $B \Rightarrow A$. In this case we can say A is true if and only if B is true.

For example, the statement "If $x = -2$ or 2, then $x^2 = 4$" is true. The statement "If $x^2 = 4$ then $x = -2$ or 2" is also true. Therefore, $x = -2$ or $2 \Leftrightarrow x^2 = 4$.

EXERCISE 13A

1 For each statement, state its negation:

  a The cat is black.   **b** x is prime.   **c** The tree is deciduous.

2 State, with justification, whether each statement is true or false:

  a If $x^2 = 9$ then $x = 3$.   **b** If $x = 3$ then $x^2 = 9$.   **c** $x = 3$ if and only if $x^2 = 9$.

3 State, with justification, whether each statement is true or false:

  a If x is positive then $\sqrt{x} \in \mathbb{R}$.   **b** If $\sqrt{x} \in \mathbb{R}$ then x is positive.

  c x is positive if and only if $\sqrt{x} \in \mathbb{R}$.

4 **a** Write the converse of the statement "If Socrates is a cat then Socrates is an animal".

  b Is this converse true or false?

5 Determine whether A and B are equivalent:

   a A: $xyz = 0$, B: $(x = 0) \vee (y = 0) \vee (z = 0)$

   b A: x is even, B: x^2 is even

6 There are four cards on a table. Every card has a letter on one side and a number on the other. With the cards placed, you see:

D   3   K   7

Identify the cards you need to turn over, to establish the truth of the statement: "Every card which has a D on one side has a 7 on the other".

This problem is a well studied logic test, devised in 1966 by Peter Wason.

B   PROOF BY DEDUCTION

When we apply a chain of implications to prove a result, we call this *proof by deduction*.

In geometry it is very common to use deductive reasoning to prove theorems.

For example, Thales' theorem appears in Euclid, book III, part of Proposition 31. It is a result which you should already be familiar with.

Example 1   ◀》 Self Tutor

Thales' theorem states: Consider a circle of any diameter [AB], and any other point P on the circle. The triangle APB is a right angle triangle, with the right angle at P.

Prove Thales' theorem.

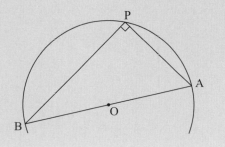

Proof:

Add the radius [OP] to the diagram.

Now OP = OA and OP = OB, so we have two isosceles triangles AOP and BOP.

In any isosceles triangle, the base angles are equal. We call the base angles of the two triangles α and β respectively.

Since the interior angles of any triangle sum to $180°$, from triangle ABP we find $2\alpha + 2\beta = 180°$

$$\therefore \quad \alpha + \beta = 90°$$

Hence $\widehat{APB}$ is a right angle.

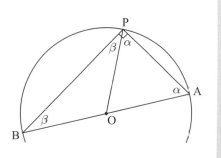

EXERCISE 13B

1 By adding extra lines to the figure shown, prove that $\beta = 2\alpha$.

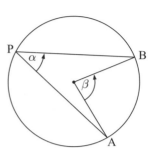

2 In the diagram alongside, three semi-circles have been constructed using the sides of a right angled triangle as diameters. The areas of the semi-circles are A, B, and C as shown. Prove that $A + B = C$.

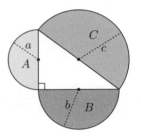

Investigation   **Pythagoras' Theorem**

One of the most famous results in mathematics is known as Pythagoras' Theorem:

> In a right angled triangle with sides a, b and hypotenuse c, $a^2 + b^2 = c^2$.

Proof by pictures:

The pictures below each show four copies of the original triangle, in different arrangements.

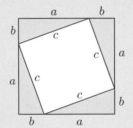

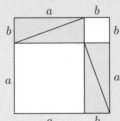

In each figure, the total area is $(a + b)^2$, and the shaded area is $4 \times \frac{1}{2}ab = 2ab$.

$\therefore$ the unshaded areas are equal

$\therefore$ $c^2 = a^2 + b^2$

In 1968, E. Loomis collected around 365 different proofs in his book *The Pythagorean Proposition* (National Council of Teachers of Mathematics, Washington). It might seem strange to have so many different proofs of the same thing, given that just one correct proof establishes the theorem. However, one purpose of proof is to help us understand the result, and different proofs can help develop this understanding.

The *converse* of Pythagoras' theorem is also true:

> Given a triangle with sides a, b, c such that $a^2 + b^2 = c^2$,
> then the angle between a and b is a right angle.

This result has practical use in the construction of right angles.

What to do:

1 The sequence of pictures below shows shears and translations of parallelograms. Explain how the sequence proves Pythagoras' Theorem.

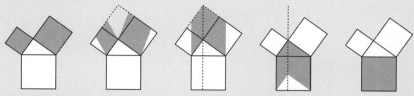

2 The sequence of pictures below shows shears and rotations of triangles. Explain how the sequence proves Pythagoras' Theorem.

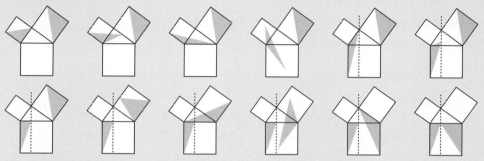

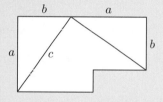

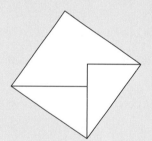

3 The figure below shows a jigsaw made from three pieces, in two arrangements. Explain how these prove Pythagoras' Theorem.

4 Suppose $a, b \in \mathbb{N}$. Let $x = a^2 - b^2$, $y = 2ab$, and $z = a^2 + b^2$. Prove that $x^2 + y^2 = z^2$.

> This result allows us to make right angled triangles with sides which are all integers.

C   PROOF BY EQUIVALENCE

Many proofs include some calculation. Calculations have the advantage of being easier to check than reasoning written out in language.

When we solve equations, we commonly use *reasoning by equivalence*. This is a formal name for the process where we correctly "do the same thing" to both sides of an equation.

Reasoning by equivalence requires deduction at each step. However, it is stronger because at every step the converse must also be true.

For example, to deduce the solutions of $(x + 1)^3 = x^3 + 1$ we can write the following series of equivalent statements:

$$
\begin{aligned}
&& (x + 1)^3 &= x^3 + 1 \\
&\Leftrightarrow & x^3 + 3x^2 + 3x + 1 &= x^3 + 1 \\
&\Leftrightarrow & 3x^2 + 3x &= 0 \\
&\Leftrightarrow & 3x(x + 1) &= 0 \\
&\Leftrightarrow & x = 0 \ \lor \ x &= -1
\end{aligned}
$$

This chain of reasoning relies on the facts that:

- two equations are equivalent if they have precisely the same solutions
- polynomials $p(x)$ and $q(x)$ are equivalent if $p(x) = q(x)$ for all $x \in \mathbb{R}$.

> To maintain mathematical equivalence, we can:
>
> - add or subtract the same term from both sides of an equation
> - multiply or divide both sides of an equation by a non-zero term
> - substitute for an equivalent sub-term, for example by replacing a term by its factored or expanded form.

There are some other operations which maintain equivalence, for example some of the rules of logarithms with positive terms.

However, squaring or taking square roots of both sides of an equation does not maintain equivalence!

Given $a^2 = b^2$, taking the square root of both sides gives $a = b$. However, in doing this we have ignored the possibility that $a = -b$.

Instead, we use the difference between two squares result as follows:

$$
\begin{aligned}
&& a^2 &= b^2 \\
&\Leftrightarrow & a^2 - b^2 &= 0 \\
&\Leftrightarrow & (a - b)(a + b) &= 0 && \{\text{difference between two squares}\} \\
&\Leftrightarrow & a - b = 0 \ \lor \ a + b &= 0 && \{\text{Null factor law}\} \\
&\Leftrightarrow & a = b \ \lor \ a &= -b
\end{aligned}
$$

Using this procedure, equivalence is maintained. With experience, mathematicians *compress* this working into a single step.

Example 2
◀) **Self Tutor**

Find the smallest positive integer a for which $x^2 + (a - 2)x + a = 0$ has real solutions.

$$
\begin{aligned}
&& x^2 + (a - 2)x + a &= 0 \\
&\Leftrightarrow & \left(x + \frac{a - 2}{2}\right)^2 - \left(\frac{a - 2}{2}\right)^2 + a &= 0 && \{\text{completing the square}\} \\
&\Leftrightarrow & \left(x + \frac{a - 2}{2}\right)^2 &= \frac{(a - 2)^2}{4} - a
\end{aligned}
$$

The equation has real solutions if and only if $\dfrac{(a-2)^2}{4} - a \geqslant 0$

$$\Leftrightarrow \quad (a-2)^2 - 4a \geqslant 0$$
$$\Leftrightarrow \quad a^2 - 8a + 4 \geqslant 0$$
$$\Leftrightarrow \quad (a-4)^2 - 16 + 4 \geqslant 0$$
$$\Leftrightarrow \quad (a-4)^2 \geqslant 12$$
$$\Leftrightarrow \quad a - 4 \geqslant \sqrt{12} \ \lor \ a - 4 \leqslant -\sqrt{12}$$

But $a > 0$, so we reject the non-positive solutions. Hence $a \geqslant 4 + \sqrt{12} \approx 7.46$.

$\therefore$ the smallest positive integer a for which the equation has real solutions is $a = 8$.

The proof above is called a **direct proof** because we start with the hypothesis and work forward to the conclusion.

ALGEBRAIC MANIPULATION

The word "simplify" is often over-used when describing algebraic manipulations. We tend to use it to describe several different processes, when actually it would be helpful to be more specific.

Simplification describes the most basic algebraic manipulations such as $1x = x$.

Isolation is a sequence of steps to "undo" a function so a variable is left on its own on one side of an equation.

Collection is the process of gathering terms together so the number of times the variable is mentioned is reduced. We collect "like" terms such as $2x + 3x = 5x$, and we can also "collect" the unknown from factors using the difference between squares expansion $(x + a)(x - a) = x^2 - a^2$.

Completing the square is a special form of collection, which uses the difference between squares expansion in reverse:

$$x^2 - 2ax = x(x - 2a)$$
$$= ((x - a) + a)((x - a) - a)$$
$$= (x - a)^2 - a^2$$

Attraction is a process of moving terms "closer" together.

For example:
$$\ln(x + 1) + \ln(x - 1) = 3$$
$$\Leftrightarrow \quad \ln((x + 1)(x - 1)) = 3 \qquad \text{\{attraction\}}$$
$$\Leftrightarrow \quad \ln(x^2 - 1) = 3 \qquad \text{\{collection\}}$$
$$\Leftrightarrow \quad x^2 - 1 = e^3$$
$$\Leftrightarrow \quad x^2 = e^3 + 1$$
$$\Leftrightarrow \quad x = \sqrt{e^3 + 1} \ \lor \ x = -\sqrt{e^3 + 1}$$

After the attraction and collection processes, the remainder of this procedure involves isolating x.

Many equations can be solved by using only attraction, collection, and isolation.

EXERCISE 13C

1 Prove that:

   a $(a + b)^2 - (a - b)^2 = 4ab$ **b** $(a + b)^2 - 4(a - b)^2 = (3b - a)(3a - b)$

2 The product of three consecutive integers is increased by the middle integer. Prove that the result is a perfect cube.

3 Prove that if p and q are odd integers then $p^2 - q^2$ is divisible by 8.

4 Prove that $(x - y)^5 + (x - y)^3 = 0$ if and only if $x = y$.

5 **a** Expand and collect like terms: $(n^2 - 2n + 2)(n^2 + 2n + 2)$

  b Hence find all integers n such that $n^4 + 4$ is prime.

6 Consider a 3-digit number "abc", $a \neq c$. Written backwards, it is "cba". Let S be the result when the smaller of the two numbers is subtracted from the larger. When S is written backwards and the result is added to S, prove that the sum is always 1089.

For example: 276 backwards is 672, so $S = 396$ and $396 + 693 = 1089$.

7 Prove that $\dfrac{a^2 + b^2}{2} \geqslant ab$ for all $a, b \in \mathbb{R}$.

8 The following "proofs" end in nonsensical results. Identify the incorrect step(s) in each case:

  a
$$a = b$$
$$\Leftrightarrow \quad a^2 = ab$$
$$\Leftrightarrow \quad a^2 - b^2 = ab - b^2$$
$$\Leftrightarrow \quad (a - b)(a + b) = b(a - b)$$
$$\Leftrightarrow \quad a + b = b$$
$$\Leftrightarrow \quad 2a = a$$
$$\Leftrightarrow \quad 2 = 1$$

  b
$$\frac{x + 10}{x - 6} - 5 = \frac{4x - 40}{13 - x}$$
$$\Leftrightarrow \quad \frac{x + 10 - 5(x - 6)}{x - 6} = \frac{4x - 40}{13 - x}$$
$$\Leftrightarrow \quad \frac{4x - 40}{6 - x} = \frac{4x - 40}{13 - x}$$
$$\Leftrightarrow \quad 6 - x = 13 - x$$
$$\Leftrightarrow \quad 6 = 13$$

9 The following "proofs" give correct results but their methods are incorrect. Identify the incorrect step(s) in each case:

  a
$$6x - 12 = 3(x - 2)$$
$$\Leftrightarrow \quad 6x - 12 + 3(x - 2) = 0$$
$$\Leftrightarrow \quad 12x - 24 = 0$$
$$\Leftrightarrow \quad x = 2$$

  b
$$x^2 - 6x + 9 = 0$$
$$\Leftrightarrow \quad x^2 - 6x = -9$$
$$\Leftrightarrow \quad x(x - 6) = 3(-3)$$
$$\Leftrightarrow \quad x = 3 \ \lor \ x - 6 = -3$$
$$\Leftrightarrow \quad x = 3$$

  c
$$(x + 3)(2 - x) = 4$$
$$\Leftrightarrow \quad x + 3 = 4 \ \lor \ 2 - x = 4$$
$$\Leftrightarrow \quad x = 1 \ \lor \ x = -2$$

10 Use the Factor Theorem to prove that $x + y + z$ is a factor of $x^3 + y^3 + z^3 - 3xyz$.

D   DEFINITIONS

Proofs normally make use of formal *definitions*.

For example:

A **rational number** is a number which can be written in the form $\dfrac{p}{q}$ where $p, q \in \mathbb{Z}$, $q \neq 0$.

An integer n is **even** if $n = 2k$ for some integer k.

An integer n is **odd** if $n = 2k + 1$ for some integer k.

Example 3
◄ﮤ **Self Tutor**

Prove that the sum of any two rational numbers is also a rational number.

Proof:

Let x and y be two rational numbers.

By definition, there exists $p, q \in \mathbb{Z}$, $q \neq 0$ so that $x = \dfrac{p}{q}$.

By definition, there exists $r, s \in \mathbb{Z}$, $s \neq 0$ so that $y = \dfrac{r}{s}$.

So, $x + y = \dfrac{p}{q} + \dfrac{r}{s} = \dfrac{ps + rq}{qs}$

Since p, q, r, s are all integers, $ps + rq$ is an integer which we call P.

Since q, s are non-zero integers, qs is a non-zero integer which we call Q.

$\therefore \quad x + y = \dfrac{ps + rq}{qs} = \dfrac{P}{Q}$ where $P, Q \in \mathbb{Z}$, $Q \neq 0$

$\therefore$ by definition, $x + y$ is a rational number.

We have written this proof in great detail. However, the whole point of a proof is that you should be able to check each step easily.

Mathematicians sometimes choose to leave out steps to make the argument shorter and easier to read. If the reader trusts the writer this is fine. However, it should always be possible to fill in the missing steps.

Learning which steps to include is part of learning how to write a mathematical proof.

Try to include steps of about the same "size". Sudden large jumps in the proof make people suspicious!

EXERCISE 13D

1 Prove that the difference between any two rational numbers is also a rational number.

2 Prove that the product of any two rational numbers is also a rational number.

3 Prove that the product of two odd integers is odd.

4 If a, b, c are integers and $ax^2 + bx + c = 0$ has rational root $\dfrac{r}{s}$ in lowest terms, prove that s is a factor of a, and r is a factor of c.

Discussion

Mathematical definitions are very difficult to write. They are often the result of careful thought by many experienced mathematicians. Once commonly accepted, they rarely change, because if they did it would cause great confusion.

Definitions collect similar examples together. When attempting to understand something, it is always worth building up a collection of examples which do and do not satisfy the definition.

Discuss how you could define a *chair*.

E   PROOF BY EXHAUSTION

A proof can sometimes be split into a finite number of cases, each of which is then proven separately. It is important to justify why the list of cases covers *all* possible cases. Since the list *exhausts* all possibilities, we call this style of proof a **proof by exhaustion**.

For example, every natural number $n \in \mathbb{Z}$ is either even or odd.

- If n is even it is divisible by two, and so $n = 2k$ for some $k \in \mathbb{Z}$.
- If n is odd, it has remainder 1 when divided by 2. In this case $n = 2k + 1$ for some $k \in \mathbb{Z}$.

Example 4   ◀⅛ **Self Tutor**

Given that $n^5 - n = (n-1)n(n+1)(n^2+1)$, prove that $n^5 - n$ is divisible by 5 for all $n \in \mathbb{Z}$.

Proof by exhaustion:

If we divide n by 5 then the remainder will be 0, 1, 2, 3, or 4. Hence every integer can be written in one of the forms $5k$, $5k+1$, $5k+2$, $5k+3$, or $5k+4$, for some $k \in \mathbb{Z}$.

Let $N = n^5 - n = (n-1)n(n+1)(n^2+1)$.

If $n = 5k$ then the factor n is divisible by 5, and so N is divisible by 5.

If $n = 5k+1$ then the factor $(n-1) = 5k$ is divisible by 5, so N is divisible by 5.

If $n = 5k+2$ then the factor $(n^2+1) = (5k+2)^2 + 1$
$$= 25k^2 + 20k + 5$$
$$= 5(5k^2 + 4k + 1)$$

which is divisible by 5, so N is divisible by 5.

If $n = 5k+3$ then the factor $(n^2+1) = (5k+3)^2 + 1$
$$= 25k^2 + 30k + 10$$
$$= 5(5k^2 + 6k + 2)$$

which is divisible by 5, so N is divisible by 5.

If $n = 5k+4$ then the factor $(n+1) = 5(k+1)$ which is divisible by 5, so N is divisible by 5.

In all cases, N is divisible by 5, so $n^5 - n$ is divisible by 5 for all $n \in \mathbb{Z}$.

EXERCISE 13E

1 Prove that if n is an integer such that n^2 is even, then n is even.

2 Prove that $n^3 - n$ is divisible by 3 for all $n \in \mathbb{Z}$.

3 Prove that $n^3 + 2n$ is divisible by 3 for all $n \in \mathbb{Z}$.

4 Prove that $n^2 - 1$ is divisible by 8 for all odd integers n.

5 Prove that 7 never divides $n^2 + 4$ for all $n \in \mathbb{Z}$.

6 Let n be a positive integer and define $x = (n+1)! + 2$. Prove that none of x, $x+1$, $x+2$, ..., $x+n-1$ are prime.

> "*a divides b*" means that b is divisible by a.

7 You are presented with 3 boxes, one of which contains a prize. On the lid of each box there is a statement, and you are told that only one of the statements is true. They say:

A The prize is in this box.

B The prize is not in this box.

C The prize is in box **A**.

Which box contains the prize?

F ▌ DISPROOF BY COUNTER EXAMPLE

Experimental evidence is very convincing, and scientific research relies on experimental evidence. However, in mathematics we do not consider experimental evidence to be sufficient to constitute a *proof*. The reason for this is that one single **counter example** which shows a general statement to be false, is sufficient to *disprove* the statement.

Example 5   ◀) **Self Tutor**

The values of $n^2 - n + 41$ for some values of $n \in \mathbb{N}$ are shown in the table alongside. We observe that all of these values are primes, so we conjecture that:

$n^2 - n + 41$ is prime for all $n \in \mathbb{N}$.

Find an example which proves this conjecture is false.

n	$n^2 - n + 41$
1	41
2	43
3	47
4	53
5	61
6	71
7	83
8	97
9	113
10	131
11	151
12	173
13	197
⋮	⋮
30	911
⋮	⋮
99	9743
⋮	⋮

For $n = 41$, we have $n^2 - n + 41 = 41^2 - 41 + 41 = 41^2$ which is not prime.

∴ the conjecture is false.

EXERCISE 13F

1 Find a counter example which disproves:

    a $(a + b)^2 = a^2 + b^2$

    b If p is prime then $2p + 1$ is prime.

    c For each k, at least one of $6k - 1$ or $6k + 1$ is prime.

2 Find a counter example which disproves:

    a If $p_1, p_2, ..., p_n$ are distinct prime numbers then $p = (p_1 \times p_2 \times .... \times p_n) + 1$ is also prime

    b If $p_1, p_2, ..., p_n$ is the list of the first n prime numbers then $p = (p_1 \times p_2 \times .... \times p_n) + 1$ is also prime.

3 Suppose n distinct dots are placed around the outside of a circle, and every pair of dots is joined with a straight line segment. We can then count the number of regions in which the circle has been divided. The first five cases are illustrated below. We observe that the circle is divided into 1, 2, 4, 8, and 16 regions, and therefore conjecture that for the case of n dots, the circle will be divided into 2^{n-1} regions.

    By considering the case $n = 6$, prove the conjecture is false.

4 Consider the sequence 31, 331, 3331, ... from which we conjecture that each number in the sequence is prime. Find a counter example to disprove this conjecture.

5 Prime numbers of the form $2^n - 1$, $n \in \mathbb{Z}^+$ are called **Mersenne primes** after **Marin Mersenne** (1588 - 1647). As of September 2015 the largest known Mersenne prime was $2^{74\,207\,281} - 1$ which has $22\,338\,618$ digits.

    a Calculate $2^n - 1$ for $n = 1, 2, ..., 10$. For what values of n is $2^n - 1$ prime?

    b Consider the conjecture: If n is prime then $2^n - 1$ is prime. Find a counter example to disprove this conjecture.

    c Consider the conjecture: If n is composite then $2^n - 1$ is composite. Prove this conjecture is true by expanding the brackets and calculating $(2^b - 1)(1 + 2^b + 2^{2b} + 2^{3b} + ... + 2^{(a-1)b})$.

Review set 13A

1 The roots of $f(x) = x^2 + px + q$ are a and b. Prove that $q = ab$ and $p = -(a+b)$.

2 Prove that $n^3 - n$ is divisible by 6 for all $n \in \mathbb{Z}$.

3   **a** Prove that the fifth powers of the numbers $k = 1, 2, 3, ..., 9$ all have last digit k.

    b Hence prove that n always has the same last digit as its 5th power n^5, for all $n \in \mathbb{Z}$.
    Hint: Consider writing an integer in the form $10m + k$.

4 Find a counter example which disproves: If p is prime then $p! + 1$ is prime.

Review set 13B

1 Let $p(x) = x^2 + 2bx + c$ and define $q(x) = p(x - b)$. Prove that $q(x) = q(-x)$ for all x.

2 Prove that $\dfrac{a+b}{2} \geqslant \sqrt{ab}$ for all $a, b \in \mathbb{R}^+$.

3 Prove that the product of 3 consecutive integers is divisible by 6.

4 Find a counter example which disproves: If 10 divides n and 15 divides n then 150 divides n.

14

Introduction to differential calculus

Contents:

Opening problem

Tina is cycling to school. This graph shows the distance she has travelled against time.

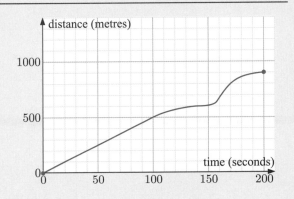

Things to think about:

a For the first 100 seconds, Tina cycles at constant speed.

   i What feature of the graph indicates that her speed was constant?

   ii What was Tina's speed during this time?

b Look at the graph for the period from $t = 100$ to $t = 200$ seconds.

   i Did Tina travel at constant speed during this time?

   ii Was there a time when Tina was stationary? Explain your answer.

   iii How can we find Tina's *average speed* from $t = 100$ to $t = 200$ seconds?

   iv How can we determine Tina's *instantaneous speed* when $t = 170$ seconds?

In previous years you will have seen travel graphs which have been made up of straight line segments. You will have calculated *average* speeds of travel between two points, and only talked about the *instantaneous* speed if the speed happens to be constant.

In the real world, we know that the speeds of objects are constantly changing. Their travel graphs are curves rather than straight lines. In order to calculate the instantaneous speed of an object, we need a branch of mathematics called **differential calculus**.

Differential calculus deals with **rates of change**. It has widespread applications in science, engineering, and finance.

Historical note

The word "calculus" is a Latin word referring to the small pebbles the ancient Romans used for counting.

The first known description of calculus is found on the **Egyptian Moscow papyrus** from about 1850 BC. Here, it was used to calculate areas and volumes.

Ancient Greek mathematicians such as **Democritus** and **Eudoxus** developed these ideas further by dividing objects into an infinite number of sections. This led to the study of **infinitesimals**, and allowed **Archimedes of Syracuse** to find the tangent to a curve other than a circle.

The methods of Archimedes were the foundation for modern calculus developed almost 2000 years later by mathematicians such as **Johann Bernoulli** and **Isaac Barrow**.

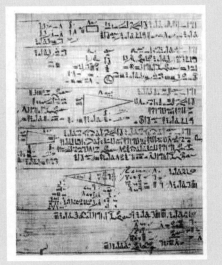

Egyptian Moscow papyrus

A ┃ RATES OF CHANGE

A **rate** is a comparison between two quantities with different units.

We often judge performances by rates. For example:

- Sir Donald Bradman's average batting rate at Test cricket level was 99.94 runs per innings.
- Michael Jordan's average basketball scoring rate was 30.1 points per game.
- Rangi's average typing rate is 63 words per minute with an error rate of 2.3 errors per page.

Speed is a commonly used rate. It is the rate of change in distance per unit of time.

CONSTANT RATES OF CHANGE

Suppose water from a hose is used to fill a swimming pool. The volume of water in the pool is recorded at 1 minute intervals in the table alongside.

Time (minutes)	0	1	2	3	4	5
Volume (litres)	0	15	30	45	60	75

+15 +15 +15 +15 +15

Notice that the volume of water increases by the same amount each time interval. This is an example of a **constant rate of change**.

The graph of the volume of water against time is a straight line because the rate of change is constant.

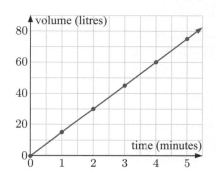

The **gradient** of the line gives the rate of change:

$$\text{rate of flow} = \frac{15 - 0}{1 - 0}$$

$$= 15 \text{ litres per minute}$$

EXERCISE 14A.1

1 The table alongside shows the distance travelled by a jogger at 30-second intervals.

Time (seconds)	0	30	60	90	120	150
Distance (metres)	0	90	180	270	360	450

   a Is the jogger travelling at a constant speed? Explain your answer.

   b Draw the graph of distance against time.

   c Find the speed of the jogger in metres per second.

2 This graph shows the height of a seedling during its first 10 weeks.

   a Is the height changing at a constant rate? Explain your answer.

   b Find the rate of change in height.

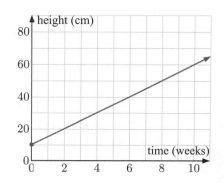

3 Find the rate of change for each function. Do not include units in your answer.

a
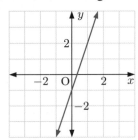

b
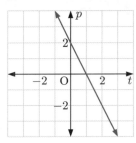

c
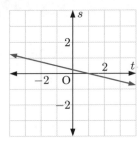

4 Find the rate of change for the function $f(x) = \frac{5}{2}x - 3$.

VARYING RATES OF CHANGE

In most real-world situations, rates of change are not constant, but rather vary over time.

For example, this graph shows the temperature of a glass of water which is left in the sun. The graph is not a straight line, which means the rate of change in temperature is not constant. The temperature increases quickly at first, and then more slowly as time goes by.

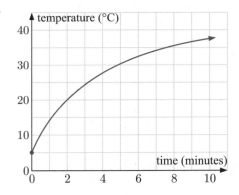

In such cases, we can find an **average rate of change** over a particular time interval. For example, from time $t = 0$ to $t = 2$ minutes, the temperature increases from $5°C$ to $20°C$.

So, the average rate of change is $\dfrac{20 - 5}{2 - 0} = 7.5°C$ per minute.

In the context of functions, we say that:

> The **average rate of change** in $f(x)$ from $x = a$ to $x = b$ is $\dfrac{f(b) - f(a)}{b - a}$.
>
> This is the **gradient of the chord [AB]**.

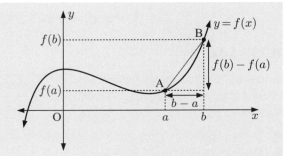

EXERCISE 14A.2

1 Aileen is driving from Amsterdam to Zurich. This graph shows the distance travelled against time.

   a Did Aileen travel at constant speed? Explain your answer.

   b Find Aileen's average speed for:

   i the first 5 hours

   ii the final 5 hours.

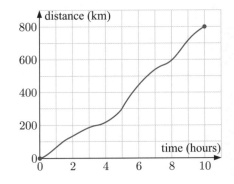

2 Chris went hiking in the mountains. His elevation above sea level is shown on this graph.

Find Chris' average rate of change in elevation from:

  a $t = 1$ hour to $t = 2.5$ hours

  b $t = 3.5$ hours to $t = 6$ hours.

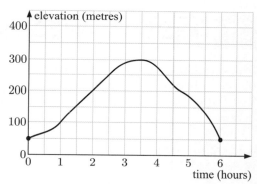

3 For each function, find the average rate of change in $f(x)$ from A to B:

a

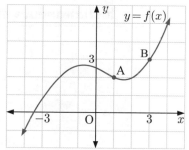

b

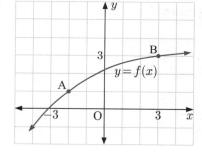

c

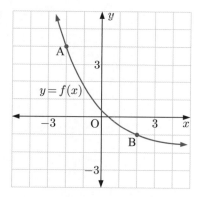

d

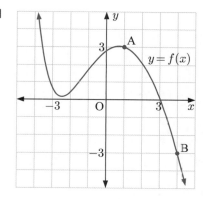

4 Consider the graph of $f(x) = x^2$.

  a Find the average rate of change in $f(x)$ from:

   i $x = 1$ to $x = 2$

   ii $x = 1$ to $x = 1.5$

   iii $x = 1$ to $x = 1.1$

   iv $x = 1$ to $x = 1.01$

   v $x = 1$ to $x = 1.001$

  b Comment on your answers in **a**.

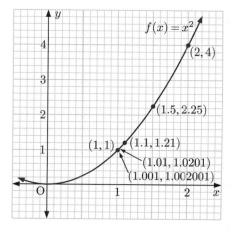

B   INSTANTANEOUS RATES OF CHANGE

Suppose the speedometer in a car indicates that you are travelling at 60 km per hour. This is not an average speed, but an *instantaneous speed*. It is the speed at which you are travelling at that particular instant.

Investigation 1   Instantaneous speed

A ball bearing is dropped from the top of a tall building. The distance D it has fallen after t seconds is recorded, and the following graph of distance against time is obtained.

We choose a fixed point F on the curve when $t = 2$ seconds. We then choose another point M on the curve, and draw the line segment or **chord** [FM] between the two points. To start with, we let M be the point when $t = 4$ seconds.

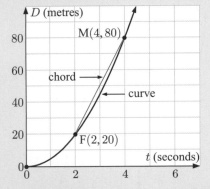

The *average* speed in the time interval $2 \leqslant t \leqslant 4$

$$= \frac{\text{distance travelled}}{\text{time taken}}$$

$$= \frac{(80 - 20)\,\text{m}}{(4 - 2)\,\text{s}}$$

$$= \tfrac{60}{2}\,\text{m s}^{-1}$$

$$= 30\,\text{m s}^{-1}$$

In this Investigation we will try to measure the *instantaneous* speed of the ball bearing when $t = 2$ seconds.

What to do:

1 Click on the icon to start the demonstration.

F is the point where $t = 2$ seconds, and M is another point on the curve. To start with, M is at $t = 4$ seconds.

The number in the box marked *gradient* is the gradient of the chord [FM]. This is the *average speed* of the ball bearing in the interval from F to M. For M at $t = 4$ seconds, you should see that the average speed is 30 m s^{-1}.

DEMO

2 Click on M and drag it slowly towards F. Copy and complete the table alongside with the gradient of the chord [FM], for M being the points on the curve at the given varying times t.

3 Observe what happens as M reaches F. Explain why this is so.

4 For $t = 2$ seconds, what do you suspect will be the instantaneous speed of the ball bearing?

t	gradient of [FM]
3	
2.5	
2.1	
2.01	

5 Move M to the origin, and then slide it towards F from the left. Copy and complete the table with the gradient of the chord [FM] for various times t.

6 Do your results agree with those in **4**?

t	gradient of [FM]
0	
1.5	
1.9	
1.99	

If A and B are two points on a function, the gradient of the chord [AB] is the average rate of change between these points.

From the **Investigation**, if we let B get closer and closer to A, then the average rate of change from A to B will approach the *instantaneous* rate of change at A.

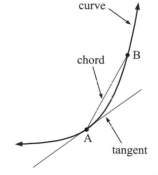

However, as B gets closer to A, the chord [AB] approaches the line which *touches* the curve at A. This line is called the **tangent** to the curve at A.

DEMO

In particular, as B approaches A, the gradient of [AB] approaches the gradient of the tangent at A.

The **instantaneous rate of change** in $f(x)$ at any point A on the curve is the **gradient of the tangent** at A.

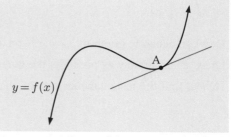

$y = f(x)$

Example 1 🔊 **Self Tutor**

Use the tangents drawn to find the instantaneous rate of change in $y = f(x)$ at:

a A **b** B

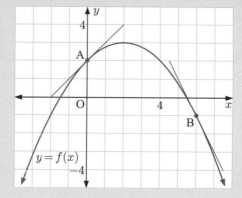

$y = f(x)$

a The tangent at A has gradient 1.
∴ the instantaneous rate of change at A is 1.

b The tangent at B has gradient -2.
∴ the instantaneous rate of change at B is -2.

EXERCISE 14B

1 This graph shows the distance travelled by a swimmer in a pool.

Use the tangents drawn to find the swimmer's instantaneous speed after:

    a 30 seconds

    b 90 seconds.

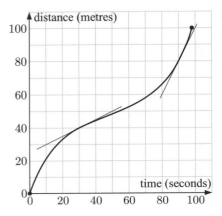

2

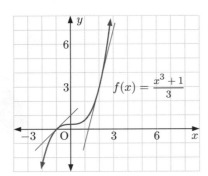

The graph of $f(x) = \dfrac{x^3 + 1}{3}$ is shown alongside.

Use the tangents drawn to find the instantaneous rate of change in $f(x)$ at:

    a $x = -1$

    b $x = 2$.

3 **a** Draw an accurate graph of $y = x^2$ on a fine grid.

    b Draw, as accurately as possible, the tangent to $y = x^2$ at $x = -1$.

    c Hence, find the instantaneous rate of change in $y = x^2$ when $x = -1$.

PRINTABLE GRAPH

C   FINDING THE GRADIENT OF THE TANGENT

Drawing a tangent on a graph and measuring its gradient can be time-consuming and inaccurate. We therefore seek a more efficient and accurate method for finding the gradient of a tangent.

We cannot find the gradient of the tangent at point A by direct calculation, because we only know one point on the tangent. However, if B is another point on the function $y = f(x)$, we can find an expression for the gradient of the chord [AB].

The gradient is $\dfrac{f(a + h) - f(a)}{h}$.

Another way to express this gradient is using the **Leibniz notation** $\dfrac{\delta y}{\delta x}$

where $\delta y = f(a + h) - f(a)$ is the vertical step

and $\delta x = h$ is the horizontal step.

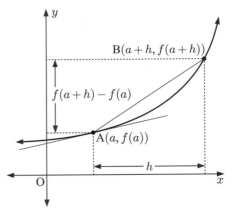

δx reads as "delta x", and refers to the *change* in x.

To calculate the gradient of the tangent at A, we let the point B get closer and closer to A. This means that the horizontal step $\delta x = h$ becomes infinitely small.

To understand what happens when this occurs, we use a mathematical principle called **limits**.

LIMITS

The following definition of a limit is informal but adequate for the purposes of this course:

> If $f(x)$ is as close as we like to some real number A for all x sufficiently close to (but not equal to) a, then we say that $f(x)$ has a **limit** of A as x approaches a, and we write
>
> $$\lim_{x \to a} f(x) = A.$$
>
> In this case, $f(x)$ is said to **converge** to A as x approaches a.

Notice that the limit is defined for x close to but *not equal to a*. Whether the function f is defined or not at $x = a$ is not important to the definition of the limit of f as x approaches a. What *is* important is the behaviour of the function as x gets *very close to a*.

Limits are very important in the study of calculus.

For example, suppose we wish to find the limit of $f(x) = \dfrac{5x + x^2}{x}$ as $x \to 0$.

It is tempting for us to simply substitute $x = 0$ into $f(x)$. However, in doing this, not only do we get the meaningless value of $\frac{0}{0}$, but also we ignore the basic limit definition.

Instead, observe that if $f(x) = \dfrac{5x + x^2}{x} = \dfrac{x(5 + x)}{x}$

then $f(x) = \begin{cases} 5 + x & \text{if } x \neq 0 \\ \text{is undefined if } x = 0. \end{cases}$

This enables us to draw the graph of $y = f(x)$. It is the straight line $y = x + 5$ with the point $(0, 5)$ missing, called a **point of discontinuity** of the function.

However, even though this point is missing, the *limit* of $f(x)$ as x approaches 0 does exist. In particular, as $x \to 0$ from either direction, $f(x) \to 5$.

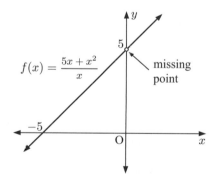

We write $\lim\limits_{x \to 0} \dfrac{5x + x^2}{x} = 5$ which reads:

"the limit as x approaches 0, of $\dfrac{5x + x^2}{x}$, is 5".

Note that we could define a function $g(x) = 5 + x$ for all x, and that in this case $f(x) = g(x)$ for all $x \neq 0$. However, since $f(x)$ is not defined at $x = 0$, f and g are different functions.

In practice we do not need to graph functions each time to determine limits, and most can be found algebraically.

Example 2

◀)) **Self Tutor**

Evaluate:

a $\lim\limits_{x \to 2} x^2$

b $\lim\limits_{x \to 0} \dfrac{x^2 + 3x}{x}$

c $\lim\limits_{x \to 3} \dfrac{x^2 - 9}{x - 3}$

a x^2 can be made as close as we like to 4 by making x sufficiently close to 2.

$\therefore \quad \lim\limits_{x \to 2} x^2 = 4$.

b
$$\lim\limits_{x \to 0} \dfrac{x^2 + 3x}{x}$$
$$= \lim\limits_{x \to 0} \dfrac{x(x + 3)}{x}$$
$$= \lim\limits_{x \to 0} (x + 3) \qquad \{\text{since } x \neq 0\}$$
$$= 3 \qquad\qquad \{\text{as } x \to 0, \ x + 3 \to 3\}$$

c
$$\lim\limits_{x \to 3} \dfrac{x^2 - 9}{x - 3}$$
$$= \lim\limits_{x \to 3} \dfrac{(x + 3)(x - 3)}{x - 3}$$
$$= \lim\limits_{x \to 3} (x + 3) \qquad \{\text{since } x \neq 3\}$$
$$= 6 \qquad\qquad \{\text{as } x \to 3, \ x + 3 \to 6\}$$

EXERCISE 14C.1

1 Evaluate:

a $\lim\limits_{x \to 3} (x + 4)$

b $\lim\limits_{x \to -1} (5 - 2x)$

c $\lim\limits_{x \to 4} (3x - 1)$

d $\lim\limits_{x \to 2} (5x^2 - 3x + 2)$

e $\lim\limits_{h \to 0} h^2(1 - h)$

f $\lim\limits_{x \to 0} (x^2 + 5)$

2 Evaluate:

a $\lim\limits_{x \to 0} 5$

b $\lim\limits_{h \to 2} 7$

c $\lim\limits_{x \to 0} c, \quad c$ a constant

3 Evaluate:

a $\lim\limits_{x \to 1} \dfrac{x^2 - 3x}{x}$

b $\lim\limits_{h \to 2} \dfrac{h^2 + 5h}{h}$

c $\lim\limits_{x \to 0} \dfrac{x - 1}{x + 1}$

d $\lim\limits_{x \to 0} \dfrac{x}{x}$

4 Evaluate:

a $\lim\limits_{x \to 0} \dfrac{x^2 - 3x}{x}$

b $\lim\limits_{x \to 0} \dfrac{x^2 + 5x}{x}$

c $\lim\limits_{x \to 0} \dfrac{2x^2 - x}{x}$

d $\lim\limits_{h \to 0} \dfrac{2h^2 + 6h}{h}$

e $\lim\limits_{h \to 0} \dfrac{3h^2 - 4h}{h}$

f $\lim\limits_{h \to 0} \dfrac{h^3 - 8h}{h}$

g $\lim\limits_{x \to 1} \dfrac{x^2 - x}{x - 1}$

h $\lim\limits_{x \to 2} \dfrac{x^2 - 2x}{x - 2}$

i $\lim\limits_{x \to 3} \dfrac{x^2 - x - 6}{x - 3}$

Discussion

1 Do limits always exist?

2 Consider the graph of $f(x) = \dfrac{1}{x}$.

    a What happens to the graph as $x \to 0$ from the:

        i left

        ii right?

    b Does $f(x) = \dfrac{1}{x}$ have a limit as $x \to 0$?

GRADIENT OF THE TANGENT AT A PARTICULAR POINT

We have seen that for two points A$(a, f(a))$ and B$(a + h, f(a + h))$ on a function, the gradient of the chord [AB] is $\dfrac{f(a+h) - f(a)}{h}$.

Letting B get infinitely close to A is equivalent to taking the limit of $h \to 0$.

The gradient of the tangent to the curve $y = f(x)$
at the point where $x = a$ is

$$\lim_{h \to 0} \frac{f(a+h) - f(a)}{h}.$$

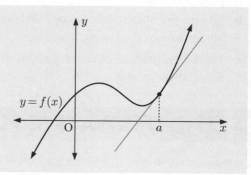

Using Leibniz notation, we write $\displaystyle\lim_{\delta x \to 0} \frac{\delta y}{\delta x}$.

Example 3   ◀)) Self Tutor

Find the gradient of the tangent to $f(x) = x^2$ at the point $(2, 4)$.

Let F be the point $(2, 4)$ and M have the x-coordinate $2 + h$, so M is $(2 + h, (2 + h)^2)$.

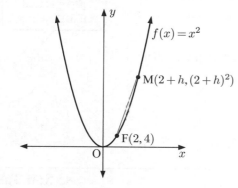

The gradient of the tangent at F

$$= \lim_{h \to 0} \frac{f(2 + h) - f(2)}{h}$$

$$= \lim_{h \to 0} \frac{(2 + h)^2 - 4}{h}$$

$$= \lim_{h \to 0} \frac{\cancel{4} + 4h + h^2 - \cancel{4}}{h}$$

$$= \lim_{h \to 0} \frac{\cancel{h}(4 + h)}{\cancel{h}}$$

$$= \lim_{h \to 0} (4 + h) \qquad \{\text{as } h \neq 0\}$$

$$= 4$$

EXERCISE 14C.2

1 F$(3, 9)$ lies on the graph of $f(x) = x^2$. M also lies on the graph, and has x-coordinate $3 + h$.

   a State the y-coordinate of M.

   b Show that the gradient of the line segment [FM] is $6 + h$.

   c Hence find the gradient of [FM] where M has coordinates:

       i $(4, 16)$ **ii** $(3.5, 12.25)$ **iii** $(3.1, 9.61)$ **iv** $(3.01, 9.0601)$

   d Use limits to find the gradient of the tangent to $f(x) = x^2$ at the point $(3, 9)$.

2 Find the gradient of the tangent to:

    a $f(x) = x^2 + x$ at the point $(2, 6)$

    b $f(x) = x^3$ at the point where $x = 1$

    c $f(x) = \dfrac{4}{x}$ at the point where $x = 2$

    d $f(x) = x^4$ at the point where $x = 1$.

3 **a** Find the gradient of the tangent to $f(x) = x^2$ at the point where $x = 4$.

    b Use the previous results to copy and complete the table alongside for $f(x) = x^2$.

    c Predict the gradient of the tangent to $f(x) = x^2$ at the point where $x = a$.

x-coordinate	Gradient of tangent
1	
2	
3	
4	

D THE DERIVATIVE FUNCTION

For a non-linear curve $y = f(x)$, the gradient of the tangent changes as we move along the curve.

We can therefore write a **gradient function** which gives the gradient of the tangent for any given value of x.

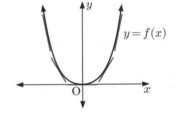

> The gradient function of $y = f(x)$ is called its **derivative function** and is labelled $f'(x)$.

For example, in question **3** of the previous **Exercise**, you should have observed that for $f(x) = x^2$, the gradient of the tangent is always double the x-coordinate. So, for $f(x) = x^2$ we write $f'(x) = 2x$.

$f'(x)$ is read "eff dashed of x".

Substituting a real number a into $f'(x)$ gives us $f'(a)$, which is the gradient of the tangent to $y = f(x)$ at the point where $x = a$.

For $f(x) = x^2$, we have $f'(x) = 2x$

$$\therefore \quad f'(3) = 6$$

$\therefore$ the gradient of the tangent to $f(x) = x^2$ at the point where $x = 3$, is 6.

Example 4 ◀ᴕ Self Tutor

For the given graph, find $f'(4)$.

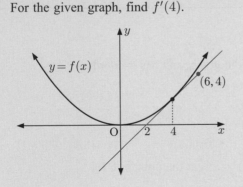

The graph shows the tangent to the curve $y = f(x)$ at the point where $x = 4$.

The tangent passes through $(2, 0)$ and $(6, 4)$.

$$\therefore \quad f'(4) = \text{gradient of the tangent}$$
$$= \frac{4 - 0}{6 - 2}$$
$$= 1$$

Alternatively, in Leibniz notation, since $f'(x) = \lim\limits_{\delta x \to 0} \dfrac{\delta y}{\delta x}$, we can write the derivative function as $\dfrac{dy}{dx}$.

This is called the derivative of y with respect to x, and is read "dee y by dee x".

For example, for $y = x^2$ we have $\dfrac{dy}{dx} = 2x$.

EXERCISE 14D.1

1 Using the graph below, find:

    a $f(0)$ **b** $f'(0)$

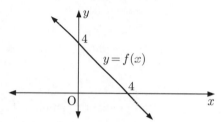

2 Use the graph below to find $f'(2)$.

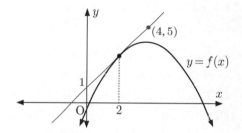

3 For the graph of $y = f(x)$ alongside, decide whether the following are positive or negative:

    a $f(3)$ **b** $f'(1)$

    c $f(-4)$ **d** $f'(-2)$

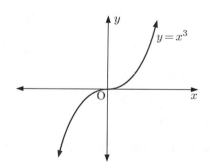

4

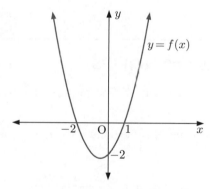

For the graph of $y = f(x)$ alongside, the derivative function is $f'(x) = 2x + 1$.

    a Find and interpret $f'(-2)$ and $f'(0)$.

    b Copy the graph, and include the information in **a**.

5 Consider the graph of $y = x^3$.

Which of the functions below could be the derivative function $\dfrac{dy}{dx}$? Explain your answer.

    A $\dfrac{dy}{dx} = -x^2$ **B** $\dfrac{dy}{dx} = 4x$ **C** $\dfrac{dy}{dx} = 3x^2$

    D $\dfrac{dy}{dx} = 3$ **E** $\dfrac{dy}{dx} = 3(x-2)^2$

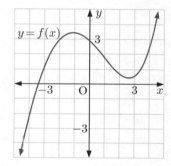

Investigation 2   Gradient functions

The software, accessible using the icon alongside, can be used to find the gradient of the tangent to a function $f(x)$ at any point. By sliding the point along the graph, we observe the changing gradient of the tangent and hence generate the gradient function $f'(x)$.

GRADIENT FUNCTIONS

What to do:

1 Consider the functions $f(x) = 0$, $f(x) = 2$, and $f(x) = 4$.

   a For each of these functions, what is the gradient?

   b Is the gradient constant for all values of x?

2 Consider the function $f(x) = mx + c$.

   a State the gradient of the function.

   b Is the gradient constant for all values of x?

   c Use the software to graph the following functions and observe the gradient function $f'(x)$. Hence verify your answer to **b**.

      i $f(x) = x - 1$ **ii** $f(x) = 3x + 2$ **iii** $f(x) = -2x + 1$

3 **a** Observe the function $f(x) = x^2$ using the software. What *type* of function is the gradient function $f'(x)$?

   b Observe the following quadratic functions using the software:

      i $f(x) = x^2 + x - 2$ **ii** $f(x) = 2x^2 - 3$

      iii $f(x) = -x^2 + 2x - 1$ **iv** $f(x) = -3x^2 - 3x + 6$

   c What *type* of function is each of the gradient functions $f'(x)$ in **b**?

4 **a** Observe the function $f(x) = e^x$ using the software.

   b What is the gradient function $f'(x)$?

FINDING THE DERIVATIVE FUNCTION FROM FIRST PRINCIPLES

To find the derivative function $f'(x)$ for a function $f(x)$, we use limit theory to find the gradient of the tangent to the curve at a general point $(x,\ f(x))$.

Consider a general function $y = f(x)$ where A is the point $(x,\ f(x))$ and B is the point $(x+h,\ f(x+h))$.

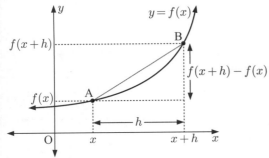

The chord [AB] has gradient $= \dfrac{f(x+h) - f(x)}{x + h - x}$

$$= \dfrac{f(x+h) - f(x)}{h}$$

If we let B approach A, then the gradient of [AB] approaches the gradient of the tangent at A.

So, the gradient of the tangent at the general point $(x,\ f(x))$ is $\displaystyle \lim_{h \to 0} \dfrac{f(x+h) - f(x)}{h}$.

This formula is valid for any value of x for which this limit exists.

Since there is at most one value of the gradient for each value of x, the formula is actually a function.

> The **derivative function** or simply **derivative** of $y = f(x)$ is defined as
>
> $$f'(x) \text{ or } \frac{dy}{dx} = \lim_{h \to 0} \frac{f(x+h) - f(x)}{h}$$

When we evaluate this limit to find a derivative function, we say we are **differentiating from first principles**.

Example 5   ◀ঠ **Self Tutor**

Use first principles to find the gradient function $f'(x)$ of $f(x) = x^2$.

$$\begin{aligned}
f'(x) &= \lim_{h \to 0} \frac{f(x+h) - f(x)}{h} \\
&= \lim_{h \to 0} \frac{(x+h)^2 - x^2}{h} \\
&= \lim_{h \to 0} \frac{\cancel{x^2} + 2hx + h^2 - \cancel{x^2}}{h} \\
&= \lim_{h \to 0} \frac{\cancel{h}(2x + h)}{\cancel{h}} \\
&= \lim_{h \to 0} (2x + h) \quad \{\text{as } h \neq 0\} \\
&= 2x
\end{aligned}$$

THE DERIVATIVE WHEN $x = a$

The derivative at the point where $x = a$, denoted $f'(a)$, can be found using $f'(a) = \lim_{h \to 0} \frac{f(a+h) - f(a)}{h}$.
We did this in **Section C** on page **323**.

Alternatively, we can find the derivative function $f'(x)$, and then substitute $x = a$ to find $f'(a)$.

Example 6   ◀ঠ **Self Tutor**

a Given $f(x) = x^4$, find $f'(x)$.

b Find $f'(-1)$, and interpret your answer.

a $$\begin{aligned}
f'(x) &= \lim_{h \to 0} \frac{f(x+h) - f(x)}{h} \\
&= \lim_{h \to 0} \frac{(x+h)^4 - x^4}{h} \\
&= \lim_{h \to 0} \frac{\cancel{x^4} + 4x^3 h + 6x^2 h^2 + 4xh^3 + h^4 - \cancel{x^4}}{h} \quad \{\text{binomial expansion}\} \\
&= \lim_{h \to 0} \frac{\cancel{h}(4x^3 + 6x^2 h + 4xh^2 + h^3)}{\cancel{h}} \\
&= \lim_{h \to 0} (4x^3 + 6x^2 h + 4xh^2 + h^3) \quad \{\text{since } h \neq 0\} \\
&= 4x^3
\end{aligned}$$

b $f'(-1) = 4(-1)^3$
$\qquad = -4$

The tangent to $f(x) = x^4$ at the point where
$x = -1$, has gradient -4.

gradient $= -4$

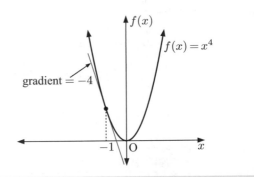

You can also use a graphics calculator to find the gradient of the tangent at a given
point on a function. Instructions for doing this can be found by clicking on the
icon.

**GRAPHICS
CALCULATOR
INSTRUCTIONS**

EXERCISE 14D.2

1 Find, from first principles, the gradient function of $f(x)$ where $f(x)$ is:

    a x **b** 1 **c** x^3

2 Find $f'(x)$ from first principles, given that $f(x)$ is:

    a $2x + 5$ **b** $x^2 - 3x$ **c** $-x^2 + 5x - 3$

3 Find $\dfrac{dy}{dx}$ from first principles given:

    a $y = 4 - x$ **b** $y = 2x^2 + x - 1$ **c** $y = x^3 - 2x^2 + 3$

4 Use the first principles formula $f'(a) = \displaystyle\lim_{h \to 0} \dfrac{f(a+h) - f(a)}{h}$ to find:

    a $f'(2)$ for $f(x) = x^3$ **b** $f'(3)$ for $f(x) = x^4$.

5 **a** Find $f'(x)$ given $f(x) = \dfrac{1}{x}$.   **b** Find $f'(-1)$ and $f'(3)$, and interpret your answers.

6 The graph of $f(x) = -x^2 + 3x$ is shown alongside.

    a Use the graph to estimate the gradient of the tangent to
       the curve at the point where:

       i $x = 0$ **ii** $x = 2$.

    b Find $f'(x)$ from first principles.

    c Find $f'(0)$ and $f'(2)$, and hence check your estimates
       in **a**.

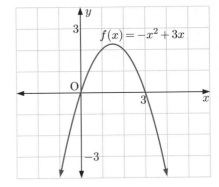

7 **a** Given $y = x^3 - 3x$, find $\dfrac{dy}{dx}$ from first principles.

    b Hence find the points on the graph at which the tangent has zero gradient.

8 The graph of $f(x) = 2x^2 + 2x - 12$ is shown alongside.

   a Find $f'(x)$.

   b Hence, find the point where the tangent has gradient -2.

   c Copy the graph, and include the information in **b**.

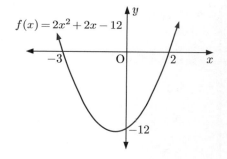

9

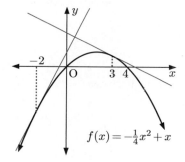

The graph of $f(x) = -\frac{1}{4}x^2 + x$ is shown alongside.

   a Find $f'(x)$.

   b Hence, show that the illustrated tangents are perpendicular.

10   **a** Use the previous results to copy and complete the table alongside.

    b Copy and complete:

       If $f(x) = x^n$, then $f'(x) = \ \text{......}$

$f(x)$	$f'(x)$
x^1	
x^2	
x^3	
x^4	
x^{-1}	
x^0	

Discussion

  1 Does a function always have a derivative function?

  2 Are the domains of a function and its derivative always the same?

Review set 14A

1 Find the average rate of change in $f(x)$ from A to B.

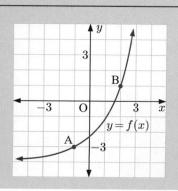

2 Chantelle is riding in a ski-lift. Her height above the base of the mountain is shown on the graph below.

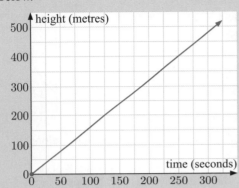

  a Is the ski-lift increasing in height at a constant rate? Explain your answer.

  b Find the rate at which the ski-lift is increasing in height.

3 Evaluate:

  a $\lim\limits_{x \to 1} (6x - 7)$

  b $\lim\limits_{h \to 0} \dfrac{2h^2 - h}{h}$

  c $\lim\limits_{x \to 4} \dfrac{x^2 - 16}{x - 4}$

4 Consider $f(x) = 2x^2$.

  a Show that $\dfrac{f(x + h) - f(x)}{h} = 4x + 2h$ provided $h \neq 0$.

  b Hence evaluate $\dfrac{f(3 + h) - f(3)}{h}$:

   i when $h = 0.1$

   ii when $h = 0.01$

   iii in the limit as h approaches zero.

  c Give a geometric interpretation of your result from **b**.

5 Use the graph alongside to find $f'(3)$.

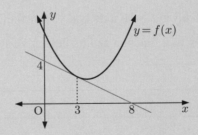

6 Find, from first principles, the derivative of:

  a $f(x) = x^2 + 2x$

  b $y = 4 - 3x^2$

7 **a** Given $y = 2x^2 - 1$, find $\dfrac{dy}{dx}$ from first principles.

  b Hence state the gradient of the tangent to $y = 2x^2 - 1$ at the point where $x = 4$.

  c For what value of x is the gradient of the tangent to $y = 2x^2 - 1$ equal to -12?

8 The graph of $f(x) = x^3 - 3x^2$ is shown alongside.

   a Find $f'(x)$.

   b Hence, show that the illustrated tangents are parallel.

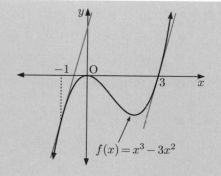

Review set 14B

1

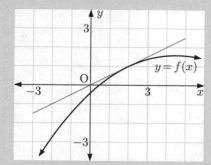

Use the tangent drawn to find the instantaneous rate of change in $f(x)$ at $x = 2$.

2 This graph shows the temperature in Berlin from 6 am to 6 pm on a particular day.

Find the average rate of change in temperature from:

   a 7 am to noon

   b 3 pm to 5 pm.

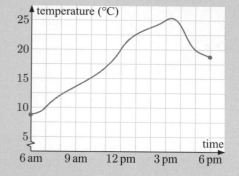

3 Evaluate the limits:

   a $\displaystyle\lim_{h \to 0} \frac{h^3 - 3h}{h}$

   b $\displaystyle\lim_{x \to 1} \frac{3x^2 - 3x}{x - 1}$

   c $\displaystyle\lim_{x \to 2} \frac{x^2 - 3x + 2}{2 - x}$

4

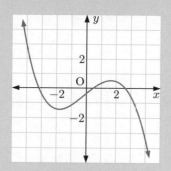

Decide whether the following are positive or negative:

   a $f(-1)$ **b** $f'(0)$

   c $f(2)$ **d** $f'(3)$

5 **a** Draw an accurate graph of $f(x) = x^2 - 2$.

   b Draw, as accurately as possible, the tangent to $f(x) = x^2 - 2$ at $x = 2$.

   c Hence, find the instantaneous rate of change in $f(x) = x^2 - 2$ when $x = 2$.

   d Check your answer using $f'(a) = \lim\limits_{h \to 0} \dfrac{f(a+h) - f(a)}{h}$.

6 **a** Find $f'(x)$ given $f(x) = x^4 - 2x$.

   b Find $f'(-2)$ and interpret your answer.

7 **a** Given $y = x^2 + 5x - 2$, find $\dfrac{dy}{dx}$ from first principles.

   b Hence find the point on the graph at which the tangent has gradient -3.

8 In a BASE jumping competition from the Petronas Towers in Kuala Lumpur, the altitude of a professional jumper in the first 3 seconds is given by $f(t) = 452 - 4.8t^2$ metres, where $0 \leqslant t \leqslant 3$ seconds.

   a Find the height of the jumper after:

   i 1 second   **ii** 2 seconds.

   b Find $f'(t)$ from first principles.

   c Find the speed of the jumper after:

   i 1 second   **ii** 2 seconds.

15

Derivatives and their applications

Contents:

Opening problem

Consider the curve $y = x^2$.

In the previous Chapter we found that the gradient function of

this curve is $\dfrac{dy}{dx} = 2x$.

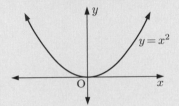

Things to think about:

a At which point on the graph of $y = x^2$ is the tangent to the curve horizontal?

b Consider the transformation of $y = x^2$ onto $y = x^2 + 3$.

  i What transformation has taken place?

  ii For a given value of x, has the gradient of the tangent to the function changed?

  iii What is the gradient function of $y = x^2 + 3$?

  DEMO

c Consider the transformation of $y = x^2$ onto $y = (x - 2)^2$.

  i What transformation has taken place?

  ii How does the gradient function of $y = (x - 2)^2$ relate to the gradient function of $y = x^2$?

  iii Can you write down the gradient function of $y = (x - 2)^2$?

d Consider the transformation of $y = x^2$ onto $y = 2x^2$.

  i What transformation has taken place?

  ii How does the gradient function of $y = 2x^2$ relate to the gradient function of $y = x^2$? If necessary, use the software to help you.

In this Chapter we will discover rules which make it easier to find derivative functions. We will also see how derivatives can be used to analyse graphs, and to solve problems involving **kinematics** (movement) and **optimisation**.

A   SIMPLE RULES OF DIFFERENTIATION

Differentiation is the process of finding a derivative or gradient function.

Given a function $f(x)$, we obtain $f'(x)$ by **differentiating with respect to** the variable x.

There are a number of rules associated with differentiation. These rules can be used to differentiate more complicated functions without having to use first principles.

Investigation   Simple rules of differentiation

In this Investigation we attempt to differentiate functions of the form cx^n where c is a constant, and functions which are a sum or difference of polynomial terms of the form cx^n.

What to do:

1 Differentiate using first principles:

   a x^2 **b** x^3 **c** x^4

2 Consider the binomial expansion:
$$(x + h)^n = \binom{n}{0} x^n + \binom{n}{1} x^{n-1}h + \binom{n}{2} x^{n-2}h^2 + ... + \binom{n}{n} h^n$$
$$= x^n + nx^{n-1}h + \binom{n}{2} x^{n-2}h^2 + ... + h^n$$

Use the first principles formula $f'(x) = \lim\limits_{h \to 0} \dfrac{f(x + h) - f(x)}{h}$ to find the derivative of $f(x) = x^n$ for $x \in \mathbb{N}$.

3 **a** Differentiate using first principles: **i** $4x^2$ **ii** $2x^3$ **iii** $7x^4$

    b By comparison with **1**, copy and complete: "If $f(x) = cx^n$, then $f'(x) = $ ......"

4 **a** Use first principles to find $f'(x)$ for:

      i $f(x) = x^2 + 3x$ **ii** $f(x) = x^3 - 2x^2$

    b Copy and complete: "If $f(x) = u(x) + v(x)$, then $f'(x) = $ ......"

The rules you found in the **Investigation** can actually be used much more widely than the cases you just considered.

For example, the rule "if $f(x) = x^n$ then $f'(x) = nx^{n-1}$" is true not just for all $n \in \mathbb{N}$, but actually for all $n \in \mathbb{R}$.

We can summarise the following rules:

$f(x)$	$f'(x)$	Name of rule
c (a constant)	0	**differentiating a constant**
x^n	nx^{n-1}	**differentiating x^n**
$c\,u(x)$	$c\,u'(x)$	**constant times a function**
$u(x) + v(x)$	$u'(x) + v'(x)$	**addition rule**

The last two rules can be proved using the first principles definition of $f'(x)$.

- If $f(x) = c\,u(x)$,
  then $f'(x) = c\,u'(x)$.

  Proof:

  $f'(x)$

  $= \lim\limits_{h \to 0} \dfrac{f(x + h) - f(x)}{h}$

  $= \lim\limits_{h \to 0} \dfrac{c\,u(x + h) - c\,u(x)}{h}$

  $= \lim\limits_{h \to 0} c \left[\dfrac{u(x + h) - u(x)}{h} \right]$

  $= c \lim\limits_{h \to 0} \dfrac{u(x + h) - u(x)}{h}$

  $= c\,u'(x)$

- If $f(x) = u(x) + v(x)$,
  then $f'(x) = u'(x) + v'(x)$

  Proof:

  $f'(x)$

  $= \lim\limits_{h \to 0} \dfrac{f(x + h) - f(x)}{h}$

  $= \lim\limits_{h \to 0} \left(\dfrac{u(x + h) + v(x + h) - [u(x) + v(x)]}{h} \right)$

  $= \lim\limits_{h \to 0} \left(\dfrac{u(x + h) - u(x) + v(x + h) - v(x)}{h} \right)$

  $= \lim\limits_{h \to 0} \dfrac{u(x + h) - u(x)}{h} + \lim\limits_{h \to 0} \dfrac{v(x + h) - v(x)}{h}$

  $= u'(x) + v'(x)$

Using the rules we have now developed, we can differentiate sums of powers of x.

For example,   if $f(x) = 3x^4 + 2x^3 - 5x^2 + 7x + 6$ then

$$f'(x) = 3(4x^3) + 2(3x^2) - 5(2x) + 7(1) + 0$$
$$= 12x^3 + 6x^2 - 10x + 7$$

Example 1
◀) **Self Tutor**

Find $f'(x)$ for $f(x)$ equal to:

a $5x^3 + 6x^2 - 3x + 2$

b $7x - \dfrac{4}{x} + \dfrac{3}{x^3}$

a $f(x) = 5x^3 + 6x^2 - 3x + 2$

$\therefore$ $f'(x) = 5(3x^2) + 6(2x) - 3(1)$

$\qquad = 15x^2 + 12x - 3$

b $f(x) = 7x - \dfrac{4}{x} + \dfrac{3}{x^3}$

$\qquad = 7x - 4x^{-1} + 3x^{-3}$

$\therefore$ $f'(x) = 7(1) - 4(-1x^{-2}) + 3(-3x^{-4})$

$\qquad = 7 + 4x^{-2} - 9x^{-4}$

$\qquad = 7 + \dfrac{4}{x^2} - \dfrac{9}{x^4}$

EXERCISE 15A

1 Find $f'(x)$ given that $f(x)$ is:

a x^3
b x^8
c x^{11}
d $6x$

e $2x^3$
f $7x^2$
g $3x^5$
h $5x^6$

i $x^2 + x$
j $x^2 + 3x - 5$
k $5x - 2$
l $x^2 + 3$

m $2x^2 + x - 1$
n $3x^2 - 7x + 8$
o $4 - 2x^2$
p $\frac{1}{2}x^4 - 6x^2$

q $x^3 - 4x^2 + 6x$
r $7 - x - 4x^3$
s $\frac{1}{5}x^3 - \frac{7}{2}x^2 - 2$
t $(2x - 1)^2$

2 Differentiate with respect to x:

a $\dfrac{1}{x^2}$
b $\dfrac{1}{x^5}$
c $\dfrac{1}{x^8}$

d $\dfrac{3}{x}$
e $\dfrac{4}{x^3}$
f $-\dfrac{7}{x^4}$

g $2x + \dfrac{3}{x^2}$
h $x^2 - \dfrac{6}{x}$
i $9 - \dfrac{2}{x^3}$

j $\dfrac{1}{x} - \dfrac{5}{x^3}$
k $\dfrac{2}{x^2} + \dfrac{9}{x^4}$
l $3x - \dfrac{1}{x} + \dfrac{2}{x^2}$

m $5 - \dfrac{8}{x^2} + \dfrac{4}{x^3}$
n $\dfrac{1}{5x^2}$
o $4x - \dfrac{1}{4x}$

p $\dfrac{x^2 - 3}{x}$
q $\dfrac{x^3 + 4}{x}$
r $\dfrac{2x - 5}{x^2}$

Remember that
$\dfrac{1}{x^n} = x^{-n}$.

Example 2
◆ **Self Tutor**

Find the gradient function for:

a $f(x) = 3\sqrt{x} + \dfrac{2}{x}$

b $g(x) = x^2 - \dfrac{4}{\sqrt{x}}$

a $f(x) = 3\sqrt{x} + \dfrac{2}{x}$

$\qquad = 3x^{\frac{1}{2}} + 2x^{-1}$

$\therefore \ f'(x) = 3(\tfrac{1}{2}x^{-\frac{1}{2}}) + 2(-1x^{-2})$

$\qquad = \tfrac{3}{2}x^{-\frac{1}{2}} - 2x^{-2}$

$\qquad = \dfrac{3}{2\sqrt{x}} - \dfrac{2}{x^2}$

b $g(x) = x^2 - \dfrac{4}{\sqrt{x}}$

$\qquad = x^2 - 4x^{-\frac{1}{2}}$

$\therefore \ g'(x) = 2x - 4(-\tfrac{1}{2}x^{-\frac{3}{2}})$

$\qquad = 2x + 2x^{-\frac{3}{2}}$

$\qquad = 2x + \dfrac{2}{x\sqrt{x}}$

3 Find the gradient function for $f(x)$ where $f(x)$ is:

a $\sqrt{x}$

b $\sqrt[3]{x}$

c $\dfrac{1}{\sqrt{x}}$

d $\dfrac{1}{x^2} + 6\sqrt{x}$

e $2x - \sqrt{x}$

f $x\sqrt{x}$

g $2x^2 - \dfrac{3}{\sqrt{x}}$

h $\dfrac{x+5}{\sqrt{x}}$

i $\dfrac{7 - x^2}{\sqrt{x}}$

j $3x^2 - x\sqrt{x}$

k $\dfrac{4}{x^2\sqrt{x}}$

l $2x - \dfrac{3}{x\sqrt{x}}$

4 Find $\dfrac{dy}{dx}$ for:

a $y = 100x$

b $y = \pi x^2$

c $y = 6\sqrt{x} + \dfrac{5}{x}$

d $y = 2.5x^3 - 1.4x^2 - 1.3$

e $y = 10(x + 1)$

f $y = 4\pi x^3$

g $y = (x + 1)(x - 2)$

h $y = (5 - x)^2$

i $y = x(x + 1)(2x - 5)$

Example 3
◆ **Self Tutor**

Find the derivative of $y = x^2 - \dfrac{4}{x}$, and hence find the gradient of the tangent to the function at the point where $x = 2$.

$y = x^2 - \dfrac{4}{x} = x^2 - 4x^{-1}$

$\therefore \ \dfrac{dy}{dx} = 2x - 4(-1x^{-2})$

$\qquad = 2x + 4x^{-2}$

$\qquad = 2x + \dfrac{4}{x^2}$

When $x = 2$, $\dfrac{dy}{dx} = 4 + 1 = 5$. So, the tangent has gradient 5.

5 Find the gradient of the tangent to:

a $y = x^2$ at $x = 2$

b $y = x^3 - 5x + 2$ at the point $(3, 14)$

c $y = \dfrac{8}{x^2}$ at the point $\left(9, \frac{8}{81}\right)$

d $y = 2x^2 - 3x + 7$ at $x = -1$

e $y = 3\sqrt{x}$ at the point $(1, 3)$

f $y = 2x - \dfrac{5}{x}$ at the point $\left(2, \frac{3}{2}\right)$

g $y = \dfrac{x^2 - 4}{x^2}$ at the point $\left(4, \frac{3}{4}\right)$

h $y = \dfrac{x^3 - 4x - 8}{x^2}$ at $x = -1$

6 Suppose $f(x) = x^2 + (b+1)x + 2c$, $f(2) = 4$, and $f'(-1) = 2$. Find the constants b and c.

Example 4   ◀)) **Self Tutor**

If $y = 3x^2 - 4x$, find $\dfrac{dy}{dx}$ and interpret its meaning.

As $y = 3x^2 - 4x$, $\dfrac{dy}{dx} = 6x - 4$.

$\dfrac{dy}{dx}$ is the gradient function or derivative of $y = 3x^2 - 4x$ from which the gradient of the tangent at any point on the curve can be found. It is also the instantaneous rate of change of y with respect to x.

---

7 If $y = 4x - \dfrac{3}{x}$, find $\dfrac{dy}{dx}$ and interpret its meaning.

8 Consider the function $f(x) = \sqrt{x} - \dfrac{4}{\sqrt{x}}$.

a State the domain of $f(x)$.

b Find the derivative function $f'(x)$.

c State the domain of $f'(x)$.

d Find $f'(1)$ and interpret your answer.

9 The position of a car moving along a straight road is given by $S = 2t^2 + 4t$ metres where t is the time in seconds.

a Find $\dfrac{dS}{dt}$ and interpret its meaning.

b Find the value of $\dfrac{dS}{dt}$ when $t = 3$, and interpret your answer.

10 The cost of producing x toasters each week is given by $C = 1785 + 3x + 0.002x^2$ pounds. Find the value of $\dfrac{dC}{dx}$ when $x = 1000$, and interpret its meaning.

B   SECOND DERIVATIVES

Given a function $f(x)$, the derivative $f'(x)$ is known as the **first derivative**.

The **second derivative** of $f(x)$ is the derivative of $f'(x)$, or **the derivative of the first derivative**.

We use $f''(x)$, y'', or $\dfrac{d^2y}{dx^2}$ to represent the second derivative.

$f''(x)$ reads "f *double dashed* x".

$\dfrac{d^2y}{dx^2} = \dfrac{d}{dx}\left(\dfrac{dy}{dx}\right)$ reads "*dee two y by dee x squared*".

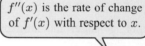 $f''(x)$ is the rate of change of $f'(x)$ with respect to x.

Example 5 🔊 Self Tutor

Find $f''(x)$ given that $f(x) = x^3 - \dfrac{3}{x}$.

Now $f(x) = x^3 - 3x^{-1}$

$\therefore\ f'(x) = 3x^2 + 3x^{-2}$

$\therefore\ f''(x) = 6x - 6x^{-3}$

$ = 6x - \dfrac{6}{x^3}$

EXERCISE 15B

1 Find $f''(x)$ given that:

   a $f(x) = 3x^2 - 6x + 2$ **b** $f(x) = \dfrac{2}{\sqrt{x}} - 1$ **c** $f(x) = 2x^3 - 3x^2 - x + 5$

   d $f(x) = \dfrac{2 - 3x}{x^2}$ **e** $f(x) = (1 - 2x)^2$

2 Find $\dfrac{d^2y}{dx^2}$ given that:

   a $y = x - x^3$ **b** $y = x^2 - \dfrac{5}{x^2}$ **c** $y = 2 - \dfrac{3}{\sqrt{x}}$

   d $y = \dfrac{4 - x}{x}$ **e** $y = (x^2 - 3x)^2$

3 Given $f(x) = x^3 - 2x + 5$, find: **a** $f(2)$ **b** $f'(2)$ **c** $f''(2)$

4 Find the value(s) of x such that $f''(x) = 0$, given:

   a $f(x) = 2x^3 - 6x^2 + 5x + 1$ **b** $f(x) = x^4 - 10x^3 + 36x^2 - 72x + 108$

5 Consider the function $f(x) = 2x^3 - x$.

Copy and complete the table alongside by indicating whether $f(x)$, $f'(x)$, and $f''(x)$ are positive $(+)$, negative $(-)$, or zero (0) at the given values of x.

x	-1	0	1
$f(x)$	$-$		
$f'(x)$			
$f''(x)$			

6 Given $f(x) = x^2 - \dfrac{1}{x}$, find: **a** $f(1)$ **b** $f'(1)$ **c** $f''(1)$

C   TANGENTS AND NORMALS

TANGENTS

> The **tangent** to a curve at point A is the best approximating straight line to the curve at A.

In cases we have seen already, the tangent *touches* the curve.

For example, consider the tangents to the circle and quadratic shown.

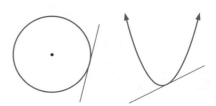

However, we note that for some functions:

- The tangent may intersect the curve again somewhere else.
- It is possible for the tangent to pass through the curve at the point of tangency. If this happens, we call it a **point of inflection**.

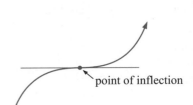

point of inflection

Consider a curve $y = f(x)$.

If A is the point with x-coordinate a, then the gradient of the tangent to the curve at this point is $f'(a)$.

The equation of the tangent is

$$y - f(a) = f'(a)(x - a)$$

or $\boxed{y = f'(a)(x - a) + f(a).}$

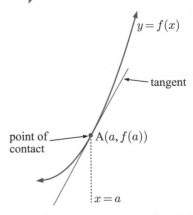

$y = f(x)$

tangent

point of contact

A$(a, f(a))$

$x = a$

Example 6   ◀》 **Self Tutor**

Find the equation of the tangent to $f(x) = x^2 + 1$ at the point where $x = 1$.

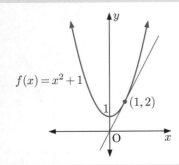

$f(x) = x^2 + 1$

$(1, 2)$

Since $f(1) = 1^2 + 1 = 2$, the point of contact is $(1, 2)$.

Now $f'(x) = 2x$, so at $x = 1$ the tangent has gradient $f'(1) = 2$.

∴   the tangent has equation $y = 2(x - 1) + 2$

which is $y = 2x$.

NORMALS

A **normal** to a curve is a line which is perpendicular to the tangent at the point of contact.

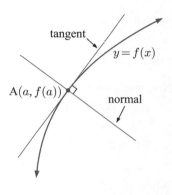

The gradients of perpendicular lines are negative reciprocals of each other, so:

The gradient of the normal to the curve at $x = a$ is $-\dfrac{1}{f'(a)}$.

The equation of the normal to the curve at $x = a$ is

$$y = -\dfrac{1}{f'(a)}(x - a) + f(a).$$

Example 7   🔊 Self Tutor

Find the equation of the normal to $y = \dfrac{8}{\sqrt{x}}$ at the point where $x = 4$.

When $x = 4$, $y = \dfrac{8}{\sqrt{4}} = \dfrac{8}{2} = 4$.   So, the point of contact is $(4, 4)$.

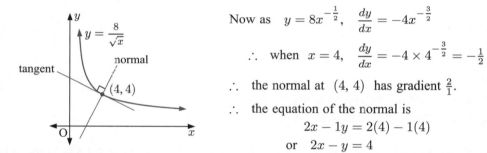

Now as $y = 8x^{-\frac{1}{2}}$, $\dfrac{dy}{dx} = -4x^{-\frac{3}{2}}$

$\therefore$ when $x = 4$, $\dfrac{dy}{dx} = -4 \times 4^{-\frac{3}{2}} = -\dfrac{1}{2}$

$\therefore$ the normal at $(4, 4)$ has gradient $\dfrac{2}{1}$.

$\therefore$ the equation of the normal is
$$2x - 1y = 2(4) - 1(4)$$
or $2x - y = 4$

EXERCISE 15C

1 Find the equation of the tangent to:

   a $y = x - 2x^2 + 3$ at $x = 2$

   b $y = \sqrt{x} + 1$ at $x = 4$

   c $y = x^3 - 5x$ at $x = 1$

   d $y = \dfrac{4}{\sqrt{x}}$ at $(1, 4)$

   e $y = \dfrac{3}{x} - \dfrac{1}{x^2}$ at $(-1, -4)$

   f $y = 3x^2 - \dfrac{1}{x}$ at $x = -1$.

2 Find the equation of the normal to:

   a $y = x^2$ at the point $(4, 16)$

   b $y = x^3 - 5x + 2$ at $x = -2$

   c $y = \dfrac{5}{\sqrt{x}} - \sqrt{x}$ at the point $(1, 4)$

   d $y = 8\sqrt{x} - \dfrac{1}{x^2}$ at $x = 1$.

Example 8

◀) **Self Tutor**

Find the equations of any horizontal tangents to $y = x^3 - 12x + 2$.

Since $y = x^3 - 12x + 2$, $\dfrac{dy}{dx} = 3x^2 - 12$

Horizontal tangents have gradient 0,

$\qquad$ so $\quad 3x^2 - 12 = 0$

$\qquad \therefore \ \ 3(x^2 - 4) = 0$

$\therefore \ \ 3(x + 2)(x - 2) = 0$

$\qquad\qquad \therefore \ \ x = -2$ or 2

When $x = 2$, $\quad y = 8 - 24 + 2 = -14$

When $x = -2$, $\ y = -8 + 24 + 2 = 18$

$\therefore \quad$ the points of contact are $(2, -14)$ and $(-2, 18)$

$\therefore \quad$ the tangents are $y = -14$ and $y = 18$.

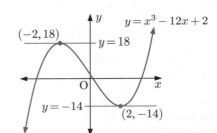

3 Find the equations of any horizontal tangents to:

$\quad$ **a** $\ y = 2x^3 + 3x^2 - 12x + 1$ $\qquad\qquad$ **b** $\ y = -x^3 + 3x^2 + 9x - 4$

4 Find the equation of the horizontal tangent to the curve $y = \sqrt{x} + \dfrac{1}{\sqrt{x}}$.

5 The tangent to $y = 2x^3 + kx^2 - 3$ at the point where $x = 2$ has gradient 4.

$\quad$ **a** Find k.

$\quad$ **b** Find the equation of the tangent at the point where $x = 2$.

$\quad$ **c** Find the equation of the normal at the point where $x = 2$.

6 Find the equation of another tangent to $y = 1 - 3x + 12x^2 - 8x^3$ which is parallel to the tangent at $(1, 2)$.

7 Consider the curve $y = x^2 + ax + b$ where a and b are constants. The tangent to this curve at the point where $x = 1$ is $2x + y = 6$. Find the values of a and b.

8 Consider the curve $y = a\sqrt{x} + \dfrac{b}{\sqrt{x}}$ where a and b are constants. The normal to this curve at the point where $x = 4$ is $4x + y = 22$. Find the values of a and b.

9 Show that the equation of the tangent to $y = 2x^2 - 1$ at the point where $x = a$, is $4ax - y = 2a^2 + 1$.

10 Consider the function $f(x) = x^2 + \dfrac{4}{x^2}$.

$\quad$ **a** Find $f'(x)$.

$\quad$ **b** Find the values of x at which the tangent to the curve is horizontal.

$\quad$ **c** Show that the tangents at these points are the same line.

Example 9

🔊 **Self Tutor**

Find where the tangent to $y = x^3 + x + 2$ at $(1, 4)$ meets the curve again.

Let $f(x) = x^3 + x + 2$

$\therefore \ f'(x) = 3x^2 + 1$ and $\therefore \ f'(1) = 3 + 1 = 4$

$\therefore$ the equation of the tangent at $(1, 4)$ is $4x - y = 4(1) - 4$

or $y = 4x$.

$(x - 1)^2$ must be a factor since we are using the tangent at $x = 1$.

The curve meets the tangent again when $x^3 + x + 2 = 4x$

$\therefore \ x^3 - 3x + 2 = 0$

$\therefore \ (x - 1)^2(x + 2) = 0$

When $x = -2$, $y = (-2)^3 + (-2) + 2 = -8$

$\therefore$ the tangent meets the curve again at $(-2, -8)$.

11   Find where the tangent to the curve $y = x^3$ at the point where $x = 2$, meets the curve again.

12   Find where the tangent to the curve $y = -x^3 + 2x^2 + 1$ at the point where $x = -1$, meets the curve again.

Example 10

🔊 **Self Tutor**

Find the equations of the tangents to $y = x^2$ from the external point $(2, 3)$.

Let (a, a^2) be a general point on $f(x) = x^2$.

Now $f'(x) = 2x$, so $f'(a) = 2a$

$\therefore$ the equation of the tangent at (a, a^2) is

$y = 2a(x - a) + a^2$

which is $y = 2ax - a^2$

Thus the tangents which pass through $(2, 3)$ satisfy

$3 = 2a(2) - a^2$

$\therefore \ a^2 - 4a + 3 = 0$

$\therefore \ (a - 1)(a - 3) = 0$

$\therefore \ a = 1$ or 3

$\therefore$ two tangents pass through the external point $(2, 3)$.

If $a = 1$, the tangent has equation $y = 2x - 1$ with point of contact $(1, 1)$.

If $a = 3$, the tangent has equation $y = 6x - 9$ with point of contact $(3, 9)$.

13   **a**   Find the equation of the tangent to $y = x^2 - x + 9$ at the point where $x = a$.

b   Hence, find the equations of the two tangents from $(0, 0)$ to the curve. State the coordinates of the points of contact.

14 Find the equations of the tangents to $y = x^3$ from the external point $(-2, 0)$.

15 Consider the function $y = 2x^2$.

a Find the equations of the tangents to the function from the external point $(1, -6)$.

b Find the points of contact for the tangents.

c Show that no tangents to the function pass through the point $(1, 4)$.

d Draw a graph of $y = 2x^2$ showing the information above.

16 Find the equation of the normal to $y = \sqrt{x}$ from the external point $(4, 0)$.

Hint: There is no normal at the point where $x = 0$, as this is the end point of the function.

17 Consider $f(x) = \dfrac{8}{x^2}$.

a Sketch the graph of the function.

b Find the equation of the tangent at the point where $x = a$.

c If the tangent in **b** cuts the x-axis at A and the y-axis at B, find the coordinates of A and B.

d Find the area of triangle OAB and discuss the area of the triangle as $a \to \infty$.

D   INCREASING AND DECREASING FUNCTIONS

The concepts of increasing and decreasing functions are closely linked to **intervals** or subsets of a function's domain.

We commonly use the algebraic notation shown in the table to describe subsets of the real numbers corresponding to intervals of the real number line.

Algebraic form	Interval notation	Geometric form
$x \geqslant 2$	$x \in [2, \infty)$	●——→ 2 ... x
$x > 2$	$x \in (2, \infty)$	○——→ 2 ... x
$x \leqslant 4$	$x \in (-\infty, 4]$	←——● 4 x
$x < 4$	$x \in (-\infty, 4)$	←——○ 4 x
$2 \leqslant x \leqslant 4$	$x \in [2, 4]$	●——● 2 ... 4 x
$2 \leqslant x < 4$	$x \in [2, 4)$	●——○ 2 ... 4 x

Suppose S is an interval in the domain of $f(x)$, so $f(x)$ is defined for all x in S.

- $f(x)$ is **increasing** on S $\Leftrightarrow$ $f(a) \leqslant f(b)$ for all $a, b \in S$ such that $a < b$.
- $f(x)$ is **decreasing** on S $\Leftrightarrow$ $f(a) \geqslant f(b)$ for all $a, b \in S$ such that $a < b$.

For example:

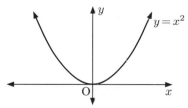

$y = x^2$ is decreasing for $x \leqslant 0$ and increasing for $x \geqslant 0$.

Note that in this example, people will often get confused about the point $x = 0$. They wonder how the curve can be both increasing and decreasing at the same point. The answer is that increasing and decreasing are associated with *intervals*, not particular values for x. We see that $y = x^2$ is decreasing *on the interval* $x \leqslant 0$ and increasing *on the interval* $x \geqslant 0$. The point $x = 0$ is included in both of these intervals because the definitions of increasing and decreasing include $\leqslant$ and $\geqslant$ rather than strict inequalities.

Example 11 ◀)) Self Tutor

Find intervals where $f(x)$ is:

a increasing

b decreasing.

a $f(x)$ is increasing for $x \leqslant -1$ and for $x \geqslant 2$.

b $f(x)$ is decreasing for $-1 \leqslant x \leqslant 2$.

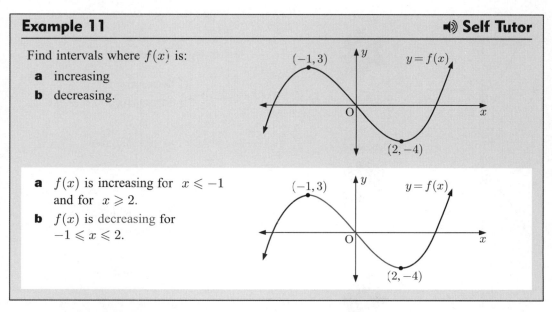

We can determine intervals where a curve $y = f(x)$ is increasing or decreasing by considering $f'(x)$ on the interval in question.

For most functions that we deal with in this course:

- $f(x)$ is **increasing** on S $\Leftrightarrow$ $f'(x) \geqslant 0$ for all x in S
- $f(x)$ is **decreasing** on S $\Leftrightarrow$ $f'(x) \leqslant 0$ for all x in S.

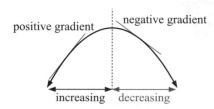

We can also describe intervals where a function is **strictly increasing** or **strictly decreasing**:

- $f(x)$ is **strictly increasing** on S $\Leftrightarrow$ $f'(x) > 0$ for all x in S
- $f(x)$ is **strictly decreasing** on S $\Leftrightarrow$ $f'(x) < 0$ for all x in S.

The word "strictly" allows us to make statements like:

- for a **strictly increasing** function, an increase in x produces an increase in y

- for a **strictly decreasing** function, an increase in x produces a decrease in y.

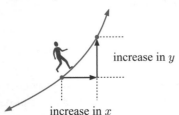

increase in y

increase in x

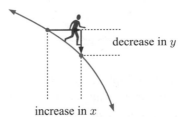

decrease in y

increase in x

Sign diagrams for the derivative are extremely useful for determining intervals where a function is increasing or decreasing. Consider the following examples:

- $f(x) = x^2$

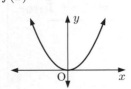

   DEMO

$f'(x) = 2x$ which has sign diagram

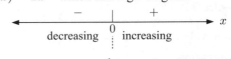

decreasing   increasing

$\therefore$ $f(x) = x^2$ is $\begin{cases} \text{decreasing for } x \leqslant 0 \\ \text{increasing for } x \geqslant 0. \end{cases}$

- $f(x) = -x^2$

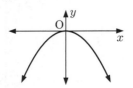

   DEMO

$f'(x) = -2x$ which has sign diagram

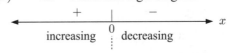

increasing   decreasing

$\therefore$ $f(x) = -x^2$ is $\begin{cases} \text{increasing for } x \leqslant 0 \\ \text{decreasing for } x \geqslant 0. \end{cases}$

- $f(x) = x^3$

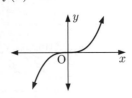

   DEMO

$f'(x) = 3x^2$ which has sign diagram

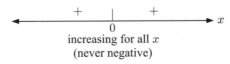

increasing for all x
(never negative)

$\therefore$ $f(x) = x^3$ is increasing for all $x \in \mathbb{R}$.

- $f(x) = x^3 - 3x + 4$

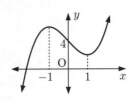

   DEMO

$f'(x) = 3x^2 - 3$
$\qquad = 3(x^2 - 1)$
$\qquad = 3(x + 1)(x - 1)$

which has sign diagram

$\qquad + \qquad | \qquad - \qquad | \qquad + \qquad \longrightarrow x$
$\qquad\qquad\quad -1 \qquad\quad 1$
increasing   decreasing   increasing

$\therefore$ $f(x) = x^3 - 3x + 4$ is $\begin{cases} \text{increasing for } x \leqslant -1 \text{ and for } x \geqslant 1 \\ \text{decreasing for } -1 \leqslant x \leqslant 1. \end{cases}$

Example 12

Find the intervals where the following functions are increasing or decreasing:

a $f(x) = -x^3 + 3x^2 + 5$ **b** $f(x) = 3x^4 - 8x^3 + 2$

a $f(x) = -x^3 + 3x^2 + 5$

$\therefore \ f'(x) = -3x^2 + 6x$

$\qquad \quad = -3x(x - 2)$

which has sign diagram

TI-84 Plus CE

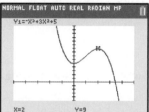

So, $f(x)$ is decreasing for $x \leqslant 0$ and for $x \geqslant 2$, and increasing for $0 \leqslant x \leqslant 2$.

b $f(x) = 3x^4 - 8x^3 + 2$

$\therefore \ f'(x) = 12x^3 - 24x^2$

$\qquad \quad = 12x^2(x - 2)$

which has sign diagram

Casio fx-CG20

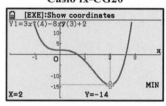

So, $f(x)$ is decreasing for $x \leqslant 2$, and increasing for $x \geqslant 2$.

Remember that $f(x)$ must be defined for all x on an interval before we can classify the function as increasing or decreasing on that interval. We need to take care with vertical asymptotes and other values for x where the function is not defined.

EXERCISE 15D

1 Write down the intervals where the graphs are: **i** increasing   **ii** decreasing.

a

b

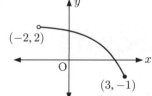

c

d

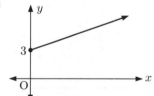

e

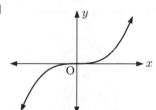

f

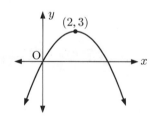

2 The graph of $f(x) = x^3 - 6x^2 + 9x + 2$ is shown alongside.

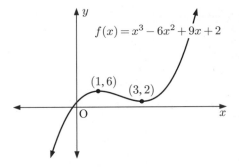

a Use the graph to write down the intervals where the function is:

    i increasing   **ii** decreasing.

b Check your answer by finding $f'(x)$ and constructing its sign diagram.

3 Find the intervals where $f(x)$ is increasing or decreasing:

a $f(x) = x^2$

b $f(x) = -x^3$

c $f(x) = 2x^2 + 3x - 4$

d $f(x) = \dfrac{1}{x}$

e $f(x) = \dfrac{2}{\sqrt{x}}$

f $f(x) = x^3 - 6x^2$

g $f(x) = -2x^3 + 4x$

h $f(x) = -4x^3 + 15x^2 + 18x + 3$

i $f(x) = 3x^4 - 16x^3 + 24x^2 - 2$

j $f(x) = 2x^3 + 9x^2 + 6x - 7$

k $f(x) = x^3 - 6x^2 + 3x - 1$

l $f(x) = x + \dfrac{2}{x}$

4 Let $f(x) = x + \dfrac{9}{x}$.

a Show that $f'(x) = \dfrac{(x+3)(x-3)}{x^2}$, and draw its sign diagram.

b Hence, find intervals where $y = f(x)$ is increasing or decreasing.

5 Consider the function $f(x) = x^3 - 3x^2 + 5x + 2$.

a Find $f'(x)$.

b Show that $f'(x) > 0$ for all x, and explain the significance of this result.

c Use technology to sketch $y = f(x)$, and check your answer to **b**.

E   STATIONARY POINTS

A **stationary point** of a function is a point where $f'(x) = 0$.

It could be a **local maximum** or **local minimum**, or else a **stationary inflection**.

At a stationary point, the tangent is horizontal.

TURNING POINTS (MAXIMA AND MINIMA)

The graph shown has the restricted
domain $-5 \leqslant x \leqslant 6$.

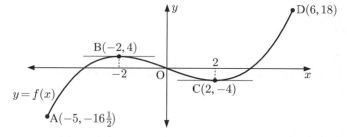

A is a **global minimum** as it has the minimum value of y on the entire domain.

B is a **local maximum** as it is a turning point where $f'(x) = 0$ and the curve has shape ⌢ .

C is a **local minimum** as it is a turning point where $f'(x) = 0$ and the curve has shape ⌣ .

D is a **global maximum** as it is the maximum value of y on the entire domain.

For many functions, a local maximum or minimum is also the global maximum or minimum.

For example, for $y = x^2$ the point $(0, 0)$ is a local minimum and is also the global minimum.

STATIONARY POINTS OF INFLECTION

It is not always true that whenever we find a value of x where $f'(x) = 0$, we have a local maximum or minimum.

For example, $f(x) = x^3$ has $f'(x) = 3x^2$, so $f'(x) = 0$ when $x = 0$.

The tangent to the curve crosses over the curve at $O(0, 0)$. This tangent is horizontal, but $O(0, 0)$ is neither a local maximum nor a local minimum.

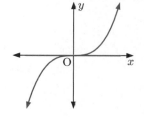

Rather, this point is called a **stationary inflection** (or **inflexion**) as the curve changes its curvature or shape.

SIGN DIAGRAMS

In calculus we commonly use sign diagrams of the *derivative function* $f'(x)$ so we can determine the nature of a stationary point.

Consider the graph alongside.

The sign diagram of its gradient function is shown directly beneath it.

We can use the sign diagram to describe the stationary points of the function.

The signs on the sign diagram of $f'(x)$ indicate whether the gradient of $y = f(x)$ is positive or negative on that interval.

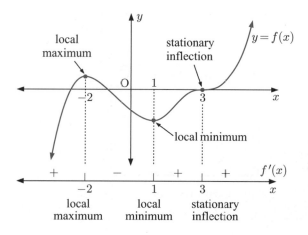

DEMO

We observe the following properties:

Stationary point where $f'(a) = 0$	Sign diagram of $f'(x)$ near $x = a$	Shape of curve near $x = a$
local maximum		
local minimum		
stationary inflection		

To find the stationary points of a function $f(x)$, we find the values of x for which $f'(x) = 0$. The sign diagram of $f'(x)$ tells us whether each stationary point is a local maximum, local minimum, or stationary inflection.

Example 13   ◄♦) Self Tutor

Find and classify all stationary points of $f(x) = x^3 - 3x^2 - 9x + 5$.

$$f(x) = x^3 - 3x^2 - 9x + 5$$
$$\therefore \ f'(x) = 3x^2 - 6x - 9$$
$$= 3(x^2 - 2x - 3)$$
$$= 3(x - 3)(x + 1)$$
$$\therefore \ f'(x) = 0 \quad \text{when} \quad x = 3 \text{ or } -1$$

The sign diagram of $f'(x)$ is

So, we have a local maximum at $x = -1$ and a local minimum at $x = 3$.

$$f(-1) = (-1)^3 - 3(-1)^2 - 9(-1) + 5 \qquad\qquad f(3) = 3^3 - 3 \times 3^2 - 9 \times 3 + 5$$
$$= 10 \qquad\qquad\qquad\qquad\qquad\qquad\qquad = -22$$

TI-84 Plus CE

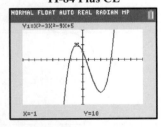

Casio fx-CG20

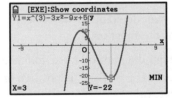

There is a local maximum at $(-1, 10)$.   There is a local minimum at $(3, -22)$.

If we are asked to find the greatest or least value of a function on an interval, then we must also check the value of the function at the end points. We seek the *global* maximum or minimum on the given domain.

Example 14   ◆ **Self Tutor**

Find the greatest and least value of $y = x^3 - 6x^2 + 5$ on the interval $-2 \leqslant x \leqslant 5$.

Now $\dfrac{dy}{dx} = 3x^2 - 12x$

$\qquad\quad = 3x(x - 4)$

$\therefore \ \dfrac{dy}{dx} = 0$ when $x = 0$ or 4.

The sign diagram of $\dfrac{dy}{dx}$ is:

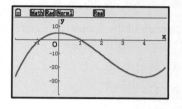

$\therefore$ there is a local maximum at $x = 0$, and a local minimum at $x = 4$.

Critical value (x)	y
-2 (end point)	-27
0 (local maximum)	5
4 (local minimum)	-27
5 (end point)	-20

The greatest of these values is 5 when $x = 0$.
The least of these values is -27 when $x = -2$ and when $x = 4$.

EXERCISE 15E

1 The tangents at points A, O, and B are horizontal.

   a Classify points A, O, and B.

   b Draw a sign diagram for the gradient function $f'(x)$ for all x.

   c State intervals where $y = f(x)$ is:

      i increasing   **ii** decreasing.

   d Draw a sign diagram for $f(x)$ for all x.

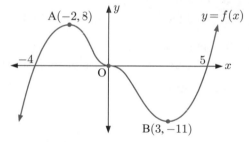

2

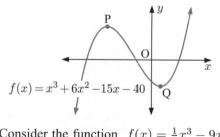

The graph of $f(x) = x^3 + 6x^2 - 15x - 40$ is shown alongside. P and Q are stationary points.

   a Classify points P and Q.

   b Find $f'(x)$.

   c Find the coordinates of P and Q.

3 Consider the function $f(x) = \frac{1}{3}x^3 - 9x + 4$.

   a Find $f'(x)$, and draw its sign diagram.

   b Find intervals where the function is increasing and decreasing.

   c Find and classify any stationary points.

   d Describe the behaviour of the function as $x \to \infty$ and $x \to -\infty$.

   e Sketch the graph of $y = f(x)$, showing the features you have found.

4 Consider the function $g(x) = -2x^3 + 6x^2 + 18x - 7$.

    a Find $g'(x)$, and draw its sign diagram.

    b Find intervals where the function is increasing and decreasing.

    c Find and classify any stationary points.

    d Describe the behaviour of the function as $x \to \infty$ and $x \to -\infty$.

    e Sketch the graph of $y = g(x)$, showing the features you have found.

5 For each of the following functions, find and classify any stationary points. Sketch the function, showing all important features.

    a $f(x) = x^2 - 2$ **b** $f(x) = x^3 + 1$

    c $f(x) = x^3 - 3x + 2$ **d** $f(x) = x^4 - 2x^2$

    e $f(x) = x^3 - 6x^2 + 12x + 1$ **f** $f(x) = \sqrt{x} + 2$

    g $f(x) = x - \sqrt{x}$ **h** $f(x) = x^4 - 6x^2 + 8x - 3$

    i $f(x) = 1 - x\sqrt{x}$ **j** $f(x) = x^4 - 2x^2 - 8$

6 **a** At what value of x does the quadratic function $f(x) = ax^2 + bx + c, \ a \neq 0$, have a stationary point?

    b Under what conditions is the stationary point a local maximum or a local minimum?

7 $f(x) = 2x^3 + ax^2 - 24x + 1$ has a local maximum at $x = -4$.

    a Find a.

    b Find the coordinates of the local maximum.

8 $f(x) = x^3 + ax + b$ has a stationary point at $(-2, 3)$.

    a Find the values of a and b.

    b Find the position and nature of all stationary points.

9 The cubic polynomial $P(x) = ax^3 + bx^2 + cx + d$ touches the line with equation $y = 9x + 2$ at the point $(0, 2)$, and has a stationary point at $(-1, -7)$. Find $P(x)$.

10 Find the greatest and least value of:

    a $x^3 - 12x - 2$ for $-3 \leqslant x \leqslant 5$ **b** $4 - 3x^2 + x^3$ for $-2 \leqslant x \leqslant 3$

    c $x^2 + \dfrac{16}{x}$ for $1 \leqslant x \leqslant 4$ **d** $x - 4\sqrt{x}$ for $0 \leqslant x \leqslant 5$.

F   SHAPE

We have seen that the first derivative $f'(x)$ gives the gradient of the curve $y = f(x)$ for any value of x.

The second derivative $f''(x)$ tells us the rate of change of the gradient $f'(x)$. It therefore gives us information about the *shape* of the curve $y = f(x)$.

When a curve, or part of a curve, has shape:

    we say that the curve is **concave downwards**

    we say that the curve is **concave upwards**.

For example:

- the curve $f(x) = -x^2$ is **concave downwards**

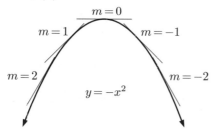

Wherever we are on the curve, as x increases, the gradient of the tangent decreases.

$\therefore$ $f'(x)$ is decreasing

$\therefore$ $f''(x) < 0$.

- the curve $f(x) = x^2$ is **concave upwards**.

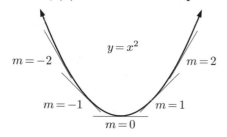

Wherever we are on the curve, as x increases, the gradient of the tangent increases.

$\therefore$ $f'(x)$ is increasing

$\therefore$ $f''(x) > 0$.

We conclude that:

- A curve is **concave downwards** on an interval $S \Leftrightarrow f''(x) \leqslant 0$ for all $x \in S$.

- A curve is **concave upwards** on an interval $S \Leftrightarrow f''(x) \geqslant 0$ for all $x \in S$.

- A curve changes shape when the sign of $f''(x)$ changes.

Example 15   ◀ৗ **Self Tutor**

Consider the function $f(x) = x^3 - 3x^2 + 12x - 5$.

a Find $f''(x)$ and draw its sign diagram.

b State the interval on which the function is:
   i concave upwards   **ii** concave downwards.

c Find the point at which the shape of $f(x)$ changes.

a $f(x) = x^3 - 3x^2 + 12x - 5$

$\therefore$ $f'(x) = 3x^2 - 6x + 12$

$\therefore$ $f''(x) = 6x - 6$

$\qquad = 6(x - 1)$

$\therefore$ $f''(x) = 0$ when $x = 1$

$$\xleftarrow{\qquad\underset{1}{-}\ \ \ |\ \ \underset{}{+}\quad} \overset{f''(x)}{\underset{x}{\longrightarrow}}$$

b   **i** $f(x)$ is concave upwards for $x \geqslant 1$.   **ii** $f(x)$ is concave downwards for $x \leqslant 1$.

c $f(1) = 1 - 3(1) + 12(1) - 5 = 5$

$\therefore$ $f(x)$ changes shape at $(1, 5)$.

EXERCISE 15F

1   **a**   Complete the table by indicating whether each
value is zero, positive, or negative:

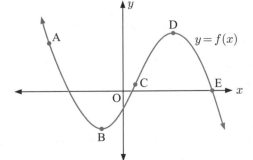

Point	$f(x)$	$f'(x)$	$f''(x)$
A	+		
B			
C			
D		0	
E			

b   Describe the turning points of $y = f(x)$.

c   At which point does the shape of $y = f(x)$ change?

2   The graph of $f(x) = x^3 + 3x^2 - 5x + 2$ is shown
alongside.

a   Find $f'(x)$ and $f''(x)$.

b   Draw the sign diagram of $f''(x)$.

c   State the interval on which the function is:

   i   concave up   **ii**   concave down.

d   Find the point at which the shape of $f(x)$ changes.

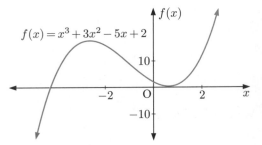

3   Determine the shape of each of the following quadratic functions:

a $y = 2x^2 - 3x + 4$

b $y = -2(x - 3)(x + 1)$

c $y = -4 - x^2 + 6x$

d $y = (5 - x)(1 - 2x)$

4   Determine the interval(s) on which the gradient of the function is increasing:

a $y = x^3 - 2x + 4$

b $y = x + \dfrac{1}{x}$

5   Determine the interval(s) on which the gradient of the function is decreasing:

a $y = -x^3 + 2x^2 - 5x$

b $y = -\dfrac{1}{\sqrt{x}}$

6   For each of the following functions, determine the interval(s) on which the function is:

   i   increasing   **ii**   decreasing   **iii**   concave upwards   **iv**   concave downwards.

a $f(x) = x^2 + 1$

b $f(x) = -x^3$

c $f(x) = \sqrt{x} - 2$

d $f(x) = x^4 - 12x^2$

G   OPTIMISATION

There are many problems for which we need to find the **maximum** or **minimum** value of a function. The
solution is often referred to as the **optimal** solution, and the process is called **optimisation**.

The maximum or minimum value does not always occur when the first derivative is zero.

It is essential to also examine the values of the function at the end point(s) of the interval under consideration
for global maxima and minima.

For example:

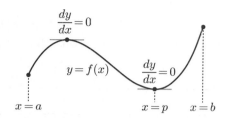

$\frac{dy}{dx} = 0$

$y = f(x)$

$\frac{dy}{dx} = 0$

$x = a$ $x = p$ $x = b$

The maximum value of y occurs at the end point $x = b$.

The minimum value of y occurs at the local minimum $x = p$.

OPTIMISATION PROBLEM SOLVING METHOD

Step 1:   Draw a large, clear diagram of the situation.

Step 2:   Construct a **formula** with the variable to be optimised as the subject. It should be written in terms of one convenient variable, for example x. You should write down what domain restrictions there are on x.

Step 3:   Find the **first derivative** and find the value(s) of x which make the first derivative **zero**.

Step 4:   For each stationary point, use a sign diagram to determine if you have a local maximum or local minimum.

Step 5:   Identify the optimal solution, also considering end points where appropriate.

Step 6:   Write your answer in a sentence, making sure you specifically answer the question.

Example 16
◀) **Self Tutor**

A rectangular cake dish is made by cutting out squares from the corners of a 25 cm by 40 cm rectangle of tin-plate, and then folding the metal to form the container.

What size squares must be cut out to produce the cake dish of maximum volume?

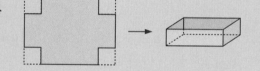

Step 1:   Let x cm be the side lengths of the squares that are cut out.

Step 2:   Volume = length × width × depth
$$= (40 - 2x)(25 - 2x)x$$
$$= (1000 - 80x - 50x + 4x^2)x$$
$$= 1000x - 130x^2 + 4x^3 \ \text{cm}^3$$

Since the side lengths must be positive, $x > 0$ and $25 - 2x > 0$.
∴ $0 < x < 12.5$

x cm

$(25 - 2x)$ cm

$(40 - 2x)$ cm

Step 3: $\frac{dV}{dx} = 12x^2 - 260x + 1000$
$$= 4(3x^2 - 65x + 250)$$
$$= 4(3x - 50)(x - 5)$$

∴ $\frac{dV}{dx} = 0$ when $x = \frac{50}{3} = 16\frac{2}{3}$ or $x = 5$

DEMO

Step 4: $\frac{dV}{dx}$ has sign diagram:

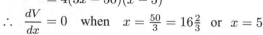

Step 5:   There is a local maximum when $x = 5$. This is the global maximum for the given domain.

Step 6:   The maximum volume is obtained when $x = 5$, which is when 5 cm squares are cut from the corners.

Example 17
◀)) **Self Tutor**

A 4 litre container must have a square base, vertical sides, and an open top. Find the most economical shape which minimises the surface area of material needed.

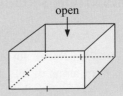
open

Step 1:   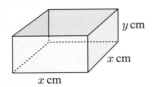   Let the base lengths be x cm and the depth be y cm.

The volume $V =$ length $\times$ width $\times$ depth

$$\therefore \quad V = x^2 y$$

$$\therefore \quad 4000 = x^2 y \quad \text{.... (1)} \quad \{1 \text{ litre} \equiv 1000 \text{ cm}^3\}$$

Step 2:   The total surface area

$$A = \text{area of base} + 4(\text{area of one side})$$

$$= x^2 + 4xy$$

$$= x^2 + 4x\left(\frac{4000}{x^2}\right) \qquad \{\text{using (1)}\}$$

$$\therefore \quad A(x) = x^2 + 16\,000x^{-1} \quad \text{where} \quad x > 0$$

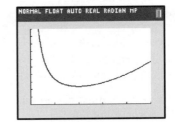

Step 3: $A'(x) = 2x - 16\,000x^{-2}$

$$\therefore \quad A'(x) = 0 \quad \text{when} \quad 2x = \frac{16\,000}{x^2}$$

$$\therefore \quad 2x^3 = 16\,000$$

$$\therefore \quad x = \sqrt[3]{8000} = 20$$

Step 4: $A'(x)$ has sign diagram:

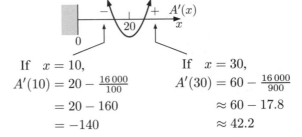

If $x = 10$,
$A'(10) = 20 - \frac{16\,000}{100}$
$= 20 - 160$
$= -140$

If $x = 30$,
$A'(30) = 60 - \frac{16\,000}{900}$
$\approx 60 - 17.8$
≈ 42.2

Step 5:   The minimum material is used to make the container when $x = 20$ and $y = \frac{4000}{20^2} = 10$.

Step 6:   The most economical shape has a square base 20 cm $\times$ 20 cm, and height 10 cm.

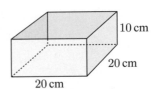

Use **calculus techniques** to answer the following problems.

In cases where finding the zeros of the derivatives is difficult you may use the **graphing package** to help you.

EXERCISE 15G

1 When a manufacturer makes x items per day, the profit function is
$P(x) = -0.022x^2 + 11x - 720$ pounds. Find the production level that will maximise profits.

2 A duck farmer wishes to build a rectangular enclosure of area 100 m². The farmer must purchase wire netting for three of the sides, as the fourth side is an existing fence. Naturally, the farmer wishes to minimise the length (and therefore cost) of fencing required to complete the job.

   a If the shorter sides have length x m, show that the required length of wire netting to be purchased is
$$L = 2x + \frac{100}{x}.$$

   b Find the minimum value of L and the corresponding value of x when this occurs.

   c Sketch the optimal situation, showing all dimensions.

3 The total cost of producing x blankets per day is $\frac{1}{4}x^2 + 8x + 20$ pounds, and for this production level each blanket may be sold for $\left(23 - \frac{1}{2}x\right)$ pounds.
How many blankets should be produced per day to maximise the total profit?

4 Radioactive waste is to be disposed of in fully enclosed lead boxes of inner volume 200 cm³. The base of the box has dimensions in the ratio $2 : 1$.

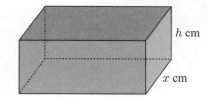

   a Show that $x^2h = 100$.

   b Show that the inner surface area of the box is given by
$A(x) = 4x^2 + \dfrac{600}{x}$ cm².

   c Find the minimum inner surface area of the box and the corresponding value of x.

   d Sketch the optimal box shape, showing all dimensions.

5

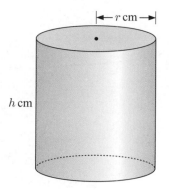

Brenda is designing a cylindrical tin can for a canned fruit company. The cans must have capacity 1 litre, and they must use as little metal as possible.

   a Explain why the height h is given by $h = \dfrac{1000}{\pi r^2}$ cm.

   b Show that the total surface area A is given by
$A = 2\pi r^2 + \dfrac{2000}{r}$ cm².

   c Find the dimensions of the can which make A as small as possible.

6 Sam has sheets of metal which are 36 cm by 36 cm square. He wants to cut out identical squares which are x cm by x cm from the corners of each sheet. He will then bend the sheets along the dashed lines to form an open container.

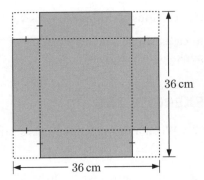

36 cm

a Show that the volume of the container is given by
$V(x) = x(36 - 2x)^2$ cm^3.

b What sized squares should be cut out to produce the container of greatest capacity?

36 cm

7 An athletics track has two "straights" of length l m, and two semi-circular ends of radius x m. The perimeter of the track is 400 m.

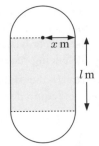

x m

l m

a Show that $l = 200 - \pi x$ and write down the possible values that x may have.

b What values of l and x maximise the shaded rectangle inside the track? What is this maximum area?

Review set 15A

1 Find $f'(x)$ given that $f(x)$ is:

   a $5x^3$ 　　　　**b** $7x^2 - \dfrac{3}{x}$ 　　　　**c** $3x - \dfrac{4}{x^2}$ 　　　　**d** $4\sqrt{x} - \dfrac{1}{\sqrt{x}}$

2 Find $\dfrac{d^2y}{dx^2}$ for:

   a $y = 3x^2 - x^4$ 　　　　**b** $y = \dfrac{x^3 - x}{x^2}$ 　　　　**c** $y = \dfrac{1}{x} - 3x^2$

3 Find the gradient of the tangent to $f(x) = -x^2 + 4x - 2$ at the point $(-3, -23)$.

4 Find all points on the curve $y = 2x^3 + 3x^2 - 10x + 3$ where the gradient of the tangent is 2.

5 Find the equation of the tangent to $y = -2x^2$ at the point where $x = -1$.

6 Find the coordinates of P and Q if (PQ) is the tangent to $y = \dfrac{5}{\sqrt{x}}$ at $(1, 5)$.

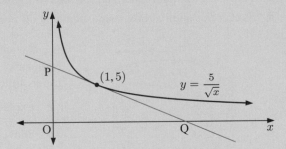

y

P

$(1, 5)$

$y = \dfrac{5}{\sqrt{x}}$

O 　　　　 Q 　　　　 x

7 A rectangular gutter is formed by bending a 24 cm wide sheet of metal as shown.
Where must the bends be made in order to maximise the capacity of the gutter?

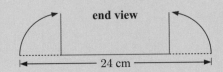

end view

24 cm

8 Find intervals where $f(x) = -x^3 - 6x^2 + 36x - 17$ is:

   a increasing   **b** decreasing.

9 Consider the function $f(x) = 2x^3 - 3x^2 - 36x + 7$.

   a Find and classify all stationary points.

   b Find intervals where the function is increasing and decreasing.

   c Describe the behaviour of the function as $x \to \infty$ and $x \to -\infty$.

   d Sketch the graph of $y = f(x)$ showing the features you have found.

10 The graph of $f(x) = 2x^3 - 3x^2 + x - 12$ is shown alongside.

   a Find $f'(x)$ and $f''(x)$.

   b Draw the sign diagram of $f''(x)$.

   c State the interval on which the function is concave down.

   d Find the point at which the shape of $f(x)$ changes.

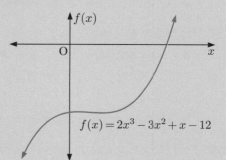

$f(x) = 2x^3 - 3x^2 + x - 12$

11

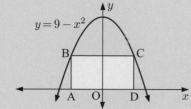

$y = 9 - x^2$

Rectangle ABCD is inscribed within the parabola $y = 9 - x^2$ and the x-axis, as shown.

   a If $OD = x$, show that the rectangle ABCD has area function $A(x) = 18x - 2x^3$.

   b Find the coordinates of C when rectangle ABCD has maximum area.

12 A 200 m fence is placed around a lawn which has the shape of a rectangle with a semi-circle on one of its sides.

   a Using the dimensions shown on the figure, show that $y = 100 - x - \frac{\pi}{2}x$.

   b Find the area of the lawn A in terms of x only.

   c Find the dimensions of the lawn of maximum area.

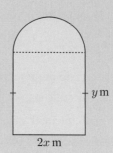

y m

$2x$ m

Review set 15B

1 Find $f'(x)$ given that $f(x)$ is:

   a $3x^2 - 7x + 4$ **b** $(x + 5)^2$ **c** $2\sqrt{x} - \dfrac{3}{x}$ **d** $6x^2\sqrt{x}$

2 Find $\dfrac{d^2y}{dx^2}$ for:

   a $y = -2x^3 + x^2 - 4x + 1$ **b** $y = x + 2x^{\frac{3}{2}}$ **c** $y = \dfrac{2x - x^2 + 3}{x}$

3 Find the equation of the normal to $y = \dfrac{1}{x^2} - \dfrac{2}{x}$ at the point where $x = 1$.

4 The curve $y = 2x^3 + ax + b$ has a tangent with gradient 10 at the point $(-2, 33)$. Find the values of a and b.

5 Determine the equation of any horizontal tangents to the curve with equation $y = x^3 - 3x^2 - 9x + 2$.

6 The tangent to $y = x^3 + ax^2 - 4x + 3$ at $x = 1$ is parallel to the line $y = 3x$.

   a Find a.

   b Find the equation of the tangent at $x = 1$.

   c Where does the tangent cut the curve again?

7 Find intervals where $f(x) = x^4 - 4x^3 - 8x^2 + 5$ is:

   a increasing   **b** decreasing.

8 $f(x) = x^3 - 3x^2 + ax + 50$ has a stationary point at $x = 3$.

   a Find a.

   b Find the position and nature of all stationary points.

9 Find the greatest and least values of $x + \dfrac{32}{x^2}$ for $2 \leqslant x \leqslant 10$.

10 Consider the function $f(x) = x^3 - 4x^2 + 4x$.

   a Find all axes intercepts.

   b Find and classify all stationary points.

   c Find intervals where the function is increasing and decreasing.

   d Describe the behaviour of the function as $x \to \infty$ and $x \to -\infty$.

   e Sketch the graph of $y = f(x)$ showing the features you have found.

11 Determine the interval(s) on which the gradient of the function is increasing:

   a $y = 3x^3 - 4x^2 + 6$ **b** $y = \dfrac{1 - x}{\sqrt{x}}$

12 Determine the interval(s) on which the function $f(x) = -\frac{1}{2}x^4 + x^3 + 6x^2 - 3x + 2$ is:

   a increasing   **b** decreasing   **c** concave upwards   **d** concave downwards.

13 A manufacturer of open steel boxes has to make one with a square base and a capacity of 1 m^3. The steel costs £2 per square metre.

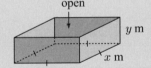

   a If the base measures x m by x m and the height is y m, find y in terms of x.

   b Hence, show that the total cost of the steel is $C(x) = 2x^2 + \dfrac{8}{x}$ pounds.

   c Find the dimensions of the steel box which would cost the least to make.

16

Integration

Contents:

Opening problem

The function $f(x) = x^2 + 1$ lies above the x-axis for all $x \in \mathbb{R}$.

Things to think about:

a How can we calculate the shaded area A, which is the area under the curve for $1 \leqslant x \leqslant 4$?

b What function has $x^2 + 1$ as its derivative?

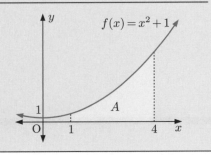

In the previous Chapters we used differential calculus to find the derivatives of many types of functions. We also used it to find the gradients of tangents to curves and to solve optimisation problems.

In this Chapter we consider **integral calculus**. This involves **antidifferentiation**, which is the reverse process of differentiation.

A   THE AREA UNDER A CURVE

The task of finding the area under a curve has been important to mathematicians for thousands of years. In the history of mathematics it was fundamental to the development of integral calculus. We will therefore begin our study by calculating the area under a curve using the same methods as the ancient mathematicians.

LOWER AND UPPER RECTANGLES

Consider the function $f(x) = x^2 + 1$ in the **Opening Problem**.

We wish to estimate the area A enclosed by $y = f(x)$, the x-axis, and the vertical lines $x = 1$ and $x = 4$.

Suppose we divide the interval $1 \leqslant x \leqslant 4$ into 3 strips of width 1 unit as shown. We obtain 3 subintervals of equal width.

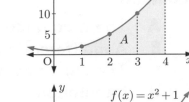

The diagram alongside shows **lower rectangles**, which are rectangles with height equal to the *minimum* value of the curve on that subinterval.

The total area of the lower rectangles is
$$A_L = 1 \times f(1) + 1 \times f(2) + 1 \times f(3)$$
$$= 2 + 5 + 10$$
$$= 17 \text{ units}^2$$

The next diagram shows **upper rectangles**, which are rectangles with height equal to the *maximum* value of the curve on that subinterval.

The total area of the upper rectangles is
$$A_U = 1 \times f(2) + 1 \times f(3) + 1 \times f(4)$$
$$= 5 + 10 + 17$$
$$= 32 \text{ units}^2$$

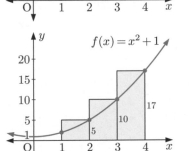

Now clearly $A_L < A < A_U$, so the area A lies between 17 units^2 and 32 units^2.

If the interval $1 \leqslant x \leqslant 4$ was divided into 6 subintervals, each of width $\frac{1}{2}$, then

$$A_L = \tfrac{1}{2}f(1) + \tfrac{1}{2}f(1\tfrac{1}{2}) + \tfrac{1}{2}f(2) + \tfrac{1}{2}f(2\tfrac{1}{2}) + \tfrac{1}{2}f(3) + \tfrac{1}{2}f(3\tfrac{1}{2})$$
$$= \tfrac{1}{2}(2 + \tfrac{13}{4} + 5 + \tfrac{29}{4} + 10 + \tfrac{53}{4})$$
$$= 20.375 \text{ units}^2$$

$$\text{and } A_U = \tfrac{1}{2}f(1\tfrac{1}{2}) + \tfrac{1}{2}f(2) + \tfrac{1}{2}f(2\tfrac{1}{2}) + \tfrac{1}{2}f(3) + \tfrac{1}{2}f(3\tfrac{1}{2}) + \tfrac{1}{2}f(4)$$
$$= \tfrac{1}{2}(\tfrac{13}{4} + 5 + \tfrac{29}{4} + 10 + \tfrac{53}{4} + 17)$$
$$= 27.875 \text{ units}^2$$

From this refinement we conclude that the area A lies between 20.375 units^2 and 27.875 units^2.

As we create more subintervals, the estimates A_L and A_U will become more and more accurate. In fact, as the subinterval width is reduced further and further, both A_L and A_U will **converge** to A.

We illustrate this process by considering another example, this time estimating the area A between the graph of $y = x^2$ and the x-axis for $0 \leqslant x \leqslant 1$.

This example is of historical interest. **Archimedes** (287 - 212 BC) found the exact area. In an article that contains 24 propositions, he developed the essential theory for what is now known as integral calculus.

Consider $f(x) = x^2$ and divide the interval $0 \leqslant x \leqslant 1$ into 4 subintervals of equal width.

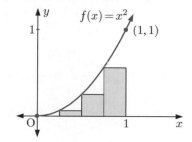 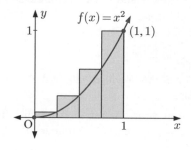

$$A_L = \tfrac{1}{4}(0)^2 + \tfrac{1}{4}(\tfrac{1}{4})^2 + \tfrac{1}{4}(\tfrac{1}{2})^2 + \tfrac{1}{4}(\tfrac{3}{4})^2 \qquad \text{and} \qquad A_U = \tfrac{1}{4}(\tfrac{1}{4})^2 + \tfrac{1}{4}(\tfrac{1}{2})^2 + \tfrac{1}{4}(\tfrac{3}{4})^2 + \tfrac{1}{4}(1)^2$$
$$\approx 0.219 \qquad\qquad\qquad\qquad\qquad\qquad\qquad \approx 0.469$$

Now suppose there are n subintervals between $x = 0$ and $x = 1$, each of width $\dfrac{1}{n}$.

We can use the **area finder** software or our **graphics calculator** to help calculate A_L and A_U for large values of n.

 AREA FINDER

 GRAPHICS CALCULATOR INSTRUCTIONS

The table alongside summarises the results you should obtain for $n = 4,\ 10,\ 25,$ and 50.

The exact value of A is in fact $\frac{1}{3}$, as we will discover later in the Chapter. Notice how both A_L and A_U *converge* to this value as n increases.

n	A_L	A_U	*Average*
4	0.218 75	0.468 75	0.343 75
10	0.285 00	0.385 00	0.335 00
25	0.313 60	0.353 60	0.333 60
50	0.323 40	0.343 40	0.333 40

EXERCISE 16A.1

1 Consider the area between $y = x$ and the x-axis from $x = 0$ to $x = 1$.

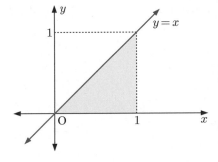

  a Divide the interval into 5 subintervals of equal width, then estimate the area using:

  i lower rectangles   **ii** upper rectangles.

  b Calculate the actual area and compare it with your answers in **a**.

2 Consider the area between $y = \dfrac{1}{x}$ and the x-axis from $x = 2$ to $x = 4$. Divide the interval into 6 subintervals of equal width, then estimate the area using:

  a lower rectangles   **b** upper rectangles.

3 Use rectangles to find lower and upper sums for the area between the graph of $y = x^2$ and the x-axis for $1 \leqslant x \leqslant 2$. Use $n = 10, 25, 50, 100,$ and 500. Give your answers to 4 decimal places.

As n gets larger, both A_L and A_U converge to the same rational number. What is it?

AREA FINDER

4 **a** Use lower and upper rectangle sums to estimate the area between each of the following functions and the x-axis for $0 \leqslant x \leqslant 1$. Use $n = 5, 10, 50, 100, 500, 1000,$ and $10\,000$. Give your answer to 5 decimal places in each case.

  i $y = x^3$ **ii** $y = x$ **iii** $y = x^{\frac{1}{2}}$ **iv** $y = x^{\frac{1}{3}}$

  b For each case in **a**, A_L and A_U converge to a rational number. Write down the number for each case.

  c Using your answer to **b**, predict the area between the graph of $y = x^a$ and the x-axis for $0 \leqslant x \leqslant 1$ and any number $a > 0$.

5 Consider the quarter circle with centre $(0, 0)$ and radius 2 units illustrated.

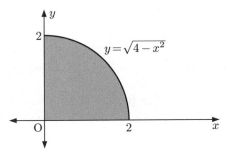

Its area is $\frac{1}{4}$(full circle with radius 2 units)

$= \frac{1}{4} \times \pi \times 2^2$

$= \pi$ units^2

  a Estimate the area using lower and upper rectangles for $n = 10, 50, 100, 200, 1000,$ and $10\,000$. Hence, find rational bounds for π.

  b Archimedes found the famous approximation $3\frac{10}{71} < \pi < 3\frac{1}{7}$.

  For what value of n is your estimate for π better than that of Archimedes?

THE DEFINITE INTEGRAL

Consider the lower and upper rectangle sums for a function which is positive and increasing on the interval $a \leqslant x \leqslant b$.

We divide the interval into n subintervals, each of width $w = \dfrac{b-a}{n}$.

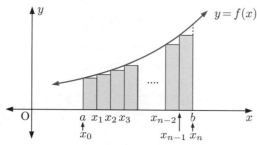 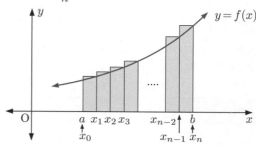

Since the function is increasing:

$$A_L = w\,f(x_0) + w\,f(x_1) + \ldots + w\,f(x_{n-2}) + w\,f(x_{n-1}) = w\sum_{i=0}^{n-1} f(x_i)$$

$$A_U = w\,f(x_1) + w\,f(x_2) + \ldots + w\,f(x_{n-1}) + w\,f(x_n) \quad = w\sum_{i=1}^{n} f(x_i)$$

$$\sum_{i=1}^{n} a_i = a_1 + a_2 + \ldots + a_n$$

Notice that $A_U - A_L = w\,(f(x_n) - f(x_0))$

$$= \frac{1}{n}(b-a)\,(f(b) - f(a))$$

$\therefore \quad \lim_{n \to \infty} (A_U - A_L) = 0 \qquad \{\text{since} \ \lim_{n \to \infty} \dfrac{1}{n} = 0\}$

$\therefore \quad \lim_{n \to \infty} A_L = \lim_{n \to \infty} A_U \quad \{\text{when both limits exist}\}$

$\therefore \quad$ since $A_L < A < A_U$ for all values of n, it follows that

$$\lim_{n \to \infty} A_L = A = \lim_{n \to \infty} A_U$$

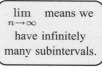

$\lim\limits_{n \to \infty}$ means we have infinitely many subintervals.

We can obtain a result like this for every increasing and decreasing interval of a positive function provided the function is *continuous*. This means that the function must have a defined value $f(k)$ for all $a \leqslant k \leqslant b$, and that $\lim\limits_{x \to k} f(x) = f(k)$ for all $a \leqslant k \leqslant b$.

A formal definition of continuous functions is not required for this course.

The value A is known as the "**definite integral** of $f(x)$ from a to b", written $A = \displaystyle\int_a^b f(x)\,dx$.

If $f(x) \geqslant 0$ for all $a \leqslant x \leqslant b$, then

$\displaystyle\int_a^b f(x)\,dx$ is equal to the shaded area.

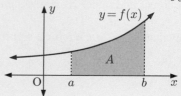

Historical note

The word **integration** means "*to put together into a whole*". An **integral** is the "whole" produced from integration, since the areas of the thin rectangular strips are put together into one whole area.

The symbol $\int$ is called an **integral sign**. In the time of **Newton** and **Leibniz** it was the stretched out letter s, but it is no longer part of the alphabet.

Example 1   ◀) Self Tutor

a   Sketch the graph of $y = x^4$ for $0 \leqslant x \leqslant 1$. Shade the area described by $\int_0^1 x^4 \, dx$.

b   Use technology to calculate the lower and upper rectangle sums for n equal subintervals where $n = 5, 10, 50, 100,$ and 500.

c   Hence evaluate $\int_0^1 x^4 \, dx$ to 2 significant figures.

a

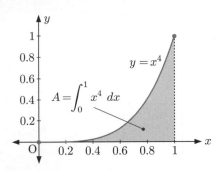

b

n	A_L	A_U
5	0.1133	0.3133
10	0.1533	0.2533
50	0.1901	0.2101
100	0.1950	0.2050
500	0.1990	0.2010

c   When $n = 500$, $A_L \approx A_U \approx 0.20$, to 2 significant figures.

$\therefore$ since $A_L < \int_0^1 x^4 \, dx < A_U$, $\quad \int_0^1 x^4 \, dx \approx 0.20$

EXERCISE 16A.2

1   **a**   Sketch the graph of $y = \sqrt{x}$ for $0 \leqslant x \leqslant 1$.

Shade the area described by $\int_0^1 \sqrt{x} \, dx$.

b   Find the lower and upper rectangle sums for $n = 5, 10, 50, 100,$ and 500.

c   Hence evaluate $\int_0^1 \sqrt{x} \, dx$ to 2 significant figures.

AREA FINDER

2 Consider the region enclosed by $y = \sqrt{1 + x^3}$ and the x-axis for $0 \leqslant x \leqslant 2$.

a Write expressions for the lower and upper rectangle sums using n subintervals where $n \in \mathbb{N}$.

b Find the lower and upper rectangle sums for $n = 50$, 100, and 500.

c Hence estimate $\displaystyle\int_0^2 \sqrt{1 + x^3}\, dx$.

3 The integral $\displaystyle\int_{-3}^3 e^{-\frac{x^2}{2}}\, dx$ is of considerable interest to statisticians.

a Use the graphing package to help sketch $y = e^{-\frac{x^2}{2}}$ for $-3 \leqslant x \leqslant 3$.

b Calculate the lower and upper rectangle sums for the interval $0 \leqslant x \leqslant 3$ using $n = 2250$.

c Use the symmetry of $y = e^{-\frac{x^2}{2}}$ to find lower and upper rectangle sums for $-3 \leqslant x \leqslant 0$ for $n = 2250$.

d Hence estimate $\displaystyle\int_{-3}^3 e^{-\frac{x^2}{2}}\, dx$.

Example 2

◀)) **Self Tutor**

Use graphical evidence and known area facts to find:

a $\displaystyle\int_0^2 (2x + 1)\, dx$

b $\displaystyle\int_0^1 \sqrt{1 - x^2}\, dx$

a

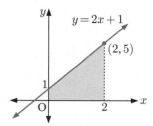

$\displaystyle\int_0^2 (2x + 1)\, dx$

$= \text{shaded area}$

$= \left(\dfrac{1 + 5}{2}\right) \times 2$

$= 6$

b If $y = \sqrt{1 - x^2}$ then $y^2 = 1 - x^2$ and so $x^2 + y^2 = 1$. This is the equation of the unit circle, and $y = \sqrt{1 - x^2}$ is the upper half.

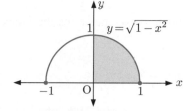

$\displaystyle\int_0^1 \sqrt{1 - x^2}\, dx$

$= \text{shaded area}$

$= \frac{1}{4} \times \pi \times 1^2$

$= \frac{\pi}{4}$

---

4 Use graphical evidence and known area facts to find:

a $\displaystyle\int_1^3 (1 + 4x)\, dx$

b $\displaystyle\int_{-1}^2 (2 - x)\, dx$

c $\displaystyle\int_{-2}^2 \sqrt{4 - x^2}\, dx$

5 **a** Use the diagram alongside to show that for any
positive function $f(x)$:

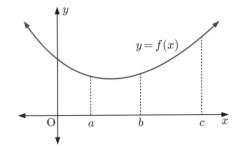

   i $\displaystyle\int_a^a f(x)\,dx = 0$

   ii $\displaystyle\int_a^b f(x)\,dx + \int_b^c f(x)\,dx = \int_a^c f(x)\,dx$

b For a positive function $f(x)$, $\displaystyle\int_2^5 f(x) = 10$, and $\displaystyle\int_5^9 f(x) = 12$. Find:

   i $\displaystyle\int_5^5 f(x)\,dx$ **ii** $\displaystyle\int_2^9 f(x)\,dx$

B   ANTIDIFFERENTIATION

In many problems in calculus, we know the rate of change of one variable with respect to another, but we
do not have a formula which directly relates the variables. In other words, we know $\dfrac{dy}{dx}$, but we need to
know y in terms of x.

> The process of finding y from $\dfrac{dy}{dx}$, or $f(x)$ from $f'(x)$, is the reverse process of
> differentiation. We call it **antidifferentiation**.

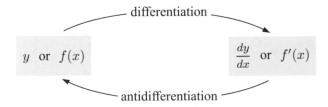

Consider $\dfrac{dy}{dx} = x^2$.

From our work on differentiation, we know that when we differentiate power functions the index reduces
by 1. We hence know that y must involve x^3.

Now if $y = x^3$ then $\dfrac{dy}{dx} = 3x^2$, so if we start with $y = \frac{1}{3}x^3$ then $\dfrac{dy}{dx} = x^2$.

This is the correct result. However, for *all* of the cases $y = \frac{1}{3}x^3 + 2$, $y = \frac{1}{3}x^3 + 100$, and $y = \frac{1}{3}x^3 - 7$,
we find that $\dfrac{dy}{dx} = x^2$.

In fact, there are infinitely many functions of the form $y = \frac{1}{3}x^3 + c$ where c is an arbitrary constant, which will give $\frac{dy}{dx} = x^2$. Ignoring the arbitrary constant, we say that $\frac{1}{3}x^3$ is the **antiderivative** of x^2. It is the simplest function which, when differentiated, gives x^2.

If $F(x)$ is a function where $F'(x) = f(x)$ we say that:

- the **derivative** of $F(x)$ is $f(x)$ and
- the **antiderivative** of $f(x)$ is $F(x)$.

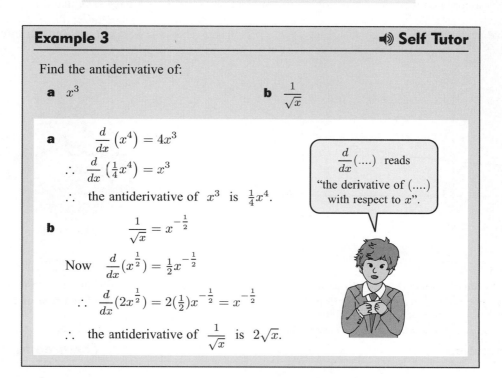

Example 3 ◀)) Self Tutor

Find the antiderivative of:

a x^3

b $\dfrac{1}{\sqrt{x}}$

a
$$\frac{d}{dx}\left(x^4\right) = 4x^3$$
$$\therefore \frac{d}{dx}\left(\frac{1}{4}x^4\right) = x^3$$
$$\therefore \text{ the antiderivative of } x^3 \text{ is } \frac{1}{4}x^4.$$

$\frac{d}{dx}(....)$ reads "the derivative of (....) with respect to x".

b
$$\frac{1}{\sqrt{x}} = x^{-\frac{1}{2}}$$
$$\text{Now } \frac{d}{dx}(x^{\frac{1}{2}}) = \frac{1}{2}x^{-\frac{1}{2}}$$
$$\therefore \frac{d}{dx}(2x^{\frac{1}{2}}) = 2(\frac{1}{2})x^{-\frac{1}{2}} = x^{-\frac{1}{2}}$$
$$\therefore \text{ the antiderivative of } \frac{1}{\sqrt{x}} \text{ is } 2\sqrt{x}.$$

EXERCISE 16B

1 a Find the antiderivative of:

i x **ii** x^2 **iii** x^5 **iv** x^{-2}

v x^{-4} **vi** $x^{\frac{1}{3}}$ **vii** $x^{-\frac{1}{2}}$ **viii** $x^{\frac{2}{3}}$

b Predict a general rule for the antiderivative of x^n, for $n \neq -1$.

2 Find the antiderivative of:

a $6x^2 + 4x$ by first differentiating $x^3 + x^2$

b $\sqrt{x}$ by first differentiating $x\sqrt{x}$

c $\dfrac{1}{x\sqrt{x}}$ by first differentiating $\dfrac{1}{\sqrt{x}}$.

C   THE FUNDAMENTAL THEOREM OF CALCULUS

Historical note

Following the work of Newton and Leibniz, integration was rigorously formalised using limits by the German mathematician **Bernhard Riemann** (1826 - 1866).

If $f(x)$ is a continuous positive function on the interval $a \leqslant x \leqslant b$, we have seen that the area under

the curve between $x = a$ and $x = b$ is $A = \displaystyle\int_a^b f(x)\,dx$. This is known as the **Riemann integral**.

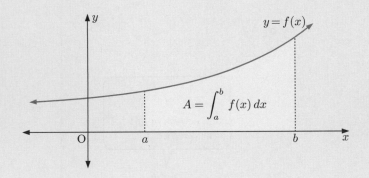

Bernhard Riemann

We now use this Riemann integral to explain the link between differential calculus and the definite integral or limit of an area sum we saw in **Section A**. This link is called the **Fundamental Theorem of Calculus**.

Investigation   The area function

Consider the constant function $f(t) = 5$.

We wish to find an **area function** which will give the area under the function between $t = a$ and some other value of t which we will call x.

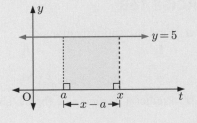

The area function is $A(x) = \displaystyle\int_a^x 5\,dt$

$\quad\quad\quad\quad\quad\ = \text{shaded area}$

$\quad\quad\quad\quad\quad\ = (x - a)5$

$\quad\quad\quad\quad\quad\ = 5x - 5a$

Notice that $f(t) = 5$ has $F(t) = 5t$ as an antiderivative. We can therefore write $A(x)$ in the form $F(x) - F(a)$.

What to do:

1 What is the derivative $F'(t)$ of the function $F(t) = 5t$? How does this relate to the function $f(t)$?

2 Consider the simplest linear function $f(t) = t$. The corresponding area function is

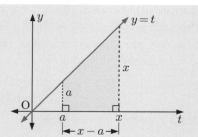

$$A(x) = \int_a^x t \, dt$$

$$= \text{shaded area}$$

$$= \left(\frac{x+a}{2}\right)(x-a)$$

    a Write $A(x)$ in the form $F(x) - F(a)$.

    b What is the derivative $F'(t)$? How does it relate to the function $f(t)$?

3 Consider $f(t) = 2t + 3$. The corresponding area function is

$$A(x) = \int_a^x (2t + 3) \, dt$$

$$= \text{shaded area}$$

$$= \left(\frac{2x + 3 + 2a + 3}{2}\right)(x-a)$$

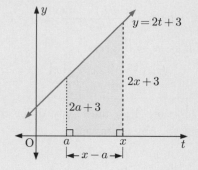

    a Write $A(x)$ in the form $F(x) - F(a)$.

    b What is the derivative $F'(t)$?
       How does it relate to the function $f(t)$?

4 Repeat the procedure in **2** and **3** to find area functions for:

    a $f(t) = \frac{1}{2}t + 3$ **b** $f(t) = 5 - 2t$

Do your results fit with your earlier observations?

5 If $f(t) = 3t^2 + 4t + 5$, predict what $F(t)$ will be without performing the algebraic procedure.

From the **Investigation** you should have found that, for $f(t) \geqslant 0$,

$$\int_a^x f(t) \, dt = F(x) - F(a) \quad \text{where} \quad F'(t) = f(t). \quad F(t) \text{ is the } \textbf{antiderivative} \text{ of } f(t).$$

The following argument shows why this is true for all functions $f(t) \geqslant 0$.

Consider a function $y = f(t)$ which has antiderivative $F(t)$ and an area function $A(x) = \int_a^x f(t) \, dt$ which is the area from $t = a$ to $t = x$.

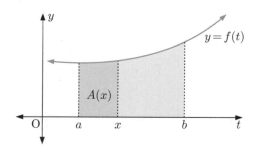

$A(x)$ is an increasing function since $f(x) \geqslant 0$, and $A(a) = 0$ .... (1)

Consider the narrow strip between $t = x$ and $t = x + h$.
The area of this strip is $A(x + h) - A(x)$, but we also
know it must lie between a lower and upper rectangle on
the interval $x \leqslant t \leqslant x + h$ of width h.

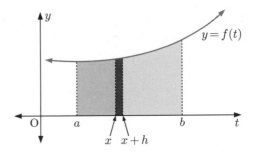

$$\text{area of lower} \atop \text{rectangle} \;\leqslant\; A(x+h) - A(x) \;\leqslant\; {\text{area of upper} \atop \text{rectangle}}$$

If $f(t)$ is increasing on this interval then

$$hf(x) \leqslant A(x+h) - A(x) \leqslant hf(x+h)$$

$$\therefore \;\; f(x) \leqslant \frac{A(x+h) - A(x)}{h} \leqslant f(x+h)$$

Equivalently, if $f(t)$ is decreasing on this interval then

$$f(x+h) \leqslant \frac{A(x+h) - A(x)}{h} \leqslant f(x)$$

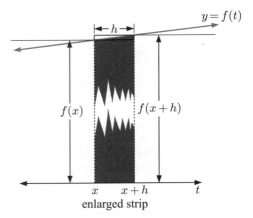

enlarged strip

Taking the limit as $h \to 0$ gives

$$f(x) \leqslant A'(x) \leqslant f(x)$$
$$\therefore \;\; A'(x) = f(x)$$

So, the area function $A(x)$ must only differ from the
antiderivative of $f(x)$ by a constant.

$$\therefore \;\; A(x) = F(x) + c$$

Letting $x = a$, $A(a) = F(a) + c$

But from (1), $A(a) = 0$ $\therefore$ $c = -F(a)$

$$\therefore \;\; A(x) = F(x) - F(a)$$

and so $\displaystyle \int_a^x f(t)\, dt = F(x) - F(a)$

Letting $x = b$, $\displaystyle \int_a^b f(t)\, dt = F(b) - F(a)$

This result is in fact true for all continuous functions $f(t)$.

However, in situations where a function is negative, the area between the curve and the x-axis is counted as
negative. We therefore refer to $A(x)$ as a **signed area function**.

THE FUNDAMENTAL THEOREM OF CALCULUS

From the argument above, the Fundamental Theorem of Calculus can be stated in two forms:

1 For a continuous function $f(t)$, if we define the signed area function from $t = a$ to $t = x$ as

$$A(x) = \int_a^x f(t)\, dt, \;\; \text{then} \;\; A'(x) = \frac{d}{dx}\left(\int_a^x f(t)\, dt \right) = f(x).$$

or more commonly, exchanging the variable t for the more familiar x:

2 For a continuous function $f(x)$ with antiderivative $F(x)$, $\displaystyle \int_a^b f(x)\, dx = F(b) - F(a)$.

PROPERTIES OF DEFINITE INTEGRALS

The following properties of definite integrals can all be deduced from the Fundamental Theorem of Calculus:

- $\displaystyle\int_a^a f(x)\,dx = 0$

- $\displaystyle\int_a^b k\,dx = k(b-a)$ {k is a constant}

- $\displaystyle\int_b^a f(x)\,dx = -\int_a^b f(x)\,dx$

- $\displaystyle\int_a^b k\,f(x)\,dx = k\int_a^b f(x)\,dx$

- $\displaystyle\int_a^b f(x)\,dx + \int_b^c f(x)\,dx = \int_a^c f(x)\,dx$

- $\displaystyle\int_a^b [f(x) \pm g(x)]\,dx = \int_a^b f(x)\,dx \pm \int_a^b g(x)\,dx$

Example proof:

$$\int_a^b f(x)\,dx + \int_b^c f(x)\,dx$$
$$= F(b) - F(a) + F(c) - F(b)$$
$$= F(c) - F(a)$$
$$= \int_a^c f(x)\,dx$$

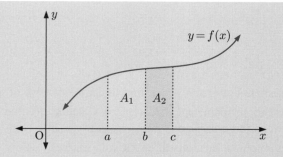

In particular, for the case where $a \leqslant b \leqslant c$ and $f(x) \geqslant 0$ for $a \leqslant x \leqslant c$, we observe that

$$\int_a^b f(x)\,dx + \int_b^c f(x)\,dx = A_1 + A_2 = \int_a^c f(x)\,dx$$

The Fundamental Theorem of Calculus allows us to calculate areas under curves that we could previously only estimate.

Example 4   ◀ッ Self Tutor

Use the Fundamental Theorem of Calculus to find the area between:
a the x-axis and $y = x^2$ from $x = 0$ to $x = 1$
b the x-axis and $y = \sqrt{x}$ from $x = 1$ to $x = 9$.

a

$f(x) = x^2$ has antiderivative $F(x) = \dfrac{x^3}{3}$

$\therefore$ shaded area $= \displaystyle\int_0^1 x^2\,dx$

$= F(1) - F(0)$

$= \tfrac{1}{3} - 0$

$= \tfrac{1}{3}$ units^2

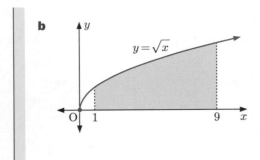

$f(x) = \sqrt{x} = x^{\frac{1}{2}}$ has antiderivative

$$F(x) = \frac{x^{\frac{3}{2}}}{\frac{3}{2}} = \frac{2}{3}x\sqrt{x}$$

$\therefore$ shaded area $= \displaystyle\int_1^9 x^{\frac{1}{2}}\, dx$

$$= F(9) - F(1)$$
$$= \frac{2}{3} \times 27 - \frac{2}{3} \times 1$$
$$= 17\frac{1}{3} \text{ units}^2$$

Instructions for evaluating definite integrals on your calculator can be found by clicking on the icon.

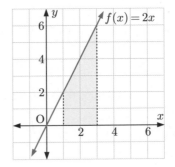

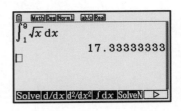

EXERCISE 16C

1 **a** Differentiate x^2, and hence find the antiderivative of $2x$.

b Use the Fundamental Theorem of Calculus to find the area between the x-axis and $f(x) = 2x$ from $x = 1$ to $x = 3$.

c Use graphical methods to check your answer.

2 **a** Find the antiderivative of $\sqrt{x}$.

b Use the Fundamental Theorem of Calculus to find the area between the x-axis and $y = \sqrt{x}$ from $x = 0$ to $x = 1$.

c Compare your answer to **Exercise 16A.2** question **1**.

3 **a** Use the Fundamental Theorem of Calculus to find the area between the x-axis and $y = x^3$ from:

   i $x = 0$ to $x = 2$ **ii** $x = 2$ to $x = 3$ **iii** $x = 0$ to $x = 3$.

b Comment on your answers in **a**.

4 Use the Fundamental Theorem of Calculus to find the area between the x-axis and:

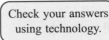

Check your answers using technology.

a $y = x^3$ from $x = 1$ to $x = 2$

b $y = x^2$ from $x = 1$ to $x = 3$

c $y = \sqrt{x}$ from $x = 1$ to $x = 2$

d $y = \dfrac{1}{\sqrt{x}}$ from $x = 1$ to $x = 4$.

5 Use the Fundamental Theorem of Calculus to show that:

a $\displaystyle\int_a^a f(x)\,dx = 0$ and explain the result graphically

b $\displaystyle\int_a^b k\,dx = k(b-a)$ where k is a constant

c $\displaystyle\int_b^a f(x)\,dx = -\int_a^b f(x)\,dx$

d $\displaystyle\int_a^b k\,f(x)\,dx = k\int_a^b f(x)\,dx$ where k is a constant

e $\displaystyle\int_a^b [f(x)+g(x)]\,dx = \int_a^b f(x)\,dx + \int_a^b g(x)\,dx$

6 **a** Use the Fundamental Theorem of Calculus to show that

$$\int_a^b (-f(x))\,dx = -\int_a^b f(x)\,dx$$

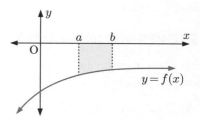

b Hence show that if $f(x) \leqslant 0$ for all x on $a \leqslant x \leqslant b$

then the shaded area $= -\displaystyle\int_a^b f(x)\,dx.$

c Calculate the following integrals, and give graphical interpretations of your answers:

i $\displaystyle\int_0^1 (-x^2)\,dx$ **ii** $\displaystyle\int_0^1 (x^2 - x)\,dx$ **iii** $\displaystyle\int_{-2}^0 3x\,dx$

d Use graphical evidence and known area facts to find $\displaystyle\int_0^2 \left(-\sqrt{4-x^2}\right) dx.$

Example 5 🔊 Self Tutor

Find $A'(x)$ given $A(x) = \displaystyle\int_1^x 2t\sqrt{t}\,dt.$

$A(x) = \displaystyle\int_1^x f(t)\,dt$ where $f(t) = 2t\sqrt{t}.$

If $f(t)$ has antiderivative $F(t)$ then

$$A(x) = F(x) - F(1) \qquad \text{\{Fundamental Theorem of Calculus\}}$$
$$\therefore \;\; A'(x) = F'(x) \qquad\qquad \text{\{}F(1) \text{ is a constant\}}$$
$$= f(x)$$
$$= 2x\sqrt{x}$$

---

7 Find $A'(x)$ given:

a $A(x) = \displaystyle\int_0^x (t^2 + 2)\,dt$ **b** $A(x) = \displaystyle\int_1^x (t^3 + 2t)\,dt$

D   INTEGRATION

Earlier, we showed that the **antiderivative** of x^2 is $\frac{1}{3}x^3$, and that any function of the form $\frac{1}{3}x^3 + c$ where c is a constant, has derivative x^2.

We say that the **indefinite integral** or **integral** of x^2 is $\frac{1}{3}x^3 + c$, and write $\int x^2 \, dx = \frac{1}{3}x^3 + c$.

We read this as "the integral of x^2 with respect to x is $\frac{1}{3}x^3 + c$, where c is a constant".

$$\text{If } F'(x) = f(x) \text{ then } \int f(x) \, dx = F(x) + c.$$

This process is known as **indefinite integration**. It is indefinite because it is not being applied to a particular interval.

DISCOVERING INTEGRALS

Since integration is the reverse process of differentiation, we can sometimes discover integrals by differentiation. For example:

- if $F(x) = x^4$ then $F'(x) = 4x^3$

$$\therefore \quad \int 4x^3 \, dx = x^4 + c$$

- if $F(x) = \sqrt{x} = x^{\frac{1}{2}}$ then $F'(x) = \frac{1}{2}x^{-\frac{1}{2}} = \frac{1}{2\sqrt{x}}$

$$\therefore \quad \int \frac{1}{2\sqrt{x}} \, dx = \sqrt{x} + c$$

The following rules may prove useful:

- Any constant within the integral may be written in front of the integral sign.

$$\int k \, f(x) \, dx = k \int f(x) \, dx, \quad k \text{ is a constant}$$

Proof: Consider differentiating $k F(x)$ where $F'(x) = f(x)$.

$$\frac{d}{dx} (k \, F(x)) = k \, F'(x) = k \, f(x)$$

$$\therefore \quad \int k \, f(x) \, dx = k \, F(x)$$

$$= k \int f(x) \, dx$$

- The integral of a sum is the sum of the separate integrals. This rule enables us to integrate term by term.

$$\int [f(x) + g(x)] \, dx = \int f(x) \, dx + \int g(x) \, dx$$

Example 6

🔊 Self Tutor

If $y = x^4 + 2x^3$, find $\dfrac{dy}{dx}$. Hence find $\displaystyle\int (2x^3 + 3x^2)\, dx$.

If $y = x^4 + 2x^3$ then $\dfrac{dy}{dx} = 4x^3 + 6x^2$

$$\therefore \int (4x^3 + 6x^2)\, dx = x^4 + 2x^3 + c$$

$$\therefore \int 2(2x^3 + 3x^2)\, dx = x^4 + 2x^{3\prime} + c$$

$$\therefore 2 \int (2x^3 + 3x^2)\, dx = x^4 + 2x^3 + c$$

$$\therefore \int (2x^3 + 3x^2)\, dx = \tfrac{1}{2}x^4 + x^3 + c$$

c represents an arbitrary constant, so is simply any value $c \in \mathbb{R}$. Instead of writing $\frac{c}{2}$, we can therefore still write just c.

EXERCISE 16D.1

1 If $y = x^7$, find $\dfrac{dy}{dx}$. Hence find $\displaystyle\int x^6\, dx$.

2 If $y = x^3 + x^2$, find $\dfrac{dy}{dx}$. Hence find $\displaystyle\int (3x^2 + 2x)\, dx$.

3 If $y = x\sqrt{x}$, find $\dfrac{dy}{dx}$. Hence find $\displaystyle\int \sqrt{x}\, dx$.

4 If $y = \dfrac{1}{\sqrt{x}}$, find $\dfrac{dy}{dx}$. Hence find $\displaystyle\int \dfrac{1}{x\sqrt{x}}\, dx$.

5 Prove the rule $\displaystyle\int [f(x) + g(x)]\, dx = \int f(x)\, dx + \int g(x)\, dx$.

We can check that an integral is correct by differentiating the answer. It should give us the **integrand**, the function we originally integrated.

RULES FOR INTEGRATION

In **Chapter 15** we developed some rules to help us differentiate functions more efficiently:

Function	Derivative	Name
c, a constant	0	
$mx + c$, m and c are constants	m	
x^n	nx^{n-1}	**power rule**
$cu(x)$	$cu'(x)$	
$u(x) + v(x)$	$u'(x) + v'(x)$	**addition rule**

By applying these general rules, we can develop rules for integration:

- For k a constant, $\dfrac{d}{dx}(kx + c) = k$ $\therefore$ $\boxed{\displaystyle\int k\,dx = kx + c}$

  c is an arbitrary constant called the **constant of integration** or **integrating constant**.

- If $n \neq -1$, $\dfrac{d}{dx}\left(\dfrac{x^{n+1}}{n+1} + c\right) = \dfrac{(n+1)x^n}{n+1} = x^n$

  $\therefore$ $\boxed{\displaystyle\int x^n\,dx = \dfrac{x^{n+1}}{n+1} + c,\ n \neq -1}$

- $\dfrac{d}{dx}(u(x) + v(x) + c) = u'(x) + v'(x)$

  $\therefore$ $\boxed{\displaystyle\int (u'(x) + v'(x))\,dx = u(x) + v(x) + c}$

Remember that you can always check your integration by differentiating the resulting function.

Example 7   ◀) Self Tutor

Find: **a** $\displaystyle\int (x^3 - 2x^2 + 5)\,dx$ **b** $\displaystyle\int \left(\dfrac{1}{x^3} - \sqrt{x}\right)dx$

a $\displaystyle\int (x^3 - 2x^2 + 5)\,dx$

$= \dfrac{x^4}{4} - \dfrac{2x^3}{3} + 5x + c$

b $\displaystyle\int \left(\dfrac{1}{x^3} - \sqrt{x}\right)dx = \displaystyle\int \left(x^{-3} - x^{\frac{1}{2}}\right)dx$

$= \dfrac{x^{-2}}{-2} - \dfrac{x^{\frac{3}{2}}}{\frac{3}{2}} + c$

$= -\dfrac{1}{2x^2} - \dfrac{2}{3}x^{\frac{3}{2}} + c$

Example 8   ◀) Self Tutor

Find: **a** $\displaystyle\int \left(3x + \dfrac{2}{x}\right)^2 dx$ **b** $\displaystyle\int \dfrac{x^2 - 2}{\sqrt{x}}\,dx$

a $\displaystyle\int \left(3x + \dfrac{2}{x}\right)^2 dx$

We expand the brackets and simplify to a form that can be integrated.

$= \displaystyle\int \left(9x^2 + 12 + \dfrac{4}{x^2}\right)dx$

$= \displaystyle\int (9x^2 + 12 + 4x^{-2})\,dx$

$= \dfrac{9x^3}{3} + 12x + \dfrac{4x^{-1}}{-1} + c$

$= 3x^3 + 12x - \dfrac{4}{x} + c$

b $\displaystyle\int \dfrac{x^2 - 2}{\sqrt{x}}\,dx$

$= \displaystyle\int \left(\dfrac{x^2}{\sqrt{x}} - \dfrac{2}{\sqrt{x}}\right)dx$

$= \displaystyle\int \left(x^{\frac{3}{2}} - 2x^{-\frac{1}{2}}\right)dx$

$= \dfrac{x^{\frac{5}{2}}}{\frac{5}{2}} - \dfrac{2x^{\frac{1}{2}}}{\frac{1}{2}} + c$

$= \dfrac{2}{5}x^2\sqrt{x} - 4\sqrt{x} + c$

EXERCISE 16D.2

1 Find:

a $\displaystyle\int (x^2 + 3x - 2)\, dx$

b $\displaystyle\int (x^4 - x^2 - x + 2)\, dx$

c $\displaystyle\int (5x^4 - 4x^3 - 6x^2 - 7)\, dx$

d $\displaystyle\int \left(\sqrt{x} + \frac{1}{\sqrt{x}} \right) dx$

e $\displaystyle\int (x\sqrt{x} - 2)\, dx$

f $\displaystyle\int \left(\frac{1}{x\sqrt{x}} + 4x \right) dx$

2 Find:

a $\displaystyle\int \left(\tfrac{1}{2}x^3 - x^4 + x^{\frac{1}{3}} \right) dx$

b $\displaystyle\int \left(\frac{4}{x^2} + x^2 - \tfrac{1}{4}x^3 \right) dx$

c $\displaystyle\int \left(5x^4 + \tfrac{1}{3}x^3 - \sqrt{x} \right) dx$

3 Find:

a $\displaystyle\int (2x + 1)^2\, dx$

b $\displaystyle\int \left(x + \frac{1}{x} \right)^2 dx$

c $\displaystyle\int \frac{1 - 4x}{x\sqrt{x}}\, dx$

d $\displaystyle\int \frac{2x - 1}{\sqrt{x}}\, dx$

e $\displaystyle\int (x + 1)^3\, dx$

f $\displaystyle\int (x - 1)^4\, dx$

4 Find y if:

a $\dfrac{dy}{dx} = 6$

b $\dfrac{dy}{dx} = 4x^2$

c $\dfrac{dy}{dx} = \dfrac{1}{x^2}$

d $\dfrac{dy}{dx} = 2x^3 - 4$

e $\dfrac{dy}{dx} = 4x^3 + 3x^2$

f $\dfrac{dy}{dx} = \dfrac{(x + 2)^3}{\sqrt{x}}$

5 Find $f(x)$ if:

a $f'(x) = (1 - 2x)^2$

b $f'(x) = \sqrt{x} - \dfrac{2}{\sqrt{x}}$

c $f'(x) = \dfrac{x^2 - 5}{x^2}$

Discussion

In the rule $\displaystyle\int x^n\, dx = \frac{x^{n+1}}{n+1} + c, \ n \neq -1,$ why did we exclude the value $n = -1$?

PARTICULAR VALUES

We can find the constant of integration c if we are given a particular value of the function.

Example 9   ◀ Self Tutor

Find $f(x)$ given that $f'(x) = x^3 - 2x^2 + 3$ and $f(0) = 2$.

$$f'(x) = x^3 - 2x^2 + 3$$

$$\therefore \ f(x) = \int (x^3 - 2x^2 + 3)\, dx$$

$$\therefore \ f(x) = \frac{x^4}{4} - \frac{2x^3}{3} + 3x + c$$

But $\ f(0) = 2, \ $ so $\ c = 2$

Thus $\ f(x) = \frac{x^4}{4} - \frac{2x^3}{3} + 3x + 2$

EXERCISE 16D.3

1 Find $f(x)$ given that:

a $f'(x) = 2x - 1$ and $f(0) = 3$

b $f'(x) = 3x^2 + 2x$ and $f(2) = 5$

c $f'(x) = 2 + \dfrac{1}{\sqrt{x}}$ and $f(1) = 1$

d $f'(x) = x - \dfrac{2}{\sqrt{x}}$ and $f(1) = 2$

2 A curve has gradient function $\dfrac{dy}{dx} = x - 2x^2$ and passes through $(2, 4)$. Find the equation of the curve.

3 A curve has gradient function $f'(x) = ax + 1$ where a is a constant. Find $f(x)$ given that $f(0) = 3$ and $f(3) = -3$.

4 Consider a function $f(x)$ with second derivative $f''(x) = 2 - x$. If $f(0) = -1$ and $f(1) = 4$, find $f(x)$.

E   DEFINITE INTEGRALS

Earlier we saw the **Fundamental Theorem of Calculus**:

> If $F(x)$ is the antiderivative of $f(x)$ where $f(x)$ is continuous on the interval $a \leqslant x \leqslant b$, then the **definite integral** of $f(x)$ on this interval is $\displaystyle\int_a^b f(x)\,dx = F(b) - F(a)$.

$\displaystyle\int_a^b f(x)\,dx$ reads "the integral from $x = a$ to $x = b$ of $f(x)$ with respect to x"
or "the integral from a to b of $f(x)$ with respect to x".

It is called a **definite** integral because there are lower and upper limits for the integration, and it therefore results in a numerical answer.

When calculating definite integrals we can omit the constant of integration c as this will always cancel out in the subtraction process.

It is common to write $F(b) - F(a)$ as $[F(x)]_a^b$, and so

$$\int_a^b f(x)\,dx = [F(x)]_a^b = F(b) - F(a)$$

Earlier in the Chapter we proved the following properties of definite integrals using the Fundamental Theorem of Calculus:

- $\displaystyle\int_a^b f(x)\,dx = -\int_b^a f(x)\,dx$

- $\displaystyle\int_a^b k f(x)\,dx = k \int_a^b f(x)\,dx, \quad k$ is any constant

- $\displaystyle\int_a^b f(x)\,dx + \int_b^c f(x)\,dx = \int_a^c f(x)\,dx$

- $\displaystyle\int_a^b [f(x) + g(x)]\,dx = \int_a^b f(x)\,dx + \int_a^b g(x)\,dx$

Example 10

◀) **Self Tutor**

Find $\displaystyle\int_1^3 (x^2 + 2)\, dx$.

$$\int_1^3 (x^2 + 2)\, dx = \left[\frac{x^3}{3} + 2x\right]_1^3$$
$$= \left(\frac{3^3}{3} + 2(3)\right) - \left(\frac{1^3}{3} + 2(1)\right)$$
$$= (9 + 6) - \left(\frac{1}{3} + 2\right)$$
$$= 12\tfrac{2}{3}$$

EXERCISE 16E

Use questions **1** to **4** to check the properties of definite integrals.

1 Find:

a $\displaystyle\int_1^4 \sqrt{x}\, dx$ and $\displaystyle\int_1^4 (-\sqrt{x})\, dx$

b $\displaystyle\int_0^1 x^7\, dx$ and $\displaystyle\int_0^1 (-x^7)\, dx$

2 Find:

a $\displaystyle\int_0^1 x^2\, dx$

b $\displaystyle\int_1^2 x^2\, dx$

c $\displaystyle\int_0^2 x^2\, dx$

d $\displaystyle\int_0^1 3x^2\, dx$

3 Find:

a $\displaystyle\int_0^2 (x^3 - 4x)\, dx$

b $\displaystyle\int_2^3 (x^3 - 4x)\, dx$

c $\displaystyle\int_0^3 (x^3 - 4x)\, dx$

4 Find:

a $\displaystyle\int_0^1 x^2\, dx$

b $\displaystyle\int_0^1 \sqrt{x}\, dx$

c $\displaystyle\int_0^1 (x^2 + \sqrt{x})\, dx$

5 Evaluate:

a $\displaystyle\int_0^1 x^3\, dx$

b $\displaystyle\int_0^2 (x^2 - x)\, dx$

c $\displaystyle\int_1^4 \left(x - \frac{3}{\sqrt{x}}\right) dx$

d $\displaystyle\int_4^9 \frac{x - 3}{\sqrt{x}}\, dx$

e $\displaystyle\int_1^3 \frac{1}{x^2}\, dx$

f $\displaystyle\int_1^2 (x + 3)^2\, dx$

6 Find m such that $\displaystyle\int_m^{2m} (2x - 1)\, dx = 4$.

7 Write as a single integral:

a $\displaystyle\int_2^4 f(x)\, dx + \int_4^7 f(x)\, dx$

b $\displaystyle\int_4^5 f(x)\, dx - \int_6^5 f(x)\, dx$

c $\displaystyle\int_1^3 g(x)\, dx + \int_3^8 g(x)\, dx + \int_8^9 g(x)\, dx$

8   **a**   If $\displaystyle\int_1^3 f(x)\,dx = 2$ and $\displaystyle\int_1^6 f(x)\,dx = -3$,   find $\displaystyle\int_3^6 f(x)\,dx$.

   b   If $\displaystyle\int_0^2 f(x)\,dx = 5$, $\displaystyle\int_4^6 f(x)\,dx = -2$,   and $\displaystyle\int_0^6 f(x)\,dx = 7$,   find $\displaystyle\int_2^4 f(x)\,dx$.

9   Suppose $\displaystyle\int_{-1}^1 f(x)\,dx = -4$.   Determine the value of:

  a $\displaystyle\int_1^{-1} f(x)\,dx$
          b $\displaystyle\int_{-1}^1 (2 + f(x))\,dx$
          c $\displaystyle\int_{-1}^1 2f(x)\,dx$

  d k such that $\displaystyle\int_{-1}^1 kf(x)\,dx = 7$

10   If $g(2) = 4$ and $g(3) = 5$,   calculate $\displaystyle\int_2^3 (g'(x) - 1)\,dx$.

Review set 16A

1   **a**   Sketch the region between the curve $y = \dfrac{4}{1 + x^2}$ and the x-axis for $0 \leqslant x \leqslant 1$.

    Divide the interval into 5 equal parts and display the 5 upper and lower rectangles.

  b   Use the area finder software to find the lower and upper rectangle sums for   AREA FINDER
    $n = 5, 50, 100$, and 500.

  c   Give your best estimate for $\displaystyle\int_0^1 \dfrac{4}{1 + x^2}\,dx$ and compare this answer with π.

2   The graph of $y = f(x)$ is illustrated:

  Evaluate the following using area interpretation:

  a $\displaystyle\int_0^4 f(x)\,dx$
        b $\displaystyle\int_4^6 f(x)\,dx$

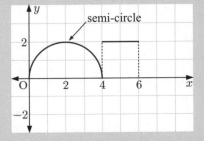

3   Find the antiderivative of:

  a x^5
          b $x^2 - 6x$
          c $\dfrac{1}{2x^2}$

4   Find:

  a $\displaystyle\int \left(\sqrt{x} - \dfrac{2}{x^2}\right) dx$
     b $\displaystyle\int \left(2x - \dfrac{3}{\sqrt[3]{x}}\right) dx$
     c $\displaystyle\int \dfrac{6x + 5}{\sqrt{x}}\,dx$

5   Integrate with respect to x:

  a $\dfrac{4}{\sqrt{x}}$
         b $\frac{1}{3}x^3 + 2x$
         c $\dfrac{1 - 2x}{x^3}$

6   Find the exact value of:

  a $\displaystyle\int_{-2}^0 (1 - 3x)\,dx$
     b $\displaystyle\int_0^{\frac{1}{2}} (x - \sqrt{x})\,dx$
     c $\displaystyle\int_1^2 (x^2 + 1)^2\,dx$

7 Find $A'(x)$ given $A(x) = \displaystyle\int_0^x \frac{3t^3 - t^2}{2t}\, dt$.

8 Given that $f'(x) = 3x^2 - 4x + 1$ and $f(0) = 2$, find $f(x)$.

9 The curve $y = f(x)$ shown alongside has gradient function $f'(x) = ax + 3$.
Find the equation of the curve.

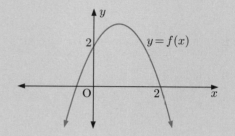

10 Find b such that $\displaystyle\int_0^b (x - b)^2\, dx = 9$.

Review set 16B

1

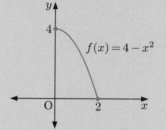

a Use *four* lower and upper rectangles to find rational numbers A and B such that:
$$A < \int_0^2 (4 - x^2)\, dx < B.$$

b Hence estimate $\displaystyle\int_0^2 (4 - x^2)\, dx$.

2 The graph of $y = f(x)$ is illustrated.
Evaluate the following using area interpretation:

a $\displaystyle\int_0^2 f(x)\, dx$ **b** $\displaystyle\int_2^6 f(x)\, dx$

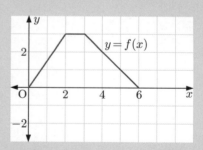

3 Integrate with respect to x:

a $\dfrac{x^2 - 2}{x^2}$ **b** $(3x - 4)^2$ **c** $4 - 2x^2$

4 Find:

a $\displaystyle\int \left(x^{\frac{1}{3}} + 3\right) dx$ **b** $\displaystyle\int (3x^2 - 2)\, dx$ **c** $\displaystyle\int (3 + 2x)^2\, dx$

5 Given that $f'(x) = x^2 - 3x + 2$ and $f(1) = 3$, find $f(x)$.

6 Find the exact value of:

a $\displaystyle\int_2^3 \frac{1}{\sqrt{3x}}\, dx$ **b** $\displaystyle\int_1^4 (x - \tfrac{1}{2}x^2)\, dx$ **c** $\displaystyle\int_0^1 (x^2 + \tfrac{1}{3})^2\, dx$

7 If $\displaystyle\int_1^4 f(x)\,dx = 3$, determine:

    a $\displaystyle\int_1^4 (f(x)+1)\,dx$
              b $\displaystyle\int_1^2 f(x)\,dx - \int_4^2 f(x)\,dx$

8 Find $A'(x)$ given $A(x) = \displaystyle\int_{\frac{1}{2}}^x (2t^2 - 3t)\,dt$.

9 Find y if:

    a $\dfrac{dy}{dx} = (x^2 - 1)^2$
              b $\dfrac{dy}{dx} = 400 - 20x^{-\frac{1}{2}}$

10 If $\displaystyle\int_0^a (x^2 - \tfrac{1}{2}x)\,dx = \tfrac{9}{16}$, find the exact value of a.

17

Kinematics

Contents:

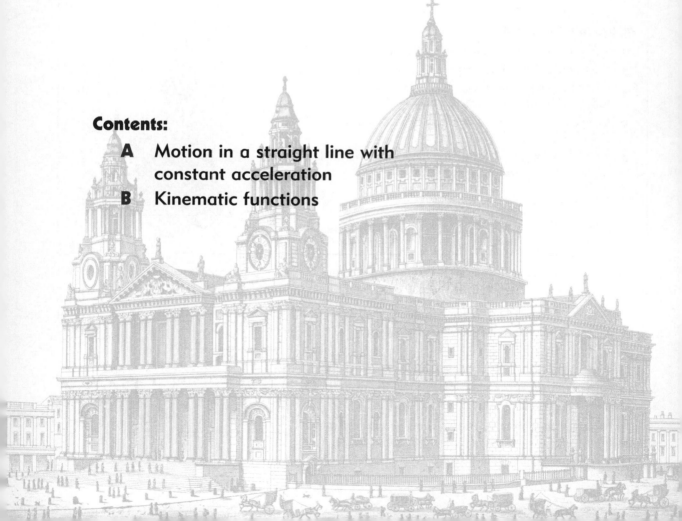

Opening problem

Michael rides up a hill and down the other side to his friend's house. The dots on the graph show Michael's position at various times t.

DEMO

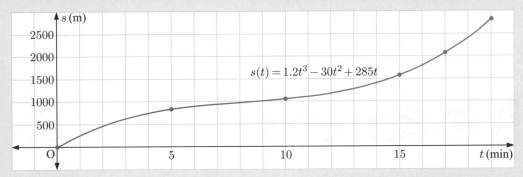

The distance Michael has travelled at various times is given by the function
$s(t) = 1.2t^3 - 30t^2 + 285t$ metres for $0 \leqslant t \leqslant 19$ minutes.

Things to think about:

a Can you find a function for Michael's *speed* at any time t?

b Michael's *acceleration* is the rate at which his speed is changing with respect to time. How can we write a function for Michael's acceleration?

c Can you find Michael's speed and acceleration at the time $t = 15$ minutes?

d At what point do you think the hill was steepest? How far had Michael travelled to this point?

In the previous Chapters we have seen how the properties of curves can be analysed using calculus. We have also seen how calculus can be used to study rates of change and optimisation.

In this Chapter we consider problems of motion called **kinematics**. These problems deal with distance and displacement, speed and velocity, and acceleration.

In the **Opening Problem** we are dealing with the movement of Michael riding his bicycle. We do not know the direction Michael is travelling, so we talk simply about the **distance** he has travelled and his **speed**.

For problems of **motion in a straight line**, we can include the *direction* the object is travelling along the line. We therefore can talk about *displacement* and *velocity*.

> Distance and speed only have size. Displacement and velocity have size and direction.

DISPLACEMENT, VELOCITY, AND ACCELERATION

Suppose an object P moves along a straight line.

- The **displacement** s of P is its position relative to a fixed origin O.
- The **velocity** v of P is its rate of change of displacement.
- The **acceleration** a of P is its rate of change of velocity.

UNITS

The SI system of units is an internationally agreed system for physical measurement. SI comes from the French *Système international d'unités* and SI is the modern form of the metric system. SI is used in most countries but not all.

SI is built on seven base units. In this course we will consider three of them: time, length, and mass. The other base units relate to electric current, temperature, an amount of matter, and luminous intensity.

The unit of time is the second, s. The original definition of a second was in terms of a day. A day was defined as 24 hours, each of 60 minutes, with each minute being 60 seconds. A second was then $\dfrac{1}{24 \times 60^2} = \dfrac{1}{86\,400}$ of a day. However, the Earth does not move in a perfectly uniform way, and so a second is now defined in terms of vibrations of a caesium-133 atom.

The unit of length is the metre, m. Originally the metre was defined as $\dfrac{1}{10\,000\,000}$ part of the distance of the line along the surface of the Earth (meridian) between the North Pole and the Equator through Paris. Currently the metre is defined as the distance travelled by light in vacuum in $\dfrac{1}{299\,792\,458}$ of a second.

The unit of mass is the kilogram, kg. The original definition was to take a volume of water at its freezing point equal to 0.1 m $\times$ 0.1 m $\times$ 0.1 m. This mass defined a kilogram. Currently the kilogram is measured against a unique physical object: the international prototype kilogram.

There are many other derived units which are formed from the base units by taking multiples and powers of the units. For example, the letter k is used for "kilo" and means 1000. Therefore, a kilometre literally means 1000 m. Some of the other SI prefixes are shown below.

SI prefix	Scientific notation	Multiplying factor
tera (T)	10^{12}	1 000 000 000 000
giga (G)	10^9	1 000 000 000
mega (M)	10^6	1 000 000
kilo (k)	10^3	1000
milli (m)	10^{-3}	0.001
micro (μ)	10^{-6}	0.000 001
nano (n)	10^{-9}	0.000 000 001
pico (p)	10^{-12}	0.000 000 000 001

The base units can also be combined together.

For example, if displacement is measured in metres, then:

- velocity, which is a ratio of speed to time, is measured in metres *per* second or $\mathrm{m\,s^{-1}}$
- acceleration, which is a ratio of velocity to time, is measured in metres per second per second, or $\mathrm{m\,s^{-2}}$.

A MOTION IN A STRAIGHT LINE WITH CONSTANT ACCELERATION

In this Section we consider an object moving along a straight line under constant acceleration. This may sound simplistic, but it provides a good approximation to the vertical motion of an object under gravity, and is therefore quite useful.

Suppose the object moves displacement s in time t under acceleration a. Let its initial velocity be u and its final velocity be v.

We will now derive a set of four equations relating these variables: s, u, v, a, t. Together they are often referred to as the **suvat equations**.

Since acceleration is assumed to be constant, acceleration is the change in velocity divided by the time taken.

> You should remember the *suvat* equations only apply for constant acceleration.

$$\therefore \quad a = \frac{v - u}{t}$$

This can be rearranged to the form $v = u + at.$

The average velocity $\frac{u + v}{2}$ is the change in displacement over time.

$$\therefore \quad \frac{u + v}{2} = \frac{s}{t}$$

This can be rearranged to give $s = \dfrac{u + v}{2} t$

and substituting $v = u + at$ we obtain $s = ut + \frac{1}{2}at^2.$

Rearranging $v = u + at$ to the form $t = \dfrac{v - u}{a}$ and substituting into $s = \dfrac{u + v}{2} t$, we find

$$s = \frac{u + v}{2} \frac{v - u}{a}$$

$$\therefore \quad s = \frac{v^2 - u^2}{2a}$$

We rearrange this to the form $v^2 = u^2 + 2as.$

Example 1
◀)) **Self Tutor**

An object accelerates from rest at 10 m s^{-2}. Find how long it will take to move:

  a   5 m   **b**   10 m   **c**   15 m   **d**   20 m

$s = ut + \frac{1}{2}at^2$ where $u = 0 \text{ m s}^{-1}$ and $a = 10 \text{ m s}^{-2}$

$\therefore \quad s = 0 + 5t^2$

$\therefore \quad t^2 = \dfrac{s}{5}$

$\therefore \quad t = \sqrt{\dfrac{s}{5}}$ {since $t > 0$}

  a $t = \sqrt{\frac{5}{5}} = 1$ s   **b** $t = \sqrt{\frac{10}{5}} \approx 1.41$ s   **c** $t = \sqrt{\frac{15}{5}} \approx 1.73$ s   **d** $t = \sqrt{\frac{20}{5}} = 2$ s

Example 2

◀ᴐ) **Self Tutor**

A car accelerates constantly from rest to 100 km h^{-1} in 12 seconds. Find:

  a the acceleration   **b** the distance travelled.

  a $100 \text{ km h}^{-1} = \dfrac{100 \times 1000}{60^2} \text{ m s}^{-1} = \dfrac{1000}{36} \text{ m s}^{-1}$

    $\therefore \quad u = 0 \text{ m s}^{-1}, \ v = \frac{1000}{36} \text{ m s}^{-1}, \ \text{and} \ t = 12 \text{ s}$

    Now $v = u + at$

    $\therefore \quad a = \dfrac{v - u}{t} = \dfrac{1000}{36 \times 12} \approx 2.31 \text{ m s}^{-2}$

  b $s = \dfrac{u + v}{2}\, t = \frac{1}{2} \times \frac{1000}{36} \times 12 \approx 167 \text{ m}$

    or $s = ut + \frac{1}{2}at^2 \approx \frac{1}{2} \times 2.31 \times 12^2 \approx 167 \text{ m}$

EXERCISE 17A.1

1 An object accelerates from rest at 3.6 m s^{-2}. Find how long it will take to move:

  a 3.6 m   **b** 10 m   **c** 100 m.

2 An object accelerates from rest at 10 m s^{-2}. Find the speed at which the object will be travelling after:

  a 2 s   **b** 5 s   **c** 10 s.

3 An object accelerating at 6 m s^{-2} travels 300 m in 8 seconds. Find the:

  a initial speed of the object   **b** final speed of the object.

4 A train accelerates constantly from rest to 200 km h^{-1} in 38 seconds. Find:

  a the acceleration   **b** the distance travelled.

5 A car brakes with constant acceleration. It stops in 4.8 seconds, and travels 65 m in this time. Find:

  a the initial speed   **b** the acceleration.

6 As a speed skater rounds the bend of the track, she begins the straight travelling at 15 m s^{-1}. She accelerates constantly at 2 m s^{-2} for the next 50 m. Find:

  a the final speed of the skater

  b the time taken to travel the 50 m.

Activity   Stopping distances

The diagram below includes information from the UK Highway Code. It shows the typical stopping distances required for a car to stop in normal conditions from various speeds. It includes the distance travelled while the driver thinks to react, and the distance travelled once the brakes are applied.

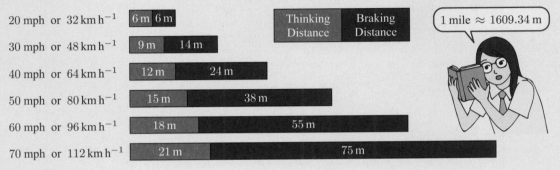

20 mph or $32 \, \text{km h}^{-1}$ 6 m 6 m

30 mph or $48 \, \text{km h}^{-1}$ 9 m   14 m

40 mph or $64 \, \text{km h}^{-1}$ 12 m   24 m

50 mph or $80 \, \text{km h}^{-1}$ 15 m   38 m

60 mph or $96 \, \text{km h}^{-1}$ 18 m   55 m

70 mph or $112 \, \text{km h}^{-1}$ 21 m   75 m

Thinking Distance   Braking Distance

1 mile $\approx 1609.34 \, \text{m}$

What to do:

1 Estimate the thinking time for a driver to react.

2 Explain why it is reasonable to apply the suvat equations for the "thinking" period and for the "braking" period, but *not* over the whole period.
State the assumptions you are making in your response.

3 Estimate the braking acceleration of a car.

4 A car travelling at 30 mph stops in 23 m. Imagine each of the faster cars brake to try to avoid an unexpected obstruction 25 m away. At what speeds, in miles per hour, will they be travelling when they reach the obstruction?

5 Find the maximum speed (in mph) that a car may be travelling at, such that it can stop short of an unexpected obstruction 30 m away?

FREE FALL UNDER GRAVITY

Near the Earth's surface, acceleration due to gravity is approximately constant. It is denoted by the symbol g, where $g \approx 9.8 \, \text{m s}^{-2}$.

Acceleration due to gravity is downwards towards the centre of the Earth. So, if the upwards direction is taken to be positive acceleration, we need to use $g \approx -9.8 \, \text{m s}^{-2}$. When solving a problem, you are often free to choose which direction is positive. However, you must state which direction is positive, and you should check the algebraic sign of each quantity carefully so that they are all consistent.

Historical note

In 1589 the scientist **Galileo Galilei** is said to have carried out a very famous experiment. It is claimed he dropped two objects with different masses from the Leaning Tower of Pisa. Both objects hit the ground at the same time, demonstrating that their time of descent was independent of their mass.

We do not know if Galileo really carried out this experiment. However, what Galileo demonstrated was contrary to the previously held theory of **Aristotle**. Aristotle taught that heavy objects fall faster than lighter ones, in direct proportion to weight. Galileo's theory was an important advance which **Sir Isaac Newton** later expanded upon.

Example 3

◀) **Self Tutor**

On 14 October 2012 Felix Baumgartner jumped from a balloon over eastern New Mexico from an altitude of $38\,969.3$ m. Baumgartner was in free fall for 4 minutes and 19 seconds. During his jump, Baumgartner set a world record for fastest speed of free fall at 377.1 $\text{m\,s}^{-1}$, making him the first human to break the sound barrier outside of a vehicle.

Without air resistance and assuming a constant acceleration of 9.8 $\text{m\,s}^{-2}$, how long would it have taken him to reach the ground?

Using the equation $s = ut + \frac{1}{2}at^2$ with $s = 38\,969.3$ m, $u = 0$ $\text{m\,s}^{-1}$, $a = 9.8$ $\text{m\,s}^{-2}$

{where the downwards direction is positive}

$$t^2 = \frac{2s}{a}$$

$$\therefore \quad t = \sqrt{\frac{2s}{a}} \quad \text{\{since } t > 0\}$$

$$\therefore \quad t \approx 89 \text{ s}$$

Example 4

◀) **Self Tutor**

A ball is thrown vertically upwards with velocity 6.86 $\text{m\,s}^{-1}$ from a platform 5.88 m high.
  a   When will it hit the ground?
  b   What is the maximum height reached by the ball above the ground?

Letting the upwards direction be positive,
$u = 6.86$ $\text{m\,s}^{-1}$, $a = -9.8$ $\text{m\,s}^{-2}$, $s = -5.88$ m   {below the starting point}

a
$$s = ut + \tfrac{1}{2}at^2$$
$$\therefore \quad -5.88 = 6.86t - \tfrac{1}{2} \times 9.8t^2$$
$$\therefore \quad 4.9t^2 - 6.86t - 5.88 = 0$$
$$\therefore \quad t^2 - 1.4t - 1.2 = 0$$
$$\therefore \quad 5t^2 - 7t - 6 = 0$$
$$\therefore \quad (t - 2)(5t + 3) = 0$$
$$\therefore \quad t = 2 \quad \text{\{since } t > 0\}$$

The ball hits the ground after 2 seconds.

b When the maximum height is reached, $v = 0 \text{ m s}^{-1}$.

Now $v^2 = u^2 + 2as$

$\therefore \quad 2as = v^2 - u^2$

$\therefore \quad 2(-9.8)s = -6.86^2$

$\therefore \quad s = \dfrac{6.86^2}{2 \times 9.8} \approx 2.40 \text{ m from the initial location}$

$\therefore$ the maximum height reached $\approx 2.40 + 5.88$

≈ 8.28 m above the ground.

EXERCISE 17A.2

1 A stone is dropped from a bridge 20.6 m above a river. Assuming constant acceleration of 9.8 m s^{-2} and the downwards direction being positive, find:

    a the time for the stone to reach the river

    b the speed at which the stone is travelling when it hits the water.

2 Dashing Darryl has just visited his girlfriend. He is standing outside her apartment block. His girlfriend is standing on her balcony 18.5 m above, waving goodbye. Darryl suddenly realises he picked up the wrong set of keys from the table when he left.

    a With what speed does Darryl need to throw his girlfriend's keys up to her, so that they will at least reach her?

    b If Darryl throws the keys at this speed, how long will they take to reach her?

    c Darryl's girlfriend throws his keys back down to him in exchange with the same initial speed as he threw hers.

        i How long will it take them to reach him?

        ii What will be their speed when they reach him?

3 The table alongside gives the approximate values of acceleration due to gravity on various objects in the Solar System.

    a Suppose you throw a ball vertically in the air with initial velocity 3.5 m s^{-1}. How high would the ball go if you are on the surface of:

        i the Earth   **ii** the moon   **iii** Pluto?

    b Suppose you take a flight to Titan, the largest moon of Saturn. You throw a ball vertically up at 5 m s^{-1}. It takes 7.3 s to return to the surface. Estimate the value of the gravitational constant on Titan.

	Surface gravity (m s^{-2})
Sun	274.78
Mercury	3.73
Venus	8.87
Earth	9.81
Moon	1.62
Mars	3.69
Jupiter	24.81
Saturn	10.49
Uranus	8.73
Neptune	11.18
Pluto	0.66

B | KINEMATIC FUNCTIONS

DISPLACEMENT

Suppose an object P moves along a straight line. The position of P
relative to an origin O is called the **displacement** of P.

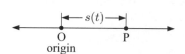

We can define a **displacement function** $s(t)$ which gives the
displacement of the object at any time $t \geqslant 0$ as it moves along
the line.

When $s(t) > 0$, P is to the right of the origin. When $s(t) < 0$, P is to the left of the origin.

For example, consider $s(t) = 2t^2 - 5t - 2$ cm.

$s(0) = -2$ cm, $s(1) = -5$ cm, $s(2) = -4$ cm, $s(3) = 1$ cm, $s(4) = 10$ cm.

To appreciate the motion of P we draw a **motion graph**.

DEMO

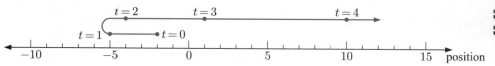

VELOCITY

The **velocity** of an object is its rate of change of displacement.

If $s(t)$ is the displacement function of an object moving in a straight line, then:

- the **average velocity** of the object moving in the time interval from $t = t_1$ to $t = t_2$ is given by

$$\text{average velocity} = \frac{s(t_2) - s(t_1)}{t_2 - t_1}$$

On a graph of $s(t)$ against t, the
average velocity is the gradient of the
chord through the points $P_1(t_1, s(t_1))$
and $P_2(t_2, s(t_2))$.

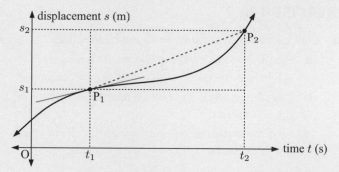

- the **instantaneous velocity** or **velocity function** of the object at time t is $v(t) = s'(t)$. It is the
  gradient of the tangent to the function $s(t)$ at any given time.
  - When $v(t) > 0$, the object is moving to the right.
  - When $v(t) < 0$, the object is moving to the left.
  - When $v(t) = 0$, the object is instantaneously at rest. A change in the sign of $v(t)$ at this time
    indicates that the object has changed direction.

ACCELERATION

The **acceleration** of an object is its rate of change of velocity.

If an object moves in a straight line with displacement function $s(t)$ and velocity function $v(t)$, then:

- the **average acceleration** for the time interval from $t = t_1$ to $t = t_2$ is given by

$$\text{average acceleration} = \frac{v(t_2) - v(t_1)}{t_2 - t_1}$$

- The **acceleration function** $a(t)$ of the object is given by $a(t) = v'(t) = s''(t)$.

Example 5   ◀)) Self Tutor

A particle moves in a straight line with displacement from O given by $s(t) = 3t - t^2$ metres at time t seconds. Find:

a the average velocity for the time interval from $t = 2$ to $t = 5$ seconds

b the instantaneous velocity at $t = 2$ seconds

c the acceleration function $a(t)$.

a   average velocity

$$= \frac{s(5) - s(2)}{5 - 2}$$

$$= \frac{(15 - 25) - (6 - 4)}{3}$$

$$= \frac{-10 - 2}{3}$$

$$= -4 \text{ m s}^{-1}$$

b $s(t) = 3t - t^2$

$\therefore$ $v(t) = s'(t) = 3 - 2t$

$\therefore$ $v(2) = 3 - 2(2)$

$\qquad = -1 \text{ m s}^{-1}$

c $a(t) = v'(t)$

$\qquad = -2 \text{ m s}^{-2}$

EXERCISE 17B.1

1 Consider the displacement-time graph alongside.

a Find the displacement of the object when:

i $t = 2$ seconds   **ii** $t = 8$ seconds.

b Find the average velocity of the object from $t = 2$ to $t = 3$ seconds.

c Find the instantaneous velocity of the object when $t = 5$ seconds.

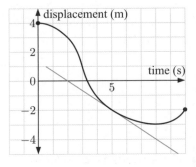

2 A particle moves in a straight line with displacement from O given by $s(t) = t^2 - 6t + 1$ metres at time t seconds, $t \geqslant 0$.

a Find the average velocity from $t = 1$ to $t = 3$ seconds.

b Find $v(t)$.

c Hence find the instantaneous velocity at:

i $t = 1$ second   **ii** $t = 5$ seconds.

3 A particle moves with velocity function $v(t) = 10t - t^2$ cm s^{-1}, $t \geq 0$. Find:

    a the velocity of the particle when $t = 2$ seconds

    b the average acceleration of the particle from $t = 1$ to $t = 3$ seconds

    c the acceleration function $a(t)$

    d the instantaneous acceleration of the particle when $t = 3$ seconds.

4 An object moves in a straight line with displacement function $s(t) = t^3 + t^2 - 5$ metres at time t seconds, $t \geq 0$. Find the object's displacement, velocity, and acceleration when $t = 2$ seconds.

SIGN INTERPRETATION

Suppose a particle P moves in a straight line with displacement function $s(t)$ relative to an origin O. Its velocity function is $v(t)$ and its acceleration function is $a(t)$.

We can use **sign diagrams** to interpret:

- where the particle is located relative to O
- the direction of motion and where a change of direction occurs
- when the particle's velocity is increasing or decreasing.

SIGNS OF $s(t)$:

$s(t)$	Interpretation
$= 0$	P is at O
> 0	P is located to the right of O
< 0	P is located to the left of O

SIGNS OF $v(t)$:

$v(t)$	Interpretation
$= 0$	P is instantaneously at rest
> 0	P is moving to the right
< 0	P is moving to the left

SIGNS OF $a(t)$:

$a(t)$	Interpretation
> 0	velocity is increasing
< 0	velocity is decreasing
$= 0$	velocity may be a maximum or minimum or possibly constant

ZEROS:

Phrase used in a question	t	s	v	a
initial conditions	0			
at the origin		0		
stationary			0	
reverses			0	
maximum or minimum displacement			0	
constant velocity				0
maximum or minimum velocity				0

When a particle reverses direction, its velocity must change sign.
This corresponds to a local maximum or local minimum distance from the origin O.

SPEED

As we have seen, velocities have size (magnitude) and sign (direction). In contrast, speed simply measures *how fast* something is travelling, regardless of the direction of travel. Speed is a *scalar* quantity which has size but no sign. Speed cannot be negative.

> The **speed** at any instant is the magnitude of the object's velocity.

For example, an object with velocity -5 m s^{-1} is moving to the left with speed 5 m s^{-1}.

To determine when the speed of an object P with displacement $s(t)$ is increasing or decreasing, we use a **sign test**.

- If the signs of $v(t)$ and $a(t)$ are the same (both positive or both negative), then the speed of P is increasing.
- If the signs of $v(t)$ and $a(t)$ are opposite, then the speed of P is decreasing.

Example 6   ◀⬮ **Self Tutor**

A particle moves in a straight line with position relative to O given by $s(t) = t^3 - 3t + 1$ cm, where t is the time in seconds, $t \geqslant 0$.

a Find expressions for the particle's velocity and acceleration, and draw sign diagrams for each of them.

b Find the initial conditions and hence describe the motion at this instant.

c Describe the motion of the particle at $t = 2$ seconds.

d Find the position of the particle when it changes direction.

e Draw a motion diagram for the particle.

f For what time interval is the particle's speed increasing?

g What is the total distance travelled in the time from $t = 0$ to $t = 2$ seconds?

> The *initial conditions* describe the particle's motion when $t = 0$.

a $s(t) = t^3 - 3t + 1$ cm

$\quad\therefore\ v(t) = 3t^2 - 3 \qquad\qquad \{v(t) = s'(t)\}$

$\qquad\qquad = 3(t^2 - 1)$

$\qquad\qquad = 3(t + 1)(t - 1)$ cm s^{-1}

which has sign diagram:

and $\ a(t) = 6t$ cm s^{-2} $\qquad\quad \{a(t) = v'(t)\}$

which has sign diagram:

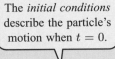

> Since $t \geqslant 0$, the stationary point at $t = -1$ is not required.

b When $t = 0$, $\ s(0) = 1$ cm

$\qquad\qquad\qquad\quad v(0) = -3$ cm s^{-1}

$\qquad\qquad\qquad\quad a(0) = 0$ cm s^{-2}

$\quad\therefore\ $ the particle is 1 cm to the right of O, moving to the left at a speed of 3 cm s^{-1}.

c When $t = 2$, $s(2) = 8 - 6 + 1 = 3$ cm
$$v(2) = 12 - 3 = 9 \text{ cm s}^{-1}$$
$$a(2) = 12 \text{ cm s}^{-2}$$

$\therefore$ the particle is 3 cm to the right of O, moving to the right at a speed of 9 cm s^{-1}.
Since a and v have the same sign, the speed of the particle is increasing.

d Since $v(t)$ changes sign when $t = 1$, a change of direction occurs at this instant.
$s(1) = 1 - 3 + 1 = -1$,   so the particle changes direction when it is 1 cm to the left of O.

e

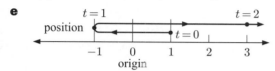

The motion is actually **on the line**, not above it as shown.

f Speed is increasing when $v(t)$ and $a(t)$ have the same sign. This is for $t \geqslant 1$.

g Total distance travelled $= 2 + 4 = 6$ cm.

EXERCISE 17B.2

1 Consider the displacement-time graph alongside.

a Describe the initial position of the object.

b At what time is the object at the origin?

c In which direction is the object moving when $t = 5$ seconds?

d At what times does the object change direction?

e Draw a sign diagram for:

  i the displacement function $s(t)$

  ii the velocity function $v(t)$.

f Find the instantaneous velocity of the object when $t = 7$ seconds.

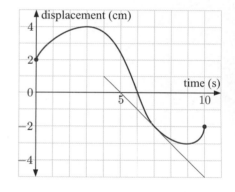

2 An object moves in a straight line with position given by $s(t) = t^3 - 11t^2 + 24t$ m from O, where t is in seconds, $t \geqslant 0$.

a Describe the initial conditions of the object.

b Find the velocity function $v(t)$.

c Draw a sign diagram for $s(t)$ and $v(t)$.

d At what times is the object at O?

e At which times does the object reverse direction? Find the position of the object at each of these times.

f Describe in words the motion of the object.

g Draw a motion diagram for the object.

3 An object moves in a straight line with position from O given by $s(t) = t^2 - 4t + 3$ cm, where t is in seconds, $t \geqslant 0$.

   a Find expressions for the object's velocity and acceleration, and draw sign diagrams for each function.

   b Find the initial conditions and explain what is happening to the object at that instant.

   c Describe the motion of the object at time $t = 4$ seconds.

   d At what time does the object reverse direction? Find the position of the object at this instant.

   e Draw a motion diagram for the object.

   f For what time intervals is the speed of the object decreasing?

4 A stone is fired from a catapult so that its position above ground level after t seconds is given by $s(t) = 98t - 4.9t^2$ metres, $t \geqslant 0$.

   a Find the velocity and acceleration functions for the stone, and draw sign diagrams for each function.

   b Find the initial position and velocity of the stone.

   c Describe the stone's motion at times $t = 5$ and $t = 12$ seconds.

   d Find the maximum height reached by the stone.

   e Find the time taken for the stone to hit the ground.

5 When a ball is thrown, its height above the ground is given by $s(t) = 1.2 + 28.1t - 4.9t^2$ metres, where t is the time in seconds.

   a From what distance above the ground was the ball released?

   b Find $s'(t)$ and state what it represents.

   c Find t when $s'(t) = 0$. What is the significance of this result?

   d What is the maximum height reached by the ball?

   e Find the ball's speed:

      i when released   **ii** at $t = 2$ s   **iii** at $t = 5$ s.

      State the significance of the sign of the derivative $s'(t)$.

   f How long will it take for the ball to hit the ground?

6 The position of a particle moving along the x-axis is given by $x(t) = t^3 - 9t^2 + 24t$ metres where t is in seconds, $t \geqslant 0$.

   a Draw sign diagrams for the particle's velocity and acceleration functions.

   b Find the position of the particle at the times when it reverses direction, and hence draw a motion diagram for the particle.

   c At what times is the particle's:

      i speed decreasing   **ii** velocity decreasing?

   d Find the total distance travelled by the particle in the first 5 seconds of motion.

> When finding the total distance travelled, always look for direction reversals first.

Investigation   Projectile motion

Suppose you are operating a cannon, and are trying to fire a cannonball as far as possible. At what angle to the ground should you fire the cannonball?

- If the angle is too high, the cannonball will go high into the air, but will not travel very far horizontally.

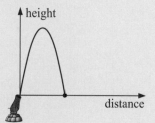

- If the angle is too low, the cannonball will hit the ground too soon, and will not travel very far.

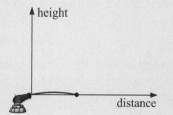

Suppose the cannonball is fired at an angle θ to the ground, with initial velocity v_0 m s^{-1}. The motion of the cannonball has both a **vertical component** and a **horizontal component**. We will consider these components separately.

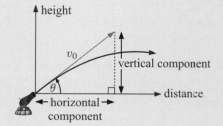

What to do:

1　**a**　If the cannon is fired from ground level, what is the initial vertical height of the cannonball?

　　b　Use the diagram above to show that the initial vertical velocity of the cannonball is $v_0 \sin \theta$ m s^{-1}.

　　c　The path of the cannonball is affected by gravity, which acts downwards on the cannonball at a rate of 9.8 m s^{-2}.
　　　Explain why the vertical acceleration of the cannonball is given by $a(t) = -9.8$ m s^{-2}.

　　d　Show that the vertical displacement function $s(t) = -4.9t^2 + [v_0 \sin \theta]t$ satisfies the properties in **a**, **b**, and **c**.

　　e　Hence, show that the cannonball takes $\dfrac{v_0 \sin \theta}{4.9}$ seconds to hit the ground.

2　**a**　Show that the horizontal velocity of the cannonball is $v_0 \cos \theta$ m s^{-1}.

　　b　Hence, show that the horizontal distance travelled by the cannonball before it hits the ground is $\dfrac{v_0^2 \sin 2\theta}{9.8}$ metres.

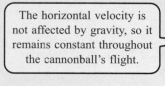

The horizontal velocity is not affected by gravity, so it remains constant throughout the cannonball's flight.

　　c　Suppose a cannonball is fired with initial velocity 200 m s^{-1}. Find the horizontal distance travelled by the cannonball if it is fired at an angle of:
　　　i　$20°$　　　　　　　　**ii**　$50°$　　　　　　　　**iii**　$80°$

　　d　Find the angle θ which maximises the range of the cannonball.
　　　Hint:　What are the possible values that $\sin 2\theta$ can take?

3　Click on the icon to run a cannon simulation.
　　Change the initial velocity and angle of trajectory, and observe the effect these have on the path of the cannonball.
　　Use the simulation to check that your answer to **2 d** is correct.

SIMULATION

DISTANCE AND DISPLACEMENT FROM VELOCITY GRAPHS

Suppose a car travels at a constant positive velocity of 60 km h^{-1} for 15 minutes.

We know the distance travelled $=$ speed $\times$ time
$$= 60 \text{ km h}^{-1} \times \tfrac{1}{4} \text{ h}$$
$$= 15 \text{ km}.$$

When we graph *velocity* against *time*, the graph in this case is a horizontal line, and we can see that the distance travelled is the area shaded.

So, the distance travelled can also be found by the definite

integral $\displaystyle\int_0^{\frac{1}{4}} 60 \, dt = 15$ km.

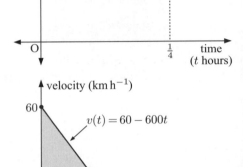

Now suppose the velocity decreases at a constant rate, so that the car, initially travelling at 60 km h^{-1}, stops in 6 minutes or $\frac{1}{10}$ hour.

In this case the *average* speed is 30 km h^{-1}, so the distance travelled $= 30 \text{ km h}^{-1} \times \tfrac{1}{10} \text{ h}$
$$= 3 \text{ km}.$$

But the triangle has area $= \tfrac{1}{2} \times$ base $\times$ altitude
$$= \tfrac{1}{2} \times \tfrac{1}{10} \times 60 = 3.$$

So, once again the shaded area gives us the distance travelled, and we can find it using the definite integral

$$\int_0^{\frac{1}{10}} (60 - 600t) \, dt = 3 \text{ km}.$$

These results suggest that we can calculate the distance travelled by integrating the velocity function. We can prove this using the Fundamental Theorem of Calculus.

By definition, the instantaneous velocity is the derivative of the position
$$v(t) = s'(t)$$

Using the Fundamental Theorem of Calculus, $s(t_1) = s(t_0) + \displaystyle\int_{t_0}^{t_1} s'(t) \, dt$

$$\therefore \quad s(t_1) = s(t_0) + \int_{t_0}^{t_1} v(t) \, dt$$

So, given a velocity function we can determine the displacement function using the integral:

$$s(t) = \int v(t) \, dt$$

The constant of integration can be found if we know the position of the object at any particular time.

We can determine the change in displacement in a time interval $t_1 \leqslant t \leqslant t_2$ using the integral:

$$\text{Change in displacement} = s(t_2) - s(t_1) = \int_{t_1}^{t_2} v(t) \, dt$$

For a velocity-time function $v(t)$ where $v(t) \geqslant 0$ on the interval $t_1 \leqslant t \leqslant t_2$,

$$\text{distance travelled} = \int_{t_1}^{t_2} v(t)\,dt.$$

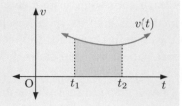

If we have a change of direction within the time interval then the velocity will change sign. We therefore need to add the components of area above and below the t-axis to find the total distance travelled.

Example 7   ◆》 Self Tutor

The velocity-time graph for a train journey is illustrated in the graph alongside. Find the total distance travelled by the train.

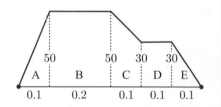

Total distance travelled

= total area under the graph

= area A + area B + area C + area D + area E

= $\frac{1}{2}(0.1)50 + (0.2)50 + \left(\frac{50+30}{2}\right)(0.1) + (0.1)30 + \frac{1}{2}(0.1)30$

= $2.5 + 10 + 4 + 3 + 1.5$

= 21 km

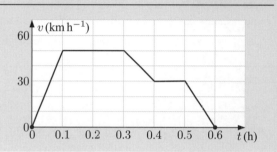

EXERCISE 17B.3

1 A runner has the velocity-time graph shown. Find the total distance travelled by the runner.

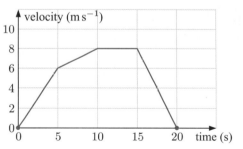

2

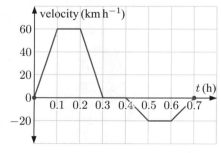

A car travels along a straight road with the velocity-time graph illustrated.

  a What is the significance of the graph:
  i above the t-axis
  ii below the t-axis?

  b Find the total *distance* travelled by the car.

  c Find the final *displacement* of the car from its starting point.

3 After leaving a station, a train accelerates at a constant rate
for 40 seconds until its speed reaches 15 m s^{-1}. The train
then travels at this speed for 160 seconds. On its approach to
the next station, the train slows down at a constant rate for
80 seconds until it is at rest.

  a Draw a graph to show the train's motion.

  b How far did the train travel between the stations?

4 A cyclist rides off from rest, accelerating at a constant rate for 3 minutes until she reaches 40 km h^{-1}.
She then maintains a constant speed for 4 minutes until reaching a hill. She slows down at a constant
rate over one minute to 20 km h^{-1}, then continues at this speed for 5 minutes. At the top of the hill
she reduces her speed uniformly, and she is stationary 2 minutes later.

  a Draw a graph to show the cyclist's motion.   **b** How far has the cyclist travelled?

Example 8   ◀) **Self Tutor**

A particle P moves in a straight line with velocity function $v(t) = t^2 - 3t + 2 \text{ m s}^{-1}$.

  a How far does P travel in the first 4 seconds of motion?

  b Find the displacement of P after 4 seconds.

  a $v(t) = s'(t) = t^2 - 3t + 2$
$$= (t-1)(t-2)$$

$\therefore$ the sign diagram of v is:

Since the signs change, P reverses direction at $t = 1$ and $t = 2$ seconds.

Now $s(t) = \displaystyle\int (t^2 - 3t + 2)\, dt = \dfrac{t^3}{3} - \dfrac{3t^2}{2} + 2t + c$

Hence $s(0) = c$ $s(1) = \frac{1}{3} - \frac{3}{2} + 2 + c = c + \frac{5}{6}$

        $s(2) = \frac{8}{3} - 6 + 4 + c = c + \frac{2}{3}$ $s(4) = \frac{64}{3} - 24 + 8 + c = c + 5\frac{1}{3}$

Motion diagram:

$\therefore$ total distance travelled

     $= (c + \frac{5}{6} - c) + (c + \frac{5}{6} - [c + \frac{2}{3}]) + (c + 5\frac{1}{3} - [c + \frac{2}{3}])$

     $= \frac{5}{6} + \frac{5}{6} - \frac{2}{3} + 5\frac{1}{3} - \frac{2}{3}$

     $= 5\frac{2}{3}$ m

> For problems involving
> total distance travelled,
> the constant of integration
> should always cancel.

  b Displacement $=$ final position $-$ original position

                   $= s(4) - s(0)$

                   $= c + 5\frac{1}{3} - c$

                   $= 5\frac{1}{3}$ m

So, the displacement is $5\frac{1}{3}$ m to the right.

5 A particle has velocity function $v(t) = 1 - 2t$ cm s^{-1} as it moves in a straight line.

   a Find the total distance travelled in the first second of motion.

   b Find the displacement of the particle after one second.

6 Particle P is initially at the origin O. It moves with the velocity function $v(t) = t^2 - t - 2$ cm s^{-1}.

   a Write a formula for the displacement function $s(t)$.

   b Find the total distance travelled in the first 3 seconds of motion.

   c Find the particle's displacement from its starting position after three seconds.

7 A ball is thrown from 1 m above ground level. Its velocity is
$v(t) = 29.4 - 9.8t$ m s^{-1}.

   a Find the displacement function $s(t)$.

   b Find the maximum height reached by the ball.

VELOCITY AND ACCELERATION FUNCTIONS

We know that the acceleration function is the derivative of the velocity function, so $a(t) = v'(t)$.

So, given an acceleration function, we can determine the velocity function by integration:

$$v(t) = \int a(t)\, dt$$

The displacement, velocity, and acceleration functions are therefore connected as follows:

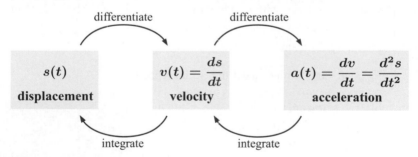

EXERCISE 17B.4

1 The velocity of a moving object is given by $v(t) = 32 + 4t$ m s^{-1}.

   a If $s = 16$ m when $t = 0$ seconds, find the displacement function.

   b Explain why the displacement of the object and its total distance travelled in the interval
$0 \leqslant t \leqslant t_1$, can both be represented by the definite integral $\displaystyle\int_0^{t_1} (32 + 4t)\, dt$.

   c Show that the object is travelling with constant acceleration.

Example 9
◀️)) **Self Tutor**

A particle is initially at the origin and moving to the right at 5 cm s^{-1}. It accelerates with time according to $a(t) = 4 - 2t \text{ cm s}^{-2}$.

a Find the velocity function of the particle, and sketch its graph for $0 \leqslant t \leqslant 6$.

b For the first 6 seconds of motion, determine the:

    i displacement of the particle   **ii** total distance travelled.

a $v(t) = \displaystyle\int a(t)\,dt = \int (4 - 2t)\,dt = 4t - t^2 + c$

But $v(0) = 5$, so $c = 5$

$\therefore \quad v(t) = -t^2 + 4t + 5 \text{ cm s}^{-1}$

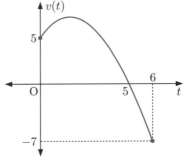

b $s(t) = \displaystyle\int v(t)\,dt = \int (-t^2 + 4t + 5)\,dt$

$\qquad = -\tfrac{1}{3}t^3 + 2t^2 + 5t + c \text{ cm}$

But $s(0) = 0$, so $c = 0$

$\therefore \quad s(t) = -\tfrac{1}{3}t^3 + 2t^2 + 5t \text{ cm}$

i   Displacement

$= s(6) - s(0)$

$= -\tfrac{1}{3}(6)^3 + 2(6)^2 + 5(6)$

$= 30 \text{ cm}$

ii The particle changes direction when $t = 5$ s.

Now $s(5) = -\tfrac{1}{3}(5)^3 + 2(5)^2 + 5(5) = 33\tfrac{1}{3} \text{ cm}$

Motion diagram:

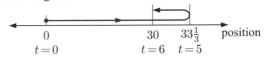

$\therefore$ the total distance travelled $= 33\tfrac{1}{3} + 3\tfrac{1}{3} = 36\tfrac{2}{3} \text{ cm}$

---

2 A train moves along a straight track with acceleration $\dfrac{t}{10} - 3 \text{ m s}^{-2}$. The initial velocity of the train is 45 m s^{-1}.

    a Determine the velocity function $v(t)$.

    b Evaluate $\displaystyle\int_0^{60} v(t)\,dt$ and explain what this value represents.

3 A stunt motorcyclist rides towards a ramp. His velocity after t seconds is given by $v(t) = 10\sqrt{t} \text{ m s}^{-1}$.

    a Find the motorcyclist's velocity after:

        i 1 second   **ii** 2 seconds.

    b Write a function $s(t)$ for the distance travelled by the motorcyclist after t seconds.

    c Find $\displaystyle\int_0^2 v(t)\,dt$, and interpret your answer.

    d In order to perform his stunt, the motorcyclist needs to be travelling at 20 m s^{-1} or faster when he reaches the ramp.

        i How long will he take to reach a speed of 20 m s^{-1}?

        ii The motorcyclist started his approach 55 m from the ramp. Has he given himself enough distance to reach the required speed?

Review set 17A

1 An object accelerates from rest at 5.3 m s^{-2}.

   a Find the speed at which the object will be travelling after 4.7 seconds.

   b How far will the object travel in the first 2 seconds?

   c Find how long it will take for the object to move 38 m.

2 Lucy is standing on a lookout at the top of a waterfall. She tosses a pebble into the air with initial speed 6.2 m s^{-1}. She fails to catch it on the way down, so it falls all the way to the pool at the bottom. The pebble hits the water 4.6 seconds after Lucy threw it. Assuming constant acceleration of 9.8 m s^{-2} downwards, find:

   a the maximum height reached by the pebble above the lookout

   b the height of the lookout above the pool

   c the speed of the pebble when it hits the water.

3 A particle moves in a straight line with displacement from O given by $s(t) = 2t^2 + t - 5$ cm at time t seconds, $t \geqslant 0$.

   a Find the average velocity from $t = 1$ to $t = 5$ seconds.

   b Find the instantaneous velocity at:

      i $t = 2$ seconds   **ii** $t = 4$ seconds.

   c Find the acceleration function $a(t)$.

4 A particle P moves in a straight line with position relative to the origin O given by $s(t) = 2t^3 - 9t^2 + 12t - 5$ cm, where t is the time in seconds, $t \geqslant 0$.

   a Find the velocity and acceleration functions, and draw a sign diagram for each.

   b Find the initial conditions.

   c Describe the motion of the particle at time $t = 2$ seconds.

   d Find the times and positions where the particle changes direction.

   e Draw a diagram to illustrate the motion of P.

   f Determine the time intervals when the particle's speed is increasing.

5 A particle moves in a straight line with velocity $v(t) = t^2 - 6t + 8$ m s^{-1}, $t \geqslant 0$ seconds.

   a Draw a sign diagram for $v(t)$.

   b Describe what happens to the particle in the first 5 seconds of motion.

   c After 5 seconds, how far is the particle from its original position?

   d Find the total distance travelled in the first 5 seconds of motion.

6 When a kayaker stops paddling, the velocity of the kayak in the following 6 seconds is given by $v(t) = 2.75 - t + 0.5t^{1.2}$ m s^{-1}, where t is the time in seconds.

   a Find the velocity of the kayak:

      i when the kayaker stops paddling   **ii** after 3 seconds.

   b Show that the kayak's speed is decreasing during the 6 second period.

   c Find $\displaystyle\int_0^2 v(t)\, dt$ and interpret your answer.

Review set 17B

1 A bicycle brakes with constant acceleration from 9.14 m s^{-1} to rest in 5.2 seconds.

  a Find the acceleration.

  b How far does the bicycle travel before it stops?

2 A car travelling at 14.2 m s^{-1} accelerates at 1.5 m s^{-2} for the next 450 m.

  a Find the final speed of the car.

  b How long will it take to travel this distance?

  c Find the average speed of the car during this time.

3 A jogger has the velocity-time graph shown. Find the total distance travelled by the jogger.

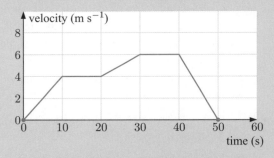

4 A particle moves along the x-axis with position relative to origin O given by $x(t) = 3t - t\sqrt{t}$ cm, where t is the time in seconds, $t \geqslant 0$.

  a Find the velocity and acceleration functions, and draw a sign diagram for each.

  b Find the initial position and velocity of the particle and hence describe the motion at that instant.

  c Describe the motion of the particle at $t = 2$ seconds.

  d Find the time and position when the particle reverses direction.

  e Determine the time interval when the particle's speed is decreasing.

  f Draw a motion diagram for the particle.

  g Find the distance travelled by the particle in the first 6 seconds of motion.

5 At time $t = 0$ a particle passes through the origin with velocity 27 cm s^{-1}. Its acceleration t seconds later is $6t - 30 \text{ cm s}^{-2}$.

  a Write an expression for the particle's velocity.

  b Calculate the displacement from the origin after 6 seconds.

6 The velocity of a human cannonball is given by $v(t) = 4.8t^2 - 0.8t^3 \text{ m s}^{-1}$ for $0 \leqslant t \leqslant 6$ seconds.

  a Find the acceleration of the human cannonball after:

    i 1 s   **ii** 2 s   **iii** 4 s   **iv** 5 s

  b Find $\displaystyle\int_0^3 v(t)\,dt$ and interpret your answer.

  c How long does it take for the human cannonball to travel 30 m?

18

Vectors

Contents:

Opening problem

An aeroplane in calm conditions is flying at 800 km h^{-1} due east. A cold wind suddenly blows from the south-west at 35 km h^{-1}, pushing the aeroplane slightly off course.

Things to think about:

a How can we illustrate the plane's movement and the wind using a scale diagram?

b What operation do we need to perform to find the effect of the wind on the aeroplane?

c Can you use a scale diagram to determine the resulting speed and direction of the aeroplane?

A   VECTORS AND SCALARS

In the **Opening Problem**, the effect of the wind on the aeroplane is determined by both its speed *and* its direction. The effect would be different if the wind was blowing against the aeroplane rather than from behind it.

Quantities which have only magnitude are called **scalars**.

Quantities which have both magnitude and direction are called **vectors**.

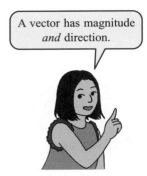

A vector has magnitude *and* direction.

The *speed* of the plane is a scalar. It describes its size or strength.

The *velocity* of the plane is a vector. It includes both its speed and also its direction.

Other examples of vector quantities are:

- acceleration
- displacement
- force
- momentum

For example, farmer Giles needs to remove a fence post. He starts by pushing on the post sideways to loosen the ground. Giles has a choice of how hard to push the post and in which direction. The force he applies is therefore a vector.

DIRECTED LINE SEGMENT REPRESENTATION

We can represent a vector quantity using a **directed line segment** or **arrow**.

The **length of the arrow** represents the size or magnitude of the quantity, and the **arrowhead** shows its direction.

For example, if farmer Giles pushes the post with a force of 50 Newtons (N) to the north-east, we can draw a scale diagram of the force relative to the north line.

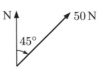

Scale: 1 cm represents 25 N

Example 1

◆)) **Self Tutor**

Draw a scale diagram to represent a force of 40 Newtons in a north-easterly direction.

N

Scale:
1 cm ≡ 10 N

40 N

45°

O

E

EXERCISE 18A.1

1 Using a scale of 1 cm represents 10 units, sketch a vector to represent:

  a 30 Newtons in a south-easterly direction

  b 25 m s^{-1} in a northerly direction

  c an excavator digging a tunnel at a rate of 30 cm min^{-1} at an angle of 30° to the ground

  d an aeroplane taking off at an angle of 10° to the runway with a speed of 50 m s^{-1}.

2 If   ⎯⎯⎯⎯⎯▸   represents a velocity of 50 m s^{-1} due east, draw a directed line segment
        25 mm
representing a velocity of:

  a 100 m s^{-1} due west   **b** 75 m s^{-1} north-east.

3 Draw a scale diagram to represent:

  a a force of 30 Newtons in a north-westerly direction

  b a velocity of 36 m s^{-1} vertically downwards

  c a displacement of 4 units at an angle of 15° to the positive x-axis

  d the velocity of an aeroplane taking off at an angle of 8° to the runway at a speed of 150 km h^{-1}.

VECTOR NOTATION

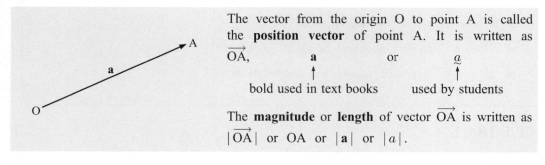

The vector from the origin O to point A is called the **position vector** of point A. It is written as

$\overrightarrow{OA}$,   **a**   or $\underset{\sim}{a}$
             ↑   ↑
   bold used in text books   used by students

The **magnitude** or **length** of vector $\overrightarrow{OA}$ is written as $|\overrightarrow{OA}|$ or OA or $|\mathbf{a}|$ or $|\underset{\sim}{a}|$.

For

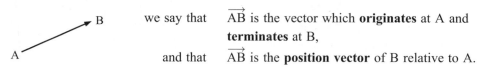

we say that $\overrightarrow{AB}$ is the vector which **originates** at A and **terminates** at B,

and that $\overrightarrow{AB}$ is the **position vector** of B relative to A.

GEOMETRIC VECTOR EQUALITY

> Two vectors are **equal** if they have the same magnitude *and* direction.

Equal vectors are **parallel** and **in the same direction**, and are **equal in length**. The arrows that represent them are translations of one another.

We can draw a vector with given magnitude and direction from *any* point, so we consider vectors to be **free**. They are sometimes referred to as **free vectors**.

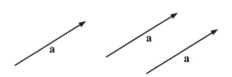

GEOMETRIC NEGATIVE VECTORS

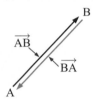

$\overrightarrow{AB}$ and $\overrightarrow{BA}$ have the same length, but they have opposite directions.

We say that $\overrightarrow{BA}$ is the **negative** of $\overrightarrow{AB}$, and write $\overrightarrow{BA} = -\overrightarrow{AB}$.

a and $-\mathbf{a}$ are parallel and equal in length, but opposite in direction.

Example 2   ◀)) **Self Tutor**

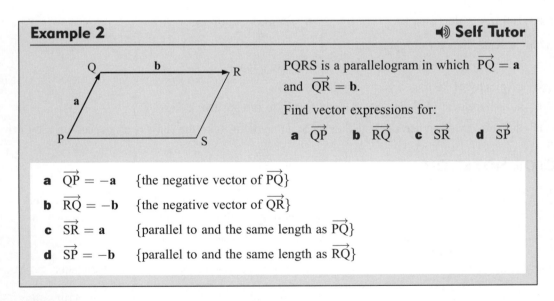

PQRS is a parallelogram in which $\overrightarrow{PQ} = \mathbf{a}$ and $\overrightarrow{QR} = \mathbf{b}$.

Find vector expressions for:

a $\overrightarrow{QP}$ **b** $\overrightarrow{RQ}$ **c** $\overrightarrow{SR}$ **d** $\overrightarrow{SP}$

a $\overrightarrow{QP} = -\mathbf{a}$ {the negative vector of $\overrightarrow{PQ}$}

b $\overrightarrow{RQ} = -\mathbf{b}$ {the negative vector of $\overrightarrow{QR}$}

c $\overrightarrow{SR} = \mathbf{a}$ {parallel to and the same length as $\overrightarrow{PQ}$}

d $\overrightarrow{SP} = -\mathbf{b}$ {parallel to and the same length as $\overrightarrow{RQ}$}

EXERCISE 18A.2

1 State the vectors which are:

   a equal in magnitude   **b** parallel

   c in the same direction   **d** equal

   e negatives of one another.

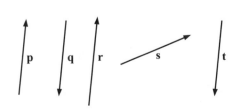

2 The figure shown consists of two equilateral triangles. A, B, and C are collinear.

$\overrightarrow{AB} = \mathbf{p}$, $\overrightarrow{AE} = \mathbf{q}$,   and $\overrightarrow{DC} = \mathbf{r}$.

Which of the following statements are true?

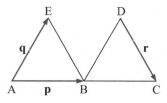

a $\overrightarrow{EB} = \mathbf{r}$	**b** $\lvert\mathbf{p}\rvert = \lvert\mathbf{q}\rvert$	**c** $\overrightarrow{BC} = \mathbf{r}$	
d $\overrightarrow{DB} = \mathbf{q}$	**e** $\overrightarrow{ED} = \mathbf{p}$	**f** $\mathbf{p} = \mathbf{q}$	

3 ABCDEF is a regular hexagon.

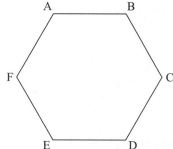

a Write down the vector which:

 i originates at B and terminates at C

 ii is equal to $\overrightarrow{AB}$.

b Write down *all* vectors which:

 i are the negative of $\overrightarrow{EF}$

 ii have the same length as $\overrightarrow{ED}$.

c Write down a vector which is parallel to $\overrightarrow{AB}$ and twice its length.

Discussion

- Does a vector of length 0 have a direction?
- Is it possible to represent such a vector geometrically?

B │ GEOMETRIC OPERATIONS WITH VECTORS

In previous years we have often used trigonometry and Pythagoras' theorem to solve problems involving distances and directions.

A typical problem could be:

A runner runs east for 4 km and then south for 2 km.

How far is she from her starting point and in what direction?

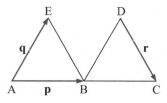

Problems like these can be well represented by vectors. In this case, the vectors are displacements. There is a displacement of 4 km to the east followed by a displacement of 2 km to the south. We want to know the *sum* of these displacements, including distance *and* direction.

GEOMETRIC VECTOR ADDITION

Suppose we have three towns P, Q, and R.

A trip from P to Q followed by a trip from Q to R has the same origin and destination as a trip from P to R.

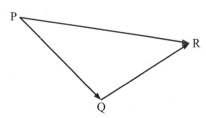

This can be expressed in vector form as the sum $\overrightarrow{PQ} + \overrightarrow{QR} = \overrightarrow{PR}$.

The triangular diagram could take all sorts of shapes, but in each case the sum would be true.

For example:

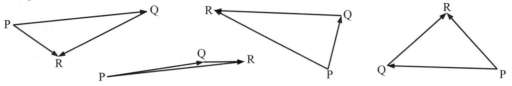

After considering diagrams like those above, we can now define vector addition geometrically:

> To construct **a** + **b**:
>
> *Step 1*:   Draw **a**.
>
> *Step 2*:   At the arrowhead end of **a**, draw **b**.
>
> *Step 3*:   Join the beginning of **a** to the arrowhead end of **b**.
>   This is vector **a** + **b**.

DEMO

Example 3   ◀) Self Tutor

Given vectors **a** and **b** shown, construct **a** + **b**.

THE ZERO VECTOR

Having defined vector addition, we are now able to state that:

> The **zero vector 0** is a vector of length 0.
>
> For any vector **a**: $\mathbf{a} + \mathbf{0} = \mathbf{0} + \mathbf{a} = \mathbf{a}$
>
> $\mathbf{a} + (-\mathbf{a}) = (-\mathbf{a}) + \mathbf{a} = \mathbf{0}.$

When we write the zero vector by hand, we usually write $\underset{\sim}{0}$.

Example 4   ◀) Self Tutor

Find a single vector which is equal to:

a $\overrightarrow{BC} + \overrightarrow{CA}$

b $\overrightarrow{BA} + \overrightarrow{AE} + \overrightarrow{EC}$

c $\overrightarrow{AB} + \overrightarrow{BC} + \overrightarrow{CA}$

d $\overrightarrow{AB} + \overrightarrow{BC} + \overrightarrow{CD} + \overrightarrow{DE}$

a $\overrightarrow{BC} + \overrightarrow{CA} = \overrightarrow{BA}$ **b** $\overrightarrow{BA} + \overrightarrow{AE} + \overrightarrow{EC} = \overrightarrow{BC}$

c $\overrightarrow{AB} + \overrightarrow{BC} + \overrightarrow{CA} = \overrightarrow{AA} = \mathbf{0}$ **d** $\overrightarrow{AB} + \overrightarrow{BC} + \overrightarrow{CD} + \overrightarrow{DE} = \overrightarrow{AE}$

EXERCISE 18B.1

1 Use the given vectors **p** and **q** to construct **p** + **q**:

a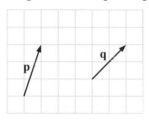

b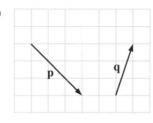

c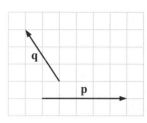

d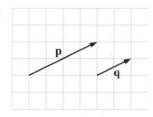

e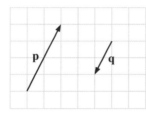

f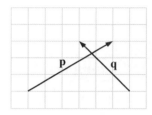

2 Find a single vector which is equal to:

a $\overrightarrow{AB} + \overrightarrow{BC}$

b $\overrightarrow{BC} + \overrightarrow{CD}$

c $\overrightarrow{AB} + \overrightarrow{BA}$

d $\overrightarrow{AB} + \overrightarrow{BC} + \overrightarrow{CD}$

e $\overrightarrow{AC} + \overrightarrow{CB} + \overrightarrow{BD}$

f $\overrightarrow{BC} + \overrightarrow{CA} + \overrightarrow{AB}$

3 a Given and use vector diagrams to find:

   i **p** + **q**
   ii **q** + **p**.

b For any two vectors **p** and **q**, is **p** + **q** = **q** + **p**? Illustrate your answer.

4 Consider:

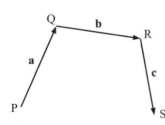

One way of finding $\overrightarrow{PS}$ is:
$$\overrightarrow{PS} = \overrightarrow{PR} + \overrightarrow{RS}$$
$$= (\mathbf{a} + \mathbf{b}) + \mathbf{c}.$$

Use the diagram to show that
$(\mathbf{a} + \mathbf{b}) + \mathbf{c} = \mathbf{a} + (\mathbf{b} + \mathbf{c})$.

5 Answer the **Opening Problem** on page **408**.

6 Susan and Cathy are pushing a heavy trolley containing groceries. Susan pushes the trolley with force 40 N in the direction 017°. Cathy pushes the trolley with force 35 N in the direction 335°.

a Use a scale diagram to estimate the resultant force from the two girls pushing.

b Use trigonometry to find the resultant force more accurately.

GEOMETRIC VECTOR SUBTRACTION

To subtract one vector from another, we simply **add its negative**. $a - b = a + (-b)$

For example,

given   and   then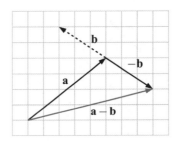

Example 5   ◀) **Self Tutor**

For the vectors illustrated,
show how to construct:

  a $r - s$
  b $s - t - r$

a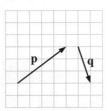

b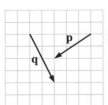

EXERCISE 18B.2

1 For the following vectors **p** and **q**, show how to construct $p - q$:

  a   **b**   **c**   **d**

2 For the vectors illustrated,
show how to construct:

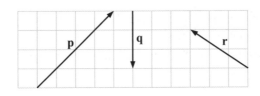

  a $p + q - r$ **b** $p - q - r$ **c** $r - q - p$

Example 6

◀)) **Self Tutor**

For points A, B, C, and D, simplify the following vector expressions:

a $\overrightarrow{AB} - \overrightarrow{CB}$

b $\overrightarrow{AC} - \overrightarrow{BC} - \overrightarrow{DB}$

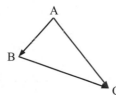

a $\overrightarrow{AB} - \overrightarrow{CB}$	**b** $\overrightarrow{AC} - \overrightarrow{BC} - \overrightarrow{DB}$
$= \overrightarrow{AB} + \overrightarrow{BC}$ {as $\overrightarrow{BC} = -\overrightarrow{CB}$}	$= \overrightarrow{AC} + \overrightarrow{CB} + \overrightarrow{BD}$
$= \overrightarrow{AC}$	$= \overrightarrow{AD}$

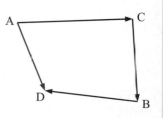

3 For points A, B, C, and D, simplify the following vector expressions:

a $\overrightarrow{AC} + \overrightarrow{CB}$

b $\overrightarrow{AD} - \overrightarrow{BD}$

c $\overrightarrow{AC} + \overrightarrow{CA}$

d $\overrightarrow{AB} + \overrightarrow{BC} + \overrightarrow{CD}$

e $\overrightarrow{BA} - \overrightarrow{CA} + \overrightarrow{CB}$

f $\overrightarrow{AB} - \overrightarrow{CB} - \overrightarrow{DC}$

VECTOR EQUATIONS

Whenever we have vectors which form a closed polygon, we can write a **vector equation**. The vector equation can usually be written in several ways, but they are all equivalent.

Example 7

◀)) **Self Tutor**

Construct vector equations for:

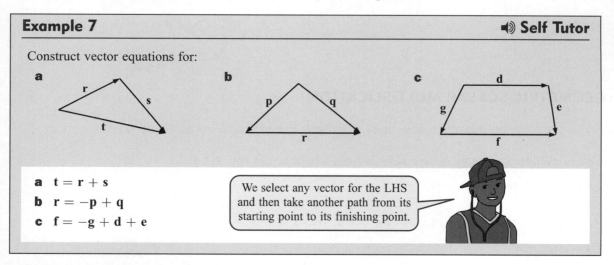

a $\mathbf{t} = \mathbf{r} + \mathbf{s}$

b $\mathbf{r} = -\mathbf{p} + \mathbf{q}$

c $\mathbf{f} = -\mathbf{g} + \mathbf{d} + \mathbf{e}$

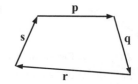

We select any vector for the LHS and then take another path from its starting point to its finishing point.

EXERCISE 18B.3

1 Construct vector equations for:

a

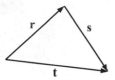

b

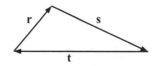

c

d 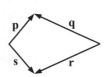   **e**   **f**

Example 8

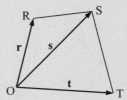

Find, in terms of **r**, **s**, and **t**:

  a $\overrightarrow{RS}$ **b** $\overrightarrow{SR}$ **c** $\overrightarrow{ST}$

 ◀) **Self Tutor**

a $\overrightarrow{RS} = \overrightarrow{RO} + \overrightarrow{OS}$	**b** $\overrightarrow{SR} = \overrightarrow{SO} + \overrightarrow{OR}$	**c** $\overrightarrow{ST} = \overrightarrow{SO} + \overrightarrow{OT}$
$\phantom{\overrightarrow{RS}} = -\overrightarrow{OR} + \overrightarrow{OS}$	$\phantom{\overrightarrow{SR}} = -\overrightarrow{OS} + \overrightarrow{OR}$	$\phantom{\overrightarrow{ST}} = -\overrightarrow{OS} + \overrightarrow{OT}$
$\phantom{\overrightarrow{RS}} = -\mathbf{r} + \mathbf{s}$	$\phantom{\overrightarrow{SR}} = -\mathbf{s} + \mathbf{r}$	$\phantom{\overrightarrow{ST}} = -\mathbf{s} + \mathbf{t}$
$\phantom{\overrightarrow{RS}} = \mathbf{s} - \mathbf{r}$	$\phantom{\overrightarrow{SR}} = \mathbf{r} - \mathbf{s}$	$\phantom{\overrightarrow{ST}} = \mathbf{t} - \mathbf{s}$

---

2   **a**   Find, in terms of **r**, **s**, and **t**:   **b**   Find, in terms of **p**, **q**, and **r**:

      i $\overrightarrow{OB}$ **ii** $\overrightarrow{CA}$ **iii** $\overrightarrow{OC}$ **i** $\overrightarrow{AD}$ **ii** $\overrightarrow{BC}$ **iii** $\overrightarrow{AC}$

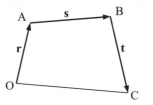   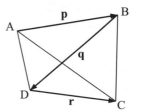

GEOMETRIC SCALAR MULTIPLICATION

> A **scalar** is a non-vector quantity. It has magnitude but no direction.

We can multiply vectors by scalars such as 2 and -3, or in fact any $k \in \mathbb{R}$.

If **a** is a vector, we define $2\mathbf{a} = \mathbf{a} + \mathbf{a}$

$\phantom{If \mathbf{a} is a vector, we define} 3\mathbf{a} = \mathbf{a} + \mathbf{a} + \mathbf{a}$

$\phantom{If \mathbf{a} is a vector, we} \text{and} \quad -3\mathbf{a} = 3(-\mathbf{a}) = (-\mathbf{a}) + (-\mathbf{a}) + (-\mathbf{a}).$

If **a** is

then

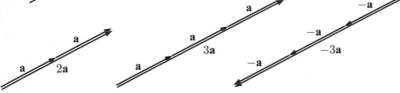

A scalar multiple of a vector is always **parallel** to the vector.

So, $2\mathbf{a}$ is in the same direction as **a** but is twice as long as **a**

      $3\mathbf{a}$ is in the same direction as **a** but is three times longer than **a**

    $-3\mathbf{a}$ has the opposite direction to **a** and is three times longer than **a**.

If **a** is a vector and k is a scalar, then k**a** is also a vector and we are performing **scalar multiplication**.

- If $k > 0$, k**a** and **a** have the same direction.
- If $k < 0$, k**a** and **a** have opposite directions.
- If $k = 0$, k**a** = **0**, the zero vector.

VECTOR SCALAR MULTIPLICATION

Example 9   ◀) **Self Tutor**

Given vectors [**r**] and [**s**], construct:

a $2\mathbf{r} + \mathbf{s}$ **b** $\mathbf{r} - 3\mathbf{s}$

a   **b**

Example 10   ◀) **Self Tutor**

Sketch vectors **p** and **q** if: **a** $\mathbf{p} = 3\mathbf{q}$ **b** $\mathbf{p} = -\tfrac{1}{2}\mathbf{q}$

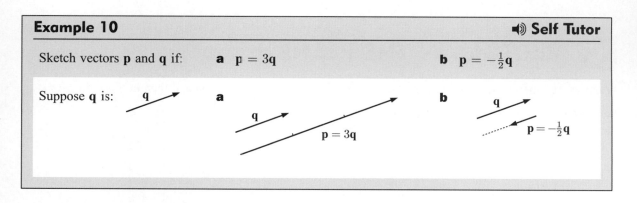

Suppose **q** is:

EXERCISE 18B.4

1 Given vectors and , construct geometrically:

   a $-\mathbf{r}$ **b** $2\mathbf{s}$ **c** $\tfrac{1}{2}\mathbf{r}$ **d** $-\tfrac{3}{2}\mathbf{s}$

   e $2\mathbf{r} - \mathbf{s}$ **f** $2\mathbf{r} + 3\mathbf{s}$ **g** $\tfrac{1}{2}\mathbf{r} + 2\mathbf{s}$ **h** $\tfrac{1}{2}(\mathbf{r} + 3\mathbf{s})$

2 Sketch vectors **p** and **q** if:

   a $\mathbf{p} = \mathbf{q}$ **b** $\mathbf{p} = -\mathbf{q}$ **c** $\mathbf{p} = 2\mathbf{q}$ **d** $\mathbf{p} = \tfrac{1}{3}\mathbf{q}$ **e** $\mathbf{p} = -3\mathbf{q}$

3   **a** Copy this diagram and on it mark the points:

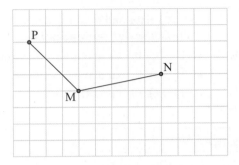

   i X such that $\overrightarrow{MX} = \overrightarrow{MN} + \overrightarrow{MP}$

   ii Y such that $\overrightarrow{MY} = \overrightarrow{MN} - \overrightarrow{MP}$

   iii Z such that $\overrightarrow{PZ} = 2\overrightarrow{PM}$

   b What type of figure is MNYZ?

4

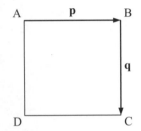

ABCD is a square. Its diagonals [AC] and [BD] intersect at M.

If $\overrightarrow{AB} = \mathbf{p}$ and $\overrightarrow{BC} = \mathbf{q}$, find in terms of $\mathbf{p}$ and $\mathbf{q}$:

   a $\overrightarrow{CD}$ **b** $\overrightarrow{AC}$ **c** $\overrightarrow{AM}$ **d** $\overrightarrow{BM}$

5

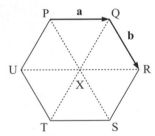

PQRSTU is a regular hexagon.

If $\overrightarrow{PQ} = \mathbf{a}$ and $\overrightarrow{QR} = \mathbf{b}$, find in terms of $\mathbf{a}$ and $\mathbf{b}$:

   a $\overrightarrow{PX}$ **b** $\overrightarrow{PS}$ **c** $\overrightarrow{QX}$ **d** $\overrightarrow{RS}$

C   VECTORS IN THE PLANE

When we plot points in the Cartesian plane, we move first in the x-direction and then in the y-direction.

For example, to plot the point P(2, 5), we start at the origin, move 2 units in the x-direction, and then 5 units in the y-direction.

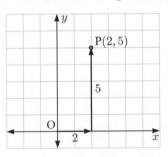

We have previously seen in transformation geometry that translating a point a units in the x-direction and b units in the y-direction can be achieved using the *translation vector* $\begin{pmatrix} a \\ b \end{pmatrix}$.

So, the vector from O to P is $\overrightarrow{OP} = \begin{pmatrix} 2 \\ 5 \end{pmatrix}$.

Suppose that $\mathbf{i} = \begin{pmatrix} 1 \\ 0 \end{pmatrix}$ is a translation 1 unit in the positive x-direction

and that $\mathbf{j} = \begin{pmatrix} 0 \\ 1 \end{pmatrix}$ is a translation 1 unit in the positive y-direction.

We can see that moving from O to P is equivalent to two lots of **i** plus 5 lots of **j**.

$$\overrightarrow{OP} = 2\mathbf{i} + 5\mathbf{j}$$

$$\therefore \quad \begin{pmatrix} 2 \\ 5 \end{pmatrix} = 2 \begin{pmatrix} 1 \\ 0 \end{pmatrix} + 5 \begin{pmatrix} 0 \\ 1 \end{pmatrix}$$

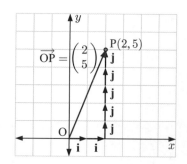

The point $P(x, y)$ has **position vector**

$$\overrightarrow{OP} = \begin{pmatrix} x \\ y \end{pmatrix} = \underbrace{x\mathbf{i} + y\mathbf{j}}$$

component form   unit vector form

where $\mathbf{i} = \begin{pmatrix} 1 \\ 0 \end{pmatrix}$ is the **base unit vector** in the x-direction

and $\mathbf{j} = \begin{pmatrix} 0 \\ 1 \end{pmatrix}$ is the **base unit vector** in the y-direction.

i and **j** are **unit vectors** because they have length 1.

VECTOR EQUALITY

Two vectors are **equal** if their components are equal.

Example 11

🔊 **Self Tutor**

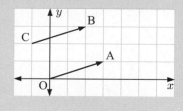

a   Write vectors $\overrightarrow{OA}$ and $\overrightarrow{CB}$ in component form and in unit vector form.

b   Comment on your answers in **a**.

a $\overrightarrow{OA} = \begin{pmatrix} 3 \\ 1 \end{pmatrix} = 3\mathbf{i} + \mathbf{j}$ $\overrightarrow{CB} = \begin{pmatrix} 3 \\ 1 \end{pmatrix} = 3\mathbf{i} + \mathbf{j}$

b   The vectors $\overrightarrow{OA}$ and $\overrightarrow{CB}$ are equal.

EXERCISE 18C

1   Write the illustrated vectors in component form and in unit vector form:

a
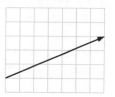

b
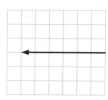

c
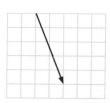

d 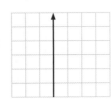   **e**    **f**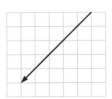

2 Write each vector in unit vector form, and illustrate it using an arrow diagram:

a $\begin{pmatrix} 3 \\ 4 \end{pmatrix}$ **b** $\begin{pmatrix} 2 \\ 0 \end{pmatrix}$ **c** $\begin{pmatrix} 2 \\ -5 \end{pmatrix}$ **d** $\begin{pmatrix} -1 \\ -3 \end{pmatrix}$

3

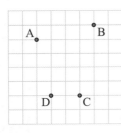

Find in component form and in unit vector form:

a $\overrightarrow{BA}$ **b** $\overrightarrow{BC}$ **c** $\overrightarrow{DC}$

d $\overrightarrow{AC}$ **e** $\overrightarrow{CA}$ **f** $\overrightarrow{DB}$

4 Write in component form and illustrate using a directed line segment:

a $\mathbf{i} + 2\mathbf{j}$ **b** $-\mathbf{i} + 3\mathbf{j}$ **c** $-5\mathbf{j}$ **d** $4\mathbf{i} - 2\mathbf{j}$

5 Write the zero vector $\mathbf{0}$ in component form.

D │ THE MAGNITUDE OF A VECTOR

Consider vector $\mathbf{v} = \begin{pmatrix} 2 \\ 3 \end{pmatrix} = 2\mathbf{i} + 3\mathbf{j}$.

The **magnitude** or **length** of $\mathbf{v}$ is represented by $|\mathbf{v}|$.

By Pythagoras, $|\mathbf{v}|^2 = 2^2 + 3^2 = 4 + 9 = 13$

$\therefore\ |\mathbf{v}| = \sqrt{13}$ units   {since $|\mathbf{v}| > 0$}

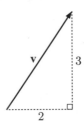

If $\mathbf{v} = \begin{pmatrix} v_1 \\ v_2 \end{pmatrix} = v_1\mathbf{i} + v_2\mathbf{j}$,   the **magnitude** or **length** of $\mathbf{v}$ is $|\mathbf{v}| = \sqrt{v_1{}^2 + v_2{}^2}$.

Example 12   ◀) **Self Tutor**

If $\mathbf{p} = \begin{pmatrix} 3 \\ -5 \end{pmatrix}$ and $\mathbf{q} = 2\mathbf{i} - 5\mathbf{j}$ find:

a $|\mathbf{p}|$ **b** $|\mathbf{q}|$

a $\mathbf{p} = \begin{pmatrix} 3 \\ -5 \end{pmatrix}$ **b**   As $2\mathbf{i} - 5\mathbf{j} = \begin{pmatrix} 2 \\ -5 \end{pmatrix}$,

$\therefore\ |\mathbf{p}| = \sqrt{3^2 + (-5)^2}$ $|\mathbf{q}| = \sqrt{2^2 + (-5)^2}$

$= \sqrt{34}$ units $= \sqrt{29}$ units.

UNIT VECTORS

> A **unit vector** is any vector which has a length of one unit.

For example, we have seen that $\mathbf{i} = \begin{pmatrix} 1 \\ 0 \end{pmatrix}$ and $\mathbf{j} = \begin{pmatrix} 0 \\ 1 \end{pmatrix}$ are the base unit vectors in the positive x and y-directions respectively.

Example 13   ◀)) Self Tutor

Find k given that $\begin{pmatrix} -\frac{1}{3} \\ k \end{pmatrix}$ is a unit vector.

Since $\begin{pmatrix} -\frac{1}{3} \\ k \end{pmatrix}$ is a unit vector,

$$\sqrt{(-\tfrac{1}{3})^2 + k^2} = 1$$
$$\therefore \ \sqrt{\tfrac{1}{9} + k^2} = 1$$
$$\therefore \ \tfrac{1}{9} + k^2 = 1 \qquad \{\text{squaring both sides}\}$$
$$\therefore \ k^2 = \tfrac{8}{9}$$
$$\therefore \ k = \pm \frac{\sqrt{8}}{3}$$

EXERCISE 18D

1 Find the magnitude of:

a $\begin{pmatrix} 3 \\ 4 \end{pmatrix}$ **b** $\begin{pmatrix} -4 \\ 3 \end{pmatrix}$ **c** $\begin{pmatrix} 2 \\ 0 \end{pmatrix}$ **d** $\begin{pmatrix} -2 \\ 2 \end{pmatrix}$ **e** $\begin{pmatrix} 0 \\ -3 \end{pmatrix}$

2 Find the length of:
   a $\mathbf{i} + \mathbf{j}$ **b** $5\mathbf{i} - 12\mathbf{j}$ **c** $-\mathbf{i} + 4\mathbf{j}$ **d** $3\mathbf{i}$ **e** $k\mathbf{j}$

3 Which of the following are unit vectors?

a $\begin{pmatrix} 0 \\ -1 \end{pmatrix}$ **b** $\begin{pmatrix} -\frac{1}{\sqrt{2}} \\ \frac{1}{\sqrt{2}} \end{pmatrix}$ **c** $\begin{pmatrix} \frac{2}{3} \\ \frac{1}{3} \end{pmatrix}$ **d** $\begin{pmatrix} -\frac{3}{5} \\ -\frac{4}{5} \end{pmatrix}$ **e** $\begin{pmatrix} \frac{2}{7} \\ -\frac{5}{7} \end{pmatrix}$

4 Find k such that the given vector is a unit vector:

a $\begin{pmatrix} 0 \\ k \end{pmatrix}$ **b** $\begin{pmatrix} k \\ 0 \end{pmatrix}$ **c** $\begin{pmatrix} k \\ 1 \end{pmatrix}$ **d** $\begin{pmatrix} k \\ k \end{pmatrix}$ **e** $\begin{pmatrix} \frac{1}{2} \\ k \end{pmatrix}$

5 Given $\mathbf{v} = \begin{pmatrix} 8 \\ p \end{pmatrix}$ and $|\mathbf{v}| = \sqrt{73}$ units, find the possible values of p.

E | OPERATIONS WITH PLANE VECTORS

ALGEBRAIC VECTOR ADDITION

Consider adding vectors $\mathbf{a} = \begin{pmatrix} a_1 \\ a_2 \end{pmatrix}$ and $\mathbf{b} = \begin{pmatrix} b_1 \\ b_2 \end{pmatrix}$.

Notice that:
- the horizontal step for $\mathbf{a} + \mathbf{b}$ is $a_1 + b_1$
- the vertical step for $\mathbf{a} + \mathbf{b}$ is $a_2 + b_2$.

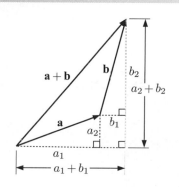

> If $\mathbf{a} = \begin{pmatrix} a_1 \\ a_2 \end{pmatrix}$ and $\mathbf{b} = \begin{pmatrix} b_1 \\ b_2 \end{pmatrix}$ then $\mathbf{a} + \mathbf{b} = \begin{pmatrix} a_1 + b_1 \\ a_2 + b_2 \end{pmatrix}$.

Example 14

◀》 **Self Tutor**

If $\mathbf{a} = \begin{pmatrix} 1 \\ -3 \end{pmatrix}$ and $\mathbf{b} = \begin{pmatrix} 4 \\ 7 \end{pmatrix}$, find $\mathbf{a} + \mathbf{b}$. Check your answer graphically.

$$\mathbf{a} + \mathbf{b} = \begin{pmatrix} 1 \\ -3 \end{pmatrix} + \begin{pmatrix} 4 \\ 7 \end{pmatrix}$$

$$= \begin{pmatrix} 1 + 4 \\ -3 + 7 \end{pmatrix}$$

$$= \begin{pmatrix} 5 \\ 4 \end{pmatrix}$$

Graphical check:

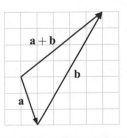

ALGEBRAIC NEGATIVE VECTORS

In the diagram we see the vector $\mathbf{a} = \begin{pmatrix} 2 \\ 3 \end{pmatrix}$

and its negative $-\mathbf{a} = \begin{pmatrix} -2 \\ -3 \end{pmatrix}$.

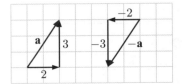

If $\mathbf{a} = \begin{pmatrix} a_1 \\ a_2 \end{pmatrix}$ then $-\mathbf{a} = \begin{pmatrix} -a_1 \\ -a_2 \end{pmatrix}$.

ALGEBRAIC VECTOR SUBTRACTION

To subtract one vector from another, we simply **add its negative**.

So, if $\mathbf{a} = \begin{pmatrix} a_1 \\ a_2 \end{pmatrix}$ and $\mathbf{b} = \begin{pmatrix} b_1 \\ b_2 \end{pmatrix}$

then $\mathbf{a} - \mathbf{b} = \mathbf{a} + (-\mathbf{b})$

$$= \begin{pmatrix} a_1 \\ a_2 \end{pmatrix} + \begin{pmatrix} -b_1 \\ -b_2 \end{pmatrix}$$

$$= \begin{pmatrix} a_1 - b_1 \\ a_2 - b_2 \end{pmatrix}$$

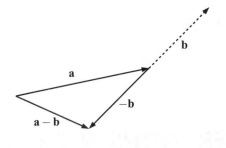

If $\mathbf{a} = \begin{pmatrix} a_1 \\ a_2 \end{pmatrix}$ and $\mathbf{b} = \begin{pmatrix} b_1 \\ b_2 \end{pmatrix}$, then $\mathbf{a} - \mathbf{b} = \begin{pmatrix} a_1 - b_1 \\ a_2 - b_2 \end{pmatrix}$.

Example 15

◀》 **Self Tutor**

Given $\mathbf{p} = \begin{pmatrix} 3 \\ -2 \end{pmatrix}$, $\mathbf{q} = \begin{pmatrix} 1 \\ 4 \end{pmatrix}$, and $\mathbf{r} = \begin{pmatrix} -2 \\ -5 \end{pmatrix}$, find:

  a $\mathbf{q} - \mathbf{p}$ **b** $\mathbf{p} - \mathbf{q} - \mathbf{r}$

a $\mathbf{q} - \mathbf{p}$

$$= \begin{pmatrix} 1 \\ 4 \end{pmatrix} - \begin{pmatrix} 3 \\ -2 \end{pmatrix}$$

$$= \begin{pmatrix} 1 - 3 \\ 4 + 2 \end{pmatrix}$$

$$= \begin{pmatrix} -2 \\ 6 \end{pmatrix}$$

b $\mathbf{p} - \mathbf{q} - \mathbf{r}$

$$= \begin{pmatrix} 3 \\ -2 \end{pmatrix} - \begin{pmatrix} 1 \\ 4 \end{pmatrix} - \begin{pmatrix} -2 \\ -5 \end{pmatrix}$$

$$= \begin{pmatrix} 3 - 1 + 2 \\ -2 - 4 + 5 \end{pmatrix}$$

$$= \begin{pmatrix} 4 \\ -1 \end{pmatrix}$$

ALGEBRAIC SCALAR MULTIPLICATION

We have already seen a geometric approach for integer scalar multiplication:

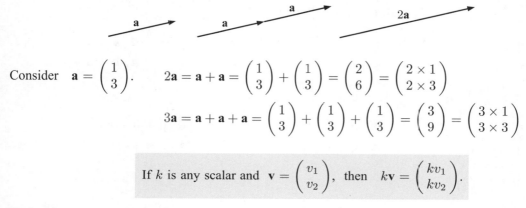

Consider $\mathbf{a} = \begin{pmatrix} 1 \\ 3 \end{pmatrix}$.

$$2\mathbf{a} = \mathbf{a} + \mathbf{a} = \begin{pmatrix} 1 \\ 3 \end{pmatrix} + \begin{pmatrix} 1 \\ 3 \end{pmatrix} = \begin{pmatrix} 2 \\ 6 \end{pmatrix} = \begin{pmatrix} 2 \times 1 \\ 2 \times 3 \end{pmatrix}$$

$$3\mathbf{a} = \mathbf{a} + \mathbf{a} + \mathbf{a} = \begin{pmatrix} 1 \\ 3 \end{pmatrix} + \begin{pmatrix} 1 \\ 3 \end{pmatrix} + \begin{pmatrix} 1 \\ 3 \end{pmatrix} = \begin{pmatrix} 3 \\ 9 \end{pmatrix} = \begin{pmatrix} 3 \times 1 \\ 3 \times 3 \end{pmatrix}$$

If k is any scalar and $\mathbf{v} = \begin{pmatrix} v_1 \\ v_2 \end{pmatrix}$, then $k\mathbf{v} = \begin{pmatrix} kv_1 \\ kv_2 \end{pmatrix}$.

Notice that:

- $(-1)\mathbf{v} = \begin{pmatrix} (-1)\,v_1 \\ (-1)\,v_2 \end{pmatrix} = \begin{pmatrix} -v_1 \\ -v_2 \end{pmatrix} = -\mathbf{v}$

- $(0)\mathbf{v} = \begin{pmatrix} (0)\,v_1 \\ (0)\,v_2 \end{pmatrix} = \begin{pmatrix} 0 \\ 0 \end{pmatrix} = \mathbf{0}$

Example 16

◀))) **Self Tutor**

For $\mathbf{p} = \begin{pmatrix} 4 \\ 1 \end{pmatrix}$, $\mathbf{q} = \begin{pmatrix} 2 \\ -3 \end{pmatrix}$ find:

a $3\mathbf{q}$

b $\mathbf{p} + 2\mathbf{q}$

c $\frac{1}{2}\mathbf{p} - 3\mathbf{q}$

a $3\mathbf{q}$

$$= 3 \begin{pmatrix} 2 \\ -3 \end{pmatrix}$$

$$= \begin{pmatrix} 6 \\ -9 \end{pmatrix}$$

b $\mathbf{p} + 2\mathbf{q}$

$$= \begin{pmatrix} 4 \\ 1 \end{pmatrix} + 2 \begin{pmatrix} 2 \\ -3 \end{pmatrix}$$

$$= \begin{pmatrix} 4 + 2(2) \\ 1 + 2(-3) \end{pmatrix}$$

$$= \begin{pmatrix} 8 \\ -5 \end{pmatrix}$$

c $\frac{1}{2}\mathbf{p} - 3\mathbf{q}$

$$= \frac{1}{2} \begin{pmatrix} 4 \\ 1 \end{pmatrix} - 3 \begin{pmatrix} 2 \\ -3 \end{pmatrix}$$

$$= \begin{pmatrix} \frac{1}{2}(4) - 3(2) \\ \frac{1}{2}(1) - 3(-3) \end{pmatrix}$$

$$= \begin{pmatrix} -4 \\ 9\frac{1}{2} \end{pmatrix}$$

> ### Example 17   ◀) Self Tutor
>
> If $\mathbf{p} = 3\mathbf{i} - 5\mathbf{j}$ and $\mathbf{q} = -\mathbf{i} - 2\mathbf{j}$, find $|\mathbf{p} - 2\mathbf{q}|$.
>
> $$\begin{aligned} \mathbf{p} - 2\mathbf{q} &= 3\mathbf{i} - 5\mathbf{j} - 2(-\mathbf{i} - 2\mathbf{j}) \\ &= 3\mathbf{i} - 5\mathbf{j} + 2\mathbf{i} + 4\mathbf{j} \\ &= 5\mathbf{i} - \mathbf{j} \end{aligned}$$
> $$\begin{aligned} \therefore \quad |\mathbf{p} - 2\mathbf{q}| &= \sqrt{5^2 + (-1)^2} \\ &= \sqrt{26} \text{ units} \end{aligned}$$

EXERCISE 18E

1 If $\mathbf{a} = \begin{pmatrix} -3 \\ 2 \end{pmatrix}$, $\mathbf{b} = \begin{pmatrix} 1 \\ 4 \end{pmatrix}$, and $\mathbf{c} = \begin{pmatrix} -2 \\ -5 \end{pmatrix}$ find:

   a $\mathbf{a} + \mathbf{b}$ **b** $\mathbf{b} + \mathbf{a}$ **c** $\mathbf{b} + \mathbf{c}$ **d** $\mathbf{c} + \mathbf{b}$

   e $\mathbf{a} + \mathbf{c}$ **f** $\mathbf{c} + \mathbf{a}$ **g** $\mathbf{a} + \mathbf{a}$ **h** $\mathbf{b} + \mathbf{a} + \mathbf{c}$

2 Given $\mathbf{p} = \begin{pmatrix} -4 \\ 2 \end{pmatrix}$, $\mathbf{q} = \begin{pmatrix} -1 \\ -5 \end{pmatrix}$, and $\mathbf{r} = \begin{pmatrix} 3 \\ -2 \end{pmatrix}$ find:

   a $\mathbf{p} - \mathbf{q}$ **b** $\mathbf{q} - \mathbf{r}$ **c** $\mathbf{p} + \mathbf{q} - \mathbf{r}$

   d $\mathbf{p} - \mathbf{q} - \mathbf{r}$ **e** $\mathbf{q} - \mathbf{r} - \mathbf{p}$ **f** $\mathbf{r} + \mathbf{q} - \mathbf{p}$

3 Consider $\mathbf{a} = \begin{pmatrix} a_1 \\ a_2 \end{pmatrix}$.

   a Use vector addition to show that $\mathbf{a} + \mathbf{0} = \mathbf{a}$.

   b Use vector subtraction to show that $\mathbf{a} - \mathbf{a} = \mathbf{0}$.

4 For $\mathbf{p} = \begin{pmatrix} 1 \\ 5 \end{pmatrix}$, $\mathbf{q} = \begin{pmatrix} -2 \\ 4 \end{pmatrix}$, and $\mathbf{r} = \begin{pmatrix} -3 \\ -1 \end{pmatrix}$ find:

   a $-3\mathbf{p}$ **b** $\frac{1}{2}\mathbf{q}$ **c** $2\mathbf{p} + \mathbf{q}$ **d** $\mathbf{p} - 2\mathbf{q}$

   e $\mathbf{p} - \frac{1}{2}\mathbf{r}$ **f** $2\mathbf{p} + 3\mathbf{r}$ **g** $2\mathbf{q} - 3\mathbf{r}$ **h** $2\mathbf{p} - \mathbf{q} + \frac{1}{3}\mathbf{r}$

5 Consider $\mathbf{p} = \begin{pmatrix} 1 \\ 1 \end{pmatrix}$ and $\mathbf{q} = \begin{pmatrix} 2 \\ -1 \end{pmatrix}$.

   a Find geometrically:

      i $\mathbf{p} + \mathbf{p} + \mathbf{q} + \mathbf{q} + \mathbf{q}$ **ii** $\mathbf{p} + \mathbf{q} + \mathbf{p} + \mathbf{q} + \mathbf{q}$ **iii** $\mathbf{q} + \mathbf{p} + \mathbf{q} + \mathbf{p} + \mathbf{q}$

   b Comment on your results in **a**.

6 If $\mathbf{r} = \begin{pmatrix} 2 \\ 3 \end{pmatrix}$ and $\mathbf{s} = \begin{pmatrix} -1 \\ 4 \end{pmatrix}$, find:

   a $|\mathbf{r}|$ **b** $|\mathbf{s}|$ **c** $|\mathbf{r} + \mathbf{s}|$ **d** $|\mathbf{r} - \mathbf{s}|$ **e** $|\mathbf{s} - 2\mathbf{r}|$

7 If $\mathbf{p} = \begin{pmatrix} 1 \\ 3 \end{pmatrix}$ and $\mathbf{q} = \begin{pmatrix} -2 \\ 4 \end{pmatrix}$, find:

   a $|\mathbf{p}|$ **b** $|2\mathbf{p}|$ **c** $|-2\mathbf{p}|$ **d** $|3\mathbf{p}|$ **e** $|-3\mathbf{p}|$

   f $|\mathbf{q}|$ **g** $|4\mathbf{q}|$ **h** $|-4\mathbf{q}|$ **i** $|\frac{1}{2}\mathbf{q}|$ **j** $|-\frac{1}{2}\mathbf{q}|$

8 Suppose $\mathbf{x} = \begin{pmatrix} x_1 \\ x_2 \end{pmatrix}$ and $\mathbf{a} = \begin{pmatrix} a_1 \\ a_2 \end{pmatrix}$. Show by equating components, that if $k\mathbf{x} = \mathbf{a}$ then $\mathbf{x} = \frac{1}{k}\mathbf{a}$.

9 From your answers in **7**, you should have noticed that $|k\mathbf{v}| = |k|\,|\mathbf{v}|$.
So, (the length of $k\mathbf{v}$) = (the modulus of k) $\times$ (the length of $\mathbf{v}$).

By letting $\mathbf{v} = \begin{pmatrix} v_1 \\ v_2 \end{pmatrix}$, prove that $|k\mathbf{v}| = |k|\,|\mathbf{v}|$.

> The *modulus* of k is its *size*.

Activity   Vector race

Click on the icon to practise your skills with vectors.

VECTOR RACE GAME

F   THE VECTOR BETWEEN TWO POINTS

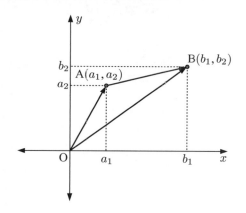

In the diagram, point A has position vector $\overrightarrow{OA} = \begin{pmatrix} a_1 \\ a_2 \end{pmatrix}$,
and point B has position vector $\overrightarrow{OB} = \begin{pmatrix} b_1 \\ b_2 \end{pmatrix}$.

$$\therefore\ \ \overrightarrow{AB} = \overrightarrow{AO} + \overrightarrow{OB}$$
$$= -\overrightarrow{OA} + \overrightarrow{OB}$$
$$= \overrightarrow{OB} - \overrightarrow{OA}$$
$$= \begin{pmatrix} b_1 \\ b_2 \end{pmatrix} - \begin{pmatrix} a_1 \\ a_2 \end{pmatrix}$$
$$= \begin{pmatrix} b_1 - a_1 \\ b_2 - a_2 \end{pmatrix}$$

> The **position vector of B relative to A** is $\overrightarrow{AB} = \overrightarrow{OB} - \overrightarrow{OA} = \begin{pmatrix} b_1 - a_1 \\ b_2 - a_2 \end{pmatrix}$.

We can also observe this in terms of transformations.

In translating point A to point B in the diagram, the translation vector is $\begin{pmatrix} b_1 - a_1 \\ b_2 - a_2 \end{pmatrix}$.

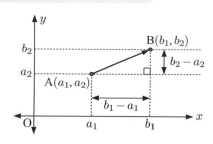

For two points A and B with position vectors **a** and **b** respectively:

$$\overrightarrow{AB} = -\mathbf{a} + \mathbf{b} \qquad \text{and} \qquad \overrightarrow{BA} = -\mathbf{b} + \mathbf{a}$$
$$= \mathbf{b} - \mathbf{a} \qquad\qquad\qquad = \mathbf{a} - \mathbf{b}$$
$$= \begin{pmatrix} b_1 - a_1 \\ b_2 - a_2 \end{pmatrix} \qquad\qquad = \begin{pmatrix} a_1 - b_1 \\ a_2 - b_2 \end{pmatrix}$$

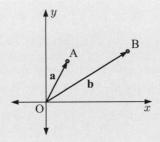

Example 18   ◀)) Self Tutor

Given points A$(-1, 2)$, B$(3, 4)$, and C$(4, -5)$, find the position vector of:

a B from O   **b** B from A   **c** A from C

a The position vector of B relative to O is $\overrightarrow{OB} = \begin{pmatrix} 3 - 0 \\ 4 - 0 \end{pmatrix} = \begin{pmatrix} 3 \\ 4 \end{pmatrix}$.

b The position vector of B relative to A is $\overrightarrow{AB} = \begin{pmatrix} 3 - -1 \\ 4 - 2 \end{pmatrix} = \begin{pmatrix} 4 \\ 2 \end{pmatrix}$.

c The position vector of A relative to C is $\overrightarrow{CA} = \begin{pmatrix} -1 - 4 \\ 2 - -5 \end{pmatrix} = \begin{pmatrix} -5 \\ 7 \end{pmatrix}$.

Example 19   ◀)) Self Tutor

[AB] is the diameter of a circle with centre C$(-1, 2)$. If B is $(3, 1)$, find:

a $\overrightarrow{BC}$ **b** the coordinates of A.

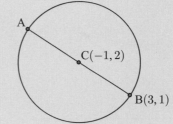

a $\overrightarrow{BC} = \begin{pmatrix} -1 - 3 \\ 2 - 1 \end{pmatrix} = \begin{pmatrix} -4 \\ 1 \end{pmatrix}$

b If A has coordinates (a, b), then $\overrightarrow{CA} = \begin{pmatrix} a - (-1) \\ b - 2 \end{pmatrix} = \begin{pmatrix} a + 1 \\ b - 2 \end{pmatrix}$

But $\overrightarrow{CA} = \overrightarrow{BC}$, so $\begin{pmatrix} a + 1 \\ b - 2 \end{pmatrix} = \begin{pmatrix} -4 \\ 1 \end{pmatrix}$

$\therefore \ a + 1 = -4 \ \text{ and } \ b - 2 = 1$

$\therefore \ a = -5 \ \text{ and } \ b = 3$

$\therefore$ A is $(-5, 3)$.

EXERCISE 18F

1 Find $\overrightarrow{AB}$ given:

    a A(2, 3) and B(4, 7)   **b** A(3, −1) and B(1, 4)   **c** A(−2, 7) and B(1, 4)

    d B(3, 0) and A(2, 5)   **e** B(6, −1) and A(0, 4)   **f** B(0, 0) and A(−1, −3).

2 Consider the point A(1, 4). Find the coordinates of:

    a B given $\overrightarrow{AB} = \begin{pmatrix} 3 \\ -2 \end{pmatrix}$
                 b C given $\overrightarrow{CA} = \begin{pmatrix} -1 \\ 2 \end{pmatrix}$.

3 [PQ] is the diameter of a circle with centre C.

    a Find $\overrightarrow{PC}$.

    b Hence find the coordinates of Q.

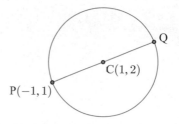

4

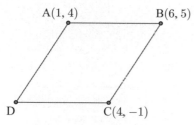

    ABCD is a parallelogram.

    a Find $\overrightarrow{AB}$.

    b Find $\overrightarrow{CD}$.

    c Hence find the coordinates of D.

5 A(−1, 3) and B(3, k) are two points which are 5 units apart.

    a Find $\overrightarrow{AB}$ and $|\overrightarrow{AB}|$.

    b Hence, find the two possible values of k.

    c Show, by illustration, why k should have two possible values.

> $|\overrightarrow{AB}|$ is the magnitude of $\overrightarrow{AB}$.

6

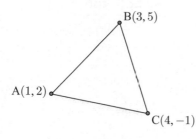

    a Find $\overrightarrow{AB}$ and $\overrightarrow{AC}$.

    b Explain why $\overrightarrow{BC} = -\overrightarrow{AB} + \overrightarrow{AC}$.

    c Hence find $\overrightarrow{BC}$.

    d Check your answer to **c** by direct evaluation.

7 **a** Given $\overrightarrow{BA} = \begin{pmatrix} 2 \\ -3 \end{pmatrix}$ and $\overrightarrow{BC} = \begin{pmatrix} -3 \\ 1 \end{pmatrix}$, find $\overrightarrow{AC}$.

    b Given $\overrightarrow{AB} = \begin{pmatrix} -1 \\ 3 \end{pmatrix}$ and $\overrightarrow{CA} = \begin{pmatrix} 2 \\ -1 \end{pmatrix}$, find $\overrightarrow{CB}$.

    c Given $\overrightarrow{PQ} = \begin{pmatrix} -1 \\ 4 \end{pmatrix}$, $\overrightarrow{RQ} = \begin{pmatrix} 2 \\ 1 \end{pmatrix}$, and $\overrightarrow{RS} = \begin{pmatrix} -3 \\ 2 \end{pmatrix}$, find $\overrightarrow{SP}$.

8

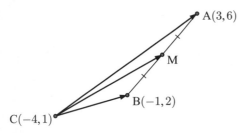

a Find the coordinates of M.

b Find vectors $\overrightarrow{CA}$, $\overrightarrow{CM}$, and $\overrightarrow{CB}$.

c Verify that $\overrightarrow{CM} = \frac{1}{2}\overrightarrow{CA} + \frac{1}{2}\overrightarrow{CB}$.

G   PARALLELISM

   are parallel vectors of different length.

Two non-zero vectors are **parallel** if and only if one is a scalar multiple of the other.

Given any non-zero vector **a** and non-zero scalar k, the vector $k\mathbf{a}$ is parallel to **a**.

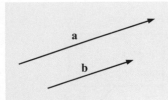

- If **a** is parallel to **b**, then there exists a scalar k such that $\mathbf{a} = k\mathbf{b}$.
- If $\mathbf{a} = k\mathbf{b}$ for some scalar k, then
  - ▸ **a** is parallel to **b**, and
  - ▸ $|\mathbf{a}| = |k||\mathbf{b}|$.

$|k|$ is the modulus of k, whereas $|\mathbf{a}|$ is the length of vector **a**.

Example 20   ◀) Self Tutor

Find s given that $\mathbf{a} = \begin{pmatrix} 2 \\ -1 \end{pmatrix}$ is parallel to $\mathbf{b} = \begin{pmatrix} s \\ 2 \end{pmatrix}$.

Since **a** and **b** are parallel, $\mathbf{a} = k\mathbf{b}$ for some scalar k.

$$\therefore \quad \begin{pmatrix} 2 \\ -1 \end{pmatrix} = k \begin{pmatrix} s \\ 2 \end{pmatrix}$$

$\therefore \ 2 = ks \ $ and $\ -1 = 2k$

Consequently, $\ k = -\frac{1}{2} \ $ and $\ \therefore \ 2 = -\frac{1}{2}s$

$\therefore \ s = -4$

UNIT VECTORS

Given a non-zero vector **a**, its magnitude $|\mathbf{a}|$ is a scalar quantity.

If we multiply **a** by the scalar $\dfrac{1}{|\mathbf{a}|}$, we obtain the parallel vector $\dfrac{1}{|\mathbf{a}|}\mathbf{a}$.

The length of this vector is $\left|\dfrac{1}{|\mathbf{a}|}\right||\mathbf{a}| = \dfrac{|\mathbf{a}|}{|\mathbf{a}|} = 1$, so $\dfrac{1}{|\mathbf{a}|}\mathbf{a}$ is a unit vector in the direction of **a**. We write this unit vector as $\widehat{\mathbf{a}}$.

- A unit vector in the direction of **a** is $\widehat{\mathbf{a}} = \dfrac{1}{|\mathbf{a}|}\mathbf{a}$.

- A vector **b** of length k in the same direction as **a** is $\mathbf{b} = k\widehat{\mathbf{a}} = \dfrac{k}{|\mathbf{a}|}\mathbf{a}$.

- A vector **b** of length k which is *parallel to* **a** could be $\mathbf{b} = \pm k\widehat{\mathbf{a}} = \pm\dfrac{k}{|\mathbf{a}|}\mathbf{a}$.

Example 21   ◀) Self Tutor

If $\mathbf{a} = 3\mathbf{i} - \mathbf{j}$ find:

a $\widehat{\mathbf{a}}$ **b** a vector of length 4 units in the direction of **a**

c vectors of length 4 units which are parallel to **a**.

a $|\mathbf{a}| = \sqrt{3^2 + (-1)^2}$ $\therefore \ \widehat{\mathbf{a}} = \frac{1}{\sqrt{10}}(3\mathbf{i} - \mathbf{j})$
$\phantom{|\mathbf{a}|} = \sqrt{9+1}$ $\phantom{\therefore \ \widehat{\mathbf{a}}} = \frac{3}{\sqrt{10}}\mathbf{i} - \frac{1}{\sqrt{10}}\mathbf{j}$
$\phantom{|\mathbf{a}|} = \sqrt{10}$ units

b A vector of length 4 units in the direction of **a** is $4\widehat{\mathbf{a}} = \frac{4}{\sqrt{10}}(3\mathbf{i} - \mathbf{j})$
$\phantom{\text{A vector of length 4 units in the direction of a is } 4\widehat{\mathbf{a}}} = \frac{12}{\sqrt{10}}\mathbf{i} - \frac{4}{\sqrt{10}}\mathbf{j}$

c The vectors of length 4 units which are parallel to **a** are
$4\widehat{\mathbf{a}} = \frac{12}{\sqrt{10}}\mathbf{i} - \frac{4}{\sqrt{10}}\mathbf{j}$ and $-4\widehat{\mathbf{a}} = -\frac{12}{\sqrt{10}}\mathbf{i} + \frac{4}{\sqrt{10}}\mathbf{j}$.

EXERCISE 18G.1

1 Find a such that:

a $\begin{pmatrix} 2 \\ -1 \end{pmatrix}$ and $\begin{pmatrix} -6 \\ a \end{pmatrix}$ are parallel   **b** $\begin{pmatrix} a \\ 2 \end{pmatrix}$ and $\begin{pmatrix} 3 \\ -1 \end{pmatrix}$ are parallel.

2 What can be deduced from the following?

a $\overrightarrow{AB} = 3\overrightarrow{CD}$ **b** $\overrightarrow{RS} = -\frac{1}{2}\overrightarrow{KL}$ **c** $\overrightarrow{AB} = 2\overrightarrow{BC}$

3 If $\mathbf{a} = \begin{pmatrix} 2 \\ 4 \end{pmatrix}$, write down the vector:

a in the same direction as **a** and twice its length

b in the opposite direction to **a** and half its length.

4 Find the unit vector in the direction of:

    a $i + 2j$ **b** $2i - 3j$ **c** $-2i + 2j$

5 Find a vector **v** which has:

    a the same direction as $\begin{pmatrix} 2 \\ -1 \end{pmatrix}$ and length 3 units

    b the opposite direction to $\begin{pmatrix} -1 \\ -4 \end{pmatrix}$ and length 2 units.

6 A is (3, 2) and point B is 4 units from A in the direction $\begin{pmatrix} 1 \\ -1 \end{pmatrix}$.

    a Find $\overrightarrow{AB}$.

    b Find $\overrightarrow{OB}$ using $\overrightarrow{OB} = \overrightarrow{OA} + \overrightarrow{AB}$.

    c Hence deduce the coordinates of B.

7 Find the coordinates of point X which is 5 units from $P(1, -5)$ in the direction $\begin{pmatrix} 3 \\ 4 \end{pmatrix}$.

8 The **triangle inequality** states that:

"In any triangle, the sum of any two sides must always be greater than the third side."

Prove that $|a + b| \leqslant |a| + |b|$ using a geometrical argument.

Hint: Consider:

    • **a** not parallel to **b** and use the triangle inequality

    • **a** and **b** parallel   • any other cases.

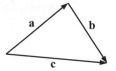

COLLINEAR POINTS

Three or more points are said to be **collinear** if they lie on the same straight line.

A, B, and C are **collinear** if $\overrightarrow{AB} = k\overrightarrow{BC}$ for some scalar k.

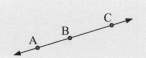

RATIO OF DIVISION

Suppose point P lies on the line segment [AB], so the three points are collinear.

We say that P **divides** [AB] **in the ratio** $AP : PB$.

EXERCISE 18G.2

1 Show that the following sets of points are collinear.

    a A(−1, 1), B(4, 6), and C(1, 3)   **b** P(3, 3), Q(6, −3), and R(1, 7)

Example 22

◀) **Self Tutor**

Given A$(-3, 2)$ and B$(5, -1)$, find the point P which divides [AB] in the ratio $2 : 5$.

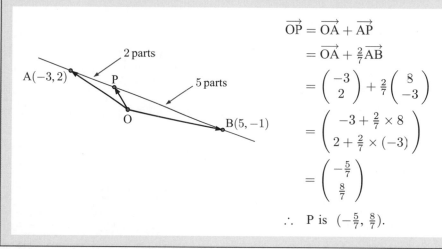

$$\overrightarrow{OP} = \overrightarrow{OA} + \overrightarrow{AP}$$

$$= \overrightarrow{OA} + \tfrac{2}{7}\overrightarrow{AB}$$

$$= \begin{pmatrix} -3 \\ 2 \end{pmatrix} + \tfrac{2}{7}\begin{pmatrix} 8 \\ -3 \end{pmatrix}$$

$$= \begin{pmatrix} -3 + \tfrac{2}{7} \times 8 \\ 2 + \tfrac{2}{7} \times (-3) \end{pmatrix}$$

$$= \begin{pmatrix} -\tfrac{5}{7} \\ \tfrac{8}{7} \end{pmatrix}$$

$\therefore$ P is $(-\tfrac{5}{7}, \tfrac{8}{7})$.

2   Given A$(3, -1)$ and B$(-3, 4)$, find Q which divides [AB] in the ratio $1 : 3$.

3   Given C$(-2, 7)$ and D$(6, -1)$, find R which divides [CD] in the ratio $5 : 3$.

4   **a**   Show that P$(3, 2)$, Q$(7, -3)$, and R$(1, \tfrac{9}{2})$ are collinear.

    b   Find the ratio in which the middle point divides the outer two.

Investigation

Linear combinations

Suppose we are standing at the origin, and we want to move to the point $(-4, -22)$.

However, we cannot move directly there. We are only allowed to move using scalar multiples of the vectors

$\begin{pmatrix} 3 \\ -1 \end{pmatrix}$ and $\begin{pmatrix} 2 \\ 4 \end{pmatrix}$.

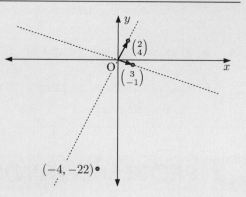

In this case, we can write the vector equation

$$r\begin{pmatrix} 3 \\ -1 \end{pmatrix} + s\begin{pmatrix} 2 \\ 4 \end{pmatrix} = \begin{pmatrix} -4 \\ -22 \end{pmatrix}.$$

If we can find values of r and s which satisfy the equation, then we can say that $\begin{pmatrix} -4 \\ -22 \end{pmatrix}$ is expressed

as a **linear combination** of the vectors $\begin{pmatrix} 3 \\ -1 \end{pmatrix}$ and $\begin{pmatrix} 2 \\ 4 \end{pmatrix}$.

Using vector addition, $\begin{pmatrix} 3r + 2s \\ -r + 4s \end{pmatrix} = \begin{pmatrix} -4 \\ -22 \end{pmatrix}$

$\therefore$ the scalars r and s must satisfy the simultaneous equations $\begin{cases} 3r - 2s = -4 \\ -r + 4s = -22 \end{cases}$.

Solving these equations simultaneously, we find that $r = 2$ and $s = -5$.

So, $2\begin{pmatrix} 3 \\ -1 \end{pmatrix} - 5\begin{pmatrix} 2 \\ 4 \end{pmatrix} = \begin{pmatrix} -4 \\ -22 \end{pmatrix}$.

What to do:

1 **a** Find scalars r and s such that:

   i $r\begin{pmatrix} 1 \\ 0 \end{pmatrix} + s\begin{pmatrix} 0 \\ 1 \end{pmatrix} = \begin{pmatrix} -4 \\ -22 \end{pmatrix}$ **ii** $r\begin{pmatrix} 1 \\ 0 \end{pmatrix} + s\begin{pmatrix} 0 \\ 1 \end{pmatrix} = \begin{pmatrix} 7 \\ -19 \end{pmatrix}$

   b Can *any* vector $\begin{pmatrix} x \\ y \end{pmatrix}$ in the plane be written as a linear combination of $\begin{pmatrix} 1 \\ 0 \end{pmatrix}$ and $\begin{pmatrix} 0 \\ 1 \end{pmatrix}$?

   Justify your answer.

2 **a** Find scalars r and s such that:

   i $r\begin{pmatrix} 1 \\ 0 \end{pmatrix} + s\begin{pmatrix} 1 \\ 1 \end{pmatrix} = \begin{pmatrix} -4 \\ -22 \end{pmatrix}$ **ii** $r\begin{pmatrix} 1 \\ 0 \end{pmatrix} + s\begin{pmatrix} 1 \\ 1 \end{pmatrix} = \begin{pmatrix} 7 \\ -19 \end{pmatrix}$

   b Can *any* vector $\begin{pmatrix} x \\ y \end{pmatrix}$ in the plane be written as a linear combination of $\begin{pmatrix} 1 \\ 0 \end{pmatrix}$ and $\begin{pmatrix} 1 \\ 1 \end{pmatrix}$?

   Justify your answer.

3 **a** Try to find scalars r and s such that:

   i $r\begin{pmatrix} 2 \\ 1 \end{pmatrix} + s\begin{pmatrix} -4 \\ -2 \end{pmatrix} = \begin{pmatrix} 8 \\ 4 \end{pmatrix}$ **ii** $r\begin{pmatrix} 2 \\ 1 \end{pmatrix} + s\begin{pmatrix} -4 \\ -2 \end{pmatrix} = \begin{pmatrix} 7 \\ -19 \end{pmatrix}$

   b What property of the vectors $\begin{pmatrix} 2 \\ 1 \end{pmatrix}$ and $\begin{pmatrix} -4 \\ -2 \end{pmatrix}$ makes it impossible to write *all* vectors

   in the plane as a linear combination of them? Use a diagram to justify your answer.

4 **a** Find scalars r and s such that $r\begin{pmatrix} 4 \\ 1 \end{pmatrix} + s\begin{pmatrix} 3 \\ 5 \end{pmatrix} = \begin{pmatrix} -6 \\ 7 \end{pmatrix}$.

   b Can *any* vector in the plane be written as a linear combination of $\begin{pmatrix} 4 \\ 1 \end{pmatrix}$ and $\begin{pmatrix} 3 \\ 5 \end{pmatrix}$?

   Justify your answer.

H   PROBLEMS INVOLVING VECTOR OPERATIONS

When we apply vectors to problems in the real world, we often consider the combined effect when vectors are added together. This sum is called the **resultant vector**.

We have an example of vector addition when two tug boats are used to pull a ship into port. If the tugs tow with forces $\mathbf{F}_1$ and $\mathbf{F}_2$ then the resultant force is $\mathbf{F}_1 + \mathbf{F}_2$.

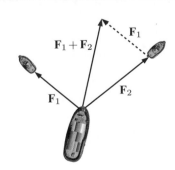

Example 23

◀ϴ **Self Tutor**

In still water, Jacques can swim at 1.5 m s^{-1}. Jacques is at point A on the edge of a canal, and considers point B directly opposite. A current is flowing from the left at a constant speed of 0.5 m s^{-1}.

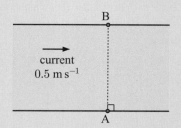

a If Jacques dives in straight towards B, and swims without allowing for the current, what will his actual speed and direction be?

b Jacques wants to swim directly across the canal to point B.

    i At what angle should Jacques *aim* to swim in order that the current will correct his direction?

    ii What will Jacques' actual speed be?

Suppose **c** is the current's velocity vector,
            s is the velocity vector Jacques would have if the water was still, and
            $\mathbf{f} = \mathbf{c} + \mathbf{s}$ is Jacques' resultant velocity vector.

a Jacques aims directly across the river, but the current takes him downstream to the right.

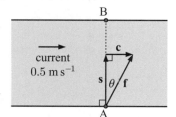

$$|\mathbf{f}|^2 = |\mathbf{c}|^2 + |\mathbf{s}|^2 \qquad \tan\theta = \frac{0.5}{1.5}$$
$$= 0.5^2 + 1.5^2 \qquad \therefore \ \theta \approx 18.4°$$
$$= 2.5$$
$$\therefore \ |\mathbf{f}| \approx 1.58$$

Jacques has an actual speed of approximately 1.58 m s^{-1} and his direction of motion is approximately $18.4°$ to the right of his intended line.

b Jacques needs to aim to the left of B so the current will correct his direction.

    i $\sin\phi = \dfrac{0.5}{1.5}$

    $\therefore \ \phi \approx 19.5°$

    Jacques needs to aim approximately $19.5°$ to the left of B.

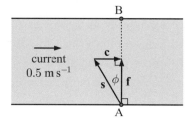

    ii $\quad |\mathbf{f}|^2 + |\mathbf{c}|^2 = |\mathbf{s}|^2$

    $\therefore \ |\mathbf{f}|^2 + 0.5^2 = 1.5^2$

    $\therefore \ |\mathbf{f}|^2 = 2$

    $\therefore \ |\mathbf{f}| \approx 1.41$

In these conditions, Jacques' actual speed towards B is approximately 1.41 m s^{-1}.

Another example of vector addition occurs when an aircraft is affected by wind. A pilot needs to know how to compensate for the wind, especially during take-off and landing.

SIMULATION

EXERCISE 18H

1 A bird can normally fly with constant speed 6 m s^{-1}. Using a vector diagram to illustrate each situation, find the bird's speed if:

    a it is assisted by a wind of 1 m s^{-1} from directly behind it

    b it flies directly into a head wind of 1 m s^{-1}.

2 In still water, Mary can swim at 1.2 m s^{-1}. She is standing at point P on the edge of a canal, directly opposite point Q. The water is flowing to the right at a constant speed of 0.6 m s^{-1}.

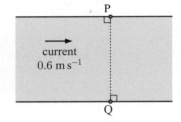

    a If Mary tries to swim directly from P to Q without allowing for the current, what will her actual velocity be?

    b Mary wants to swim directly across the canal to point Q.

        i At what angle should she *aim* to swim in order that the current corrects her direction?

        ii What will Mary's actual speed be?

3 An ocean liner is supposed to be travelling at 16 km h^{-1} on a course of 072°. However, it is drifting off-course due to a 3 km h^{-1} ocean current which is flowing due west. What is the actual speed and direction of the liner?

4 A boat needs to travel south at a speed of 20 km h^{-1}. However a constant current of 6 km h^{-1} is flowing from the south-east. Use vectors to find:

    a the equivalent speed in still water for the boat to achieve the actual speed of 20 km h^{-1}

    b the direction in which the boat must head to compensate for the current.

5 An aeroplane needs to fly due east from one city to another at a speed of 400 km h^{-1}. However, a 50 km h^{-1} wind blows constantly from the north-east.

    a How does the wind affect the speed of the aeroplane?

    b In what direction must the aeroplane head to compensate for the wind?

6 Find the resultant force when these three forces are applied to point A.

Force is a vector so it requires a direction.

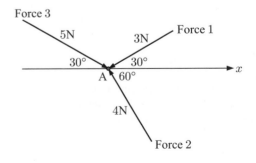

7   As part of an endurance race, Stephanie needs to swim from X to Y across a wide river.

Stephanie swims at 1.8 m s^{-1} in still water.

The river flows with a consistent current of 0.3 m s^{-1} as shown.

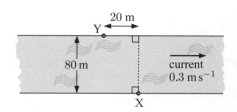

a   Find the distance from X to Y.

b   In which direction should Stephanie *aim* so that the current will push her onto a path directly towards Y?

c   How long will it take Stephanie to cross the river?

Puzzle   **Plain sailing**

In a yacht race, each boat has to sail around a set of 5 buoys and then return to the starting position.

Buoy 1 is 4 km from the start on a bearing of $325°$.

Buoy 2 is 6 km from Buoy 1 on a bearing of $072°$.

Buoy 3 is 10 km from Buoy 2 on a bearing of $168°$.

Buoy 4 is 5 km from Buoy 3 on a bearing of $238°$.

Buoy 5 is 5 km from Buoy 4 on a bearing of $315°$.

Find the distance and bearing of the starting position from Buoy 5.

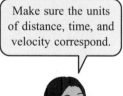

I   CONSTANT VELOCITY PROBLEMS

An object moving with a constant velocity will travel in a straight line. To model the position using vectors:

- the **velocity vector** of the motion gives the direction vector of the line
- **time** is the parameter
- the **initial position** of the object gives a fixed point on the line.

If an object has initial position vector **a** and moves with constant velocity **b**, its position at time t is given by

$$\mathbf{r} = \mathbf{a} + t\mathbf{b} \quad \text{for } t \geqslant 0.$$

The **speed** of the object is $|\mathbf{b}|$.

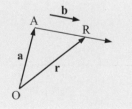

Make sure the units of distance, time, and velocity correspond.

Example 24

◀)) **Self Tutor**

$\begin{pmatrix} x \\ y \end{pmatrix} = \begin{pmatrix} 1 \\ 9 \end{pmatrix} + t \begin{pmatrix} 3 \\ -4 \end{pmatrix}$ is the vector equation of the path of an object.

The time t is in seconds, $t \geqslant 0$. The distance units are metres.

a Find the object's initial position.

b Plot the path of the object for $t = 0, 1, 2, 3$.

c Find the velocity vector of the object.

d Find the object's speed.

e If the object continues in the same direction but increases its speed to 30 m s^{-1}, state its new velocity vector.

a At $t = 0$, $\begin{pmatrix} x \\ y \end{pmatrix} = \begin{pmatrix} 1 \\ 9 \end{pmatrix}$

∴ the object is at $(1, 9)$.

DEMO

b

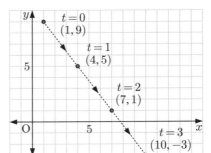

c The velocity vector is $\begin{pmatrix} 3 \\ -4 \end{pmatrix}$.

d The speed is $\left| \begin{pmatrix} 3 \\ -4 \end{pmatrix} \right| = \sqrt{3^2 + (-4)^2}$

$= 5 \text{ m s}^{-1}$.

Velocity is a vector.
Speed is a scalar.

e Previously, the speed was 5 m s^{-1} and the velocity vector was $\begin{pmatrix} 3 \\ -4 \end{pmatrix}$.

∴ the new velocity vector is $\frac{30}{5} \begin{pmatrix} 3 \\ -4 \end{pmatrix} = \begin{pmatrix} 18 \\ -24 \end{pmatrix}$.

EXERCISE 18I

1 A particle at $P(x(t), y(t))$ moves such that $x(t) = 1 + 2t$ and $y(t) = 2 - 5t$, $t \geqslant 0$.
The distances are in centimetres and t is in seconds.

a Find the initial position of P.

b Plot the path of P for $t = 0, 1, 2, 3$.

c Find the velocity vector of P.

d Find the speed of P.

Example 25

◀) **Self Tutor**

An object is initially at $(5, 10)$ and moves with velocity vector $3\mathbf{i} - \mathbf{j}$ metres per minute. Find:

a the position of the object at time t minutes

b the speed of the object

c the position of the object at $t = 3$ minutes

d the time when the object is due east of $(0, 0)$.

a

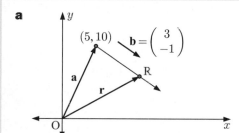

$$\mathbf{r} = \mathbf{a} + t\mathbf{b}$$

$$\therefore \begin{pmatrix} x \\ y \end{pmatrix} = \begin{pmatrix} 5 \\ 10 \end{pmatrix} + t \begin{pmatrix} 3 \\ -1 \end{pmatrix}, \quad t \in \mathbb{R}$$

$$\therefore \begin{pmatrix} x \\ y \end{pmatrix} = \begin{pmatrix} 5 + 3t \\ 10 - t \end{pmatrix}$$

After t minutes, the object is at $(5 + 3t, \ 10 - t)$.

b The speed of the object is $|\mathbf{b}| = \sqrt{3^2 + (-1)^2} = \sqrt{10}$ metres per minute.

c At $t = 3$ minutes, $5 + 3t = 14$ and $10 - t = 7$. The object is at $(14, 7)$.

d When the object is due east of $(0, 0)$, y must be zero.

$$\therefore \quad 10 - t = 0$$
$$\therefore \quad t = 10$$

The object is due east of $(0, 0)$ after 10 minutes.

---

2 **a** Find the vector equation of a boat initially at $(2, 3)$, which travels with velocity vector $\begin{pmatrix} 4 \\ -5 \end{pmatrix}$. The grid units are kilometres, and the time is in hours.

  b Locate the boat's position after 90 minutes.

  c How long will it take for the boat to reach the point $(5, -0.75)$?

3 A remote controlled toy car is initially at the point $(-3, -2)$. It moves with constant velocity $2\mathbf{i} + 4\mathbf{j}$. The distance units are centimetres, and the time is in seconds.

  a Write an expression for the position vector of the car at any time $t \geqslant 0$.

  b Hence find the position vector of the car at time $t = 2.5$.

  c Find when the car is   **i** due north   **ii** due west   of the observation point $(0, 0)$.

  d Plot the car's positions at times $t = 0, 0.5, 1, 1.5, 2, 2.5$.

4 Find the velocity vector of:

  a a speed boat moving parallel to $\begin{pmatrix} 4 \\ -3 \end{pmatrix}$ with speed 150 km h^{-1}

  b a jogger moving parallel to $\begin{pmatrix} -5 \\ 12 \end{pmatrix}$ with speed 7.8 km h^{-1}

  c a ferry moving parallel to $\begin{pmatrix} 6 \\ 7 \end{pmatrix}$ with speed 25 km h^{-1}.

5 Yacht A moves according to $x_A(t) = 4 + t$, $y_A(t) = 5 - 2t$, $t \geqslant 0$. Yacht B moves according to $x_B(t) = 1 + 2t$, $y_B(t) = -8 + t$, $t \geqslant 0$. The distance units are kilometres, and the time units are hours.

　　a Find the initial position of each yacht.　　　**b** Find the velocity vector of each yacht.

　　c Show that the speed of each yacht is constant, and state these speeds.

6 At 1:34 pm, submarine P fires a torpedo with velocity vector $\begin{pmatrix} 3 \\ -1 \end{pmatrix}$ from the point $(-5, 4)$.

a minutes later submarine Q fires a torpedo with velocity vector $\begin{pmatrix} -4 \\ -3 \end{pmatrix}$ from the point $(15, 7)$.

Distances are measured in kilometres, and time is in minutes.

　　a Show that the position of P's torpedo can be written as $P(x_1(t), y_1(t))$ where $x_1(t) = -5 + 3t$ and $y_1(t) = 4 - t$.

　　b What is the speed of P's torpedo?

　　c Show that the position of Q's torpedo can be written as $Q(x_2(t), y_2(t))$ where $x_2(t) = 15 - 4(t - a)$ and $y_2(t) = 7 - 3(t - a)$.

　　d Q's torpedo is successful in knocking out P's torpedo. At what time did Q fire its torpedo and at what time did the explosion occur?

J　PROOF USING VECTOR GEOMETRY

We can use vectors to prove important geometrical facts. The use of vectors in such proofs provides us with an alternative to using deductive or coordinate arguments, and can often simplify the proofs.

Example 26　　　　　　　　　　　　◀) **Self Tutor**

If M is the midpoint of [AB], prove that $\overrightarrow{OM} = \frac{1}{2}\mathbf{a} + \frac{1}{2}\mathbf{b}$.

$$\begin{aligned} \overrightarrow{OM} &= \overrightarrow{OA} + \overrightarrow{AM} \\ &= \overrightarrow{OA} + \tfrac{1}{2}\overrightarrow{AB} \\ &= \mathbf{a} + \tfrac{1}{2}(\mathbf{b} - \mathbf{a}) \\ &= \tfrac{1}{2}\mathbf{a} + \tfrac{1}{2}\mathbf{b} \end{aligned}$$

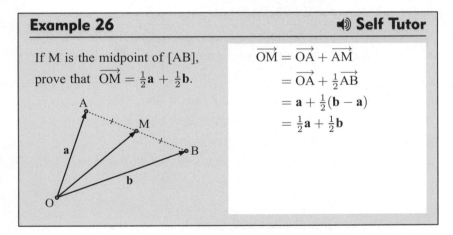

USEFUL TOOLS IN VECTOR PROOF

　　● If $\mathbf{a} = k\mathbf{b}$ where k is a scalar then $\mathbf{a}$ and $\mathbf{b}$ are parallel, and $|\mathbf{a}| = |k||\mathbf{b}|$.

　　● If M is the midpoint of [AB] then $\overrightarrow{OM} = \frac{1}{2}\mathbf{a} + \frac{1}{2}\mathbf{b}$.

Example 27
◀) **Self Tutor**

Use vector geometry to prove the midpoint theorem:

The line joining the midpoints of two sides of a triangle is parallel to the third side and half its length.

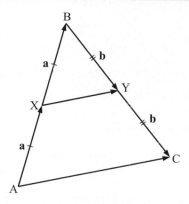

In triangle ABC, X and Y are midpoints of [AB] and [BC] respectively.

Let $\overrightarrow{AX} = \overrightarrow{XB} = \mathbf{a}$ and $\overrightarrow{BY} = \overrightarrow{YC} = \mathbf{b}$.

Now $\overrightarrow{XY} = \overrightarrow{XB} + \overrightarrow{BY} = \mathbf{a} + \mathbf{b}$

and $\overrightarrow{AC} = \overrightarrow{AB} + \overrightarrow{BC} = 2\mathbf{a} + 2\mathbf{b}$

$\therefore \quad \overrightarrow{XY} = \frac{1}{2}\overrightarrow{AC}$

Thus $\overrightarrow{XY} \parallel \overrightarrow{AC}$ and $|\overrightarrow{XY}| = \frac{1}{2}|\overrightarrow{AC}|$

Hence the line joining the midpoints of two sides of the triangle is parallel to the third side and half its length.

EXERCISE 18J

1 Prove that: *If a pair of opposite sides of a quadrilateral are parallel and equal in length, then the quadrilateral is a parallelogram.*

Hint:

Let $\overrightarrow{AB} = \mathbf{r}$ and $\overrightarrow{AD} = \mathbf{s}$.
Find $\overrightarrow{DC}$ and $\overrightarrow{BA} + \overrightarrow{AD} + \overrightarrow{DC}$
in terms of $\mathbf{r}$ and $\mathbf{s}$.

2 Prove that: *The diagonals of a parallelogram bisect each other.*

Hint:

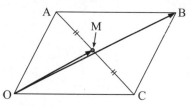

M is the midpoint of [AC].

Let $\overrightarrow{OA} = \mathbf{a}$ and $\overrightarrow{OC} = \mathbf{c}$.

Find $\overrightarrow{OB}$ and $\overrightarrow{OM}$ in terms of $\mathbf{a}$ and $\mathbf{c}$.

3 ABCD is a quadrilateral in which BP = PD and AP = PC.

Let $\overrightarrow{AP} = \mathbf{r}$ and $\overrightarrow{PB} = \mathbf{s}$.

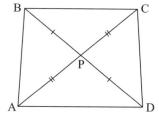

a Find, in terms of $\mathbf{r}$ and $\mathbf{s}$:

   i $\overrightarrow{PC}$ and $\overrightarrow{DP}$ **ii** $\overrightarrow{AB}$ and $\overrightarrow{DC}$.

b Discuss the significance of your answers to **a ii**.

c Copy and complete: *If the diagonals of a quadrilateral bisect each other ......*

4 P, Q, R, and S are the midpoints of [AB], [BC], [CD], and
[DA] respectively.

Let $\overrightarrow{AP} = \mathbf{p}$, $\overrightarrow{BQ} = \mathbf{q}$, and $\overrightarrow{CR} = \mathbf{r}$.

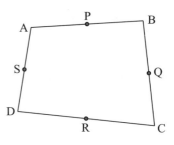

   a Find vector expressions for:

   i $\overrightarrow{AD}$ **ii** $\overrightarrow{AS}$ **iii** $\overrightarrow{PQ}$ **iv** $\overrightarrow{SR}$.

   b What can be deduced from **a iii** and **iv**?

5 OABC is a parallelogram and M is the midpoint of [OC]. T lies on [AM] such that AT : TM $= 2 : 1$.

   a Prove that O, T, and B are collinear.   **b** Find the ratio in which T divides [OB].

Review set 18A

1 Using a scale of $1 \text{ cm} \equiv 10$ units, sketch a vector to represent:

   a an aeroplane taking off at an angle of $8°$ to a runway with a speed of 60 m s^{-1}

   b a displacement of 45 m in a north-easterly direction.

2 Simplify:

   a $\overrightarrow{AB} - \overrightarrow{CB}$

   b $\overrightarrow{AB} + \overrightarrow{BC} - \overrightarrow{DC}$.

3 Construct a vector equation for:

   a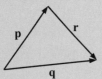

   b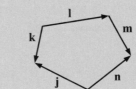

4 Write the illustrated vectors in component form and in unit vector form:

   a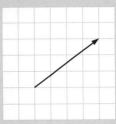

   b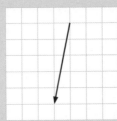

5 If $\overrightarrow{PQ} = \begin{pmatrix} -4 \\ 1 \end{pmatrix}$, $\overrightarrow{RQ} = \begin{pmatrix} -1 \\ 2 \end{pmatrix}$, and $\overrightarrow{RS} = \begin{pmatrix} 2 \\ -3 \end{pmatrix}$, find $\overrightarrow{SP}$.

6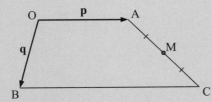

[BC] is parallel to [OA] and is twice its length.
Find, in terms of **p** and **q**, vector expressions for:

   a $\overrightarrow{AC}$ **b** $\overrightarrow{OM}$.

7 Find m if $\begin{pmatrix} 3 \\ m \end{pmatrix}$ and $\begin{pmatrix} -12 \\ -20 \end{pmatrix}$ are parallel vectors.

8 Consider points X$(-2, 5)$, Y$(3, 4)$, W$(-3, -1)$, and Z$(4, 10)$. Use vectors to show that WYZX is a parallelogram.

9 In this question you may *not* assume any diagonal properties of parallelograms.

OABC is a parallelogram with $\overrightarrow{CA} = \mathbf{p}$ and $\overrightarrow{OC} = \mathbf{q}$. M is the midpoint of [AC].

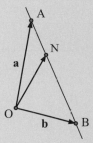

  a Find in terms of $\mathbf{p}$ and $\mathbf{q}$:

   i $\overrightarrow{OB}$ **ii** $\overrightarrow{OM}$

  b Hence show that O, M, and B are collinear, and that M is the midpoint of [OB].

10 Find the values of k such that the following are unit vectors: **a** $\begin{pmatrix} \frac{4}{7} \\ \frac{1}{k} \end{pmatrix}$ **b** $\begin{pmatrix} k \\ k \end{pmatrix}$

11 [AB] and [CD] are diameters of a circle with centre O.

  a If $\overrightarrow{OC} = \mathbf{q}$ and $\overrightarrow{OB} = \mathbf{r}$, find:

   i $\overrightarrow{DB}$ in terms of $\mathbf{q}$ and $\mathbf{r}$ **ii** $\overrightarrow{AC}$ in terms of $\mathbf{q}$ and $\mathbf{r}$.

  b What can be deduced about [DB] and [AC]?

12 Point N divides [AB] in the ratio $1 : 2$.

  a Write $\overrightarrow{ON}$ in terms of $\mathbf{a}$ and $\mathbf{b}$.

  b Find the coordinates of N given A is $(1, 6)$ and B is $(4, -1)$.

13 A small plane can fly at 350 km h^{-1} in still conditions. Its pilot needs to fly due north, but needs to deal with a 70 km h^{-1} wind from the east.

  a In what direction should the pilot face the plane to ensure that his resultant velocity is due north?

  b What will the speed of the plane be?

14 A yacht is sailing at 35 km h^{-1} in the direction $246°$. It suddenly encounters a current of 11 km h^{-1} pushing the boat in the direction $183°$. If the captain makes no correction, what will be the new speed and direction of the yacht?

15 A moving particle has coordinates P$(x(t), y(t))$ where $x(t) = -4 + 8t$, and $y(t) = 3 + 6t$. The distance units are metres, and $t \geqslant 0$ is the time in seconds. Find the:

  a initial position of the particle

  b position of the particle after 4 seconds

  c particle's velocity vector

  d speed of the particle.

16 A jetboat begins a tour across a lake at 11:30 am. The tour begins at point $(7, 16)$ on the map. The grid units are kilometres.

The jetboat travels in a straight line at 25 km h^{-1} across the lake to the lunch stop, which has coordinates $(4, -5)$.

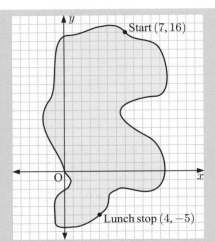

  a Write down the direction vector for the jetboat's movement.

  b Write a vector equation for the straight line between the starting point and the lunch stop.

  c At what time will the jetboat reach the lunch stop?

17 In parallelogram OABC, M is the midpoint of [OA] and N is the midpoint of [AB]. X lies on [MB] such that $MX : XB = 3 : 2$.

  a Show that C, X, and N are collinear.

  b Find the ratio in which X divides [CN].

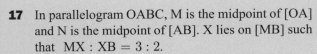

Review set 18B

1 Copy the given vectors and find geometrically:

  a $\mathbf{x} + \mathbf{y}$ **b** $\mathbf{y} - 2\mathbf{x}$

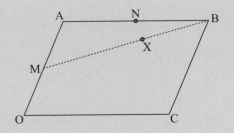

2 Find a single vector which is equal to:

  a $\overrightarrow{PR} + \overrightarrow{RQ}$ **b** $\overrightarrow{PS} + \overrightarrow{SQ} + \overrightarrow{QR}$

3 Find in component form and in unit vector form:

  a $\overrightarrow{PQ}$ **b** $\overrightarrow{RP}$

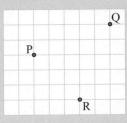

4 For $\mathbf{m} = \begin{pmatrix} 6 \\ -3 \end{pmatrix}$, $\mathbf{n} = \begin{pmatrix} 2 \\ 3 \end{pmatrix}$, and $\mathbf{p} = \begin{pmatrix} -1 \\ 3 \end{pmatrix}$, find:

  a $\mathbf{m} - \mathbf{n} + \mathbf{p}$ **b** $2\mathbf{n} - 3\mathbf{p}$ **c** $|\mathbf{m} + \mathbf{p}|$

5 What geometrical facts can be deduced from the equations:

  a $\overrightarrow{AB} = \tfrac{1}{2}\overrightarrow{CD}$ **b** $\overrightarrow{AB} = 2\overrightarrow{AC}$?

6 Given P(2, −5) and Q(−1, 7), find:

a the position vector of Q relative to P

b the distance from P to Q

c the distance from P to the x-axis.

7

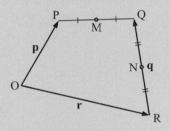

In the figure alongside, $\overrightarrow{OP} = \mathbf{p}$, $\overrightarrow{OR} = \mathbf{r}$, and $\overrightarrow{RQ} = \mathbf{q}$. M and N are the midpoints of [PQ] and [QR] respectively. Find, in terms of $\mathbf{p}$, $\mathbf{q}$, and $\mathbf{r}$:

a $\overrightarrow{OQ}$ **b** $\overrightarrow{PQ}$ **c** $\overrightarrow{ON}$ **d** $\overrightarrow{MN}$

8 Find k if the following are unit vectors: **a** $\begin{pmatrix} \frac{5}{13} \\ k \end{pmatrix}$ **b** $\begin{pmatrix} k \\ -2k \end{pmatrix}$

9 Given P(3, −1) and Q(4, 2), find:

a $\overrightarrow{PQ}$ **b** the distance between P and Q   **c** the midpoint of [PQ].

10   **a** Find $t > 0$ such that A(−1, 2t + 1), B(5, −4), and C(t − 2, 1) are collinear.

b Find the ratio in which the middle point divides the outer two.

11 When an archer fires an arrow, he is suddenly aware of a breeze which pushes his shot off-target. The speed of the shot $|\mathbf{v}|$ is *not* affected by the wind, but the arrow's flight is 2° off-line.

a Draw a vector diagram to represent the situation.

b Hence explain why:

i the breeze must be 91° to the intended direction of the arrow

ii the speed of the breeze must be $2\,|\mathbf{v}|\sin 1°$.

12 An eagle is trying to return to her nest, which is 7.4 km away. She needs to fly in the direction 098°, but there is wind blowing at 48 km h⁻¹ in the direction 305°. Her speed in still air is 56 km h⁻¹.

a In what direction should the eagle face in order that the wind will blow her onto the correct course?

b How long will it take for the eagle to reach her nest?

13 A yacht is sailing with constant speed $5\sqrt{10}$ km h⁻¹ in the direction $-\mathbf{i} - 3\mathbf{j}$. Initially it is at point (−6, 10). A beacon is at (0, 0) at the centre of a tiny atoll. Distances are in kilometres.

a Find, in terms of $\mathbf{i}$ and $\mathbf{j}$:

i the initial position vector of the yacht

ii the direction vector of the yacht

iii the position vector of the yacht after t hours, $t \geqslant 0$.

b Find the time when the yacht is due west of the beacon. How far away from the beacon is the yacht at this time?

14 Submarine X23 is at $(2, 4)$. It fires a torpedo with velocity vector $\begin{pmatrix} 1 \\ -3 \end{pmatrix}$ at exactly 2:17 pm.

Submarine Y18 is at $(11, 3)$. It fires a torpedo with velocity vector $\begin{pmatrix} -1 \\ a \end{pmatrix}$ at 2:19 pm to

intercept the torpedo from X23. Distance units are kilometres, and time units are minutes.

a Find $x_1(t)$ and $y_1(t)$ for the torpedo fired from submarine X23.

b Find $x_2(t)$ and $y_2(t)$ for the torpedo fired from submarine Y18.

c At what time does the interception occur?

d What was the direction and speed of the interception torpedo?

15 ABCD is a trapezium in which [BC] and [AD] are parallel. X and Y are the midpoints of [AB] and [CD] respectively. If $\overrightarrow{XB} = \mathbf{p}$, $\overrightarrow{BC} = \mathbf{q}$, and $\overrightarrow{CY} = \mathbf{r}$:

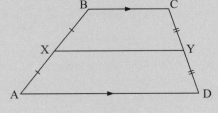

a Show that $\overrightarrow{AD} = 2\mathbf{p} + \mathbf{q} + 2\mathbf{r}$.

b If $\overrightarrow{AD} = k\,\overrightarrow{BC}$, find another vector expression for $\overrightarrow{AD}$.

c Deduce that $\mathbf{p} + \mathbf{r} = \left(\dfrac{k-1}{2}\right)\mathbf{q}$ and that $\overrightarrow{XY} = \left(\dfrac{k+1}{2}\right)\mathbf{q}$.

d What conclusion can be drawn from **c** concerning *the line joining the midpoints of the non-parallel sides of a trapezium?*

19

Mechanics: Forces and Newton's Laws

Contents:

Opening problem

Imagine a hot air balloon rising gently from the ground at a constant speed.

Suspended below the balloon is a basket containing the pilot and the passengers.

Things to think about:

a What causes the balloon to move upwards?

b What stops the people falling downwards?

Scientists use the word **force** to describe something which will change the motion of an object. The work of **Sir Isaac Newton** clarified this vague idea in an important, precise, and useful way.

Historical note   Newton's Laws

Before Newton, many other people tried to understand what caused bodies to move, including Aristotle and Galileo. They observed the world around them and tried various experiments.

Aristotle argued that forces cause movement and movement means *velocity*. This seems intuitive because everyday experience suggests that pushing something makes it move. However, if you have ever pushed a car, you will know that it takes a lot of effort to make the car move, and then once it is moving it is relatively easy to keep it moving. Therefore, Aristotle's model does not correspond well to the world we observe.

Galileo made many important advances and Newton built upon these to create the theory which is now referred to as **Newton's Laws**.

By contrast to Aristotle, Newton argued that a force causes *acceleration*. He published his work on forces in his book *Mathematical Principles of Natural Philosophy*. His model is still commonly used today.

A   NEWTON'S FIRST LAW OF MOTION

Newton's First Law of Motion states:

> A body will remain at rest, or will continue to move with a constant velocity, unless an external force acts upon it.

If a body is moving with a constant velocity then there can be no resultant force acting upon it.

For example:

- A book is sitting on a table. The book is at rest, and so there is no overall force. The weight of the book is balanced by the contact force between the book and the table.

- In the **Opening Problem**, the balloon is rising with constant velocity. The balloon is moving, but there is no acceleration and therefore no overall force. Whatever forces are acting must be *balanced*. In particular, the weight of the people, basket, and balloon are balanced by a force called buoyancy.

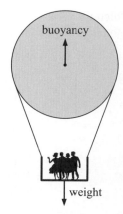

Conversely, we can say that if the velocity of a body changes, then a force must have caused it.

For example, suppose a book is sliding across a table. It slows down and stops, which means its velocity decreases to zero. We conclude that some force must have acted on the book to bring it to rest. We call this force *friction* or resistance.

Forces are *vector* quantities, having both magnitude and direction. The standard unit of force is the Newton, N.

For example, suppose a glider flies through still air at a constant velocity. There are three forces acting on the glider:

- the force of weight acting vertically downwards
- the force of lift acting perpendicular to the velocity, and
- a force of drag acting parallel to the velocity.

These forces must balance for the velocity to be constant.

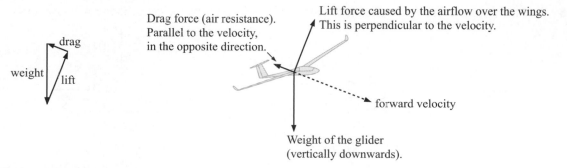

EXERCISE 19A

1 For each of the situations below, draw a clear modelling diagram showing all of the forces acting on the object in italics.

A modelling diagram does not need to include a realistic picture of the object, only an accurate representation of the physical situation.

    a a *cup* sits at rest on a table

    b a *crate* being lifted by a crane

    c a *person* is sitting still on a chair

    d a *spaceship* flying steadily through interstellar space

    e a *skydiver* in freefall

    f a *hockey puck* is freely sliding across a smooth ice skating rink with constant velocity

    g a *car* is rolling down a hill.

2   Which three forces act on a glider as it flies through still air? Under what conditions will the glider's velocity remain constant?

3   Each body below is at rest and subjected to the forces shown. Find x and y.

a

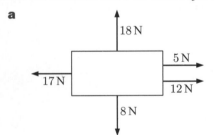

b

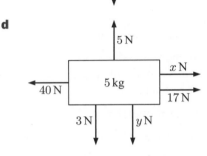

c

d

4   A spaceship in interstellar space is accelerating under rocket power. If it shuts off its rockets, which of the following is most likely to happen? Explain your answer.

A   The spaceship slows down and stops.

B   The spaceship continues at a constant velocity.

C   The spaceship continues to accelerate.

5   Find the resultant force on each object. Hence decide whether the object's motion will change.

a

b

B   NEWTON'S SECOND LAW OF MOTION

The vector sum of all the forces acting on a point is called the **resultant force**.

Newton's Second Law tells us what happens when there is an overall resultant force acting on a body:

> For a body with constant mass m, a resultant force F causes an acceleration a which is proportional to the force.
>
> $$F = ma.$$

The Newton is a derived unit, and from this equation of motion we see that one Newton is equivalent to the product of the units for mass and acceleration. Hence $1 \text{ N} \equiv 1 \text{ kg m s}^{-2}$.

Example 1

Thrust SSC is a British jet-propelled car which set a land speed record on 15 October 1997. It was the first land vehicle to officially break the sound barrier, achieving a speed of 1228 km h^{-1}.

The mass of Thrust SSC is approximately 10 600 kg. It took about 16 s to reach 1000 km h^{-1}, which is about 278 m s^{-1}.

Find the corresponding force from the engines.

Assuming constant acceleration, we use the *suvat* equations.

$$v = u + at$$
$$\therefore \quad 278 = 0 + a \times 16$$
$$\therefore \quad a \approx 17.4 \text{ m s}^{-2}$$

Using Newton's Second Law, the engines generated force
$$F = ma$$
$$\approx 10\,600 \times 17.4$$
$$\approx 184\,000 \text{ N}$$

In fact, the Twin Rolls-Royce Spey powered jet-car engines produced a total thrust of 222 000 N. The difference in thrust was used to overcome air resistance.

EXERCISE 19B

1 A body of mass 10 kg accelerates at $a = 5$ m s^{-2}. Find the resultant force acting on the body.

2 A particle of mass 6 kg is acted upon by a force of 12 N. Find the resulting acceleration.

3 The Class 390 Pendolino train has mass 466 tonnes and a top working speed of 200 km h^{-1} or approximately 55.6 m s^{-1}.

The optimal brake force gives a deceleration of about 0.9 m s^{-2}. Applying a greater force will lock the wheels and the train will skid along the rails. This would damage the wheels and result in a much longer stopping distance.

What force should be applied to give optimal braking?

4 A body is subjected to the forces shown. It accelerates to the right with acceleration a. Find:

   a the overall force on the body

   b the acceleration a.

5

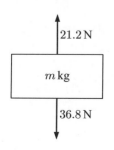

A body is subjected to the forces shown. It is falling with acceleration 9.8 m s^{-2}. Find:

   a the overall force on the body

   b the mass of the body.

6 A cyclist and her bike have total mass 86 kg. She wishes to accelerate at 0.5 m s^{-2} along a horizontal road.

    a Find the magnitude of the resultant force that needs to be applied.

    b In which direction must this force be applied?

7 Find the resulting acceleration of each object:

    a
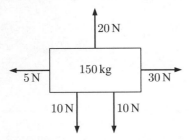

    b
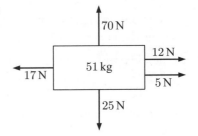

8 Find the mass of the object given that it is:

    a accelerating 0.2 m s^{-2} to the left

    b accelerating 3 m s^{-2} upwards.

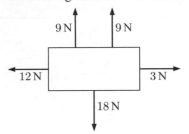
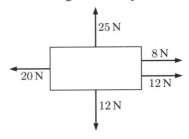

9 The AMT-USA AT-180 jet engine developed for radio-controlled aircraft produces 90 N of thrust. A model aircraft full of fuel has mass 7.6 kg.

    a Calculate the initial acceleration.

    b As the fuel is used up, what happens to the acceleration?

    c Estimate how long it will take for the aircraft to reach a speed of 45 m s^{-1} from rest.

10 In 2010, the Bugatti Veyron (Super Sport World Record Edition) set a world record as the fastest production car to reach 60 mph (27 m s^{-1}) from rest, taking about 2.46 seconds. The Bugatti Veyron has a mass of 1888 kg.

    a Calculate the acceleration required to reach 27 m s^{-1} in 2.46 s from rest.

    b Calculate the force required to cause this acceleration in the Bugatti Veyron.

C   WEIGHT

The **mass** of an object is a physical property related to the quantity of matter which it consists of. Mass is a *scalar* quantity.

Objects with mass attract each other, and the force of attraction is called **gravity**. This force is a *vector* quantity.

> Consider two objects with masses m_1 and m_2 which are r m apart. The force of attraction between the objects acts along the line between them, with magnitude given by $\dfrac{Gm_1m_2}{r^2}$ where G is the universal gravitational constant.

In this course we consider the force of gravity on a relatively small mass m close to the surface of the Earth or other planet. The radius of the Earth is approximately 6370 km, and most of the atmosphere is within 20 km of the surface, so it is reasonable to assume r is constant. The magnitude of the force due to gravity on the mass m is therefore $\dfrac{Gm_1}{r^2} m$. We call this the **weight** of the object, and it is directed "downwards" towards the centre of the planet.

We define $g = \dfrac{Gm_1}{r^2}$ to be the acceleration due to gravity which is dependent on the mass and radius of a planet. At this point weight is simply given by $W = mg$.

On Earth, acceleration due to gravity actually varies between 9.76 m s^{-2} and 9.83 m s^{-2} depending on the latitude and height above sea level. The standard acceleration due to gravity is internationally agreed to be 9.80665 m s^{-2}, but the approximation of 9.8 m s^{-2} is commonly used.

Strictly speaking, an object with mass 1 kg does not *weigh* 1 kg. Weight is a force measured in Newtons, so a mass of 1 kg actually weighs 9.8 N. For scientific work, this difference matters. The same object would still have mass 1 kg on the moon, but because the force of gravity on the moon is considerably less, it will have a smaller weight.

Example 2   ◀) Self Tutor

A balloon with total mass 400 kg starts from rest, and rises from the ground with uniform acceleration. After 20 s, the height is 25 m.

Find the lifting force needed.

Let the positive direction be up, and let L be the lifting force on the balloon.

The forces on the balloon are:

- lift $= L$ (upwards)
- weight $= -mg = -400g$ (downwards)

If a is the overall acceleration, then the resultant force $= ma = 400a$ (upwards)

$\therefore$ $L - 400g = 400a$

$\qquad \therefore$ $L = 400(a + g)$

Using the *suvat* equations: $s = ut + \frac{1}{2}at^2$

$\qquad\qquad\qquad \therefore$ $25 = 0 \times 20 + \frac{1}{2} \times a \times 20^2$

$\qquad\qquad\qquad\qquad \therefore$ $a = 0.125$ m s^{-2}

$\therefore$ the lifting force $L = 400(0.125 + 9.8) = 3970$ N.

EXERCISE 19C

1 Find the weight of a particle of mass

  a 6 kg   **b** 15 kg   **c** 24 kg

2 Find the mass of a particle with weight:

  a 24.5 N   **b** 88.2 N   **c** 101 N

3 A person has mass of 75 kg. Find their weight:

    a on Earth where $g = 9.8 \text{ m s}^{-2}$ **b** on the moon where $g = 1.6 \text{ m s}^{-2}$.

4 A body is subjected to the forces shown. It accelerates to the right with acceleration a. Find:

    a the force c

    b the acceleration a.

5 A farmer is travelling to the market with his donkey to sell some radishes. The donkey is pulling a cart with total weight 2350 N.

    a Find the mass of the fully laden cart.

    b Find the force the donkey needs to apply to accelerate the cart by 0.4 m s^{-2}.

6 The lunar rover was a battery-powered four-wheeled rover used on the moon during the Apollo 15 mission in 1971. On Earth it weighed 2058 N when unloaded.

    a Calculate the mass of the lunar rover.

    b On Earth, the electric motors delivered 150 N of thrust to move the vehicle. Calculate the resulting acceleration along a horizontal road.

    c Find the acceleration of the lunar rover on the moon along a horizontal road.

7 A drop tower is an amusement ride made with a large central tower. Riders are dropped from the top and experience freefall followed by rapid deceleration.

The Giant Drop in Dreamworld, Queensland, Australia has a drop of 119 m. The maximum speed is advertised as 37.5 m s^{-1} before the brakes are applied to bring the ride to rest.

Calculate:

    a the time taken to reach 37.5 m s^{-1}

    b the distance travelled in freefall

    c the braking force applied to a person of mass m to bring the person to rest within the 119 m before they hit the ground.

8 A rocket with total mass 29 tonnes takes off from the ground with uniform acceleration for the first 20 seconds. After 15 seconds it has reached height 270 m. Find the lifting force on the rocket.

9 A party balloon is filled with helium. It is tied to a long string which is not tied to anything else. Initially it starts to rise, but eventually it stops rising and remains at rest with some of the string hanging down and some of the string laying on the floor. Explain why the balloon has stopped moving upwards.

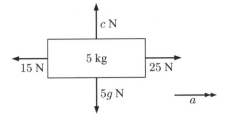

D   NEWTON'S THIRD LAW OF MOTION

If you push against an object, then the object pushes back. **Newton's Third Law** tells us exactly how much this happens:

Every action has an equal and opposite reaction.

CONTACT FORCES

Contact forces occur when solid objects press against each other. They occur because of atomic forces which hold particles together in solid objects. A contact force exerted by a flat surface is *perpendicular* to the surface.

In the **Opening Problem**, the people standing in the basket experience two forces: the force of their weight acting downwards, and the contact force between the people and the basket. The contact force acts upwards on the person, and there is an equal and opposite contact force which acts downwards on the basket. The upwards contact force on the person is opposite to their weight.

Example 3 ◀) Self Tutor

Alice has mass 70 kg. She is standing in a lift which is accelerating downwards at 2 m s^{-2}. Find the contact force exerted by the floor on Alice.

Let the positive direction be down, and let C be the contact force between Alice and the floor. The forces on Alice are:

- weight $= mg = 70g$ (downwards)
- contact force $= -C$ (upwards)

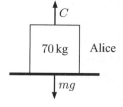

Overall, Alice accelerates downwards at 2 m s^{-2}.

Using $F = ma$ we find $70g - C = 70 \times 2$

$$\therefore \quad C = 70 \times 9.8 - 140 = 546 \text{ N}$$

The contact force is 546 N upwards.

EXERCISE 19D

1 Greg has several objects on his desk. Find the contact force exerted by the desk on:

   a a book with mass 1.2 kg   **b** a coffee mug with mass 0.38 kg

   c a monitor with mass 5.1 kg.

2 Georgina has mass 52 kg. She is standing in a lift which is accelerating downwards at 2.5 m s^{-2}. Find the contact force exerted by the floor on Georgina.

3 Bob has mass 85 kg. He is standing in a lift which is accelerating upwards at 3 m s^{-2}. Find the contact force exerted by the floor on Bob.

4 Kim is standing in a lift. When the lift is stationary, it exerts contact force F N upwards on Kim. State whether the force will be greater than, less than, or equal to F when the lift is:

   a moving upwards and speeding up   **b** moving downwards and speeding up

   c moving upwards at constant speed   **d** moving downwards at constant speed

   e moving upwards and slowing down   **f** moving downwards and slowing down.

5 A grand piano with mass 485 kg is on a stage which can be raised and lowered. Find the contact force exerted by the stage onto the piano if the stage is:

    a moving downwards with constant speed

    b accelerating upwards at 0.16 m s^{-2}

    c accelerating downwards at 0.16 m s^{-2}.

6 A balloon is gradually filling with hot air, creating a steadily increasing buoyancy force. The basket underneath the balloon is at rest on the ground until the buoyancy balances the weight.

Sketch a graph of the forces acting on the balloon against time. Label the three forces: weight, buoyancy, and the contact force between the balloon and the ground. Indicate the point at which the balloon starts to take off.

E   DRIVING AND RESISTANCE FORCES

Driving forces cause objects to move. They are commonly produced by engines. For example, **thrust** is the force which moves an aircraft through the air. Thrust is created by an engine which converts fuel into mechanical movement.

In every day life, the motion of an object does not go on forever. It will eventually slow down and stop due to **resistance** forces.

Objects sliding across surfaces experience **friction**.

Aeroplanes need to move air out of their way, so there is **air resistance**. Likewise, boats need to move water out of the way. These resistance forces are called **drag**.

For example, consider an aeroplane flying along horizontally with constant velocity. The aeroplane experiences a number of balancing forces:

- *weight* due to gravity acting vertically downwards
- *lift* from the wings acting vertically upwards equal and opposite to the weight
- *thrust* from the engines pushing the aeroplane forwards
- *drag* or air resistances which is equal and opposite to the thrust.

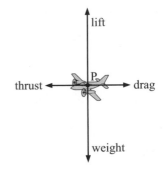

Notice how there are pairs of perpendicular forces. Each pair balances so there is zero overall force.

Discussion   Terminal velocity

When a skydiver jumps from a plane, they initially accelerate towards the centre of the earth at about 9.8 m s^{-2}. The force of gravity continues to act on the skydiver, but their acceleration reduces to zero and they reach a *terminal velocity*. What forces are acting which cause this to happen?

Discussion	**Mechanics modelling**

Mechanics allows us to create models of the real world. These models are approximations of the true situation because of assumptions we make.

When creating a simple model, we often choose to ignore resistance forces. This simplifies the model, making the mathematical equations possible to solve, but the predictions from the model will be less accurate.

When creating a model, it is *essential* to draw a picture. Label carefully all the vector quantities.

Mechanics has a number of *keywords* which mean specific things. You will often be posed a question which contains these keywords, and they communicate to you the modelling assumptions you are allowed to make.

Discuss each of the following keywords, considering situations where the assumption being made might be reasonable or unreasonable:

light	You may assume the object has no mass.
smooth	You may ignore friction.
rough	You may not ignore friction.
uniform	Something does not change, either in space or time. For example, "a particle moves under uniform acceleration" means "the acceleration is constant".
particle	You may assume the particle has no size. You do not need to worry about which direction the object is pointing in, or whether it is spinning.
thin	You may assume the object has very small width compared with its length.
inextensible or **inelastic**	You may assume the object cannot be stretched or squashed. If we cannot make this assumption then we may need to model the object as a spring of some kind, which is much more complicated.
rigid	You may assume the object does not bend.
long term	We are concerned about what happens for very large values of time.

For most questions in this course, we assume we are considering the motion of an inelastic, rigid particle.

Newton's laws are superbly effective in modelling the physical world we find ourselves in. Sometimes we cannot solve the resulting equations, and sometimes the equations have no simple solution (just as when a quadratic equation has no real roots). A failure to solve the equations is not a failure of the laws! However, the physical world is in reality more subtle, and Einstein's theory of relativity and other more modern theories have proved to be more useful models of the world for velocities closer to the speed of light, and for forces on a sub-atomic scale.

EXERCISE 19E

1 **a** Some great thinkers including Aristotle and Archimedes believed that a force was required to maintain motion, even at a constant velocity. How does this differ from Newton's theory?

  b If you push a book along a table and let go, why does it slow down and stop?

2 Aristotle suggested that heavier objects will fall faster than light ones. Ignoring air resistance, what do Newton's laws suggest? Explain your answer.

3 A skydiver jumps from an aeroplane. She falls to earth, accelerating due to the force of weight. As her velocity increases, so does the air resistance until the drag balances with gravity. Her speed tends to a constant value called the *terminal velocity*. If the skydiver has mass 70 kg and her terminal velocity is 55 m s^{-1}, find the wind resistance force at this terminal velocity.

Historical note   **London Millennium Footbridge**

All large engineering design relies on a mathematical model.

The London Millennium Footbridge was opened across the River Thames in London in June 2000.   This is a steel suspension bridge for pedestrians and is located between Southwark Bridge and Blackfriars Railway Bridge.

When the bridge was first opened, people walking over the bridge felt an unexpected swaying motion of up to 70 mm and so the bridge was nicknamed the "Wobbly Bridge". The effect was so alarming that the bridge was closed later on its opening day and remained closed for nearly two years while engineers modified the bridge to stop the vibration.

The side-to-side vibration is caused by **resonance**. This is a feedback process which occurs commonly in all kinds of structures. In this case, the resonance was caused by the people walking on the bridge.

It is unusual for resonance not to show up in the original model, but all modelling has its limitations.

After the vibration was discovered, the bridge engineers developed a more sophisticated model of the bridge. Their new calculations enabled them to design shock absorbers to dampen the vibration, thus solving the problem.

F   TENSION

Imagine a mass which is hanging in equilibrium suspended from a point P by a string. We assume the string is not elastic.

Since the mass is in equilibrium, there is no overall acceleration.

By Newton's First Law, the forces on the mass must balance. The weight of the mass mg must therefore be balanced by a **tension force** in the string. The tension will always act parallel to the string.

By Newton's Third Law, the tension T also acts in an equal and opposite manner on the suspension point P.

In the diagram alongside, we show the forces acting on the mass.

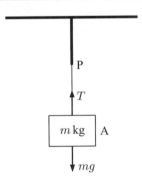

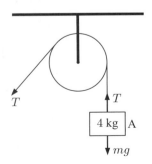

We can use a **pulley** to transfer the tension to a different direction.

For example, in the diagram alongside, the 4 kg mass is supported by a smooth light pulley. The tension T balances the weight of A, and the direction of the tension is transferred by the pulley so it remains parallel to the string.

CONNECTED OBJECTS

When two or more objects are connected together, we have to be very careful in identifying which force acts on which object.

For example, in the **Opening Problem**, the basket containing the people is connected to the balloon by ropes.

The tension in the ropes acts on the basket, pulling upwards. An equal and opposite force of tension acts to pull the balloon downwards.

In this example we can think in two ways:

- the balloon, people, and basket as a single object
- splitting the objects up so we consider just the balloon, just the basket, and just the people separately.

Splitting the system into smaller parts allows us to calculate the individual forces. When doing this you should draw a picture to show each part separately.

For example, imagine we have two masses which are hanging in equilibrium and suspended from P by a string.

In a situation like this it is clearer to draw a small separate diagram for each object, and list all the forces which act on it.

The forces on B are the weight m_2g, and the tension T_2 in the string between A and B. Since B is in equilibrium, $T_2 = m_2g$.

The forces on A are the weight m_1g, the tension T_2 which acts downward, and the tension T_1 which acts upwards. Since A is in equilibrium, $T_1 = m_1g + T_2 = (m_1 + m_2)g$.

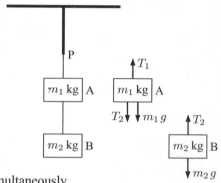

To find the overall forces we can solve the resulting equations simultaneously.

Example 4   ◀ **Self Tutor**

Two particles are suspended from a frictionless pulley by a light inextensible string. Particle A has mass 4 kg. Particle B has mass 2 kg. If the particles are released from rest, find:

a the resulting acceleration a **b** the tension T in the string.

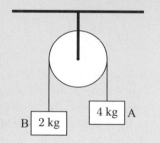

a Let the positive direction be *downwards*.

Since the string is inextensible, if A moves down a distance x, then B will move up a distance x.

Hence if A accelerates by a then B will accelerate at $-a$.

Adding the forces on each object, we find:

Forces on A: $4g - T = 4a$ .... (1)

Forces on B: $2g - T = -2a$ .... (2)

$(1) - (2)$ gives $2g = 6a$

$\therefore \quad a = \tfrac{1}{3}g$

b Using (1), $T = 4g - 4a = \left(4 - \tfrac{4}{3}\right)g = \tfrac{8}{3}g \approx 26.1$ N.

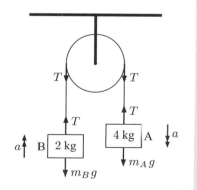

EXERCISE 19F

1 Calculate:

   a the force on P

   b the tension in the string between A and B.

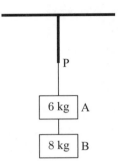

2

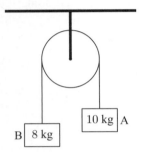

Two particles are suspended from a frictionless pulley by a light inextensible string. A has mass 10 kg, and B has mass 8 kg. The particles hang freely, and are released from rest. Find:

   a the resulting acceleration a

   b the tension T in the string.

3 Two particles are suspended from a frictionless pulley by a light inextensible string. A has mass 5 kg, and you are free to choose the mass m of B. The particles hang freely, and are released from rest. Find the mass m such that the resulting acceleration of A is:

   a 2 m s^{-2} downwards   **b** 2 m s^{-2} upwards.

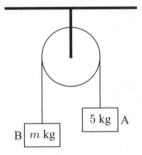

4 A 5 kg mass A lies on a smooth horizontal table. A light inextensible string attached to A passes over a smooth pulley. On its other end it carries a mass B of m kg which is suspended freely. Find the mass m needed to generate an overall acceleration of the particles in the system of 1 m s^{-2}.

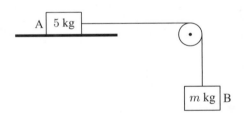

5

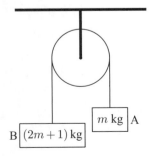

Two particles are suspended from a frictionless pulley by a light inextensible string. A has mass m kg and B has mass $(2m + 1)$ kg. The particles hang freely, and are released from rest.

Find the mass m such that the resulting acceleration of A is 4 m s^{-2} upwards.

Example 5

◀ Self Tutor

In the frictionless pulley system shown, A and B are fixed, and C is movable. The objects are connected by a light, inextensible string.

Let the positive direction be downwards.

Find the acceleration of C and the tension T in the string. Leave your answers in terms of g.

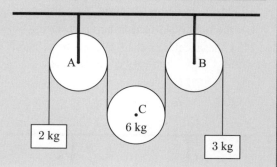

Let a_1 be the acceleration of mass $m_1 = 2$ kg on the left.

Let a_2 be the acceleration of mass $m_2 = 3$ kg on the right.

Since the string is inextensible, if the mass m_1 moves down a distance x, then the pulley C moves up a distance $\frac{1}{2}x$.

Likewise, if the mass m_2 moves down a distance y, then the pulley C moves up a distance $\frac{1}{2}y$.

∴   overall the pulley C moves up a distance $\frac{1}{2}(x + y)$.

∴   the acceleration of C must be $-\frac{1}{2}(a_1 + a_2)$ downwards.

Equating forces on the left hand mass:

$m_1 g - T = m_1 a_1$
∴ $2g - T = 2a_1$ .... (1)

Equating forces on the right hand mass:

$m_2 g - T = m_2 a_2$
∴ $3g - T = 3a_2$ .... (2)

Equating forces on the pulley C:

$mg - 2T = m \times \left[-\frac{1}{2}(a_1 + a_2)\right]$
∴ $6g - 2T = -3(a_1 + a_2)$ .... (3)

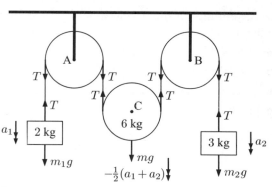

We need to solve (1), (2), and (3) simultaneously.

(2) − (1) gives $g = -2a_1 + 3a_2$ .... (4)

(3) − 2× (1) gives $2g = -7a_1 - 3a_2$ .... (5)

(4) + (5) gives $3g = -9a_1$
∴ $a_1 = -\frac{1}{3}g$

Using (4), $3a_2 - 2\left(-\frac{1}{3}g\right) = g$
∴ $3a_2 = \left(1 - \frac{2}{3}\right)g$
∴ $a_2 = \frac{1}{9}g$

So, the acceleration of C is $-\frac{1}{2}(a_1 + a_2) = -\frac{1}{2}\left(-\frac{1}{3}g + \frac{1}{9}g\right) = -\frac{1}{2}\left(-\frac{2}{9}g\right) = \frac{1}{9}g$

Using (1), $T = 2g - 2a_1$
$= 2g - 2\left(-\frac{1}{3}g\right)$
$= \frac{8}{3}g$

6 In the frictionless pulley system shown, A and B are
fixed, and C is movable. The objects are connected by
a light, inextensible string.

Let the positive direction be downwards.

Find the acceleration of C and the tension T in the
string. Leave your answers in terms of g.

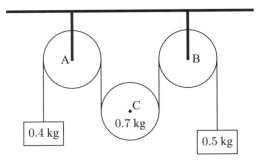

7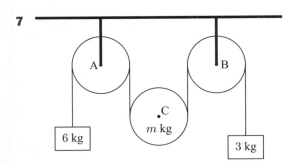

In the frictionless pulley system shown, A and B are
fixed, and C is movable. The objects are connected by
a light, inextensible string.

Find the load m given that pulley C does not move
when released from rest.

Review set 19A

1 For each of the situations below, draw a clear modelling diagram showing all of the forces acting
on the object(s) in italics.

  a a *book* lies at rest on a table

  b a *box* is hanging from a chain

  c a crane is picking up a *container* from a cargo ship

  d a *car* is towing a *trailer*.

2 The body subjected to the forces shown is at rest.
Find x and y.

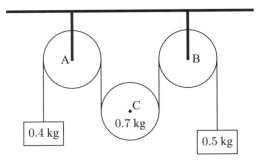

3 Clare has mass 65 kg. She is standing in a lift which is accelerating upwards at 2 m s^{-2}. Find the
contact force exerted by the floor on Clare.

4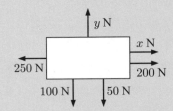

A 15 kg mass A lies on a smooth horizontal table.
A light inextensible string attached to A, passes
over a smooth fixed pulley. On the other end is an
18 kg mass B suspended freely. Find the overall
acceleration of the particles in the system.

5 A car driver fails to wear their seat belt and unfortunately has a crash during which the car stops
suddenly. The driver flies forward and hits the car windscreen, breaking it from the inside. Discuss
the forces resulting in the broken windscreen.

6 An 11 tonne meteor plummets through the atmosphere towards Earth, reaching terminal velocity 180 m s^{-1}. Find the wind resistance force at this terminal velocity.

7 Two particles A and B are suspended from a frictionless pulley by a light inextensible string.

A has mass 20 kg, and B has mass 18 kg. The particles hang freely and are released from rest.

   a Find the resulting acceleration and the tension in the string.

   b How long will it take for A to move 2 m?

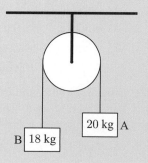

Review set 19B

1 For each of the situations below, draw a clear modelling diagram showing all of the forces acting on the object(s) in italics.

   a a *ladder* is leaning against a wall

   b a jet powered *rocket* is launched

   c a *parachutist* is descending under his *parachute*

   d a *bridge* is supported by two pillars.

2 A body is subjected to the forces shown. It accelerates to the left with acceleration a. Find:

   a the force c

   b the acceleration a.

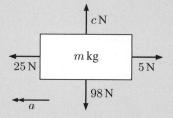

3 Louise is travelling in a lift which is accelerating upwards at 4.5 m s^{-2}. The floor of the lift is exerting a contact force of 586 N. Find Louise's mass.

4 You are inside a train without windows, which is travelling on a straight horizontal track. You place a heavy ball on the floor at rest. Explain how watching the ball will help you decide if the train in accelerating or decelerating.

5 Two particles are suspended from a frictionless pulley by a light inextensible string.

A has mass 3 kg, and B has mass 2 kg. The particles hang freely and are released from rest.

   a Find the resulting acceleration and the tension in the string.

   b After travelling 5 m, A hits the ground and comes to rest.

     i Find the velocity of B at this time.

     ii Describe the subsequent motion of B.

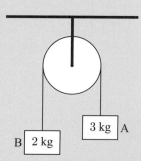

6 After a profitable day, a farmer has sold all of his goods. He returns home to his farm, his donkey pulling an empty cart with mass 83 kg.

　a Find the weight of the cart.

　b Find the force the donkey needs to exert to accelerate the cart by 0.5 m s^{-2}.

　c Discuss the assumptions you have made in your answer to **b**. How do the wheels on the cart help the donkey?

7 In the frictionless pulley system shown, A and B are fixed, and C is moveable. The objects are connected by a light, inextensible string.

　a Find the acceleration of C and the tension in the string. Leave your answers in terms of g.

　b What extra mass would need to be added to C in order that it will not move when released from rest?

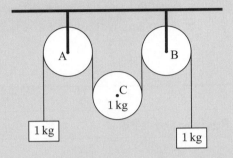

20

Single-variable statistics

Contents:

Opening problem

A supermarket sells 1 kg bags of grapes.

Things to think about:

a Would you expect every bag of grapes to weigh *exactly* 1 kg?

b In what range of weights would you expect most of the bags of grapes to lie?

c If you weighed many bags of grapes and graphed the results on the set of axes alongside, what would you expect the graph to look like?

d Do you think the graph would look different if we were analysing the weights of 1 kg bags of sugar? Explain your answer.

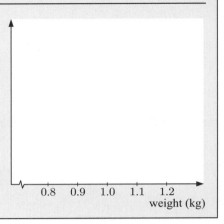

In statistics we collect information about a group of individuals, then analyse this information to draw conclusions about those individuals.

You should already be familiar with these words which are commonly used in statistics:

Data:	information about the characteristics of a group of individuals
Categorical variable:	describes a particular characteristic which can be divided into categories
Numerical variable:	describes a characteristic which has a numerical value that can be counted or measured
Population:	an entire collection of individuals about which we want to draw conclusions
Census:	the collection of information from the **whole population**
Parameter:	a numerical quantity measuring some aspect of a population
Sample:	a group of individuals selected from a population
Survey:	the collection of information from a **sample**
Statistic:	a quantity calculated from data gathered from a sample, usually used to estimate a population parameter
Distribution:	the pattern of variation of data, which may be described as:

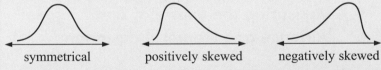

symmetrical   positively skewed   negatively skewed

Outliers:	data values that are either much larger or much smaller than the general body of data; they should be included in analysis *unless* they are the result of human or other known error

A   SAMPLING

A **census** is the most accurate way to investigate a population of interest. However, in most situations it is impractical or impossible to obtain data from the entire population. Instead, we can conduct a **survey** of a well-chosen **sample** of the population.

In this Section we will investigate what it means for a sample to be "well-chosen" by considering **sources of error** that arise in surveys and the merits of different **sampling methods**.

SOURCES OF ERROR IN SURVEYS

When we collect data to estimate a characteristic of a population, our estimate will almost certainly be different to the actual characteristic of the population. This difference is referred to as **error**.

There are four main categories of error: **sampling error**, **measurement error**, **coverage error**, and **non-response error**.

Sampling error occurs when a characteristic of a sample differs from that of the whole population. This error is random, and will occur even for samples which are well chosen to avoid bias.

Measurement error refers to inaccuracies in measurement at the data collection stage. For example, when we record a person's height to the nearest centimetre, the recorded height is slightly different from the person's *exact* height.

Measurement error can also arise from the way survey questions are asked. The question may be worded to lead the respondent to answer in a certain way.   For example, the question "Do you support the dangerous practice of cycling without a helmet?" invites the respondent to answer "no", since the question contains the judgement that riding without a helmet is dangerous. To avoid this type of error, questions should be worded clearly, and in a neutral tone.

Coverage errors occur when a sample does not truly reflect the population we are trying to find information about.

To avoid coverage errors, samples should be **sufficiently large** and **unbiased**.

For example, suppose you are interested in the health of bees on a particular island.

- If you only collect data from 10 bees, you will not get a reliable idea of the health of all bees on the island.

- If you only collect data from one particular bee hive, the sample may not be **representative** of all of the bees on the island. For example, the hive you pick may be stressed and preparing to swarm, whereas its neighbouring hives may be healthy. The sample would therefore be a **biased sample**, and would be unreliable for forming conclusions about the whole population.

Non-response errors occur when a large number of people selected for a survey choose not to respond to it.

For example:

- An online survey is less likely to be completed by elderly people who are unfamiliar with technology. This means that elderly people will be under-represented in the survey.

- In surveys on customer satisfaction, people are more likely to respond if they are unsatisfied.

EXERCISE 20A.1

1 A new drug called Cobrasyl has been developed for the treatment of high blood pressure in humans. A derivative of cobra venom, it is able to reduce blood pressure to an acceptable level. Before its release, a research team treated 7 high blood pressure patients with the drug, and in 5 cases it reduced their blood pressure to an acceptable level.

Do you think this sample can be used to draw reliable conclusions about the drug's effectiveness for all patients? Explain your answer.

2   50 people in a London shopping mall were surveyed. It was found that 20 of them had been to a football match in the past year. From this survey, it was concluded that "40% of people living in England have been to a football match in the past year".

Give *two* reasons why this conclusion is unreliable.

3   A polling agency is employed to investigate the voting intention of residents in a particular electorate. From the data collected, they want to predict the election result for that electorate in the next election. Explain why each of the following situations may produce a biased sample:

   a   A random selection of people in the local large shopping complex is surveyed between 1 pm and 3 pm on a weekday.

   b   The members of the local golf club are surveyed.

   c   A random sample of people at the local train station between 7 am and 9 am are surveyed.

   d   A door to door visit is undertaken, surveying every voter in a particular street.

4   Jennifer wants to estimate the average weight of the 2000 sheep on her farm. She selects a sample of 10 sheep, and weighs them.

Explain why this approach may produce a:

   a   coverage error   **b**   measurement error.

5   The government has released a new proposal to move funding from education to health. A journalist wants to understand the public's feelings about this proposal. She asks 100 people the question "Do you support the Government's proposed cuts to education?".

   a   Explain why this survey may produce a measurement error.

   b   How could the question be worded so the public's feelings about the proposal would be more accurately measured?

6   Jack owns 800 apple trees. To determine how many apples the trees are producing, he instructs his four sons to each count the apples from 200 trees.

   a   Explain why there will be no sampling error in this process.

   b   Two of the sons only count the apples on the tree itself, whilst the other two sons also count the apples on the ground beneath the tree. What type of error is this?

7   A survey company is interested in whether people feel overworked at their jobs. They mail out a survey to 5000 workers, and ask the workers to mail back the survey.

   a   Explain why this survey may produce a significant non-response error.

   b   What would be the advantages and disadvantages of conducting the survey online instead of by mail?

Discussion

Why do you think companies offer incentives for people to complete their surveys?

COMPLETE OUR SURVEY
FOR YOUR CHANCE TO
WIN
A £50 GIFT CARD

SAMPLING METHODS

In general, the best way to avoid bias when selecting a sample is to make sure the sample is **randomly selected**. This means that each member of the population has the same chance of being selected in the sample.

We will look at four sampling methods:

- simple random sampling
- stratified sampling
- systematic sampling
- self-selected sampling.

SIMPLE RANDOM SAMPLING

Suppose 3 students are to be sampled from a class of 30 students. The names of each student in the class are placed in a barrel, and 3 names are drawn from the barrel.

Notice that:

- Each student has the same chance ($\frac{1}{10}$) of being selected.
- Each set of 3 students is just as likely to be selected as any other. For example, the selection {Bruce, Jane, Sean} is just as likely to occur as {Jane, Peter, Vanessa}.

This type of sampling is called **simple random sampling**.

> For a **simple random sample** of size n from a population:
>
> - Each member of the population has the same chance of being selected in the sample.
> - Each set of n members of the population has the same chance of being selected as any other set of n members.

Instead of drawing names from a barrel, it is usually more practical to number the members of the population, and use a random number generator to select the sample.

You can use your calculator to generate random numbers. In this case, the 10th, 17th, and 25th students would be selected for the sample.

GRAPHICS
CALCULATOR
INSTRUCTIONS

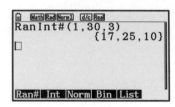

SYSTEMATIC SAMPLING

In **systematic sampling**, the sample is created by selecting members of the population at regular intervals.

For example, an accountancy firm may wish to sample the files of $\frac{1}{10}$th of their clients. They choose a starting file from 1 to 10 (for example, 3), and then select every 10th file after that. So, they would select the 3rd file, then the 13th, 23rd, 33rd, and so on.

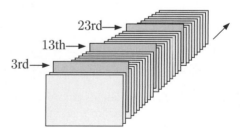

Systematic sampling is useful when not all members of the population are available for sampling at the same time. An example of this is the sampling of cars which pass through a particular intersection during the day.

Example 1
◄) **Self Tutor**

Management of a large city store wishes to find out whether potential customers like the look of a new product. They decide to sample 5% of the customers using a systematic sample. Show how this sample would be selected.

$5\% = \frac{5}{100} = \frac{1}{20}$

So, every 20th person will be sampled.

A starting customer is selected from 1 to 20. In this case it is customer 7.

So, the store would select the 7th customer, then the 27th, 47th, 67th, and so on.

```
NORMAL FLOAT AUTO REAL RADIAN MP
randInt(1,20)
                            7
```

STRATIFIED SAMPLING

Stratified sampling is useful when the population can be divided into subgroups, and you want to make sure each subgroup is represented fairly in the sample.

For example, a school may want to know the opinions of its students on which charities it should support in the school fun run. To make sure each year level is represented fairly, the number of students sampled from each year level should be proportional to the fraction of the total number of students that year level represents.

Strata	Random Samples
Year 8s	
Year 9s	
Year 10s	
Year 11s	
Year 12s	

Example 2
◄) **Self Tutor**

In our school there are 137 students in Year 8, 152 in Year 9, 174 in Year 10, 168 in Year 11, and 121 in Year 12. A stratified sample of 50 students is needed. How many should be randomly selected from each year?

Total number of students in the school $= 137 + 152 + 174 + 168 + 121 = 752$

For the sample, we want:

number of Year 8 students $= \frac{137}{752} \times 50 \approx 9$

number of Year 9 students $= \frac{152}{752} \times 50 \approx 10$

number of Year 10 students $= \frac{174}{752} \times 50 \approx 12$

number of Year 11 students $= \frac{168}{752} \times 50 \approx 11$

number of Year 12 students $= \frac{121}{752} \times 50 \approx 8$

Year 8 students represent $\frac{137}{752}$ of the school, so they should also represent $\frac{137}{752}$ of the sample.

We should select 9 students from Year 8, 10 from Year 9, 12 from Year 10, 11 from Year 11, and 8 from Year 12.

SELF-SELECTED SAMPLES

In many situations, it is impractical to simply select people to participate in a survey. For instance, people may be required to go on a special diet for weeks at a time, or the study may need people with a specific medical condition.

In cases like these, the usual procedure for selecting a sample is to advertise for volunteers to participate. This is known as a **self-selected sample**.

Self-selected samples will almost certainly be **biased**, but in these cases we accept the bias because it means the sample we are taking has particular **relevance** to what we are studying.

EXERCISE 20A.2

1 Use your calculator to select a random sample of:

You may need to generate additional random numbers if a number appears more than once.

    a 6 different numbers between 5 and 25 inclusive

    b 10 different numbers between 1 and 25 inclusive

    c 6 different numbers between 1 and 45 inclusive

    d 5 different numbers between 100 and 499 inclusive.

2 Click on the icon to obtain a printable calendar for 2016 showing the weeks of the year. Each day is numbered.

CALENDAR

Using a random number generator, choose a sample from the calendar of:

    a five different dates   **b** a complete week starting with a Monday

    c a month   **d** three different months   **e** three consecutive months

    f five different dates during winter   **g** four different Wednesdays.

Explain your method of selection in each case.

January	February	March	April	May
1 Fr (1) Wk 1	1 Mo (32)	1 Tu (61)	1 Fr (92) Wk 14	1 Su (122)
2 Sa (2)	2 Tu (33)	2 We (62)	2 Sa (93)	2 Mo (123)
3 Su (3)	3 We (34)	3 Th (63)	3 Su (94)	3 Tu (124)
4 Mo (4)	4 Th (35)	4 Fr (64) Wk 10	4 Mo (95)	4 We (125)
5 Tu (5)	5 Fr (36) Wk 6	5 Sa (65)	5 Tu (96)	5 Th (126)
6 We (6)	6 Sa (37)	6 Su (66)	6 We (97)	6 Fr (127) Wk 19
7 Th (7)	7 Su (38)	7 Mo (67)	7 Th (98)	7 Sa (128)
8 Fr (8) Wk 2	8 Mo (39)	8 Tu (68)	8 Fr (99) Wk 15	8 Su (129)
9 Sa (9)	9 Tu (40)	9 We (69)	9 Sa (100)	9 Mo (130)
10 Su (10)	10 We (41)	10 Th (70)	10 Su (101)	10 Tu (131)
11 Mo (11)	11 Th (42)	11 Fr (71) Wk 11	11 Mo (102)	11 We (132)
...	...	...	...	...

3 A chocolate factory produces 80 000 blocks of chocolate per day. Today, the factory operator wants to sample 2% of the blocks for quality testing. He uses a systematic sample, starting from the 17th block.

    a List the first five blocks to be sampled.   **b** Find the total size of the sample.

4 An annual dog show averages 3540 visitors. The catering manager is conducting a survey to investigate the proportion of visitors who will spend more than £20 on food and drinks at the show. He decides to survey the first 40 people through the gate.

    a Discuss any problems with the sampling method.

    b Suggest a better sampling method that includes a suitable sample size and which better represents the population.

5 A library manager is interested in the number of people using the library each day. She decides to perform a count every 28th day for one year, starting next Monday.

   a What type of sampling method is this?

   b How many days will be in her sample?

   c Explain why the sample may be biased.

6 A sporting club wants to ask its members some questions about the clubhouse. The club has 80 tennis members, 60 lawn bowls members, and 20 croquet members.

   a How many members does the club have in total?

   b The club decides to use a stratified sample of 40. How many members of each sport should be sampled?

7 A large retail store has 10 departmental managers, 24 supervisors, 65 senior sales staff, 98 junior sales staff, and 28 shelf packers. The company director wishes to interview a sample of 30 staff to obtain their view of operating procedures. How many of each group should be selected for the sample?

8 A local council wants to know whether residents are in favour of reducing the size of a local park to make room for road upgrades. The council invites the public to voice their opinions at an information seminar about the project.

   a What type of sampling method is this?

   b In what way might the sample be biased?

9 A medical school wants to trial a new diabetes medication. They advertise in a medical journal for volunteers aged 60 and over with diabetes.

50 of the 80 volunteers reported an improvement in health after using the medication.

   a Explain why a self-selected sample is appropriate in this situation.

   b What percentage of the volunteers reported an improvement in health?

   c In what way might the sample be biased? Discuss whether you think this is a problem.

10 The 200 students in Years 11 and 12 at a high school were asked whether or not they had ever smoked a cigarette. The replies received were:

nnnny	nnnyn	ynnnn	yynyy	ynyny	ynnyn	nyynn	yynyn
ynnyn	yynyy	nnyyy	yyyyy	nnnyy	nnnnn	nnyny	yynny
nynnn	ynyyn	nnyny	ynyyy	ynnnn	yyyyn	yynnn	nynyn
nynnn	yynny	nyynn	yynyn	ynynn	nyyyn	ynnyy	nyyny
ynynn	nyynn	nnnyy	ynyyn	yyyny	ynnyy	nnyny	ynnnn

   a Why is this considered to be a census?

   b Find the actual proportion of all students who said they had smoked.

c Discuss the validity and usefulness of the following sampling methods which could have been used to estimate the proportion in **b**:

    i   sampling the first five replies

    ii   sampling the first ten replies

    iii   sampling every second reply

    iv   sampling the fourth member of every group of five

    v   randomly selecting 30 numbers from 1 to 200 and choosing the response corresponding to that number

    vi   sampling 20% of Year 11 students and 20% of Year 12 students.

d Are any of the methods in **c** examples of simple random sampling, systematic sampling, or stratified sampling?

Discussion

The so-called "Brexit" referendum of 2016 to determine whether the United Kingdom should remain part of the European Union is one of the most controversial democratic referendums in recent history.

1 Was the referendum a census or a sample?

2 What sampling errors may have been present? In what ways might the sample have been biased?

3 Do you think it is a good idea to have a non-compulsory referendum which can be carried with only a simple majority?

B   NUMERICAL DATA

In this course we will focus on data from **numerical variables**.

The methods we use to organise and display numerical data depend on the *type* of numerical variable from which it was collected.

There are two types of numerical variable that we will consider:

- A **discrete numerical variable** takes exact numerical values and is often a result of **counting**.

  Examples of discrete numerical variables are:
  - *The number of people in a car*:   the variable could take the values 1, 2, 3, ...
  - *The score out of 20 for a test*:   the variable could take the values 0, 1, 2, 3, ..., 20.

- A **continuous numerical variable** takes numerical values within a certain continuous range. It is usually a result of **measuring**.

  Examples of continuous numerical variables are:
  - *The height of Year 12 students*:   the variable can take any value from about 140 cm to 200 cm.
  - *The speed of cars on a stretch of highway*:   the variable can take any value from 0 mph to the fastest speed that a car can travel, but is most likely to be in the range 30 mph to 100 mph.

ORGANISING NUMERICAL DATA

One of the simplest ways to organise data is using a **tally and frequency table** or just **frequency table**.

For example, consider the data set:

$$
\begin{array}{lllll}
1\ 3\ 1\ 2\ 4 & 2\ 4\ 1\ 5\ 3 & 1\ 3\ 2\ 2\ 4 \\
1\ 3\ 4\ 1\ 2 & 3\ 2\ 4\ 1\ 3 & 2\ 1\ 2\ 5\ 2
\end{array}
$$

A **tally** is used to count the number of 1s, 2s, 3s, and so on. As we read the data from left to right, we place a vertical stroke in the tally column. We use ┼┼┼ to represent 5 occurrences.

The **frequency** column summarises the number of occurrences of each particular data value.

Value	Tally	Frequency (f)
1	┼┼┼ |||	8
2	┼┼┼ ||||	9
3	┼┼┼		6
4	┼┼┼	5
5				2
	Total	30

When data from a continuous numerical variable is measured, it is usually recorded to a certain level of accuracy, such as 1 decimal place. This makes the data appear to be discrete.

For example, the data below shows the lengths in centimetres, rounded to 1 decimal place, of pencils in a pencil case.

9.2	14.6	12.5	13.7	12.1	11.7
10.4	13.8	11.0	12.6	11.3	12.6
11.8	10.6	13.4	11.3	14.2	12.3
10.7	11.7	9.8	13.4	11.6	10.0
9.4	12.6	11.4	10.9	14.5	9.2

We can organise this data by grouping it into **class intervals** of **equal width**. In this case we let the length be l and choose the class intervals $9 \leqslant l < 10$, $10 \leqslant l < 11$, ..., $14 \leqslant l < 15$.

Length (l cm)	Tally	Frequency
$9 \leqslant l < 10$	||||	4
$10 \leqslant l < 11$	┼┼┼	5
$11 \leqslant l < 12$	┼┼┼ |||	8
$12 \leqslant l < 13$	┼┼┼		6
$13 \leqslant l < 14$	||||	4
$14 \leqslant l < 15$	|||	3
	Total	30

Example 3

◀)) **Self Tutor**

25 students sat a Mathematics test. The marks they received for the test are given below:

$$8 \quad 5 \quad 3 \quad 7 \quad 5 \quad 8 \quad 5 \quad 8 \quad 6 \quad 8 \quad 7 \quad 6 \quad 6$$
$$3 \quad 6 \quad 5 \quad 7 \quad 7 \quad 8 \quad 9 \quad 8 \quad 9 \quad 6 \quad 6 \quad 8$$

  a Is the *number of marks* a discrete or continuous variable?

  b Record this information in a tally and frequency table.

  c What proportion of students received more than 6 marks for the test?

  a The *number of marks* is a discrete variable.

  b

Number of marks	Tally	Frequency
3			1
4		0
5	‖‖	4
6	⧸⧸⧸⧸		6
7	‖‖	4
8	⧸⧸⧸⧸ ‖|	8
9	‖	2

  c $\dfrac{4+8+2}{25} = \dfrac{14}{25} = 56\%$ of students received more than 6 marks for the test.

EXERCISE 20B

1 Classify the following numerical variables as discrete or continuous:

    a the number of students in a classroom   **b** the weights of cows in a field

    c the maximum temperature of a city   **d** the number of hairs on a person's head

    e the scores obtained by gymnasts in a competition

    f the amount of water you consume each day.

2 Consider the following statistics for a tennis player:

    Age: 28

    Height: 191 cm

    Tournament wins: 14

    Average serving speed: 185 km h^{-1}

    Ranking: 6

    Career prize money: £3 720 000

Classify each variable as discrete or continuous.

3 Lucas owns a hobby shop. In the last fortnight, his store had the following numbers of customers each day:

$$10 \quad 6 \quad 11 \quad 9 \quad 8 \quad 7 \quad 8 \quad 10 \quad 11 \quad 8 \quad 9 \quad 12 \quad 9 \quad 8$$

    a Is the *number of customers* a discrete or continuous variable?

    b Construct a tally and frequency table to organise the data.

    c Find the percentage of days for which Lucas' shop had:

      i 8 customers   **ii** more than 10 customers.

4 A school asked a group of 60 parents to fill in a questionnaire about the school. The times they took to fill in the questionnaire are given below in minutes, rounded to 1 decimal place:

6.1	7.6	8.3	4.1	5.3	12.9	16.7	21.0	9.2	12.3	9.3	8.7
22.3	16.4	17.7	23.1	20.2	3.0	10.7	6.1	5.4	5.2	13.2	8.0
18.1	22.7	7.8	8.3	13.1	16.2	17.3	4.3	7.1	9.3	7.9	14.2
9.7	16.0	3.5	6.2	7.1	10.4	5.3	8.1	7.0	14.2	15.7	10.7
12.8	4.4	16.0	23.1	7.4	7.6	10.2	9.2	4.4	5.1	12.6	11.3

a Is the time taken t a discrete or continuous variable?

b Copy and complete the tally and frequency table alongside.

c Find the number of parents who took:

  i between 10 and 15 minutes to fill in the questionnaire

  ii between 15 and 20 minutes to fill in the questionnaire

  iii more than 10 minutes to fill in the questionnaire.

Time (t min)	Tally	Frequency
$0 \leqslant t < 5$		
$5 \leqslant t < 10$		
$10 \leqslant t < 15$		
$15 \leqslant t < 20$		
$20 \leqslant t < 25$		

C DISPLAYING NUMERICAL DATA

DISPLAYING DISCRETE NUMERICAL DATA

Discrete numerical data can be displayed using a **bar chart**.

For example, we can construct a bar chart for the data on page **472** using the frequency table:

Value	Frequency
1	8
2	9
3	6
4	5
5	2

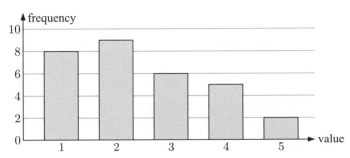

DESCRIBING THE DISTRIBUTION OF A DATA SET

A bar chart allows us to quickly observe the **distribution** or **shape** of the data set. We can describe the distribution as:

- **Symmetric**

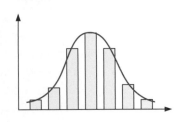

- **Negatively skewed**

negative side is stretched

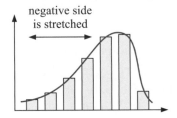

- **Positively skewed**

positive side is stretched

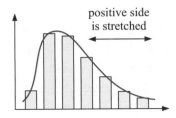

Outliers are data values that are either much larger or much smaller than the general body of data.

Outliers appear separated from the body of data on a bar chart.

If an outlier is a genuine piece of data, it should be retained for analysis. However, if it is found to be the result of an error in the data collection process, it should be removed from the data.

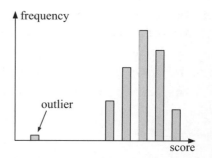

Example 4   ◄)) **Self Tutor**

The scores out of 10 for a Mathematics test are shown in the table.

a Construct a bar chart to display the data.

b Describe the distribution of the data. Are there any outliers?

Number of marks	Frequency
3	1
4	0
5	4
6	6
7	4
8	8
9	2

a
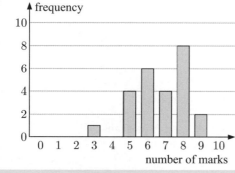

b The data is negatively skewed. The data value "3" is an outlier.

EXERCISE 20C.1

1 Consider the bar chart alongside.

a Describe the distribution of the data.

b Are there any outliers?

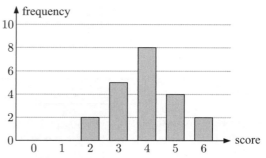

2 The number of matches in 30 match boxes were recorded. The results are given in the table below:

Number of matches per box	47	49	50	51	52	53	55
Frequency	1	1	9	12	4	2	1

a Construct a bar chart to display the data.   **b** Describe the distribution of the data.

3 The data alongside shows the number of guests staying in each room of a hotel on a particular night.

2	1	0	1	2	3	0	2
3	2	2	1	2	2	1	0
2	3	1	4	0	2	2	1
2	1	0	3	2	2	1	2
4	1	3	2	0	1	2	1

  a Organise the data using a frequency table.

  b Draw a bar chart to display the data.

  c Describe the distribution of the data.

4 24 archery students each took 15 shots at a target. The number of times they hit the target are recorded below:

$$10 \quad 8 \quad 11 \quad 10 \quad 9 \quad 8 \quad 12 \quad 9 \quad 10 \quad 9 \quad 10 \quad 11$$
$$7 \quad 9 \quad 10 \quad 8 \quad 11 \quad 9 \quad 18 \quad 10 \quad 11 \quad 12 \quad 8 \quad 11$$

  a Construct a tally and frequency table to organise the data.

  b Draw a bar chart to display the data.

  c Identify the outlier in the data. Explain why this outlier must be the result of a recording error.

DISPLAYING CONTINUOUS NUMERICAL DATA

Continuous numerical data can be displayed using a **histogram**. This is similar to a bar chart, except:

- the "bars" are joined together to account for the continuous nature of the variable
- the frequency of a class interval is not the height of the bar, but rather the *area* of the bar.

$$\text{area} = \text{bar height} \times \text{bar width}$$
$$\therefore \quad \text{frequency} = \text{bar height} \times \text{class interval width}$$

We call the bar height of a class interval its **frequency density**. This should be labelled on the vertical axis of a histogram.

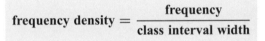

$$\text{frequency density} = \frac{\text{frequency}}{\text{class interval width}}$$

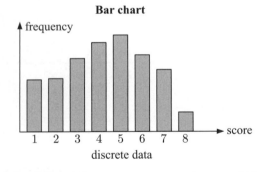

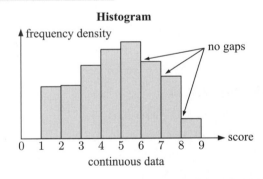

Example 5   ◀)) **Self Tutor**

30 customers were asked how long they spent waiting in a queue. The results are summarised in the table alongside:

  a Calculate the frequency density for each class interval.

  b Construct a histogram for the data.

  c Describe the distribution of the data.

Time (t minutes)	Frequency
$0 \leqslant t < 2$	9
$2 \leqslant t < 4$	10
$4 \leqslant t < 6$	5
$6 \leqslant t < 8$	3
$8 \leqslant t < 10$	2
$10 \leqslant t < 12$	1

a The width of each class interval is 2 minutes.

∴   the frequency density for each class interval $= \dfrac{\text{frequency}}{2}$.

Time (t minutes)	Frequency	Frequency density
$0 \leqslant t < 2$	9	4.5
$2 \leqslant t < 4$	10	5
$4 \leqslant t < 6$	5	2.5
$6 \leqslant t < 8$	3	1.5
$8 \leqslant t < 10$	2	1
$10 \leqslant t < 12$	1	0.5

b

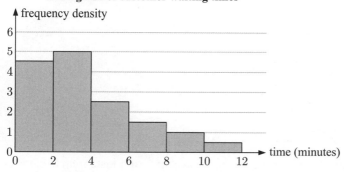

Histogram of customer waiting times

c The data is positively skewed. There are no outliers.

In some situations we may choose to use class intervals with different widths. For example:

- There may be a smaller number of data values which are spread out away from the centre of the data. This may include outliers. In such cases where the frequency density is low, a wider class interval may be used.

- The data may be naturally grouped in the context of the problem.

Example 6
◀⑴ Self Tutor

A post office charges different postage fees for parcels that fall in different weight categories.

Over the last fortnight, the number of parcels the post office received in each weight category was recorded. The results are shown in the table alongside.

Weight (w kg)	Frequency
$0 \leqslant w < 1$	5
$1 \leqslant w < 2$	7
$2 \leqslant w < 5$	9
$5 \leqslant w < 10$	5
$10 \leqslant w < 20$	2

a How many parcels did the post office receive in the last fortnight?

b Calculate the frequency density for each class interval.

c Construct a histogram for the data.

d Describe the distribution of the data.

a The post office received $5 + 7 + 9 + 5 + 2 = 28$ parcels in total.

b

Weight (w kg)	Frequency	Class interval width	Frequency density
$0 \leqslant w < 1$	5	1	5
$1 \leqslant w < 2$	7	1	7
$2 \leqslant w < 5$	9	3	3
$5 \leqslant w < 10$	5	5	1
$10 \leqslant w < 20$	2	10	0.2

c

Histogram of parcel weights

It is natural to use the same groups as the postage fees, so this gives us class intervals with different widths.

d   The data is positively skewed.

Using the frequency density rather than the frequency on the vertical axis of a histogram becomes important when we have class intervals of different widths. For instance in **Example 6**, although the classes $0 \leqslant w < 1$ and $5 \leqslant w < 10$ have the same frequency, $5 \leqslant w < 10$ is less *dense* because it is a wider interval. With wider class intervals, we are less certain of the exact original data values, since they are spread out over a larger range.

EXERCISE 20C.2

1   Consider the histogram alongside.

   a   Describe the distribution of the data.

   b   State the width of each class interval.

   c   Calculate the frequency of each class interval.

   d   Determine the number of scores:

      i   between 10 and 20

      ii   greater than or equal to 15.

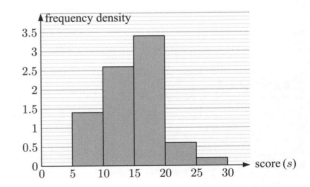

2   The heights of 25 junior hockey players are summarised in the table below:

Height (h cm)	$120 \leqslant h < 130$	$130 \leqslant h < 140$	$140 \leqslant h < 150$	$150 \leqslant h < 160$	$160 \leqslant h < 170$
Frequency	1	2	7	14	1

   a   Calculate the frequency density for each class interval.

   b   Construct a histogram for the data.

   c   Describe the distribution of the data.

3 The following table shows the cost of parking at a shopping centre car park:

Time (t hours)	Cost
$0 \leqslant t < 0.5$	£2.00
$0.5 \leqslant t < 1$	£3.00
$1 \leqslant t < 2$	£4.00
$2 \leqslant t < 3$	£6.00
$3 \leqslant t < 5$	£11.50
$5 \leqslant t < 8$	£20.00

35 customers were randomly selected. The length of time each customer stayed at the car park, in hours, was recorded:

1.5 1.4 2.4 2.2 1.0 5.1 2.6 2.2 2.1 5.3 1.9 2.8 2.2 1.4 2.5 1.6 3.0 2.2
4.6 1.6 3.1 1.6 3.5 3.4 1.3 2.1 4.8 3.0 2.7 1.2 3.4 1.4 2.8 1.4 0.3

a Organise the data using the class intervals shown in the table.

b How many customers spent at least £6 on parking?

c Draw a histogram to display the data.

d Describe the distribution of the data.

4 Patrick recorded the time it took to drive to work over 20 days. The following data shows his results in minutes, rounded to 2 decimal places:

9.75   10.42   9.62   10.02   15.32   9.82   9.86   9.81   9.91   10.04
10.37   9.76   9.68   9.95   9.68   9.96   9.82   9.34   10.07   9.92

a Identify the outlier. Explain why the outlier should *not* be removed.

b Copy and complete each frequency table for the data:

i

Time (t minutes)	Frequency
$9 \leqslant t < 10$	
$10 \leqslant t < 11$	
$11 \leqslant t < 12$	
$12 \leqslant t < 13$	
$13 \leqslant t < 14$	
$14 \leqslant t < 15$	
$15 \leqslant t < 16$	

ii

Time (t minutes)	Frequency
$9.25 \leqslant t < 9.5$	
$9.5 \leqslant t < 9.75$	
$9.75 \leqslant t < 10$	
$10 \leqslant t < 10.25$	
$10.25 \leqslant t < 10.5$	
$10.5 \leqslant t < 16$	

c Construct a histogram for each frequency table in **b**. Use the histogram to describe the shape of the distribution in each case.

d Which histogram do you think illustrates the distribution better? Explain your answer.

Discussion

- Is it possible for someone to be *exactly* 150 cm tall?
- If a person describes their height as 150 cm, in what range do you think it will be?
- Erin is approximately 149.7 cm tall. When Georgio records her height in a survey, he writes down 150 cm. When he constructs a frequency table and histogram for the data, he incorrectly places Erin in the class $150 \leqslant h < 155$ cm. What could Georgio have done to make sure his rounding did not spoil his data?

D   MEASURING THE CENTRE OF DATA

We can get a better understanding of a data set if we can locate the **middle** or **centre** of the data, and also get an indication of its **spread** or dispersion. Knowing one of these without the other is often of little use.

There are three statistics that are used to measure the **centre** of a data set. These are the **mode**, the **mean**, and the **median**.

THE MODE

- For discrete numerical data, the **mode** is the most frequently occurring value in the data set.
- For continuous numerical data, we cannot talk about a mode in this way because no two data values will be *exactly* equal. Instead we talk about a **modal class**, which is the class or group that has the highest *frequency density*. It is not necessarily the class with the highest frequency.

If a data set has two values which both occur most frequently, we say it is **bimodal**.

If a data set has three or more values which all occur most frequently, the mode is not an appropriate measure of centre to use.

THE MEAN

The **mean** of a data set is the statistical name for the arithmetic average.

For the data set $\{x_1, x_2, x_3, ..., x_n\}$,

$$\text{mean} = \frac{\textbf{sum of all data values}}{\textbf{the number of data values}}$$

$$= \frac{x_1 + x_2 + x_3 + ... + x_n}{n}$$

$$= \frac{\sum\limits_{i=1}^{n} x_i}{n}$$

We use $\overline{x}$ to represent the mean of a **sample**, and μ to represent the mean of a **population**.

In many cases we do not have data from all of the members of a population, so the exact value of μ is unknown. Instead we collect data from a sample of the population, and use the mean of the sample $\overline{x}$ as an approximation for μ.

μ is the Greek letter "mu" which we pronounce as "mew".

THE MEDIAN

The **median** is the *middle value* of an ordered data set.

An ordered data set is obtained by listing the data from the smallest to the largest value.

The median splits the data in halves. Half of the data values are less than or equal to the median, and half are greater than or equal to it.

For example, if the median mark for a test is 73% then you know that half the class scored less than or equal to 73% and half scored greater than or equal to 73%.

For an **odd number** of data values, the median is one of the original data values.

For an **even number** of data values, the median is the average of the two middle values, and hence may not be in the original data set.

> If there are n data values listed in order from smallest to largest,
> the median is the $\left(\dfrac{n+1}{2}\right)$th data value.

For example:

DEMO

If $n = 13$, $\dfrac{n+1}{2} = 7$, so the median is the 7th ordered data value.

If $n = 14$, $\dfrac{n+1}{2} = 7.5$, so the median is the average of the 7th and 8th ordered data values.

THE MERITS OF THE MEAN AND MEDIAN AS MEASURES OF CENTRE

The **median** is the only measure of centre that will locate the true centre regardless of the data set's features. It is unaffected by the presence of extreme values. It is called a *resistant* measure of centre.

The **mean** is a reliable measure of centre if the distribution is symmetrical or approximately symmetrical. If it is not, then unbalanced high or low values will *drag* the mean toward them, and it may not be appropriate to still use the mean as a measure of centre. The mean is called a *non-resistant* measure of centre because it is influenced by *all* data values in the set.

THE RELATIONSHIP BETWEEN THE MEAN AND THE MEDIAN FOR DIFFERENT DISTRIBUTIONS

For distributions that are **symmetric** about the centre, the mean and median will be equal.

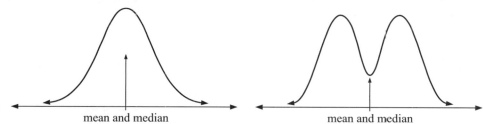

If the data set is not symmetric, it may be positively or negatively skewed:

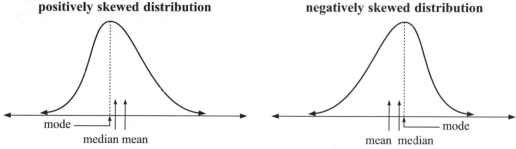

Notice that the mean and median are clearly different for these skewed distributions.

However, for some asymmetric distributions the mean and median may be similar or even equal, so care must be taken when drawing conclusions.

Example 7
◄)) **Self Tutor**

The numbers of faulty products returned to an electrical goods store each day over a 21 day period are:

$$3 \quad 4 \quad 4 \quad 9 \quad 8 \quad 8 \quad 6 \quad 4 \quad 7 \quad 9 \quad 1 \quad 3 \quad 5 \quad 3 \quad 5 \quad 9 \quad 8 \quad 6 \quad 3 \quad 7 \quad 1$$

a For this data set, find:

i the mean   **ii** the median   **iii** the mode.

b On the 22nd day there were 9 faulty products returned. How does this affect the measures of the centre?

a **i** mean $= \dfrac{3 + 4 + 4 + \,....\, + 3 + 7 + 1}{21}$ ◄── sum of all the data values

$$= \dfrac{113}{21}$$ ◄────── 21 data values

$$\approx 5.38 \text{ faulty products}$$

ii As $n = 21$, $\dfrac{n+1}{2} = 11$

The ordered data set is: ~~1 1 3 3 3 3 4 4 4 5~~ 5 ~~6 6 7 7 8 8 8 9 9 9~~

11th value

∴ median $= 5$ faulty products

iii 3 is the data value which occurs the most often, so the mode is 3 faulty products.

b We expect the mean to increase since the new data value is greater than the old mean.

In fact, the new mean $= \dfrac{113 + 9}{22} = \dfrac{122}{22} \approx 5.55$ faulty products.

Since $n = 22$, $\dfrac{n+1}{2} = 11.5$

The new ordered data set is:

~~1 1 3 3 3 3 4 4 4 5~~ 5 6 ~~6 7 7 8 8 8 9 9 9~~

two middle data values

∴ the new median $= \dfrac{5 + 6}{2} = 5.5$ faulty products.

The new data set has two modes which are 3 and 9 faulty products.

You can use your **graphics calculator** or the **statistics package** to find measures of centre.

 GRAPHICS CALCULATOR INSTRUCTIONS

 STATISTICS PACKAGE

EXERCISE 20D.1

1 For each data set, find the: **i** mean   **ii** median   **iii** mode.

a 2, 3, 3, 3, 4, 4, 4, 5, 5, 5, 5, 6, 6, 6, 6, 6, 7, 7, 8, 8, 8, 9, 9

b 10, 12, 12, 15, 15, 16, 16, 17, 18, 18, 18, 18, 19, 20, 21

c 22.4, 24.6, 21.8, 26.4, 24.9, 25.0, 23.5, 26.1, 25.3, 29.5, 23.5

Check your answers using technology.

2 The annual salaries of ten office workers are:

£23 000, £46 000, £23 000, £38 000, £24 000,
£23 000, £23 000, £38 000, £23 000, £32 000

a Find the mean, median, and modal salaries for this group of office workers.

b Explain why the mode is an unsatisfactory measure of the centre in this case.

c Is the median a satisfactory measure of the centre of this data set?

3 The following raw data is the daily rainfall (to the nearest millimetre) for the month of July in a desert:

3, 1, 0, 0, 0, 0, 0, 2, 0, 0, 3, 0, 0, 0, 7, 1, 1, 0, 3, 8, 0, 0, 0, 42, 21, 3, 0, 3, 1, 0, 0

a Find the mean, median, and mode for the data.

b Explain why the median is not the most suitable measure of centre for this data set.

c Explain why the mode is not the most suitable measure of centre for this data set.

d Are there any outliers in this data set?

e On some occasions outliers are removed because they must be due to measurement errors. In this case the outliers in the data set are accurate. Should they be removed before finding the measures of the centre?

4 A bakery keeps a record of how many pies and pasties they sell each day for a month:

Pies									**Pasties**							
62	76	55	65	49	78	71	82		37	52	71	59	63	47	56	68
79	47	60	72	58	82	76	67		43	67	38	73	54	55	61	49
50	61	70	85	77	69	48	74		50	48	53	39	45	60	46	51
63	56	81	75	63	74	54			38	57	41	72	50	44	76	

a Find the:

i mean number of pies and pasties sold

ii median number of pies and pasties sold.

b Which bakery item was more popular? Explain your answer.

5 The selling prices of the last 10 houses sold in a certain district were:

£146 400,   £127 600,   £211 000,   £192 500,
£456 400,   £132 400,   £148 000,   £129 500,
£131 400,   £162 500

a Calculate the mean and median selling prices.

b Which measure was most affected by the outlier?

c Which measure is the best indicator of typical house prices in the district?

Example 8   ◀》 **Self Tutor**

If 6 people have a mean mass of 53.7 kg, find their total mass.

$$\frac{\text{sum of masses}}{6} = 53.7 \text{ kg}$$

∴ sum of masses $= 53.7 \times 6$

∴ the total mass $= 322.2$ kg

6 This year, the mean monthly sales for a clothing store have been £15 467. Calculate the total sales for the store for the year.

7 While on a 12 day outback safari, Bill drove an average of 262 km per day. How far did Bill drive in total while on the safari?

8 Towards the end of a season, a netballer had played 14 matches and scored an average of 16.5 goals per game. In the final two matches of the season she scored 21 goals and 24 goals. Find the netballer's average for the whole season.

9 Find x if 5, 9, 11, 12, 13, 14, 17, and x have a mean of 12.

10 Over the entire assessment period, Aruna averaged 35 out of a possible 40 marks for her Mathematics tests. However, when checking her files, she could only find 7 of the 8 tests. For these she scored 29, 36, 32, 38, 35, 34, and 39. How many marks out of 40 did she score for the eighth test?

11 A sample of 10 measurements has a mean of 15.7, and a sample of 20 measurements has a mean of 14.3. Find the mean of all 30 measurements.

12 The mean and median of a set of 9 measurements are both 12. Seven of the measurements are 7, 9, 11, 13, 14, 17, and 19. Find the other two measurements.

MEASURES OF THE CENTRE FROM A FREQUENCY TABLE

When the same values appear several times in a data set, we often summarise the data in a frequency table.

Consider the data in the table alongside:

We can find the measures of the centre directly from the table.

Value (x)	Frequency (f)	Product (xf)
3	1	$3 \times 1 = 3$
4	1	$4 \times 1 = 4$
5	3	$5 \times 3 = 15$
6	7	$6 \times 7 = 42$
7	15	$7 \times 15 = 105$
8	8	$8 \times 8 = 64$
9	5	$9 \times 5 = 45$
Total	$\sum f = 40$	$\sum xf = 278$

THE MODE

The value 7 has the highest frequency.

The mode is therefore 7.

THE MEAN

Adding a "Product" column to the table helps to add the data values.

For example, the value 7 occurs 15 times, and these add to $15 \times 7 = 105$.

Remembering that the mean $= \dfrac{\text{sum of all data values}}{\text{the number of data values}}$, we find

$$\overline{x} = \frac{x_1 f_1 + x_2 f_2 + x_3 f_3 + ... + x_k f_k}{f_1 + f_2 + f_3 + ... + f_k} \qquad \text{where } k \text{ is the number of } \textit{different} \text{ values in the data.}$$

$$\therefore \quad \overline{x} = \frac{\displaystyle\sum_{j=1}^{k} x_j f_j}{\displaystyle\sum_{j=1}^{k} f_j} \qquad \text{which we often abbreviate as } \quad \frac{\sum xf}{\sum f}.$$

In this case the mean $= \dfrac{278}{40} = 6.95$.

THE MEDIAN

Since $\dfrac{n+1}{2} = \dfrac{41}{2} = 20.5$, the median is the average of the 20th and 21st ordered data values.

In the table, the blue numbers show the accumulated frequency values, or **cumulative frequency**.

We can see that the 20th and 21st ordered data values are both 7s.

∴   the median $= \dfrac{7+7}{2} = 7$

Value	Frequency	Cumulative frequency	
3	1	1	← one number is 3
4	1	2	← two numbers are 4 or less
5	3	5	← five numbers are 5 or less
6	7	12	← 12 numbers are 6 or less
7	15	27	← 27 numbers are 7 or less
8	8	35	← 35 numbers are 8 or less
9	5	40	← all numbers are 9 or less
Total	40		

Notice that we have a skewed distribution even though the mean, median, and mode are nearly equal. So, we must be careful if we use measures of the centre to call a distribution symmetric.

WELL, IF YOU COMPARE AVERAGES...

I DON'T BELIEVE IN AVERAGES!

WHY NOT?

WELL, WHAT HAPPENS IF YOU HAVE YOUR HEAD IN THE OVEN AND YOUR FEET IN THE FREEZER...

DO YOU FEEL PRETTY GOOD, ON AVERAGE?

Example 9

◀)) **Self Tutor**

The table below shows the number of aces served by a sample of tennis players in their first sets of a tournament.

Number of aces	1	2	3	4	5	6
Frequency	4	11	18	13	7	2

Determine the: **a** mean   **b** median   **c** mode   for this data.

Number of aces (x)	Frequency (f)	Product (xf)	Cumulative frequency
1	4	4	4
2	11	22	15
3	18	54	33
4	13	52	46
5	7	35	53
6	2	12	55
Total	$\sum f = 55$	$\sum xf = 179$	

a $\overline{x} = \dfrac{\sum xf}{\sum f}$

$= \dfrac{179}{55}$

≈ 3.25 aces

In this case $\dfrac{\sum xf}{\sum f}$ is short for $\dfrac{\displaystyle\sum_{j=1}^{6} x_j f_j}{\displaystyle\sum_{j=1}^{6} f_j}$.

b There are 55 data values, so $n = 55$. $\dfrac{n+1}{2} = 28$, so the median is the 28th ordered data value.

From the cumulative frequency column, the 16th to 33rd ordered data values are 3 aces.

∴ the 28th ordered data value is 3 aces.

∴ the median is 3 aces.

c Looking down the frequency column, the highest frequency is 18. This corresponds to 3 aces, so the mode is 3 aces.

EXERCISE 20D.2

1 The table alongside shows the number of people in cars on a road.

Calculate the:

   a mode   **b** median   **c** mean.

Check your answers using your graphics calculator.

Number of people	Frequency
1	13
2	8
3	4
4	5
Total	30

GRAPHICS CALCULATOR INSTRUCTIONS

2 The frequency table alongside shows the number of phone calls made in a day by 50 fifteen-year-olds.

   a For this data set, find the:

      i mean   **ii** median   **iii** mode.

   b Construct a bar chart for the data and show the position of the mean, median, and mode on the horizontal axis.

   c Describe the distribution of the data.

   d Why is the mean larger than the median?

   e Which measure of centre would be the most suitable for this data set?

Number of phone calls	Frequency
0	5
1	8
2	13
3	8
4	6
5	3
6	3
7	2
8	1
11	1

3

Number of matches	Frequency
47	5
48	4
49	11
50	6
51	3
52	1
Total	30

A company claims that their match boxes contain 50 matches on average. The Consumer Protection Society conducts a survey to assess the company's claim. The results of the survey are shown alongside.

   a Calculate the:

      i mode   **ii** median   **iii** mean.

   b Do the results support the company's claim?

   c In a court for "false advertising", the company won their case against the Consumer Protection Society. Suggest how they did this.

4 Families at a school in Manchester were surveyed, and the number of children in each family recorded. The results of the survey are shown alongside.

Number of children	Frequency
1	5
2	28
3	15
4	8
5	2
6	1
Total	59

  a Calculate the:
   i mean   **ii** mode   **iii** median.

  b The average British family has 2.075 children. How does this school compare to the national average?

  c Describe the skewness of the data.

  d How has the skewness of the data affected the measures of the centre of the data set?

5 The bar chart shows the weekly pocket money for a class of children.

  a Construct a frequency table from the graph.

  b Determine the total number of children in the class.

  c Find the:
   i mean   **ii** median   **iii** mode   of the data.

  d Which of the measures of centre can be found easily using the graph only?

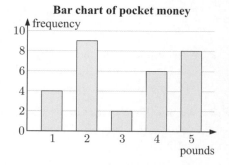

Bar chart of pocket money

6 Out of 31 measurements, 15 are below 10 cm and 12 are above 11 cm. Find the median if the other 4 measurements are 10.1 cm, 10.4 cm, 10.7 cm, and 10.9 cm.

7 The table shows the test scores for a class of students. A pass is a score of 5 or more.

Score	2	3	4	5	6	7	8
Frequency	0	2	3	5	x	4	1

  a Given that the mean score was 5.45, find x.

  b Find the percentage of students who passed.

8 In an office of 20 people there are only 4 salary levels paid:

  £100 000 (1 person),   £84 000 (3 people),
  £70 000 (6 people),   £56 000 (10 people).

  a Calculate:
   i the median salary
   ii the modal salary
   iii the mean salary.

  b Which measure of central tendency might be used by the boss who is against a pay rise for the other employees?

GROUPED DATA

When information has been gathered in groups or classes, we use the **midpoint** or **mid-interval value** to represent all data values within each interval.

We are assuming that the data values within each class are evenly distributed throughout that interval. The mean calculated is an **approximation** of the actual value, and we cannot do better than this without knowing each individual data value.

Investigation   Mid-interval values

When mid-interval values are used to represent all data values within each interval, what effect will this have on estimating the mean of the grouped data?

The table alongside summarises the marks out of 50 received by students who sat a Physics examination. The exact results for each student have been lost.

Marks	Frequency
0 - 9	2
10 - 19	31
20 - 29	73
30 - 39	85
40 - 49	28

What to do:

1   Suppose that all of the students scored the lowest possible result in their class interval, so 2 students scored 0, 31 students scored 10, and so on. Calculate the mean of these results, and hence complete:
"The mean Physics examination mark must be *at least* ......"

2   Now suppose that all of the students scored the highest possible result in their class interval. Calculate the mean of these results, and hence complete:
"The mean Physics examination mark must be *at most* ......"

3   We now have two extreme values between which the actual mean must lie.
Now suppose that all of the students scored the mid-interval value in their class interval. We assume that 2 students scored 4.5, 31 students scored 14.5, and so on.

   a   Calculate the mean of these results.

   b   How does this result compare with lower and upper limits found in **1** and **2**?

   c   Copy and complete:
   "The mean Physics examination mark was approximately ......"

4   Discuss with your class how accurate you think an estimate of the mean using mid-interval values will be. How is this accuracy affected by the number and width of the class intervals?

Example 10   ◀ͫ) Self Tutor

The table below shows the ages of bus drivers. Estimate the mean age, to the nearest year.

Age (years)	21 - 25	26 - 30	31 - 35	36 - 40	41 - 45	46 - 50	51 - 55
Frequency	11	14	32	27	29	17	7

Age (years)	Frequency (f)	Midpoint (x)	xf
21 - 25	11	23	253
26 - 30	14	28	392
31 - 35	32	33	1056
36 - 40	27	38	1026
41 - 45	29	43	1247
46 - 50	17	48	816
51 - 55	7	53	371
Total	$\sum f = 137$		$\sum xf = 5161$

$$\overline{x} = \frac{\sum xf}{\sum f}$$

$$= \frac{5161}{137}$$

$$\approx 37.7$$

∴   the mean age of the drivers is about 38 years.

EXERCISE 20D.3

1   Simone recorded the lengths of her phone
    calls for one week. The results are shown
    in the table alongside.

Time (t min)	Frequency
$0 \leqslant t < 10$	17
$10 \leqslant t < 20$	10
$20 \leqslant t < 30$	9
$30 \leqslant t < 40$	4

The midpoint of an
interval is the average
of its endpoints.

   a   How many phone calls did she make
       during the week?

   b   Estimate the mean length of the calls.

2   50 students sat a Mathematics test. Estimate the mean score given these results:

Score	0 - 9	10 - 19	20 - 29	30 - 39	40 - 49
Frequency	2	5	7	27	9

   Check your answers using your calculator.

3   The table shows the petrol sales in one day by a number of city service stations.

Amount of petrol (L L)	Frequency
$2000 < L \leqslant 3000$	4
$3000 < L \leqslant 4000$	4
$4000 < L \leqslant 5000$	9
$5000 < L \leqslant 6000$	14
$6000 < L \leqslant 7000$	23
$7000 < L \leqslant 8000$	16

   a   How many service stations were involved in the survey?

   b   Estimate the total amount of petrol sold for the day by the service stations.

   c   Estimate the mean amount of petrol sold for the day.

   d   Find the modal class for this distribution. Explain your answer.

4   The data below shows the runs scored by Jeff over an entire cricket season

```
17   5   22   13   6    0    15   20
14   7   28   36   13   28   9    18
 2   23  12   27   5    22   3    0
32   8   13   25   9
```

   a   Organise the data into the groups 0 - 9, 10 - 19, 20 - 29,
       30 - 39.

   b   Use your grouped data to estimate the mean number of runs
       scored.

   c   Use the raw data to find the exact mean number of runs
       scored. How accurate was your estimate in **b**?

5 This histogram illustrates the results of an aptitude test given to a group of people seeking positions in a company.

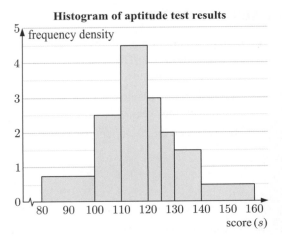

Histogram of aptitude test results

  a State the modal class for the distribution.

  b Calculate the frequency of each class interval.

  c How many people took the test?

  d What fraction of the people scored less than 110 for the test?

  e What percentage of the people scored 130 or more for the test?

  f By using the midpoint of each class interval, estimate the mean score for the test.

E VARIANCE AND STANDARD DEVIATION

To provide a more complete description of the distribution of a data set, we need to measure not only its **centre** but also its **spread** or **dispersion**.

In previous years you should have studied the **range** and **interquartile range (IQR)**, which are two simple measures of the spread of a data set.

The problem with using the range and the IQR as measures of spread or dispersion is that both of them only use two values in their calculation. As a result, some data sets can have their spread characteristics hidden when only the range or IQR are quoted.

So we need to consider alternative measures of spread which take into account all data values of a data set. We therefore turn to the **variance** and **standard deviation**.

POPULATION VARIANCE AND STANDARD DEVIATION

The **population variance** of a data set $\{x_1, x_2, x_3, ..., x_n\}$ is

$$\sigma^2 = \frac{\sum\limits_{i=1}^{n} (x_i - \mu)^2}{n}$$

where μ is the population mean
and n is the number of data values.

> The variance is the average of the squares of the distances from the mean.

We observe that if the data values x_i are situated close together around the mean μ, then the values $(x_i - \mu)^2$ will be small, and so the variance will be small.

The **standard deviation** is the square root of the variance.

The **population standard deviation** of a data set $\{x_1, x_2, x_3, ..., x_n\}$ is

$$\sigma = \sqrt{\frac{\sum\limits_{i=1}^{n} (x_i - \mu)^2}{n}}.$$

> The standard deviation measures the degree to which the data *deviates* from the mean.

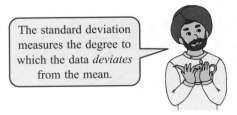

The square root in the standard deviation is used to correct the units. For example, if x_i is the weight of a student in kg, the variance σ^2 would be in kg^2, and σ would be in kg.

Example 11

◀) **Self Tutor**

Find the population variance and standard deviation for the data set:

$$3 \quad 12 \quad 8 \quad 15 \quad 7$$

The mean $\mu = \dfrac{3 + 12 + 8 + 15 + 7}{5} = 9$

The population variance $\sigma^2 = \dfrac{\sum (x - \mu)^2}{n}$

$$= \dfrac{86}{5}$$

$$= 17.2$$

The population standard deviation $\sigma = \sqrt{17.2}$

$$\approx 4.15$$

x	$x - \mu$	$(x - \mu)^2$
3	-6	36
12	3	9
8	-1	1
15	6	36
7	-2	4
Total		86

SAMPLE VARIANCE AND STANDARD DEVIATION

If we are only given a *sample* of data from a larger population, we calculate a statistic called the **sample standard deviation**. This statistic is used to *estimate* the standard deviation of the population.

For a sample of n data values $\{x_1, x_2, x_3, ..., x_n\}$ with sample mean $\overline{x}$:

- The **sample variance** is $s^2 = \dfrac{\displaystyle\sum_{i=1}^{n} (x_i - \overline{x})^2}{n - 1}$.

- The **sample standard deviation** is $s = \sqrt{\dfrac{\displaystyle\sum_{i=1}^{n} (x_i - \overline{x})^2}{n - 1}}$.

CALCULATING STANDARD DEVIATION

We commonly use technology to find the standard deviation. If we are given the whole population we use σ_x, and if we are given a sample we use s_x. We can then square these values to find the population and sample variance, σ_x^2 and s_x^2 respectively.

GRAPHICS CALCULATOR INSTRUCTIONS

```
1-Variable
x̄     =30.0333333
Σx    =901
Σx²   =33211
σx    =14.3189462
sx    =14.5637323
n     =30              ↓
```

Example 12

◀ Self Tutor

Kylie is interested in the ages of spectators at a rugby match. She selects a sample of 30 spectators. Their ages are shown below:

17 24 30 10 42 48 37 19 28 53 29 40 11 21 9
43 22 59 46 52 31 13 7 26 32 47 22 15 26 42

Use technology to find the sample standard deviation.

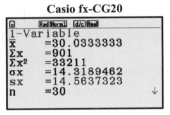
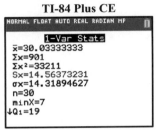

Casio fx-9860G PLUS	Casio fx-CG20	TI-84 Plus CE

```
1-Variable
x̄      =30.0333333
Σx     =901
Σx²    =33211
σx     =14.3189462
sx     =14.5637323
n      =30            ↓
```

```
         Rad Normal d/c Real
1-Variable
x̄      =30.0333333
Σx     =901
Σx²    =33211
σx     =14.3189462
sx     =14.5637323
n      =30            ↓
```

```
NORMAL FLOAT AUTO REAL RADIAN MP
            1-Var Stats
x̄=30.03333333
Σx=901
Σx²=33211
Sx=14.56373231
σx=14.31894627
n=30
minX=7
↓Q₁=19
```

The sample standard deviation $s \approx 14.6$ years.

EXERCISE 20E.1

1 Consider the following data sets:

Data set A: 10   7   5   8   10

Data set B: 4   12   11   14   1   6

a Show that each data set has mean 8.

b Which data set appears to have the greater spread? Explain your answer.

c Find the population variance and standard deviation of each data set. Use technology to check your answers.

2 Skye recorded the number of pets owned by each student in her class:

0 2 3 1 2 4 0 0 1 5 2 3 6
2 3 1 1 0 4 1 1 0 2 1 2 0

a Use technology to find the population standard deviation of the data.

b Find the population variance of the data.

3 The ages of members of an Olympic water polo team are: 22, 25, 23, 28, 29, 21, 20, 26.

a Calculate the mean and population standard deviation for this group.

b The same team members are chosen to play in the next Olympic Games 4 years later. Calculate the mean and population standard deviation of their ages at the next Olympic Games.

c Comment on your results in general terms.

4 A hospital selected a sample of 20 patients and asked them how many glasses of water they had consumed that day. The results were:

$$5 \quad 2 \quad 1 \quad 0 \quad 4 \quad 1 \quad 0 \quad 2 \quad 7 \quad 4$$
$$8 \quad 2 \quad 7 \quad 6 \quad 1 \quad 2 \quad 3 \quad 8 \quad 0 \quad 2$$

Use technology to find the sample standard deviation of the data.

5 Danny and Jennifer recorded how many hours they spent on homework each day for 14 days.

Danny: $3\frac{1}{2}, \ 3\frac{1}{2}, \ 4, \ 2\frac{1}{2}, \ 3, \ 3\frac{1}{2}, \ 3, \ 1\frac{1}{2}, \ 3, \ 4, \ 2\frac{1}{2}, \ 4, \ 4, \ 3$

Jennifer: $2\frac{1}{2}, \ 1, \ 2\frac{1}{2}, \ 2, \ 2, \ 2\frac{1}{2}, \ 1\frac{1}{2}, \ 2, \ 2, \ 2\frac{1}{2}, \ 2, \ 2, \ 2, \ 1\frac{1}{2}$

  a Calculate the mean number of hours each person spent on homework.

  b Which person generally studies for longer?

  c Calculate the sample standard deviation s for each data set.

  d Which person studies more consistently?

6 Tyson wants to compare the swimming speeds of boys and girls at his school. He randomly selects 10 boys and 10 girls, and records the time, in seconds, each person takes to swim two laps of the school pool.

Boys: 42, 26, 51, 30, 28, 62, 24, 57, 40, 31

Girls: 50, 55, 48, 63, 42, 37, 49, 52, 57, 43

  a Copy and complete the table:

	Boys	Girls
Mean $\bar{x}$		49.6
Median	35.5	
Standard deviation s		7.69
Range	38	

  b Which group:

    i generally swims faster   **ii** has the greater spread of swimming speeds?

  c How could Tyson improve the reliability of his findings?

7 The number of visitors to a museum and an art gallery each day during December are shown.

Museum: 1108 1019 850 1243 1100 923 964 847 918 820 781
               963 814 881 742 911 1101 952 864 943 1087 1132
               906 1050 0 826 986 1040 1127 1084 981

Art gallery: 1258 1107 1179 1302 1236 1386 1287 1313 1269 1332 1094
                 1153 1275 1168 1086 1276 1342 1153 1227 1305 1187 1249
                 1300 1156 1074 1168 1299 1257 1134 1259 1366

  a For each data set, calculate the:

    i mean   **ii** sample standard deviation.

  b Which place had the greater spread of visitor numbers?

  c **i** Identify the outlier in the *Museum* data.

    ii Give a reason why this outlier may have occurred.

    iii Do you think it is reasonable to remove the outlier when comparing the numbers of visitors to these places? Explain your answer.

    iv Recalculate the mean and sample standard deviation with the outlier removed.

    v Discuss the effect of the outlier on the sample standard deviation.

8 A set of 8 integers $\{1, 3, 5, 7, 4, 5, p, q\}$ has mean 5 and population variance 5.25. Find p and q given that $p < q$.

9 A set of 10 integers $\{3, 9, 5, 5, 6, 4, a, 6, b, 8\}$ has mean 6 and population variance 3.2. Find a and b given that $a > b$.

10 **a** Prove that $\sum\limits_{i=1}^{n}(x_i - \mu)^2 = \sum\limits_{i=1}^{n}\left(x_i^2\right) - n\mu^2$.

  b The data set $\{x_1, x_2, ..., x_{25}\}$ has $\sum\limits_{i=1}^{25}x_i^2 = 2568.25$ and population standard deviation 5.2. Find the mean of the data set.

VARIANCE AND STANDARD DEVIATION FROM A FREQUENCY TABLE

Suppose there are n data values in a data set with mean μ.

If the different values are $x_1, x_2, ..., x_k$, with corresponding frequencies $f_1, f_2, ..., f_k$, then:

- the population variance is given by $\quad \sigma^2 = \dfrac{\sum\limits_{j=1}^{k}(x_j - \mu)^2 f_j}{n} = \dfrac{\sum\limits_{j=1}^{k}x_j{}^2 f_j}{n} - \mu^2$

- the population standard deviation is given by $\quad \sigma = \sqrt{\dfrac{\sum\limits_{j=1}^{k}(x_j - \mu)^2 f_j}{n}}.$

Example 13
◀ **Self Tutor**

Find the population standard deviation of the following data using:

a the standard deviation formula   **b** technology.

GRAPHICS
CALCULATOR
INSTRUCTIONS

Value	1	2	3	4	5
Frequency	1	2	4	2	1

a

Value (x)	Frequency (f)	xf	$x - \mu$	$(x - \mu)^2$	$(x - \mu)^2 f$
1	1	1	-2	4	4
2	2	4	-1	1	2
3	4	12	0	0	0
4	2	8	1	1	2
5	1	5	2	4	4
Total	10	30			12

$$\mu = \frac{\sum xf}{n} \qquad \sigma = \sqrt{\frac{\sum(x - \mu)^2 f}{n}}$$

$$= \frac{30}{10} \qquad\qquad = \sqrt{\frac{12}{10}}$$

$$= 3 \qquad\qquad\quad \approx 1.10$$

b

Casio fx-9860G PLUS	Casio fx-CG20	TI-84 Plus CE

```
1-Variable
x̄      =3
Σx    =30
Σx²   =102
σx    =1.09544511
sx    =1.15470053
n     =10         ↓
```

```
       Rad Norm1 d/c Real
1-Variable
x̄      =3
Σx    =30
Σx²   =102
σx    =1.09544511
sx    =1.15470053
n     =10            ↓
```

```
NORMAL FLOAT AUTO REAL RADIAN MP
        1-Var Stats
x̄=3
Σx=30
Σx²=102
Sx=1.154700538
σx=1.095445115
n=10
minX=1
↓Q₁=2
```

EXERCISE 20E.2

1 Find the population standard deviation of the data alongside using:

   a the standard deviation formula

   b technology.

Value	Frequency
3	1
4	3
5	11
6	5

2 The table shows the ages of squash players at the Junior National Squash Championship.

Age	11	12	13	14	15	16	17	18
Frequency	2	1	4	5	6	4	2	1

Use technology to find the mean and population standard deviation of the ages.

3 The table alongside shows the results obtained by female and male students in a test out of 20 marks.

   a Looking at the table:

      i Which group appears to have scored better in the test?

      ii Which group appears to have a greater spread of scores?

   Justify your answers.

   b Use technology to calculate the mean and population standard deviation for each group.

Score	Females	Males
12	0	1
13	0	0
14	0	2
15	0	3
16	2	4
17	6	2
18	5	0
19	1	1
20	1	0

Activity   **Estimating the variance and standard deviation of a population**

The Year 12 students at a school were asked to record how many minutes they spent travelling to school. The results were collected in a survey the following morning.

There are a total of 150 Year 12 students at the school, and these are split into 6 classes.

What to do:

1 Click on the icon to obtain a spreadsheet containing all of the responses to the survey.   **SPREADSHEET**

   a Use the frequency table in the spreadsheet to draw a histogram for the data. Describe this distribution.

   b The summary statistics in the spreadsheet are calculated using all of the survey responses, and hence are the *true* population values. Find the true population variance.

2 10 students were randomly selected from each class to form 6 samples. Their responses to the survey are shown below:

Sample 1:   10 14 16   9 16 15 15 21   9 21
Sample 2:   11   9 11 16 16 13 10 12 21 16
Sample 3:   12 10 14   7 13 11 21 20 15   9
Sample 4:   20 19 19 19 13 19 22 15 10 19
Sample 5:   19 13 23 11 17   4 14 21 13 11
Sample 6:   19 11 16   6   8 13 10 22 20 11

a Calculate the *sample* statistics s and s^2 for each sample.

b Calculate the *population* statistics σ and σ^2 for each sample.

c Which set of estimates from **a** and **b** are generally closer to the true population variance and standard deviation?

d Does your answer to **c** explain why we have different variance and standard deviation formulae for a sample as opposed to a population?

3 To see which set of estimators (population or sample) are better at estimating the true population variance and standard deviation, we will consider a simulation based on the survey responses from the school.

Click on the icon to obtain a spreadsheet with 1000 simulations of the survey results. The values s, s^2, σ, and σ^2 are calculated for each simulated sample. The average values for each estimator are shown in the table on the sheet labelled "Summary".

SPREADSHEET

	A	B	C	D	E	F
1	**Actual values**				**Estimator**	**Average estimate**
2	μ	15		*Variance*	σ^2	23.794
3	σ	5			s^2	25.046
4	σ^2	25		*Standard*	σ	4.814
5	n	20		*deviation*	s	4.939

Based on the calculations in the spreadsheet, which set of estimates (population or sample) are generally closer to the true values? Does your conclusion agree with your answer to **2 c**?

4 Change the values for μ and σ in the spreadsheet. This will now effectively simulate the results for a different distribution, perhaps the travel times for the students at a different school. Does your choice of μ or σ affect your conclusion regarding the choice of estimators?

5 Why is it important to have accurate estimates of the variance and standard deviation of a population?

Review set 20A

1 Andrew is interested in the cultural background of the students at his school. He puts together a survey which he hands out to students in his Italian class.

a Explain why Andrew's sample may be biased.

b Suggest an alternative sampling method that Andrew can use so that his results will be more representative of his population of interest.

2 A golf club has 1800 members with ages shown alongside. A member survey is to be undertaken to determine the proportion of members who are in favour of changes to dress regulations.

Age range	Members
under 18	257
18 - 39	421
40 - 54	632
55 - 70	356
over 70	134

   a Explain why the golf club would not question all members on the proposed changes to dress regulations.

   b If a stratified sample size of 350 is used, how many of each age group will be surveyed?

3 This bar chart shows the number of goals scored by a football team in each game of a season.

   a Is the *number of goals scored* a discrete or continuous variable?

   b Describe the distribution of the data.

   c Find the:

      i mode   **ii** mean   **iii** median.

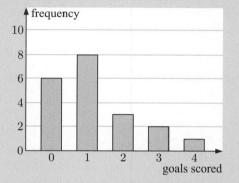

4 Ryan measured the heights of 87 randomly selected boys at his school. His results are summarised alongside.

   a Calculate the frequency density for each class interval.

   b Construct a histogram to display the data.

   c Identify the modal class.

   d Describe the distribution of the data.

Height (h cm)	Frequency
$130 \leqslant h < 150$	1
$150 \leqslant h < 160$	13
$160 \leqslant h < 165$	22
$165 \leqslant h < 170$	18
$170 \leqslant h < 175$	20
$175 \leqslant h < 180$	10
$180 \leqslant h < 190$	3
Total	87

5 For each of the following data sets, find the:

      i mean   **ii** median.

   a 0, 2, 3, 3, 4, 5, 5, 6, 6, 7, 7, 8

   b 2.9, 3.1, 3.7, 3.8, 3.9, 3.9, 4.0, 4.5, 4.7, 5.4

6 Heike is preparing for an athletics carnival. She records her times in seconds for the 100 m sprint each day for 4 weeks.

                    Week 1: 16.4 15.2 16.3 16.3 17.1 15.5 14.9

                    Week 2: 14.9 15.7 15.1 15.1 14.7 14.7 15.3

                    Week 3: 14.3 14.2 14.6 14.6 14.3 14.3 14.4

                    Week 4: 14.0 14.0 13.9 14.0 14.1 13.8 14.2

   a Calculate Heike's mean and median time for each week.

   b Do you think Heike's times have improved over the 4 week period? Explain your answer.

7 The data set 4, 6, 9, a, 3, b has a mean and mode of 6. Find the values of a and b given that $a > b$.

8 The winning margins in 100 basketball games were recorded. The results are summarised alongside.

Margin (points)	Frequency
1 - 10	13
11 - 20	35
21 - 30	27
31 - 40	18
41 - 50	7

   a Is the *winning margin* a discrete or continuous variable?

   b Find the modal class.

   c Explain why you cannot calculate the mean winning margin from the table exactly.

   d Estimate the mean winning margin.

9 Find the population standard deviation of the data alongside using:

   a the standard deviation formula

   b technology.

$$5 \quad 8 \quad 15 \quad 11$$
$$12 \quad 9 \quad 8 \quad 4$$

10 Friends Kevin and Felicity each selected a sample of 20 crossword puzzles. The times they took, in minutes, to complete each puzzle were:

Kevin				
37	53	47	33	39
49	37	48	32	36
39	42	34	29	52
48	33	56	39	41

Felicity				
33	36	41	26	52
38	49	57	39	44
48	25	34	27	53
38	34	35	50	31

   a Find the mean of each data set.

   b Find the sample standard deviation of each data set.

   c Who generally solves crossword puzzles faster?

   d Who is more consistent in their time taken to solve the puzzles?

11 A data set has $s^2 = 4.1$ and $\sigma^2 = 3.69$. How many data values does the data set have?

Review set 20B

1 Classify the following variables as discrete or continuous:

   a the number of pages in a book   **b** the distance travelled by hikers in one day

   c the attendance figures for a music festival.

2 A sales promoter decides to visit 10 houses in a street and offer special discounts on a new window treatment. The street has 100 houses numbered from 1 to 100. The sales promoter selects a random number between 1 and 10 inclusive and calls on the house with that street number. After this the promoter calls on every tenth house.

   a What sampling technique is used by the sales promoter?

   b Explain why every house in the street has an equal chance of being visited.

   c Explain why this is not a simple random sample.

3 Petra emailed a questionnaire to her teacher colleagues about general student behaviour in their classes.

   a Explain why Petra's questionnaire may produce a high non-response error.

   b Of the 20 teachers who were emailed the questionnaire, 10 responded. Petra decides to use these 10 responses as her sample. Explain why Petra is likely to encounter a coverage error.

4 A parking inspector recorded the number of parking tickets she issued each day for four weeks. Her results are shown below:

$$\begin{array}{ccccccc} 2 & 4 & 2 & 3 & 5 & 0 & 3 \\ 3 & 2 & 4 & 6 & 3 & 3 & 3 \\ 4 & 1 & 3 & 3 & 4 & 5 & 2 \\ 3 & 1 & 3 & 1 & 2 & 5 & 4 \end{array}$$

  a Construct a tally and frequency table to organise the data.

  b Draw a bar chart to display the data.

  c Describe the distribution of the data. Are there any outliers?

5 The data supplied below is the diameter (in cm) of a number of bacteria colonies as measured by a microbiologist 12 hours after seeding.

$$\begin{array}{ccccccccccccccc} 0.4 & 2.1 & 3.4 & 3.9 & 4.7 & 3.7 & 0.8 & 3.6 & 4.1 & 4.9 & 2.5 & 3.1 & 1.5 & 2.6 & 4.0 \\ 1.3 & 3.5 & 0.9 & 1.5 & 4.2 & 3.5 & 2.1 & 3.0 & 1.7 & 3.6 & 2.8 & 3.7 & 2.8 & 3.2 & 3.3 \end{array}$$

  a Is the *diameter of bacteria colonies* a discrete or continuous variable?

  b Organise the data into 5 class intervals of equal width.

  c Draw a histogram to display the data.

  d State the modal class.

  e Describe the distribution.

6 A die was rolled 50 times. The results are shown in the table alongside. Find the:

  a mode   **b** mean   **c** median.

Number	Frequency
1	10
2	7
3	8
4	5
5	12
6	8

7 The data in the table alongside has mean 5.7.

  a Find the value of x.

  b Find the median of the distribution.

Value	2	5	x	$x+6$
Frequency	3	2	4	1

8 Jana took seven spelling tests, each with ten words, but she could only find the results of five of them. These were 9, 5, 7, 9, and 10. Jana's teacher tells her that the mode of her scores was 9 and the mean was 8. Given that Jana remembers she only scored one 10, find the two missing results.

9 Consider the histogram alongside.

  a State the modal class.

  b For each class interval, determine:

    i the class interval width

    ii the frequency

    iii the midpoint.

  c Hence estimate the mean of the data.

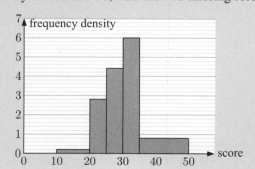

10 The table alongside shows the number of matches in each box in a carton of match boxes.

Number	47	48	49	50	51	52
Frequency	21	29	35	42	18	31

    a Find the mean and population standard deviation for this data.

    b Does this result justify the claim that the average number of matches per box is 50?

11 A data set $\{x_1, x_2, ..., x_n\}$ has mean $\overline{x}$ and population variance σ^2. Consider the new data set $\{ax_1, ax_2, ..., ax_n\}$, where a is a constant. For this new data set, prove that:

    a the mean is $a\overline{x}$

    b the population variance is $a^2\sigma^2$.

21

Bivariate statistics

Contents:

Opening problem

At a junior tournament, a group of young athletes throw a discus. The *age* and *distance thrown* are recorded for each athlete.

Athlete	A	B	C	D	E	F	G	H	I	J	K	L
Age (years)	12	16	16	18	13	19	11	10	20	17	15	13
Distance thrown (m)	20	35	23	38	27	47	18	15	50	33	22	20

Things to think about:

a   Do you think the distance an athlete can throw is related to the person's age?

b   What happens to the distance thrown as the age of the athlete increases?

c   How could you graph the data to more clearly see the relationship between the variables?

d   How can we *measure* the relationship between the variables?

In the **Opening Problem**, each athlete has had *two* variables (*age* and *distance thrown*) recorded about them. This type of data is called **bivariate data**.

By studying the bivariate data, we can explore the **relationship** between the two variables. For example, we can establish how differences in the *ages* of athletes *explain* the differences in the *distance thrown*. In this case *age* is the **explanatory variable**, and *distance thrown* is the **response variable**.

> The **explanatory** and **response** variables are sometimes called the **independent** and **dependent** variables respectively.

In this Chapter we **describe** and **model** relationships between pairs of numerical variables.

A   ASSOCIATION BETWEEN NUMERICAL VARIABLES

We can observe the relationship between two numerical variables using a **scatter diagram**. We usually place the explanatory variable on the horizontal axis, and the response variable on the vertical axis.

In the **Opening Problem**, the explanatory variable *age* is placed on the horizontal axis, and the response variable *distance thrown* is placed on the vertical axis.

We then graph each data value as a point on the scatter diagram. For example, the red point represents athlete H, who is 10 years old and threw the discus 15 metres.

From the general shape formed by the dots, we can see that as the *age* increases, so does the *distance thrown*.

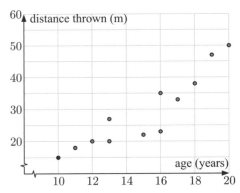

CORRELATION

> **Correlation** refers to the relationship or association between two numerical variables.

There are several characteristics we consider when describing the correlation between two variables: direction, linearity, strength, outliers, and causation.

DIRECTION

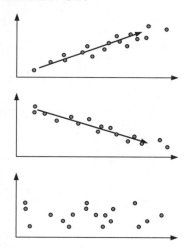

For a generally *upward* trend, we say that the correlation is **positive**. An increase in the explanatory variable generally results in an increase in the response variable.

For a generally *downward* trend, we say that the correlation is **negative**. An increase in the explanatory variable generally results in a decrease in the response variable.

For *randomly scattered* points, with no upward or downward trend, we say there is **no correlation**.

LINEARITY

When a trend exists, if the points approximately form a straight line, we say the trend is **linear**.

These points are roughly linear.

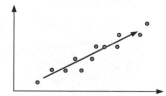

These points do not follow a linear trend.

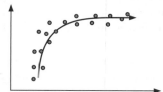

STRENGTH

To describe how closely the data follows a pattern or trend, we talk about the **strength** of correlation. It is usually described as either **strong**, **moderate**, or **weak**.

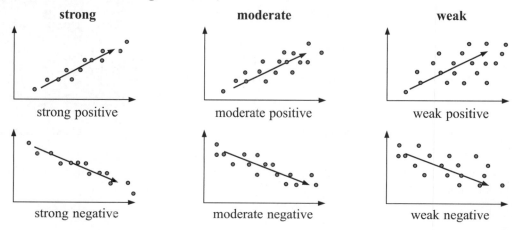

strong	moderate	weak
strong positive	moderate positive	weak positive
strong negative	moderate negative	weak negative

OUTLIERS

Outliers are isolated points which do not follow the trend formed by the main body of data.

If an outlier is the result of a recording or graphing error, it should be discarded. However, if the outlier is a genuine piece of data, it should be kept.

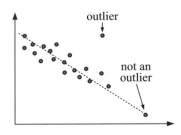

For the scatter diagram of the data in the **Opening Problem**, we can say that there is a strong positive correlation between *age* and *distance thrown*. The relationship appears to be linear, with no outliers.

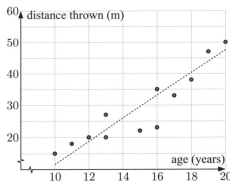

CAUSALITY

Correlation between two variables does not necessarily mean that one variable *causes* the other.

For example:

- The *arm length* and *running speed* of a sample of young children were measured, and a strong, positive correlation was found between the variables.

  This does *not* mean that short arms cause a reduction in running speed, or that a high running speed causes your arms to grow long.

  Rather, there is a strong, positive correlation between the variables because both *arm length* and *running speed* are closely related to a third variable, *age*. Up to a certain age, both *arm length* and *running speed* increase with *age*.

- The number of television sets sold in London and the number of stray dogs collected in Edinburgh were recorded over several years. A strong, positive correlation was found between the variables.

  Obviously the number of television sets sold in London was not influencing the number of stray dogs collected in Edinburgh. It is coincidental that the variables both increased over this period of time.

If a change in one variable *causes* a change in the other variable then we say that a **causal relationship** exists between them.

In cases where a causal relationship is not apparent, we cannot conclude that a causal relationship exists based on high correlation alone.

EXERCISE 21A

1 For each scatter diagram, describe the relationship between the variables. Consider the direction, linearity, and strength of the relationship, as well as the presence of any outliers.

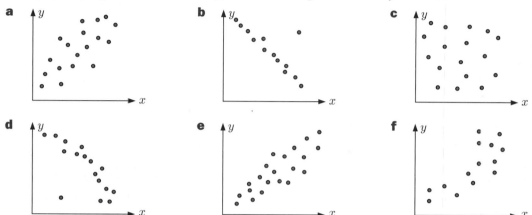

2 Tiffany is a hairdresser. The table below shows the number of hours she worked each day last week, and the number of customers she had.

Day	Mon	Tue	Wed	Thu	Fri	Sat	Sun
Hours worked	8	4	5	10	8	3	6
Number of customers	9	6	5	12	7	4	5

a Which is the explanatory variable, and which is the response variable?

b Draw a scatter diagram of the data.

c On which two days did Tiffany:
  i work the same number of hours
  ii have the same number of customers?

d Explain why you would expect a positive correlation between the variables.

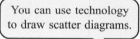

GRAPHICS
CALCULATOR
INSTRUCTIONS

3 The scores awarded by two judges at an ice skating competition are shown in the table.

Competitor	P	Q	R	S	T	U	V	W	X	Y
Judge A	5	6.5	8	9	4	2.5	7	5	6	3
Judge B	6	7	8.5	9	5	4	7.5	5	7	4.5

a Construct a scatter diagram for the data, with Judge A's scores on the horizontal axis and Judge B's scores on the vertical axis.

b Copy and complete the following comments about the scatter diagram:
There appears to be ......, ..., ... correlation between Judge A's scores and Judge B's scores. This means that as Judge A's scores increase, Judge B's scores ......

c Would it be reasonable to conclude that an increase in Judge A's scores *causes* an increase in Judge B's scores? Explain your answer.

4 Paul owns a company which installs industrial air conditioners. The table below shows the number of workers at the company's last 10 jobs, and the time it took to complete the job.

Job	A	B	C	D	E	F	G	H	I	J
Number of workers	5	3	8	2	5	6	1	4	2	7
Time (hours)	4	6	2.5	9	3	4	10	4	7.5	3

    a Which job:

       i took the longest

       ii involved the most workers?

    b Draw a scatter diagram to display the data.

    c Describe the relationship between the variables *number of workers* and *time*.

5 Choose the scatter diagram which would best illustrate the relationship between the variables x and y.

    a $x =$ the number of apples bought by customers, $y =$ the total cost of apples bought

    b $x =$ the number of pushups a student can perform in one minute,
       $y =$ the time taken for the student to run 100 metres

    c $x =$ the height of a person, $y =$ the weight of the person

    d $x =$ the distance a student travels to school, $y =$ the height of the student's uncle

A
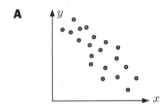

B
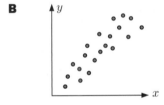

C
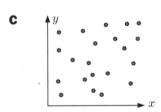

D
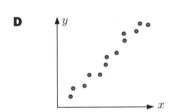

6 The scatter diagram shows the marks obtained by students in a test out of 50 marks, plotted against the number of hours each student studied for the test.

    a Describe the correlation between the variables.

    b How should the outlier be treated? Explain your answer.

    c Do you think there is a causal relationship between the variables? Explain your answer.

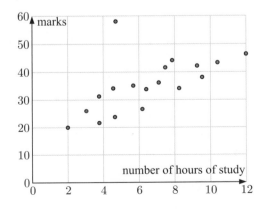

7   When the following pairs of variables were measured, a strong, positive correlation was found between each pair. Discuss whether a causal relationship exists between the variables. If not, suggest a third variable to which they may both be related.

    a   The lengths of one's left and right feet.

    b   The damage caused by a fire and the number of firefighters who attend it.

    c   A company's expenditure on advertising, and the sales they make the following year.

    d   The heights of parents and the heights of their adult children.

    e   The numbers of hotels and numbers of service stations in rural towns.

B   MEASURING CORRELATION

In the previous Section, we classified the strength of the correlation between two variables as either strong, moderate, or weak. We observed the points on a scatter diagram, and judged how clearly the points formed a linear relationship.

Since this method is *subjective* and relies on the observer's opinion, it is important to get a more precise measure of the strength of linear correlation between the variables. We achieve this using the **product moment correlation coefficient** r.

> For a set of n data given as ordered pairs (x_1, y_1), (x_2, y_2), (x_3, y_3), ..., (x_n, y_n),
>
> the **product moment correlation coefficient** is $r = \dfrac{\sum (x - \overline{x})(y - \overline{y})}{\sqrt{\sum (x - \overline{x})^2 \sum (y - \overline{y})^2}}$
>
> where $\overline{x}$ and $\overline{y}$ are the means of the x and y data respectively, and $\sum$ means the sum over all the data values.

You are not required to learn this formula, but you should be able to calculate the value of r using technology.

GRAPHICS CALCULATOR INSTRUCTIONS

PROPERTIES OF THE PRODUCT MOMENT CORRELATION COEFFICIENT

- The values of r range from -1 to $+1$.
- The **sign** of r indicates the **direction** of the correlation.
  - ▸ A positive value for r indicates the variables are **positively correlated**. An increase in one variable results in an increase in the other.
  - ▸ A negative value for r indicates the variables are **negatively correlated**. An increase in one variable results in a decrease in the other.
  - ▸ If $r = 0$ then there is **no correlation** between the variables.
- The **size** of r indicates the **strength** of the correlation.
  - ▸ A value of r close to $+1$ or -1 indicates strong correlation between the variables.
  - ▸ A value of r close to zero indicates weak correlation between the variables.

The following table is a guide for describing the strength of linear correlation using r.

Positive correlation		Negative correlation	
$r = 1$	perfect positive correlation	$r = -1$	perfect negative correlation
$0.95 \leqslant r < 1$	very strong positive correlation	$-1 < r \leqslant -0.95$	very strong negative correlation
$0.87 \leqslant r < 0.95$	strong positive correlation	$-0.95 < r \leqslant -0.87$	strong negative correlation
$0.7 \leqslant r < 0.87$	moderate positive correlation	$-0.87 < r \leqslant -0.7$	moderate negative correlation
$0.5 \leqslant r < 0.7$	weak positive correlation	$-0.7 < r \leqslant -0.5$	weak negative correlation
$0 < r < 0.5$	very weak positive correlation	$-0.5 < r < 0$	very weak negative correlation

Example 1   ◀) Self Tutor

The Department of Road Safety wants to know if there is any association between *average speed* in the metropolitan area and the *age of drivers*. They commission a device to be fitted in the cars of drivers of different ages.

The results are shown in the scatter diagram.
The r-value for this association is $+0.027$.
Describe the association.

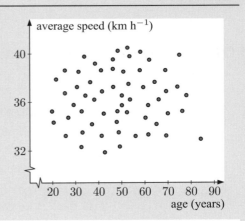

Since $0 < r < 0.5$, there is a very weak positive correlation between the two variables.
We observe this in the graph as the points are randomly scattered.

EXERCISE 21B.1

1 In a recent survey, the Department of International Commerce compared the *number of employees of a company* with its *export earnings*. A scatter diagram of their data is shown alongside. The corresponding value of r is 0.556.

Describe the association between the variables.

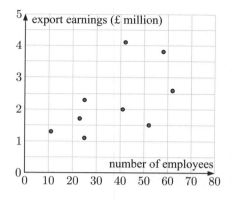

2 Match each scatter diagram with the correct value of r.

a
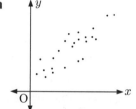

b
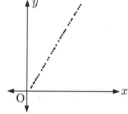

c
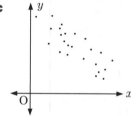

d
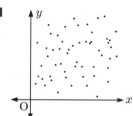

e
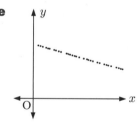

A $r = 1$ **B** $r = 0.6$ **C** $r = 0$ **D** $r = -0.7$ **E** $r = -1$

Example 2   ◀)) Self Tutor

The botanical gardens have been trying a new chemical to control the number of beetles infesting their plants. The results of one of their tests are shown in the table.

Sample	Quantity of chemical (g)	Number of surviving beetles
A	2	11
B	5	6
C	6	4
D	3	6
E	9	3

a Draw a scatter diagram for the data.

b Determine the correlation coefficient r.

c Describe the correlation between the *quantity of chemical* and the *number of surviving lawn beetles*.

We first enter the data into separate lists:

Casio fx-9860G PLUS	Casio fx-CG20	TI-84 Plus CE
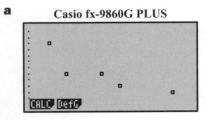	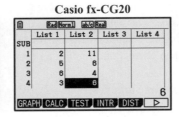	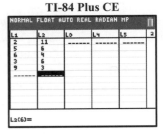

a

Casio fx-9860G PLUS	Casio fx-CG20	TI-84 Plus CE
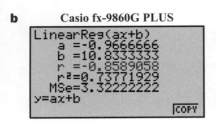	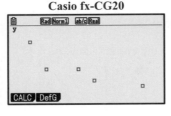	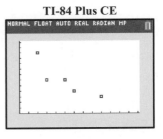

b

Casio fx-9860G PLUS	Casio fx-CG20	TI-84 Plus CE
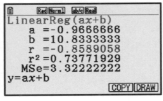		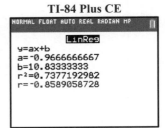

So, $r \approx -0.859$.

c There is a moderate negative correlation between the *quantity of chemical used* and the *number of surviving beetles*.

In general, the more chemical that is used, the fewer beetles that survive.

3 For each of the following data sets:

   i Draw a scatter diagram for the data.

   ii Calculate the product moment correlation coefficient r.

   iii Describe the linear correlation between x and y.

a

x	1	2	3	4	5	6
y	3	2	5	5	9	6

b

x	3	8	5	14	19	10	16
y	17	12	15	6	1	10	4

c

x	3	6	11	7	5	6	8	10	4
y	2	8	8	4	7	9	11	1	5

4 A selection of students were asked how many phone calls and text messages they received the previous day. The results are shown alongside.

Student	A	B	C	D	E	F	G	H
Phone calls received	4	7	1	0	3	2	2	4
Text messages received	6	9	2	2	5	8	4	7

   a Draw a scatter diagram for the data.
       b Calculate r.

   c Describe the linear correlation between *phone calls received* and *text messages received*.

   d Give a reason why this correlation may occur.

5 Consider the **Opening Problem** on page **502**.

   a Calculate r for the data.

   b Hence describe the association between the variables.

6 Jill does her washing every Saturday and hangs her clothes out to dry. She notices that the clothes dry faster some days than others. She investigates the relationship between the temperature and the time her clothes take to dry:

Temperature ($x\,°$C)	25	32	27	39	35	24	30	36	29	35
Drying time (y minutes)	100	70	95	25	38	105	70	35	75	40

   a Draw a scatter diagram for the data.   **b** Calculate r.

   c Describe the correlation between *temperature* and *drying time*.

7 This table shows the number of supermarkets in 10 towns, and the number of car accidents that have occurred in these towns in the last month.

Number of supermarkets	5	8	12	7	6	2	15	10	7	3
Number of car accidents	10	13	27	19	10	6	40	30	22	37

   a Draw a scatter diagram for the data.   **b** Calculate r.

   c Identify the outlier in the data.

   d It was found that the outlier was due to an error in the data collection process.

      i Recalculate r with the outlier removed.

      ii Describe the relationship between the variables.

      iii Discuss the effect of removing the outlier on the value of r.

   e Do you think there is a causal relationship between the variables? Explain your answer.

8 A health researcher notices that the incidence of Multiple Sclerosis (MS) is higher in some parts of the world than in others.

To investigate further, she records the *latitude* and *incidence of MS per 100 000 people* of 20 countries.

Latitude (degrees)	55	25	41	22	47	37	56	14	34	25
MS incidence per 100 000	165	95	75	20	180	140	230	15	45	65

Latitude (degrees)	27	65	10	24	4	56	46	8	50	40
MS incidence per 100 000	30	140	5	15	2	290	95	8	160	105

   a Draw a scatter diagram for the data.

   b Calculate the value of r.

   c Describe the relationship between the variables.

   d Is the incidence of MS higher near the equator, or near the poles?

Higher latitudes occur near the poles. Lower latitudes occur near the equator.

Activity 1   Comparing height and foot length

In this Activity, you will explore the relationship between the *height* and *foot length* of the students in your class.

You will need: ruler, tape measure

What to do:

1   Predict whether there will be positive correlation, no correlation, or negative correlation between the *height* and *foot length* of the students in your class.

2   Measure the height and foot length of each student in your class. Record your measurements in a table like the one alongside.

Student	Height (cm)	Foot length (cm)

3   Use technology to draw a scatter diagram for the data.

4   Calculate the product moment correlation coefficient r for the data.

5   Describe the relationship between *height* and *foot length*. Was your prediction correct?

6   Do you think that a high value of r indicates a causal relationship in this case?

THE COEFFICIENT OF DETERMINATION r^2

To help describe the correlation between two variables, we can also calculate the **coefficient of determination** r^2. This is simply the square of the product moment correlation coefficient r, so the direction of correlation is eliminated.

We can find r^2 using technology, or if r is already known, we can simply square this value.

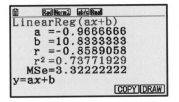

INTERPRETATION OF THE COEFFICIENT OF DETERMINATION

If there is a causal relationship, then r^2 indicates the degree to which change in the explanatory variable explains change in the response variable.

For example, an investigation into many different brands of muesli found that there is strong positive correlation between the variables *fat content* and *kilojoule content*. It was found that $r \approx 0.862$ and $r^2 \approx 0.743$.

An interpretation of this r^2 value is:

response variable   explanatory variable

74.3% of the variation in *kilojoule content* of muesli can be explained by the variation in *fat content* in the muesli.

In this case, we assume that the other $100\% - 74.3\% = 25.7\%$ of the variation in *kilojoule content* in the muesli can be explained by other factors.

Example 3   ◀)) Self Tutor

At a father-son camp, the heights of the fathers and their sons were measured.

Father's height (x cm)	175	183	170	167	179	180	183	185	170	181	185
Son's height (y cm)	167	178	158	162	171	167	180	177	152	164	172

a Draw a scatter diagram for the data.

b Calculate r^2 for the data, and interpret its value.

a
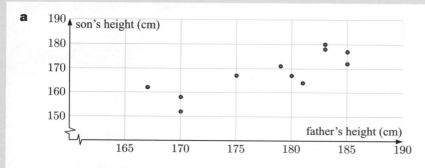

b
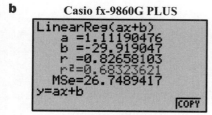
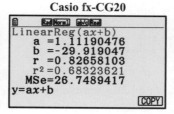
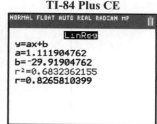

So, $r^2 \approx 0.683$.

$\therefore$ 68.3% of the variation in the son's height can be explained by variation in the father's height.

EXERCISE 21B.2

1 From an investigation at an aquatic centre, the coefficient of determination between the variables *number of visitors* and *maximum temperature* is found to be 0.578. Complete the following interpretation of the coefficient of determination:

...... % of the variation in the ...... can be explained by the variation in ......

2 An investigation has found the association between the variables *time spent gambling* and *money lost* has correlation coefficient 0.7732. Find the coefficient of determination and interpret its meaning.

3 For a group of children, the correlation coefficient -0.365 is found between the variables *heart rate* and *age*. Find the coefficient of determination and interpret its meaning.

4 For a particular species of bear, the variables *weight* and *running speed* are found to be negatively correlated with coefficient of determination $r^2 = 0.821$. Find the correlation coefficient r.

5 Joanne is a real estate agent. This table shows the *distance from the city* and the *selling price* of the last 12 houses she has sold.

Distance from city (km)	10	4	23	16	3	35	8	7	12	24	14	12
Selling price (£ × 1000)	380	495	350	420	540	260	480	340	350	310	470	350

a Draw a scatter diagram for the data.

b Calculate the coefficient of determination r^2.

c What percentage of the variation in selling price can be explained by the variation in the distance from the city?

d What other factors could explain the variation in selling price?

6 A sample of 8 tyres was taken to examine the association between the *tread depth* and the *distance travelled*.

Distance (x km × 1000)	14	17	24	34	35	37	38	39
Tread depth (y mm)	5.7	6.5	4.0	3.0	1.9	2.7	1.9	2.3

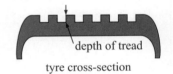

depth of tread

tyre cross-section

a Draw a scatter diagram for the data.

b Calculate r^2 for the data, and interpret its meaning.

C   LINEAR MODELS

If there is a sufficiently strong linear correlation between two variables, we can draw a "line of best fit" to illustrate their relationship. This is known as a **linear model**.

In previous years, you should have constructed lines of best fit by eye. This involved drawing a line through the *mean point* on a scatter diagram to follow the trend of the data.

The problem with drawing a line of best fit by eye is that the line drawn will vary from one person to another. For consistency, we instead use a method known as **linear regression** to find the equation of the line which best fits the data.

Finding the equation of the **regression line** by hand is time consuming, so we use technology to find the equation of the line.

GRAPHICS
CALCULATOR
INSTRUCTIONS

STATISTICS
PACKAGE

INTERPOLATION AND EXTRAPOLATION

Consider the data in the scatter diagram alongside. The data with the highest and lowest values are called the **poles**.

The regression line for the data is also drawn on the scatter diagram. We can use this line to predict the value of one variable for a given value of the other.

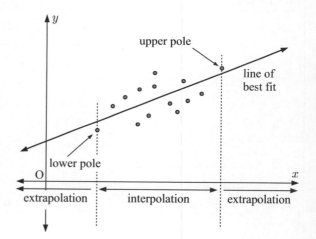

- If we predict a y value for an x value **in between** the poles, we say we are **interpolating** in between the poles.

- If we predict a y value for an x value **outside** the poles, we say we are **extrapolating** outside the poles.

The accuracy of an interpolation depends on how well the linear model fits the data. This can be gauged by the correlation coefficient and by ensuring that the data is randomly scattered around the line of best fit.

The accuracy of an extrapolation depends not only on how well the model fits, but also on the assumption that the linear trend will continue past the poles. The validity of this assumption depends greatly on the situation we are looking at.

For example, consider the regression line for the data in the **Opening Problem**. It can be used to predict the distance a discus will be thrown by an athlete of a particular age.

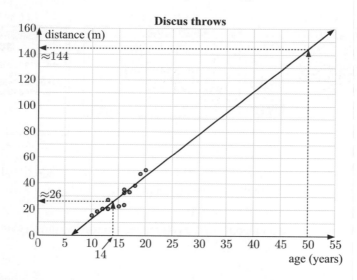

The age 14 is within the range of ages in the original data, so it is reasonable to predict that a 14 year old will be able to throw the discus 26 m.

However, it is unlikely that the linear trend shown in the data will continue far beyond the poles. For example, according to the model, a 50 year old might throw the discus 144 m. This is almost twice the current world record of 76.8 m, so it would clearly be an unreasonable prediction.

Example 4

◀⑴ **Self Tutor**

The annual income and average weekly grocery bill for a selection of families is shown below:

Income (x thousand pounds)	55	36	25	47	60	64	42	50
Grocery bill (y pounds)	120	90	60	160	190	250	110	150

a Construct a scatter diagram to illustrate the data.

b Use technology to find the regression line.

c State and interpret the gradient of the regression line.

d Estimate the weekly grocery bill for a family with an annual income of £95 000.

e Estimate the annual income of a family whose weekly grocery bill is £100.

f Comment on whether the estimates in **d** and **e** are likely to be reliable.

a

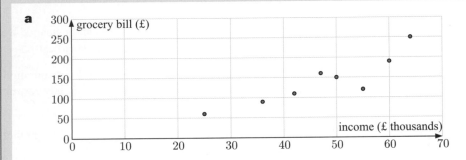

b

Casio fx-9860G PLUS	Casio fx-CG20	TI-84 Plus CE

Using technology, the regression line is $y \approx 4.18x - 56.7$

c The gradient of the regression line ≈ 4.18. This means that for every additional £1000 of income, a family's weekly grocery bill will increase by an average of £4.18.

d When $x = 95$, $y \approx 4.18(95) - 56.7 \approx 340$

So, we expect a family with an income of £95 000 to have a weekly grocery bill of approximately £340.

e When $y = 100$, $100 \approx 4.18x - 56.7$

$\therefore \quad 156.7 \approx 4.18x$ {adding 56.7 to both sides}

$\therefore \quad x \approx 37.5$ {dividing both sides by 4.18}

So, we expect a family with a weekly grocery bill of £100 to have an annual income of approximately £37 500.

f The estimate in **d** is an extrapolation, so the estimate may not be reliable.

The estimate in **e** is an interpolation and there is strong linear correlation between the variables. We therefore expect this estimate to be reliable.

EXERCISE 21C

1 Consider the data set below.

x	10	4	6	8	9	5	7	1	2	3
y	20	6	8	13	20	12	13	4	2	7

GRAPHICS
CALCULATOR
INSTRUCTIONS

a Draw a scatter diagram for the data.

b Use technology to find the equation of the regression line, and plot the line on your calculator.

c Use **b** to draw the regression line on your scatter plot.

2 Steve wanted to see whether there was any relationship between the temperature when he leaves for work in the morning, and the time it takes for him to get to work.

He collected data over a 14 day period:

Temperature (x °C)	25	19	23	27	32	35	29	27	21	18	16	17	28	34
Time (y minutes)	35	42	49	31	37	33	31	47	42	36	45	33	48	39

a Draw a scatter diagram for the data.

b Calculate r.

c Describe the relationship between the variables.

d Is it reasonable to fit a linear model to this data? Explain your answer.

3 The table below shows the price of petrol and the number of customers per hour for sixteen petrol stations.

Petrol price (x pence per litre)	105.9	106.9	109.9	104.5	104.9	111.9	110.5	112.9
Number of customers (y)	45	42	25	48	43	15	19	10

Petrol price (x pence per litre)	107.5	108.0	104.9	102.9	110.9	106.9	105.5	109.5
Number of customers (y)	30	23	42	50	12	24	32	17

a Calculate the correlation coefficient r for the data.

b Describe the relationship between the *petrol price* and the *number of customers*.

c Use technology to find the regression line.

d State and interpret the gradient of the regression line.

e Estimate the number of customers per hour for a petrol station which sells petrol at 115.9 pence per litre.

f Estimate the petrol price at a petrol station which has 40 customers per hour.

g Comment on the reliability of your estimates in **e** and **f**.

4 To investigate whether speed cameras have an impact on road safety, data was collected from several cities. The number of speed cameras in operation was recorded for each city, as well as the number of accidents over a 7 day period.

Number of speed cameras (x)	7	15	20	3	16	17	28	17	24	25	20	5	16	25	15	19
Number of car accidents (y)	48	35	31	52	40	35	28	30	34	19	29	42	31	21	37	32

   a Construct a scatter diagram to display the data.
   b Calculate r for the data.
   c Describe the relationship between the *number of speed cameras* and the *number of car accidents*.
   d Find the equation of the regression line.
   e State and interpret the gradient and y-intercept of the regression line.
   f Estimate the number of car accidents in a city with 10 speed cameras.

5 The table below contains information about the *maximum speed* and *ceiling* (maximum altitude obtainable) for nineteen World War II fighter planes. The maximum speed is given in $km\,h^{-1}$, and the ceiling is given in km.

Maximum speed	Ceiling
460	8.84
420	10.06
530	10.97
530	9.906
490	9.448
530	10.36
680	11.73

Maximum speed	Ceiling
680	10.66
720	11.27
710	12.64
660	11.12
780	12.80
730	11.88

Maximum speed	Ceiling
670	12.49
570	10.66
440	10.51
670	11.58
700	11.73
520	10.36

   a Draw a scatter diagram for the data.   **b** Calculate r.
   c Describe the association between *maximum speed* (x) and *ceiling* (y).
   d Use technology to find the regression line, and draw the line on your scatter diagram.
   e State and interpret the gradient of the regression line.
   f Estimate the ceiling for a fighter plane with a maximum speed of $600\ km\,h^{-1}$.
   g Estimate the maximum speed for a fighter plane with a ceiling of 11 km.

6 A group of children was asked the numbers of hours they spent exercising and watching television each week.

Exercise (x hours per week)	4	1	8	7	10	3	3	2
Television (y hours per week)	12	24	5	9	1	18	11	16

   a Draw a scatter diagram for the data.   **b** Calculate r.
   c Describe the correlation between *time exercising* and *time watching television*.
   d Find the equation of the regression line, and draw the line on your scatter diagram.

e State and interpret the gradient and y-intercept of the regression line.

f   i One of the children in the group exercised for 7 hours each week. How much television does this child watch weekly?

  ii Use the regression line to predict the amount of television watched each week by a child who exercises for 7 hours each week.

  iii Compare your answers to **i** and **ii**.

7 The yield of pumpkins on a farm depends on the quantity of fertiliser used.

Fertiliser (x g per m^2)	4	13	20	26	30	35	50
Yield (y kg)	1.8	2.9	3.8	4.2	4.7	5.7	4.4

a Draw a scatter diagram for the data, and identify the outlier.

b What effect do you think the outlier has on:

  i the strength of correlation of the data

  ii the gradient of the regression line?

c Calculate the correlation coefficient:

  i with the outlier included

  ii without the outlier.

d Calculate the equation of the regression line:

  i with the outlier included

  ii without the outlier.

e If you wish to estimate the yield when 15 g per m^2 of fertiliser is used, which regression line from **d** should be used? Explain your answer.

f Can you explain what may have caused the outlier? Do you think the outlier should be kept when analysing the data?

Historical note

Anscombe's quartet was first described in 1973 by the English statistician **Francis Anscombe** (1918 - 2001). At the time, computers were becoming increasingly popular in statistics, as they allowed for more large scale and complex computations to be done within a reasonable amount of time. However, many common statistical packages primarily performed numerical calculations rather than produce graphs. Such output was often limited to those with advanced programming skills.

In his 1973 article, Anscombe stressed that:

  "*A computer should make* both *calculations* and *graphs. Both sorts of output should be studied; each will contribute to understanding.*"

Francis Anscombe
Photo courtesy of
Yale University.

Activity 2   Anscombe's quartet

Anscombe's quartet is a collection of four bivariate data sets which have interesting statistical properties. The data values are given in the tables below:

Data set A:

x	10	8	13	9	11	14	6	4	12	7	5
y	8.04	6.95	7.58	8.81	8.33	9.96	7.24	4.26	10.84	4.82	5.68

Data set B:

x	10	8	13	9	11	14	6	4	12	7	5
y	9.14	8.14	8.74	8.77	9.26	8.1	6.13	3.1	9.13	7.26	4.74

Data set C:

x	10	8	13	9	11	14	6	4	12	7	5
y	7.46	6.77	12.74	7.11	7.81	8.84	6.08	5.39	8.15	6.42	5.73

Data set D:

x	8	8	8	8	8	8	8	19	8	8	8
y	6.58	5.76	7.71	8.84	8.47	7.04	5.25	12.5	5.56	7.91	6.89

Enter the data into your **graphics calculator** or click on the icon to access the data in the **statistics package**.

STATISTICS
PACKAGE

What to do:

1 For each data set, use technology to calculate:

    a the mean of each variable   **b** the sample variance of each variable.

    Comment on your answers.

2 Find the regression line for each data set. What do you notice?

3 Construct a scatter diagram for each data set, and plot the corresponding regression line on the same set of axes.

4 How do your calculations in **1** and **2** compare to your graphs in **3**? Is a linear model necessarily appropriate for each data set?

5 Why is it important to consider both graphs *and* descriptive statistics when analysing data?

Activity 3   Residual plots

In addition to the *correlation coefficient* and the *linearity* of a scatter diagram, we can use a **residual plot** to decide whether a linear model is appropriate. Click on the icon to explore these graphs.

RESIDUAL
PLOTS

D ■ EXPONENTIAL AND POWER MODELS

For data which is clearly non-linear, it is not sensible to fit a linear model directly to the data. However, for some relationships between variables we can **transform** the data into data which *is* linearly related. We can then use linear regression to find a model connecting the transformed variables.

In this Section we will use **logarithmic transformations** to fit **exponential models** and **power models** to data.

EXPONENTIAL MODELS

> An **exponential model** has the form $y = kb^x$ where k and b are constants.

Using the laws of logarithms, notice that:

If $y = kb^x$, then $\ln y = \ln(kb^x)$ {taking the logarithm of both sides}
$$= \ln k + \ln(b^x)$$
$$= \ln k + x \ln b$$

Since $\ln k$ and $\ln b$ are constants, there is a linear relationship between the variables $\ln y$ and x.

> If the variables x and y are connected by an exponential model, the graph of $\ln y$ against x is linear.

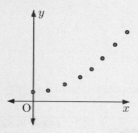 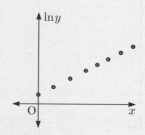

Once we have used linear regression to find an equation connecting $\ln y$ and x, we can rearrange the equation to make y the subject.

Example 5
◀) Self Tutor

Find the exponential model connecting x and y.

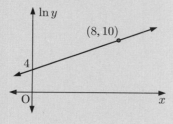

The graph of $\ln y$ against x is linear with

gradient $m = \dfrac{10 - 4}{8 - 0} = 0.75$ and y-intercept $c = 4$.

$\therefore \ \ln y = 0.75x + 4$

$\quad \therefore \ y = e^{0.75x + 4}$

$\quad \therefore \ y = e^{0.75x} \times e^4$

$\quad \therefore \ y = e^4 \times (e^{0.75})^x$

$\quad \therefore \ y \approx 54.6 \times 2.12^x$

Example 6

◀) **Self Tutor**

The mass of bacteria in a culture is measured each day for five days.

t (days)	1	2	3	4	5
M (grams)	3.6	5.7	9.1	14.6	23.3

a Draw scatter diagrams of M against t and $\ln M$ against t.

b Explain why M and t are related by an exponential model.

c Find the equation connecting M and t.

d Estimate the original mass of the bacteria.

GRAPHICS CALCULATOR INSTRUCTIONS

a

t (days)	1	2	3	4	5
M (grams)	3.6	5.7	9.1	14.6	23.3
$\ln M$	1.28	1.74	2.21	2.68	3.15

The logarithm of a variable is *not* given units.

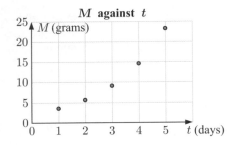

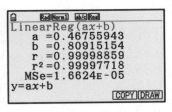

b The graph of $\ln M$ against t appears linear, so an exponential model is appropriate.

c

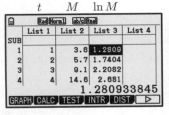

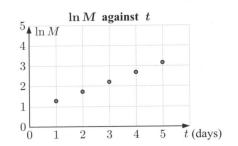

Using technology, the linear model connecting $\ln M$ and t is

$$\ln M \approx 0.468t + 0.809$$

$$\therefore \quad M \approx e^{0.468t + 0.809}$$

$$\therefore \quad M \approx e^{0.468t} \times e^{0.809}$$

$$\therefore \quad M \approx e^{0.809} \times (e^{0.468})^t$$

$$\therefore \quad M \approx 2.25 \times (1.60)^t$$

d When $t = 0$, $M \approx 2.25 \times (1.60)^0 \approx 2.25$

So, the original mass of the bacteria was approximately 2.25 g.

EXERCISE 21D.1

1 For each of the following graphs, find the exponential model connecting the variables.

a
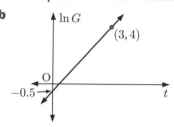

b

c
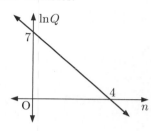

2 The population of a buffalo herd was recorded every 5 years after 1990.

Years since 1990 (x)	5	10	15	20	25
Population (y)	440	597	819	1120	1540

a Draw a scatter diagram of $\ln y$ against x.

b Explain why x and y are related by an exponential model.

c Find the linear model connecting $\ln y$ and x.

d Find the exponential model connecting x and y.

e Estimate the population of the herd in: **i** 1998   **ii** 2025.

3 The table below shows the concentration of venom in the blood of a snake bite victim at various times after an injection was administered to neutralise it.

Time (t minutes)	10	20	30	40	50	60	70
Venom concentration (V units)	104.6	36.5	12.7	4.43	1.55	0.539	0.188

a Draw scatter diagrams of V against t and $\ln V$ against t.

b Explain why the model connecting V and t is exponential.

c Find the linear model connecting $\ln V$ and t.

d Find the exponential model connecting V and t.

e The victim is considered to be "safe" when the venom concentration is less than 0.01 units. How long will it take to reach this "safe" level?

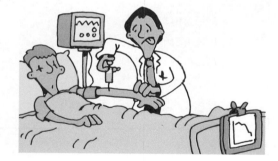

POWER MODELS

A **power model** has the form $y = ax^n$ where a and n are constants.

Using the laws of logarithms, notice that:

If $y = ax^n$, then $\ln y = \ln(ax^n)$ {taking the logarithm of both sides}
$$= \ln a + \ln(x^n)$$
$$= \ln a + n \ln x$$

Since $\ln a$ and n are constants, there is a linear relationship between the variables $\ln y$ and $\ln x$.

If the variables x and y are connected by a **power model**, the graph of $\ln y$ against $\ln x$ is linear.

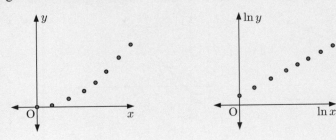

Since $y = ax^n$, all power models pass through the origin. However, since we cannot take the logarithm of 0, we will need to remove data such as $(0, 0)$ before starting our analysis.

Example 7   ◀)) **Self Tutor**

Find the power model connecting F and t.

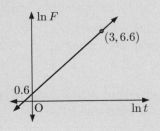

The graph of $\ln F$ against $\ln t$ is linear with

gradient $m = \dfrac{6.6 - 0.6}{3 - 0} = 2$ and y-intercept $c = 0.6$.

$\therefore \ \ln F = 2 \ln t + 0.6$

$\therefore \ \ln F = \ln(t^2) + \ln(e^{0.6})$

$\therefore \ \ln F = \ln(t^2 \times e^{0.6})$

$\therefore \ \ \ F = t^2 \times e^{0.6}$

$\therefore \ \ \ F \approx 1.82t^2$

> Knowing the laws of logarithms is essential.

Example 8   ◀)) **Self Tutor**

The maximum speed of a canoe with different numbers of rowers is recorded in the table below:

Number of rowers (n)	4	6	10	14	18
Maximum speed (S km h^{-1})	8.7	10.3	12.6	14.2	15.9

a Draw scatter diagrams of S against n and $\ln S$ against $\ln n$.

b Explain why S and n are related by a power model.

c Find the equation connecting n and S.

d Predict the maximum speed of the canoe if there are 8 rowers.

a

n	4	6	10	14	18
S	8.7	10.3	12.6	14.2	15.9
$\ln n$	1.39	1.79	2.30	2.64	2.89
$\ln S$	2.16	2.33	2.53	2.65	2.77

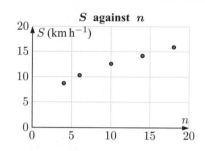

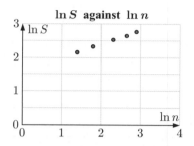

b The graph of $\ln S$ against $\ln n$ appears linear, so a power model is appropriate.

c

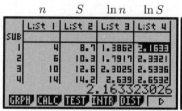

Using technology, the linear model connecting $\ln S$ and $\ln n$ is

$$\ln S \approx 0.396 \ln n + 1.618$$

$\therefore \ \ln S \approx \ln(n^{0.396}) + \ln(e^{1.618})$

$\therefore \ \ln S \approx \ln(n^{0.396} \times e^{1.618})$

$\therefore \ \ S \approx n^{0.396} \times e^{1.618}$

$\therefore \ \ S \approx 5.04 \times n^{0.396}$

d When $n = 8$, $S \approx 5.04 \times 8^{0.396} \approx 11.5$

So, we would expect the maximum speed of a canoe with 8 rowers to be approximately 11.5 km h^{-1}.

EXERCISE 21D.2

1 For each of the following graphs, find the power model connecting the variables.

a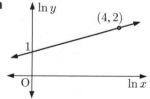

b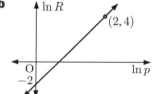

c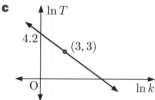

2 A tennis ball is dropped from the top of a cliff. The distance fallen after various times is measured. The results are:

Time (t seconds)	1.4	2.1	2.9	3.3	3.6	4.3	4.9
Distance fallen (D m)	10.0	21.3	40.6	52.1	63.4	89.2	117.7

   a Draw a scatter diagram of $\ln D$ against $\ln t$.

   b Explain why D and t are related by a power model.

   c Find the linear model connecting $\ln D$ and $\ln t$.

   d Find the power model connecting D and t.

3 When a force is applied to an object, the *pressure* of the object depends on the *surface area* where the force is applied. The pressure that results when 100 newtons of force is applied over various areas, is recorded below.

Area (a m^2)	4	7	15	20	24	30	35	40	45
Pressure (P pascals)	25	14.3	6.7	5	4.2	3.3	2.9	2.5	2.2

   a Draw scatter diagrams of P against a and $\ln P$ against $\ln a$.

   b Explain why P and a are related by a power model.

   c Find the linear model connecting $\ln P$ and $\ln a$.

   d Find the power model connecting P and a.

   e Estimate the pressure that results when the 100 newton force is applied over an area of 10 m^2. Comment on the reliability of this estimate.

E   PROBLEM SOLVING

When we obtain a set of data, we generally do not know which type of model connects the variables. We must use the techniques we have learnt to assess which model is the most appropriate fit for the data.

To determine whether a **linear**, **exponential**, or **power** model is most appropriate to connect variables x and y:

  Step 1:   Draw scatter diagrams of y against x, $\ln y$ against x, and $\ln y$ against $\ln x$.

  Step 2:   Find the regression line for each scatter diagram in which the variables appear linearly related. If more than one model appears appropriate, choose the one with the highest r^2 value.

  Step 3:   Write the equation connecting the variables without logarithms.

EXERCISE 21E

1 When Tristan went fishing, he caught ten salmon. He measured and weighed each one:

Length (x cm)	32	28	15	42	39	22	25	45	35	47
Weight (y g)	300	200	33	680	540	100	150	830	400	950

   a Draw scatter diagrams of:

     i y against x **ii** $\ln y$ against x **iii** $\ln y$ against $\ln x$.

   b Explain why a power model is most appropriate.

   c Find the linear model connecting $\ln y$ and $\ln x$. State the value of r^2.

   d Find the power model connecting x and y.

2 The area affected by a forest fire t minutes after a lightning strike is recorded in the table below.

Time (t minutes)	2	3	5	7	9	10	12
Area affected (A hectares)	1.6	2.5	4.9	9.3	18.2	27.3	55

a Draw scatter diagrams of:

   i A against t **ii** $\ln A$ against t **iii** $\ln A$ against $\ln t$.

b Explain why an exponential model is most appropriate.

c Find the linear model connecting $\ln A$ and t. State the value of r^2.

d Find the exponential model connecting t and A.

3 A water balloon is filled from a hose. The diameter of the balloon after t seconds is recorded in the table:

Time (t seconds)	1	2	3	4	5	6	7	8
Diameter (D cm)	5.1	6.4	7.2	8.0	8.6	9.2	9.8	10

a Draw scatter diagrams of:

   i D against t **ii** $\ln D$ against t **iii** $\ln D$ against $\ln t$.

b Which model is most appropriate for the data? Explain your answer.

c Find the model connecting D and t.

d Estimate the diameter of the water balloon after 3.5 seconds. Comment on the reliability of your estimate.

4 A driver was timed to see how long he took to bring his car to rest from varying speeds:

Speed (v km h^{-1})	10	20	30	40	50	60	70	80	90
Stopping time (t seconds)	1.23	1.54	1.88	2.20	2.52	2.83	3.15	3.45	3.83

a Draw scatter diagrams of:

   i t against v **ii** $\ln t$ against v **iii** $\ln t$ against $\ln v$.

b Which model is most appropriate for the data? Explain your answer.

c Find the model connecting t and v.

d Estimate the stopping time from speed 110 km h^{-1}.

5 The table below shows the value of a house t years after it is built.

Time (t years)	1	4	6	10	12	15	20
Value (£$V \times 1000$)	257	281	299	335	354	390	450

a Find an appropriate model connecting V and t.

b Predict the value of the house after 25 years.

6 The German mathematician and astronomer **Johannes Kepler** (1571 - 1630) was an important figure in the 17th century scientific revolution. He used data from observations of planetary orbits to show that these motions are not random, that they obey certain mathematical laws, and that these laws can be written in algebraic form. He took the Earth as his "base unit", so that orbital periods are given as multiples of one Earth year, and orbital radii as multiples of one Earth orbit. Some of his observations are given in this table.

Planet	Mercury	Venus	Earth	Mars	Jupiter	Saturn
Orbital radius (r)	0.387	0.723	1.000	1.542	5.202	9.539
Orbital period (T)	0.241	0.615	1.000	1.881	11.862	29.457

Kepler showed that this data could be summarised by an equation of the form $T = ar^k$ where a and k are constants.

a Find values for a and k.

b Determine whether this is an appropriate model for the data.

c Kepler stated the relationship as "The square of the planet's year is proportional to the cube of its distance from the sun." Show that your results agree with this conclusion.

Activity 4   The pendulum

A **pendulum** can be made by tying a solid object to a piece of string and allowing the object to swing back and forth.

The **period** of a pendulum is the time taken for one complete oscillation.

The **length** of the pendulum is the distance from the point of support to the object's centre of mass.

Our aim is to determine a rule which connects the period of the pendulum (T s) with its length (l cm).

The period is independent of the angle θ, so for the purposes of the experiment, use $\theta \approx 15°$.

What to do:

1 Discuss which of the following ideas have merit when finding the period of the pendulum for a particular length:
- several students should time the period using their stopwatches
- timing 8 complete swings and finding the average is better than timing one complete swing
- if several students do the timing, the highest and lowest scores should be removed and the remaining scores averaged.

2 Discuss possible factors which could lead to inaccurate results.

3 After deciding on a method for determining the period, measure the period for pendulum lengths 20 cm, 30 cm, 40 cm, ..., 100 cm. Record your results in a table.

Length (l cm)	Period (T s)
20	
30	
40	
⋮	
100	

4 Determine the law connecting T and l.

Activity 5   Surge, terminal velocity, and logistic models

Click on the icon to investigate other types of models which can all be studied by transforming variables and using linear regression.

ACTIVITY

Review set 21A

1 For each scatter diagram, describe the relationship between the variables. Consider the direction, linearity, and strength of the relationship, as well as the presence of any outliers.

a

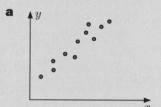

b

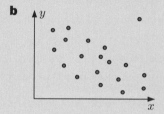

c

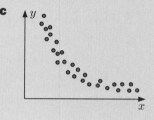

2 Kerry wants to investigate the relationship between the *water bill* and the *electricity bill* for the houses in her neighbourhood.

   a Do you think the correlation between the variables is likely to be positive or negative? Explain your answer.

   b Is there a causal relationship between the variables? Justify your answer.

3 The table below shows the ticket and beverage sales for each day of a 12 day music festival:

Ticket sales (£$x \times 1000$)	25	22	15	19	12	17	24	20	18	23	29	26
Beverage sales (£$y \times 1000$)	9	7	4	8	3	4	8	10	7	7	9	8

   a Draw a scatter diagram for the data.

   b Calculate the product moment correlation coefficient r.

   c Describe the correlation between *ticket sales* and *beverage sales*.

4 Jamie is a used car salesman. This table shows the age and selling price of the last 10 cars he has sold.

Age (years)	2	10	5	4	3	4	7	12	15	8
Selling price (£ $\times 1000$)	25	10	12	7	17	15	4	3	2	7

   a Draw a scatter diagram for the data.

   b Describe the correlation between *age* and *selling price*.

   c Calculate the coefficient of determination r^2.

   d What percentage of the variation in selling price can be explained by variation in age?

   e What other factors could explain the variation in selling price?

5   Tomatoes are sprayed with a pesticide-fertiliser mix. The table below shows the *yield of tomatoes* per bush for various *spray concentrations*.

Spray concentration (x mL per L)	3	5	6	8	9	11	15
Yield of tomatoes per bush (y)	67	90	103	120	124	150	82

a Draw a scatter diagram to display the data.

b Determine the value of r and interpret your answer.

c Is there an outlier present that is affecting the correlation?

d The outlier was found to be a recording error. Remove the outlier from the data set, and recalculate r. Is it reasonable to now fit a linear model?

e Determine the equation of the regression line.

f State and interpret the gradient and y-intercept of the regression line.

g Use your line to estimate:

  i the yield if the spray concentration is 7 mL per L

  ii the spray concentration if the yield is 200 tomatoes per bush.

h Comment on the reliability of your estimates in **g**.

6   The ages and heights of children at a playground are given below:

Age (x years)	3	9	7	4	4	12	8	6	5	10	13
Height (y cm)	94	132	123	102	109	150	127	110	115	145	157

a Draw a scatter diagram for the data.

b Use technology to find the regression line.

c State and interpret the gradient of the regression line.

d Use the line to predict the height of a 5 year old child.

e Based on the given data, at what age would you expect a child to reach 140 cm in height?

7   Thomas rode his bicycle for an hour each day for eleven days. He recorded the number of kilometres he rode, along with the temperature that day:

Temperature (T °C)	22.9	23.9	25.2	27.1	28.9	20.3
Distance (d km)	26.5	26.7	24.4	22.8	23.5	32.6

Temperature (T °C)	22.5	21.7	25.7	26.3	24.7
Distance (d km)	28.7	29.4	24.2	23.2	29.7

a Using technology, construct a scatter diagram for the data.

b Find and interpret the product moment correlation coefficient.

c Find the equation of the regression line.

d How far would you expect Thomas to ride on a 30°C day?

8 Find the exponential model connecting the variables:

a
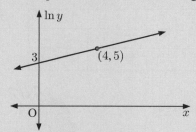

b
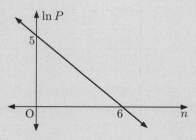

9 The rate of a chemical reaction decreases with time as the reactants are slowly consumed.

Time (t seconds)	75	100	125	150	175	200
Rate of reaction (R)	45.4	42.2	39.3	36.5	34.1	31.8

a Draw scatter diagrams of:
  i R against t **ii** $\ln R$ against t **iii** $\ln R$ against $\ln t$.

b Which model for R and t is most appropriate? Explain your answer.

c Find the model connecting R and t.

d Hence estimate the rate of reaction after 160 seconds. Comment on the reliability of your answer.

10 The table below shows the alarm volume required to wake a sleeping person under the influence of alcohol.

Alcohol reading (a g per 100 mL)	0.02	0.04	0.06	0.08
Volume (V dB)	35.5	40	43	45

a Draw scatter diagrams of:
  i V against a **ii** $\ln V$ against a **iii** $\ln V$ against $\ln a$.

b Which model is most appropriate for the data? Explain your answer.

c Find the model connecting V and a.

d Estimate the alarm volume required to wake a person with an alcohol reading of:
  i 0.15 g per 100 mL   **ii** 0.05 g per 100 mL.

Review set 21B

1 For each pair of variables, discuss whether the correlation between the variables is likely to be positive or negative, and whether a causal relationship exists between the variables:

  a *price of tickets* and *number of tickets sold*

  b *ice cream sales* and *number of shark attacks*.

2 For a group of foods, a correlation coefficient of 0.787 is found between the *fat content* and *energy*.

  a Describe the relationship between the variables.

  b Calculate the coefficient of determination, and interpret your answer.

3 A group of students is comparing their results for a Mathematics test and an Art project:

Student	A	B	C	D	E	F	G	H	I	J
Mathematics test	64	67	69	70	73	74	77	82	84	85
Art project	85	82	80	82	72	71	70	71	62	66

a Construct a scatter diagram for the data.

b Describe the relationship between the Mathematics and Art marks.

c Given that the coefficient of determination $r^2 \approx 0.864$, find the correlation coefficient r.

4 A craft shop sells canvasses in a variety of sizes. The table below shows the area and price of each canvas type.

Area (x cm^2)	100	225	300	625	850	900
Price (£y)	6	12	13	24	30	35

a Construct a scatter diagram for the data.

b Calculate the correlation coefficient r.

c Describe the correlation between *area* and *price*.

d Find the regression line, then draw the line on the scatter diagram.

e Estimate the price of a canvas with area 1200 cm^2. Discuss whether your estimate is likely to be reliable.

5 A drinks vendor varies the price of Supa-fizz on a daily basis. He records the number of sales of the drink as shown:

Price (p)	£2.50	£1.90	£1.60	£2.10	£2.20	£1.40	£1.70	£1.85
Sales (s)	389	450	448	386	381	458	597	431

a Produce a scatter diagram for the data.

b Are there any outliers? If so, should they be included in the analysis?

c Calculate the equation of the regression line.

d State and interpret the gradient of the regression line.

e Do you think the regression line would give a reliable prediction of sales if Supa-fizz was priced at 50 pence? Explain your answer.

6 Find the power model connecting x and y.

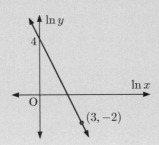

7 Winter frosts are important for producing good harvests of cherries and apples. The following data shows the *annual cherry yield* and *incidence of frosts* data for a cherry growing farm over a 7 year period.

Number of frosts (x)	27	23	7	37	32	14	16
Cherry yield (y tonnes)	5.6	4.8	3.1	7.2	6.1	3.7	3.8

   a Draw a scatter diagram for the data.

   b Determine the r and r^2 values.

   c Describe the association between *cherry yield* and the *number of frosts*.

   d Determine the equation of the regression line.

   e Use the equation of the line to predict:

      i the cherry yield in a year when 29 frosts were recorded

      ii the number of frosts in a year when the cherry yield was 4 tonnes.

8 Eight identical flower beds contain petunias. The different beds were watered different numbers of times each week, and the number of flowers each bed produced was recorded in the table below:

Number of waterings (n)	0	1	2	3	4	5	6	7
Flowers produced (f)	18	52	86	123	158	191	228	250

   a Draw a scatter diagram for the data, and describe the correlation between the variables.

   b Find the equation of the regression line.

   c Is it likely that a causal relationship exists between these two variables? Explain your answer.

   d Plot the regression line on the scatter diagram.

   e Violet has two beds of petunias. She waters one of the beds 5 times a fortnight and the other 10 times a week.

      i How many flowers can she expect from each bed?

      ii Discuss which of your estimates is likely to be more reliable.

9 A bird bath is filled with water. Over time, the water evaporates as shown in the table below:

Time (t hours)	3	6	9	12	15	18	21	24
Water remaining (V litres)	6.7	3.6	2	1.1	0.6	0.32	0.18	0.10

   a Draw scatter diagrams of:

      i V against t **ii** $\ln V$ against t

      iii $\ln V$ against $\ln t$.

   b Find an appropriate model connecting V and t.

   c Estimate the amount of water remaining in the bird bath after 5 hours.

   d Estimate the amount of water which has evaporated after 10 hours.

10 Gravity is the force of attraction which exists between any
two objects in the universe. The force of attraction F between
two spherical masses at various distances d apart is shown
below:

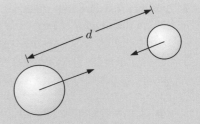

d (cm)	24	26	28	30	32	34	36	38	40
F (newtons)	237	202	174	152	133	118	105	95	85

a Find the model which best fits the data. Give reasons for your choice.

b Estimate the force of attraction between the two spheres if they are:

i 29 cm apart   **ii** 20 cm apart   **iii** 50 m apart.

22

Probability

Contents:

Opening problem

Roulette is a game in which a wheel labelled with the numbers from 0 to 36 is spun in one direction and a ball is spun within the wheel in the opposite direction. Players place bets on the number that the ball will land on.

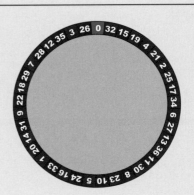

For one particular game of roulette:

- André bets on the number 16
- Beth bets on the numbers 0, 1, 2, and 3
- Charlie bets on all the even numbers.

Things to think about:

a What are the chances that:
   i Beth wins   **ii** both Beth and Charlie win?

b Is is *possible* for André and Beth to win at the same time?

c Let A, B, and C be the events that André, Beth, and Charlie win respectively. How can we draw a Venn diagram to illustrate these events?

From previous courses you should know that we measure the chance of an event happening using a number between 0 and 1 inclusive. We call this number a **probability**.

The number line below shows how we could interpret different probabilities:

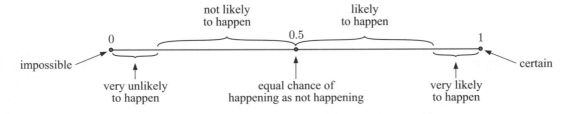

A   OUTCOMES AND SAMPLE SPACES

> In an experiment involving chance, we call any possible result from one trial of the experiment an **outcome**.
>
> A **sample space** $\mathcal{E}$ is the set of all possible outcomes of an experiment. It is also referred to as the **universal set** $\mathcal{E}$.

There are a variety of ways of representing or illustrating sample spaces, including:

- lists   • 2-dimensional grids   • tree diagrams   • Venn diagrams.

We will use Venn diagrams later in the Chapter.

LISTING OUTCOMES

Example 1
◀⑨ **Self Tutor**

List the sample space of possible outcomes for:

a tossing a coin

b rolling a normal die.

a When a coin is tossed, there are two possible outcomes.

∴   sample space = {H, T}

b When a normal die is rolled, there are 6 possible outcomes.

∴   sample space = {1, 2, 3, 4, 5, 6}

2-DIMENSIONAL GRIDS

When an experiment involves more than one operation we can still list the sample space. However, illustrating the sample space on a grid is often more efficient.

Example 2
◀⑨ **Self Tutor**

Use a 2-dimensional grid to illustrate the possible outcomes when two coins are tossed.

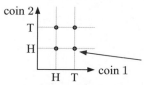

Each of the points on the grid represents one of the possible outcomes: {HH, HT, TH, TT}.

For example, this point represents "a tail with coin 1 and a head with coin 2", or TH.

TREE DIAGRAMS

The sample space in **Example 2** could also be illustrated using a tree diagram. The advantage of tree diagrams is that they can be used when more than two operations are involved.

Example 3
◀⑨ **Self Tutor**

Illustrate, using a tree diagram, the possible outcomes when:

a tossing two coins

b drawing two marbles from a bag containing many red, green, and yellow marbles.

a

coin 1	coin 2	possible outcomes
H	H	HH
	T	HT
T	H	TH
	T	TT

Each 'branch' gives a different outcome from the sample space {HH, HT, TH, TT}.

b

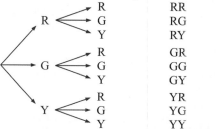

EXERCISE 22A

1 List the sample space for:

   a twirling a square spinner labelled A, B, C, D   **b** the sexes of a 2-child family

   c the order in which 4 blocks A, B, C, and D can be lined up

   d the 8 different 3-child families.

2 Illustrate on a 2-dimensional grid the sample space for:

   a rolling a die and tossing a coin simultaneously

   b rolling two dice

   c rolling a die and spinning a spinner with sides A, B, C, D

   d twirling two square spinners, one labelled A, B, C, D and the other 1, 2, 3, 4.

3 Illustrate on a tree diagram the sample space for:

   a tossing a 5-pence and a 10-pence coin simultaneously

   b tossing a coin and twirling an equilateral triangular spinner labelled A, B, C

   c twirling two equilateral triangular spinners labelled 1, 2, 3, and X, Y, Z

   d drawing two tickets from a hat containing a large number of pink, blue, and white tickets

   e tossing three coins simultaneously.

4 From the whole numbers 1 to 7, Adam selects an even number and Bill selects an odd number.

   a Illustrate the sample space:

      i by listing outcomes   **ii** on a 2-dimensional grid   **iii** on a tree diagram.

   b How many possible outcomes are there?

B   THEORETICAL PROBABILITY

Consider the octagonal spinner shown. Since the spinner is symmetrical, each spin could finish with equal likelihood on each of the sections marked 1 to 8.

The likelihood of obtaining a "4" would be 1 chance in 8, which equals $\frac{1}{8}$, $12\frac{1}{2}\%$, or 0.125.

This is a **mathematical** or **theoretical** probability of that outcome occurring in any trial of the experiment. It is based on what we theoretically expect to occur.

EVENTS

> An **event** is a set of outcomes with a particular property.

For example, for the octagonal spinner above, there are three outcomes (6, 7, and 8) which correspond to the event of spinning "6 or more". Since these are three of the eight total possible outcomes, and the outcomes are equally likely to occur, P(6 or more) $= \frac{3}{8}$.

We read $\frac{3}{8}$ as "3 chances in 8".

In general, for an event A containing **equally likely** possible outcomes, the probability of A occurring is

$$P(A) = \frac{\text{the number of outcomes in event } A}{\text{the total number of possible outcomes}} = \frac{n(A)}{n(\mathcal{E})}.$$

Example 4

◀» **Self Tutor**

A ticket is *randomly selected* from a basket containing 3 green, 4 yellow, and 5 blue tickets. Determine the probability of getting:

a   a green ticket

b   a green or yellow ticket

c   an orange ticket

d   a green, yellow, or blue ticket.

There are $3 + 4 + 5 = 12$ tickets which could be selected with equal chance.

a   P(G)

$= \frac{3}{12}$

$= \frac{1}{4}$

b   P(G or Y)

$= \frac{3+4}{12}$

$= \frac{7}{12}$

c   P(O)

$= \frac{0}{12}$

$= 0$

d   P(G, Y, or B)

$= \frac{3+4+5}{12}$

$= 1$

From **Example 4**, notice that:

- In **c** an orange result cannot occur. The probability is 0 because the event is *impossible*.
- In **d** a green, yellow, or blue is certain to occur. It is 100% likely, so the probability is 1.

For any event A, the probability $P(A)$ of A occurring satisfies $0 \leqslant P(A) \leqslant 1$.

Example 5

◀» **Self Tutor**

An ordinary six-sided die is rolled once. Determine the chance of:

a   getting a 6

b   not getting a 6

c   getting a 1 or 2

d   not getting a 1 or 2.

The sample space of possible outcomes is $\{1, 2, 3, 4, 5, 6\}$.

a   P(6)

$= \frac{1}{6}$

b   P(not a 6)

$= P(1, 2, 3, 4, \text{ or } 5)$

$= \frac{5}{6}$

c   P(1 or 2)

$= \frac{2}{6}$

$= \frac{1}{3}$

d   P(not a 1 or 2)

$= P(3, 4, 5, \text{ or } 6)$

$= \frac{4}{6}$

$= \frac{2}{3}$

COMPLEMENTARY EVENTS

Two events are **complementary** if exactly one of the events *must* occur.
If A is an event, then A' is the complementary event of A, or "not A".

$$P(A) + P(A') = 1$$

For example, in **Example 5** we notice that $P(6) + P(\text{not a } 6) = 1$

and that $P(1 \text{ or } 2) + P(\text{not a } 1 \text{ or } 2) = 1$.

This is no surprise as "6" and "not a 6" are complementary events. It is certain that one of the events will occur, and impossible for both of them to occur at the same time.

EXERCISE 22B.1

1 A marble is randomly selected from a box containing 5 green, 3 red, and 7 blue marbles. Determine the probability that the marble is:

   a red   **b** green   **c** blue

   d not red   **e** neither green nor blue   **f** green or red.

2 A carton of a dozen eggs contains eight brown eggs.
The rest are white.

   a How many white eggs are there in the carton?

   b Find the probability that an egg selected at random is:

      i brown   **ii** white.

3 A dart board has 36 sectors labelled 1 to 36. Determine the probability that a dart thrown at the centre of the board will hit a sector labelled with:

   a a multiple of 4

   b a number between 6 and 9 inclusive

   c a number greater than 20

   d 9   **e** a multiple of 13

   f an odd number that is a multiple of 3

   g a multiple of both 4 and 6

   h a multiple of 4 or 6, or both.

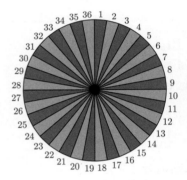

4 What is the probability that a randomly chosen person has his or her next birthday:

   a on a Tuesday   **b** on a weekend   **c** in July   **d** in January or February?

5   **a** List the six different orders in which Antti, Kai, and Neda may sit in a row.

   b If the three of them sit randomly in a row, determine the probability that:

      i Antti sits in the middle   **ii** Antti sits at the left end

      iii Antti does not sit at the right end   **iv** Kai and Neda are seated together.

6   **a** List the 8 possible 3-child families according to the gender of the children. For example, GGB means "*the first is a girl, the second is a girl, the third is a boy*".

   b Assuming that each of these is equally likely to occur, determine the probability that a randomly selected 3-child family consists of:

      i all boys   **ii** all girls   **iii** boy then girl then girl

      iv two girls and a boy   **v** a girl for the eldest   **vi** at least one boy.

7   **a** List, in systematic order, the 24 different orders in which four people A, B, C, and D may sit in a row.

   b Determine the probability that when the four people sit at random in a row:

      i A sits on one of the end seats

     ii B sits on one of the two middle seats

    iii A and B are seated together

     iv A, B, and C are seated together, not necessarily in that order.

USING GRIDS TO FIND PROBABILITIES

2-dimensional grids can give us excellent visual displays of sample spaces. We can use them to count favourable outcomes and hence calculate probabilities.

Example 6
🔊 **Self Tutor**

Use a 2-dimensional grid to illustrate the sample space for tossing a coin and rolling a die simultaneously. Hence determine the probability of:

a tossing a head   **b** tossing a tail and rolling a 5   **c** tossing a tail or rolling a 5.

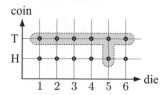

In probability, we take "a tail or a 5" to mean "a tail or a 5, or both".

There are 12 members in the sample space.

a $P(\text{head}) = \frac{6}{12} = \frac{1}{2}$

b $P(\text{tail and a '5'}) = \frac{1}{12}$

c $P(\text{tail or a '5'}) = \frac{7}{12}$ {the points in the shaded region}

EXERCISE 22B.2

1 Draw the grid of the sample space when a 5-pence and a 20-pence coin are tossed simultaneously. Hence determine the probability of tossing:

    a two heads   **b** two tails   **c** exactly one tail   **d** at most one tail.

2 A coin and a pentagonal spinner with sectors 1, 2, 3, 4, and 5 are tossed and spun respectively.

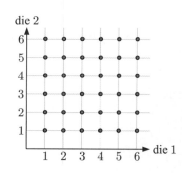

    a Draw a grid to illustrate the sample space of possible outcomes.

    b Use your grid to determine the chance of getting:

"A head or a 4" means "a head or a 4, or both".

       i a head and a 5

      ii a tail and a prime number

     iii an even number

     iv a head or a 4.

3 The 36 different possible results from rolling two dice are illustrated on the 2-dimensional grid.

    Use the grid to find the probability of rolling:

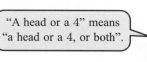

    a two 3s   **b** a 5 and a 6

    c a 5 or a 6 (or both)   **d** at least one 6

    e exactly one 6   **f** no sixes

    g a sum of 7   **h** a sum greater than 8

    i a sum of 7 or 11   **j** a sum of no more than 8.

Discussion

Three children have been tossing a coin in the air and recording the outcomes. They have done this 10 times and have recorded 10 tails. Before the next toss they make these statements:

Jackson: "It's got to be a head next time!"

Sally: "No, it always has an equal chance of being a head or a tail. The coin cannot remember what the outcomes have been."

Amy: "Actually, I think it will probably be a tail again, because I think the coin must be biased. It might be weighted so it is more likely to give a tail."

Discuss the statements of each child. Who do you think is correct?

C   COMPOUND EVENTS

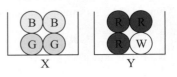

Suppose box X contains 2 blue and 2 green balls, and box Y contains 1 white and 3 red balls. A ball is randomly selected from each of the boxes. Determine the probability of selecting "a blue ball from X *and* a red ball from Y".

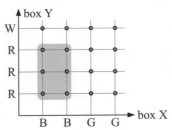

By illustrating the sample space on the 2-dimensional grid shown, we can see that 6 of the 16 possibilities are blue from X and red from Y. Each of the outcomes is equally likely, so

$$P(\text{blue from X } and \text{ red from Y}) = \tfrac{6}{16}.$$

We call this situation a **compound event** because two selections are being made at the same time.

INDEPENDENT EVENTS

> Events are **independent** if the occurrence of each of them does not affect the probability that the other occurs.

Consider again the example above.

Suppose we happen to choose a blue ball from box X. This does not affect the outcome when we choose a ball from box Y. The probability of selecting a red ball from box Y is $\frac{3}{4}$ regardless of which colour ball is selected from box X.

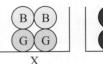

Similarly, the selection from box Y does not affect the outcome of the selection from box X.

So, the two events "a blue ball from X" and "a red ball from Y" are independent.

> If A and B are **independent events** then $P(A \text{ and } B) = P(A) \times P(B).$

This rule can be extended for any number of independent events.

For example: If A, B, and C are all **independent events**, then
$P(A \text{ and } B \text{ and } C) = P(A) \times P(B) \times P(C).$

Example 7
🔊 **Self Tutor**

A coin and a die are tossed and rolled simultaneously. Determine the probability of getting a head and a 3 without using a grid.

P(a head and a 3) = P(H) × P(3)   {events are independent}

$$= \tfrac{1}{2} \times \tfrac{1}{6}$$

$$= \tfrac{1}{12}$$

Events that are *not* independent are called **dependent events**. In this course we will only consider probability calculations for independent events.

EXERCISE 22C

1 Suppose these spinners are each spun once. Find the probability of spinning:

   a a green with spinner 1 and a blue with spinner 2

   b a red with both spinners.

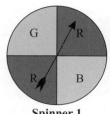 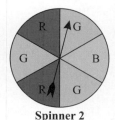

     Spinner 1   Spinner 2

2 A coin is tossed 3 times. Determine the probability of getting the following sequences of results:

   a head, head, head

   b tail, head, tail.

3 A school has two photocopiers. On any one day, machine A has an 8% chance of malfunctioning and machine B has a 12% chance of malfunctioning. Determine the probability that on any one day both machines will:

   a malfunction

   b work effectively.

4 A couple would like to have 4 children, none of whom will be adopted. If the couple are given their wish, find the probability that the children will:

   a be born in the order boy, girl, boy, girl

   b *not* be born in the order boy, girl, boy, girl.

5 Two marksmen fire at a target simultaneously. Jiri hits the target 70% of the time and Benita hits it 80% of the time. Determine the probability that:

   a they both hit the target

   b they both miss the target

   c Jiri hits but Benita misses

   d Benita hits but Jiri misses.

6

An archer hits the bullseye on average 2 out of every 5 shots. If 3 arrows are fired at the target, determine the probability that the bullseye is hit:

   a every time

   b the first two times, but not on the third shot

   c on no occasion.

D | TREE DIAGRAMS

Tree diagrams can be used to illustrate sample spaces provided the possible outcomes are not too numerous. The tree diagram can then be used to determine probabilities.

Consider two archers Li and Yuka firing simultaneously at a target. The results are independent events. Li has probability $\frac{3}{4}$ of hitting the target, and Yuka has probability $\frac{4}{5}$.

The tree diagram for this information is given below using $H = $ hit and $M = $ miss.

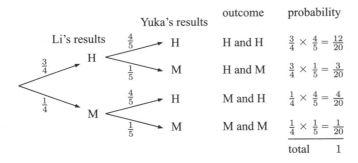

	outcome	probability
	H and H	$\frac{3}{4} \times \frac{4}{5} = \frac{12}{20}$
	H and M	$\frac{3}{4} \times \frac{1}{5} = \frac{3}{20}$
	M and H	$\frac{1}{4} \times \frac{4}{5} = \frac{4}{20}$
	M and M	$\frac{1}{4} \times \frac{1}{5} = \frac{1}{20}$
	total	1

Notice that:

- The probabilities for hitting and missing are marked on the branches.
- There are *four* alternative branches, each showing a particular outcome.
- All outcomes are represented.
- The probability of each outcome is obtained by **multiplying** the probabilities along its branch.

Example 8   ◀) Self Tutor

Carl is not having much luck lately. His car will only start 80% of the time and his motorbike will only start 60% of the time, independently of one another.

a Draw a tree diagram to illustrate this situation.

b Use the tree diagram to determine the chance that on the next attempt:
  i both will start   **ii** Carl can only use his car.

a Let C be the event that Carl's car starts, and M be the event that his motorbike starts.

car	motorbike	outcome	probability
	M	C and M	$0.8 \times 0.6 = 0.48$
C	M'	C and M'	$0.8 \times 0.4 = 0.32$
	M	C' and M	$0.2 \times 0.6 = 0.12$
C'	M'	C' and M'	$0.2 \times 0.4 = 0.08$
		total	1.00

b i   P(both start)
       $= $ P(C and M)
       $= 0.8 \times 0.6$
       $= 0.48$

ii   P(car starts but motorbike does not)
       $= $ P(C and M')
       $= 0.8 \times 0.4$
       $= 0.32$

If there is more than one outcome that results in an event occurring, then we need to **add** the probabilities of these outcomes.

Example 9

◄)) **Self Tutor**

Liam rolls a six-sided die twice. Determine the probability that exactly 1 four is rolled.

Let A be the event that a four is rolled on the first roll, and B be the event that a four is rolled on the second roll.

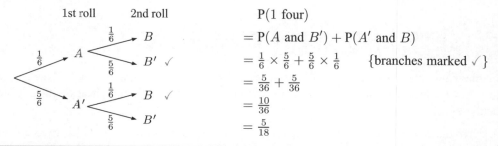

1st roll   2nd roll

$P(1 \text{ four})$

$= P(A \text{ and } B') + P(A' \text{ and } B)$

$= \frac{1}{6} \times \frac{5}{6} + \frac{5}{6} \times \frac{1}{6}$ {branches marked ✓}

$= \frac{5}{36} + \frac{5}{36}$

$= \frac{10}{36}$

$= \frac{5}{18}$

EXERCISE 22D

1 For a particular household, there is a 90% chance that at the end of the week the rubbish bin is full, and a 50% chance that the recycling bin is full, independently of one another.

   a Draw a tree diagram to illustrate this situation.

   b Find the probability that at the end of the week:

     i both bins are full   **ii** only 1 bin is full.

2 Suppose this spinner is spun twice.

   a Copy and complete the branches on the tree diagram:

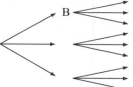

   b Find the probability that:

     i black appears on both spins

     ii yellow appears on both spins

     iii different colours appear on the two spins

     iv black appears on either of the spins.

3 One ball is drawn from each of the bags shown.

   a Draw a tree diagram to illustrate this situation.

   b Find the probability that:

     i 3 blue balls are drawn

     ii green balls are drawn from bags Y and Z

     iii at least one blue ball is drawn.

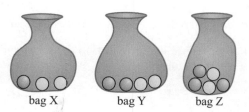

bag X   bag Y   bag Z

4 Kane plays 3 matches in a darts challenge, alternating between Penny and Quentin as his opponents.

Kane must win 2 matches in a row to win the challenge.

Kane is allowed to choose whether he plays against Penny - Quentin - Penny, or against Quentin - Penny - Quentin. He knows that Penny is the better darts player.

Which strategy should Kane use to maximise his chances of winning the challenge? Justify your answer.

E   SETS AND VENN DIAGRAMS

Venn diagrams are a useful way of representing the events in a sample space. These diagrams usually consist of a rectangle which represents the complete sample space $\mathcal{E}$, and circles within it which represent particular events.

Venn diagrams can be used to solve certain types of probability questions and also to establish a number of probability laws. In these cases, the universal set $\mathcal{E}$ is the set of all possible outcomes, and an event A of outcomes with a particular property is a set within $\mathcal{E}$.

For example, when we roll an ordinary die, the sample space or universal set is $\mathcal{E} = \{1, 2, 3, 4, 5, 6\}$.

If the event A is "a number less than 3", then there are two outcomes which satisfy event A. We can write $A = \{1, 2\}$.

The Venn diagram alongside illustrates the event A within the universal set $\mathcal{E}$.

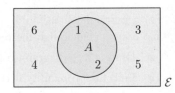

$n(\mathcal{E}) = 6$ and $n(A) = 2$,   so $\text{P}(A) = \dfrac{n(A)}{n(\mathcal{E})} = \dfrac{2}{6} = \dfrac{1}{3}$.

SET NOTATION

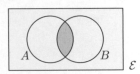

The **universal set** or **sample space** $\mathcal{E}$ is represented by a rectangle. A set within the universal set is usually represented by a circle.

A' (shaded green) is the **complement** of A (shaded purple). A' represents the non-occurrence of A, so $\text{P}(A) + \text{P}(A') = 1$.

For example, if $\mathcal{E} = \{1, 2, 3, 4, 5, 6, 7\}$ and $A = \{2, 4, 6\}$ then $A' = \{1, 3, 5, 7\}$.

- $x \in A$ reads "x is in A" and means that x is an element of the set A.

- $n(A)$ reads "the number of elements in set A".

- $A \cap B$ is the **intersection** of sets A and B. This set contains all elements common to **both** sets.

$A \cap B$ is shaded in purple.

$$A \cap B = \{x : x \in A \ \textbf{and} \ x \in B\}$$

- $A \cup B$ is the **union** of sets A and B. This set contains all elements belonging to A **or** B (**or both** A **and** B).

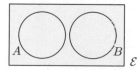

$A \cup B$ is shaded in purple.

$$A \cup B = \{x : x \in A \ \textbf{or} \ x \in B\}$$

- **Disjoint sets** are sets which do not have elements in common.

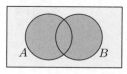

These two sets are disjoint.

$A \cap B = \varnothing$ where $\varnothing$ denotes the **empty set**.

A and B are said to be **mutually exclusive**.

Example 10 ◄⑴ Self Tutor

Suppose A is the set of all factors of 24, and B is the set of all factors of 28.
$\mathcal{E} = \{x : 1 \leqslant x \leqslant 28, \ x \in \mathbb{Z}\}$

a Find $A \cap B$.   **b** Illustrate A and B on a Venn diagram.   **c** Find $A \cup B$.

$A = \{1, 2, 3, 4, 6, 8, 12, 24\}$ and $B = \{1, 2, 4, 7, 14, 28\}$

a $A \cap B$ is the set of factors common to both 24 **and** 28 $= \{1, 2, 4\}$

b

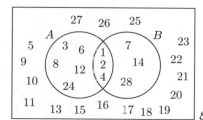

c $A \cup B$ is the set of factors of 24 **or** 28 (or both)
$= \{1, 2, 3, 4, 6, 7, 8, 12, 14, 24, 28\}$

Example 11 ◄⑴ Self Tutor

On separate Venn diagrams containing two events A and B that intersect, shade the region representing:

a in A but not in B **b** neither in A nor B.

a The set "in A but not in B" is shaded green.

b The set "neither in A nor B" is shaded green.

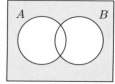

$A \cap B'$ $(A \cup B)'$

To practise shading the regions represented by various subsets, click on the icon.

VENN DIAGRAMS

EXERCISE 22E

1 Let A be the set of all factors of 6, B be the set of all positive even integers less than 11, and $\mathcal{E} = \{x : 1 \leqslant x \leqslant 10, \ x \in \mathbb{Z}\}$.

   a List the elements of A and B.

   b Illustrate A and B on a Venn diagram.

   c Find:

      i $n(A)$　　　**ii** $A \cup B$　　　**iii** $A \cap B$

2 On separate Venn diagrams containing two events A and B that intersect, shade the region representing:

   a in A　　　　　　　　　　　**b** in B

   c in both A and B　　　　　**d** in A or B

   e in B but not in A　　　　**f** in exactly one of A or B.

PRINTABLE VENN DIAGRAMS

3 If A and B are two intersecting sets, shade the region on separate Venn diagrams representing:

   a A'　　　　　**b** $A' \cap B$　　　　　**c** $A \cup B'$　　　　　**d** $A' \cap B'$

4 The diagram alongside is the most general case for three events in the same sample space $\mathcal{E}$.

On separate Venn diagrams, shade:

   a A　　　　　　**b** B'　　　　　　**c** $B \cap C$

   d $A \cup C$　　　　**e** $A \cap B \cap C$　　　**f** $(A \cup B) \cap C$

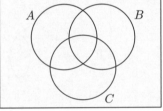

PRINTABLE VENN DIAGRAMS

Example 12

◀)) **Self Tutor**

The Venn diagram alongside illustrates the number of people in a sporting club who play tennis (T) and hockey (H).

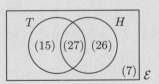

We use brackets to indicate the number of elements in a region.

Determine the number of people:

   a in the club　　　　　　　　　**b** who play hockey

   c who play both sports　　　　**d** who play neither of these sports

   e who play at least one of these sports.

a Number in the club $= 15 + 27 + 26 + 7 = 75$
b Number who play hockey $= 27 + 26 = 53$
c Number who play both sports $= 27$
d Number who play neither of these sports $= 7$
e Number who play at least one of these sports
$= 15 + 27 + 26 = 68$

5 The Venn diagram alongside illustrates the number of students in a particular class who study Chemistry (C) and History (H). Determine the number of students:

a in the class   **b** who study both of these subjects
c who study at least one of these subjects
d who only study Chemistry.

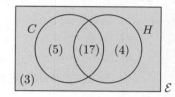

Example 13   ◄)) **Self Tutor**

The Venn diagram alongside represents the set $\mathcal{E}$ of all children in a class. Each dot represents a student. The event E shows all those students with blue eyes.

Determine the probability that a randomly selected child:
a has blue eyes   **b** does not have blue eyes.

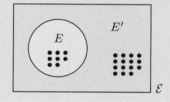

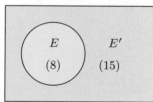

$n(\mathcal{E}) = 23$, $n(E) = 8$

a P(blue eyes) $= \dfrac{n(E)}{n(\mathcal{E})}$
$= \dfrac{8}{23}$

b   P(not blue eyes) $= \dfrac{n(E')}{n(\mathcal{E})}$
$= \dfrac{15}{23}$

or   P(not blue eyes) $= 1 - $ P(blue eyes)
$= 1 - \dfrac{8}{23}$
$= \dfrac{15}{23}$

---

6 The Venn diagram alongside represents the set $\mathcal{E}$ of all cars in a car park. The event R corresponds to cars that are red. Determine the probability that a randomly selected car:

a is red   **b** is not red.

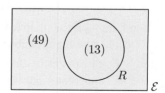

7 In a survey at an alpine resort, people were asked whether they liked skiing (S) or snowboarding (B .

Determine the probability that a randomly chosen person at the resort likes:

a both activities

b neither activity

c exactly one activity.

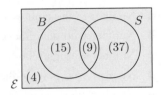

Example 14   ◀) Self Tutor

In a class of 30 students, 19 study Physics, 17 study Chemistry, and 15 study both of these subjects.

a Display this information on a Venn diagram.

b Hence determine the probability that a randomly selected class member studies:

   i both subjects   **ii** at least one of the subjects

  iii Physics but not Chemistry   **iv** exactly one of the subjects

   v neither subject.

a

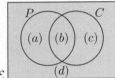

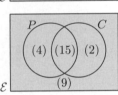

Let P represent the event of 'studying Physics' and C represent the event of 'studying Chemistry'.

Now
$$a + b = 19 \quad \{19 \text{ study Physics}\}$$
$$b + c = 17 \quad \{17 \text{ study Chemistry}\}$$
$$b = 15 \quad \{15 \text{ study both}\}$$
$$a + b + c + d = 30 \quad \{\text{there are 30 in the class}\}$$
$$\therefore \quad b = 15, \ a = 4, \ c = 2, \ d = 9.$$

b **i** P(studies both)

    $= \frac{15}{30}$ or $\frac{1}{2}$

ii P(studies at least one subject)

  $= \frac{4+15+2}{30}$

  $= \frac{7}{10}$

iii P(P but not C)

  $= \frac{4}{30}$

  $= \frac{2}{15}$

iv P(studies exactly one)

  $= \frac{4+2}{30}$

  $= \frac{1}{5}$

v P(studies neither)

  $= \frac{9}{30}$

  $= \frac{3}{10}$

---

8 50 married men were asked whether they gave their wife flowers or chocolates for her last birthday.   31 gave chocolates, 12 gave flowers, and 5 gave both chocolates and flowers.

a Display this information on a Venn diagram.

b If one of the married men was chosen at random, determine the probability that he gave his wife:

   i chocolates or flowers

  ii chocolates but not flowers

  iii neither chocolates nor flowers.

9 In a class of 40 students, 19 play tennis, 20 play netball, and 8 play neither of these sports. A student is randomly chosen from the class. Determine the probability that the student:

    a plays tennis   **b** does not play netball

    c plays at least one of the sports   **d** plays exactly one of the sports

    e plays netball but not tennis.

10 The medical records for a class of 30 children showed that 24 had previously had measles, 12 had previously had measles and mumps, and 26 had previously had at least one of measles or mumps. If one child from the class is selected at random, determine the probability that he or she has had:

    a mumps   **b** mumps but not measles   **c** neither mumps nor measles.

11 The Venn diagram opposite indicates the types of programs a group of 40 individuals watched on television last night.

M represents movies, S represents sports, and D represents dramas.

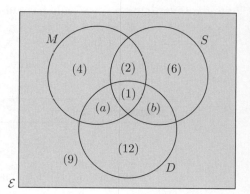

    a Given that 10 people watched a movie last night, calculate a and b.

    b Find the probability that one of these individuals, selected at random, watched:

        i sport   **ii** drama and sport

        iii a movie but not sport

        iv drama but not a movie

        v drama or a movie.

F THE ADDITION LAW OF PROBABILITY

Suppose there are two events A and B in a sample space $\mathcal{E}$.

In the following **Investigation** we look for a formula for the probability of *at least one* of the events occurring. We write this as $\mathrm{P}(A \cup B)$.

Investigation   The addition law of probability

What to do:

1 Suppose $\mathcal{E} = \{x : x \text{ is a positive integer less than } 100\}$.

    Let $A = \{\text{multiples of 7 in } \mathcal{E}\}$ and $B = \{\text{multiples of 5 in } \mathcal{E}\}$.

    a How many elements are there in:

        i A **ii** B **iii** $A \cap B$ **iv** $A \cup B$?

    b Show that $n(A \cup B) = n(A) + n(B) - n(A \cap B)$.

2 By comparing shaded regions of Venn diagrams, verify that $n(A \cup B) = n(A) + n(B) - n(A \cap B)$ for all sets A and B in a universal set $\mathcal{E}$.

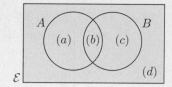

3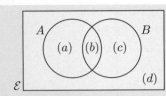

a From the Venn diagram, explain why

$$P(A) = \frac{a+b}{a+b+c+d}.$$

b Use the Venn diagram to find:

   i $P(B)$ **ii** $P(A \cap B)$ **iii** $P(A \cup B)$ **iv** $P(A) + P(B) - P(A \cap B)$

c State the connection between $P(A \cup B)$ and $P(A) + P(B) - P(A \cap B)$.

From the **Investigation** you should have discovered the **addition law of probability**:

For two events A and B, $P(A \cup B) = P(A) + P(B) - P(A \cap B)$

which means: $P(\textbf{either } A \textbf{ or } B \textbf{ or } \text{both}) = P(A) + P(B) - P(\textbf{both } A \textbf{ and } B)$.

Example 15   ◀ﻪ) Self Tutor

If $P(A) = 0.6$, $P(A \cup B) = 0.7$, and $P(A \cap B) = 0.3$, find $P(B)$.

$$P(A \cup B) = P(A) + P(B) - P(A \cap B)$$
$$\therefore \quad 0.7 = 0.6 + P(B) - 0.3$$
$$\therefore \quad P(B) = 0.4$$

If A and B are disjoint **mutually exclusive** events then $P(A \cap B) = 0$ and so the addition law becomes $P(A \cup B) = P(A) + P(B)$.

Example 16   ◀ﻪ) Self Tutor

A class of 30 students was given a History test. 7 students scored an A and 11 students scored a B.

A student is randomly selected. Let A be the event that the student scored an A, and B be the event that the student scored a B.

a Are A and B mutually exclusive?

b Find:

   i $P(A)$ **ii** $P(B)$ **iii** $P(A \cap B)$ **iv** $P(A \cup B)$

a It is impossible for a student to score both an A and a B for the test.

   $\therefore$ A and B are mutually exclusive.

b **i** $P(A) = \frac{7}{30}$ **ii** $P(B) = \frac{11}{30}$

    iii $P(A \cap B) = 0$ **iv** $P(A \cup B) = P(A) + P(B)$

        $\{A$ and B are mutually exclusive$\}$ $= \frac{7}{30} + \frac{11}{30}$

                                                      $= \frac{3}{5}$

EXERCISE 22F

1 If $P(A) = 0.2$, $P(B) = 0.4$, and $P(A \cap B) = 0.05$, find $P(A \cup B)$.

2 If $P(A) = 0.4$, $P(A \cup B) = 0.9$, and $P(A \cap B) = 0.1$, find $P(B)$.

3 If $P(X) = 0.6$, $P(Y) = 0.5$, and $P(X \cup Y) = 0.9$, find $P(X \cap Y)$.

4 Suppose $P(A) = 0.25$, $P(B) = 0.45$, and $P(A \cup B) = 0.7$.

   a Find $P(A \cap B)$.   **b** What can you say about A and B?

5 A and B are mutually exclusive events.
   If $P(B) = 0.45$ and $P(A \cup B) = 0.8$, find $P(A)$.

6 20 swimmers are selected for a national swimming team.
5 of the swimmers were born in Birmingham, and 3 of the
swimmers were born in Manchester.
A swimmer is selected at random. Let B be the event that
the swimmer was born in Birmingham, and M be the event
that the swimmer was born in Manchester.

   a Are B and M mutually exclusive?

   b Find:

     i $P(B)$ **ii** $P(M)$ **iii** $P(B \cap M)$ **iv** $P(B \cup M)$

7 Suppose A and B are mutually exclusive, and that A' and B' are mutually exclusive. Find $P(A \cup B)$.

Review set 22A

1 **a** List the different orders in which 4 people A, B, C, and D could line up.

   b If they line up at random, determine the probability that:

     i A is next to C   **ii** there is exactly one person between A and C.

2 A coin is tossed and a square spinner labelled A, B, C, D, is twirled. Determine the probability of
obtaining:

   a a head and consonant   **b** a tail and C   **c** a tail or a vowel (or both).

3 The probability that a man will be alive in 25 years is $\frac{3}{5}$, and the probability that his wife will be
alive is $\frac{2}{3}$. Determine the probability that in 25 years:

   a both will be alive   **b** at least one will be alive   **c** only the wife will be alive.

4 Given $P(Y) = 0.35$ and $P(X \cup Y) = 0.8$, and that X and Y are mutually exclusive events, find:

   a $P(X \cap Y)$ **b** $P(X)$ **c** $P(X$ or Y but not both).

5 **a** Graph the sample space of all possible outcomes when a pair of dice is rolled.

   b Hence, determine the probability of getting:

     i a sum of 7 or 11   **ii** a sum of at least 8.

6 In a group of 40 students, 22 study Economics, 25 study Law, and 3 study neither of these subjects.

   a Draw a Venn diagram to display this information.

   b Determine the probability that a randomly chosen student studies:

     i both Economics and Law   **ii** at least one of these subjects.

7 A school photocopier has a 95% chance of working on any particular day. Find the probability that it will be working on at least one of the next two days.

8 Suppose A and B are independent events, $P(A) = 0.4$, and $P(B) = 0.7$.

  a Calculate $P(A \cap B)$. Hence explain why A and B cannot be mutually exclusive.

  b Calculate $P(A \cup B)$.

Review set 22B

1 Suppose $P(A) = m$ is the probability of event A occurring in any given trial.

  a Write $P(A')$ in terms of m.

  b State the range of possible values of m.

  c Suppose two trials are performed independently. Find, in terms of m, the probability of A occurring:

    i exactly once   **ii** at least once.

2 **a** Systematically list the possible sexes of a 4-child family.

  b Hence, determine the probability that a randomly selected 4-child family has two children of each sex.

3 A bag contains 3 red, 4 yellow, and 5 blue marbles. Two marbles are randomly selected from the bag with replacement. Find the probability that:

  a both are blue   **b** they are the same colour

  c at least one is red   **d** exactly one is yellow.

4 A class contains 25 students. 13 play tennis, 14 play volleyball, and 1 plays neither of these sports. A student is randomly selected from the class. Determine the probability that the student:

  a plays both tennis and volleyball   **b** plays at least one of these sports.

5 The students A, B, and C have 10%, 20%, and 30% chance of independently solving a certain maths problem. If they all try independently of one another, what is the probability that at least one of them will solve the problem?

6 Two events are defined such that $P(A) = 0.11$ and $P(B) = 0.7$.

  a Calculate $P(A')$.

  b Find $P(A \cap B)$ given A and B are independent events.

  c If instead, A and B are mutually exclusive events, find $P(A \cup B)$.

7 Suppose $P(A) = 0.2$ and $P(B) = 0.5$. Find $P(A \cup B)$ given that A and B are:

  a mutually exclusive   **b** independent.

8 A and B are independent events. Prove that A' and B' are also independent events.
  Hint: $A' \cap B' = (A \cup B)'$

23

Statistical distributions

Contents:

Opening problem

Theresa flipped a coin 20 times and got 15 heads.

Things to think about:

a   If we assume Theresa's coin is a *fair* coin, what was the probability of getting this outcome?

b   Theresa suspects that the coin might be *biased*.

   i   How can we write Theresa's claim as a mathematical statement?

   ii   How can we test to see whether Theresa's claim is justified?

Many variables in the world around us depend on chance events. Examples of such variables are:

- the number of players in your football team who will score a goal in the next match
- the time it will take you to travel to school tomorrow
- the sum of the values when three dice are rolled.

Because of the element of chance in these variables, we cannot predict the exact value they will take when next measured. However, we can often determine the *possible values* the variable can take, and we can assign to each possible value the **probability** of it occurring. This allows us to determine which outcomes are most likely, and to assess whether claims made about a set of data are reasonable.

In this Chapter we will extend the ideas of probability covered in **Chapter 22** to model the random variation or **distribution** of numerical variables.

A   RANDOM VARIABLES

> A **random variable** uses numbers to describe the possible outcomes which could result from a random experiment.

A random variable is often represented by a capital letter such as X.

Random variables can be either **discrete** or **continuous**.

> A **discrete random variable** X has a set of distinct possible values.

For example, X could be:

- the number of wickets a bowler takes in an innings of cricket, so X could take the values 0, 1, 2, ..., 10
- the number of defective light bulbs in a purchase order of 50, so X could take the values 0, 1, 2, ..., 50.

To determine the value of a discrete random variable, we need to **count**.

> A **continuous random variable** X can take any value within some interval on the number line.

For example, X could be:

- the heights of men, which would all lie in the interval $50 \text{ cm} < X < 250 \text{ cm}$
- the volume of water in a rainwater tank, which could lie in the interval $0 \text{ m}^3 < X < 100 \text{ m}^3$.

To determine the value of a continuous random variable, we need to **measure**.

DISCRETE RANDOM VARIABLES

In this course we will only consider discrete random variables with a finite number of outcomes, so we label them $x_1, x_2, x_3, ..., x_n$.

Example 1 ◀) **Self Tutor**

A supermarket has three checkouts A, B, and C. A government inspector checks the weighing scales for accuracy at each checkout. The random variable X is the number of accurate weighing scales at the supermarket.

a List the possible outcomes and the corresponding values of X.

b What value(s) of X correspond to there being:

    i one accurate scale   **ii** at least one accurate scale?

a Possible outcomes:

A	B	C	X
✗	✗	✗	0
✓	✗	✗	1
✗	✓	✗	1
✗	✗	✓	1
✗	✓	✓	2
✓	✗	✓	2
✓	✓	✗	2
✓	✓	✓	3

b   **i** $X = 1$

    ii $X = 1, 2,$ or 3

EXERCISE 23A

1 Classify each random variable as continuous or discrete:

  a the quantity of fat in a sausage

  b the mark out of 50 for a geography test

  c the weight of a Year 12 student

  d the volume of water in a cup of coffee

  e the number of trout in a lake

  f the number of hairs on a cat

  g the length of a horse's mane

  h the height of a sky-scraper.

2 For each scenario:

    i Identify the random variable being considered.

    ii State whether the variable is continuous or discrete.

    iii Give possible values for the random variable.

  a To measure the rainfall over a 24-hour period in Singapore, water is collected in a rain gauge.

  b To investigate the stopping distance for a tyre with a new tread pattern, a braking experiment is carried out.

  c To check the reliability of a new type of light switch, switches are repeatedly turned off and on until they fail.

3 Suppose the spinners alongside are spun, and X is the sum of the numbers.

  a Explain why X is a discrete random variable.

  b State the possible values of X.

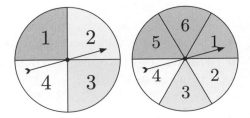

4 In the finals series of a baseball championship, the first team to win 4 games wins the championship.

Let X represent the number of games played in the finals series.

  a State the possible values of X.

  b What value(s) of X correspond to the series lasting:

    i exactly 5 games   **ii** at least 6 games?

5 A supermarket has four checkouts A, B, C, and D. Management checks the weighing devices at each checkout. The random variable X is the number of weighing devices which are accurate.

  a What values can X have?

  b List the possible outcomes and the corresponding values of X.

  c What value(s) of X correspond to:

    i exactly two devices being accurate

    ii at least two devices being accurate?

6 Suppose three coins are tossed simultaneously. The random variable X is the number of heads that result.

  a State the possible values of X.

  b List the possible outcomes and the corresponding values of X.

  c Are the possible values of X equally likely to occur? Explain your answer.

B DISCRETE PROBABILITY DISTRIBUTIONS

For any random variable, there is a corresponding **probability distribution** which describes the probability that the variable will take a particular value.

The probability that the variable X takes value x is denoted $P(X = x)$.

If X is a random variable with possible values $\{x_1, x_2, x_3, ..., x_n\}$ and corresponding probabilities $\{p_1, p_2, p_3, ..., p_n\}$ such that $P(X = x_i) = p_i$, $i = 1, ..., n$, then:

- $0 \leqslant p_i \leqslant 1$ for all $i = 1, ..., n$

- $\sum_{i=1}^{n} p_i = p_1 + p_2 + p_3 + ... + p_n = 1$

- $\{p_1, ..., p_n\}$ describes the **probability distribution** of X.

For example, suppose X is the number of heads obtained when 2 coins are tossed. The possible values for X are $\{0, 1, 2\}$ with corresponding probabilities $\{\frac{1}{4}, \frac{1}{2}, \frac{1}{4}\}$. We see that $0 \leqslant p_i \leqslant 1$ for each value of i, and that the probabilities add up to 1.

We can display this probability distribution in a **table** or a **graph**.

x	0	1	2
$P(X = x)$	$\frac{1}{4}$	$\frac{1}{2}$	$\frac{1}{4}$

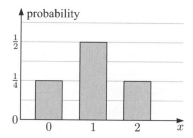

UNIFORM DISCRETE RANDOM VARIABLES

If the possible values $x_1, x_2, ..., x_n$ of a discrete random variable X all have the same probability $\frac{1}{n}$ of occurring, then X is a **uniform discrete random variable**.

An example of a uniform discrete random variable is the result X when a die is rolled. The possible values of X are 1, 2, 3, 4, 5, and 6, and each value has probability $\frac{1}{6}$ of occurring.

By contrast, if two dice are rolled, the sum of the resulting numbers Y is *not* a uniform discrete random variable.

THE MODE AND MEDIAN

The **mode** of a discrete probability distribution is the most frequently occurring value of the variable. This is the data value x_i whose probability p_i is the highest.

The **median** of the distribution corresponds to the 50th percentile. If the possible values $\{x_1, x_2, x_3, ..., x_n\}$ are listed in ascending order, the median is the value x_j when the cumulative sum $p_1 + p_2 + ... + p_j$ reaches 0.5.

Example 2
◀) **Self Tutor**

A magazine store recorded the number of magazines purchased by its customers in one week. 23% purchased one magazine, 38% purchased two, 21% purchased three, 13% purchased four, and 5% purchased five. Let X be the number of magazines sold to a randomly selected customer.

a State the possible values of X.

b Construct a probability table for X.

c Graph the probability distribution.

d Find the mode and median of the distribution.

a $X = 1, 2, 3, 4,$ or 5

b

x	1	2	3	4	5
$P(X = x)$	0.23	0.38	0.21	0.13	0.05

c

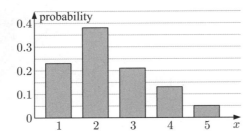

d Customers are most likely to buy 2 magazines, so this is the mode of the distribution.

$$p_1 = 0.23$$
$$p_1 + p_2 = 0.23 + 0.38 = 0.61$$

Since $p_1 + p_2 \geqslant 0.5$, the median is 2 magazines.

We can also describe the probability distribution of a random variable using a **probability function** $p(x) = P(X = x)$. The domain of the probability function is the set of possible values of the variable, and the range is the set of values in the probability distribution.

Example 3
◀) **Self Tutor**

Show that $p(x) = \dfrac{x^2 + 1}{34}$, $x = 1, 2, 3, 4$ is a valid probability function.

$p(1) = \frac{2}{34}$, $p(2) = \frac{5}{34}$, $p(3) = \frac{10}{34}$, $p(4) = \frac{17}{34}$

All of these obey $0 \leqslant p(x_i) \leqslant 1$, and $\displaystyle\sum_{i=1}^{n} p(x_i) = \frac{2}{34} + \frac{5}{34} + \frac{10}{34} + \frac{17}{34} = 1$

$\therefore$ $p(x)$ is a valid probability function.

EXERCISE 23B

1 **a** State whether each of the following is a valid probability distribution:

i

x	1	2	3	4
P($X = x$)	0.2	0.4	0.15	0.25

ii

x	0	1	2	3
P($X = x$)	0.2	0.3	0.4	0.2

iii

x	0	1	2	3	4
P($X = x$)	0.2	0.2	0.2	0.2	0.2

iv

x	2	3	4	5
P($X = x$)	0.3	0.4	0.5	-0.2

b For which of the probability distributions in **a** is X a uniform random variable?

2 Find k in each of these probability distributions:

a

x	0	1	2
P($X = x$)	0.3	k	0.5

b

x	0	1	2	3
P($X = x$)	k	$2k$	$3k$	k

3 Consider the probability distribution alongside.

x	0	1	2	3
P($X = x$)	0.1	0.25	0.45	a

    a Find the value of a.

    b Is X a uniform discrete random variable? Explain your answer.

    c Find the mode of the distribution.

    d Find P($X \geqslant 2$).

4 The probability distribution for Jason scoring X home runs in each game during his baseball career is given in the following table:

x	0	1	2	3	4	5
$p(x)$	a	0.3333	0.1088	0.0084	0.0007	0.0000

    a State the value of $p(2)$.

    b Find the value of a. Explain what this number means.

    c Find the value of $p(1) + p(2) + p(3) + p(4) + p(5)$. Explain what this means.

    d Draw a graph of $p(x)$ against x.

    e Find the mode and median of the distribution.

5 A policeman inspected the safety of tyres on cars passing through a checkpoint. The number of tyres X which needed replacing on each car followed the probability distribution below.

x	0	1	2	3	4
P($X = x$)	0.68	0.2	0.06	k	0.02

    a Find the value of k.

    b Find the mode of the distribution.

    c Find P($X > 1$), and interpret this value.

6 Let X be the result when the spinner alongside is spun.

   a Display the probability distribution of X in a table.

   b Graph the probability distribution.

   c Find the mode and median of the distribution.

   d Find $P(X \leqslant 3)$.

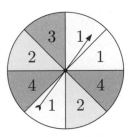

7 100 people were surveyed about the number of bedrooms in their house. 24 people had one bedroom, 35 people had two bedrooms, 27 people had three bedrooms, and 14 people had four bedrooms. Let X be the number of bedrooms a randomly selected person has in their house.

   a State the possible values of X.

   b Construct a probability table for X.

   c Find the mode and median of the distribution.

8 A group of 25 basketballers took shots from the free throw line until they scored a goal. 12 of the players only needed one shot, 7 players took two shots, 2 players took three shots, and the rest took four shots. Let X be the number of shots a randomly selected player needs to score a goal.

   a State the possible values of X.

   b Construct a probability table for X.

   c Find the mode and median of the distribution.

9 Show that the following are valid probability functions:

   a $p(x) = \dfrac{x+1}{10}$ for $x = 0, 1, 2, 3$

   b $p(x) = \dfrac{6}{11x}$ for $x = 1, 2, 3$.

10 Find k for the following probability functions:

   a $p(x) = k(x+2)$ for $x = 1, 2, 3$

   b $p(x) = \dfrac{k}{x+1}$ for $x = 0, 1, 2, 3$.

11 A discrete random variable X has the probability function $p(x) = \dfrac{4x - x^2}{a}$ for $x = 0, 1, 2, 3$.

   a Find the value of a.

   b Find $P(X = 1)$.

   c Find the mode of the distribution.

C | THE BINOMIAL DISTRIBUTION

Suppose $X =$ the number of blues which result from spinning this spinner *once*.

The probability distribution of X is as follows:

x	0	1
$P(X = x)$	$\frac{1}{4}$	$\frac{3}{4}$

Now suppose we spin the spinner n times and count the number of blues that result. The probability that we get a blue is the same for each spin, and each spin is independent of every other spin. This is an example of a **binomial experiment**.

In a **binomial experiment**:
- there are a fixed number of **independent trials**
- there are only *two* possible results for each trial:
  success if some event occurs, or **failure** if the event does not occur
- the probability of success is the same for each trial.

If X is the number of successes in a binomial experiment with n trials, each with probability of success p, then X is a **binomial random variable.**

THE PROBABILITY DISTRIBUTION OF A BINOMIAL RANDOM VARIABLE

Consider the spinner on the previous page with 3 blue sectors and 1 white sector. Suppose a "success" is a blue result and let X be the number of "successes" in 3 spins of the spinner. X is a binomial random variable with $n = 3$ and $p = \frac{3}{4}$, and can take the values 0, 1, 2, or 3.

To help determine the probability distribution of X, we first draw a tree diagram and find the probabilities associated with each possible outcome. We let B represent blue and W represent white.

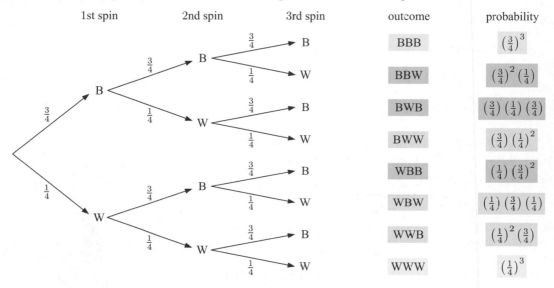

The outcomes have been shaded according to the value of X.

The probabilities associated with each value of X are:

$P(X = 0) = P(\text{WWW})$

$\qquad = \left(\frac{1}{4}\right)^3 \qquad\qquad$ {outcome shaded green}

$P(X = 1) = P(\text{BWW or WBW or WWB})$

$\qquad = \left(\frac{3}{4}\right)\left(\frac{1}{4}\right)^2 + \left(\frac{1}{4}\right)\left(\frac{3}{4}\right)\left(\frac{1}{4}\right) + \left(\frac{1}{4}\right)^2\left(\frac{3}{4}\right)$

$\qquad = ③ \times \left(\frac{3}{4}\right)\left(\frac{1}{4}\right)^2 \quad$ {outcomes shaded orange}

$P(X = 2) = P(\text{BBW or BWB or WBB})$

$\qquad = \left(\frac{3}{4}\right)^2\left(\frac{1}{4}\right) + \left(\frac{3}{4}\right)\left(\frac{1}{4}\right)\left(\frac{3}{4}\right) + \left(\frac{1}{4}\right)\left(\frac{3}{4}\right)^2$

$\qquad = 3 \times \left(\frac{3}{4}\right)^2\left(\frac{1}{4}\right) \quad$ {outcomes shaded red}

$P(X = 3) = P(\text{BBB})$

$\qquad = \left(\frac{3}{4}\right)^3 \qquad\qquad$ {outcome shaded blue}

Notice that for any particular value of X, each outcome with this property will have the same probability of occurring. The *order* in which blues and whites appear does not matter.

In **Chapter 9** we saw that $nCr = \binom{n}{r} = \dfrac{n!}{r!(n-r)!}$ is the number of ways in which we can obtain r successes from n trials, ignoring order.

For example, the circled factor ③ is the number of ways of getting 1 success out of 3 trials. This is $\binom{3}{1}$.

We can use this notation to write:

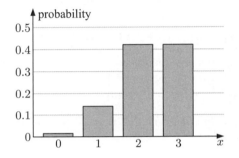

$$P(X = 0) = \left(\tfrac{1}{4}\right)^3 \qquad = \binom{3}{0}\left(\tfrac{3}{4}\right)^0 \left(\tfrac{1}{4}\right)^3 \approx 0.0156$$

$$P(X = 1) = 3\left(\tfrac{1}{4}\right)^2 \left(\tfrac{3}{4}\right)^1 = \binom{3}{1}\left(\tfrac{3}{4}\right)^1 \left(\tfrac{1}{4}\right)^2 \approx 0.1406$$

$$P(X = 2) = 3\left(\tfrac{1}{4}\right)^1 \left(\tfrac{3}{4}\right)^2 = \binom{3}{2}\left(\tfrac{3}{4}\right)^2 \left(\tfrac{1}{4}\right)^1 \approx 0.4219$$

$$P(X = 3) = \left(\tfrac{3}{4}\right)^3 \qquad = \binom{3}{3}\left(\tfrac{3}{4}\right)^3 \left(\tfrac{1}{4}\right)^0 \approx 0.4219$$

So, $P(X = x) = \binom{3}{x}\left(\tfrac{3}{4}\right)^x \left(\tfrac{1}{4}\right)^{3-x}$ where $x = 0, 1, 2, 3$.

The sum of the probabilities $\qquad P(X = 0) + P(X = 1) + P(X = 2) + P(X = 3)$

$$= \left(\tfrac{1}{4}\right)^3 + 3\left(\tfrac{1}{4}\right)^2 \left(\tfrac{3}{4}\right) + 3\left(\tfrac{1}{4}\right)\left(\tfrac{3}{4}\right)^2 + \left(\tfrac{3}{4}\right)^3$$

which is the binomial expansion of $\left(\tfrac{1}{4} + \tfrac{3}{4}\right)^3$, and $\left(\tfrac{1}{4} + \tfrac{3}{4}\right)^3 = 1$ since all possibilities are covered.

Suppose X is a binomial random variable with n independent trials and probability of success p. The **probability function** of X is:

$$p(x) = P(X = x) = \underbrace{\binom{n}{x}}_{} \underbrace{p^x(1-p)^{n-x}}_{} \quad \text{where} \quad x = 0, 1, 2, ..., n.$$

number of ways x successes can be ordered amongst the n trials

probability of obtaining x successes and $n - x$ failures in a particular order

The probability distribution of X is called the **binomial distribution**, and we write $X \sim B(n, p)$.

"~" reads "is distributed as".

Example 4   ◀◉ Self Tutor

a Expand $\left(\tfrac{9}{10} + \tfrac{1}{10}\right)^5$.

b An archer has a 90% chance of hitting a target with each arrow. If 5 arrows are fired, determine the chance of hitting the target:

   i twice only   **ii** at most 3 times.

a $\left(\tfrac{9}{10} + \tfrac{1}{10}\right)^5$

$$= \sum_{k=0}^{5} \binom{5}{k}\left(\tfrac{9}{10}\right)^k \left(\tfrac{1}{10}\right)^{5-k}$$

$$= \left(\tfrac{1}{10}\right)^5 + 5\left(\tfrac{9}{10}\right)\left(\tfrac{1}{10}\right)^4 + 10\left(\tfrac{9}{10}\right)^2\left(\tfrac{1}{10}\right)^3 + 10\left(\tfrac{9}{10}\right)^3\left(\tfrac{1}{10}\right)^2 + 5\left(\tfrac{9}{10}\right)^4\left(\tfrac{1}{10}\right) + \left(\tfrac{9}{10}\right)^5$$

b The probability of success with each arrow is $p = \frac{9}{10}$.

Let X be the number of arrows that hit the target.

The expansion in **a** gives the probability distribution for X.

$$\underbrace{\left(\tfrac{1}{10}\right)^5}_{\substack{P(X=0) \\ 5 \text{ misses}}} + \underbrace{5\left(\tfrac{9}{10}\right)\left(\tfrac{1}{10}\right)^4}_{\substack{P(X=1) \\ 1 \text{ hit} \\ 4 \text{ misses}}} + \underbrace{10\left(\tfrac{9}{10}\right)^2\left(\tfrac{1}{10}\right)^3}_{\substack{P(X=2) \\ 2 \text{ hits} \\ 3 \text{ misses}}} + \underbrace{10\left(\tfrac{9}{10}\right)^3\left(\tfrac{1}{10}\right)^2}_{\substack{P(X=3) \\ 3 \text{ hits} \\ 2 \text{ misses}}} + \underbrace{5\left(\tfrac{9}{10}\right)^4\left(\tfrac{1}{10}\right)}_{\substack{P(X=4) \\ 4 \text{ hits} \\ 1 \text{ miss}}} + \underbrace{\left(\tfrac{9}{10}\right)^5}_{\substack{P(X=5) \\ 5 \text{ hits}}}$$

i $P(\text{hits twice only}) = P(X = 2)$

$$= 10\left(\tfrac{9}{10}\right)^2\left(\tfrac{1}{10}\right)^3$$

$$= 0.0081$$

ii $P(\text{hits at most 3 times}) = P(X \leqslant 3)$

$$= P(X = 0) + P(X = 1) + P(X = 2) + P(X = 3)$$

$$= \left(\tfrac{1}{10}\right)^5 + 5\left(\tfrac{9}{10}\right)\left(\tfrac{1}{10}\right)^4 + 10\left(\tfrac{9}{10}\right)^2\left(\tfrac{1}{10}\right)^3 + 10\left(\tfrac{9}{10}\right)^3\left(\tfrac{1}{10}\right)^2$$

$$\approx 0.0815$$

EXERCISE 23C.1

1 For which of these probability experiments does the binomial distribution apply? Explain your answers.

  a A coin is thrown 100 times. The variable is the number of heads.

  b One hundred coins are each thrown once. The variable is the number of heads.

  c A box contains 5 blue and 3 red marbles. I draw out 5 marbles one at a time, replacing the marble before the next is drawn. The variable is the number of red marbles drawn.

  d A box contains 5 blue and 3 red marbles. I draw out 5 marbles without replacement. The variable is the number of red marbles drawn.

  e A large bin contains ten thousand bolts, 1% of which are faulty. I draw a sample of 10 bolts from the bin. The variable is the number of faulty bolts.

2 **a** Expand $(p + q)^4$.

  b If a coin is tossed *four* times, what is the probability of getting 3 heads?

3 **a** Expand $(p + q)^5$.

  b If *five* coins are tossed simultaneously, what is the probability of getting:

    i 4 heads and 1 tail in any order

    ii 2 heads and 3 tails in any order

    iii 4 heads and then 1 tail?

4 **a** Expand $\left(\tfrac{2}{3} + \tfrac{1}{3}\right)^4$.

  b A box of chocolates contains strawberry creams and almond centres in the ratio $2 : 1$. Four chocolates are selected at random, with replacement. Find the probability of getting:

    i all strawberry creams

    ii two of each type

    iii at least 2 strawberry creams.

5 a Expand $\left(\frac{3}{4} + \frac{1}{4}\right)^5$.

b In New Zealand in 1946 there were two different coins of value one florin. These were "normal" kiwis and "flat back" kiwis, in the ratio $3 : 1$. From a very large batch of 1946 florins, five were selected at random with replacement. Find the probability that:

  i two were "flat backs"

  ii at least 3 were "flat backs"

  iii at most 3 were "normal" kiwis.

USING TECHNOLOGY TO FIND BINOMIAL PROBABILITIES

We can quickly calculate binomial probabilities using a graphics calculator.

For example:

GRAPHICS CALCULATOR INSTRUCTIONS

- To find the probability $P(X = k)$ that the variable takes the value k, we use the **binomial probability function**.

- To find the probability that the variable takes a *range* of values, such as $P(X \leqslant k)$ or $P(X \geqslant k)$, we use the **binomial cumulative probability function**.

Some calculator models, such as the **Casio fx-9860G PLUS** and the **TI-84 Plus CE**, only allow you to calculate $P(X \leqslant k)$. To find the probability $P(X \geqslant k)$ for these models, it is often easiest to find the complement $P(X \leqslant k - 1)$ and use $P(X \geqslant k) = 1 - P(X \leqslant k - 1)$.

Example 5
◀)) **Self Tutor**

72% of union members are in favour of a certain change to their conditions of employment. A random sample of five members is taken. Find the probability that:

a three members are in favour of the change in conditions

b at least three members are in favour of the changed conditions.

Let X denote the number of members in the sample in favour of the change.

$n = 5$, so $X = 0, 1, 2, 3, 4$, or 5, and $p = 72\% = 0.72$

$\therefore \ X \sim B(5, 0.72)$.

a $P(X = 3) = \binom{5}{3} (0.72)^3 (0.28)^2$

        ≈ 0.293

Casio fx-9860G PLUS	Casio fx-CG20	TI-84 Plus CE
Binomial P.D p=0.29262643	`Rad Norm1 ab/c Real` Binomial P.D p=0.29262643	NORMAL FLOAT AUTO REAL RADIAN MP binompdf(5,0.72,3) 0.292626432

b $P(X \geqslant 3) \approx 0.862$

Casio fx-9860G PLUS	Casio fx-CG20	TI-84 Plus CE

BinominalCD(2,5,0.72)
          0.1376478208
1-Ans
          0.8623521792
▯
 	
JUMP DEL ▸MAT MATH
	Rad Norm1 ab/c Real
	Binomial C.D
	  p=0.86235217
		NORMAL FLOAT AUTO REAL RADIAN MP
		binomcdf(5,0.72,2)
		          0.1376478208
		1-Ans
		          0.8623521792

EXERCISE 23C.2

1 5% of electric light bulbs are defective at manufacture. 6 bulbs are randomly tested, with each one being replaced before the next is chosen. Determine the probability that:

    a two are defective   **b** at least one is defective.

2 Records show that 6% of the items assembled on a production line are faulty. A random sample of 12 items is selected with replacement. Find the probability that:

    a none will be faulty   **b** at most one will be faulty

    c at least two will be faulty   **d** less than four will be faulty.

3 The local bus service does not have a good reputation. The 8 am bus will run late on average two days out of every five. For any week of the year taken at random, find the probability of the 8 am bus being on time:

    a all 7 days   **b** only on Monday

    c on any 6 days   **d** on at least 4 days.

4 In a multiple choice test there are 10 questions. Each question has 5 choices, one of which is correct. Raj knows absolutely nothing about the subject, and guesses each answer at random. Given that the pass mark is 70%, determine the probability that he will pass.

5 An infectious flu virus is spreading through a school. The probability of a randomly selected student having the flu next week is 0.3. Mr C has a class of 25 students.

    a Calculate the probability that 2 or more students from Mr C's class will have the flu next week.

    b If more than 20% of the students have the flu next week, a class test will have to be cancelled. What is the probability that the test will be cancelled?

6 During a season, a basketball player has an 85% success rate in shooting from the free throw line. In one match the basketballer has 20 shots from the free throw line.

Find the probability that the basketballer is successful with:

    a all 20 throws   **b** at least 18 throws

    c between 14 and 17 (inclusive) throws.

7 Martina beats Jelena in 2 games out of 3 at tennis. What is the probability that Jelena wins a set of tennis 6 games to 4?

Hint: What does the score after 9 games need to be?

8   A fair coin is tossed 200 times. Find the probability of obtaining:

    a   between 90 and 110 (inclusive) heads   **b**   more than 95 but less than 105 heads.

9   **a**   Find the probability of rolling double sixes with a pair of dice.

    b   Suppose a pair of dice is rolled 500 times. Find the probability of rolling between 10 and 20 (inclusive) double sixes.

10   Shelley must pass through 15 traffic lights on her way to work. She has probability 0.6 of being stopped at any given traffic light. If she is stopped at more than 11 traffic lights, she will be late for work.

    a   Find the probability that Shelley will be late for work on a given day.

    b   Find the probability that Shelley is on time for work each day of a 5 day week.

    c   Shelley wants to increase the probability in **b** to at least 80%. She decides to leave home a little earlier, so she must now be stopped at more than 12 traffic lights in order to be late. Has Shelley achieved her goal? Justify your answer.

11   A hot water unit relies on 20 solar components for its power, and will operate provided at least one of its 20 components is working. The probability that an individual solar component will fail in a year is 0.85, and the failure of each individual component is independent of the others.

    a   Find the probability that the hot water unit will fail within one year.

    b   Find the smallest number of solar components required to ensure that a hot water service like this one is operating at the end of one year with a probability of at least 0.98.

Investigation 1   The graph of a binomial distribution

In this Investigation we will explore the shape of the graph of binomial distributions.

What to do:

1   Click on the icon to open a spreadsheet. It shows the graph of the binomial distribution for $X \sim B(20, 0.1)$.

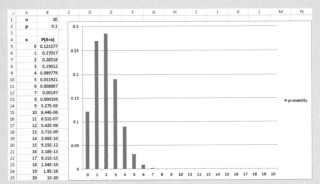

SPREADSHEET

    a   What is the mode of X?

    b   Describe the shape of the distribution.

2   Change p to 0.5, and then to 0.9. Describe the shape of the distribution in each case.

3 Reset p to 0.1. Increase n to 50 and then 100.

    a How does this affect the shape of the distribution?

    b What do you think happens to the shape of the binomial distribution as the number of trials n increases?

D | STATISTICAL HYPOTHESIS TESTING

We often hear claims about **population proportions**.

For example, a light bulb manufacturer might claim that only 1% of the bulbs they make are faulty. In statistics, we call this a **statistical hypothesis**.

We can decide whether a statistical hypothesis is reasonable or justified using a formal procedure called a **statistical hypothesis test**.

HYPOTHESES

Suppose a claim is made that a population proportion p has the value p_0. We call this the **null hypothesis** H_0, and we write

$$H_0: \ p = p_0.$$

This statement is assumed to be true unless we have enough evidence to reject it.

If H_0 is not rejected, we accept that the population proportion is p_0. So, the null hypothesis is a statement that there is *no difference* between p and p_0.

If H_0 is rejected, we accept that there *is a difference* between p and p_0. This statement is called the **alternative** hypothesis H_1.

1-TAILED AND 2-TAILED ALTERNATIVE HYPOTHESES

Given the null hypothesis $H_0: \ p = p_0$, the alternative hypothesis could be:

- $H_1: \ p > p_0$ **(1-tailed)**
- $H_1: \ p < p_0$ **(1-tailed)**
- $H_1: \ p \neq p_0$ **(2-tailed**, as $p \neq p_0$ could mean $p > p_0$ or $p < p_0$).

For example, consider the manufacturer's claim that only 1% of the light bulbs they make are faulty.

> The null hypothesis H_0 always states that p is **equal** to a specific value.

- If the manufacturer changes the manufacturing process to *reduce* the proportion of faulty bulbs and wants evidence to support this, the hypotheses would be:

    $H_0: \ p = 0.01$ {the new manufacturing process is the same as the old one}

    $H_1: \ p < 0.01$ {the new process is better than the old one}

- If a consumer advocacy group wants evidence that the manufacturer is producing a *higher* proportion of faulty bulbs than advertised, the hypotheses would be:

  H_0: $p = 0.01$ {the manufacturer's claim is true}

  H_1: $p > 0.01$ {the manufacturer is producing a higher proportion of faulty bulbs than advertised}

- If a quality inspector wants to determine if the proportion of faulty bulbs has *changed* over the last few years, but is not concerned about whether this change is an increase or decrease, the hypotheses would be:

  H_0: $p = 0.01$ {the proportion of faulty bulbs has remained constant}

  H_1: $p \neq 0.01$ {the proportion of faulty bulbs has changed}

EXERCISE 23D.1

1   In 2010, 21% of the British population smoked. A researcher wants to know if there has been any significant decrease in the proportion of smokers in the population since 2010. What set of hypotheses should the researcher consider?

Remember to specify what p is in context.

2   A pharmaceutical company conducts a clinical trial to test the effectiveness of a new cancer treatment. Only 30% of patients using the currently best available treatment survive more than 5 years after diagnosis. What set of hypotheses should the company consider?

3   At the last election, 42% of voters voted for Party A. An independent polling agency wants to gauge voting trends for the next election. What set of hypotheses should the polling agency consider if they are interested:

a   only in an increase in the proportion of Party A supporters

b   in *any* change in the proportion of Party A supporters?

TEST STATISTICS

When we collect data from a sample, we calculate statistics which can be used to test our hypotheses.

For example, suppose we took a random sample of 50 light bulbs from the manufacturer. The number of faulty light bulbs found in the sample, X, is a **test statistic**.

The total number of light bulbs is much larger than the sample size. We assume that:

- the probability of each bulb being faulty is the same
- the bulbs are independent of one another.

If the manufacturer's claim is true, then X would be a binomial random variable where the number of trials is 50 and the probability of "success" is 0.01. Hence $X \sim B(50, 0.01)$.

If the manufacturer's claim is false, the probability of "success" is not 0.01, and X is not distributed as $B(50, 0.01)$.

We can therefore study the distribution we observe in the sample to test the manufacturer's claim. We call this sample distribution the **null distribution**.

OBTAINING EVIDENCE

"Extreme" values of the test statistic are unlikely, so observing such a value is evidence against the null hypothesis. However, we need a measure of just *how* extreme a value should be before we conclude that the null hypothesis should be rejected.

> The **p-value** of a test statistic is the probability of that result being observed if H_0 is true.

The meaning of "extreme" depends on whether the alternative hypothesis is 1-tailed or 2-tailed:

- If the alternative hypothesis is H_1: $p < p_0$, extreme results are values which are *less* than the observed test statistic. We can visualise this as the **lower tail** of the null distribution.

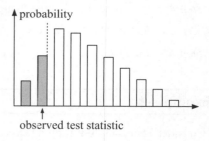

- Similarly, if H_1: $p > p_0$, extreme results correspond to the **upper tail** of the null distribution.

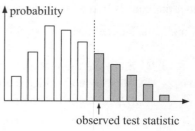

- If H_1: $p \neq p_0$, extreme results can be values in the same tail *or* opposite tail to the observed test statistic. There are several ways to do this, but the simplest approach is to define extreme results as values which have a probability less than or equal to the probability of the observed test statistic.

  By summing all the probabilities below the dotted line shown in the diagram, we obtain a p-value which covers **both** tails of the null distribution.

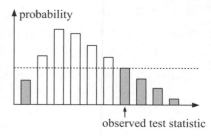

MAKING DECISIONS

Although "extreme" values are unlikely to occur, it is still *possible* to observe such values in a sample. We therefore need a rule which defines how much evidence is required to reject the null hypothesis.

> The **significance level** α of a statistical hypothesis test is the largest p-value that would result in rejecting H_0. Any p-value less than or equal to α results in H_0 being rejected.
>
> If a statistical hypothesis test has significance level α, the probability of *incorrectly* rejecting H_0 is α.

For example, for a significance level of $\alpha = 0.05$, a p-value of 0.02 would result in H_0 being rejected, whereas a p-value of 0.06 would not.

Important: We **must** choose a significance level **before** we test the hypothesis. It is *not* appropriate to calculate a p-value and then select a value of α so that H_0 will be rejected.

TESTING PROCEDURE

Now that we have all the components of a statistical hypothesis test, we can define the testing procedure as follows:

Step 1:   State the **null hypothesis** H_0 and **alternative hypothesis** H_1.

Step 2:   State the **significance level** α.

Step 3:   Identify the **test statistic** and state the **null distribution**.

Step 4:   Calculate the **p-value** using the null distribution and the observed value of the test statistic.

Step 5:   Reject H_0 if p-value $< \alpha$.

Step 6:   Interpret your decision in context, and write your conclusion as a sentence.

Example 6   ◀ㅮ **Self Tutor**

Consider Theresa's coin flipping experiment from the **Opening Problem** on page **556**. Theresa suspects that the coin is biased towards heads.

Conduct a 1-tailed test with significance level $\alpha = 0.05$ to determine if Theresa's claim is justified.

Step 1:   Let p be the probability of obtaining a head when the coin is tossed. The hypotheses that should be considered are:

H_0: $p = 0.5$ {the coin is fair}

H_1: $p > 0.5$ {the coin is biased towards heads}

Step 2:   The significance level is $\alpha = 0.05$.

Step 3:   Let X be the number of heads in 20 tosses of the coin.

$\therefore$ $X \sim B(20, 0.5)$

Step 4:   The alternative hypothesis is H_1: $p > 0.5$, so we use the upper tail of the null distribution.

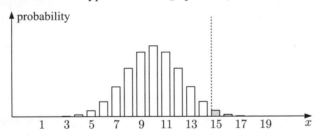

p-value $= P(X \geqslant 15)$

≈ 0.0207 {using technology}

Step 5:   Since p-value $< 0.05 = \alpha$, we have enough evidence to reject H_0 in favour of H_1 on the $\alpha = 0.05$ significance level.

Step 6:   Since we have accepted H_1, we conclude that the coin is indeed biased towards heads. Theresa's claim is justified.

Example 7   ◀) **Self Tutor**

Again consider the experiment from the **Opening Problem**.
Theresa's friend Peter claims that the coin is biased one way
or the other.

Is Peter's claim justified on the 5% level?

The significance level
may also be given as
a percentage.

Step 1: H_0: $p = 0.5$ {the coin is fair}
         H_1: $p \neq 0.5$ {the coin is biased}

Step 2: The significance level is $\alpha = 0.05$.

Step 3: Let X be the number of heads in 20 tosses of the coin.
         $\therefore$ $X \sim B(20, 0.5)$

Step 4: The alternative hypothesis is H_1: $p \neq 0.5$, so we sum all the probabilities which are
         less than or equal to $P(X = 15) \approx 0.0148$.

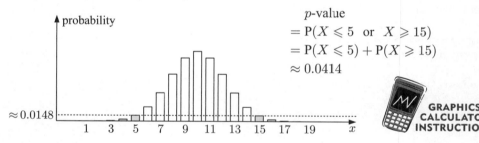

p-value
$= P(X \leqslant 5 \text{ or } X \geqslant 15)$
$= P(X \leqslant 5) + P(X \geqslant 15)$
≈ 0.0414

**GRAPHICS
CALCULATOR
INSTRUCTIONS**

Step 5: Since p-value $< 0.05 = \alpha$, we have enough evidence to reject H_0 in favour of H_1 on the
         5% significance level.

Step 6: Since we have accepted H_1, we conclude that the coin is biased. Peter's claim is justified.

EXERCISE 23D.2

1 A magician claims that he can roll a six with a fair die on average nine times out of ten. To test the
   magician's claim, he is invited to roll the die six times. His claim will be accepted if he rolls at least
   four sixes.

   a State the hypothesis to be tested.

   b What is the significance level of this test?

2 A student suspects that her six-sided die is biased towards the number four. She decides to conduct a
   statistical hypothesis test with a 5% level of significance. She rolls the die 30 times and 8 fours appear.

   a State the null and alternative hypotheses to be tested.

   b State the significance level α of the test.

   c Define the test statistic and write down the null distribution.

   d Calculate the p-value.

   e Does the student have sufficient evidence to conclude that her die is biased towards the number
      four?

3 To test if a coin is biased, it was tossed 80 times. 37 heads appeared.

    a State the null and alternative hypotheses to be tested.

    b Define the test statistic and write down the null distribution.

    c Calculate the p-value.

    d Is there enough evidence to conclude that the coin is biased with a 5% level of significance?

4 Sixty migraine sufferers were asked to change from their old medication to a new one. Thirty eight said the medication improved their condition. The remaining participants said it made their condition worse. Is there enough evidence on a 5% level to say that the new medication is better than the old?

    Hint: If the medication made no difference, the probability that a person improves is the same as the probability that a person becomes worse.

5 A lotto company produces instant scratch lottery tickets. They claim that 5% of its tickets win a prize. A consumer group wants to test this claim.

    In a randomly selected sample of 200 tickets, 8 were found to be winning tickets. Does this support the manufacturer's claim on a 2% significance level?

6 In 2006, 20.6% of people over the age of 16 said they expected to be better off in 5 years' time. To see if this proportion had changed in 2016, a pollster surveyed a random selection of 300 people. 66 said they expected to be better off in 5 years' time. Does this support the hypothesis that people's feelings about their future well-being have changed on a 1% significance level?

Historical note

Sir Ronald Aylmer Fisher (1890 - 1962) was an English statistician and biologist. He was known for his work in both agriculture and statistics, combining the disciplines with his work in classical statistics and significance testing.

In 1952 Fisher published a book titled *Statistical Methods for Research Workers* which is best known for the following statement about p-values:

Sir Ronald Fisher

    "The value for which $p = 0.05$, or 1 in 20 [....] it is convenient to take this point as a limit in judging whether a deviation is to be considered significant or not."

Today, a significance level of $\alpha = 0.05$ is still widely quoted in scientific journals and is often used as a de facto standard when testing for significance.

Discussion

A researcher tested the same hypothesis H_0 20 times at a significance level $\alpha = 0.05$. He only rejected H_0 once, but he then only published the results from the test where H_0 was rejected.

1 Explain why the researcher should have published the results of the other 19 tests as well.

2 Are the researcher's results likely to be replicable?

3 Discuss the cartoon on the next page. Do you think the claim that "green jelly beans are linked to acne" is justified?

4 Funding for research often hinges on producing significant results. Do you think this might *bias* decisions made by researchers?

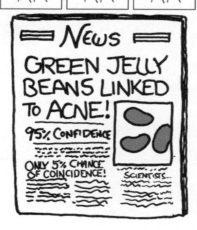

CRITICAL REGIONS

> The **critical region** C of a statistical hypothesis test is the set of all values of the test statistic which result in H_0 being rejected.
>
> The **acceptance region** A is the set of all values of the test statistic which result in H_0 being accepted.

For a 1-tailed test, instead of using a p-value we can test H_0 by seeing if the observed value of the test statistic lies in the critical region. We can do this using the **critical value** of the test.

> The **critical value** c of a statistical hypothesis test is the value in the critical region C which has the largest p-value associated with it.

Example 8   ◀) **Self Tutor**

Let p be the probability of rolling a one with a four-sided die.

Consider the hypotheses: H_0: $p = 0.25$
                              H_1: $p > 0.25$

The hypotheses will be tested using a sample of 6 rolls of the die, with significance level $\alpha = 0.05$.

a Find:

    i the critical region C **ii** the acceptance region A **iii** the critical value c.

b The die was rolled 6 times and 3 ones appeared. Is this sufficient evidence to reject H_0?

---

a The test statistic is the number of ones that appear in 6 rolls of the die, X.

    $\therefore$ $X \sim B(6,\, 0.25)$

X	p-value
0	1
1	≈ 0.822
2	≈ 0.466
3	≈ 0.169
4	≈ 0.0376
5	≈ 0.00464
6	$\approx 2.44 \times 10^{-4}$

The critical region is the set of all x-values with p-value $\leqslant \alpha = 0.05$.

    i $C = \{4,\, 5,\, 6\}$

    ii $A = \{0,\, 1,\, 2,\, 3\}$

    iii The value in C with the largest p-value is 4.

        $\therefore$ the critical value $c = 4$

b $3 \notin C$, so we do not have sufficient evidence to reject H_0.

EXERCISE 23D.3

1 For each statistical hypothesis test below, find:

  i the critical region C **ii** the acceptance region A **iii** the critical value c.

  a H_0: $p = 0.6$ against H_1: $p < 0.6$ using a sample of 5 individuals and a significance level of $\alpha = 0.05$.

  b H_0: $p = 0.35$ against H_1: $p > 0.35$ using a sample of 8 individuals and a significance level of $\alpha = 0.01$.

  c H_0: $p = 0.74$ against H_1: $p < 0.74$ using a sample of 10 individuals and a significance level of $\alpha = 0.02$.

2 Judeau wishes to test if a coin is biased. Let p be the probability of a head.

Judeau's hypotheses are: H_0: $p = 0.5$
H_1: $p > 0.5$

To test these hypotheses on the 5% significance level, Judeau counts the number of heads in 4 tosses of the coin.

  a For Judeau's test, find: **i** the critical region   **ii** the acceptance region.

  b Is it *possible* to reject H_0 in this situation?

  c What should Judeau do if he wants to test his hypotheses more accurately?

Discussion

Many statisticians prefer to say that they "failed to reject H_0" when the observed p-value is greater than the significance level, rather than saying they "accepted H_0".

- Why do you think they might do this?
- Why do you think more emphasis is placed on failing to reject H_0 rather than failing to reject H_1?

Investigation 2   Randomised tests

Since binomial random variables are discrete, even though we may state a significance level of α, the actual significance level may not be *exactly* equal to α.

What to do:

1 Consider testing a coin for bias. Let p be the probability of a head. The hypotheses to be tested are:
$$H_0: \ p = 0.5$$
$$H_1: \ p < 0.5$$

Let X be the number of heads in 10 tosses of the coin.

  a State the null distribution.

  b Copy and complete:

X	0	1	2	3	4	5	6	7	8	9	10
p-value											

  c Find the critical region for the significance level:

    i $\alpha = 0.1$ **ii** $\alpha = 0.05$ **iii** $\alpha = 0.01$.

  d For each critical region in **c**, state the probability that H_0 will be incorrectly rejected.

  e Hence explain why the *actual* significance level of this test is always less than or equal to α.

2 The following procedure is a **randomised test** which we can use to achieve a significance level of exactly α:

Consider the hypotheses in **1** tested with significance level $\alpha = 0.05$. Let a be the smallest value of X such that H_0 is *not* rejected.

a Find the value of a.

b Suppose when $X = a$, we flip a *biased* coin which has probability θ of resulting in a head. If we get a head, H_0 is rejected.

   i Explain why: $P(\text{incorrectly reject } H_0) = P(X < a) + \theta \times P(X = a)$

   ii Find the value of θ such that $P(\text{incorrectly reject } H_0) = \alpha$.

3 Construct randomised tests for the hypotheses in **1** with significance levels $\alpha = 0.1$ and 0.01. What happens to the value of θ as α changes?

4 How might you modify the randomised test in **2** for the alternative hypothesis:

a H_1: $p > 0.5$ **b** H_1: $p \neq 0.5$?

5 Discuss the critical and acceptance regions of a randomised test. Would you say they are well defined?

6 Do you think it is reasonable to "flip a coin" to decide the outcome of a statistical hypothesis test? Discuss this question in the context of the following scenarios:

a a polling agency determining the proportion of voters that will vote for a particular political party

b a clinical trial testing the effectiveness of a new treatment

c a quality inspector testing the strength of bolts using different materials.

Review set 23A

1 Determine whether the following variables are discrete or continuous:

a the number of attempts to pass a driving test

b the length of time before a phone loses its battery charge

c the number of phone calls made before a salesperson has sold 3 products.

2 **a** State whether each of the following is a valid probability distribution:

i

x	1	2	3
$P(X = x)$	0.6	0.25	0.15

ii

x	0	2	5	10
$P(X = x)$	0.3	0.5	0.1	0.2

iii

x	0	1	2	3
$P(X = x)$	0.4	-0.2	0.35	0.45

iv

x	2	3	4	5
$P(X = x)$	0.25	0.25	0.25	0.25

v

x	2	3
$P(X = x)$	0.7	0.3

vi

x	0	1
$P(X = x)$	0.28	0.72

b For which of the probability distributions in **a** is X a uniform discrete random variable?

3 $P(X = x) = \dfrac{a}{x^2 + 1}$, $x = 0, 1, 2, 3$ is a probability function.

   a Find the value of a.   **b** Find $P(X \geqslant 1)$.

4 A random variable X has the probability function $p(x)$ described in the table.

x	0	1	2	3	4
$p(x)$	0.10	0.30	0.45	0.10	k

   a Find k.   **b** Find $P(X \geqslant 3)$.

   c Find the mode of the distribution.

5   **a** Expand $\left(\frac{4}{5} + \frac{1}{5}\right)^5$.

   b With every attempt, Jack has an 80% chance of kicking a goal. In one quarter of a match he has 5 kicks for goal. Determine the probability that he scores:

     i 3 goals then misses twice   **ii** 3 goals and misses twice.

6 Consider the two spinners illustrated:

  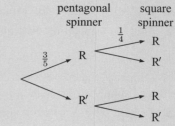

   a Copy and complete the tree diagram which shows all possible results when the two spinners are spun together.

   b Calculate the probability that exactly one red will occur.

   c The pair of spinners is now spun 10 times. Let X be the number of times that exactly one red occurs.

     i State the distribution of X.

     ii Write down expressions for $P(X = 1)$ and $P(X = 9)$. Hence determine which of these outcomes is more likely.

7 A training method for teaching people to type accurately has a success rate of 70%. A new set of exercises is proposed which is claimed to have a higher success rate.

30 people were randomly selected to try the new exercises, and 26 people successfully learned how to type accurately.

On a 5% level of significance, is this sufficient evidence to conclude that the new exercises are better?

8 The probability that a train is behind schedule is 0.3. A new engine with better acceleration is to be tried on the route to see if the arrival time can be improved.

To test the effectiveness of the engine improvements, 10 trial runs on the route are to be conducted.

   a State the hypotheses to be considered.

   b Identify the test statistic and state the null distribution.

   c The test is to be conducted with a significance level of 0.05. Find the critical region for the test.

   d Of the 10 trial runs, the train was behind schedule once. Is there sufficient evidence to support the claim that the new engine is better?

Review set 23B

1 Sally's number of hits in each softball match has the probability distribution shown.

x	0	1	2	3	4	5
P($X = x$)	0.07	0.14	k	0.46	0.08	0.02

   a State clearly what the random variable represents.

   b Find: **i** k **ii** P($X \geqslant 2$)   **iii** P($1 \leqslant X \leqslant 3$)

   c Find the mode and median number of hits.

2 Show that the following are valid probability functions:

   a $p(x) = \dfrac{x^2 + x}{40}, \quad x = 1, 2, 3, 4$ **b** $p(x) = \log\left(\dfrac{x+1}{x}\right), \quad x = 1, 2, 3, ..., 9$

3 A 6-sided and 4-sided die are rolled simultaneously. Let X be the number of twos rolled.

   a Explain why X is not a binomial random variable.

   b Find the probability distribution of X.

4 The spinner alongside is spun 20 times. Let X be the number of threes spun.

   a Explain why X is a binomial random variable.

   b Find the probability that at least 1 three is spun.

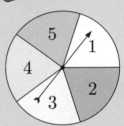

5 24% of visitors to a museum make voluntary donations. On a certain day the museum has 175 visitors. Find the probability that:

   a less than 40 visitors make a donation

   b between 50 and 60 (inclusive) visitors make a donation.

6 A school volleyball team has 9 players, each of whom has a 75% chance of turning up for any given game. The team needs at least 6 players to avoid forfeiting the game.

   a Find the probability that for a randomly chosen game, the team will:

      i have all of its players   **ii** have to forfeit the game.

   b The team plays 30 games for the season. Find the probability that the team will have to forfeit at least 3 games during the season.

7 Sebastian rolled a six-sided die 25 times and got 8 sixes. Test the fairness of the die using a 2-tailed statistical hypothesis test with a significance level of 5%.

8 An advertisement claimed that 20% of all households used Ongodo washing powder. A consumer group consulted a statistician to help test the advertisement's claim. The statistician recommended sampling 100 households at random. He said the advertisement's claim was only reasonable if the number of households in the sample that use Ongodo was between 13 and 29 inclusive.

   a For this test, write down the:

      i acceptance region   **ii** critical region.

   b Find the significance level of this test.

ANSWERS

EXERCISE 1A

1 **a** $x = 3$ **b** $x = -7$ **c** $x = 4$
d $x = 6$ **e** $x = 12$ **f** $x = 6$

2 **a** $x = 9$ **b** $x = 6$ **c** $x = -\frac{5}{2}$

3 **a** $x = 2$ **b** $x = -\frac{4}{3}$ **c** $x = \frac{8}{5}$
d $x = 6$ **e** $x = -\frac{7}{2}$ **f** $x = \frac{16}{3}$

4 **a** no solutions   **b** infinitely many solutions
c infinitely many solutions

5 **a** $x = 10$ **b** $x = -5$ **c** $x = -9\frac{1}{2}$

6 If $ax = b$, then $x = \dfrac{b}{a}$ provided $a \neq 0$.
Now the product of two rational numbers is rational

$\therefore \quad \dfrac{b}{a} = \dfrac{b}{1} \times \dfrac{1}{a}$ is rational as $a \neq 0$

$\therefore \quad x$ is rational, and the equation $ax = b$ has a rational solution for all $a, b \in \mathbb{Q}, \ a \neq 0$.

7 £16   **8** 24 students   **9** €1049.40

EXERCISE 1B

1 **a** $m = 3, \ c = 7$ **b** $m = -2, \ c = -5$
c $m = \frac{2}{3}, \ c = -\frac{1}{3}$ **d** $m = -4, \ c = 11$
e $m = -1, \ c = -6$ **f** $m = -\frac{6}{5}, \ c = \frac{9}{5}$
g $m = \frac{7}{9}, \ c = \frac{2}{9}$ **h** $m = \frac{1}{3}, \ c = -\frac{1}{2}$
i $m = -\frac{5}{8}, \ c = \frac{3}{8}$

2 **a** $y = 3x - 11$ **b** $y = -2x - 1$
c $y = \frac{1}{4}x - 4$ **d** $y = -\frac{2}{3}x - \frac{25}{3}$
e $y = 2x - 9$ **f** $y = -\frac{3}{4}x + 4$

3 **a** $4x + y - 6 = 0$ **b** $x - 2y - 13 = 0$
c $5x + 3y - 8 = 0$ **d** $7x - 6y - 17 = 0$

4 **a** $4x + y - 6 = 0$ **b** $5x - y - 3 = 0$
c $3x + 4y - 5 = 0$ **d** $2x + 9y - 8 = 0$
e $3x - 5y - 1 = 0$ **f** $5x - 6y + 18 = 0$

5 **a** $y = -5x + 2$ **b** $y = -\frac{3}{7}x + \frac{2}{7}$ **c** $y = -\frac{4}{3}x - \frac{1}{3}$
d $y = 2x - 6$ **e** $y = \frac{3}{13}x + \frac{4}{13}$ **f** $y = \frac{10}{3}x - \frac{7}{3}$

6 $Ax + By + C = 0$ can be written as $y = -\dfrac{A}{B}x - \dfrac{C}{B}$ which has the form $y = mx + c$.

$\therefore \quad m = -\dfrac{A}{B}$

7 **A** and **D**, **B** and **C**

8 **C** and **D** are both perpendicular to **A**.

9 **a** $y = 2x + 5$ **b** $y = -x + 9$ **c** $y = -5x - 12$
d $y = \frac{2}{3}x - 8$ **e** $y = \frac{7}{5}x - \frac{11}{5}$ **f** $y = -\frac{5}{6}x + \frac{19}{6}$

10 **a** $2x - y + 2 = 0$ **b** $3x + 10y - 8 = 0$
c $8x + 5y + 13 = 0$

11 **a** $y = \frac{3}{4}x - \frac{5}{4}$ **b** $-\frac{5}{4}$

12 **a** $x - y + 2 = 0$ **b** -2

13 **a** $y = 3x + 1$ **b** $2x - y - 7 = 0$
c $y = \frac{1}{2}x + \frac{11}{2}$ **d** $2x - y + 3 = 0$

EXERCISE 1C

1 **a** yes   **b** no   **2** **a** yes   **b** yes
3 **a** no   **b** yes
4 **a** $c = 7$ **b** $m = 11$ **c** $t = 8$
5 **a** $k = -3$ **b** $k = -51$ **c** $k = -12$
6 **a** $m = -\frac{1}{7}$ **b** $t = 5$

EXERCISE 1D

1 **a**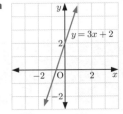
b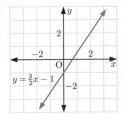

c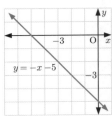
d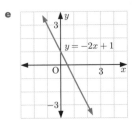

e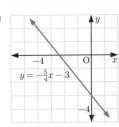
f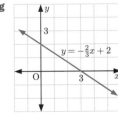

g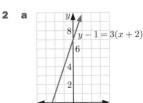
h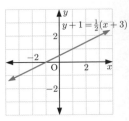

2 **a**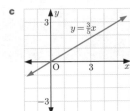
b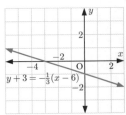

c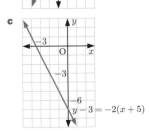
d

e
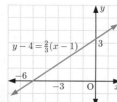
$y - 4 = \frac{2}{3}(x - 1)$

f
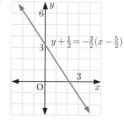
$y + \frac{1}{2} = -\frac{3}{2}(x - \frac{5}{2})$

3 a
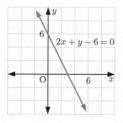
$2x + y - 6 = 0$

b
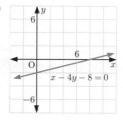
$x - 4y - 8 = 0$

c
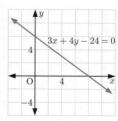
$3x + 4y - 24 = 0$

d
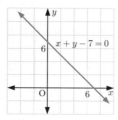
$x + y - 7 = 0$

e
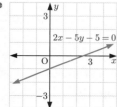
$2x - 5y - 5 = 0$

f
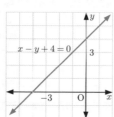
$x - y + 4 = 0$

g
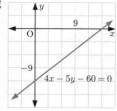
$4x - 5y - 60 = 0$

h
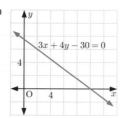
$3x + 4y - 30 = 0$

4 a i $-\frac{3}{4}$ **ii** 2
b i yes **ii** no **iii** yes
c
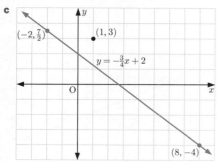
$(-2, \frac{7}{2})$ $(1, 3)$
$y = -\frac{3}{4}x + 2$
$(8, -4)$

5 a i 9 **ii** -6
b i yes **ii** no
c $c = -8$
d
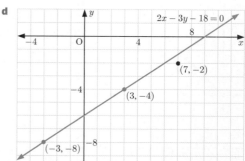
$2x - 3y - 18 = 0$
$(7, -2)$
$(3, -4)$
$(-3, -8)$

EXERCISE 1E

1 a i
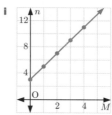
ii The points lie in a straight line so the variables are linearly related.
iii Not in direct proportion.
iv $y = 3x + 1$

b i
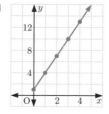
ii The points lie in a straight line so the variables are linearly related.
iii $t \propto P$
iv $t = 5P$

c i
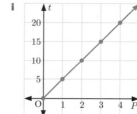
ii The points lie in a straight line so the variables are linearly related.
iii Not in direct proportion.
iv $n = 2M + 3$

2 a

Time (t hours)	0	1	2	3	4
Cost (£C)	50	130	210	290	370

b
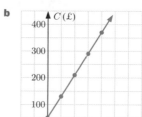

c Linearly related, not in direct proportion.
d C-intercept is 50, gradient is 80.
e $C = 80t + 50$

3 a

No. of bottles bought (x)	0	1	2	3	4
Total cost of bottles (£y)	0	2.50	5	7.50	10

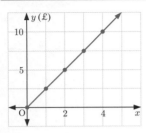

The graph is a straight line passing through the origin $\therefore$ $y \propto x$.

b 2.5   **c** $y = 2.5x$

4 a

Water used (w kL)	0	10	20	30	40
Cost (£C)	100	130	160	190	220

b

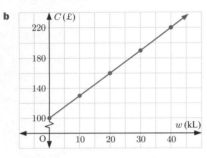

c As the graph is a straight line, C and w are linearly related. The graph does not pass through the origin so C and w are not in direct proportion.

d C-intercept is 100, gradient is 3.
£100 is the flat service fee, £3 is the charge per kL of water.

5 a y is trebled   **b** y is halved   **c** x is multiplied by 7
d x is increased by 40%   **e** y is decreased by 10%
f The relationship is only true for multiplication and division.

6 a **i** no   **ii** $P = 4n + 8$
b **i** yes, 8   **ii** $A = 8n$

7 $y \propto x$ so we let $y = k_1 x$, $k_1 \in \mathbb{R}$, $k_1 \neq 0$
$y \propto z$ so we let $y = k_2 z$, $k_2 \in \mathbb{R}$, $k_2 \neq 0$
$\therefore$ $k_1 x = k_2 z$
$\therefore$ $x = \left(\dfrac{k_2}{k_1}\right) z$ where $\dfrac{k_2}{k_1} \in \mathbb{R}$
$\therefore$ $x \propto z$

8 a $3t = 25N$ or $N = \frac{3}{25}t$ **b** 15 trees
c ≈ 167 minutes

9 a $V = 58.4d$ **b** ≈ 0.685 m   **c** 105.12 kL

EXERCISE 1F.1

1 a $x = -2$, $y = -4$ **b** $x = 1$, $y = -3$
c $x = 6$, $y = 7$

2 a $x = 3$, $y = 2$ **b** $x = 6$, $y = 1$
c $x = 2$, $y = -12$

3 a The lines are parallel, so there are no solutions.
b The lines are coincident. There are infinitely many solutions.
c The lines are parallel, so there are no solutions.

EXERCISE 1F.2

1 a $x = 3$, $y = 5$ **b** $x = 1$, $y = -1$
c $x = -1$, $y = 8$ **d** $x = \frac{1}{2}$, $y = 2\frac{1}{2}$
e $x = \frac{2}{3}$, $y = -4$ **f** $x = 3\frac{3}{25}$, $y = 1\frac{16}{25}$

2 a $x = 5$, $y = 8$ **b** $x = -7$, $y = -2$
c $x = -5$, $y = -2$ **d** $x = \frac{1}{3}$, $y = -1\frac{1}{3}$
e $x = -4$, $y = -\frac{1}{4}$ **f** $x = -1\frac{11}{31}$, $y = -\frac{4}{31}$

3 a $x = -3$, $y = 3\frac{1}{2}$ **b** $x = -2\frac{1}{4}$, $y = 3$
c $x = 8$, $y = -2\frac{1}{3}$ **d** $x = \frac{2}{3}$, $y = 2\frac{2}{3}$
e $x = \frac{1}{4}$, $y = \frac{3}{4}$ **f** $x = \frac{1}{3}$, $y = 2\frac{1}{4}$

EXERCISE 1F.3

1 a $x = 2$, $y = 1$ **b** $x = 3$, $y = -1$
c $x = -4$, $y = 5$ **d** $x = 4$, $y = -3$
e $x = 6$, $y = -2$ **f** $x = 1\frac{1}{2}$, $y = -2\frac{1}{2}$

2 a $x = 3$, $y = 7$ **b** $x = -5$, $y = 2$
c $x = -1$, $y = -6$ **d** $x = \frac{1}{3}$, $y = 4$
e $x = -3$, $y = 1\frac{1}{2}$ **f** $x = \frac{1}{4}$, $y = 1\frac{1}{4}$

3 a $x = 5$, $y = -2$ **b** $x = -3$, $y = -4$
c $x = 7$, $y = -3$ **d** $x = 1\frac{1}{4}$, $y = -\frac{3}{4}$
e $x = -4\frac{1}{2}$, $y = -2\frac{1}{2}$ **f** $x = -28\frac{2}{3}$, $y = -17\frac{2}{3}$

EXERCISE 1F.4

1 plates: £7, bowls: £9
2 waltz: 3 minutes, sonatina: 7 minutes
3 short cable: 2.5 m, long cable: 4.2 m
4 a 10 points   **b** 6 points
5 19 cans of paint   **6** £125   **7** 36 km

REVIEW SET 1A

1 a $x = 8$ **b** $x = 4$ **c** $x = 5$
2 a $x = -9\frac{1}{2}$ **b** $x = -\frac{17}{3}$ **c** $x = -32$
3 £60
4 a $y = -\frac{1}{3}x + 4$ **b** $x + 3y - 12 = 0$
5 a $3x - 2y - 12 = 0$ **b** 4
6 a yes   **b** yes   **c** no
7 a   **b**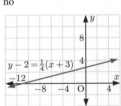

c

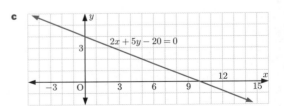

8 **a** **i**

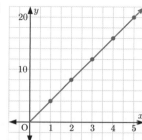

ii The points lie in a straight line so the variables are linearly related.

iii In direct proportion.

iv $y = 4x$

b **i**

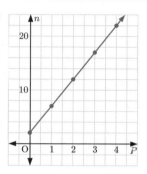

ii The points lie in a straight line so the variables are linearly related.

iii Not in direct proportion.

iv $n = 5P + 2$

9 **a** $m = -\frac{1}{2}, \quad c = 4$ **b** yes   **c** $k = -2$

d

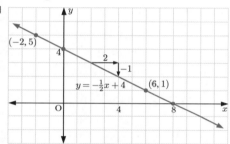

10 **a**

Time (t minutes)	0	1	2	3	4
Amount of water (A mL)	200	250	300	350	400

b

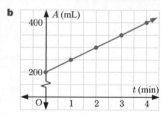

c Linearly related, not directly proportional.

d $A = 50t + 200$

11 **a** $x = 1, \quad y = 7$ **b** $x = -1, \quad y = 2$
   c $x = 3, \quad y = -1$ **d** $x = -4, \quad y = 3$
   e $x = 4, \quad y = 1$ **f** $x = -2, \quad y = -5$

12 **a** £60   **b** £35

REVIEW SET 1B

1 **a** $x = \frac{2}{3}$ **b** $x = -40$ **c** $x = 12$

2 **a** $x = 1$ **b** $x = \frac{2}{17}$ **c** $x = -\frac{2}{3}$

3 150 mL

4 **a** $5x - y - 11 = 0$ **b** $x + 4y + 19 = 0$

5 **a** $y = 3x + 1$ **b** $5x - 2y + 3 = 0$

6 **a** $k = 7$ **b** $k = -13$ **c** $k = -11$

7 **a**

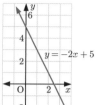

b

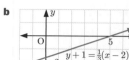

c

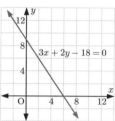

8 **a** $m = \frac{2}{3}$ **b** **i** yes   **ii** no

c

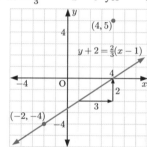

9 y is decreased by 15%

10 **a**

No. of litres bought (x)	0	1	2	3
Cost of petrol (£y)	0	1.25	2.50	3.75

Multiplying the number of litres of petrol bought by a number results in multiplying the cost by the same number.
$\therefore$ x and y are directly proportional.

b 1.25   **c** $y = 1.25x$

11 **a**

Length of call (t minutes)	0	1	2	3	4
Cost of call (£C) Plan A	0.50	1.50	2.50	3.50	4.50
Cost of call (£C) Plan B	0	1.25	2.50	3.75	5.00

b

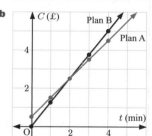

c Each plan represents a linear relationship as both graphs are straight lines.

d Plan B represents a direct proportion as it starts at the origin.

e Plan A: $C = t + 0.50$
   Plan B: $C = 1.25t$

12 **a** $x = \frac{1}{3}, \quad y = 4$ **b** $x = -2, \quad y = 4$
   c $x = 3, \quad y = -\frac{1}{2}$ **d** $x = 1\frac{1}{2}, \quad y = -3\frac{1}{2}$
   e $x = -3, \quad y = -5$ **f** $x = \frac{1}{3}, \quad y = -1\frac{1}{3}$

13 15 books

EXERCISE 2A

1 a i

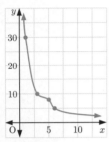

ii For each of the data pairs, $xy = 80$.
∴ x and y are inversely proportional.
The equation is $y = \dfrac{80}{x}$.

b i

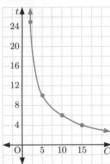

ii For each of the data pairs, xy is not constant.
∴ x and y are not inversely proportional.

c i

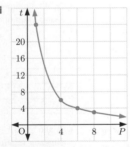

ii For each of the data pairs, Ct is not constant.
∴ C and t are not inversely proportional.

d i

ii For each of the data pairs, $Pt = 24$.
∴ P and t are inversely proportional.
The equation is $t = \dfrac{24}{P}$.

2 a

x	1	2	3	4	6
$\dfrac{1}{x}$	1	$\dfrac{1}{2}$	$\dfrac{1}{3}$	$\dfrac{1}{4}$	$\dfrac{1}{6}$
y	12	6	4	3	2

b

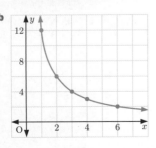

c For each of the data pairs, $xy = 12$.
∴ x and y are inversely proportional.

d

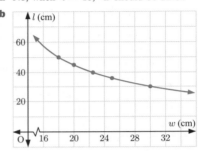

e The graph is a straight line passing through the origin.
∴ y is directly proportional to $\dfrac{1}{x}$.

3 a No, when $l = 40$, w should be 22.5.

b

c For each of the data pairs, $lw = 900$.
∴ l and w are inversely proportional.
∴ $l = \dfrac{900}{w}$

4 a Speed and time are inversely proportional.
b Distance and time are directly proportional.
c Distance and speed are directly proportional.

5 a

b No. For each of the data pairs (x, y), the product xy is not constant.
(In fact $(\text{base length})^2$ and depth are inversely proportional.)

6 a y is halved
b y is multiplied by 6
c x is divided by 10
d y is multiplied by 3.5
e x is divided by 1.2
f y is divided by 0.93

7 20 days

EXERCISE 2B.1

1 a

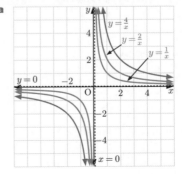

b For $k > 0$, as k becomes larger the graphs move further from the origin.

2 a

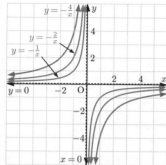

b For $k < 0$, the graph exists in the 2nd and 4th quadrants only. As $|k|$ becomes larger, the graphs move further from the origin.

3 a $y = \dfrac{6}{x}$ **b** $y = \dfrac{15}{x}$ **c** $y = -\dfrac{36}{x}$

4 a 5 cards   **b** decrease   **c** it is halved

d $nt = 40$, where n is the number of cards made and t is the time taken, in minutes, to make 1 card.

e

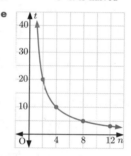

EXERCISE 2B.2

1 a

x	-3	-2	-1	-0.5	-0.2	0
y	$\frac{1}{9}$	$\frac{1}{4}$	1	4	25	undefined

x	0.2	0.5	1	2	3
y	25	4	1	$\frac{1}{4}$	$\frac{1}{9}$

b

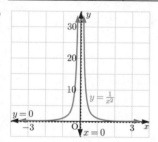

c quadrants 1 and 2
d $x = 0$
e $y = 0$

2 a

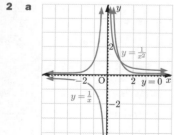

b For both graphs the horizontal asymptote is $y = 0$ and the vertical asymptote is $x = 0$. Both graphs pass through $(1, 1)$.

The graph of $y = \dfrac{1}{x}$ is in quadrants 1 and 3 and the graph of $y = \dfrac{1}{x^2}$ is in quadrants 1 and 2.

3 a

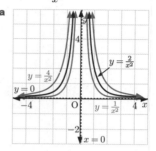

b An increase in k dilates the graph vertically.

EXERCISE 2C

1 a $x = 12$ **b** $x = \frac{1}{7}$ **c** $x = \frac{15}{4}$

d $x = \frac{15}{8}$ **e** $x = 24$ **f** $x = \pm\frac{10}{3}$

2 $5\frac{5}{8}$ hours or 5 h $37\frac{1}{2}$ min

3 a 9 minutes   **b** $t = \dfrac{25}{n-1}$ minutes

4 $2\frac{2}{9}$ days or 2 days 5 h 20 min

REVIEW SET 2A

1 a

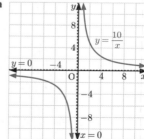

b For each of the data pairs, $pN = 1200$, which is constant, so N and p are inversely proportional.

$$\therefore \ N = \dfrac{1200}{p}$$

2 $x \propto \dfrac{1}{y}$ so $x = \dfrac{k_1}{y}$, $k_1 \in \mathbb{R}$, $k_1 \neq 0$

$y \propto \dfrac{1}{z}$ so $y = \dfrac{k_2}{z}$, $k_2 \in \mathbb{R}$, $k_2 \neq 0$

$$\therefore \ x = \dfrac{k_1}{y} = \dfrac{k_1}{\frac{k_2}{z}} = \left(\dfrac{k_1}{k_2}\right)z, \ \dfrac{k_1}{k_2} \in \mathbb{R}$$

$\therefore$ x and z are directly proportional, not inversely proportional.

3 a $d = 12s$ **b** 96 units of damage   **c** level 15 weapon

4 a

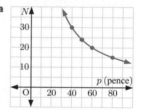

b

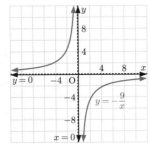

c

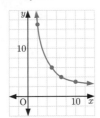

5 135 minutes

REVIEW SET 2B

1 n is divided by 2.5.

2 **a** **i**

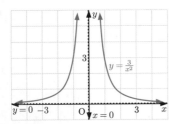

ii For each of the data pairs, xy is not constant, so the variables are not inversely proportional.

b **i**

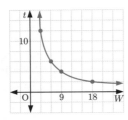

ii For each of the data pairs, $Wt = 36$, which is constant, so W and t are inversely proportional.

$$\therefore \quad t = \frac{36}{W}$$

3 60 days

4 **a** $y = \dfrac{18}{x}$ **b** $y = -\dfrac{28}{x}$ **c** $C = \dfrac{16}{t}$

5

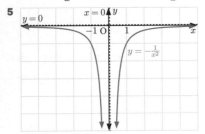

The horizontal asymptote is $y = 0$.
The vertical asymptote is $x = 0$.
The graph is symmetric about $x = 0$. The graph is in quadrants 3 and 4.

6 **a** Yes, as $l = \dfrac{36}{w}$ (or $w = \dfrac{36}{l}$ or $lw = 36$, which is constant).

b

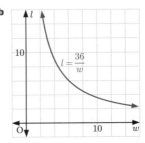

EXERCISE 3A.1

1 **a** $x = 0$ or $-\frac{7}{4}$ **b** $x = 0$ or $-\frac{1}{3}$ **c** $x = 0$ or $\frac{7}{3}$
  d $x = 0$ or $\frac{11}{2}$ **e** $x = 0$ or $\frac{8}{3}$ **f** $x = 0$ or $\frac{3}{2}$
  g $x = 2$ or 3 **h** $x = -2$ or 4 **i** $x = 3$ or 7
  j $x = 3$ **k** $x = -4$ or 3 **l** $x = -11$ or 3

2 **a** $x = \frac{2}{3}$ **b** $x = -\frac{1}{2}$ or 7 **c** $x = -\frac{2}{3}$ or 6
  d $x = \frac{1}{3}$ or -2 **e** $x = \frac{3}{2}$ or 1 **f** $x = -\frac{2}{3}$ or -2
  g $x = -\frac{2}{3}$ or 4 **h** $x = \frac{1}{2}$ or $-\frac{3}{2}$ **i** $x = -\frac{1}{4}$ or 3
  j $x = -\frac{3}{4}$ or $\frac{5}{3}$ **k** $x = \frac{1}{7}$ or -1 **l** $x = -2$ or $\frac{28}{15}$

3 **a** $x = 2$ or 5 **b** $x = -3$ or 2 **c** $x = 0$ or $-\frac{3}{2}$
  d $x = 1$ or 2 **e** $x = \frac{1}{2}$ or -1 **f** $x = 3$
  g $x = 1$ or -2 **h** $x = 6$ or -4 **i** $x = 7$ or -5
  j $x = 4$ or -2

EXERCISE 3A.2

1 **a** $x = -5 \pm \sqrt{2}$ **b** no real solutions   **c** $x = 4 \pm 2\sqrt{2}$
  d $x = 8 \pm \sqrt{7}$ **e** $x = -3 \pm \sqrt{5}$ **f** $x = 2 \pm \sqrt{6}$
  g $x = -1 \pm \sqrt{10}$ **h** $x = -\frac{1}{2} \pm \frac{\sqrt{3}}{2}$ **i** $x = \frac{1}{3} \pm \frac{\sqrt{7}}{3}$

2 **a** $x = 2 \pm \sqrt{3}$ **b** $x = -3 \pm \sqrt{7}$ **c** $x = 7 \pm \sqrt{3}$
  d $x = 2 \pm \sqrt{7}$ **e** $x = -3 \pm \sqrt{2}$ **f** $x = 1 \pm \sqrt{7}$
  g $x = -3 \pm \sqrt{11}$ **h** $x = 4 \pm \sqrt{6}$ **i** no real solutions

3 **a** $x = -1 \pm \frac{1}{\sqrt{2}}$ **b** $x = \frac{5}{2} \pm \frac{\sqrt{19}}{2}$ **c** $x = -2 \pm \sqrt{\frac{7}{3}}$
  d $x = 1 \pm \sqrt{\frac{7}{3}}$ **e** $x = \frac{3}{2} \pm \sqrt{\frac{37}{20}}$ **f** $x = -\frac{1}{2} \pm \frac{\sqrt{6}}{2}$

4 **a** $x = \frac{2}{3} \pm \frac{\sqrt{10}}{3}$ **b** $x = -\frac{1}{10} \pm \frac{\sqrt{21}}{10}$ **c** $x = -\frac{5}{6} \pm \frac{\sqrt{13}}{6}$

5 $x = \dfrac{-b \pm \sqrt{b^2 - 4ac}}{2a}$

EXERCISE 3A.3

1 **a** $x = 2 \pm \sqrt{7}$ **b** $x = -3 \pm \sqrt{2}$ **c** $x = 2 \pm \sqrt{3}$
  d $x = -2 \pm \sqrt{5}$ **e** $x = 2 \pm \sqrt{2}$ **f** $x = \frac{1}{2} \pm \frac{\sqrt{7}}{2}$
  g $x = \frac{5}{6} \pm \frac{\sqrt{37}}{6}$ **h** $x = 2 \pm \sqrt{10}$ **i** $x = \frac{7}{4} \pm \frac{\sqrt{33}}{4}$

2 **a** $x = -2 \pm 2\sqrt{2}$ **b** $x = -\frac{5}{8} \pm \frac{\sqrt{57}}{8}$ **c** $x = \frac{5}{2} \pm \frac{\sqrt{13}}{2}$
  d $x = -\frac{4}{9} \pm \frac{\sqrt{7}}{9}$ **e** $x = -\frac{7}{4} \pm \frac{\sqrt{97}}{4}$ **f** $x = \frac{1}{8} \pm \frac{\sqrt{145}}{8}$
  g $x = \frac{1}{2} \pm \frac{\sqrt{7}}{2}$ **h** $x = \frac{1}{2} \pm \frac{\sqrt{5}}{2}$ **i** $x = \frac{3}{4} \pm \frac{\sqrt{17}}{4}$

EXERCISE 3B

1 **a** $\Delta = 13$ **b** 2 distinct irrational roots   **c** $x = \frac{7}{2} \pm \frac{\sqrt{13}}{2}$

2 **a** $\Delta = 0$ **b** 1 root (repeated)   **c** $x = \frac{1}{2}$

3 **a** $x^2 = -5$, $\therefore$ no real roots   **b** $\Delta = -20$

4 **a** 2 distinct irrational roots   **b** 2 distinct rational roots
  c 2 distinct rational roots   **d** 2 distinct irrational roots
  e no real roots   **f** a repeated root

5 **a, c, d, f**

6 **a** $\Delta = 16 - 4m$

  i $m = 4$ **ii** $m < 4$ **iii** $m > 4$

  b $\Delta = 9 - 8m$

  i $m = \frac{9}{8}$ **ii** $m < \frac{9}{8}$, $m \neq 0$ **iii** $m > \frac{9}{8}$

  c $\Delta = 9 - 4m$

  i $m = \frac{9}{4}$ **ii** $m < \frac{9}{4}$, $m \neq 0$ **iii** $m > \frac{9}{4}$

EXERCISE 3C

1 **a** **i** sum $= -4$, product $= -21$ **ii** roots are -7 and 3
  b **i** sum $= 3$,   product $= \frac{5}{4}$ **ii** roots are $\frac{1}{2}$ and $\frac{5}{2}$
  c **i** sum $= \frac{4}{3}$,   product $= -\frac{2}{3}$ **ii** roots are $\frac{2}{3} \pm \frac{\sqrt{10}}{3}$

2 **a** sum $= 5$,   product $= 5$ **b** roots are $\frac{5}{2} \pm \frac{\sqrt{5}}{2}$

3 $k = -\frac{3}{5}$,   roots are -1 and $\frac{1}{3}$

4 **a** $3\alpha = \frac{6}{a}$, $2\alpha^2 = \frac{a-2}{a}$

  b $a = 4$, roots are $\frac{1}{2}$ and 1 or $a = -2$, roots are -1 and -2

5 $k = 4$, roots are $-\frac{1}{2}$ and $\frac{3}{2}$ or $k = 16$, roots are $-\frac{5}{4}$ and $\frac{3}{4}$

6 **a** $3x^2 - 2x - 4 = 0$ **b** $3x^2 + 4x - 16 = 0$

7 $7x^2 - 48x + 64 = 0$ **8** $a(8x^2 - 70x + 147) = 0$, $a \neq 0$

EXERCISE 3D.1

1 **a**   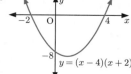   **b**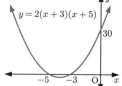

  c   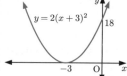   **d**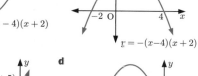

  e   **f**

2 **a** $x = 1$ **b** $x = 1$ **c** $x = -4$
  d $x = -3$ **e** $x = -3$ **f** $x = -2$

3 **a C**   **b E**   **c B**   **d F**   **e G**   **f H**
  g I   **h A**   **i D**

4 **a**   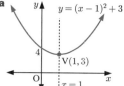   **b**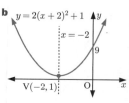

  c   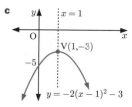   **d**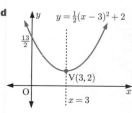

  e   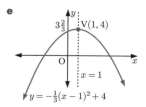   **f**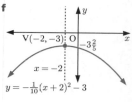

5 **a G**   **b A**   **c E**   **d B**   **e I**   **f C**
  g D   **h F**   **i H**

EXERCISE 3D.2

1 **a** $y = (x - 1)^2 + 2$ **b** $y = (x + 2)^2 - 6$

  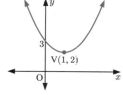   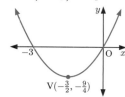

  c $y = (x - 2)^2 - 4$ **d** $y = \left(x + \frac{3}{2}\right)^2 - \frac{9}{4}$

  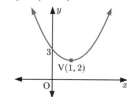   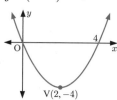

  e $y = \left(x + \frac{5}{2}\right)^2 - \frac{33}{4}$ **f** $y = \left(x - \frac{3}{2}\right)^2 - \frac{1}{4}$

  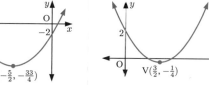   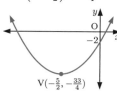

  g $y = (x - 3)^2 - 4$ **h** $y = (x + 4)^2 - 18$

  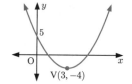   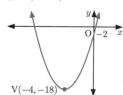

i $y = \left(x - \frac{5}{2}\right)^2 - \frac{21}{4}$

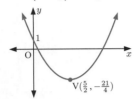

2 a i $y = 2(x+1)^2 + 3$
ii $(-1, 3)$ **iii** 5
iv

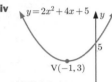

b i $y = 2(x-2)^2 - 5$
ii $(2, -5)$ **iii** 3
iv

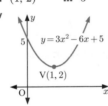

c i $y = 2(x - \frac{3}{2})^2 - \frac{7}{2}$
ii $(\frac{3}{2}, -\frac{7}{2})$ **iii** 1
iv

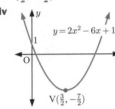

d i $y = 3(x-1)^2 + 2$
ii $(1, 2)$ **iii** 5
iv

e i $y = -(x-2)^2 + 6$
ii $(2, 6)$ **iii** 2
iv

f i $y = -2(x + \frac{5}{4})^2 + \frac{49}{8}$
ii $(-\frac{5}{4}, \frac{49}{8})$ **iii** 3
iv

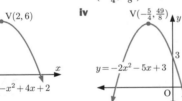

EXERCISE 3D.3

1 a $(2, -2)$ **b** $(-1, -4)$ **c** $(0, 4)$ **d** $(0, 1)$
e $(-2, -15)$ **f** $(-2, -5)$ **g** $(-\frac{3}{2}, -\frac{11}{2})$
h $(\frac{5}{2}, -\frac{19}{2})$ **i** $(1, -\frac{9}{2})$ **j** $(14, -43)$

2 a i $x = 4$
ii $(4, -9)$
iii x-intercepts 1, 7,
    y-intercept 7
iv

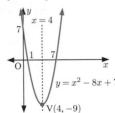

b i $x = -3$
ii $(-3, 1)$
iii x-int. -2, -4,
    y-intercept -8
iv

c i $x = 3$
ii $(3, 9)$
iii x-intercepts 0, 6,
    y-intercept 0
iv

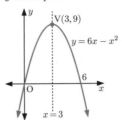

d i $x = \frac{3}{2}$
ii $(\frac{3}{2}, \frac{1}{4})$
iii x-intercepts 1, 2,
    y-intercept -2
iv

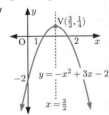

e i $x = -1$
ii $(-1, -26)$
iii x-int. $-1 \pm \sqrt{13}$,
    y-intercept -24
iv

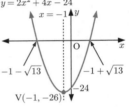

f i $x = \frac{2}{3}$
ii $(\frac{2}{3}, \frac{1}{3})$
iii x-intercepts $\frac{1}{3}$, 1,
    y-intercept -1
iv

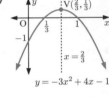

g i $x = \frac{5}{4}$
ii $(\frac{5}{4}, -\frac{9}{8})$
iii x-intercepts $\frac{1}{2}$, 2,
    y-intercept 2
iv

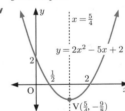

h i $x = 1$
ii $(1, -9)$
iii x-intercepts $-\frac{1}{2}$, $\frac{5}{2}$,
    y-intercept -5
iv

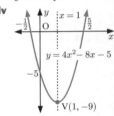

i i $x = 4$
ii $(4, 1)$
iii x-intercepts 2, 6,
    y-intercept -3
iv

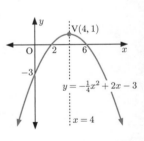

EXERCISE 3D.4

1 a cuts x-axis twice, concave up
b cuts x-axis twice, concave up
c lies entirely below the x-axis, concave down, negative definite
d cuts x-axis twice, concave up
e touches x-axis, concave up
f cuts x-axis twice, concave down
g cuts x-axis twice, concave up
h cuts x-axis twice, concave down
i touches x-axis, concave up

2 a concave up

b $\Delta = 17$ which is > 0
∴ cuts x-axis twice

c x-intercepts
≈ 0.22 and 2.28

d y-intercept is 1

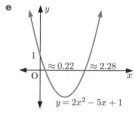
$y = 2x^2 - 5x + 1$

3 a $\Delta = -12$ which is < 0
∴ does not cut x-axis

b negative definite

c vertex is $(2, -3)$,
y-intercept is -7

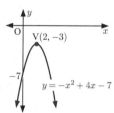
V$(2, -3)$
-7
$y = -x^2 + 4x - 7$

4 a $a = 2$ which is > 0 and $\Delta = -40$ which is < 0
∴ positive definite.

b $a = -2$ which is < 0 and $\Delta = -23$ which is < 0
∴ negative definite.

c $a = 1$ which is > 0 and $\Delta = -15$ which is < 0
∴ positive definite so $x^2 - 3x + 6 > 0$ for all x.

d $a = -1$ which is < 0 and $\Delta = -8$ which is < 0
∴ negative definite so $4x - x^2 - 6 < 0$ for all x.

5 $a = 3$ which is > 0 and $\Delta = k^2 + 12$ which is always > 0
{as $k^2 \geqslant 0$ for all k} ∴ cannot be positive definite.

6 $-4 < k < 4$

EXERCISE 3E

1 a $y = 2(x - 1)(x - 2)$ **b** $y = 3(x - 2)^2$
c $y = (x - 1)(x - 3)$ **d** $y = -(x - 3)(x + 1)$
e $y = -3(x - 1)^2$ **f** $y = -2(x + 2)(x - 3)$

2 a $y = \frac{3}{2}(x - 2)(x - 4)$ **b** $y = -\frac{1}{2}(x + 4)(x - 2)$
c $y = -\frac{4}{3}(x + 3)^2$

3 a $y = 3x^2 - 18x + 15$ **b** $y = -4x^2 + 6x + 4$
c $y = -x^2 + 6x - 9$ **d** $y = 4x^2 + 16x + 16$

4 a $y = \frac{3}{2}x^2 - 6x + \frac{9}{2}$ **b** $y = -\frac{1}{3}x^2 + \frac{2}{3}x + 5$

5 a $y = -(x - 2)^2 + 4$ **b** $y = 2(x - 2)^2 - 1$
c $y = -2(x - 3)^2 + 8$ **d** $y = \frac{2}{3}(x - 4)^2 - 6$
e $y = -2(x - 2)^2 + 3$ **f** $y = 2(x - \frac{1}{2})^2 - \frac{3}{2}$

6 $y = 3$

EXERCISE 3F

1 a $(1, 7)$ and $(2, 8)$ **b** $(4, 5)$ and $(-3, -9)$
c $(3, 0)$ (touching)   **d** graphs do not meet

2 $c = -9$ **3** $m = 0$ or -8 **4** -1 or 11

5 a $c < -9$
b example: $c = -10$

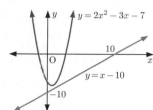
$y = 2x^2 - 3x - 7$
$y = x - 10$

6 a $c > -2$ **b** $c = -2$ **c** $c < -2$

7 a $m < -1$ or $m > 7$ **b** $m = -1$ or $m = 7$
c $-1 < m < 7$

8 Hint: A straight line through $(0, 3)$ will have an equation of the form $y = mx + 3$.

EXERCISE 3G

1 7 and -5 or -7 and 5   **2** 5 or $\frac{1}{5}$

3 18 and 20 or -18 and -20 **4** 15 sides

5 3.48 cm   **6 b** 6 cm by 6 cm by 7 cm

7 11.2 cm square   **8** no

10 a $y = -\frac{8}{9}x^2 + 8$
b No, as the tunnel is only 4.44 m high when it is the same width as the truck.

11 a $h = -5(t - 2)^2 + 80$ **b** 75 m   **c** 6 seconds

12 b The graph is a concave down parabola.   **c** 21.25 m
d $y = -0.05x^2 + 2x + 1.25$ **e** yes

EXERCISE 3H

1 a min. -1, when $x = 1$ **b** max. 8, when $x = -1$
c max. $8\frac{1}{3}$, when $x = \frac{1}{3}$ **d** min. $-1\frac{1}{8}$, when $x = -\frac{1}{4}$
e min. $4\frac{15}{16}$, when $x = \frac{1}{8}$ **f** max. $6\frac{1}{8}$, when $x = \frac{7}{4}$

2 a 40 refrigerators   **b** £4000

4 500 m by 250 m   **5 c** 100 m by 112.5 m

6 a $41\frac{2}{3}$ m by $41\frac{2}{3}$ m   **b** 50 m by $31\frac{1}{4}$ m

7 b $3\frac{1}{8}$ units   **8 a** $y = 6 - \frac{3}{4}x$ **b** 3 cm by 4 cm

REVIEW SET 3A

1 a -2 and 1   **e**
b $x = -\frac{1}{2}$
c 4
d $(-\frac{1}{2}, \frac{9}{2})$

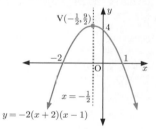
V$(-\frac{1}{2}, \frac{9}{2})$
4
-2 1
$x = -\frac{1}{2}$
$y = -2(x + 2)(x - 1)$

2 a $x = 0$ or 4   **b** $x = -\frac{5}{3}$ or 2   **c** $x = 15$ or -4

3 a $x = -\frac{5}{2} \pm \frac{\sqrt{13}}{2}$ **b** $x = -\frac{11}{6} \pm \frac{\sqrt{145}}{6}$

4 a sum $= -8$, product $= -11$
b sum $= 3$, product $= \frac{7}{5}$

5 a
$y = (x - 2)^2 - 4$
$x = 2$
V$(2, -4)$

b
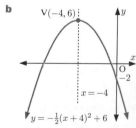
V$(-4, 6)$
-2
$x = -4$
$y = -\frac{1}{2}(x + 4)^2 + 6$

6 a $y = 3x^2 - 24x + 48$ **b** $y = \frac{2}{5}x^2 + \frac{16}{5}x + \frac{37}{5}$

7 maximum $= 5$ when $x = 1$

8 $(4, 4)$ and $(-3, 18)$ **9** $k < -3\frac{1}{8}$

10 a $m = \frac{9}{8}$ **b** $m < \frac{9}{8}$ **c** $m > \frac{9}{8}$ **11** $\frac{6}{5}$ or $\frac{5}{6}$

12 Hint: Let the line have equation $y = mx + 10$.

13 a $y = 2(x+1)^2 - 5$ **b**

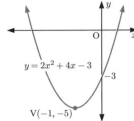

14 a $y = \frac{20}{9}(x-2)^2 - 20$ **b** $y = -\frac{2}{7}(x-1)(x-7)$

c $y = \frac{2}{9}(x+3)^2$

15 21 m

REVIEW SET 3B

1 a $x = 2$ **d**

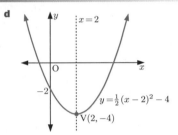

b $(2, -4)$

c -2

2 a $x = \frac{5}{2} \pm \frac{\sqrt{37}}{2}$ **b** $x = \frac{7}{4} \pm \frac{\sqrt{73}}{4}$

3 a $\Delta = 0$, a repeated root

b $\Delta = 41$, 2 distinct irrational roots

c $\Delta = -11$, no real roots

4 $y = 7x^2 - x + 3$ **5** $x = \frac{4}{3}$, $V(\frac{4}{3}, 12\frac{1}{3})$

6 a graph cuts   **b** graph cuts
x-axis twice x-axis twice

7 a $a < 0$, $\Delta > 0$, neither

b $a > 0$, $\Delta < 0$, positive definite

8 $y = -6(x-2)^2 + 25$

9 a $x = -1$ **d**

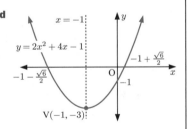

b $(-1, -3)$

c x-int. $-1 \pm \frac{\sqrt{6}}{2}$

y-intercept -1,

10 a $c > -6$

b example: $c = -2$, $(-1, -5)$ and $(3, 7)$

11 a $y = -\frac{2}{5}(x+5)(x-1)$ **b** $(-2, 3\frac{3}{5})$, $x = -2$

12 a minimum $= 5\frac{2}{3}$ when $x = -\frac{2}{3}$

b maximum $= 5\frac{1}{8}$ when $x = -\frac{5}{4}$

13 a $a > 0$ {graph opens upwards}

b $b < 0$ $\{x = -\dfrac{b}{2a} > 0$ is x-coordinate of vertex$\}$

c $c < 0$ {y-intercept is negative}

d $\Delta > 0$ {two x-intercepts $\therefore$ two real roots}

14 a i $y = (x+2)^2 - 1$ **b i** $y = (x+1)^2 - 4$

ii $y = (x+3)(x+1)$ **ii** $y = (x+3)(x-1)$

iii   **iii**

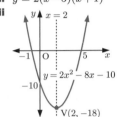   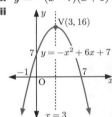

c i $y = 2(x-2)^2 - 18$ **d i** $y = -(x-3)^2 + 16$

ii $y = 2(x-5)(x+1)$ **ii** $y = -(x-7)(x+1)$

iii   **iii**

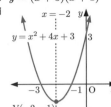

15 b $37\frac{1}{2}$ m by $33\frac{1}{3}$ m   **c** 1250 m^2

EXERCISE 4A

1 a Is a function, since for any value of x there is at most one value of y.

b Is a function, since for any value of x there is at most one value of y.

c Is not a function. If $x^2 + y^2 = 9$, then $y = \pm\sqrt{9 - x^2}$. So, for example, for $x = 2$, $y = \pm\sqrt{5}$.

2 a function   **b** function   **c** function

d not a function   **e** not a function   **f** function

g function   **h** not a function

3 Not a function as a 2-year-old child could pay £0 or £20.

4 No, because a vertical line (the y-axis) would cut the relation more than once.

5 No. A vertical line is not a function. It will not pass the "vertical line" test.

6 a

x	9	4	1	0	1	4	9
y	-3	-2	-1	0	1	2	3

b

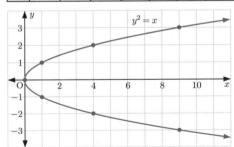

c $y^2 = x$ is a relation but not a function.
$y = x^2$ is a function (and a relation).
$y^2 = x$ has a horizontal axis of symmetry (the x-axis).
$y = x^2$ has a vertical axis of symmetry (the y-axis).
Both $y^2 = x$ and $y = x^2$ have vertex $(0, 0)$.
$y^2 = x$ is a rotation of $y = x^2$ clockwise through $90°$ about the origin *or* $y^2 = x$ is a reflection of $y = x^2$ in the line $y = x$.

d i The part of $y^2 = x$ in the first quadrant.

  ii $y = \sqrt{x}$ is a function as any vertical line cuts the graph at most once.

EXERCISE 4B

1 a 2 **b** 2 **c** -16 **d** -68 **e** $\frac{17}{4}$

2 a -3 **b** 3 **c** 3 **d** -3 **e** $\frac{15}{2}$

3 a i 1 **ii** -1 **b** $x = -4$

4 a i $-\frac{7}{2}$ **ii** $-\frac{3}{4}$ **iii** $-\frac{4}{9}$ **b** $x = 4$ **c** $x = \frac{9}{5}$

5 a $7 - 3a$ **b** $7 + 3a$ **c** $-3a - 2$ **d** $7 - 6a$
  e $1 - 3x$ **f** $7 - 3x - 3h$

6 a $2x^2 + 19x + 43$ **b** $2x^2 - 11x + 13$
  c $2x^2 - 3x - 1$ **d** $2x^4 + 3x^2 - 1$
  e $18x^2 + 9x - 1$ **f** $2x^2 + (4h + 3)x + 2h^2 + 3h - 1$

7 f is the function which converts x into $f(x)$ whereas $f(x)$ is the value of the function at any value of x.

8

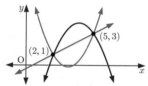

9 $f(x) = -2x + 5$

10 a $P(3) = 35$. There are 35 L of petrol in the tank after 3 minutes.
  b $t = 4.5$ After $4\frac{1}{2}$ minutes there are 50 L of petrol in the tank.
  c 5 L

11 a $H(30) = 800$. After 30 minutes the balloon is 800 m high.
  b $t = 20$ or 70. After 20 minutes and after 70 minutes the balloon is 600 m high.
  c $0 \leqslant t \leqslant 80$ **d** 0 m to 900 m

12 a $V(4) = 5400$; $V(4)$ is the value of the photocopier in pounds after 4 years.
  b $t = 6$. After 6 years the value of the photocopier is £3600.
  c £9000 **d** $0 \leqslant t \leqslant 10$

EXERCISE 4C.1

1

Set notation	Interval notation
$\{x : x < 4\}$	$x \in (-\infty, 4)$
Number line graph	Meaning
(number line with open circle at 4, arrow left)	the set of all x such that x is less than 4

Set notation	Interval notation
$\{x : x < 9\}$	$x \in (-\infty, 9)$
Number line graph	Meaning
(number line with open circle at 9, arrow left)	the set of all x such that x is less than 9

Set notation	Interval notation
$\{x : 3.2 \leqslant x < 3.7\}$	$x \in [3.2, 3.7)$
Number line graph	Meaning
(number line with filled circle at 3.2, open circle at 3.7)	the set of all x such that x is between 3.2 and 3.7, including 3.2

Set notation	Interval notation
$\{x : \frac{2}{5} \leqslant x \leqslant \frac{8}{5}\}$	$x \in [\frac{2}{5}, \frac{8}{5}]$
Number line graph	Meaning
(number line with filled circles at $\frac{2}{5}$ and $\frac{8}{5}$)	the set of all x such that x is between $\frac{2}{5}$ and $\frac{8}{5}$ inclusive

Set notation	Interval notation
$\{x : x \geqslant 17\}$	$x \in [17, \infty)$
Number line graph	Meaning
(number line with filled circle at 17, arrow right)	the set of all x such that x is greater than or equal to 17

Set notation	Interval notation
$\{x : 0 < x < 4 \cup x > 6\}$	$x \in (0, 4) \cup (6, \infty)$
Number line graph	Meaning
(number line with open circles at 0, 4, 6)	the set of all x such that x is between 0 and 4, or greater than 6

Set notation	Interval notation
$\{x : x \leqslant 1 \cup x > 2\}$	$x \in (-\infty, 1] \cup (2, \infty)$
Number line graph	Meaning
(number line with filled circle at 1 arrow left, open circle at 2 arrow right)	the set of all x such that x is less than or equal to 1 or greater than 2

Set notation	Interval notation
$\{x : x < 5, \; x \geqslant 11\}$	$x \in (-\infty, 5) \cup [11, \infty)$
Number line graph	Meaning
(number line with open circle at 5 arrow left, filled circle at 11 arrow right)	the set of all x such that x is less than 5 or greater than or equal to 11

2 a $x \in (-\infty, 0) \cup [5, 10)$ **b** $x \in [1.6, 3.2) \cup [4.2, \infty)$

EXERCISE 4C.2

1 a

b Domain $= \{x : x > 0\}$, Range $= \{2, 3, 5, 7, 9\}$

2 a At any moment in time there can be only one temperature, so the graph is a function.
  b Domain $= \{t : 0 \leqslant t \leqslant 30\}$, Range $= \{T : 15 \leqslant T \leqslant 25\}$

3 a Domain $= \{x : x \geqslant -1\}$, Range $= \{y : y \leqslant 3\}$
  b Domain $= \{x : -1 < x \leqslant 5\}$, Range $= \{y : 1 < y \leqslant 3\}$
  c Domain $= \{x : x \neq 2\}$, Range $= \{y : y \neq -1\}$
  d Domain $= \{x : x \in \mathbb{R}\}$, Range $= \{y : 0 < y \leqslant 2\}$
  e Domain $= \{x : x \in \mathbb{R}\}$, Range $= \{y : y \geqslant -1\}$
  f Domain $= \{x : x \in \mathbb{R}\}$, Range $= \{y : y \leqslant \frac{25}{4}\}$
  g Domain $= \{x : x \geqslant -4\}$, Range $= \{y : y \geqslant -3\}$

h Domain $= \{x : x \in \mathbb{R}\}$, Range $= \{y : y > -2\}$

i Domain $= \{x : x \neq \pm 2\}$,

Range $= \{y : y \leqslant -1 \ \text{or} \ y > 0\}$

4 a true   **b** false   **c** true   **d** true

5 a

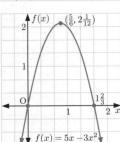

Domain $= \{x : x \in \mathbb{R}\}$,

Range $= \{y : y \geqslant -\frac{9}{4}\}$

b

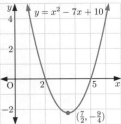

Domain $= \{x : x \in \mathbb{R}\}$,

Range $= \{y : y \leqslant 2\frac{1}{12}\}$

6 a $f(x)$ defined for $x \geqslant -6$, Domain $= \{x : x \geqslant -6\}$

b $f(x)$ defined for $x \neq 0$, Domain $= \{x : x \neq 0\}$

c $f(x)$ defined for $x < \frac{3}{2}$, Domain $= \{x : x < \frac{3}{2}\}$

7 a $x \geqslant 0$

b i 0   **ii** 1   **iii** 2

c

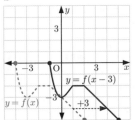

d Domain $= \{x : x \geqslant 0\}$,

Range $= \{y : y \geqslant 0\}$

8 a Domain $= \{x : x \geqslant 2\}$, Range $= \{y : y \geqslant 0\}$

b Domain $= \{x : x \neq 0\}$, Range $= \{y : y > 0\}$

c Domain $= \{x : x \leqslant 4\}$, Range $= \{y : y \geqslant 0\}$

d Domain $= \{x : x \in \mathbb{R}\}$, Range $= \{y : y \geqslant 2\}$

e Domain $= \{x : x \leqslant -2 \ \text{or} \ x \geqslant 2\}$, Range $= \{y : y \geqslant 0\}$

f Domain $= \{x : x \neq 0\}$, Range $= \{y : y \leqslant -2 \ \text{or} \ y \geqslant 2\}$

g Domain $= \{x : x \neq 2\}$, Range $= \{y : y \neq 1\}$

h Domain $= \{x : x \in \mathbb{R}\}$, Range $= \{y : y \in \mathbb{R}\}$

i Domain $= \{x : x \neq -1 \ \text{and} \ x \neq 2\}$,

Range $= \{y : y \leqslant \frac{1}{3} \ \text{or} \ y \geqslant 3\}$

j Domain $= \{x : x \neq 0\}$, Range $= \{y : y \geqslant 2\}$

k Domain $= \{x : x \neq 0\}$, Range $= \{y : y \leqslant -2 \ \text{or} \ y \geqslant 2\}$

l Domain $= \{x : x \in \mathbb{R}\}$, Range $= \{y : y \geqslant -8\}$

EXERCISE 4D.1

1 a

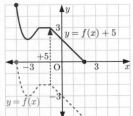

b

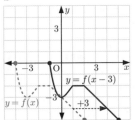

c

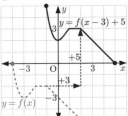

2 a

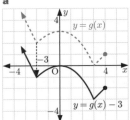

b

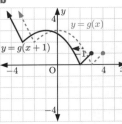

c

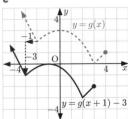

d

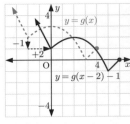

3 a $g(x) = f(x - 4)$ **b** $g(x) = f(x + 1) + 3$

4 a $g(x) = 2x - 1$ **b** $g(x) = 3x + 2$

c $g(x) = -x^2 + 5x - 4$ **d** $g(x) = x^2 - 6x + 4$

5 $g(x) = (x - h)^2 + k$ has vertex (h, k).

$f(x) = x^2$ has vertex $(0, 0)$, and $(0, 0)$ translated through

$\begin{pmatrix} h \\ k \end{pmatrix}$ is (h, k).

6 $(1, -9)$

7 a y-intercept is -1 **b** x-intercepts are -2 and 5

c inconclusive

EXERCISE 4D.2

1 a

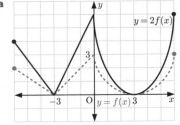

b

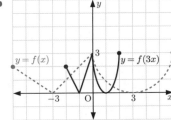

2 a

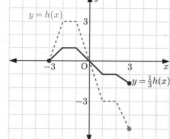

b

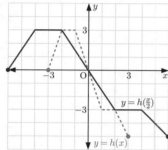

3 a $g(x) = 2f(x)$ **b** $g(x) = f\left(\dfrac{x}{3}\right)$

4 cm **5 a** $(2, 25)$ **b** $(-25, -15)$

6 a $g(x) = 2x^2 + 4$ **b** $g(x) = 5 - x$
  c $g(x) = \frac{1}{4}x^3 + 2x^2 - \frac{1}{2}$ **d** $g(x) = 8x^2 + 2x - 3$

7

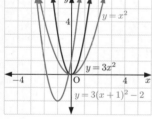

$y = x^2$ is transformed to $y = 3(x + 1)^2 - 2$ by vertically dilating with scale factor 3 and then translating through $\begin{pmatrix} -1 \\ -2 \end{pmatrix}$.

8

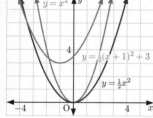

$y = x^2$ is transformed to $y = \frac{1}{2}(x + 1)^2 + 3$ by vertically dilating with scale factor $\frac{1}{2}$ and then translating through $\begin{pmatrix} -1 \\ 3 \end{pmatrix}$.

9

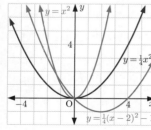

$y = x^2$ is transformed to $y = \frac{1}{4}(x - 2)^2 - 1$ by vertically dilating with scale factor $\frac{1}{4}$ and then translating through $\begin{pmatrix} 2 \\ -1 \end{pmatrix}$.

10

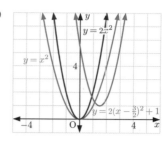

$y = x^2$ is transformed to $y = 2(x - \frac{3}{2})^2 + 1$ by vertically dilating with scale factor 2 and then translating through $\begin{pmatrix} \frac{3}{2} \\ 1 \end{pmatrix}$.

EXERCISE 4D.3

1 a

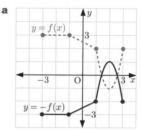

b

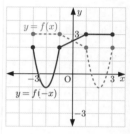

2 a

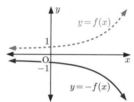

b

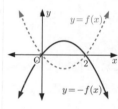

c

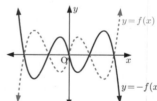

3 a

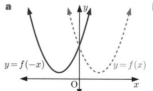

b

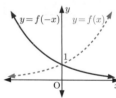

c

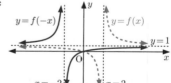

4 a $(3, 0)$ **b** $(7, 1)$

5 a $(-2, -1)$ **b** $(-5, -4)$

6 a Reflect $y = f(x)$ in the x-axis.

  b Vertically dilate $y = -f(x)$ with scale factor 3 to obtain $y = -3f(x)$.

c

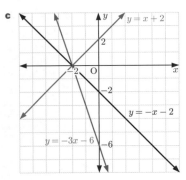

7 a Reflect $y = f(x)$ in the y-axis to obtain $y = f(-x)$.

b Horizontally dilate $y = f(-x)$ with scale factor 2 to obtain $y = f(-\frac{1}{2}x)$.

c

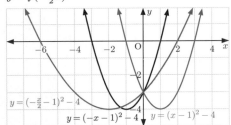

EXERCISE 4D.4

1 a

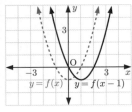

x-intercepts are ± 1, y-intercept is -1

b i

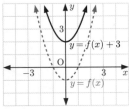

$y = f(x)$ has been translated 3 units upwards.

ii

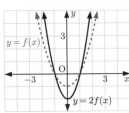

$y = f(x)$ has been translated 1 unit to the right.

iii

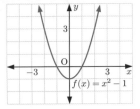

$y = f(x)$ has been vertically dilated with scale factor 2.

iv

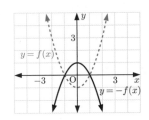

$y = f(x)$ has been reflected in the x-axis.

2 a i A vertical dilation with scale factor 3.

ii $g(x) = 3f(x)$

b i A vertical translation through $\begin{pmatrix} 0 \\ -2 \end{pmatrix}$.

ii $g(x) = f(x) - 2$

c i A vertical dilation with scale factor $\frac{1}{2}$.

ii $g(x) = \frac{1}{2}f(x)$

d i A reflection in the y-axis.

ii $g(x) = f(-x)$

3

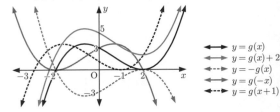

4

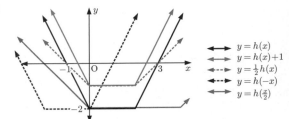

5 a $f(-x - 4) - 1$ **b** $f(-x + 4) - 1$

c $\frac{1}{2}f(x + 2) + \frac{1}{2}$ **d** $\frac{1}{2}f(x + 2) + 1$

6 a A reflection in the x-axis, then a translation through $\begin{pmatrix} -1 \\ 3 \end{pmatrix}$.

b A horizontal dilation with scale factor 2, then a translation through $\begin{pmatrix} 0 \\ -7 \end{pmatrix}$.

c A horizontal dilation with scale factor $\frac{1}{3}$, then a translation through $\begin{pmatrix} 1 \\ 0 \end{pmatrix}$.

d A horizontal dilation with scale factor 4, a vertical dilation with scale factor 2, then a translation through $\begin{pmatrix} 1 \\ -1 \end{pmatrix}$.

e A reflection in the y-axis, a vertical dilation with scale factor 2, then a translation through $\begin{pmatrix} -1 \\ 5 \end{pmatrix}$.

EXERCISE 4E

1 a $y = \dfrac{1}{2x}$ **b** $y = \dfrac{3}{x}$ **c** $y = \dfrac{1}{x + 3}$

d $y = 4 + \dfrac{1}{x} = \dfrac{4x + 1}{x}$

2 **a** $g(x) = \dfrac{3}{x-1} - 1 = \dfrac{-x+4}{x-1}$

b vertical asymptote $x = 1$,
horizontal asymptote $y = -1$

c Domain $= \{x : x \neq 1\}$,   Range $= \{y : y \neq -1\}$

d

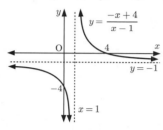

3 **a** **i** vertical asymptote is $x = 1$,
horizontal asymptote is $y = 2$

     ii A vertical dilation with scale factor 6, then a translation
through $\begin{pmatrix} 1 \\ 2 \end{pmatrix}$.

b **i** vertical asymptote is $x = -1$,
horizontal asymptote is $y = 3$

     ii A vertical dilation with scale factor 5, reflection in the
x-axis, then a translation through $\begin{pmatrix} -1 \\ 3 \end{pmatrix}$.

c **i** vertical asymptote is $x = 2$,
horizontal asymptote is $y = -2$

     ii A vertical dilation with scale factor 5, reflection in the
x-axis, then a translation through $\begin{pmatrix} 2 \\ -2 \end{pmatrix}$.

4 **a** **i** vertical asymptote is $x = -1$,
horizontal asymptote is $y = 2$

     ii as $x \to -1^-$, $y \to -\infty$
as $x \to -1^+$, $y \to \infty$
as $x \to -\infty$, $y \to 2^-$
as $x \to \infty$, $y \to 2^+$

     iii x-intercept is $-\frac{3}{2}$, y-intercept is 3

     iv

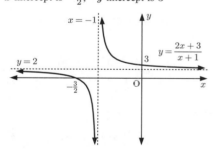

     v Translate $\begin{pmatrix} -1 \\ 2 \end{pmatrix}$.   **vi** Translate $\begin{pmatrix} 1 \\ -2 \end{pmatrix}$.

b **i** vertical asymptote is $x = 2$,
horizontal asymptote is $y = 0$

     ii as $x \to 2^-$, $y \to -\infty$
as $x \to 2^+$, $y \to \infty$
as $x \to -\infty$, $y \to 0^-$
as $x \to \infty$, $y \to 0^+$

     iii no x-intercept, y-intercept is $-1\frac{1}{2}$

iv

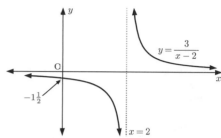

v Vertical dilation with scale factor 3, then translate $\begin{pmatrix} 2 \\ 0 \end{pmatrix}$.

vi Translate $\begin{pmatrix} -2 \\ 0 \end{pmatrix}$, then vertical dilation with scale
factor $\frac{1}{3}$.

c **i** vertical asymptote is $x = 3$,
horizontal asymptote is $y = -2$

     ii as $x \to 3^-$, $y \to \infty$
as $x \to 3^+$, $y \to -\infty$
as $x \to -\infty$, $y \to -2^+$
as $x \to \infty$, $y \to -2^-$

     iii x-intercept is $\frac{1}{2}$, y-intercept is $-\frac{1}{3}$

     iv

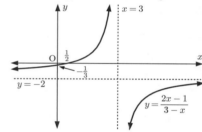

     v Vertical dilation with scale factor 5, reflect in x-axis, then
translate $\begin{pmatrix} 3 \\ -2 \end{pmatrix}$.

     vi Translate $\begin{pmatrix} -3 \\ 2 \end{pmatrix}$, reflect in x-axis, then vertical
dilation with scale factor $\frac{1}{5}$.

d **i** vertical asymptote is $x = -\frac{1}{2}$,
horizontal asymptote is $y = 2\frac{1}{2}$

     ii as $x \to -\frac{1}{2}^-$, $y \to \infty$
as $x \to -\frac{1}{2}^+$, $y \to -\infty$
as $x \to -\infty$, $y \to 2\frac{1}{2}^+$
as $x \to \infty$, $y \to 2\frac{1}{2}^-$

     iii x-intercept is $\frac{1}{5}$, y-intercept is -1

     iv

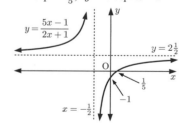

     v Vertical dilation with scale factor $\frac{7}{4}$, reflect in x-axis,
then translate $\begin{pmatrix} -\frac{1}{2} \\ \frac{5}{2} \end{pmatrix}$.

vi Translate $\begin{pmatrix} \frac{1}{2} \\ -\frac{5}{2} \end{pmatrix}$, reflect in x-axis, then vertical dilation with scale factor $\frac{4}{7}$.

5 a 70 weeds/ha   **b** 30 weeds/ha   **c** 3 days

d

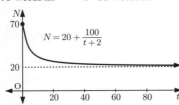

e No, the number of weeds/ha will approach 20 (from above), so at least 20 weeds per hectare will remain.

6 a $y = \dfrac{4}{x^2}$ **b** $y = \dfrac{1}{x^2}$ **c** $y = \dfrac{1}{(x-3)^2} - 1$

7 a $y = \dfrac{3}{(x+1)^2} + 6$

b

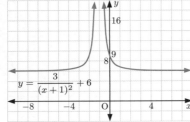

8 a

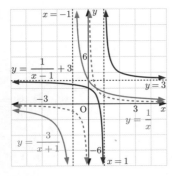

b The graphs $y = \dfrac{1}{x-1} + 3$ and $y = \dfrac{3}{x+1}$ never intersect, hence $\dfrac{1}{x-1} + 3 = \dfrac{3}{x+1}$ has no solutions.

9 a

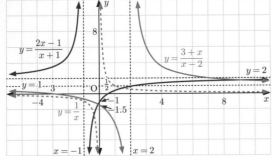

b From the graph, $x \approx -0.1$ or 9.1.   **c** $x = \dfrac{9 \pm \sqrt{85}}{2}$

REVIEW SET 4A

1 a i Domain $= \{x : x \in \mathbb{R}\}$ **ii** Range $= \{y : y > -4\}$
   iii yes

b i Domain $= \{x : x \in \mathbb{R}\}$ **ii** Range $= \{y : y = 2\}$
   iii yes

c i Domain $= \{x : x \in \mathbb{R}\}$
   ii Range $= \{y : y \leqslant -1 \text{ or } y \geqslant 1\}$ **iii** no

d i Domain $= \{x : x \in \mathbb{R}\}$
   ii Range $= \{y : -5 \leqslant y \leqslant 5\}$ **iii** yes

2 a 0   **b** -15 **c** $-\frac{5}{4}$

3 a i 2   **ii** 0   **b** $x = -1$

4 a $x \in (-2, -\frac{1}{2}] \cup (1, \infty)$ **b** $x \in [-2, 0) \cup (0, 2]$

5 Domain $= \{t : 0 \leqslant t \leqslant 140\}$,   Range $= \{N : 70 \leqslant N \leqslant 110\}$

6 a $x = 0$ **b**

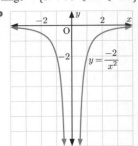

c Domain $= \{x : x \neq 0\}$
   Range $= \{y : y < 0\}$

7 a $f(-3) = (-3)^2 = 9$, $g(-\frac{4}{3}) = 1 - 6(-\frac{4}{3}) = 9$
   b $x = -4$

8

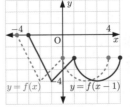

Domain $= \{x : x \in \mathbb{R}\}$,
Range $= \{y : y \geqslant -\frac{1}{4}\}$

9 $g(x)$ is the result of transforming $f(x)$ 3 units to the left and 4 units down.
   $\therefore$ domain of $g(x)$ is $\{x : -5 \leqslant x \leqslant 0\}$
   range of $g(x)$ is $\{y : -5 \leqslant y \leqslant 3\}$.

10 a

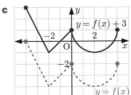

b

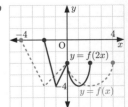

c

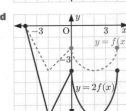

d

e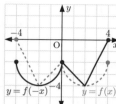

f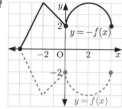

11 **a** $g(x) = 3x - x^2$ **b** $g(x) = 16 - x$
   c $g(x) = \frac{1}{12}x + 2$

12 **a** $g(x) = \dfrac{2x - 3}{x - 1}$
   b vertical asymptote $x = 1$,
      horizontal asymptote $y = 2$.
   c Domain $= \{x : x \neq 1\}$, Range $= \{y : y \neq 2\}$
   d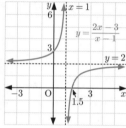

13 **a** $y = \dfrac{1}{4(x - 3)^2} + 2$
   b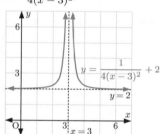

REVIEW SET 4B

1 **a** $x^2 - x - 2$ **b** $16x^2 - 12x$

2 **a** **i** Domain $= \{x : x \in \mathbb{R}\}$, Range $= \{y : y \geqslant -5\}$
      ii x-intercepts -1 and 5, y-intercept $-\frac{25}{9}$
      iii is a function
   b **i** Domain $= \{x : x \in \mathbb{R}\}$, Range $= \{y : y = 1 \text{ or } -3\}$
      ii no x-intercepts, y-intercept 1
      iii is a function

3 **a** is a function **b** is not a function

4 **a** **i** -4 **ii** $-\frac{1}{2}$ **iii** 2
   b $x = -2$ **c** $\dfrac{3x - 4}{x + 1}$ **d** $x = -9$

5

Set notation	Interval notation
$\{x : 4 < x < 9\}$	$x \in (4, 9)$
Number line graph	Meaning
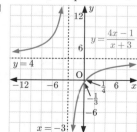	the set of all x such that x is more than 4 and less than 9

Set notation	Interval notation
$\{x : -3 < x \leqslant 7\}$	$x \in (-3, 7]$
Number line graph	Meaning
	the set of all x such that x is between -3 and 7, including 7

Set notation	Interval notation
$\{x : x < 2 \text{ or } 3 < x \leqslant 4\}$	$x \in (-\infty, 2) \cup (3, 4]$
Number line graph	Meaning
	the set of all x such that x is less than 2 or between 3 and 4, including 4

6 **a**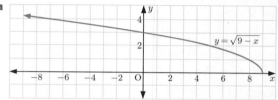
   b It is a function.
   c Domain $= \{x : x \leqslant 9\}$, Range $= \{y : y \geqslant 0\}$

7 **a** $g(x) = 4x - 10$ **b** $g(x) = 5x^2 + 30$
   c $g(x) = -3x - 5$ **d** $g(x) = \frac{2}{9}x^2 - \frac{1}{3}x + 4$
   e $g(x) = -x^3$

8 **a** $y = -f(x + 2) + 3$ **b** $y = 2f(x - 4) - 2$

9 **a** x-intercepts -9 and -3, y-intercept -3
   b x-intercepts -5 and 1, y-intercept -9
   c x-intercepts -10 and 2, y-intercept -3
   d x-intercepts -5 and 1, y-intercept 3

10 $(1, 6)$

11 **a** A vertical dilation with scale factor 2, then a translation through $\begin{pmatrix} -1 \\ 3 \end{pmatrix}$.
   b A horizontal dilation with scale factor $\frac{3}{2}$, a reflection in the x-axis, then a translation through $\begin{pmatrix} 0 \\ -6 \end{pmatrix}$.
   c A vertical dilation with scale factor $\frac{1}{3}$, a reflection in the y-axis, then a translation through $\begin{pmatrix} -2 \\ 0 \end{pmatrix}$.

12 **a** vertical asymptote $x = -3$,
      horizontal asymptote $y = 4$
   b as $x \to -3^-$, $y \to \infty$
      as $x \to -3^+$, $y \to -\infty$
      as $x \to -\infty$, $y \to 4^+$
      as $x \to \infty$, $y \to 4^-$
   c x-intercept is $\frac{1}{4}$, y-intercept is $-\frac{1}{3}$
   d

e A reflection in the x-axis, a vertical dilation with scale factor 13, then a translation through $\begin{pmatrix} -3 \\ 4 \end{pmatrix}$.

f A translation through $\begin{pmatrix} 3 \\ -4 \end{pmatrix}$, a vertical dilation with scale factor $\frac{1}{13}$, then a reflection in the x-axis.

13 a

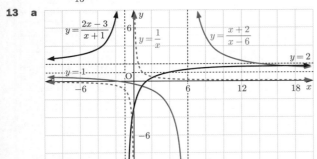

b From the graph, $x \approx 0.9$ or 17 **c** $x = 9 \pm \sqrt{65}$

EXERCISE 5A.1

1 **a** $S \leqslant 40$ **b** $A \geqslant 18$ **c** $a > 3$ **d** $b \leqslant -3$
   e $d < 5$ **f** $-20 \geqslant x$ **g** $4 < y$ **h** $z \geqslant 0$

2 **a** $x > 2$ **b** $b < 5$ **c** $c \geqslant 2\frac{1}{2}$ **d** $d \leqslant -7$
   e $a < -19$ **f** $p > -3$

3 **a** $a > 2$ **b** $b \leqslant -3$

c $s < 6$ **d** $c < 10$

e $x \geqslant 5$ **f** $b < -4$

g $t > -5$ **h** $k < -6$

i $m \leqslant -60$

4 **a** $x > 3$ **b** $m \leqslant 4$

c $a \geqslant \frac{10}{3}$ **d** $a < -2$

e $b > 5$ **f** $s > -2$

g $a \leqslant 2$ **h** $b < 3$

i $b \geqslant \frac{1}{3}$ **j** $n < -2$

k $x < 13$ **l** $b \geqslant \frac{7}{4}$

5 **a** $x > 9$ **b** $b \leqslant -5$

c $c \geqslant 16$ **d** $x < 9$

e $x \geqslant -\frac{14}{3}$ **f** $x > -6$

g $x \leqslant 20$ **h** $x > \frac{5}{2}$

i $x < \frac{28}{3}$

6 **a** $a < 15$ **b** $b \geqslant -1$

c $c \leqslant -2$ **d** $a < -6$

e $x \geqslant \frac{17}{3}$ **f** $x \leqslant 3$

7 **a** $c > \frac{5}{3}$ **b** $a \leqslant -\frac{3}{5}$ **c** $a \leqslant \frac{4}{3}$ **d** $a \leqslant -1$
   e $a > \frac{1}{8}$ **f** $a > \frac{1}{4}$

8 **a** $x < 1$ **b** $c \geqslant -2$ **c** $b < -2$ **d** $a \geqslant 21$
   e $d > 14$ **f** $p \leqslant \frac{11}{3}$

9 **a** $x > 2$ **b** $x \leqslant -3$

c $x < -1$ **d** $x < \frac{4}{5}$

e $x \leqslant -3$ **f** $x \geqslant -2$

g $x > -\frac{5}{3}$ **h** $x \leqslant \frac{23}{14}$

i $x \leqslant \frac{7}{13}$

10 Any score of 14 or more.

11 For **B**, it is better when the purchase price is more than £200.

12 It is cheaper to use Lightning Pace when the weight is less than 10 kg.

EXERCISE 5A.2

1 a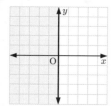

b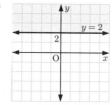

c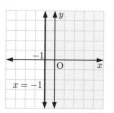

d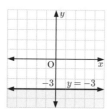

2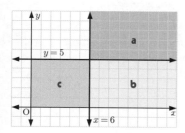

3 a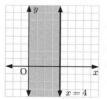

b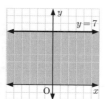

c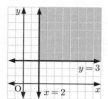

4 a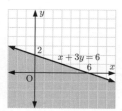

b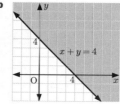

c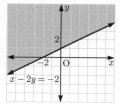

d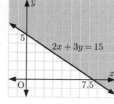

e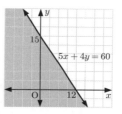

f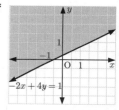

g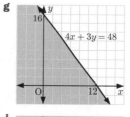

h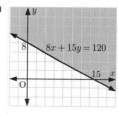

i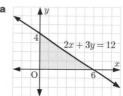

5 a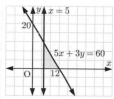

b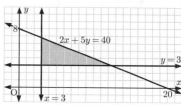

6 a $x \geqslant 3,$
$y \geqslant 3,$
$2x + 5y \leqslant 40$

b

7 a $x \geqslant 4, \;\; y \geqslant 5, \;\; 25x + 40y \leqslant 1000$

b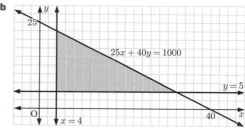

8 a $x \geqslant 3,$
$y \geqslant 0,$
$8x + 5y \leqslant 120$

b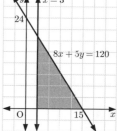

9 a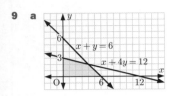

b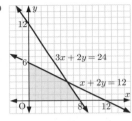

c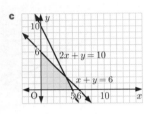

d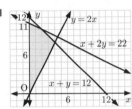

10 a $x + y \geqslant 3$, $-x + y \leqslant 3$, $x \leqslant 3$, $1 \leqslant y \leqslant 5$

b $(0, 3)$, $(2, 5)$, $(3, 5)$, $(3, 1)$, $(2, 1)$

EXERCISE 5B

1 a
```
    −  |  +
       2
```
→ x

b
```
 − | + | −
  −1   3
```
→ x

c
```
 + | − | +
   0    2
```
→ x

d
```
   + |  +
      1
```
→ x

e
```
   − |  −
     −2
```
→ x

f
```
 + | − | + | −
  −2  0   2
```
→ x

g
```
   −  ⋮  +
      0
```
→ x

h
```
 + | + | −
  −1   2
```
→ x

i
```
 − | + | + | −
  −3  0   4
```
→ x

j
```
 + ⋮ − | +
  1    2
```
→ x

k
```
 − | + | − ⋮ +
  −1  0   2
```
→ x

l
```
 − | + | − | + | −
 −2 −1  1   2
```
→ x

2 a
```
 + | − | +
  −4   2
```
→ x

b
```
 + | − | +
  −1   5
```
→ x

c
```
 + | − | +
   0    3
```
→ x

d
```
 + | − | +
  −2   0
```
→ x

e
```
 + | − | +
 −½    4
```
→ x

f
```
 − | + | −
  −1   3
```
→ x

g
```
 − | + | −
 −1   ⅔
```
→ x

h
```
 − | + | −
    ½   3
```
→ x

i
```
 + | − | +
   ½    5
```
→ x

j
```
 + | − | +
      3
```
→ x

k
```
   − |  −
     −4
```
→ x

l
```
   − |  −
    −5/2
```
→ x

3 a
```
 + | − ⋮ +
  −2   1
```
→ x

b
```
 + ⋮ − | +
 −3    0
```
→ x

c
```
 + ⋮ − | +
 −5   −1
```
→ x

d
```
 + ⋮ − | +
 −½    2
```
→ x

e
```
 − | + ⋮ −
 −3/2   4
```
→ x

f
```
 − | + ⋮ −
   ¼    2
```
→ x

g
```
 + | − | +
   0    2
```
→ x

h
```
 + | − ⋮ +
   0    3
```
→ x

i
```
 − ⋮ + | −
   0    1
```
→ x

j
```
 − ⋮ − | +
 −1    0
```
→ x

k
```
 + | − | + ⋮ −
 −2  1   3
```
→ x

l
```
 + | − | + ⋮ −
  0   1   2
```
→ x

m
```
 + | − ⋮ + | −
 −2  0   2
```
→ x

n
```
 + ⋮ − | + | −
 −3/2  2   3
```
→ x

o
```
 + | − ⋮ − | +
 −5 −2   1
```
→ x

p
```
 + | − | + ⋮ +
 −3  ½   4
```
→ x

EXERCISE 5C.1

1 a $x \in [-3, 2]$ **b** no solutions   **c** $x \in (-\tfrac{1}{2}, 3)$

 d $x \in (-\infty, 0]$ or $[1, \infty)$ **e** $x \in (-\infty, 0]$ or $[3, \infty)$

 f $x \in (-\tfrac{2}{3}, 0)$ **g** $x \in (-2, 2)$

 h $x \in (-\infty, -\sqrt{2}]$ or $[\sqrt{2}, \infty)$ **i** $x \neq -2$

 j $x \in (-\infty, -1]$ or $[\tfrac{3}{2}, \infty)$ **k** no solutions

 l $x \in (-\tfrac{3}{2}, \tfrac{1}{3})$ **m** $x \in (-\infty, -\tfrac{4}{3})$ or $(4, \infty)$

 n $x \neq 1$ **o** $x \in [\tfrac{1}{3}, \tfrac{1}{2}]$

 p $x \in (-\infty, -\tfrac{1}{6})$ or $(1, \infty)$

 q $x \in (-\infty, -\tfrac{1}{4}]$ or $[\tfrac{2}{3}, \infty)$

 r $x \in (-\infty, \tfrac{3}{2})$ or $(3, \infty)$

2 a The numbers greater than 0 and less than 3, i.e. $x \in (0, 3)$.

 b The number is less than or equal to $-\tfrac{2}{3}$, or greater than or equal to 2, i.e. $x \in (-\infty, -\tfrac{2}{3}]$ or $[2, \infty)$.

3 a $\Delta < 0$ **b** $\Delta = 0$ **c** $\Delta > 0$

EXERCISE 5C.2

1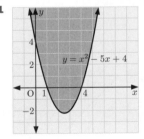

2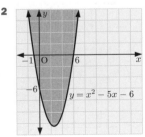

3

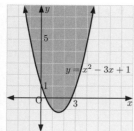

4 a

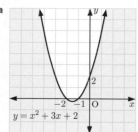

b

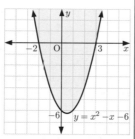

c

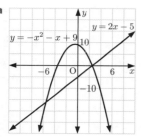

d

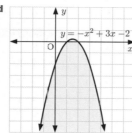

5 a

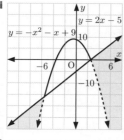

b **i**

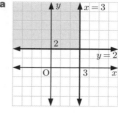

ii

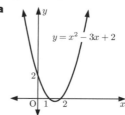

iii

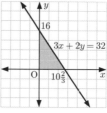

iv

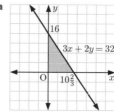

EXERCISE 5D

1 a $x < -4$ or $x > \frac{1}{2}$ **b** $x < -1$ or $x > 4$

c $x \leqslant -3$ or $x > -\frac{3}{2}$ **d** $x \leqslant -3$ or $x > 3$

e $x \leqslant \frac{1}{4}$ or $x > 1$ **f** $x < \frac{1}{2}$ **g** $0 < x < \frac{1}{100}$

h $\frac{1}{2} < x \leqslant \frac{5}{9}$ **i** $x < -1$ or $x > -\frac{3}{5}$

2 a

$x^2 - 3x + 2 < 0$ when $y = x^2 - 3x + 2$ lies below the x-axis.

$y = 0$ at $x = 1$ and $x = 2$, so the graph is below the x-axis for $1 < x < 2$.

$\therefore$ $x^2 - 3x + 2 < 0$ for $1 < x < 2$.

b Use a sign diagram.

So $x^2 - 3x + 2 < 0$ when $1 < x < 2$.

3 a $-7 < x < \frac{5}{2}$ **b** $-3 < x < 0$ or $x > 2$

c $-5 \leqslant x \leqslant -2$ or $0 \leqslant x < 2$

d $x < -2$ or $-1 < x < 0$ or $x > 2$

e $-2 < x < 0$ or $x > 2$ **f** $-1 \leqslant x < 0$ or $x \geqslant 1$

REVIEW SET 5A

1 a $x \leqslant \frac{7}{2}$ **b** $x < -\frac{9}{2}$

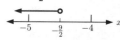

c $x \geqslant -\frac{4}{7}$

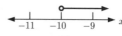

2 Any number greater than 10.

3 a $x > -10$ **b** $x \leqslant \frac{1}{3}$

c $-10 < x \leqslant \frac{1}{3}$

4 a

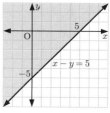

b

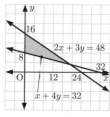

5 a

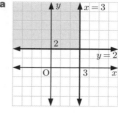

b

6 a   **b**

7 a   **b**

8 **a** $x < -2$ or $x > 3$ **b** $-1 \leqslant x \leqslant 5$

    c $x < -\frac{5}{2}$ or $x > 2$

9

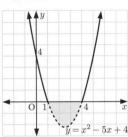

10

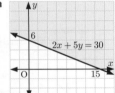

11   **a** $-2 < x < -1$ or $x > 4$ **b** $-8 < x < -\frac{1}{2}$ or $x > 1$

REVIEW SET 5B

1   **a** $x > \frac{13}{3}$

    b infinitely many

    c   **i** yes   **ii** no   **iii** no   **iv** yes

2   **a** $x \leqslant \frac{3}{2}$ **b** $x < 10$ **c** $x \geqslant 0$

3 For all calls greater than 8 minutes.

4   **a**

    b

5   **a** $x \geqslant 4$, $y \geqslant 2$, $3x + 5y \leqslant 60$

    b

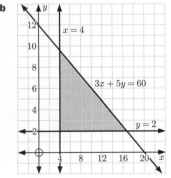

6   **a**

    b

    c

7   **a** $0 < x < \frac{3}{4}$ **b** $x \leqslant -1$ or $x \geqslant \frac{5}{2}$

    c $x \leqslant \frac{1}{3}$ or $x \geqslant \frac{3}{2}$

8   **a**

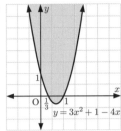

    b

9   **a** If $x = -2$, $\frac{3}{5}$ is not $< \frac{2}{-2} = -1$.

    b In Henry's method he is really multiplying both sides by $5x$. This cannot be done unless we know that $5x$ is positive.

10   **a**

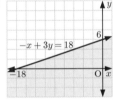

    b $x < -2$ or $1 < x < 3$

11   **a** $x < -4$ or $x \geqslant 3$ **b** $x \leqslant \frac{7}{3}$ or $x > 3$

    c $x < -3$ or $-2 < x < 0$

EXERCISE 6A.1

1   **a** 11   **b** $\sqrt{15}$ **c** 3   **d** $\sqrt{30}$

    e 4   **f** 12   **g** 42   **h** 45

    i $\sqrt{6}$ **j** $\sqrt{6}$ **k** 2   **l** $\sqrt{5}$

2   **a** $2\sqrt{2}$ **b** $2\sqrt{3}$ **c** $2\sqrt{5}$ **d** $4\sqrt{2}$

    e $3\sqrt{3}$ **f** $3\sqrt{5}$ **g** $4\sqrt{3}$ **h** $3\sqrt{6}$

    i $5\sqrt{2}$ **j** $4\sqrt{5}$ **k** $4\sqrt{6}$ **l** $6\sqrt{3}$

EXERCISE 6A.2

1   **a** $5\sqrt{2}$ **b** $-\sqrt{2}$ **c** $2\sqrt{5}$ **d** $8\sqrt{5}$

    e $-2\sqrt{5}$ **f** $9\sqrt{3}$ **g** $-3\sqrt{6}$ **h** $3\sqrt{2}$

2   **a** $3\sqrt{2} - 2$ **b** $5 + \sqrt{5}$ **c** $3\sqrt{10} + 20$

    d $21 - 4\sqrt{7}$ **e** $-5\sqrt{3} - 3$ **f** $12 - 14\sqrt{6}$

    g $-8 + 5\sqrt{8}$ **h** $-12\sqrt{2} + 36$

3   **a** $22 + 9\sqrt{2}$ **b** $34 + 15\sqrt{3}$ **c** $22 + 14\sqrt{7}$

    d $-7 - \sqrt{3}$ **e** $34 - 15\sqrt{8}$ **f** $30\sqrt{5} - 47$

4   **a** $11 + 6\sqrt{2}$ **b** $39 - 12\sqrt{3}$ **c** $6 + 2\sqrt{5}$

    d $17 - 6\sqrt{8}$ **e** $28 + 16\sqrt{3}$ **f** $46 + 6\sqrt{5}$

    g $89 - 28\sqrt{10}$ **h** $166 - 40\sqrt{6}$

5   **a** 2   **b** -23 **c** 13   **d** 7   **e** -56 **f** 218

EXERCISE 6A.3

1   **a** $\frac{\sqrt{3}}{3}$ **b** $\sqrt{3}$ **c** $3\sqrt{3}$ **d** $\frac{11\sqrt{3}}{3}$ **e** $\frac{\sqrt{6}}{9}$

    f $\sqrt{2}$ **g** $3\sqrt{2}$ **h** $6\sqrt{2}$ **i** $\frac{\sqrt{6}}{2}$ **j** $\frac{\sqrt{2}}{8}$

    k $\sqrt{5}$ **l** $3\sqrt{5}$ **m** $-\frac{3\sqrt{5}}{5}$ **n** $40\sqrt{5}$ **o** $\frac{\sqrt{5}}{15}$

    p $\sqrt{7}$ **q** $3\sqrt{7}$ **r** $\frac{2\sqrt{11}}{11}$ **s** $2\sqrt{13}$ **t** $\frac{\sqrt{3}}{9}$

2   **a** $\frac{3 - \sqrt{2}}{7}$ **b** $\frac{6 + 2\sqrt{2}}{7}$ **c** $-2 + \sqrt{5}$

    d $\sqrt{2} + 1$ **e** $2\sqrt{6} + 2$ **f** $\frac{\sqrt{21} - 2\sqrt{3}}{3}$

    g $-3 - 2\sqrt{2}$ **h** $\frac{4\sqrt{3} + 3}{13}$ **i** $2\sqrt{2} + 4$

    j $-7 - 3\sqrt{5}$ **k** $\frac{5 + 3\sqrt{3}}{2}$ **l** $\frac{-38 + 11\sqrt{10}}{6}$

m $\dfrac{7+\sqrt{5}}{11}$ **n** $\dfrac{28+\sqrt{2}}{23}$ **o** $\dfrac{17+7\sqrt{7}}{3}$

p $\dfrac{\sqrt{11}-1}{5}$

3 a $3-2\sqrt{2}$ **b** $11+6\sqrt{2}$ **c** $3-2\sqrt{2}$

d $\dfrac{14}{17}-\dfrac{1}{34}\sqrt{2}$ **e** $3-2\sqrt{2}$ **f** $\dfrac{11}{49}+\dfrac{6}{49}\sqrt{2}$

g $3-2\sqrt{2}$ **h** $-\dfrac{7}{41}-\dfrac{2}{41}\sqrt{2}$

EXERCISE 6B

1 a $2^1=2,\ 2^2=4,\ 2^3=8,\ 2^4=16,\ 2^5=32,\ 2^6=64$
 b $3^1=3,\ 3^2=9,\ 3^3=27,\ 3^4=81,\ 3^5=243,$
  $3^6=729$
 c $4^1=4,\ 4^2=16,\ 4^3=64,\ 4^4=256,\ 4^5=1024,$
  $4^6=4096$

2 a $5^1=5,\ 5^2=25,\ 5^3=125,\ 5^4=625$
 b $6^1=6,\ 6^2=36,\ 6^3=216,\ 6^4=1296$
 c $7^1=7,\ 7^2=49,\ 7^3=343,\ 7^4=2401$

3 a -1 **b** 1 **c** 1 **d** -1 **e** 1 **f** -1
 g -1 **h** -32 **i** -32 **j** -64 **k** 625 **l** -625

4 a $16\,384$ **b** 2401 **c** -3125 **d** -3125
 e $262\,144$ **f** $262\,144$ **g** $-262\,144$
 h $902.436\,039\,6$ **i** $-902.436\,039\,6$ **j** $-902.436\,039\,6$

5 a $0.\overline{1}$ **b** $0.\overline{1}$ **c** $0.02\overline{7}$ **d** $0.02\overline{7}$
 e $0.0\overline{12\,345\,679\,0}$ **f** $0.0\overline{12\,345\,679\,0}$ **g** 1 **h** 1

Notice that $a^{-n}=\dfrac{1}{a^n}$ and $a^0=1$.

6 3 **7** 7

EXERCISE 6C

1 a 5^{11} **b** d^8 **c** k^5 **d** 7^{-1} **e** x^{10} **f** 3^{16}
 g p^{-4} **h** n^{12} **i** 5^{3t} **j** 7^{x+2} **k** 10^{3-q} **l** c^{4m}

2 a 2^2 **b** 2^{-2} **c** 2^3 **d** 2^{-3} **e** 2^5 **f** 2^{-5}
 g 2^1 **h** 2^{-1} **i** 2^6 **j** 2^{-6} **k** 2^7 **l** 2^{-7}

3 a 3^2 **b** 3^{-2} **c** 3^3 **d** 3^{-3} **e** 3^1 **f** 3^{-1}
 g 3^4 **h** 3^{-4} **i** 3^0 **j** 3^5 **k** 3^{-5}

4 a 2^{1+a} **b** 2^{2+b} **c** 2^{3+t} **d** 2^{2x+2} **e** 2^{n-1}
 f 2^{c-2} **g** 2^{2m} **h** 2^{1+n} **i** 2^1 **j** 2^{3x-1}

5 a 3^{2+p} **b** 3^{3a} **c** 3^{1+2n} **d** 3^{3+d} **e** 3^{2+3t}
 f 3^{y-1} **g** 3^{1-y} **h** 3^{2-3t} **i** 3^{3a-1} **j** 3^3

6 a $4a^2$ **b** $27b^3$ **c** a^4b^4 **d** p^3q^3 **e** $\dfrac{m^2}{n^2}$
 f $\dfrac{a^3}{27}$ **g** $\dfrac{b^4}{c^4}$ **h** $1,\ a,b\neq 0$ **i** $\dfrac{m^4}{81n^4}$ **j** $\dfrac{x^3y^3}{8}$

7 a $4a^2$ **b** $36b^4$ **c** $-8a^3$ **d** $-27m^6n^6$
 e $16a^4b^{16}$ **f** $\dfrac{-8a^6}{b^6}$ **g** $\dfrac{16a^6}{b^2}$ **h** $\dfrac{9p^4}{q^6}$

8 a $\dfrac{a}{b^2}$ **b** $\dfrac{1}{a^2b^2}$ **c** $\dfrac{4a^2}{b^2}$ **d** $\dfrac{9b^2}{a^4}$ **e** $\dfrac{a^2}{bc^2}$
 f $\dfrac{a^2c^2}{b}$ **g** a^3 **h** $\dfrac{b^3}{a^2}$ **i** $\dfrac{2}{ad^2}$ **j** $12am^3$

9 a a^{-n} **b** $5a^{-m}$ **c** b^n **d** 2^{3-n}
 e 3^{n-2} **f** $3a^{m-4}$ **g** a^nb^m **h** a^{-2n-2}

10 a x^{-2} **b** $2x^{-1}$ **c** $x+x^{-1}$ **d** x^2-2x^{-3}
 e $x^{-1}+3x^{-2}$ **f** $4x^{-1}-5x^{-3}$
 g $7x-4x^{-1}+5x^{-2}$ **h** $3x^{-1}-2x^{-2}+5x^{-4}$

11 a 1 **b** $\dfrac{4}{7}$ **c** 6 **d** 27 **e** $\dfrac{9}{16}$ **f** $\dfrac{5}{2}$
 g $\dfrac{27}{125}$ **h** $\dfrac{151}{5}$

12 a 3^{-2} **b** 2^{-4} **c** 5^{-3} **d** $3^1\times 5^{-1}$ **e** $2^2\times 3^{-3}$
 f $2^{c-3}\times 3^{-2}$ **g** $3^{2k}\times 2^{-1}\times 5^{-1}$ **h** $2^p\times 3^{p-1}\times 5^{-2}$

13 a $5^3=21+23+25+27+29$
 b $7^3=43+45+47+49+51+53+55$
 c $12^3=133+135+137+139+141+143+145+147$
  $+149+151+153+155$

EXERCISE 6D

1 a $2^{\frac{1}{5}}$ **b** $2^{-\frac{1}{5}}$ **c** $2^{\frac{3}{2}}$ **d** $2^{\frac{5}{2}}$ **e** $2^{-\frac{1}{3}}$
 f $2^{\frac{4}{3}}$ **g** $2^{\frac{3}{2}}$ **h** $2^{\frac{3}{2}}$ **i** $2^{-\frac{4}{3}}$ **j** $2^{-\frac{3}{2}}$

2 a $3^{\frac{1}{3}}$ **b** $3^{-\frac{1}{3}}$ **c** $3^{\frac{1}{4}}$ **d** $3^{\frac{3}{2}}$ **e** $3^{-\frac{5}{2}}$

3 a $7^{\frac{1}{3}}$ **b** $3^{\frac{3}{4}}$ **c** $2^{\frac{4}{5}}$ **d** $2^{\frac{5}{3}}$ **e** $7^{\frac{2}{7}}$
 f $7^{-\frac{1}{3}}$ **g** $3^{-\frac{3}{4}}$ **h** $2^{-\frac{4}{5}}$ **i** $2^{-\frac{5}{3}}$ **j** $7^{-\frac{2}{7}}$

4 a $x^{\frac{1}{2}}$ **b** $x^{\frac{3}{2}}$ **c** $x^{-\frac{1}{2}}$ **d** $x^{\frac{5}{2}}$ **e** $x^{-\frac{3}{2}}$

5 a 2.28 **b** 0.435 **c** 1.68 **d** 1.93 **e** 0.523

6 a 8 **b** 32 **c** 8 **d** 125 **e** 4
 f $\dfrac{1}{2}$ **g** $\dfrac{1}{27}$ **h** $\dfrac{1}{16}$ **i** $\dfrac{1}{81}$ **j** $\dfrac{1}{25}$

EXERCISE 6E.1

1 a $x^5+2x^4+x^2$ **b** $2^{2x}+2^x$ **c** $x+1$
 d $7^{2x}+2(7^x)$ **e** $2(3^x)-1$ **f** x^2+2x+3
 g $1+5(2^{-x})$ **h** 5^x+1 **i** $x^{\frac{3}{2}}+x^{\frac{1}{2}}+1$
 j $3^{2x}+5(3^x)+1$ **k** $2x^{\frac{3}{2}}-x^{\frac{1}{2}}+5$ **l** $2^{3x}-3(2^{2x})-1$

2 a $2^{2x}+2^{x+1}-3$ **b** $3^{2x}+7(3^x)+10$
 c $5^{2x}-6(5^x)+8$ **d** $2^{2x}+6(2^x)+9$
 e $3^{2x}-2(3^x)+1$ **f** $4^{2x}+14(4^x)+49$
 g $x-4$ **h** 4^x-9 **i** $x-x^{-1}$ **j** $x^2+4+\dfrac{4}{x^2}$
 k $7^{2x}-2+7^{-2x}$ **l** $25-10(2^{-x})+2^{-2x}$

EXERCISE 6E.2

1 a $5^x(5^x+1)$ **b** $10(3^n)$ **c** $7^n(1+7^{2n})$
 d $5(5^n-1)$ **e** $6(6^{n+1}-1)$ **f** $16(4^n-1)$

2 a $(3^x+2)(3^x-2)$ **b** $(2^x+5)(2^x-5)$
 c $(4+3^x)(4-3^x)$ **d** $(5+2^x)(5-2^x)$
 e $(3^x+2^x)(3^x-2^x)$ **f** $(2^x+3)^2$
 g $(3^x+5)^2$ **h** $(2^x-7)^2$ **i** $(5^x-2)^2$

3 a $(2^x+3)(2^x+6)$ **b** $(2^x+4)(2^x-5)$
 c $(3^x+2)(3^x+7)$ **d** $(3^x+5)(3^x-1)$
 e $(5^x+2)(5^x-1)$ **f** $(7^x-4)(7^x-3)$

EXERCISE 6F

1 a $x=5$ **b** $x=2$ **c** $x=4$ **d** $x=0$

2 a $x=-1$ **b** $x=\frac{1}{2}$ **c** $x=-3$ **d** $x=2$
 e $x=-3$ **f** $x=-4$ **g** $x=2$ **h** $x=1$

3 a $x=\frac{5}{3}$ **b** $x=-\frac{3}{2}$ **c** $x=-\frac{3}{2}$ **d** $x=-\frac{1}{2}$
 e $x=-\frac{2}{3}$ **f** $x=-\frac{5}{4}$ **g** $x=\frac{3}{2}$ **h** $x=\frac{5}{2}$
 i $x=\frac{1}{8}$ **j** $x=\frac{9}{2}$ **k** $x=-4$ **l** $x=-4$
 m $x=0$ **n** $x=\frac{7}{2}$ **o** $x=-2$ **p** $x=-6$

4 a $x = \frac{1}{7}$ **b** has no solutions **c** $x = \frac{5}{2}$

5 a $x = 3$ **b** $x = 2$ **c** $x = -1$
   d $x = 2$ **e** $x = -2$ **f** $x = -2$

6 a $x = 1$ or 2 **b** $x = 1$ **c** $x = 1$ or 2
   d $x = 1$ **e** $x = 2$ **f** $x = 0$

EXERCISE 6G

1 a 1.4 **b** 1.7 **c** 2.8 **d** 0.4

2 a $x \approx 1.6$ **b** $x \approx -0.8$

3 $y = 2^x$ has a horizontal asymptote of $y = 0$

4 a
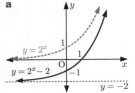
   b
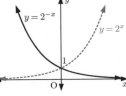

   c
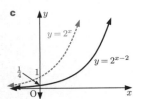
   d
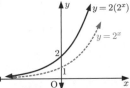

5 a
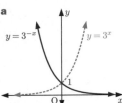
   b
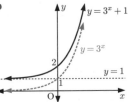

   c
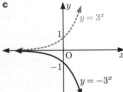
   d
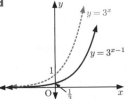

6 a i -1 **ii** 7 **iii** $-\frac{17}{9} = -1\frac{8}{9}$ **b** $y = -2$

   c
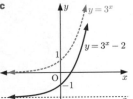
   d Domain: $\{x : x \in \mathbb{R}\}$
   Range: $\{y : y > -2\}$

7 a i
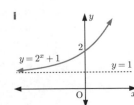
   ii Domain: $\{x : x \in \mathbb{R}\}$
   Range: $\{y : y > 1\}$
   iii $y \approx 3.67$

iv As $x \to \infty$, $y \to \infty$
   As $x \to -\infty$, $y \to 1^+$
v $y = 1$

b i
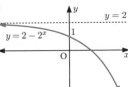
   ii Domain: $\{x : x \in \mathbb{R}\}$
   Range: $\{y : y < 2\}$
   iii $y \approx -0.665$

iv As $x \to \infty$, $y \to -\infty$
   As $x \to -\infty$, $y \to 2^-$
v $y = 2$

c i
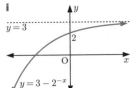
   ii Domain: $\{x : x \in \mathbb{R}\}$
   Range: $\{y : y > 3\}$
   iii $y \approx 3.38$

iv As $x \to \infty$, $y \to 3^+$
   As $x \to -\infty$, $y \to \infty$
v $y = 3$

d i
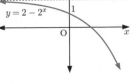
   ii Domain: $\{x : x \in \mathbb{R}\}$
   Range: $\{y : y < 3\}$
   iii $y \approx 2.62$

iv As $x \to \infty$, $y \to 3^-$
   As $x \to -\infty$, $y \to -\infty$
v $y = 3$

8 a $x \approx 3.46$ **b** $x \approx 2.46$ **c** $x \approx 1.16$
   d $x \approx -0.738$ **e** $x \approx 1.85$ **f** $x \approx 0.0959$

EXERCISE 6H.1

1 a 100 grams **c**
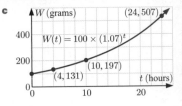
   b i ≈ 131 g
     ii ≈ 197 g
     iii ≈ 507 g

2 a $P_0 = 50$ possums
   b i ≈ 76 possums **ii** ≈ 141 possums
     iii ≈ 396 possums

   c
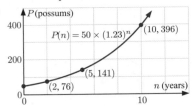

   e ≈ 11.1 years

3 a $B_0 = 12$ bears **b** ≈ 138 bears
   c $\approx 239\%$ **d** ≈ 23.0 years

4 a i V_0 **ii** $2V_0$ **b** 100%

c 183% increase, it is the percentage increase at 50°C compared with 20°C.

5 a $A(t) = 5000 \times (1.1)^t$ **b i** £6050   **ii** £8052.55

c

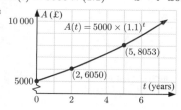

EXERCISE 6H.2

1 a 250 g   **b i** ≈ 112 g   **ii** ≈ 50.4 g   **iii** ≈ 22.6 g

c

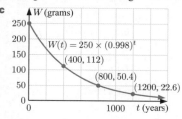

d ≈ 346 years

2 a 100°C

b i ≈ 80.9°C   **ii** ≈ 75.4°C   **iii** ≈ 33.3°C

c

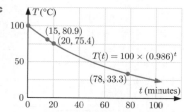

3 a 1000 g

b i ≈ 809 g   **ii** ≈ 120 g   **iii** $\approx 6.06 \times 10^{-7}$ g

c

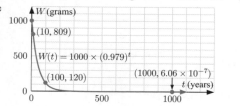

d ≈ 217 years   **e** $1000(1 - 0.979^t)$ grams

4 a $P(t) = 400 \times (0.92)^t$

b i 368 orangutans   **ii** ≈ 264 orangutans

c

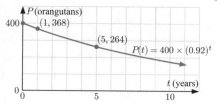

d ≈ 8.31 years, or ≈ 8 years 114 days

5 a i 22°C   **ii** 6°C   **iii** -2°C

b

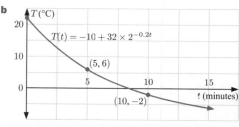

c ≈ 8.39 min or ≈ 8 min 23 s

d No, as $32 \times 2^{-0.2t} > 0$ for any value of t.

EXERCISE 6I

1

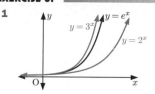

The graph of $y = e^x$ lies between $y = 2^x$ and $y = 3^x$.

2

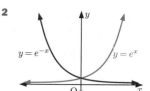

One is the other reflected in the y-axis.

3 a

4 a $e^x > 0$ for all x

b i $\approx 4.12 \times 10^{-9}$ **ii** $\approx 9.70 \times 10^8$

5 a ≈ 7.39 **b** ≈ 20.1 **c** ≈ 2.01 **d** ≈ 1.65

e ≈ 0.368

6 a $e^{\frac{1}{2}}$ **b** $e^{-\frac{1}{2}}$ **c** e^{-2} **d** $e^{\frac{3}{2}}$

7 a $e^{2x} + 2e^x + 1$ **b** $1 - e^{2x}$ **c** $1 - 3e^x$

8 a $e^x(e^x + 1)$ **b** $(e^x + 4)(e^x - 4)$ **c** $(e^x - 6)(e^x - 2)$

9 a

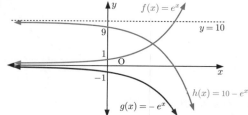

b Domain of f, g, and h is $\{x : x \in \mathbb{R}\}$
Range of f is $\{y : y > 0\}$,   Range of g is $\{y : y > 0\}$
Range of h is $\{y : y > 3\}$

10 a

b Domain of f, g, and h is $\{x : x \in \mathbb{R}\}$
Range of f is $\{y : y > 0\}$,   Range of g is $\{y : y < 0\}$
Range of h is $\{y : y < 10\}$

c For f: as $x \to \infty$, $y \to \infty$
as $x \to -\infty$, $y \to 0^+$
For g: as $x \to \infty$, $y \to -\infty$
as $x \to -\infty$, $y \to 0^-$
For h: as $x \to \infty$, $y \to -\infty$
as $x \to -\infty$, $y \to 10^-$

11 a i 2 g
ii ≈ 2.57 g
iii ≈ 4.23 g
iv ≈ 40.2 g

b
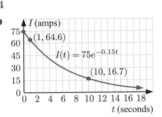

12 a $x = \frac{1}{2}$ **b** $x = -4$

13 a i ≈ 64.6 amps
ii ≈ 16.7 amps
c ≈ 28.8 seconds

b
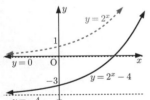

REVIEW SET 6A

1 a $20\sqrt{3} - 15$ **b** $86 - 60\sqrt{2}$ **c** 4

2 a -1 **b** 27 **c** $\frac{2}{3}$ **3 a** $a^6 b^7$ **b** $\frac{2}{3x}$ **c** $\frac{y^2}{5}$

4 a 4 **b** $\frac{1}{9}$

5 a $x = -2$ **b** $x = \frac{3}{4}$ **c** $x = -\frac{1}{4}$

6 a $1 + e^{2x}$ **b** $2^{2x} + 10(2^x) + 25$ **c** $x - 49$

7 a i ≈ 2.2 **ii** ≈ 0.6
b i $x \approx 1.45$ **ii** $x \approx -0.6$ **iii** $x \approx 1.1$

8 a 3 **b** 24 **c** $\frac{3}{4}$

9

10 a

x	-2	-1	0	1	2
y	$-4\frac{8}{9}$	$-4\frac{2}{3}$	-4	-2	4

b as $x \to \infty$,   **c, d**
$y \to \infty$;
as $x \to -\infty$,
$y \to -5^+$
d $y = -5$

11 a $80°$C
b i $\approx 26.8°$C
ii $\approx 9.00°$C
iii $\approx 3.02°$C
d ≈ 12.8 min

c
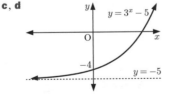

---

12 a
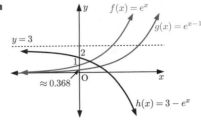

b For $f(x)$: domain is $\{x : x \in \mathbb{R}\}$
range is $\{y : y > 0\}$
For $g(x)$: domain is $\{x : x \in \mathbb{R}\}$
range is $\{y : y > 0\}$
For $h(x)$: domain is $\{x : x \in \mathbb{R}\}$
range is $\{y : y < 3\}$

c For $f(x)$: as $x \to \infty$, $f(x) \to \infty$
as $x \to -\infty$, $f(x) \to 0^+$
For $g(x)$: as $x \to \infty$, $g(x) \to \infty$
as $x \to -\infty$, $g(x) \to 0^+$
For $h(x)$: as $x \to \infty$, $h(x) \to -\infty$
as $x \to -\infty$, $h(x) \to 3^-$

REVIEW SET 6B

1 a $17 - 11\sqrt{3}$ **b** 28

2 a $\frac{2\sqrt{3}}{3}$ **b** $\frac{\sqrt{35}}{5}$ **c** $\frac{4 - \sqrt{7}}{9}$

3 a $\frac{1}{x^5}$ **b** $\frac{2}{a^2 b^2}$ **c** $\frac{2a}{b^2}$ **4 a** 3^{3-2a} **b** $3^{\frac{5}{2} - \frac{9}{2}x}$

5 a 2.28 **b** 0.517 **c** 3.16

6 a 8×3^x **b** $(2^x - 4)(2^x + 3)$ **c** $(e^x + 5)(e^x - 3)$

7 a $x = 4$ **b** $x = -4$ **c** $x = 0$

8 a i ≈ 2.3 **ii** ≈ 0.2 **b** $x \approx 0.79$

9 a $\frac{1}{\sqrt{2}} + 1 \approx 1.71$ **b** $a = -1$

10 a

x	-2	-1	0	1	2
y	15.8	6.44	3	1.74	1.27

b as $x \to \infty$, $y \to 1^+$;   as $x \to -\infty$, $y \to \infty$

c   **d** $y = 1$

11 a clock: £525, vase: £428
b clock: $V(t) = 500 \times (1.05)^t$
vase: $V(t) = 400 \times (1.07)^t$
c clock $\approx$ £1039.46, vase $\approx$ £1103.61 ∴ the vase
d $500 \times (1.05)^t = 400 \times (1.07)^t$ and solve for t.
$t \approx 11.8$ years

12 a C   **b** E   **c** A   **d** B   **e** D

EXERCISE 7A

1 a 4 **b** -3 **c** 1 **d** 0 **e** $\frac{1}{2}$ **f** $\frac{1}{3}$
g $-\frac{1}{4}$ **h** $1\frac{1}{2}$ **i** $\frac{2}{3}$ **j** $1\frac{1}{2}$ **k** $1\frac{1}{3}$ **l** $3\frac{1}{2}$

2 a n **b** $a + 2$ **c** $1 - m$ **d** $a - b$

3 a $100 < 237 < 1000$ **b** ≈ 2.37
∴ $\log 100 < \log 237 < \log 1000$
∴ $2 < \log 237 < 3$

4 a $-1 < \log 0.6 < 0$ **b** ≈ -0.22

5 a ≈ 1.88 **b** ≈ 2.06 **c** ≈ 0.48

   d ≈ 2.92 **e** ≈ -0.40 **f** ≈ 3.51

   g ≈ -2.10 **h** does not exist

6 a $x > 1$ **b** $x = 1$ **c** $0 < x < 1$ **d** $x \leqslant 0$

7 a $10^{0.7782}$ **b** $10^{1.7782}$ **c** $10^{3.7782}$ **d** $10^{-0.2218}$

   e $10^{-2.2218}$ **f** $10^{1.1761}$ **g** $10^{3.1761}$ **h** $10^{0.1761}$

   i $10^{-0.8239}$ **j** $10^{-3.8239}$

8 a **i** 0.477 **ii** 2.477 **b** $\log 300 = \log(3 \times 10^2)$

9 a **i** 0.699 **ii** -1.301 **b** $\log 0.05 = \log(5 \times 10^{-2})$

10 a $x = 100$ **b** $x = 10$ **c** $x = 1$

   d $x = \frac{1}{10}$ **e** $x = 10^{\frac{1}{2}}$ **f** $x = 10^{-\frac{1}{2}}$

   g $x = 10\,000$ **h** $x = 0.000\,01$ **i** $x \approx 6.84$

   j $x \approx 140$ **k** $x \approx 0.0419$ **l** $x \approx 0.000\,631$

EXERCISE 7B

1 a $10^2 = 100$ **b** $10^4 = 10\,000$ **c** $10^{-1} = 0.1$

   d $10^{\frac{1}{2}} = \sqrt{10}$ **e** $2^3 = 8$ **f** $3^2 = 9$

   g $2^{-2} = \frac{1}{4}$ **h** $3^{1.5} = \sqrt{27}$ **i** $5^{-\frac{1}{2}} = \frac{1}{\sqrt{5}}$

2 a $\log_2 4 = 2$ **b** $\log_4 64 = 3$ **c** $\log_5 25 = 2$

   d $\log_7 49 = 2$ **e** $\log_2 64 = 6$ **f** $\log_2(\frac{1}{8}) = -3$

   g $\log_{10}(0.01) = -2$ **h** $\log_2(\frac{1}{2}) = -1$

   i $\log_3(\frac{1}{27}) = -3$

3 a 5 **b** -2 **c** $\frac{1}{2}$ **d** 2 **e** 6 **f** 7

   g 2 **h** 3 **i** -3 **j** $\frac{1}{2}$ **k** 2 **l** $\frac{1}{2}$

   m 5 **n** $\frac{1}{3}$ **o** $\frac{1}{3}$ **p** $\frac{3}{2}$ **q** 0 **r** 1

   s -1 **t** $\frac{3}{4}$ **u** $-\frac{1}{2}$ **v** $\frac{5}{2}$ **w** $-\frac{3}{2}$ **x** $-\frac{3}{4}$

4 a 2 **b** -1 **c** $\frac{1}{2}$ **d** 3 **e** $\frac{3}{2}$ **f** -2

   g $-\frac{1}{2}$ **h** $\frac{5}{2}$

5 a $x = 8$ **b** $x = 2$ **c** $x = 3$ **d** $x = 14$

6 $\log_b a = \dfrac{1}{x}$

EXERCISE 7C

1 a $\log 16$ **b** $\log 20$ **c** $\log 8$ **d** $\log\left(\dfrac{p}{m}\right)$

   e 1 **f** $\log 2$ **g** 3 **h** 2

   i $\log 24$ **j** 1 **k** 0 **l** $\log 28$

2 a $\log 700$ **b** $\log\left(\frac{2}{5}\right)$ **c** $\log_2 6$

   d $\log_3\left(\frac{5}{9}\right)$ **e** $\log 200$ **f** $\log(0.005)$

   g $\log(10^t \times w)$ **h** $\log_m\left(\dfrac{40}{m^2}\right)$ **i** $\log_5\left(\frac{5}{2}\right)$

3 a $\log 96$ **b** $\log 72$ **c** $\log 8$ **d** $\log_3\left(\frac{25}{8}\right)$

   e 1 **f** $\log\left(\frac{1}{2}\right)$ **g** $\log 20$ **h** $\log 25$ **i** $\log_n\left(\dfrac{n^2}{10}\right)$

4 a 2 **b** $\frac{3}{2}$ **c** 3 **d** $\frac{1}{2}$ **e** -2 **f** $-\frac{3}{2}$

5 For example, for **a**, $\log 9 = \log(3^2) = 2\log 3$

6 a $p + q$ **b** $2q + r$ **c** $2p + 3q$ **d** $r + \frac{1}{2}q - p$

   e $r - 5p$ **f** $p - 2q$

7 a $x + z$ **b** $z + 2y$ **c** $x + z - y$ **d** $2x + \frac{1}{2}y$

   e $3y - \frac{1}{2}z$ **f** $2z + \frac{1}{2}y - 3x$

8 a 0.86 **b** 2.15 **c** 1.075

9 $\log 384$ **10** $4 + \log_2 45$

EXERCISE 7D.1

1 a 2 **b** 4 **c** $\frac{3}{2}$ **d** 0 **e** -1

   f $\frac{1}{3}$ **g** -2 **h** $-\frac{1}{2}$

2 a 3 **b** 9 **c** $\frac{1}{5}$ **d** $\frac{1}{4}$ **e** a

   f $1 + a$ **g** $a + b$ **h** ab

3 a ≈ 2.485 **b** ≈ 4.220 **c** ≈ 0.336

   d ≈ -0.357 **e** ≈ 6.215

4 x does not exist such that $e^x = -2$ or 0 since $e^x > 0$ for all $x \in \mathbb{R}$.

5 a $e^{1.7918}$ **b** $e^{4.0943}$ **c** $e^{8.6995}$ **d** $e^{-0.5108}$

   e $e^{-5.1160}$ **f** $e^{2.7081}$ **g** $e^{7.3132}$ **h** $e^{0.4055}$

   i $e^{-1.8971}$ **j** $e^{-8.8049}$

6 a $x \approx 20.1$ **b** $x \approx 2.72$ **c** $x = 1$

   d $x \approx 0.368$ **e** $x \approx 0.006\,74$ **f** $x \approx 2.30$

   g $x \approx 8.54$ **h** $x \approx 0.0370$

7 a **i** x **ii** x **b** They are inverses of each other.

EXERCISE 7D.2

1 a $\ln 45$ **b** $\ln 5$ **c** $\ln 4$ **d** $\ln 24$

   e $\ln 1 = 0$ **f** $\ln 30$ **g** $\ln(4e)$ **h** $\ln\left(\dfrac{6}{e}\right)$

   i $\ln 20$ **j** $\ln(4e^2)$ **k** $\ln\left(\dfrac{20}{e^2}\right)$ **l** $\ln 1 = 0$

2 a $\ln 972$ **b** $\ln 200$ **c** $\ln 1 = 0$ **d** $\ln 16$ **e** $\ln 6$

   f $\ln\left(\frac{1}{3}\right)$ **g** $\ln\left(\frac{1}{2}\right)$ **h** $\ln 2$ **i** $\ln 16$

3 For example, for **a**, $\ln 27 = \ln(3^3) = 3\ln 3$.

EXERCISE 7E

1 a $16 < 20 < 32 \Rightarrow 2^4 < 20 < 2^5$ **b** $x = \dfrac{\log 20}{\log 2}$

   c $x \approx 4.32$

2 a 3 and 4 **b** $x = \dfrac{\log 40}{\log 3}$ **c** $x \approx 3.36$

3 a **i** $x = \dfrac{1}{\log 2}$ **ii** $x \approx 3.32$

   b **i** $x = \dfrac{\log 20}{\log 3}$ **ii** $x \approx 2.73$

   c **i** $x = \dfrac{\log 50}{\log 4}$ **ii** $x \approx 2.82$

   d **i** $x = 4$ **ii** $x = 4$

   e **i** $x = -\dfrac{1}{\log\left(\frac{3}{4}\right)}$ **ii** $x \approx 8.00$

   f **i** $x = \log(0.000\,015)$ **ii** $x \approx -4.82$

4 a $x = \ln 10$ **b** $x = \ln 1000$ **c** $x = \ln 0.15$

   d $x = 2\ln 5$ **e** $x = \frac{1}{2}\ln 18$ **f** $x = 0$

5 a $x = \dfrac{\log 25}{\log 2}$ **b** $x = \dfrac{\log\left(\frac{20}{7}\right)}{\log 1.5}$ **c** $x = \dfrac{\log 0.6}{\log 0.8}$

   d $x = -\dfrac{\log(0.03)}{\log 2}$ **e** $x = \dfrac{10\log\left(\frac{10}{3}\right)}{\log 5}$ **f** $x = 4\ln 8$

6 a $x = \dfrac{\log 3}{\log 5}$ **b** $x = -\dfrac{\log 8}{\log 3}$ **c** $x = -1$

7 a Hint: If $\log_b a = x$, then $b^x = a$.

   b **i** $x = 16$ **ii** $x = \sqrt[3]{5} \approx 1.71$ **iii** $x = \log_{25} 8$

EXERCISE 7F

1 **a** ≈ 2.37 years **b** ≈ 8.36 years

2 **a** ≈ 3.90 hours **b** ≈ 15.5 hours

3 **a**, **b** see graph below

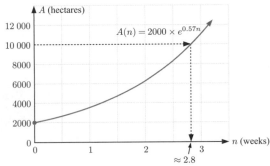

$\therefore$ approximately 2.8 weeks.

4 In ≈ 5.86 years or ≈ 5 years 10 months

5 **a**

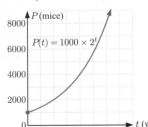

b ≈ 4.32 weeks

c $t = \dfrac{\log P - 3}{\log 2}$

6 **Hint:** Set $V = 40$, solve for t.

7 **a** decreasing **b** **i** 3900 m s^{-1} **ii** ≈ 2600 m s^{-1}

c ≈ 11.8 seconds

EXERCISE 7G

1 **a** **i** Domain $= \{x : x > 0\}$, Range $= \{y : y \in \mathbb{R}\}$

ii vertical asymptote is $x = 0$, x-intercept 4, no y-intercept

iii

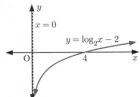

iv $x = 2$

b **i** Domain $= \{x : x > -1\}$, Range $= \{y : y \in \mathbb{R}\}$

ii vertical asymptote is $x = -1$, x and y-intercepts 0

iii

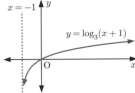

iv $x = -\frac{2}{3}$

c **i** Domain $= \{x : x > -1\}$, Range $= \{y : y \in \mathbb{R}\}$

ii vertical asymptote is $x = -1$, x-intercept 2, y-intercept 1

iii

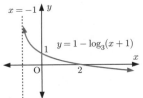

iv $x = 8$

d **i** Domain $= \{x : x > 2\}$, Range $= \{y : y \in \mathbb{R}\}$

ii vertical asymptote is $x = 2$, x-intercept 27, no y-intercept

iii

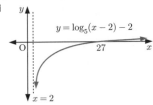

iv $x = 7$

e **i** Domain $= \{x : x > 2\}$, Range $= \{y : y \in \mathbb{R}\}$

ii vertical asymptote is $x = 2$, x-intercept 7, no y-intercept

iii

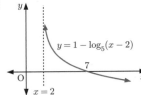

iv $x = 27$

f **i** Domain $= \{x : x > 0\}$, Range $= \{y : y \in \mathbb{R}\}$

ii vertical asymptote is $x = 0$, x-intercept $\sqrt{2}$, no y-intercept

iii

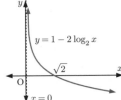

iv $x = 2$

2 **a** **i** Domain $= \{x : x > 0\}$, Range $= \{y : y \in \mathbb{R}\}$

ii vertical asymptote is $x = 0$, x-intercept e^4, no y-intercept

iii

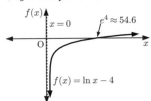

b **i** Domain $= \{x : x > 1\}$, Range $= \{y : y \in \mathbb{R}\}$

ii vertical asymptote is $x = 1$, x-intercept $1 + e^{-2}$, no y-intercept

iii

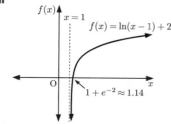

$f(x) = \ln(x-1) + 2$

$1 + e^{-2} \approx 1.14$

3 a A is $y = \ln x$ as its x-intercept is 1.

b

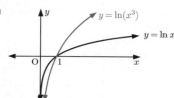

$y = \ln(x+2)$

$y = \ln(x-2)$

$y = \ln x$

c $y = \ln x$ has vertical asymptote $x = 0$
$y = \ln(x-2)$ has vertical asymptote $x = 2$
$y = \ln(x+2)$ has vertical asymptote $x = -2$

4 $y = \ln(x^2) = 2\ln x$, so she is correct.
This is because the y-values are twice as large for $y = \ln(x^2)$ as they are for $y = \ln x$.

5 a

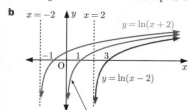

$y = \ln(x^3)$
$y = \ln x$

b

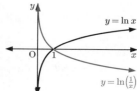

$y = \ln x$
$y = \ln\left(\frac{1}{x}\right)$

c

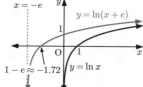

$x = -e$
$y = \ln(x+e)$
$1 - e \approx -1.72$
$y = \ln x$

d

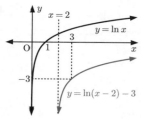

$x = 2$
$y = \ln x$
$y = \ln(x-2) - 3$

e

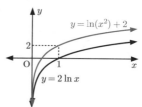

$y = \ln(x^2) + 2$
$y = 2\ln x$

6 Hint: Set $M_t = 50$ and solve for t. **7** 9 years

8 a $\dfrac{8.4\%}{12} = 0.7\% = 0.007$, $r = 1 + 0.007 = 1.007$

b after 74 months

9 a ≈ 17.3 years **b** ≈ 92.2 years **c** ≈ 115 years

10 a ≈ 50.7 min **b** ≈ 152 min

11 a

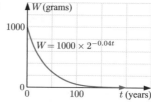

$W = 1000 \times 2^{-0.04t}$

b $t = \dfrac{3 - \log W}{0.04 \log 2}$

c i ≈ 141 years **ii** ≈ 498 years

12 a $10\,000$ years **b** $\approx 49\,800$ years

13 Hint: $t = \dfrac{-50\log(0.1)}{\log 2}$ **14** $t = \dfrac{\log\left(1 - \frac{v}{60}\right)}{-0.2\log 2}$ s

REVIEW SET 7A

1 a $\frac{1}{2}$ **b** $-\frac{1}{3}$ **c** $a + b + 1$

2 a 3 **b** 8 **c** -2 **d** $\frac{1}{2}$ **e** 0
 f $\frac{1}{4}$ **g** -1 **h** $\frac{1}{2}$, $k > 0$, $k \neq 1$

3 a ≈ 1.431 **b** ≈ -0.237 **c** ≈ 2.602 **d** ≈ 3.689

4 a $\ln 144$ **b** $\ln\left(\frac{3}{2}\right)$ **c** $\ln\left(\dfrac{25}{e}\right)$ **d** $\ln 3$

5 a $\log 144$ **b** $\log_2\left(\frac{16}{9}\right)$ **c** $\log_4 80$

6 a $2A + 2B$ **b** $A + 3B$ **c** $3A + \frac{1}{2}B$
 d $\frac{1}{2}(A + B)$ **e** $4B - 2A$ **f** $3A - 2B$

7 a $x = \frac{1}{8}$ **b** $x \approx 82.7$ **c** $x \approx 0.0316$

8 a i $x = \dfrac{\log 50}{\log 2}$ **ii** $x \approx 5.64$

 b i $x = \dfrac{\log 4}{\log 7}$ **ii** $x \approx 0.71$

 c i $x = \dfrac{-2}{\log(0.6)}$ **ii** $x \approx 9.02$

9 $\log_a\left(\dfrac{1}{b}\right) = -x$

10 a ≈ 4.96 years or ≈ 4 years $11\frac{1}{2}$ months **b** $\approx 75\%$

11 a i Domain $= \{x : x > -4\}$, Range $= \{y : y \in \mathbb{R}\}$
 ii vertical asymptote is $x = -4$, x-intercept -2, y-intercept 1

iii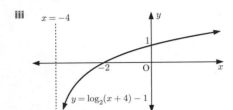

b **i** Domain $= \{x : x > 0\}$, Range $= \{y : y \in \mathbb{R}\}$
   ii vertical asymptote is $x = 0$, x-intercept e^{-2}, no y-intercept
   iii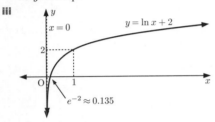

12 a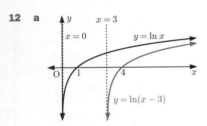

b

13 Hint: Set $T = 40$, and solve for t.

REVIEW SET 7B

1 a $\frac{3}{2}$ **b** $\frac{2}{3}$ **c** $a + b$

2 a 7   **b** -3 **c** $-\frac{1}{2}$

3 a $\approx 10^{1.5051}$ **b** $\approx 10^{-2.8861}$ **c** $\approx 10^{-4.0475}$

4 a $\frac{3}{2}$ **b** -3 **c** $2x$ **d** $1 - x$

5 a $\frac{2}{3}$ **b** $\frac{6}{5}$ **c** 8

6 a **i** $x = \dfrac{\log 7}{\log 5}$ **ii** $x \approx 1.21$

   b **i** $x = -\dfrac{1}{\log 2}$ **ii** $x \approx -3.32$

7 a $\ln 3$ **b** $\ln 4$ **c** $\ln 125$

8 a $x = \dfrac{\ln 70}{2}$ **b** $x = \dfrac{\log\left(\frac{11}{3}\right)}{\log 1.3}$ **c** $x = \dfrac{10\log\left(\frac{16}{5}\right)}{3\log 2}$

9 $x = 1$ **10 a** 2500 g   **b** ≈ 3288 years

11 a $x = \dfrac{2\log 9}{\log 5}$ **b** $x = \ln 30$ **c** $x = \dfrac{1 - \ln 2}{3}$

12 a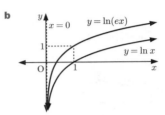

b

13 a

   b **i** ≈ 3.58 seconds   **ii** ≈ 5.55 seconds
   c ≈ 1.34 seconds longer

EXERCISE 8A

1 a **i** 3   **ii** 2   **iii** 5   **b** **i** 4   **ii** 1   **iii** -2
   c **i** 5   **ii** -3 **iii** 1   **d** **i** 3   **ii** 5   **iii** 0
   e **i** 4   **ii** -1 **iii** 8   **f** **i** 3   **ii** -4 **iii** 7

2 a 7   **b** -4 **c** 0   **d** 1   **e** -1

EXERCISE 8B

1 a $3x^2 + 6x + 9$ **b** $5x^2 + 7x + 9$ **c** $-7x^2 - 8x - 9$
   d $4x^4 + 13x^3 + 28x^2 + 27x + 18$

2 a $x^3 + x^2 - 4x + 7$ **b** $x^3 - x^2 - 2x + 3$
   c $3x^3 + 2x^2 - 11x + 19$ **d** $2x^3 - x^2 - x + 5$
   e $x^5 - x^4 - x^3 + 8x^2 - 11x + 10$
   f $x^4 - 2x^3 + 5x^2 - 4x + 4$

3 a $2x^3 - 3x^2 + 4x + 3$ **b** $x^4 + x^3 - 7x^2 + 7x - 2$
   c $x^3 + 6x^2 + 12x + 8$ **d** $4x^4 - 4x^3 + 13x^2 - 6x + 9$
   e $16x^4 - 32x^3 + 24x^2 - 8x + 1$
   f $18x^4 - 87x^3 + 56x^2 + 20x - 16$

4 a $6x^3 - 11x^2 + 18x - 5$ **b** $8x^3 + 18x^2 - x + 10$
   c $-2x^3 + 7x^2 + 13x + 10$ **d** $2x^3 - 7x^2 + 4x + 4$
   e $2x^4 - 2x^3 - 9x^2 + 11x - 2$
   f $15x^4 + x^3 - x^2 + 7x - 6$ **g** $x^4 - 2x^3 + 7x^2 - 6x + 9$
   h $4x^4 + 4x^3 - 15x^2 - 8x + 16$
   i $8x^3 + 60x^2 + 150x + 125$
   j $x^6 + 2x^5 + x^4 - 4x^3 - 4x^2 + 4$

5 degree of $Q(x)$ is 4 $\{(x - 1) \times x^3 = x^4 ....\}$

6 degree of $Q(x)$ is 3

7 degree is 6, leading coefficient is -15, constant is -10

8 a If $p \neq q$, the degree of $P(x) + Q(x)$ is the maximum of p and q since the highest power of x is the maximum of p and q.

If $p = q$, the degree of $P(x) + Q(x) \leqslant p$, since the coefficients of the higher powers of x may cancel.

b $kP(x)$ has degree p since any non-zero scalar multiple of a polynomial results in a polynomial of the same degree.

c $P(x)Q(x)$ has degree $p + q$ since the highest power of x is $x^p \times x^q = x^{p+q}$.

d $(P(x))^2$ has degree $2p$ since the highest power of x is $x^p \times x^p = x^{2p}$.

EXERCISE 8C

1 a yes   **b** no   **c** no   **d** yes

2 a -3 and 7 **b** $-\frac{3}{2}$ and 4 **c** $-3 \pm \sqrt{10}$

3 a $\frac{1}{3}$ and 4 **b** $-4 \pm \sqrt{19}$ **c** 0, 3, and -5

5 a $x(x+2)(x-2)$ **b** $x(x+3)(x-1)$
   c $x(x+3)(x-7)$ **d** $x(x-4)(x-5)$
   e $x(x+3)(x+8)$ **f** $x(2x+1)(x-2)$
   g $x(3x-2)(x+4)$ **h** $x(5x+1)(x-2)$
   i $x(3x+4)(2x-5)$

6 a $(x-8)(x+2)$; zeros are 8 and -2
   b $(2x+3)(x-5)$; zeros are $-\frac{3}{2}$ and 5
   c no real linear factors; no real zeros
   d $x(x+1+\sqrt{5})(x+1-\sqrt{5})$; zeros are 0, $-1 \pm \sqrt{5}$
   e $x(x+\sqrt{7})(x-\sqrt{7})$; zeros are 0, $\pm\sqrt{7}$
   f $z(3z-2)(2z+1)$; zeros are 0, $\frac{2}{3}$, or $-\frac{1}{2}$
   g $(z+\sqrt{5})(z-\sqrt{5})(z+1)(z-1)$; zeros are ±1, $\pm\sqrt{5}$
   h real linear factors $(z+\sqrt{3})(z-\sqrt{3})$; real zeros are $\pm\sqrt{3}$
   i real linear factor $(x+5)$; only real zero is -5

8 a $P(\alpha) = 0$, $P(\beta) = 0$, $P(\gamma) = 0$
   b If $P(x)$ has a factor of $(x-a)$, then $P(a) = 0$ which implies that $P(x)$ has x-intercept a which is distinct from the x-intercepts of α, β, and γ.
   But $P(x)$ has only three x-intercepts and since $a \neq \alpha$, β, or γ, a cannot be one of them.
   $\therefore$ $P(x)$ cannot have a factor of $(x-a)$.

9 a $P(x) = a(x+3)(x-4)(x-5)$, $a \neq 0$
   b $P(x) = a(x+2)(x-2)(x-3)$, $a \neq 0$
   c $P(x) = a(x-3)(x^2 - 2x - 4)$, $a \neq 0$
   d $P(x) = a(x+1)(x^2 + 4x + 2)$, $a \neq 0$

10 a $P(x) = a(x+2)(x-2)(x^2 - 3)$, $a \neq 0$
   b $P(x) = a(2x-1)(x+1)(x^2 - 5)$, $a \neq 0$
   c $P(x) = ax(x^2 - 4x + 2)(x - 4)$, $a \neq 0$
   d $P(x) = a(x^2 - 3)(x^2 + 2x - 1)$, $a \neq 0$

11 a $\Delta = k^2 + 8k$
    $= k(k+8)$

   i $k < -8$ or $k > 0$ **ii** $k \leqslant -8$ or $k \geqslant 0$
   iii $k = -8$ or 0 **iv** $-8 < k < 0$

   b $\Delta = 4 - 4k^2$
     $= 4(1+k)(1-k)$

   i $-1 < k < 1$, $k \neq 0$ **ii** $-1 \leqslant k \leqslant 1$, $k \neq 0$
   iii $k = \pm 1$ **iv** $k < -1$ or $k > 1$

c $\Delta = k^2 + 4k - 12$
   $= (k+6)(k-2)$

   i $k < -6$ or $k > 2$ **ii** $k \leqslant -6$ or $k \geqslant 2$
   iii $k = -6$ or 2 **iv** $-6 < k < 2$

d $\Delta = k^2 - 4k - 12$
   $= (k+2)(k-6)$

   i $k < -2$ or $k > 6$ **ii** $k \leqslant -2$ or $k \geqslant 6$
   iii $k = -2$ or 6 **iv** $-2 < k < 6$

e $\Delta = 9k^2 - 14k - 39$
   $= (9k+13)(k-3)$

   i $k < -\frac{13}{9}$ or $k > 3$ **ii** $k \leqslant -\frac{13}{9}$ or $k \geqslant 3$
   iii $k = -\frac{13}{9}$ or 3 **iv** $-\frac{13}{9} < k < 3$

f $\Delta = -3k^2 - 4k$
   $= -k(3k+4)$

   i $-\frac{4}{3} < k < 0$, $k \neq -1$ **ii** $-\frac{4}{3} \leqslant k \leqslant 0$, $k \neq -1$
   iii $k = -\frac{4}{3}$ or 0 **iv** $k < -\frac{4}{3}$ or $k > 0$

12 $-8 + \sqrt{60} \leqslant k < 0$

EXERCISE 8D

1 a $a = 2$, $b = 5$, $c = 5$ **b** $a = 4$, $b = 5$, $c = 14$
   c $a = 3$, $b = 4$, $c = 3$

2 a $a = 2$, $b = -2$ or $a = -2$, $b = 2$
   b $a = 2$, $b = -1$ or $a = -1$, $b = 2$
   c $a = 3$, $b = -1$

4 $a = -2$, $b = 2$, $x = 1 \pm i$ or $-1 \pm \sqrt{3}$

5 $c = \pm\sqrt{12}$, $d = \mp\sqrt{12}$, $x = -\sqrt{3} \pm \sqrt{2}$, $\sqrt{3} \pm \sqrt{2}$

6 a $a = 3$, zeros are -4, 1, $\frac{3}{2}$
   b $a = -4$, zeros are 2, -1, $-\frac{2}{3}$

7 a $a = -9$, $b = -1$, zeros are -1, $-\frac{1}{2}$, 2, 4
   b $a = 1$, $b = -15$, zeros are -3, $\frac{1}{2}$, $1 \pm \sqrt{2}$

8 $k = 13$

9 $x^4 - 2x^3 - 3x^2 + 4x + 3 = (x^2 - x)^2 - 4(x^2 - x) + 3$,
   zeros are $\frac{1}{2} \pm \frac{\sqrt{5}}{2}$, $\frac{1}{2} \pm \frac{\sqrt{13}}{2}$

10 a If $k = 20$, $P(x) = (x-2)^2(x+5)$
     If $k = -\frac{832}{27}$, $P(x) = \frac{1}{27}(3x-13)(3x+8)^2$
   b $P(x) = (x+3)^2(x-3)$ or $P(x) = (x-1)^2(x+5)$
   c If $m = -2$, zeros are -1 (repeated) and $\frac{2}{3}$.
     If $m = \frac{14}{243}$, zeros are $\frac{1}{9}$ (repeated) and $-\frac{14}{9}$.

EXERCISE 8E

1 a $Q(x) = x$, $R = -3$, $x^2 + 2x - 3 = x(x+2) - 3$
   b $Q(x) = x - 4$, $R = -3$, $x^2 - 5x + 1 = (x-4)(x-1) - 3$
   c $Q(x) = 2x^2 + 10x + 16$, $R = 35$,
     $2x^3 + 6x^2 - 4x + 3 = (2x^2 + 10x + 16)(x-2) + 35$

2 a $x^2 - 3x + 6 = (x+1)(x-4) + 10$
   b $x^2 + 4x - 11 = (x+1)(x+3) - 14$
   c $2x^2 - 7x + 2 = (2x-3)(x-2) - 4$
   d $2x^3 + 3x^2 - 3x - 2 = (x^2 + x - 2)(2x+1)$
   e $3x^3 + 11x^2 + 8x + 7 = (x^2 + 4x + 4)(3x-1) + 11$
   f $2x^4 - x^3 - x^2 + 7x + 4 = (x^3 - 2x^2 + \frac{5}{2}x - \frac{1}{4})(2x+3) + \frac{19}{4}$

3 a $x + 2 + \dfrac{9}{x-2}$ **b** $2x + 1 - \dfrac{1}{x+1}$

c $3x - 4 + \dfrac{3}{x+2}$ **d** $x^2 + 3x - 2$

e $2x^2 - 8x + 31 - \dfrac{124}{x+4}$ **f** $x^2 + 3x + 6 + \dfrac{7}{x-2}$

4 a $3x^2 - 8x + 4$, $(x+1)(3x-2)(x-2)$

b $2x^2 + 11x + 12$, $(x-2)(2x+3)(x+4)$

c $4x^2 + x - 3$, $(x+5)(4x-3)(x+1)$

5 a $\dfrac{x^3 + a^3}{x+a} = x^2 - ax + a^2$

b **i** $(x^2 - x + 1)(x+1)$ **ii** $(x^2 - 2x + 4)(x+2)$

iii $(x^2 - 5x + 25)(x+5)$

6 a **i** $\dfrac{x^2 - a^2}{x-a} = x + a$ **ii** $\dfrac{x^3 - a^3}{x-a} = x^2 + ax + a^2$

iii $\dfrac{x^4 - a^4}{x-a} = x^3 + ax^2 + a^2x + a^3$

iv $\dfrac{x^5 - a^5}{x-a} = x^4 + ax^3 + a^2x^2 + a^3x + a^4$

b $(x-a)(x^{n-1} + ax^{n-2} + a^2 x^{n-3} + \dots + a^{n-2}x + a^{n-1})$

c **i** $(x-2)(x^2 + 2x + 4)$

ii $(x-1)(x^3 + x^2 + x + 1)$

iii $(x-2)(x^3 + 2x^2 + 4x + 8)$

iv $(x-3)(x^4 + 3x^3 + 9x^2 + 27x + 81)$

EXERCISE 8F

1 a $P(x) = Q(x)(x-2) + 7$, $P(x)$ divided by $x - 2$ leaves a remainder of 7.

b $P(-3) = -8$, $P(x)$ divided by $x + 3$ leaves a remainder of -8.

c $P(5) = 11$, $P(x) = Q(x)(x-5) + 11$

2 a 1 **b** -19 **c** 1 **3 a** $a = 3$ **b** $a = 2$

4 $a = -5$, $b = 6$ **5** $a = -3$, $n = 4$ **6** -7

7 a $P(x) = Q(x)(2x-1) + R$

$P(\tfrac{1}{2}) = Q(\tfrac{1}{2})(2 \times \tfrac{1}{2} - 1) + R$

$= Q(\tfrac{1}{2}) \times 0 + R$

$= R$

b **i** -3 **ii** 7

8 -7 **9** $a = 3$, $b = 10$

EXERCISE 8G

1 a yes **b** no **c** yes

2 a $a = 5$ **b** $a = -\dfrac{79}{8}$

3 a $k = -8$, $P(x) = (x+2)(2x+1)(x-2)$

b $k = 2$, $P(x) = x(x-3)(x+\sqrt{2})(x-\sqrt{2})$

4 a $k = 18$ **b** $P(x) = (x-4)(3x^2 - 5x - 2)$

c $x = -\tfrac{1}{3}$, 2, or 4

5 $a = 7$, $b = -14$

6 $k = -1$ or -2

If $k = -1$, zeros are 0, -2, and 3.

If $k = -2$, zeros are $-1 \pm \sqrt{2}$, and 3.

7 $m = -\dfrac{10}{7}$

8 a $a = 7$, $b = -6$ **b** 60

c $P(x) = (x+3)(2x^2 + 3x - 2)$ **d** $-3, -2, \tfrac{1}{2}$

9 a $a = 7$, $b = 2$ **b** $x = -2 \pm \sqrt{6}$ **11** $a = 2$

EXERCISE 8H

1 a sum $= \tfrac{3}{2}$, product $= 2$ **b** sum $= \tfrac{4}{3}$, product $= \tfrac{5}{3}$

c sum $= 1$, product $= -4$ **d** sum $= \tfrac{3}{2}$, product $= 4$

e sum $= 0$, product $= 9$ **f** sum $= 0$, product $= -1$

2 a sum $= \tfrac{20}{3}$, product $= \tfrac{14}{3}$ **b** -40 **c** -28

3 a $k = 4$ **b** 5 **4** $a = \pm\sqrt{3}$ or $\pm\sqrt{2}$

5 b $p = -1$, $q = -1$, $r = 1$

EXERCISE 8I

1 a

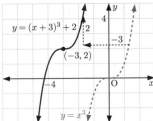

We translate $y = x^3$ 3 units left and 2 units up.

b

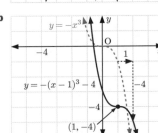

We reflect $y = x^3$ in the y-axis, then translate the graph 1 unit right and 4 units down.

c

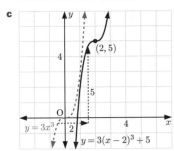

We translate $y = 3x^3$ 2 units right and 5 units up.

d

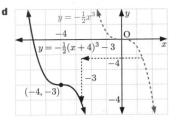

We reflect $y = \tfrac{1}{2}x^3$ in the y-axis, then translate the graph of $y = -\tfrac{1}{2}x^3$ 4 units to the left and 3 units down.

2 a **b**

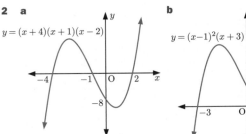

c

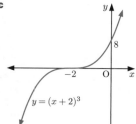

$y = (x+2)^3$

d

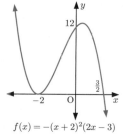

$f(x) = -(x+2)^2(2x-3)$

e

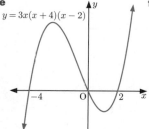

$y = 3x(x+4)(x-2)$

f

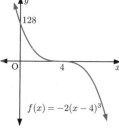

$f(x) = -2(x-4)^3$

g

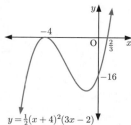

$y = \frac{1}{2}(x+4)^2(3x-2)$

h

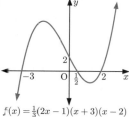

$f(x) = \frac{1}{3}(2x-1)(x+3)(x-2)$

i

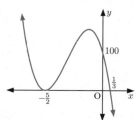

$f(x) = -4(2x+5)^2(3x-1)$

3 **a** $y = 2(x+1)(x-2)(x-3)$
   b $y = -2(x+3)(2x-1)(2x+1)$
   c $y = \frac{1}{4}(x+4)^2(x-3)$
   d $y = \frac{1}{10}(x+5)(x+2)(x-5)$
   e $y = \frac{1}{4}(x+4)(x-3)^2$
   f $y = -2(x+3)(x+2)(2x+1)$

4 **a** $f(-2) = 0$
   b $(x+2)(2x-1)(x-3)$
   d Domain $= \{x : x \in \mathbb{R}\}$
      Range $= \{y : y \in \mathbb{R}\}$
   e as $x \to \infty$, $y \to \infty$
      as $x \to -\infty$, $y \to -\infty$

   c

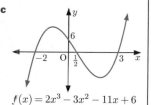

$f(x) = 2x^3 - 3x^2 - 11x + 6$

5 **a** $y = (x-3)(x-1)(x+2)$ **b** $y = 3x(x+2)(2x-1)$
   c $y = (x-1)^2(x+2)$ **d** $y = -\frac{1}{3}(3x+2)^2(x-4)$

6 **a** F   **b** G   **c** E   **d** I   **e** A   **f** C
   g B   **h** D   **i** H

7 **a** $-2(x+3)(x-1)^2$
   c as $x \to \infty$, $y \to -\infty$
      as $x \to -\infty$, $y \to \infty$

   b

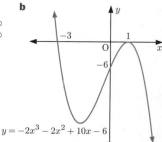

$y = -2x^3 - 2x^2 + 10x - 6$

8 **a** $P(x) = 5(2x-1)(x+3)(x-2)$
   b $P(x) = -2(x+2)^2(x-1)$
   c $P(x) = (x-2)(2x^2 - 3x + 2)$

9 **a** $a = 700$, the time at which the barrier has returned to its original position.
   b $k = \frac{85}{36\,000\,000}$, $f(t) = \frac{85}{36\,000\,000} t(t-700)^2$

10 **b** $0 < x < 15$ **c**

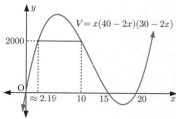

$V = x(40-2x)(30-2x)$

   d 10 cm $\times$ 10 cm   or ≈ 2.19 cm $\times$ 2.19 cm

EXERCISE 8J

1 **a**

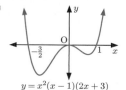

$y = x^2(x-1)(2x+3)$

   b

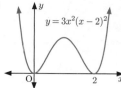

$y = 3x^2(x-2)^2$

   c

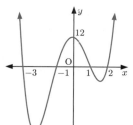

$f(x) = 2(x+3)(x+1)(x-1)(x-2)$

   d

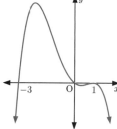

$y = -2x(x-1)^2(x+3)$

   e

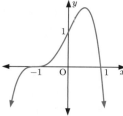

$f(x) = -(x-1)(x+1)^3$

   f

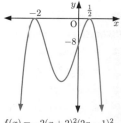

$f(x) = -2(x+2)^2(2x-1)^2$

2 a $x^2(x-2)(x+1)$

b

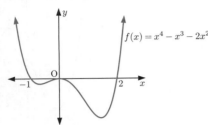

3 a $y = 2(x+1)^2(x-1)^2$
b $y = (x+3)(x+1)^2(3x-2)$
c $y = -2(x+2)(x+1)(x-2)^2$
d $y = -\frac{1}{3}(x+3)(x+1)(2x-3)(x-3)$
e $y = \frac{1}{4}(x+1)(x-4)^3$
f $y = x^2(x+2)(x-3)$

4 a $y = (x+4)(2x-1)(x-2)^2$
b $y = \frac{1}{4}(3x-2)^2(x+3)^2$
c $y = 2(2x+1)(2x-1)(x+2)(x-2)$
d $y = (x-1)^2(\frac{8}{3}x^2 + \frac{8}{3}x - 1)$

5 a C   b F   c A   d E   e B   f D

6 $y = \frac{1}{2}x^4 + \frac{7}{2}x^3 + 6x^2 - 2x - 8$

7 a $f(x) = (x-2)^2(x^2+3x+3)$ where x^2+3x+3 has $\Delta < 0$, so x^2+3x+3 has no real zeros.

b

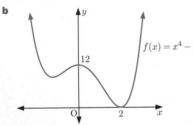

8 a $(x^2+x+1)(x^2-5x+7)$
b x^2+x+1 has $a > 0$ and $\Delta < 0$
  x^2-5x+7 has $a > 0$ and $\Delta < 0$
  $\therefore$ the graph lies entirely above the x-axis.

c

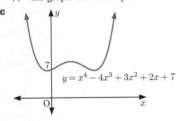

9 a ≈ 877 joules s^{-1} **b** ≈ 900 joules s^{-1}
10 a $a = 120$, $b = 200$ **b** $k = 1\,000\,000$ **c** 6.75 m

EXERCISE 8K

1 a $-1, 2 \pm \sqrt{3}$ **b** 1 **c** $\frac{7}{2}$ **d** $\frac{1}{2}$
e $\pm\frac{1}{2}, 3, -2$ **f** 2

2 a $x = -2$ **b** $x = -2, -\frac{1}{2}, 1$
c $x = 2$ (treble root)   **d** $x = -2, \frac{3}{2}, 3$
e $x = -3, 2, 1 \pm \sqrt{2}$ **f** $x = -\frac{1}{2}, 3$

3 a $x = 2$ **b** $x = -3$
c $x = \frac{1}{2}, 2 \pm \sqrt{3}$ **d** $x = 2$
e $x = -\frac{1}{2}, 1, \frac{3}{2}$ **f** $x = -2, \frac{2}{3}$
g $x = -1, \frac{1}{2}$ **h** $x = -\frac{5}{2}$

4 a $x \approx -3.27, -0.860, 2.13$ **b** $x \approx -2.52, -1.18, 2.70$

5 March

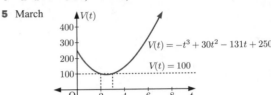

6 ≈ 1.11 m or ≈ 9.94 m

REVIEW SET 8A

1 a $2z^3 - z^2 + 2z + 6$ **b** $-2z^4 + 7z^3 - 7z^2 + 12z$
c $-2z^2 - 5z - 19 + \dfrac{57}{3-z}$

2 a $12x^4 - 9x^3 + 8x^2 - 26x + 15$
b $4x^4 - 4x^3 + 13x^2 - 6x + 9$

3 a $x^2 - 2x + 4 - \dfrac{8}{x+2}$ **b** $2x^2 + 2x - 1 + \dfrac{3}{x-1}$

4 a yes   **b** no

5 a $a = -7$, $b = 12$ **b** $a = 3$, $b = 1$

6 -2, -4, and 3

7 a $x(x-4)(x+2)$ **b** $x(3x-5)(x+2)$

8 $P(x) = a(x^4 - 6x^3 + 8x^2 + 2x - 1)$, $a \neq 0$

9 $x = -2 \pm \sqrt{6}$ **10** $(2x-3)(x+5)(x-2)$

11 $a = 7$, $b = -20$

12 a $k = 0, 4,$ or $-\dfrac{343}{8}$
b $P(x) = (x+2)^2(2x-1)$ when $k = 4$

13 $k = 11$, $(x+1)^2(2x+11)$ or $k = -16$, $(x+4)^2(2x-1)$

14 "When a polynomial $P(x)$ is divided by $x-k$ until a constant remainder R is obtained, then $R = P(k)$."

15 $267\,214$ **16** $m = 7$

17 $a = -14$, $b = -24$

18 Another hint: Show that $(\alpha\beta)^3 + (\alpha\beta)^2 - 1 = 0$

19 a sum $= \frac{4}{3}$, product $= \frac{8}{3}$ **b** sum $= 0$, product $= -5$

20

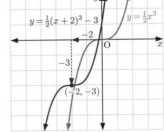

We translate $y = \frac{1}{2}x^3$ 2 units left and 3 units down.

21 a $y = (x+2)(x-2)(x-3)$
b $y = -2(x+1)^2(x-4)$

22 a

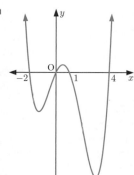

$y = x(x+2)(x-1)(x-4)$

b

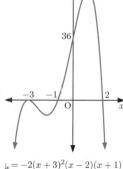

$y = -2(x+3)^2(x-2)(x+1)$

c

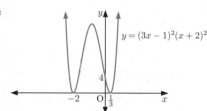

$y = (3x-1)^2(x+2)^2$

23 $P(x) = (x+2)^2(x-1)(4x-3)$

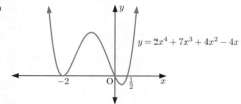

$y = (x+2)^2(x-1)(4x-3)$

24 a $P(x) = x(x+2)^2(2x-1)$

b

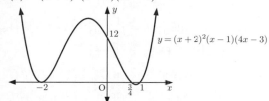

$y = 2x^4 + 7x^3 + 4x^2 - 4x$

c $x \leqslant 0$ and $x \geqslant \frac{1}{2}$

25 a $x = -3, -\frac{1}{2}, \frac{2}{3}$ **b** $x = -\frac{1}{3}, 2$

REVIEW SET 8B

1 a $f(x) - g(x) = x^4 - 3x^3 - 3x^2 + 2x - 8$
  b **i** 7   **ii** -2 **iii** -7

2 a $3x^5 + 13x^4 - 9x^3 - x^2 + 4x - 2$
  b $x^6 - 4x^5 + 4x^4 + 2x^3 - 4x^2 - 1$

3 a $(3x-2)$ and $(x-3)$, zeros are $\frac{2}{3}$ and 3
  b $(x+\sqrt{3})$, $(x-\sqrt{3})$, $(x+2)$ and $(x-2)$,
    zeros are $\pm\sqrt{3}$, ± 2

5 a $P(x) = a(x+4)(x-1)(x-6)$, $a \neq 0$
  b $P(x) = a(3x-1)(x^2 - 6x + 4)$, $a \neq 0$

6 a $k = -8$ **b** $k < -8$ or $k > 0$ **c** $-8 < k < 0$

7 $a = 1$, $b = -1$, $c = 3$

8 a $x^2 + 3x - 2 + \dfrac{5}{2x+3}$ **b** $x^3 + x^2 + 2x + 2 + \dfrac{4}{x-1}$

9 $(3x-2)(2x-1)(x+5)$

10 $x = -\frac{1}{2}$ (repeated), and $x = 3$

11 Other factor is $(x^2 - 3x + 3)$, $\Delta < 0$ $\therefore$ no real roots

12 a $k > 0$ **b** $k \leqslant 0$ **13** 2

14 $k = -2$, $n = 36$ **15** $a = -\frac{7}{2}$

16 a $a = -9$, $b = 23$ **b** -3 **c** 1, 3, and 5

17 a sum $= -\frac{3}{2}$, product $= -3$ **b** sum $= 0$, product $= \frac{3}{2}$

18 $P(x) = 2x^3 - 6x - 4$

19 a

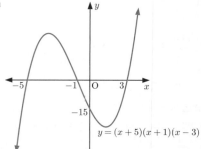

$y = (x+5)(x+1)(x-3)$

b

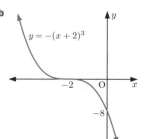

$y = -(x+2)^3$

c

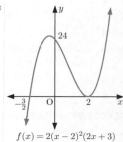

$f(x) = 2(x-2)^2(2x+3)$

20 a $f(x) = (x+5)(x^2 - 2x - 4)$
    $f(-5) = 0$ $\therefore$ -5 is an x-intercept.

  b $1 - \sqrt{5} \approx -1.24$, $1 + \sqrt{5} \approx 3.24$

  c

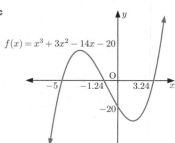

$f(x) = x^3 + 3x^2 - 14x - 20$

  d as $x \to \infty$,
    $f(x) \to \infty$
    as $x \to -\infty$,
    $f(x) \to -\infty$

21 a $0 \leqslant v < 100$
  b 4320 watts
  d ≈ 7.94 m s^{-1}

  c

P(watts)

10 000

$P = 20v^3$

≈ 7.94

v (m s^{-1})

22 $P(x) = -2x^3 + 6x^2 - 8$

23 a $y = \frac{1}{2}(x-3)^3(x+2)$ **b** $y = -3(x+1)^2(x-2)^2$

24 $(x+1)(x-4)(2x^2 - 6x + 5)$

$2x^2 - 6x + 5$ has $\Delta < 0$, so $2x^2 - 6x + 5$ has no real zeros.

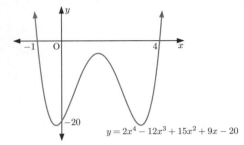

$y = 2x^4 - 12x^3 + 15x^2 + 9x - 20$

25 a $-\frac{1}{2}$ **b** $-7, -1,$ and 2

EXERCISE 9A

1 a 6 **b** 120 **c** 720 **d** 3 628 800

2 a $4!$ **b** $7!$ **c** $\dfrac{8!}{5!}$ **d** $\dfrac{15!}{11!}$ **e** $\dfrac{9!}{3!6!}$ **f** $\dfrac{13!}{4!9!}$

3 a 7 **b** 56 **c** 132 **d** 120 **e** 45 **f** 4950

4 a $n, \ n \geqslant 1$ **b** $(n+2)(n+1), \ n \geqslant 0$

   c $(n+1)n, \ n \geqslant 1$

5 a $4! \times 6$ **b** $10! \times 10$ **c** $6! \times 57$ **d** $10! \times 131$

   e $7! \times 81$ **f** $6! \times 62$ **g** $11! \times 10$ **h** $8! \times 32$

6 a $11!$ **b** $9!$ **c** $8!$ **d** 9

   e 34 **f** $n+1$ **g** $(n-1)!$ **h** $(n+1)!$

EXERCISE 9B

1 a 3 **b** 15 **c** 5 **d** 21

2 a PQ, PR, PS, PT, QR, **b** $\binom{5}{2} = \dfrac{5!}{2!3!} = 10$ ✓
       QS, QT, RS, RT, ST

3 a ABCD, ABCE, ABCF, ABDE, ABDF, ABEF, ACDE, ACDF,
       ACEF, ADEF, BCDE, BCDF, BCEF, BDEF, CDEF

   b $\binom{6}{4} = 15$ ✓

4 a i 4 **ii** 7 **iii** 10

   b $\binom{n}{1} = \dfrac{n!}{(n-1)!1!} = \dfrac{n(n-1)!}{(n-1)!} = n$

5 a i 1 **ii** 1 **iii** 1 **iv** 1

   b i $\binom{n}{0} = \dfrac{n!}{0!n!} = 1$ **ii** $\binom{n}{n} = \dfrac{n!}{n!0!} = 1$

6 a i $\binom{7}{2} = 21, \quad \binom{7}{5} = 21$

   ii $\binom{10}{3} = 120, \quad \binom{10}{7} = 120$

   b $\binom{n}{k} = \dfrac{n!}{k!(n-k)!} = \dfrac{n!}{(n-k)!k!} = \binom{n}{n-k}$

EXERCISE 9C

1 a $p^3 + 3p^2q + 3pq^2 + q^3$ **b** $x^3 + 3x^2 + 3x + 1$

   c $x^3 - 9x^2 + 27x - 27$ **d** $8 + 12x + 6x^2 + x^3$

   e $27x^3 - 27x^2 + 9x - 1$ **f** $8x^3 + 60x^2 + 150x + 125$

   g $8a^3 - 12a^2b + 6ab^2 - b^3$ **h** $27x^3 - 9x^2 + x - \frac{1}{27}$

   i $8x^3 + 12x + \dfrac{6}{x} + \dfrac{1}{x^3}$

2 a $1 + 4x + 6x^2 + 4x^3 + x^4$

   b $p^4 - 4p^3q + 6p^2q^2 - 4pq^3 + q^4$

c $x^4 - 8x^3 + 24x^2 - 32x + 16$

d $81 - 108x + 54x^2 - 12x^3 + x^4$

e $1 + 8x + 24x^2 + 32x^3 + 16x^4$

f $16x^4 - 96x^3 + 216x^2 - 216x + 81$

g $16x^4 + 32x^3b + 24x^2b^2 + 8xb^3 + b^4$

h $x^4 + 4x^2 + 6 + \dfrac{4}{x^2} + \dfrac{1}{x^4}$

i $16x^4 - 32x^2 + 24 - \dfrac{8}{x^2} + \dfrac{1}{x^4}$

3 a $x^5 + 10x^4 + 40x^3 + 80x^2 + 80x + 32$

   b $x^5 - 10x^4y + 40x^3y^2 - 80x^2y^3 + 80xy^4 - 32y^5$

   c $1 + 10x + 40x^2 + 80x^3 + 80x^4 + 32x^5$

   d $x^5 - 5x^3 + 10x - \dfrac{10}{x} + \dfrac{5}{x^3} - \dfrac{1}{x^5}$

4 a $7 + 5\sqrt{2}$ **b** $161 + 72\sqrt{5}$ **c** $232 - 164\sqrt{2}$

5 a $32 + 80x + 80x^2 + 40x^3 + 10x^4 + x^5$

   b 32.808 040 100 1

6 $2x^5 + 11x^4 + 24x^3 + 26x^2 + 14x + 3$ **7 a** 270 **b** 4320

EXERCISE 9D

1 a $1^{11} + \binom{11}{1}(2x)^1 + \binom{11}{2}(2x)^2 + \dots + \binom{11}{10}(2x)^{10} + (2x)^{11}$

   b $(3x)^{15} + \binom{15}{1}(3x)^{14}\left(\dfrac{2}{x}\right)^1 + \binom{15}{2}(3x)^{13}\left(\dfrac{2}{x}\right)^2 + \dots$
   $\dots + \binom{15}{14}(3x)^1\left(\dfrac{2}{x}\right)^{14} + \left(\dfrac{2}{x}\right)^{15}$

   c $(2x)^{20} + \binom{20}{1}(2x)^{19}\left(-\dfrac{3}{x}\right)^1 + \binom{20}{2}(2x)^{18}\left(-\dfrac{3}{x}\right)^2 + \dots$
   $\dots + \binom{20}{19}(2x)^1\left(-\dfrac{3}{x}\right)^{19} + \left(-\dfrac{3}{x}\right)^{20}$

2 a $T_6 = \binom{15}{5}(2x)^{10}5^5$ **b** $T_4 = \binom{9}{3}(x^2)^6y^3$

   c $T_{10} = \binom{17}{9}x^8\left(-\dfrac{2}{x}\right)^9$ **d** $T_9 = \binom{21}{8}(2x^2)^{13}\left(-\dfrac{1}{x}\right)^8$

3 a $T_{r+1} = \binom{8}{r}x^{8-r}2^r$ **b** 448

4 a $T_{r+1} = \binom{7}{r}x^{7-r}b^r$ **b** $b = -2$

5 a $\binom{15}{5}2^5$ **b** $\binom{9}{3}(-3)^3$

6 a $\binom{10}{5}3^5 2^5$ **b** $\binom{6}{3}2^3(-3)^3$ **c** $\binom{6}{3}2^3(-3)^3$

   d $\binom{12}{4}2^8(-1)^4$

7 $T_3 = \binom{6}{2}(-2)^2 x^8 y^8$ **8** $n = 9, \ T_4 = 84x^3$ **9** $a = 2$

10 a $\binom{6}{3}(-3)^3 + 4\binom{6}{2}(-3)^2 = 0$ **b** $\binom{8}{6} = 28$

   c $2\binom{9}{3}3^6 x^6 - \binom{9}{4}3^5 x^6 = 91\,854x^6$

11 $T_3 = \binom{6}{2}(-2)^2 x^8 y^8$ **12** $n = 6$ and $k = -2$

13 a
```
      1  1
    1  2  1
  1  3  3  1
1  4  6  4  1
1 5 10 10 5 1
```
   b i 2
      ii 4
      iii 8
      iv 16
      v 32

   c The sum of the numbers in row n of Pascal's triangle is 2^n.

   e i Hint: Let $x = 1$, in the expansion of $(1+x)^n$.
      ii Hint: Let $x = -1$, in the expansion of $(1+x)^n$.
      iii Hint: Consider the binomial expansion of $(1+1)^{2n+1}$
      and show that $\displaystyle\sum_{r=0}^{2n+1} \binom{2n+1}{r} = 2\sum_{r=0}^{n}\binom{2n+1}{r}$.

   f $\displaystyle\sum_{r=0}^{n} 2^r \binom{n}{r} = 3^n$

14 a $(3+x)^n = 3^n + \binom{n}{1}3^{n-1}x + \binom{n}{2}3^{n-2}x^2 +$
$\binom{n}{3}3^{n-3}x^3 + \ldots + \binom{n}{n-1}3^1x^{n-1} + x^n$

b 4^n

15 Hint: Equate coefficients of x^n in both expansions.

REVIEW SET 9A

1 a $8!$　**b** $\dfrac{10!}{7!}$　**2 a** $n(n-1)$, $n \geqslant 2$　**b** $n+2$

3 a $x^3 + 9x^2 + 27x + 27$

b $x^5 - 10x^4 + 40x^3 - 80x^2 + 80x - 32$

4 a $\binom{9}{4}(2x)^5 3^4$　**b** $\binom{12}{7}(3x)^5\left(-\dfrac{1}{x}\right)^7$

5 a $170 + 78\sqrt{3}$　**b** $x^5 - x^4 - 6x^3 + 14x^2 - 11x + 3$

6 $64.964\,808$

7 $(a+b)^6 = a^6 + 6a^5b + 15a^4b^2 + 20a^3b^3 + 15a^2b^4 + 6ab^5 + b^6$

a $x^6 - 18x^5 + 135x^4 - 540x^3 + 1215x^2 - 1458x + 729$

b $1 + \dfrac{6}{x} + \dfrac{15}{x^2} + \dfrac{20}{x^3} + \dfrac{15}{x^4} + \dfrac{6}{x^5} + \dfrac{1}{x^6}$

8 $\binom{12}{6}2^6(-3)^6$　**9** $8\binom{6}{2} - 6\binom{6}{1} = 84$　**10** $c = 3$

11 a $2^n + \binom{n}{1}2^{n-1}x^1 + \binom{n}{2}2^{n-2}x^2 + \binom{n}{3}2^{n-3}x^3 + \ldots$
$\ldots + \binom{n}{n-1}2^1x^{n-1} + x^n$

b 3^n　**Hint:** Let $x = 1$ in **a**.

12 $a = \pm 4$

REVIEW SET 9B

1 a 72　**b** 56　**2 a** 6　**b** 6　**c** 36

3 a $x^3 - 6x^2y + 12xy^2 - 8y^3$

b $81x^4 + 216x^3 + 216x^2 + 96x + 16$

4 $20\,000$　**5** 60

6 a $792 - 560\sqrt{2}$　**b** $8x^4 + 36x^3 + 42x^2 + 19x + 3$

7 a $(2x)^{10} + \binom{10}{1}(2x)^9(-7)^1 + \binom{10}{2}(2x)^8(-7)^2 + \ldots$
$\ldots + \binom{10}{9}(2x)^1(-7)^9 + (-7)^{10}$

b $(3x)^{13} + \binom{13}{1}(3x)^{12}\left(\dfrac{4}{x}\right)^1 + \binom{13}{2}(3x)^{11}\left(\dfrac{4}{x}\right)^2 + \ldots$
$\ldots + \binom{13}{12}(3x)^1\left(\dfrac{4}{x}\right)^{12} + \left(\dfrac{4}{x}\right)^{13}$

8 a $\binom{9}{2}3^7 = 78\,732$　**b** $\binom{9}{6}3^3 = 2268$

9 $k = -\dfrac{1}{4}$, $n = 16$　**10** $k = 180$　**11** $q = \pm\sqrt{\dfrac{3}{35}}$

EXERCISE 10A.1

1 a $(x-5)^2 + (y-1)^2 = 4$　**b** $(x+3)^2 + (y-4)^2 = 36$

c $(x+6)^2 + (y-2)^2 = 3$　**d** $x^2 + y^2 = 1$

e $(x+4)^2 + y^2 = 17$　**f** $(x+3)^2 + (y+7)^2 = 81$

2 a i $(-1, 3)$, 2 units　**ii** $(x+1)^2 + (y-3)^2 = 4$

b i $(0, -2)$, 4 units　**ii** $x^2 + (y+2)^2 = 16$

c i $(1, 2)$, $\sqrt{5}$ units　**ii** $(x-1)^2 + (y-2)^2 = 5$

d i $(-4, -1)$, $\sqrt{13}$ units

ii $(x+4)^2 + (y+1)^2 = 13$

3 a Centre $(2, 3)$, $r = 2$ units

b Centre $(0, -3)$, $r = 3$ units

c Centre $(2, 0)$, $r = \sqrt{7}$ units

4 a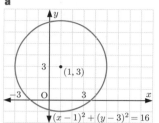

b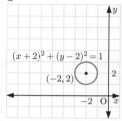

c

d

5 a $(x-3)^2 + (y+2)^2 = 4$

b $(x+4)^2 + (y-3)^2 = 16$

c $(x-5)^2 + (y-3)^2 = 17$

d $(x-2)^2 + (y-2)^2 = 17$

e $(x+3)^2 + (y-2)^2 = 7$

6 a A circle, centre $(-2, 7)$, radius $\sqrt{5}$ units.

b The point $(-2, 7)$.

7 a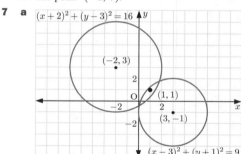

b $(1, 1)$

8 a

b No. It fails the vertical line test.

c Domain $= \{x : -5 \leqslant x \leqslant 1\}$, Range $= \{y : -2 \leqslant y \leqslant 4\}$

9 a $m = 5$ or -1　**b** $m = -2 \pm \sqrt{11}$　**c** $m = 3$ or -1

10 b the region outside the circle

c i on the circle　**ii** inside the circle

iii outside the circle　**iv** outside the circle

11 a $(3, 2)$　**b** ≈ 31.6 km　**c** no, ≈ 1.92 km

12 a $x_B = 2a - x_A$, $y_B = 2b - y_A$

b i $\dfrac{y_C - y_A}{x_C - x_A}$　**ii** $\dfrac{y_C - y_B}{x_C - x_B}$

c Hint: Expand $\left(\dfrac{y_C - y_A}{x_C - x_A}\right) \times \left(\dfrac{y_C - y_B}{x_C - x_B}\right)$ and substitute for x_B and y_B.

13 a $\dfrac{y_B - y_A}{x_B - x_A}$ **b** $y = b - \dfrac{x_B - x_A}{y_B - y_A}(x - a)$

c Hint: Substitute the x-coordinate of the midpoint of [AB] into the equation in **b**.

EXERCISE 10A.2

1 a $x^2 + y^2 - 4x - 6y + 12 = 0$
b $x^2 + y^2 - 10x + 2y + 17 = 0$
c $x^2 + y^2 + 8x + 6 = 0$
d $x^2 + y^2 + 12x + 18y + 44 = 0$

2 a $x^2 + y^2 - 2x + 2y - 14 = 0$
b $x^2 + y^2 - 6y + 1 = 0$

3 a $(-3, 1)$, $\sqrt{13}$ units   **b** $(3, 0)$, $\sqrt{11}$ units
c $(0, -2)$, $\sqrt{5}$ units   **d** $(-2, 4)$, $\sqrt{17}$ units
e $(2, 3)$, 4 units   **f** $(4, 0)$, 4 units

4 a   **b**

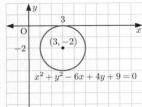   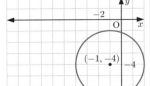

5 $x^2 + y^2 - 4x + 2y + 14 = 0$
$\Leftrightarrow (x - 2)^2 + (y + 1)^2 = -9$

But the sum of squares must be greater than or equal to 0.
∴ the equation is not the equation of a circle.

6 a $k = 36$ **b** $k = -2$ **c** $k < 5$

7 a i $(x - 3)^2 + (y - 4)^2 \leqslant 64$
ii $x^2 + y^2 - 6x - 8y - 39 \leqslant 0$

b i $(-5, -7)$ **c**
ii 6 km

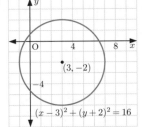

d $(-2, -2)$ is $\sqrt{61} \approx 7.8$ km from Pete's, and $\sqrt{34} \approx 5.8$ km from Pamela's shop.

8 b Centre $(-1, \frac{3}{2})$, radius $\sqrt{\frac{31}{12}}$ units

c i The equation represents the point $\left(-\dfrac{A}{2}, -\dfrac{B}{2}\right)$.

ii $\sqrt{\dfrac{A^2}{4} + \dfrac{B^2}{4} - C}$ is a non-real number
∴ the equation has no meaning.

9 a a circle, centre $(\frac{11}{2}, 0)$, radius $\frac{3}{2}$ units
b a circle, centre $(\frac{1}{2}, 0)$, radius $\frac{3}{2}$ units
c $x = 3$, which is a vertical line

EXERCISE 10B

1 a $x - 4y = -6$ **b** $y = 2$
2 a $2\sqrt{97} \approx 19.7$ m   **b** $9x + 4y = 43$
3 $y = 7$ and $12x - 5y = 61$
4 $y \approx 0.236x$ and $y \approx 1.76x$ **5** $y = \frac{11}{2}x$
6 a $(x - 3)^2 + (y + 2)^2 = 25$ **b** $(0, 2)$
7 a $k = 2 \pm 5\sqrt{5}$ **b** $2 - 5\sqrt{5} < k < 2 + 5\sqrt{5}$
c $k > 2 + 5\sqrt{5}$ or $k < 2 - 5\sqrt{5}$
8 a $\left(x - \dfrac{r}{2}\right)^2 + y^2 = \dfrac{r^2}{4}$

b a circle centre $\left(\dfrac{r}{2}, 0\right)$, radius $\dfrac{r}{2}$ units

REVIEW SET 10A

1 a $(x - 2)^2 + (y + 1)^2 = 25$
b $(x + 4)^2 + (y + 6)^2 = 7$
2 a $x^2 + y^2 + 2x - 4y - 4 = 0$
b $x^2 + y^2 + 4x + 8y + 2 = 0$
3 a   **b**

    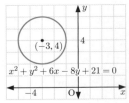

4 $m = 1 \pm \sqrt{35}$ **5** $4x - 7y = 28$
6 $y = -(2 \pm \frac{6}{\sqrt{5}})x \pm 6\sqrt{5} + 15$
7 a $k = \pm 13$ **b** $-13 < k < 13$ **c** $k < -13$ or $k > 13$

REVIEW SET 10B

1 a Centre $(-1, 3)$, radius 2 units
b Centre $(4, 2)$, radius $\sqrt{5}$ units

2 a   **b**

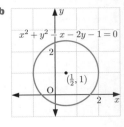

3 a $(x - 2)^2 + (y - 4)^2 = 3$
b $(x - \frac{3}{2})^2 + (y - 1)^2 = \frac{89}{4}$

4 a $(4, 2)$ **d**
b 50 km
c i yes
ii no

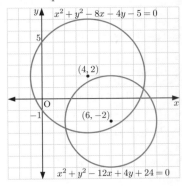

5 $k = 1$, centre $(-3, 2)$ **6** $(2, 4)$ and $(-4, -2)$

7 $y = \frac{37}{39}x$

EXERCISE 11A

1 a i A$(\cos 26°, \sin 26°)$, B$(\cos 146°, \sin 146°)$,
C$(\cos 199°, \sin 199°)$

ii A$(0.899, 0.438)$, B$(-0.829, 0.559)$,
C$(-0.946, -0.326)$

b i A$(\cos 123°, \sin 123°)$, B$(\cos 251°, \sin 251°)$,
C$(\cos(-35°), \sin(-35°))$

ii A$(-0.545, 0.839)$, B$(-0.326, -0.946)$,
C$(0.819, -0.574)$

2

θ	0°	90°	180°	270°	360°	450°
sine	0	1	0	-1	0	1
cosine	1	0	-1	0	1	0
tangent	0	undef	0	undef	0	undef

3 a i 0.985 **ii** 0.985 **iii** 0.966 **iv** 0.966
  v 0.454 **vi** 0.454

b $\sin(180° - \theta) = \sin\theta$

c $\sin\theta$ and $\sin(180° - \theta)$ have the same value, as P and Q have the same y-coordinate.

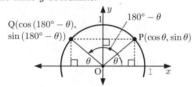

d i 135° **ii** 129°

4 a i 0.342 **ii** -0.342 **iii** 0.906 **iv** -0.906
  v 0.174 **vi** -0.174

b $\cos(180° - \theta) = -\cos\theta$

c $\cos(180° - \theta) = -\cos\theta$, as the x-coordinates of P and Q are negatives of each other.

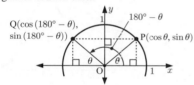

d i 140° **ii** 161°

5 a ≈ 0.6820 **b** ≈ 0.8572 **c** ≈ -0.7986
  d ≈ 0.9135 **e** ≈ 0.9063 **f** ≈ -0.6691

6 a $A\widehat{O}Q = 180° - \theta$

b [OQ] is a reflection of [OP] in the y-axis and so Q has coordinates $(-\cos\theta, \sin\theta)$.

c $\cos(180° - \theta) = -\cos\theta$, $\sin(180° - \theta) = \sin\theta$

7 b $\cos(360° - \theta) = \cos\theta$, $\sin(360° - \theta) = -\sin\theta$

EXERCISE 11B

1

	a	b	c	d	e	f	g	h
$\sin\theta$	$\frac{1}{2}$	$\frac{1}{\sqrt{2}}$	0	$\frac{1}{\sqrt{2}}$	1	$\frac{\sqrt{3}}{2}$	-1	0
$\cos\theta$	$\frac{\sqrt{3}}{2}$	$\frac{1}{\sqrt{2}}$	1	$-\frac{1}{\sqrt{2}}$	0	$-\frac{1}{2}$	0	-1
$\tan\theta$	$\frac{1}{\sqrt{3}}$	1	0	-1	undef.	$-\sqrt{3}$	undef.	0

	i	j	k	l	m	n	o	p
$\sin\theta$	$-\frac{1}{2}$	$-\frac{\sqrt{3}}{2}$	$-\frac{1}{2}$	0	$-\frac{\sqrt{3}}{2}$	$-\frac{1}{\sqrt{2}}$	$\frac{1}{\sqrt{2}}$	0
$\cos\theta$	$-\frac{\sqrt{3}}{2}$	$-\frac{1}{2}$	$\frac{\sqrt{3}}{2}$	1	$\frac{1}{2}$	$\frac{1}{\sqrt{2}}$	$-\frac{1}{\sqrt{2}}$	-1
$\tan\theta$	$\frac{1}{\sqrt{3}}$	$\sqrt{3}$	$-\frac{1}{\sqrt{3}}$	0	$-\sqrt{3}$	-1	-1	0

2 a $\frac{1}{2}$ **b** $\frac{1}{4}$ **c** $\frac{1}{3}$ **d** $\frac{3}{4}$

3 a 150° **b** 225° **c** 30° **d** 315°

EXERCISE 11C

1 a $\cos\theta = \pm\frac{\sqrt{3}}{2}$ **b** $\cos\theta = \pm\frac{2\sqrt{2}}{3}$ **c** $\cos\theta = \pm 1$
  d $\cos\theta = 0$

2 a $\sin\theta = \pm\frac{3}{5}$ **b** $\sin\theta = \pm\frac{\sqrt{7}}{4}$ **c** $\sin\theta = 0$
  d $\sin\theta = \pm 1$

3 a $\sin\theta = \frac{\sqrt{5}}{3}$ **b** $\cos\theta = -\frac{\sqrt{21}}{5}$ **c** $\cos\theta = \frac{4}{5}$
  d $\sin\theta = -\frac{12}{13}$

4 a $\tan\theta = -\frac{1}{2\sqrt{2}}$ **b** $\tan\theta = -2\sqrt{6}$ **c** $\tan\theta = \frac{1}{\sqrt{2}}$
  d $\tan\theta = -\frac{\sqrt{7}}{3}$

5 a $\sin x = \frac{2}{\sqrt{13}}$, $\cos x = \frac{3}{\sqrt{13}}$
  b $\sin x = \frac{4}{5}$, $\cos x = -\frac{3}{5}$
  c $\sin x = \sqrt{\frac{5}{14}}$, $\cos x = -\frac{3}{\sqrt{14}}$
  d $\sin x = -\frac{12}{13}$, $\cos x = \frac{5}{13}$

6 $\sin\theta = \frac{-k}{\sqrt{k^2 + 1}}$, $\cos\theta = \frac{-1}{\sqrt{k^2 + 1}}$

EXERCISE 11D

1 a $\theta \approx 76.0°$ or 256.0° **b** $\theta \approx 33.9°$ or 326.1°
  c $\theta \approx 36.9°$ or 143.1° **d** $\theta = 90°$ or 270°
  e $\theta \approx 50.2°$ or 230.2° **f** $\theta \approx 38.6°$ or 321.4°
  g $\theta \approx 5.22°$ or 174.8° **h** $\theta \approx 87.2°$ or 267.2°
  i $\theta \approx 77.2°$ or 102.8°

2 a $\theta \approx 104.5°$ or 255.5° **b** $\theta = 0°$, 180°, or 360°
  c $\theta \approx 107.9°$ or 287.9° **d** $\theta \approx 204.9°$ or 335.1°
  e $\theta \approx 98.5°$ or 278.5° **f** $\theta \approx 96.8°$ or 263.2°
  g $\theta \approx 114.1°$ or 294.1° **h** $\theta \approx 125.3°$ or 234.7°
  i $\theta \approx 219.2°$ or 320.8°

EXERCISE 11E

1 a ≈ 28.9 cm^2 **b** ≈ 384 km^2 **c** 20 m^2
  d ≈ 18.7 cm^2 **e** ≈ 28.3 cm^2 **f** ≈ 52.0 m^2

2 a yellow **b** brown **3** $x \approx 19.0$

4 18.9 cm^2 **5** 137 cm^2 **6** 374 cm^2

7 7.49 cm **8** ≈ 11.9 m

9 a $\approx 48.6°$ or $\approx 131.4°$ **b** $\approx 42.1°$ or $\approx 137.9°$

10 $\frac{1}{4}$ is not covered

11 a ≈ 35.1 cm^2 **b** ≈ 61.8 cm^2 **c** 40.4 mm^2

12 4.69 cm^2

EXERCISE 11F

1 a ≈ 3.84 cm **b** ≈ 7.99 m **c** ≈ 9.28 cm
  d ≈ 28.8 cm **e** ≈ 3.38 km **f** ≈ 14.2 m

2 a $\theta \approx 82.8°$ **b** $\theta \approx 54.8°$ **c** $\theta \approx 98.2°$

3 $\widehat{BAC} \approx 52.0°$, $\widehat{ABC} \approx 59.3°$, $\widehat{ACB} \approx 68.7°$

4 a $\approx 112°$ **b** ≈ 16.2 cm^2

5 a $\approx 40.3°$ **b** $\approx 107°$

6 a $\cos\theta = 0.65$ **b** $x \approx 3.81$

7 a $\theta \approx 75.2°$ **b** ≈ 6.30 m   **8 b** $x = 3 + \sqrt{22}$

9 $x \approx 1.41$ or 7.78 **10** ≈ 12.4 cm

EXERCISE 11G.1

1 a $x \approx 28.4$ **b** $x \approx 13.4$ **c** $x \approx 3.79$
   d $x \approx 10.3$ **e** $x \approx 4.49$ **f** $x \approx 7.07$

2 a $\widehat{BAC} = 74°$, $AB \approx 7.99$ cm, $BC \approx 9.05$ cm
   b $\widehat{PQR} = 54°$, $PQ \approx 4.67$ m, $QR \approx 7.41$ m
   c $\widehat{XZY} = 108°$, $XZ \approx 13.5$ cm, $XY \approx 26.5$ cm

3 $x \approx 17.7$, $y \approx 33.1$ **4** $x = 8 + \frac{11}{2}\sqrt{2}$

EXERCISE 11G.2

1 $C \approx 62.1°$ or $C \approx 117.9°$

2 a $\widehat{BAC} \approx 49.5°$ **b** $\widehat{ABC} \approx 72.0°$ or $108°$
   c $\widehat{ACB} \approx 44.3°$

3 No, the angle opposite the 9.8 cm side has a sine of 1.05, which
   is impossible.

4 a   i $\widehat{ACB} \approx 22.9°$ **ii** $\widehat{BAC} \approx 127°$ **b** ≈ 25.1 cm^2

5 a $\approx 69.4°$ or $\approx 110.6°$
   b
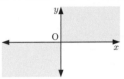
   c   i $\approx 60.6°$, $\approx 19.4°$
       ii ≈ 43.1 m^2, ≈ 16.5 m^2
       iii ≈ 30.2 m, ≈ 23.9 m

EXERCISE 11H

1 ≈ 17.7 m   **2** ≈ 207 m   **3** $\approx 23.9°$ **4** $\approx 9.38°$

5 ≈ 69.1 m   **6 a** ≈ 38.0 m   **b** ≈ 94.0 m

7 a $\approx 55.1°$ **b** $\approx 50.3°$ **8** $\approx 65.6°$

9 a ≈ 74.9 km^2 **b** ≈ 7490 hectares

10 ≈ 9.12 km   **11** ≈ 85.0 mm   **12** ≈ 10.1 km

13 ≈ 37.6 km   **14** ≈ 7400 m^2

REVIEW SET 11A

1 a $60°$ **b** $15°$ **c** $84°$ **2** $\theta = 45°$ or $315°$

3

	a	**b**	**c**	**d**
$\sin\theta$	0	$\frac{\sqrt{3}}{2}$	0	$\frac{1}{2}$
$\cos\theta$	1	$-\frac{1}{2}$	-1	$\frac{\sqrt{3}}{2}$
$\tan\theta$	0	$-\sqrt{3}$	0	$\frac{1}{\sqrt{3}}$

4 $\sin\theta = \pm\frac{\sqrt{7}}{4}$ **5** $\cos x = \frac{2}{\sqrt{13}}$, $\sin x = -\frac{3}{\sqrt{13}}$

6 a $\theta \approx 99.6°$ or $260.4°$ **b** $\theta \approx 19.5°$ or $160.5°$
   c $\theta \approx 107.4°$ or $287.4°$

7 a ≈ 26.8 cm^2 **b** 14 km^2 **c** ≈ 33.0 m^2

8 ≈ 22.7 cm^2 **9 a** ≈ 10.5 cm   **b** ≈ 11.6 m

10 a $x \approx 9.24$ **b** $\theta \approx 59.2°$ **c** $x \approx 6.28$

11 ≈ 113 cm^2 **12** ≈ 51.6 cm^2 **13** ≈ 204 m

14 $\widehat{EDG} \approx 74.4°$ **15** $x \approx 18.5$, $y \approx 13.8$

16 a $\approx 69.5°$, $\approx 110.5°$ **b** ≈ 16.3 cm^2, ≈ 8.08 cm^2

REVIEW SET 11B

1 a ≈ 0.358 **b** ≈ -0.035 **c** ≈ 0.259 **d** ≈ -0.731

2

3 a $\sin(180° - p) = m$ **b** $\sin(p + 360°) = m$
   c $\cos p = \sqrt{1 - m^2}$ **d** $\tan p = \dfrac{m}{\sqrt{1 - m^2}}$

4 $\frac{\sqrt{6}}{\sqrt{11}}$ **5** $\cos\theta = \frac{\sqrt{21}}{5}$, $\tan\theta = -\frac{2}{\sqrt{21}}$

6 a $120°$ **b** $210°$

7 a $\theta \approx 48.2°$ or $311.8°$ **b** $\theta \approx 194.5°$ or $345.5°$
   c $\theta \approx 71.6°$ or $251.6°$

8 a $x \approx 34.1$ **b** $x \approx 18.9$ **9** $\approx 47.5°$ or $132.5°$

10 a $\theta \approx 29.9°$ **b** $\theta \approx 103°$

11 a $AC \approx 12.6$ cm, $\widehat{BAC} \approx 48.6°$, $\widehat{ACB} \approx 57.4°$
   b $\widehat{PRQ} = 51°$, $PQ \approx 7.83$ cm, $QR \approx 7.25$ cm
   c $\widehat{YXZ} \approx 78.3°$, $\widehat{XYZ} \approx 55.5°$, $\widehat{XZY} \approx 46.2°$

12 a $x \approx 6.93$ **b** $x \approx 11.4$ **c** $x \approx 7.16$

13 $\widehat{BAD} \approx 90.5°$, $\widehat{BCD} \approx 94.3°$, $\widehat{ADC} \approx 70.2°$

14 $Q \approx 39.7°$ **15 a** $\approx 10\,600$ m^2 **b** ≈ 1.06 ha

16 a The information
   given could give
   two triangles:

   b ≈ 2.23 m^3
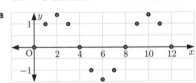

EXERCISE 12A

1 a periodic   **b** periodic   **c** periodic   **d** not periodic
   e periodic   **f** periodic   **g** not periodic   **h** not periodic

2 a
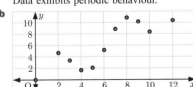

   b A curve can be fitted to the data.
   c The data is periodic.
       i $y = 32$ (approximately)   **ii** ≈ 64 cm
       iii ≈ 2 seconds   **iv** ≈ 32 cm

3 a

   Data exhibits periodic behaviour.
   b

   Not enough information to say data is periodic.

EXERCISE 12B.1

1 **a** 0

b **i** $\theta = 0°, 180°, 360°, 540°, 720°$
ii $\theta = 270°, 630°$
iii $\theta = 30°, 150°, 390°, 510°$
iv $\theta = 60°, 120°, 420°, 480°$

c $\theta \approx 17°, 163°, 377°, 523°$

d **i** $0° < \theta < 180°,\quad 360° < \theta < 540°$
ii $180° < \theta < 360°,\quad 540° < \theta < 720°$

e $\{y : -1 \leqslant y \leqslant 1\}$

2 **a** 1

b **i** $\theta = 90°, 270°, 450°, 630°$
ii $\theta = 0°, 360°, 720°$
iii $\theta = 120°, 240°, 480°, 600°$
iv $\theta = 135°, 225°, 495°, 585°$

c $\theta \approx 73°, 287°, 433°, 647°$

d **i** $0° \leqslant \theta < 90°,\quad 270° < \theta < 450°,\quad 630° < \theta \leqslant 720°$
ii $90° < \theta < 270°,\quad 450° < \theta < 630°$

e $\{y : -1 \leqslant y \leqslant 1\}$

EXERCISE 12B.2

1 **a** 4   **b** 2   **c** $\frac{1}{3}$

2 **a** $120°$ **b** $90°$ **c** $720°$

3 **a** $y = -3$ **b** $y = 5$ **c** $y = 0$

4 **a**
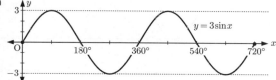

b
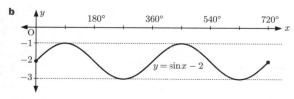

c
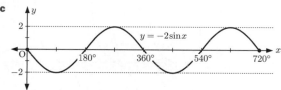

d
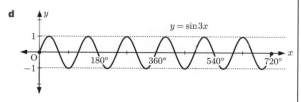

e
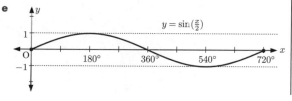

f
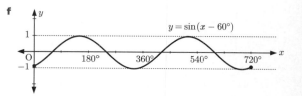

5 **a**
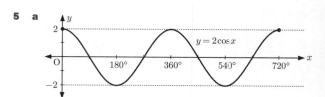

b
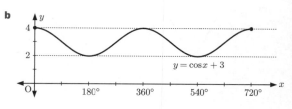

c
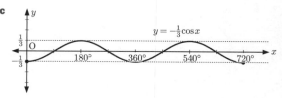

d
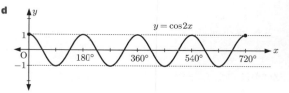

e
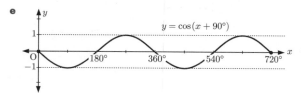

f
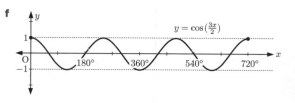

6 **a**
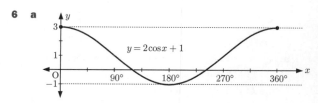

b

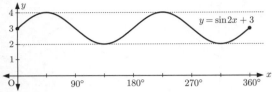

$$y = \sin 2x + 3$$

c

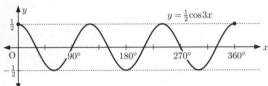

$$y = \tfrac{1}{2}\cos 3x$$

d

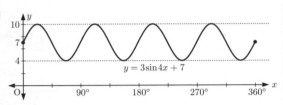

$$y = 3\sin 4x + 7$$

7 a

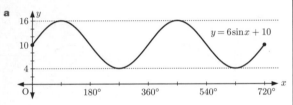

$$y = 6\sin x + 10$$

b $y = 13$

c maximum value $= 16$, when $x = 90°$ and $450°$

d minimum value $= 4$, when $x = 270°$ and $630°$

EXERCISE 12C

1 a

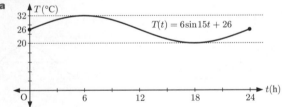

$$T(t) = 6\sin 15t + 26$$

b **i** $26°C$ **ii** $29°C$

c $32°C$, at 6 pm

2 a

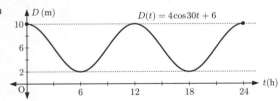

$$D(t) = 4\cos 30t + 6$$

b highest $= 10$ m, at midnight, midday, and midnight the next day

lowest $= 2$ m, at 6 am and 6 pm

c no (water height is 4 m)

3 a

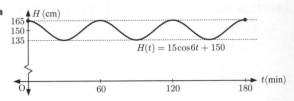

$$H(t) = 15\cos 6t + 150$$

b 15 cm

c **i** 160.0 cm **ii** 138.9 cm **iii** 158.8 cm
iv 138.9 cm

4 a

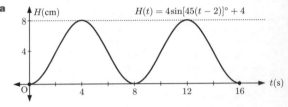

$$H(t) = 4\sin[45(t-2)]° + 4$$

b 4 cm

c no (ball diameter is 4.28 cm, gate height is ≈ 3.066 cm)

5 a The height of the spot increases and decreases in a periodic manner. It would look like a cosine curve.

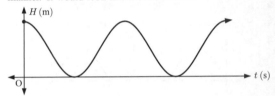

b The graph has an amplitude of 1, and the principal axis is $H = 1$.

c The graph has a period of 2 seconds.

d Yes, $H(t) = \cos(180t)° + 1$ m, where t is in seconds, $t \geqslant 0$.

EXERCISE 12D

1 a **i** $y = \tan(x - 90°)$

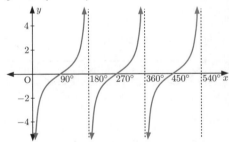

ii $y = \tan(x + 60°)$

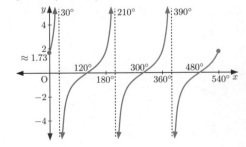

iii $y = \tan 3x$

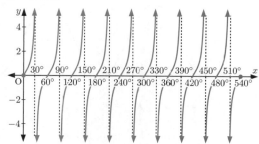

2 a horizontal translation to the right by a distance equivalent to $40°$ on the x-axis

b horizontal dilation with scale factor 4

3 a $180°$ **b** $60°$ **c** $\dfrac{180°}{n}$

4

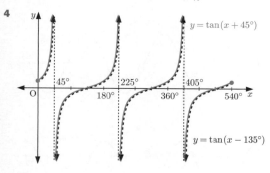

They have the same graph.

EXERCISE 12E

1 a $\theta = 90°$ or $270°$ **b** $\theta = 45°$ or $225°$
c $\theta = 240°$ or $300°$ **d** $\theta = 45°$ or $135°$
e $\theta = 180°$ **f** $\theta = 150°$ or $330°$

2 a $\theta = 45°, 315°, 405°,$ or $675°$
b $x = 90°$ or $450°$
c $x = 120°, 300°, 480°,$ or $660°$
d $\theta = 30°, 150°, -330°,$ or $-210°$
e $\theta = 150°, 210°, -210°,$ or $-150°$
f $x = 135°, 315°, 495°, 675°, 855°,$ or $1035°$

3 a $x = 15°$ or $165°$
b $x = 70°$ or $110°$
c $x = 60°$ or $150°$
d $x \approx 9.74°$ or $\approx 80.26°$
e $x \approx 27.62°, \approx 87.62°,$ or $\approx 147.62°$
f $x \approx 16.06°$ or $\approx 103.94°$

4 a $\theta = 45°, 135°, 225°,$ or $315°$
b $\theta = 60°, 120°, 240°,$ or $300°$
c $\theta = 90°, 180°,$ or $270°$
d $\theta = 0°, 60°, 120°, 180°,$ or $360°$
e $\theta = 0°, 120°, 240°,$ or $360°$
f $\theta = 45°, 135°, 225°,$ or $315°$

5 a i 300 ants   **ii** 325 ants
b 350 ants, on April 1
c July 30 and November 27

d

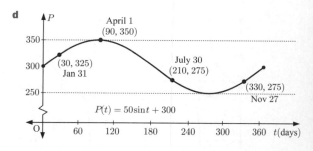

REVIEW SET 12A

1 a no   **b** yes

2 a $x \approx 115°, 245°, 475°, 605°$
b $x \approx 25°, 335°, 385°$

3 a 5   **b** $\frac{1}{4}$

4 a

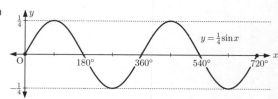

b

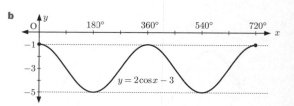

c

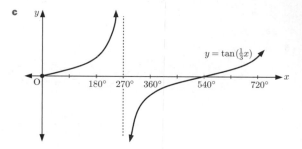

d

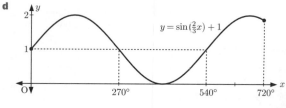

e

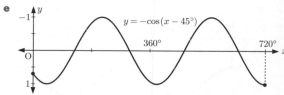

f

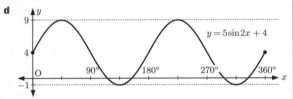

5 a

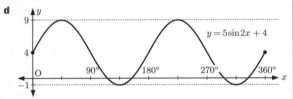

$$M(t) = \tfrac{1}{2}\cos 12t + \tfrac{1}{2}$$

b **i** 0.75   **ii** 0.25   **iii** ≈ 0.835 **iv** ≈ 0.165

c Once every 30 days.   **d** January 16, February 15

6 a $\theta = 120°, 240°, 480°,$ or $600°$

b $\theta = 30°, 210°, 390°,$ or $570°$

c $\theta = 60°, 120°, 420°,$ or $480°$

7 a $x = 60°$ or $120°$ **b** $x = 75°$ or $105°$

c $x \approx 76.72°$ or $\approx 166.72°$

8 a 5   **b** $y = 4$ **c** $180°$

d

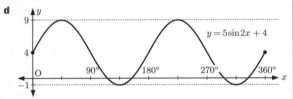

$$y = 5\sin 2x + 4$$

e $y = 9$

9 a

$$y = -2\sin x + 7$$

b $y = 6$

c maximum $= 9$, when $x = 270°$ and $630°$

d minimum $= 5$, when $x = 90°$ and $450°$

REVIEW SET 12B

1 a The function repeats itself over and over in a horizontal direction, in intervals of length 8 units.

b **i** 8   **ii** 5   **iii** -1

2 a $120°$ **b** $720°$ **3 a** $y = 5$ **b** $y = -4$

4 a

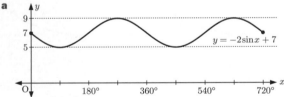

$$y = \cos x - 3$$

b

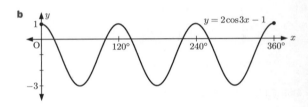

$$y = \sin(x - 90°)$$

c

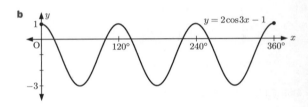

$$y = \tan(x - 135°)$$

5 a

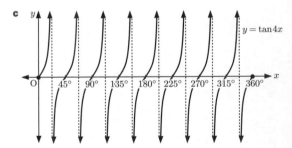

$$y = \tfrac{3}{2}\sin 3x$$

b

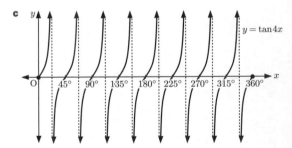

$$y = 2\cos 3x - 1$$

c

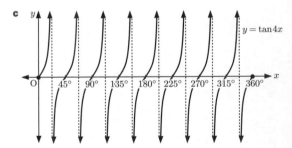

$$y = \tan 4x$$

6 a $\theta = 270°$ or $630°$ **b** $\theta = 30°, 330°, 390°,$ or $690°$

7 a $x = 30°, 150°, 210°,$ or $330°$

b $x = 60°, 90°, 270°,$ or $300°$

8 a $\theta = 135°$ **b** $\theta = 90°, 135°, 225°,$ or $270°$

c $\theta = -270°, -225°, -135°, -90°, 90°, 135°, 225°,$ $270°, 450°, 495°, 585°,$ or $630°$

9 a

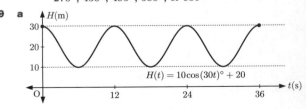

$$H(t) = 10\cos(30t)° + 20$$

b 20 m   **c** 10 m   **d** 12 seconds

EXERCISE 13A

1 a The cat is not black   **b** x is not prime.
  c The tree is not deciduous.

2 a False, x may be -3.   **b** True, $3^2 = 9$.
  c False, $x^2 = 9$ does not imply that $x = 3$.

3 a True, as the square root of any positive number is real.
  b False: for example, $\sqrt{0} = 0 \in \mathbb{R}$ but 0 is not positive.
  c False, $\sqrt{x} \in \mathbb{R} \not\Rightarrow x$ is positive.

4 a "If Socrates is an animal, then Socrates is a cat."
  b False

5 a Equivalent   **b** Not equivalent

6 Two cards - D and 3.

EXERCISE 13B

1 Hint:

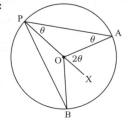

2 Hint: Use Pythagoras' Theorem.

EXERCISE 13C

1 a Hint: $(a + b)^2 - (a - b)^2$
      $= [a + b + (a - b)][a + b - (a - b)]$

2 Hint: Let the 3 consecutive integers be $x - 1$, x, and $x + 1$.

3 Hint: Let $p = 2a + 1$, $q = 2b + 1$, $a, b \in \mathbb{Z}$.

4 Hint: $(x - y)^5 + (x - y)^3 = (x - y)^3[(x - y)^2 + 1]$

5 a $n^4 + 4$ **b** $n = \pm 1$

6 Hint: The 3-digit number "abc" has value $100a + 10b + c$.

7 Hint: $(a + b)^2 \geqslant 0$

8 a $(a - b)(a + b) = b(a - b) \not\Rightarrow a + b = b$
  b $\dfrac{4x - 40}{6 - x} = \dfrac{4x - 40}{13 - x} \not\Rightarrow 6 - x = 13 - x$

9 a $6x - 12 = 3(x - 2) \not\Rightarrow 6x - 12 + 3(x - 2) = 0$,
      $6x - 12 + 3(x - 2) = 0 \not\Rightarrow 12x - 24 = 0$
  b $x(x - 6) = 3(-3) \not\Rightarrow x = 3 \ \vee \ x - 6 = -3$
  c $(x + 3)(2 - x) = 4 \not\Rightarrow x + 3 = 4 \ \vee \ 2 - x = 4$

10 Hint: Let $f(x, y, z) = x^3 + y^3 + z^3 - 3xyz$.
     Show $f(x, y, -x - y) = 0$.

EXERCISE 13D

3 Hint: Let the 2 odd integers be $2a + 1$ and $2b + 1$, $a, b \in \mathbb{Z}$.

EXERCISE 13E

3 Hint: $n^3 + 2n = (n^3 - n) + 3n$, then use the result of **2**.

5 Hint: Let $n = 7k$, $7k + 1$, ..., $7k + 6$, and show that n^2
     never leaves remainder 3 when divided by 7.

7 Box **C**

EXERCISE 13F

1 a Let $a = 1$, $b = 1$, $2^2 \neq 1 + 1$
  b Let $p = 7$, $2p + 1 = 15$ which is not prime.

c Let $k = 31$, $6k - 1 = 185 = 5 \times 37$
         $6k + 1 = 187 = 11 \times 17$

2 a Let $p_1 = 2$, $p_2 = 7$, then $p = 2 \times 7 + 1 = 15$, which is
      not prime.
  b If $n = 6$, then
      $p = 2 \times 3 \times 5 \times 7 \times 11 \times 13 + 1 = 30\,031 = 59 \times 509$

3 For $n = 6$ there are 31 regions. $31 \neq 2^5$

4 $333\,333\,331$ is not prime.

5 a

n	$2^n - 1$		n	$2^n - 1$
1	1		6	63
2	3		7	127
3	7		8	255
4	15		9	511
5	31		10	1023

  $n = 2, 3, 5, 7$

  b $n = 11$, $2^{11} - 1 = 2047 = 23 \times 89$

REVIEW SET 13A

2 Hint: $n^3 - n = n(n + 1)(n - 1)$

3 b Hint: Expand $(10m + k)^5$.

4 If $p = 5$, $5! + 1 = 121$ which is not prime.

REVIEW SET 13B

2 Hint: $(\sqrt{a} - \sqrt{b})^2 \geqslant 0$

4 10 and 15 both divide 30, but 150 does not divide 30.

EXERCISE 14A.1

1 a Yes. The distance increases by the same amount each time
      interval.
  b

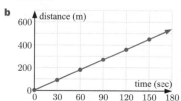

  c 3 m per s

2 a Yes. The height increases by the same amount each time
      interval.
  b 5 cm per week

3 a 3   **b** -2 **c** $-\frac{1}{4}$ **4** $\frac{5}{2}$

EXERCISE 14A.2

1 a No. The graph is not a straight line.
  b **i** 60 km per hour   **ii** 100 km per hour

2 a 100 m per hour   **b** 100 m per hour (downwards)

3 a $\frac{1}{2}$ **b** $\frac{2}{5}$ **c** $-\frac{5}{4}$ **d** -2

4 a **i** 3   **ii** 2.5   **iii** 2.1   **iv** 2.01   **v** 2.001
  b The average rate of change approaches 2.

EXERCISE 14B

1 a 0.5 m s^{-1} **b** 2 m s^{-1} **2 a** 1   **b** 4
3 a, b
  c -2

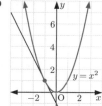

EXERCISE 14C.1

1 a 7   **b** 7   **c** 11   **d** 16   **e** 0   **f** 5

2 a 5   **b** 7   **c** c

3 a -2 **b** 7   **c** -1 **d** 1

4 a -3 **b** 5   **c** -1 **d** 6   **e** -4 **f** -8
　　g 1   **h** 2   **i** 5

EXERCISE 14C.2

1 a $(3+h)^2$ **b** $\dfrac{(3+h)^2 - 9}{(3+h) - 3} = 6 + h$ for $h \neq 0$

　c i 7   **ii** 6.5   **iii** 6.1   **iv** 6.01   **d** 6

2 a 5   **b** 3   **c** -1 **d** 4

3 a 8   **b**

x-coordinate	Gradient of tangent
1	2
2	4
3	6
4	8

　c $2a$

EXERCISE 14D.1

1 a $f(0) = 4$ **b** $f'(0) = -1$ **2** $f'(2) = 1$

3 a positive   **b** negative   **c** negative   **d** positive

4 a $f'(-2) = -3$
　　At $x = -2$, the derivative function is -3, *or* the gradient of the tangent to $y = f(x)$ at the point where $x = -2$ is -3.
　　$f'(0) = 1$
　　At $x = 0$, the derivative function is 1, *or* the gradient of the tangent to $y = f(x)$ at the point where $x = 0$ is 1.

　b

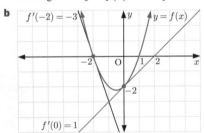

5 c

EXERCISE 14D.2

1 a $f'(x) = 1$ **b** $f'(x) = 0$ **c** $f'(x) = 3x^2$

2 a $f'(x) = 2$ **b** $f'(x) = 2x - 3$ **c** $f'(x) = -2x + 5$

3 a $\dfrac{dy}{dx} = -1$ **b** $\dfrac{dy}{dx} = 4x + 1$ **c** $\dfrac{dy}{dx} = 3x^2 - 4x$

4 a 12   **b** 108

5 a $f'(x) = -\dfrac{1}{x^2}$

　b $f'(-1) = -1$; the tangent at the point where $x = -1$ has gradient -1.
　　$f'(3) = -\frac{1}{9}$; the tangent at the point where $x = 3$ has gradient $-\frac{1}{9}$.

6 a i ≈ 3 **ii** ≈ -1 **b** $f'(x) = -2x + 3$
　c $f'(0) = 3$, $f'(2) = -1$

7 a $\dfrac{dy}{dx} = 3x^2 - 3$ **b** $(-1, 2)$ and $(1, -2)$

8 a $f'(x) = 4x + 2$
　b $(-1, -12)$

　c

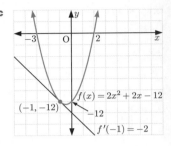

9 a $f'(x) = -\frac{1}{2}x + 1$
　b $f'(-2) = 2$, $f'(3) = -\frac{1}{2}$
　　Gradients of tangents are 2 and $-\frac{1}{2}$, and $2 \times -\frac{1}{2} = -1$
　　$\therefore$ tangents are perpendicular.

10 a

$f(x)$	$f'(x)$
x^1	1
x^2	$2x$
x^3	$3x^2$
x^4	$4x^3$
x^{-1}	$-x^{-2}$
x^0	0

　b If $f(x) = x^n$,
　　then $f'(x) = nx^{n-1}$.

REVIEW SET 14A

1 $\frac{4}{3}$

2 a Yes. The height increases by the same amount each time interval.
　b 1.6 m s^{-1}

3 a -1 **b** -1 **c** 8

4 b i 12.2   **ii** 12.02   **iii** 12
　c The gradient of the tangent to $y = 2x^2$ at $(3, 18)$ is 12.

5 $f'(3) = -\frac{1}{2}$ **6 a** $f'(x) = 2x + 2$ **b** $\dfrac{dy}{dx} = -6x$

7 a $\dfrac{dy}{dx} = 4x$ **b** gradient $= 16$ **c** when $x = -3$

8 a $f'(x) = 3x^2 - 6x$
　b $f'(-1) = 9$, $f'(3) = 9$
　　Gradients of tangents are both 9.
　　$\therefore$ the tangents are parallel.

REVIEW SET 14B

1 $\frac{1}{2}$ **2 a** $2°$C per hour   **b** $-2\frac{1}{2}°$C per hour

3 a -3 **b** 3   **c** -1

4 a negative   **b** positive   **c** positive   **d** negative

5 a, b

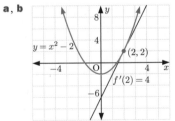

　　c 4

6 a $f'(x) = 4x^3 - 2$
　b $f'(-2) = -34$
　　The gradient of $f'(x)$ at the point where $x = -2$ is -34.

7 a $\dfrac{dy}{dx} = 2x + 5$ **b** $(-4, -6)$

8 a i 447.2 m   **ii** 432.8 m   **b** $f'(t) = -9.6t$ ms^{-1}

　c i -9.6 ms^{-1} **ii** -19.2 ms^{-1}

EXERCISE 15A

1 a $3x^2$ **b** $8x^7$ **c** $11x^{10}$ **d** 6 **e** $6x^2$

　f $14x$ **g** $15x^4$ **h** $30x^5$ **i** $2x + 1$ **j** $2x + 3$

　k 5 **l** $2x$ **m** $4x + 1$ **n** $6x - 7$ **o** $-4x$

　p $2x^3 - 12x$ **q** $3x^2 - 8x + 6$ **r** $-1 - 12x^2$

　s $\frac{3}{5}x^2 - 7x$ **t** $8x - 4$

2 a $-\frac{2}{x^3}$ **b** $-\frac{5}{x^6}$ **c** $-\frac{8}{x^9}$ **d** $-\frac{3}{x^2}$

　e $-\frac{12}{x^4}$ **f** $\frac{28}{x^5}$ **g** $2 - \frac{6}{x^3}$ **h** $2x + \frac{6}{x^2}$

　i $\frac{6}{x^4}$ **j** $-\frac{1}{x^2} + \frac{15}{x^4}$ **k** $-\frac{4}{x^3} - \frac{36}{x^5}$ **l** $3 + \frac{1}{x^2} - \frac{4}{x^3}$

　m $\frac{16}{x^3} - \frac{12}{x^4}$ **n** $-\frac{2}{5x^3}$ **o** $4 + \frac{1}{4x^2}$

　p $1 + \frac{3}{x^2}$ **q** $2x - \frac{4}{x^2}$ **r** $-\frac{2}{x^2} + \frac{10}{x^3}$

3 a $\frac{1}{2\sqrt{x}}$ **b** $\frac{1}{3\sqrt[3]{x^2}}$ **c** $-\frac{1}{2x\sqrt{x}}$

　d $-\frac{2}{x^3} + \frac{3}{\sqrt{x}}$ **e** $2 - \frac{1}{2\sqrt{x}}$ **f** $\frac{3}{2}\sqrt{x}$

　g $4x + \frac{3}{2x\sqrt{x}}$ **h** $\frac{1}{2\sqrt{x}} - \frac{5}{2x\sqrt{x}}$ **i** $-\frac{7}{2x\sqrt{x}} - \frac{3\sqrt{x}}{2}$

　j $6x - \frac{3\sqrt{x}}{2}$ **k** $\frac{-10}{x^3\sqrt{x}}$ **l** $2 + \frac{9}{2x^2\sqrt{x}}$

4 a $\frac{dy}{dx} = 100$ **b** $\frac{dy}{dx} = 2\pi x$ **c** $\frac{dy}{dx} = \frac{3}{\sqrt{x}} - \frac{5}{x^2}$

　d $\frac{dy}{dx} = 7.5x^2 - 2.8x$ **e** $\frac{dy}{dx} = 10$ **f** $\frac{dy}{dx} = 12\pi x^2$

　g $\frac{dy}{dx} = 2x - 1$ **h** $\frac{dy}{dx} = 2x - 10$ **i** $\frac{dy}{dx} = 6x^2 - 6x - 5$

5 a 4 **b** 22 **c** $-\frac{16}{729}$ **d** -7 **e** $\frac{3}{2}$

　f $\frac{13}{4}$ **g** $\frac{1}{8}$ **h** -11

6 $b = 3,\ c = -4$

7 $\frac{dy}{dx} = 4 + \frac{3}{x^2}$, $\frac{dy}{dx}$ is the gradient function of $y = 4x - \frac{3}{x}$ from which the gradient of the tangent at any point can be found.

8 a $\{x : x > 0\}$ **b** $f'(x) = \frac{1}{2\sqrt{x}} + \frac{2}{x\sqrt{x}}$

　c $\{x : x > 0\}$

　d $f'(1) = 2.5$ The gradient of the tangent to the curve

$$f(x) = \sqrt{x} - \frac{4}{\sqrt{x}}\ \text{ at } x = 1 \text{ is } 2.5.$$

9 a $\frac{dS}{dt} = 4t + 4$ ms^{-1}, $\frac{dS}{dt}$ is the instantaneous rate of change in the car's position at the time t.

　b When $t = 3$, $\frac{dS}{dt} = 16$ ms^{-1}. This is the instantaneous rate of change in position at the time $t = 3$ seconds.

10 When $x = 1000$, $\frac{dC}{dx} = 7$. When 1000 toasters per week are being produced, the cost of production is increasing by £7 per toaster.

EXERCISE 15B

1 a $f''(x) = 6$ **b** $f''(x) = \frac{3}{2x^2\sqrt{x}}$

　c $f''(x) = 12x - 6$ **d** $f''(x) = \frac{12 - 6x}{x^4}$

　e $f''(x) = 8$

2 a $\frac{d^2y}{dx^2} = -6x$ **b** $\frac{d^2y}{dx^2} = 2 - \frac{30}{x^4}$

　c $\frac{d^2y}{dx^2} = -\frac{9}{4x^2\sqrt{x}}$ **d** $\frac{d^2y}{dx^2} = \frac{8}{x^3}$

　e $\frac{d^2y}{dx^2} = 12x^2 - 36x + 18$

3 a $f(2) = 9$ **b** $f'(2) = 10$ **c** $f''(2) = 12$

4 a $x = 1$ **b** $x = 2$ or $x = 3$

5

x	-1	0	1
$f(x)$	$-$	0	$+$
$f'(x)$	$+$	$-$	$+$
$f''(x)$	$-$	0	$+$

6 a $f(1) = 0$ **b** $f'(1) = 3$ **c** $f''(1) = 0$

EXERCISE 15C

1 a $y = -7x + 11$ **b** $y = \frac{1}{4}x + 2$ **c** $y = -2x - 2$

　d $y = -2x + 6$ **e** $y = -5x - 9$ **f** $y = -5x - 1$

2 a $x + 8y = 132$ **b** $x + 7y = 26$ **c** $x - 3y = -11$

　d $x + 6y = 43$

3 a $y = 21$ and $y = -6$ **b** $y = 23$ and $y = -9$

4 $y = 2$

5 a $k = -5$ **b** $y = 4x - 15$ **c** $x + 4y = -26$

6 $y = -3x + 1$ **7** $a = -4,\ b = 7$ **8** $a = 2,\ b = 4$

10 a $f'(x) = 2x - \frac{8}{x^3}$ **b** $x = \pm\sqrt{2}$

　c When $x = \sqrt{2}$, $y = 4$ and when $x = -\sqrt{2}$, $y = 4$.
　∴ tangents are $y = 4$.

11 $(-4, -64)$ **12** $(4, -31)$

13 a $y = (2a - 1)x - a^2 + 9$

　b $y = 5x$, contact $(3, 15)$, and
　$y = -7x$, contact $(-3, 21)$

14 $y = 0$ and $y = 27x + 54$

15 a $y + 4x = -2$ and $y - 12x = -18$

　b $(-1, 2)$ for $y + 4x = -2$ and
　$(3, 18)$ for $y - 12x = -18$

　c For a tangent to pass through $(1, 4)$, $4 = 4a - 2a^2$ must have real solutions. But $\Delta < 0$, so no real solutions.

　d

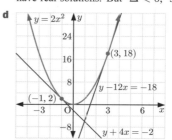

16 $y = -\sqrt{14}x + 4\sqrt{14}$

17 **a**

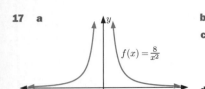

b $16x + a^3 y = 24a$

c A is $(\frac{3}{2}a, 0)$,

B is $(0, \dfrac{24}{a^2})$

d area $= \dfrac{18}{|a|}$ units^2,

as $a \to \infty$, area $\to 0$

EXERCISE 15D

1 **a** **i** $x \geqslant 0$ **ii** never   **b** **i** never **ii** $-2 < x \leqslant 3$

   c **i** $x \leqslant 2$ **ii** $x \geqslant 2$ **d** **i** $x \in \mathbb{R}$ **ii** never

   e **i** $1 \leqslant x \leqslant 5$ **ii** $x \leqslant 1, \ x \geqslant 5$

   f **i** $2 \leqslant x < 4, \ x > 4$ **ii** $x < 0, \ 0 < x \leqslant 2$

2 **a** **i** $x \leqslant 1, \ x \geqslant 3$ **ii** $1 \leqslant x \leqslant 3$

   b $f'(x) = 3x^2 - 12x + 9$

$= 3(x - 3)(x - 1)$

3 **a** increasing for $x \geqslant 0$, decreasing for $x \leqslant 0$

   b decreasing for all x

   c increasing for $x \geqslant -\frac{3}{4}$, decreasing for $x \leqslant -\frac{3}{4}$

   d decreasing for all $x \neq 0$ **e** decreasing for all $x > 0$

   f increasing for $x \leqslant 0$ and $x \geqslant 4$,

decreasing for $0 \leqslant x \leqslant 4$

   g increasing for $-\sqrt{\frac{2}{3}} \leqslant x \leqslant \sqrt{\frac{2}{3}}$,

decreasing for $x \leqslant -\sqrt{\frac{2}{3}}, \ x \geqslant \sqrt{\frac{2}{3}}$

   h increasing for $-\frac{1}{2} \leqslant x \leqslant 3$,

decreasing for $x \leqslant -\frac{1}{2}, \ x \geqslant 3$

   i increasing for $x \geqslant 0$, decreasing for $x \leqslant 0$

   j increasing for $x \geqslant -\frac{3}{2} + \frac{\sqrt{5}}{2}$ and $x \leqslant -\frac{3}{2} - \frac{\sqrt{5}}{2}$,

decreasing for $-\frac{3}{2} - \frac{\sqrt{5}}{2} \leqslant x \leqslant -\frac{3}{2} + \frac{\sqrt{5}}{2}$

   k increasing for $x \leqslant 2 - \sqrt{3}, \ x \geqslant 2 + \sqrt{3}$,

decreasing for $2 - \sqrt{3} \leqslant x \leqslant 2 + \sqrt{3}$

   l increasing for $x \leqslant -\sqrt{2}$ and $x \geqslant \sqrt{2}$,

decreasing for $-\sqrt{2} \leqslant x < 0$ and $0 < x \leqslant \sqrt{2}$

4 **a** $f'(x) = 1 - \dfrac{9}{x^2} = \dfrac{x^2 - 9}{x^2} = \dfrac{(x+3)(x-3)}{x^2}$

   b increasing for $x \leqslant -3$ and $x \geqslant 3$,

decreasing for $-3 \leqslant x < 0$ and $0 < x \leqslant 3$

5 **a** $f'(x) = 3x^2 - 6x + 5$

   b $\Delta = 36 - 60 < 0$ and $a > 0$

$\therefore \ f'(x)$ lies entirely above x-axis.

$\therefore \ f'(x) > 0$ for all x.

$\therefore \ f(x)$ is increasing for all x.

   c

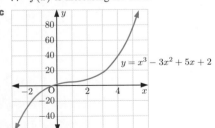

EXERCISE 15E

1 **a** A - local max,   O - stationary inflection,   B - local min.

   b

   c **i** $x \leqslant -2$ and $x \geqslant 3$ **ii** $-2 \leqslant x \leqslant 3$

   d

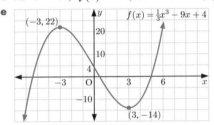

2 **a** P is a local maximum, Q is a local minimum.

   b $f'(x) = 3x^2 + 12x - 15 = 3(x + 5)(x - 1)$

   c $P(-5, 60), \quad Q(1, -48)$

3 **a** $f'(x) = x^2 - 9$

   b increasing for $x \leqslant -3$ and $x \geqslant 3$,

decreasing for $-3 \leqslant x \leqslant 3$

   c $(-3, 22)$ is a local maximum, $(3, -14)$ is a local minimum

   d As $x \to \infty, \ f(x) \to \infty$, as $x \to -\infty, \ f(x) \to -\infty$.

   e

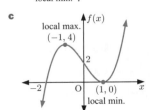

4 **a** $g'(x) = -6x^2 + 12x + 18 = -6(x - 3)(x + 1)$

   b increasing for $-1 \leqslant x \leqslant 3$,

decreasing for $x \leqslant -1$ and $x \geqslant 3$

   c $(3, 47)$ is a local maximum, $(-1, -17)$ is a local minimum

   d As $x \to \infty, \ g(x) \to -\infty$, as $x \to -\infty, \ g(x) \to \infty$.

   e

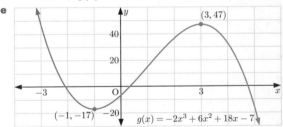

5 **a** **b**

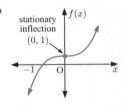

   c **d**

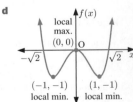

e
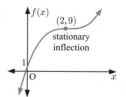
stationary inflection
(2, 9)
1

f
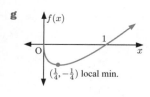
(no stationary points)
2

g
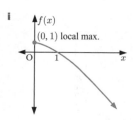
$(\frac{1}{4}, -\frac{1}{4})$ local min.
1

h
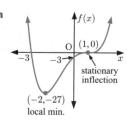
(1, 0)
stationary inflection
-3 -3
$(-2, -27)$ local min.

i
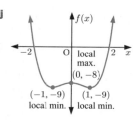
(0, 1) local max.
1

j
$f(x)$
-2 O   local max. (0, −8)   2
$(-1, -9)$ local min. $(1, -9)$ local min.

6 a $x = -\dfrac{b}{2a}$ **b** local min. if $a > 0$, local max. if $a < 0$

7 a $a = 9$ **b** $(-4, 113)$

8 a $a = -12, \ b = -13$
  b $(-2, 3)$ local maximum, $(2, -29)$ local minimum

9 $P(x) = -9x^3 - 9x^2 + 9x + 2$

10 a greatest value is 63 when $x = 5$,
    least value is -18 when $x = 2$
  b greatest value is 4 when $x = 3$ and $x = 0$,
    least value is -16 when $x = -2$
  c greatest value is 20 when $x = 4$,
    least value is 12 when $x = 2$
  d greatest value is 0 when $x = 0$,
    least value is -4 when $x = 4$

EXERCISE 15F

1 a

Point	$f(x)$	$f'(x)$	$f''(x)$
A	+	−	+
B	−	0	+
C	+	+	0
D	+	0	−
E	0	−	−

  b B is a local minimum, D is a local maximum
  c C is a non-stationary point of inflection.

2 a $f'(x) = 3x^2 + 6x - 5$ **b**
    $f''(x) = 6x + 6$

    -1
  c **i** $x \geqslant -1$ **ii** $x \leqslant -1$ **d** $(-1, 9)$

3 a concave upwards   **b** concave downwards
  c concave downwards   **d** concave upwards

4 a $x \geqslant 0$ **b** $x > 0$ **5 a** $x \geqslant \frac{2}{3}$ **b** $x > 0$

6 a i $x \geqslant 0$ **ii** $x \leqslant 0$ **iii** $x \in \mathbb{R}$ **iv** never
  b i never   **ii** $x \in \mathbb{R}$ **iii** $x \leqslant 0$ **iv** $x \geqslant 0$
  c i $x > 0$ **ii** never   **iii** never   **iv** $x > 0$

d i $-\sqrt{6} \leqslant x \leqslant 0$ and $x \geqslant \sqrt{6}$
  ii $x \leqslant -\sqrt{6}$ and $x \geqslant \sqrt{6}$
  iii $x \leqslant -\sqrt{2}$ and $x \geqslant \sqrt{2}$ **iv** $-\sqrt{2} \leqslant x \leqslant \sqrt{2}$

EXERCISE 15G

1 250 items per day

2 b $L_{\min} \approx 28.3$ m, when $x \approx 7.07$
  c

14.1 m
7.07 m

3 10 blankets

4 a $V = 200 = 2x \times x \times h$
  b **Hint:** Show $h = \dfrac{100}{x^2}$ and substitute into the surface area equation.
  c $A_{\min} \approx 213$ cm^2, when $x \approx 4.22$
  d
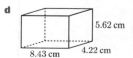
5.62 cm
8.43 cm   4.22 cm

5 a **Hint:** Recall that $V_{\text{cylinder}} = \pi r^2 h$ and that 1 L $= 1000$ cm^3.
  b **Hint:** Recall that $SA_{\text{cylinder}} = 2\pi r^2 + 2\pi rh$.
  c
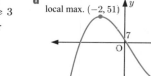
5.42 cm
10.84 cm

6 b 6 cm $\times$ 6 cm

7 a $0 \leqslant x \leqslant \dfrac{200}{\pi} \approx 63.7$
  b $l = 100$ m, $x = \dfrac{100}{\pi} \approx 31.8$ m, $A = \dfrac{20\,000}{\pi} \approx 6370$ m^2

REVIEW SET 15A

1 a $f'(x) = 15x^2$ **b** $f'(x) = 14x + \dfrac{3}{x^2}$
  c $f'(x) = 3 + \dfrac{8}{x^3}$ **d** $f'(x) = \dfrac{2}{\sqrt{x}} + \dfrac{1}{2x\sqrt{x}}$

2 a $\dfrac{d^2y}{dx^2} = 6 - 12x^2$ **b** $\dfrac{d^2y}{dx^2} = -\dfrac{2}{x^3}$
  c $\dfrac{d^2y}{dx^2} = \dfrac{2}{x^3} - 6$

3 10   **4** $(-2, 19)$ and $(1, -2)$ **5** $y = 4x + 2$
6 P(0, 7.5), Q(3, 0)   **7** 6 cm from each end
8 a $-6 \leqslant x \leqslant 2$ **b** $x \leqslant -6$ and $x \geqslant 2$
9 a local maximum at $(-2, 51)$, local minimum at $(3, -74)$
  b increasing for
    $x \leqslant -2, \ x \geqslant 3$
    decreasing for
    $-2 \leqslant x \leqslant 3$
  c as $x \to \infty$,
    $y \to \infty$,
    as $x \to -\infty$,
    $y \to -\infty$
  d

local max. $(-2, 51)$
$y = f(x)$
7
local min. $(3, -74)$

10 a $f'(x) = 6x^2 - 6x + 1$,   **b**
    $f''(x) = 12x - 6$
    $\dfrac{1}{2}$
  c $x \leqslant \frac{1}{2}$ **d** $(\frac{1}{2}, -12)$

11 b $C(\sqrt{3}, 6)$

12 b $A = 200x - 2x^2 - \frac{1}{2}\pi x^2$ **c**

28.0 m

56.0 m

REVIEW SET 15B

1 a $f'(x) = 6x - 7$ **b** $f'(x) = 2x + 10$

 c $f'(x) = \dfrac{1}{\sqrt{x}} + \dfrac{3}{x^2}$ **d** $f'(x) = 15x\sqrt{x}$

2 a $\dfrac{d^2y}{dx^2} = -12x + 2$ **b** $\dfrac{d^2y}{dx^2} = \dfrac{3}{2\sqrt{x}}$

 c $\dfrac{d^2y}{dx^2} = \dfrac{6}{x^3}$

3 $x = 1$ **4** $a = -14$, $b = 21$ **5** $y = 7$, $y = -25$

6 a $a = 2$ **b** $y = 3x - 1$ **c** $(-4, -13)$

7 a $-1 \leqslant x \leqslant 0$ and $x \geqslant 4$
 b $x \leqslant -1$ and $0 \leqslant x \leqslant 4$

8 a $a = -9$
 b local maximum at $(-1, 55)$, local minimum at $(3, 23)$

9 greatest value is ≈ 10.3 when $x = 10$,
 least value is 6 when $x = 4$

10 a x-intercepts 0 and 2, y-intercept 0
 b local maximum at $(\frac{2}{3}, \frac{32}{27})$, local minimum at $(2, 0)$
 c increasing for $x \leqslant \frac{2}{3}$ and $x \geqslant 2$,
  decreasing for $\frac{2}{3} \leqslant x \leqslant 2$
 d As $x \to \infty$, $y \to \infty$, as $x \to -\infty$, $y \to -\infty$.
 e

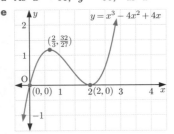

11 a $x \geqslant \frac{4}{9}$ **b** $x > 0$

12 a $x \leqslant -1.957$ and $0.2381 \leqslant x \leqslant 1.638$
 b $-1.957 \leqslant x \leqslant 0.2381$ and $x \geqslant 3.219$
 c $-1 \leqslant x \leqslant 2$ **d** $x \leqslant -1$ and $x \geqslant 2$

13 a $y = \dfrac{1}{x^2}$, $x > 0$
 c base is 1.26 m square, height 0.630 m

EXERCISE 16A.1

1 a i 0.4 units^2 **ii** 0.6 units^2 **b** 0.5 units^2

2 a ≈ 0.653 units^2 **b** ≈ 0.737 units^2

3

n	A_L	A_U
10	2.1850	2.4850
25	2.2736	2.3936
50	2.3034	2.3634
100	2.3184	2.3484
500	2.3303	2.3363

A_L and A_U converge to $\frac{7}{3}$.

4 a i

n	A_L	A_U
5	0.160 00	0.360 00
10	0.202 50	0.302 50
50	0.240 10	0.260 10
100	0.245 03	0.255 03
500	0.249 00	0.251 00
1000	0.249 50	0.250 50
10 000	0.249 95	0.250 05

ii

n	A_L	A_U
5	0.400 00	0.600 00
10	0.450 00	0.550 00
50	0.490 00	0.510 00
100	0.495 00	0.505 00
500	0.499 00	0.501 00
1000	0.499 50	0.500 50
10 000	0.499 95	0.500 05

iii

n	A_L	A_U
5	0.549 74	0.749 74
10	0.610 51	0.710 51
50	0.656 10	0.676 10
100	0.661 46	0.671 46
500	0.665 65	0.667 65
1000	0.666 16	0.667 16
10 000	0.666 62	0.666 72

iv

n	A_L	A_U
5	0.618 67	0.818 67
10	0.687 40	0.787 40
50	0.738 51	0.758 51
100	0.744 41	0.754 41
500	0.748 93	0.750 93
1000	0.749 47	0.750 47
10 000	0.749 95	0.750 05

 b i $\frac{1}{4}$ **ii** $\frac{1}{2}$ **iii** $\frac{2}{3}$ **iv** $\frac{3}{4}$ **c** area $= \dfrac{1}{a+1}$

5 a

n	Rational bounds for π
10	$2.9045 < \pi < 3.3045$
50	$3.0983 < \pi < 3.1783$
100	$3.1204 < \pi < 3.1604$
200	$3.1312 < \pi < 3.1512$
1000	$3.1396 < \pi < 3.1436$
10 000	$3.1414 < \pi < 3.1418$

 b $n = 10\,000$

EXERCISE 16A.2

1 a

$y = \sqrt{x}$

b

n	A_L	A_U
5	0.5497	0.7497
10	0.6105	0.7105
50	0.6561	0.6761
100	0.6615	0.6715
500	0.6656	0.6676

 c $\displaystyle\int_0^1 \sqrt{x}\, dx \approx 0.67$

2 a $A_L = \dfrac{2}{n} \displaystyle\sum_{i=0}^{n-1} \sqrt{1+x_i{}^3}, \quad A_U = \dfrac{2}{n} \sum_{i=1}^{n} \sqrt{1+x_i{}^3},$

where $x_i = \dfrac{2i}{n}$

b

n	A_L	A_U
50	3.2016	3.2816
100	3.2214	3.2614
500	3.2373	3.2453

c $\displaystyle\int_0^2 \sqrt{1+x^3}\,dx \approx 3.24$

3 a

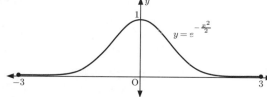

$y = e^{-\frac{x^2}{2}}$

b lower ≈ 1.2493, upper ≈ 1.2506
c lower ≈ 1.2493, upper ≈ 1.2506

d $\displaystyle\int_{-3}^3 e^{-\frac{x^2}{2}}\,dx \approx 2.4999$

4 a 18   **b** 4.5   **c** 2π **5 b i** 0   **ii** 22

EXERCISE 16B

1 a i $\dfrac{x^2}{2}$ **ii** $\dfrac{x^3}{3}$ **iii** $\dfrac{x^6}{6}$ **iv** $-\dfrac{1}{x}$

v $-\dfrac{1}{3x^3}$ **vi** $\dfrac{3}{4}x^{\frac{4}{3}}$ **vii** $2\sqrt{x}$ **viii** $\dfrac{3}{5}x^{\frac{5}{3}}$

b The antiderivative of x^n is $\dfrac{x^{n+1}}{n+1}$ $(n \neq -1)$.

2 a $\dfrac{d}{dx}(x^3 + x^2) = 3x^2 + 2x$

$\therefore$ the antiderivative of $6x^2 + 4x = 2x^3 + 2x^2$

b $\dfrac{d}{dx}(x\sqrt{x}) = \dfrac{3}{2}\sqrt{x}$

$\therefore$ the antiderivative of $\sqrt{x} = \dfrac{2}{3}x\sqrt{x}$

c $\dfrac{d}{dx}\left(\dfrac{1}{\sqrt{x}}\right) = -\dfrac{1}{2}x^{-\frac{3}{2}} = -\dfrac{1}{2x\sqrt{x}}$

$\therefore$ the antiderivative of $\dfrac{1}{x\sqrt{x}} = -\dfrac{2}{\sqrt{x}}$

EXERCISE 16C

1 a $\dfrac{d}{dx}(x^2) = 2x$

$\therefore$ the antiderivative of $2x$ is x^2.

b 8 units^2

2 a $\dfrac{2}{3}x^{\frac{3}{2}}$ **b** $\dfrac{2}{3}$ units^2

c $\dfrac{2}{3} \approx 0.67$ $\therefore$ answers are the same.

3 a i 4 units^2 **ii** $16\frac{1}{4}$ units^2 **iii** $20\frac{1}{4}$ units^2

b $\displaystyle\int_0^3 x^3\,dx = \int_0^2 x^3\,dx + \int_2^3 x^3\,dx$

4 a $3\frac{3}{4}$ units^2 **b** $8\frac{2}{3}$ units^2 **c** $\dfrac{4\sqrt{2}-2}{3}$ units^2

d 2 units^2

6 c i $\displaystyle\int_0^1 (-x^2)\,dx = -\frac{1}{3}$, the area between $y = -x^2$
and the x-axis from $x = 0$ to $x = 1$ is $\frac{1}{3}$ units^2.

ii $\displaystyle\int_0^1 (x^2 - x)\,dx = -\frac{1}{6}$, the area between $y = x^2 - x$
and the x-axis from $x = 0$ to $x = 1$ is $\frac{1}{6}$ units^2.

iii $\displaystyle\int_{-2}^0 3x\,dx = -6$, the area between $y = 3x$
and the x-axis from $x = -2$ to $x = 0$ is 6 units^2.

d $-\pi$

7 a $A'(x) = x^2 + 2$ **b** $A'(x) = x^3 + 2x$

EXERCISE 16D.1

1 $\dfrac{dy}{dx} = 7x^6$, $\displaystyle\int x^6\,dx = \frac{1}{7}x^7 + c$

2 $\dfrac{dy}{dx} = 3x^2 + 2x$, $\displaystyle\int (3x^2 + 2x)\,dx = x^3 + x^2 + c$

3 $\dfrac{dy}{dx} = \frac{3}{2}\sqrt{x}$, $\displaystyle\int \sqrt{x}\,dx = \frac{2}{3}x\sqrt{x} + c$

4 $\dfrac{dy}{dx} = -\dfrac{1}{2x\sqrt{x}}$, $\displaystyle\int \dfrac{1}{x\sqrt{x}}\,dx = -\dfrac{2}{\sqrt{x}} + c$

EXERCISE 16D.2

1 a $\frac{1}{3}x^3 + \frac{3}{2}x^2 - 2x + c$ **b** $\dfrac{x^5}{5} - \dfrac{x^3}{3} - \dfrac{x^2}{2} + 2x + c$

c $x^5 - x^4 - 2x^3 - 7x + c$ **d** $\frac{2}{3}x^{\frac{3}{2}} + 2x^{\frac{1}{2}} + c$

e $\frac{2}{5}x^{\frac{5}{2}} - 2x + c$ **f** $-\dfrac{2}{\sqrt{x}} + 2x^2 + c$

2 a $\frac{1}{8}x^4 - \frac{1}{5}x^5 + \frac{3}{4}x^{\frac{4}{3}} + c$ **b** $-\dfrac{4}{x} + \frac{1}{3}x^3 - \frac{1}{16}x^4 + c$

c $x^5 + \frac{1}{12}x^4 - \frac{2}{3}x^{\frac{3}{2}} + c$

3 a $\frac{4}{3}x^3 + 2x^2 + x + c$ **b** $\frac{1}{3}x^3 + 2x - \dfrac{1}{x} + c$

c $-\dfrac{2}{\sqrt{x}} - 8\sqrt{x} + c$ **d** $\frac{4}{3}x\sqrt{x} - 2\sqrt{x} + c$

e $\frac{1}{4}x^4 + x^3 + \frac{3}{2}x^2 + x + c$

f $\frac{1}{5}x^5 - x^4 + 2x^3 - 2x^2 + x + c$

4 a $y = 6x + c$ **b** $y = \frac{4}{3}x^3 + c$ **c** $y = -\dfrac{1}{x} + c$

d $y = \frac{1}{2}x^4 - 4x + c$ **e** $y = x^4 + x^3 + c$

f $y = \frac{2}{7}x^{\frac{7}{2}} + \frac{12}{5}x^{\frac{5}{2}} + 8x^{\frac{3}{2}} + 16x^{\frac{1}{2}} + c$

5 a $f(x) = x - 2x^2 + \frac{4}{3}x^3 + c$

b $f(x) = \frac{2}{3}x\sqrt{x} - 4\sqrt{x} + c$ **c** $f(x) = x + \dfrac{5}{x} + c$

EXERCISE 16D.3

1 a $f(x) = x^2 - x + 3$ **b** $f(x) = x^3 + x^2 - 7$

c $f(x) = 2x + 2\sqrt{x} - 3$ **d** $f(x) = \frac{1}{2}x^2 - 4\sqrt{x} + \frac{11}{2}$

2 $y = \dfrac{x^2}{2} - \dfrac{2x^3}{3} + \dfrac{22}{3}$ **3** $f(x) = -x^2 + x + 3$

4 $f(x) = -\dfrac{x^3}{6} + x^2 + \dfrac{25}{6}x - 1$

EXERCISE 16E

1 a $\int_1^4 \sqrt{x}\,dx = \frac{14}{3}$, $\int_1^4 (-\sqrt{x})\,dx = -\frac{14}{3}$

  b $\int_0^1 x^7\,dx = \frac{1}{8}$, $\int_0^1 (-x^7)\,dx = -\frac{1}{8}$

2 a $\frac{1}{3}$ **b** $\frac{7}{3}$ **c** $\frac{8}{3}$ **d** 1

3 a -4 **b** $6\frac{1}{4}$ **c** $2\frac{1}{4}$ **4 a** $\frac{1}{3}$ **b** $\frac{2}{3}$ **c** 1

5 a $\frac{1}{4}$ **b** $\frac{2}{3}$ **c** $1\frac{1}{2}$ **d** $6\frac{2}{3}$ **e** $\frac{2}{3}$ **f** $20\frac{1}{3}$

6 $m = -1$ or $\frac{4}{3}$

7 a $\int_2^7 f(x)\,dx$ **b** $\int_4^6 f(x)\,dx$ **c** $\int_1^9 g(x)\,dx$

8 a -5 **b** 4

9 a 4   **b** 0   **c** -8 **d** $k = -\frac{7}{4}$ **10** 0

REVIEW SET 16A

1 a

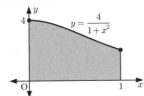

lower rectangles   upper rectangles

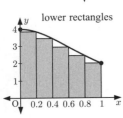

b

n	A_L	A_U
5	2.9349	3.3349
50	3.1215	3.1615
100	3.1316	3.1516
500	3.1396	3.1436

c $\int_0^1 \frac{4}{1+x^2}\,dx$

≈ 3.1416

$\approx \pi$

2 a 2π **b** 4   **3 a** $\frac{x^6}{6}$ **b** $\frac{x^3}{3} - 3x^2$ **c** $-\frac{1}{2x}$

4 a $\frac{2}{3}x\sqrt{x} + \frac{2}{x} + c$ **b** $x^2 - \frac{9}{2}x^{\frac{2}{3}} + c$

  c $4x\sqrt{x} + 10\sqrt{x} + c$

5 a $8\sqrt{x} + c$ **b** $\frac{x^4}{12} + x^2 + c$ **c** $-\frac{1}{2x^2} + \frac{2}{x} + c$

6 a 8   **b** $\frac{1}{8} - \frac{1}{3\sqrt{2}}$ **c** $11\frac{13}{15}$

7 $A'(x) = \frac{3x^3 - x^2}{2x}$ **8** $f(x) = x^3 - 2x^2 + x + 2$

9 $y = -2x^2 + 3x + 2$ **10** $b = 3$

REVIEW SET 16B

1 a $A = \frac{17}{4}$, $B = \frac{25}{4}$ **b** $\int_0^2 (4 - x^2)\,dx \approx \frac{21}{4}$

2 a 3   **b** $\frac{15}{2}$

3 a $x + \frac{2}{x} + c$ **b** $3x^3 - 12x^2 + 16x + c$ **c** $4x - \frac{2x^3}{3} + c$

---

4 a $\frac{3}{4}x^{\frac{4}{3}} + 3x + c$ **b** $x^3 - 2x + c$ **c** $9x + 6x^2 + \frac{4}{3}x^3 + c$

5 $f(x) = \frac{1}{3}x^3 - \frac{3}{2}x^2 + 2x + 2\frac{1}{6}$

6 a $2 - \frac{2\sqrt{2}}{\sqrt{3}}$ **b** -3 **c** $\frac{8}{15}$

7 a 6   **b** 3   **8** $A'(x) = 2x^2 - 3x$

9 a $y = \frac{1}{5}x^5 - \frac{2}{3}x^3 + x + c$ **b** $y = 400x - 40x^{\frac{1}{2}} + c$

10 $a = \frac{3}{2}$

EXERCISE 17A.1

1 a ≈ 1.41 s   **b** ≈ 2.36 s   **c** ≈ 7.45 s

2 a 20 m s^{-1} **b** 50 m s^{-1} **c** 100 m s^{-1}

3 a 13.5 m s^{-1} **b** 61.5 m s^{-1}

4 a ≈ 1.46 m s^{-2} **b** ≈ 1060 m

5 a ≈ 27.1 m s^{-1} **b** ≈ -5.64 m s^{-2}

6 a ≈ 20.6 m s^{-1} **b** ≈ 2.81 s

EXERCISE 17A.2

1 a ≈ 2.05 s   **b** ≈ 20.1 m s^{-1}

2 a ≈ 19.0 m s^{-1} **b** ≈ 1.94 s

  c i ≈ 0.805 s   **ii** ≈ 26.9 m s^{-1}

3 a i ≈ 0.624 m or ≈ 62.4 cm   **ii** ≈ 3.78 m

  iii ≈ 9.28 m

  b ≈ 1.37 m s^{-2}

EXERCISE 17B.1

1 a i 3 m   **ii** -3 m   **b** -2 m s^{-1} **c** $-\frac{2}{3}$ m s^{-1}

2 a -2 m s^{-1} **b** $v(t) = 2t - 6$ m s^{-1}

  c i -4 m s^{-1} **ii** 4 m s^{-1}

3 a 16 cm s^{-1} **b** 6 cm s^{-2}

  c $a(t) = 10 - 2t$ cm s^{-2} **d** 4 cm s^{-2}

4 $s(2) = 7$ m, $v(2) = 16$ m s^{-1}, $a(2) = 14$ m s^{-2}

EXERCISE 17B.2

1 a 2 cm to the right of O   **b** when $t = 6$ s

  c to the left   **d** when $t = 3$ s and $t = 9$ s

  e   **i**   **ii**

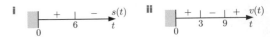

  f -1 cm s^{-1}

2 a The object is at the origin, moving to the right at 24 m s^{-1}, with decreasing speed.

  b $v(t) = 3t^2 - 22t + 24$ m s^{-1}

  c

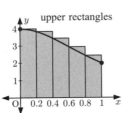

  d at 0 s, 3 s, and 8 s

  e at $\frac{4}{3}$ s and 6 s; $s(\frac{4}{3}) \approx 14.8$ m, $s(6) = -36$ m

  f The object starts at O, and moves towards the right at 24 m s^{-1}. Its velocity is decreasing. After $\frac{4}{3}$ seconds, when it is 14.8 m to the right of O, it changes direction and moves to the left, passing O after 3 seconds. After 6 seconds, when it is 36 m to the left of O, it changes direction again and moves towards the right, passing O once more after 8 seconds.

  g

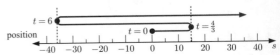

3 a $v(t) = 2t - 4$ cm s^{-1}, $a(t) = 2$ cm s^{-2}

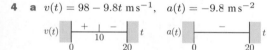

b $s(0) = 3$ cm, $v(0) = -4$ cm s^{-1}, $a(0) = 2$ cm s^{-2}
The object is initially 3 cm to the right of the origin and is moving to the left at 4 cm s^{-1}. It is accelerating at 2 cm s^{-2}.

c $s(4) = 3$ cm, $v(4) = 4$ cm s^{-1}, $a(4) = 2$ cm s^{-2}
The object is 3 cm to the right of the origin and is moving to the right at 4 cm s^{-1}. It is accelerating at 2 cm s^{-2}.

d At $t = 2$, the object is 1 cm to the left of the origin.

e 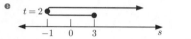   **f** $0 \leqslant t \leqslant 2$

4 a $v(t) = 98 - 9.8t$ m s^{-1}, $a(t) = -9.8$ m s^{-2}

b $s(0) = 0$ m above the ground, $v(0) = 98$ m s^{-1} upward

c At $t = 5$ s, the stone is 367.5 m above the ground and moving upward at 49 m s^{-1}. Its speed is decreasing.
At $t = 12$ s, the stone is 470.4 m above the ground and moving downward at 19.6 m s^{-1}. Its speed is increasing.

d 490 m   **e** 20 seconds

5 a 1.2 m

b $s'(t) = 28.1 - 9.8t$ represents the instantaneous velocity of the ball.

c $t \approx 2.87$ s. The ball has reached its maximum height and is instantaneously at rest.

d 41.5 m

e **i** 28.1 m s^{-1} **ii** 8.5 m s^{-1} **iii** 20.9 m s^{-1}
$s'(t) \geqslant 0$ when the ball is travelling upwards.
$s'(t) \leqslant 0$ when the ball is travelling downwards.

f 5.78 s

6 a $v(t) = 3t^2 - 18t + 24$ m s^{-1} $a(t) = 6t - 18$ m s^{-2}

b $x(2) = 20$, $x(4) = 16$

c **i** $0 \leqslant t \leqslant 2$ and $3 \leqslant t \leqslant 4$ **ii** $0 \leqslant t \leqslant 3$ **d** 28 m

EXERCISE 17B.3

1 110 m

2 a **i** travelling forwards
   ii travelling backwards (opposite direction)
b 16 km   **c** 8 km from starting point (on positive side)

3 a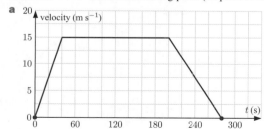

b 3.3 km

4 a    **b** $6\frac{1}{6}$ km

5 a $\frac{1}{2}$ cm   **b** 0 cm

6 a $s(t) = \frac{1}{3}t^3 - \frac{1}{2}t^2 - 2t$ cm   **b** $5\frac{1}{6}$ cm
   c $1\frac{1}{2}$ cm left of its starting point

7 a $s(t) = 29.4t - 4.9t^2 + 1$ m   **b** 45.1 m

EXERCISE 17B.4

1 a $s(t) = 32t + 2t^2 + 16$ m
b There is no change of direction,
   so displacement $= s(t_1) - s(0) = \displaystyle\int_0^{t_1} (32 + 4t)\, dt$
c acceleration $= v'(t) = 4$ m s^{-2}

2 a $v(t) = \dfrac{t^2}{20} - 3t + 45$ m s^{-1}
b $\displaystyle\int_0^{60} v(t)\, dt = 900$ The train travels a total of 900 m in the first 60 seconds.

3 a **i** 10 m s^{-1} **ii** $10\sqrt{2}$ m s^{-1} **b** $s(t) = \frac{20}{3}t^{\frac{3}{2}}$ m
c $\displaystyle\int_0^2 v(t)\, dt \approx 18.9$ The motorcyclist travels about 18.9 m in the first 2 seconds.
d **i** 4 seconds
   ii Yes, he only needs $53\frac{1}{3}$ m to reach the required speed.

REVIEW SET 17A

1 a 24.91 m s^{-1} **b** 10.6 m   **c** ≈ 3.79 s
2 a ≈ 1.96 m   **b** ≈ 75.2 m   **c** ≈ 38.9 m s^{-1}
3 a 13 cm s^{-1} **b** **i** 9 cm s^{-1} **ii** 17 cm s^{-1}
   c $a(t) = 4$ cm s^{-2}
4 a $v(t) = 6t^2 - 18t + 12$ cm s^{-1}, $a(t) = 12t - 18$ cm s^{-2}

b $s(0) = 5$ cm to left of origin
   $v(0) = 12$ cm s^{-1} towards origin
   $a(0) = -18$ cm s^{-2} (decreasing speed)
c At $t = 2$, the particle is 1 cm to the left of the origin, is instantaneously stationary, and is beginning to accelerate.
d $t = 1$, $s = 0$, and $t = 2$, $s = -1$
e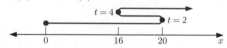

f Speed is increasing for $1 \leqslant t \leqslant 1\frac{1}{2}$ and $t \geqslant 2$.

5 a

b The particle moves in the positive direction initially, then at $t = 2$, $6\frac{2}{3}$ m from its starting point, it changes direction. It changes direction again at $t = 4$, $5\frac{1}{3}$ m from its starting point, and at $t = 5$, it is $6\frac{2}{3}$ m from its starting point again.

c $6\frac{2}{3}$ m   **d** $9\frac{1}{3}$ m

6 a   i 2.75 m s^{-1} **ii** $\approx 1.62 \text{ m s}^{-1}$

   b Hint: Show that $a(t)$ and $v(t)$ are opposite in sign for all $0 \leqslant t \leqslant 6$.

   c $\displaystyle\int_0^2 v(t)\, dt \approx 4.54$ The kayak travels approximately 4.54 m in the first 2 seconds after the kayaker stops paddling.

REVIEW SET 17B

1 a $\approx -1.76 \text{ m s}^{-2}$ **b** ≈ 23.8 m

2 a $\approx 39.4 \text{ m s}^{-1}$ **b** ≈ 16.8 s   **c** $\approx 26.8 \text{ m s}^{-1}$

3 200 m

4 a $v(t) = 3 - \frac{3}{2}\sqrt{t} \text{ cm s}^{-1}$ $a(t) = -\dfrac{3}{4\sqrt{t}} \text{ cm s}^{-2}$

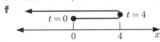

   b $x(0) = 0$, $v(0) = 3$

The particle is initially at the origin, moving to the right at 3 cm s^{-1}.

   c The particle is ≈ 3.17 cm to the right of the origin, travelling to the right at $\approx 0.879 \text{ cm s}^{-1}$, and deccelerating at $\approx 0.530 \text{ cm s}^{-2}$.

   d when $t = 4$, $x = 4$ **e** $0 \leqslant t \leqslant 4$

   f

   g ≈ 4.70 cm

5 a $v(t) = 3t^2 - 30t + 27 \text{ cm s}^{-1}$

   b -162 cm   (162 cm to the left of the origin)

6 a   i 7.2 m s^{-2} **ii** 9.6 m s^{-2} **iii** 0 m s^{-2}

   iv -12 m s^{-2}

   b $\displaystyle\int_0^3 v(t)\, dt = 27$ The human cannonball travels 27 m in the first 3 seconds.

   c ≈ 3.14 s

EXERCISE 18A.1

1 a   **b**   **c**

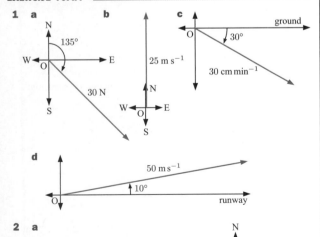

2 a

EXERCISE 18A.2

1 a p, q, s, t   **b** p, q, r, t   **c** p and r, q and t

   d q, t   **e** p and q, p and t

2 a true   **b** true   **c** false   **d** false   **e** true   **f** false

3 a   i $\overrightarrow{BC}$ **ii** $\overrightarrow{ED}$

   b   i $\overrightarrow{FE}$, $\overrightarrow{BC}$

     ii $\overrightarrow{DE}$, $\overrightarrow{EF}$, $\overrightarrow{FE}$, $\overrightarrow{FA}$, $\overrightarrow{AF}$, $\overrightarrow{AB}$, $\overrightarrow{BA}$, $\overrightarrow{BC}$, $\overrightarrow{CB}$, $\overrightarrow{CD}$, $\overrightarrow{DC}$

   c $\overrightarrow{FC}$ (or $\overrightarrow{CF}$)

EXERCISE 18B.1

1 a   **b**

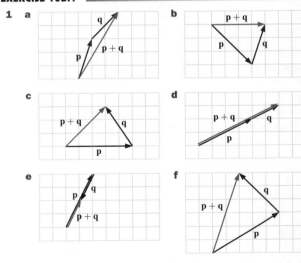

2 a $\overrightarrow{AC}$ **b** $\overrightarrow{BD}$ **c** 0   **d** $\overrightarrow{AD}$ **e** $\overrightarrow{AD}$ **f** 0

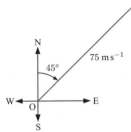

3 a   **b**   *Scale*: $1 \text{ cm} \equiv 10 \text{ m s}^{-1}$

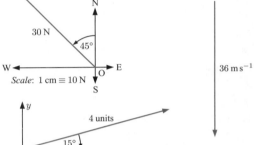

   c

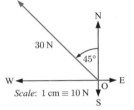

   d

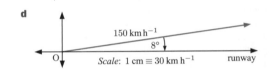

3 a i

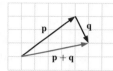

ii

b yes

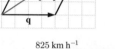

5 a

825 km h⁻¹
800 km h⁻¹
35 km h⁻¹
135°

Scale: 1 cm ≡ 125 km h⁻¹

b We use vector addition.   **c** 825 km h⁻¹, 88° east of north

6 a

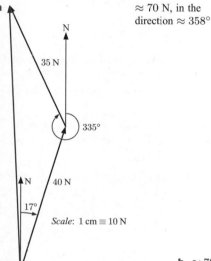

≈ 70 N, in the
direction ≈ 358°

N
35 N
335°
N   40 N
17°
Scale: 1 cm ≡ 10 N

b ≈ 70.0 N, in the
direction ≈ 357°

EXERCISE 18B.2

1 a

b

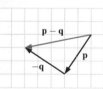

c

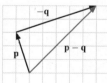

d

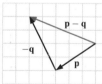

2 a

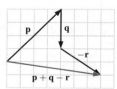

b

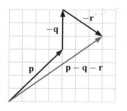

c

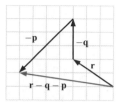

3 a $\overrightarrow{AB}$ **b** $\overrightarrow{AB}$ **c** 0   **d** $\overrightarrow{AD}$ **e** 0   **f** $\overrightarrow{AD}$

EXERCISE 18B.3

1 Note: Other answers are possible.

  a $t = r + s$ **b** $r = -s - t$
  c $r = -p - q - s$ **d** $r = q - p + s$
  e $p = t + s + r - q$ **f** $p = -u + t + s - r - q$

2 a i $r + s$ **ii** $-t - s$ **iii** $r + s + t$
  b i $p + q$ **ii** $q + r$ **iii** $p + q + r$

EXERCISE 18B.4

1 a

b

c

d

e

$2r - s$
$-s$
r
r

f

r   s
s
r   s
$2r + 3s$

g

$\frac{1}{2}r$ s
s
$\frac{1}{2}r + 2s$

h

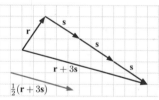

r   s
s
$r + 3s$ s
$\frac{1}{2}(r + 3s)$

2 a

p   q

b

p   q

c

p
q
$p = 2q$

d

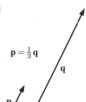

$p = \frac{1}{3}q$

e

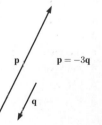

p $p = -3q$
q

3 a

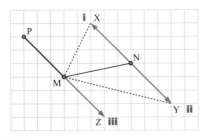

b a parallelogram

4 a $-\mathbf{p}$ **b** $\mathbf{p} + \mathbf{q}$ **c** $\frac{1}{2}(\mathbf{p} + \mathbf{q})$ **d** $\frac{1}{2}(\mathbf{q} - \mathbf{p})$

5 a $\mathbf{b}$ **b** $2\mathbf{b}$ **c** $\mathbf{b} - \mathbf{a}$ **d** $\mathbf{b} - \mathbf{a}$

EXERCISE 18C

1 a $\begin{pmatrix} 7 \\ 3 \end{pmatrix}$, $7\mathbf{i} + 3\mathbf{j}$ **b** $\begin{pmatrix} -6 \\ 0 \end{pmatrix}$, $-6\mathbf{i}$

  c $\begin{pmatrix} 2 \\ -5 \end{pmatrix}$, $2\mathbf{i} - 5\mathbf{j}$ **d** $\begin{pmatrix} 0 \\ 6 \end{pmatrix}$, $6\mathbf{j}$

  e $\begin{pmatrix} -6 \\ 3 \end{pmatrix}$, $-6\mathbf{i} + 3\mathbf{j}$ **f** $\begin{pmatrix} -5 \\ -5 \end{pmatrix}$, $-5\mathbf{i} - 5\mathbf{j}$

2 a $3\mathbf{i} + 4\mathbf{j}$ **b** $2\mathbf{i}$ **c** $2\mathbf{i} - 5\mathbf{j}$ **d** $-\mathbf{i} - 3\mathbf{j}$

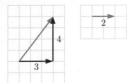

3 a $\begin{pmatrix} -4 \\ -1 \end{pmatrix}$, $-4\mathbf{i} - \mathbf{j}$ **b** $\begin{pmatrix} -1 \\ -5 \end{pmatrix}$, $-\mathbf{i} - 5\mathbf{j}$

  c $\begin{pmatrix} 2 \\ 0 \end{pmatrix}$, $2\mathbf{i}$ **d** $\begin{pmatrix} 3 \\ -4 \end{pmatrix}$, $3\mathbf{i} - 4\mathbf{j}$

  e $\begin{pmatrix} -3 \\ 4 \end{pmatrix}$, $-3\mathbf{i} + 4\mathbf{j}$ **f** $\begin{pmatrix} 3 \\ 5 \end{pmatrix}$, $3\mathbf{i} + 5\mathbf{j}$

4 a $\begin{pmatrix} 1 \\ 2 \end{pmatrix}$ **b** $\begin{pmatrix} -1 \\ 3 \end{pmatrix}$ **c** $\begin{pmatrix} 0 \\ -5 \end{pmatrix}$ **d** $\begin{pmatrix} 4 \\ -2 \end{pmatrix}$

5 $\begin{pmatrix} 0 \\ 0 \end{pmatrix}$

EXERCISE 18D

1 a 5 units **b** 5 units **c** 2 units
  d $\sqrt{8}$ units **e** 3 units

2 a $\sqrt{2}$ units **b** 13 units **c** $\sqrt{17}$ units
  d 3 units **e** $|k|$ units

3 a unit vector **b** unit vector **c** not a unit vector
  d unit vector **e** not a unit vector

4 a $k = \pm 1$ **b** $k = \pm 1$ **c** $k = 0$
  d $k = \pm \frac{1}{\sqrt{2}}$ **e** $k = \pm \frac{\sqrt{3}}{2}$

5 $p = \pm 3$

EXERCISE 18E

1 a $\begin{pmatrix} -2 \\ 6 \end{pmatrix}$ **b** $\begin{pmatrix} -2 \\ 6 \end{pmatrix}$ **c** $\begin{pmatrix} -1 \\ -1 \end{pmatrix}$ **d** $\begin{pmatrix} -1 \\ -1 \end{pmatrix}$

  e $\begin{pmatrix} -5 \\ -3 \end{pmatrix}$ **f** $\begin{pmatrix} -5 \\ -3 \end{pmatrix}$ **g** $\begin{pmatrix} -6 \\ 4 \end{pmatrix}$ **h** $\begin{pmatrix} -4 \\ 1 \end{pmatrix}$

2 a $\begin{pmatrix} -3 \\ 7 \end{pmatrix}$ **b** $\begin{pmatrix} -4 \\ -3 \end{pmatrix}$ **c** $\begin{pmatrix} -8 \\ -1 \end{pmatrix}$ **d** $\begin{pmatrix} -6 \\ 9 \end{pmatrix}$

  e $\begin{pmatrix} 0 \\ -5 \end{pmatrix}$ **f** $\begin{pmatrix} 6 \\ -9 \end{pmatrix}$

3 a $\mathbf{a} + \mathbf{0} = \begin{pmatrix} a_1 \\ a_2 \end{pmatrix} + \begin{pmatrix} 0 \\ 0 \end{pmatrix} = \begin{pmatrix} a_1 + 0 \\ a_2 + 0 \end{pmatrix} = \begin{pmatrix} a_1 \\ a_2 \end{pmatrix} = \mathbf{a}$

  b $\mathbf{a} - \mathbf{a} = \begin{pmatrix} a_1 \\ a_2 \end{pmatrix} - \begin{pmatrix} a_1 \\ a_2 \end{pmatrix} = \begin{pmatrix} a_1 - a_1 \\ a_2 - a_2 \end{pmatrix} = \begin{pmatrix} 0 \\ 0 \end{pmatrix} = \mathbf{0}$

4 a $\begin{pmatrix} -3 \\ -15 \end{pmatrix}$ **b** $\begin{pmatrix} -1 \\ 2 \end{pmatrix}$ **c** $\begin{pmatrix} 0 \\ 14 \end{pmatrix}$ **d** $\begin{pmatrix} 5 \\ -3 \end{pmatrix}$

  e $\begin{pmatrix} \frac{5}{2} \\ \frac{11}{2} \end{pmatrix}$ **f** $\begin{pmatrix} -7 \\ 7 \end{pmatrix}$ **g** $\begin{pmatrix} 5 \\ 11 \end{pmatrix}$ **h** $\begin{pmatrix} 3 \\ \frac{17}{3} \end{pmatrix}$

5 a i $\begin{pmatrix} 8 \\ -1 \end{pmatrix}$ **ii** $\begin{pmatrix} 8 \\ -1 \end{pmatrix}$ **iii** $\begin{pmatrix} 8 \\ -1 \end{pmatrix}$

  b The vector expressions are equal, as each consists of the sum of 2 $\mathbf{p}$s and 3 $\mathbf{q}$s. Each expression is equal to $2\mathbf{p} + 3\mathbf{q}$.

6 a $\sqrt{13}$ units **b** $\sqrt{17}$ units **c** $5\sqrt{2}$ units **d** $\sqrt{10}$ units
  e $\sqrt{29}$ units

7 a $\sqrt{10}$ units **b** $2\sqrt{10}$ units **c** $2\sqrt{10}$ units **d** $3\sqrt{10}$ units
  e $3\sqrt{10}$ units **f** $2\sqrt{5}$ units **g** $8\sqrt{5}$ units **h** $8\sqrt{5}$ units
  i $\sqrt{5}$ units **j** $\sqrt{5}$ units

EXERCISE 18F

1 a $\begin{pmatrix} 2 \\ 4 \end{pmatrix}$ **b** $\begin{pmatrix} -2 \\ 5 \end{pmatrix}$ **c** $\begin{pmatrix} 3 \\ -3 \end{pmatrix}$ **d** $\begin{pmatrix} 1 \\ -5 \end{pmatrix}$

  e $\begin{pmatrix} 6 \\ -5 \end{pmatrix}$ **f** $\begin{pmatrix} 1 \\ 3 \end{pmatrix}$

2 a B(4, 2) **b** C(2, 2) **3 a** $\begin{pmatrix} 2 \\ 1 \end{pmatrix}$ **b** Q(3, 3)

4 a $\begin{pmatrix} 5 \\ 1 \end{pmatrix}$ **b** $\begin{pmatrix} -5 \\ -1 \end{pmatrix}$ **c** D(−1, −2)

5 a $\overrightarrow{AB} = \begin{pmatrix} 4 \\ k-3 \end{pmatrix}$, $|\overrightarrow{AB}| = \sqrt{16 + (k-3)^2} = 5$ units
  b $k = 0$ or 6

6 a $\overrightarrow{AB} = \begin{pmatrix} 2 \\ 3 \end{pmatrix}$, $\overrightarrow{AC} = \begin{pmatrix} 3 \\ -3 \end{pmatrix}$
  b $\overrightarrow{BC} = \overrightarrow{BA} + \overrightarrow{AC} = -\overrightarrow{AB} + \overrightarrow{AC}$ **c** $\overrightarrow{BC} = \begin{pmatrix} 1 \\ -6 \end{pmatrix}$

7 a $\begin{pmatrix} -5 \\ 4 \end{pmatrix}$ **b** $\begin{pmatrix} 1 \\ 2 \end{pmatrix}$ **c** $\begin{pmatrix} 6 \\ -5 \end{pmatrix}$

8 a M(1, 4) **b** $\overrightarrow{CA} = \begin{pmatrix} 7 \\ 5 \end{pmatrix}$, $\overrightarrow{CM} = \begin{pmatrix} 5 \\ 3 \end{pmatrix}$, $\overrightarrow{CB} = \begin{pmatrix} 3 \\ 1 \end{pmatrix}$

EXERCISE 18G.1

1 a $a = 3$ **b** $a = -6$

2 a $\overrightarrow{AB} \parallel \overrightarrow{CD}$, $|\overrightarrow{AB}| = 3|\overrightarrow{CD}|$
  b $\overrightarrow{RS} \parallel \overrightarrow{KL}$, $|\overrightarrow{RS}| = \frac{1}{2}|\overrightarrow{KL}|$, $\overrightarrow{RS}$ and $\overrightarrow{KL}$ are in opposite directions.
  c $\overrightarrow{AB} \parallel \overrightarrow{BC}$, $|\overrightarrow{AB}| = 2|\overrightarrow{BC}|$

3 a $\begin{pmatrix} 4 \\ 8 \end{pmatrix}$ **b** $\begin{pmatrix} -1 \\ -2 \end{pmatrix}$

4 a $\frac{1}{\sqrt{5}}\mathbf{i} + \frac{2}{\sqrt{5}}\mathbf{j}$ **b** $\frac{2}{\sqrt{13}}\mathbf{i} - \frac{3}{\sqrt{13}}\mathbf{j}$ **c** $-\frac{1}{\sqrt{2}}\mathbf{i} + \frac{1}{\sqrt{2}}\mathbf{j}$

5 a $\begin{pmatrix} \frac{6}{\sqrt{5}} \\ -\frac{3}{\sqrt{5}} \end{pmatrix}$ **b** $\begin{pmatrix} \frac{2}{\sqrt{17}} \\ \frac{8}{\sqrt{17}} \end{pmatrix}$

6 a $\overrightarrow{AB} = \begin{pmatrix} 2\sqrt{2} \\ -2\sqrt{2} \end{pmatrix}$ **b** $\overrightarrow{OB} = \begin{pmatrix} 3 + 2\sqrt{2} \\ 2 - 2\sqrt{2} \end{pmatrix}$

c $B(3 + 2\sqrt{2}, \; 2 - 2\sqrt{2})$

7 $X(4, -1)$

EXERCISE 18G.2

1 a $\overrightarrow{AB} = -\frac{5}{3}\overrightarrow{BC}$ **b** $\overrightarrow{PQ} = -\frac{3}{5}\overrightarrow{QR}$

2 Q is $(\frac{3}{2}, \frac{1}{4})$ **3** R is $(3, 2)$

4 a $\overrightarrow{PQ} = -\frac{2}{3}\overrightarrow{QR}$ **b** P divides [QR] in the ratio $2 : 1$.

EXERCISE 18H

1 a

$\begin{array}{c} \xrightarrow{\quad 6\,\text{m\,s}^{-1}\quad} \xrightarrow{1\,\text{m\,s}^{-1}} \\ \xrightarrow{\qquad 7\,\text{m\,s}^{-1}\qquad} \end{array}$ $\therefore\; 7\,\text{m\,s}^{-1}$

b

$\begin{array}{c} \xrightarrow{\quad 6\,\text{m\,s}^{-1}\quad} \\ \xrightarrow{\quad 5\,\text{m\,s}^{-1}\quad}\xleftarrow{1\,\text{m\,s}^{-1}} \end{array}$ $\therefore\; 5\,\text{m\,s}^{-1}$

2 a $\approx 1.34\;\text{m\,s}^{-1}$ in the direction $\approx 26.6°$ to the left of her intended line.

b i $30°$ to the right of Q **ii** $\approx 1.04\;\text{m\,s}^{-1}$

3 $\approx 13.2\;\text{km\,h}^{-1}$ in the direction $\approx 068.0°$

4 a $\approx 24.6\;\text{km\,h}^{-1}$ **b** $\approx 9.93°$ east of due south

5 a The plane's speed in still air would be $\approx 437\;\text{km\,h}^{-1}$. The wind slows the plane down to $400\;\text{km\,h}^{-1}$.

b $\approx 4.64°$ north of due east

6 ≈ 0.599 N, on a bearing of $\approx 207°$ from A.

7 a ≈ 82.5 m **b** $\approx 23.3°$ to the left of straight across

c ≈ 48.4 s

EXERCISE 18I

1 a $(1, 2)$

c $\begin{pmatrix} 2 \\ -5 \end{pmatrix}$

d $\sqrt{29}\;\text{cm\,s}^{-1}$

b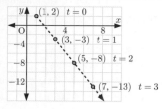

2 a $\begin{pmatrix} x \\ y \end{pmatrix} = \begin{pmatrix} 2 \\ 3 \end{pmatrix} + t\begin{pmatrix} 4 \\ -5 \end{pmatrix}, \quad t \geqslant 0$ **b** $(8, -4.5)$

c 45 minutes

3 a $\begin{pmatrix} -3 + 2t \\ -2 + 4t \end{pmatrix}$ **d**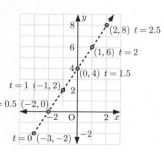

b $\begin{pmatrix} 2 \\ 8 \end{pmatrix}$

c i $t = 1.5$ s
ii $t = 0.5$ s

4 a $\begin{pmatrix} 120 \\ -90 \end{pmatrix}$ **b** $\begin{pmatrix} -3 \\ 7.2 \end{pmatrix}$ **c** $\begin{pmatrix} \frac{30\sqrt{85}}{17} \\ \frac{35\sqrt{85}}{17} \end{pmatrix}$

5 a A is at $(4, 5)$, B is at $(1, -8)$

b For A it is $\begin{pmatrix} 1 \\ -2 \end{pmatrix}$. For B it is $\begin{pmatrix} 2 \\ 1 \end{pmatrix}$.

c For A, speed is $\sqrt{5}\;\text{km\,h}^{-1}$. For B, speed is $\sqrt{5}\;\text{km\,h}^{-1}$.

6 a $\begin{pmatrix} x_1 \\ y_1 \end{pmatrix} = \begin{pmatrix} -5 \\ 4 \end{pmatrix} + t\begin{pmatrix} 3 \\ -1 \end{pmatrix}$

$\therefore\; x_1(t) = -5 + 3t, \quad y_1(t) = 4 - t$

b speed $= \sqrt{10}$ km per minute

c a minutes later, $(t - a)$ minutes have elapsed.

$\therefore\; \begin{pmatrix} x_2 \\ y_2 \end{pmatrix} = \begin{pmatrix} 15 \\ 7 \end{pmatrix} + (t - a)\begin{pmatrix} -4 \\ -3 \end{pmatrix}$

$\therefore\; x_2(t) = 15 - 4(t - a), \quad y_2(t) = 7 - 3(t - a)$

d Torpedo is fired at 1:35:28 pm and the explosion occurs at 1:37:42 pm.

EXERCISE 18J

3 a i $\overrightarrow{PC} = \mathbf{r}, \quad \overrightarrow{DP} = \mathbf{s}$

ii $\overrightarrow{AB} = \mathbf{r} + \mathbf{s}. \quad \overrightarrow{DC} = \mathbf{r} + \mathbf{s}$

b $\overrightarrow{AB} \parallel \overrightarrow{DC}, \quad |\overrightarrow{AB}| = |\overrightarrow{DC}|$

c If the diagonals of a quadrilateral bisect each other then the quadrilateral is a parallelogram.

4 a i $\overrightarrow{AD} = 2\mathbf{p} + 2\mathbf{q} + 2\mathbf{r}$ **ii** $\overrightarrow{AS} = \mathbf{p} + \mathbf{q} + \mathbf{r}$

iii $\overrightarrow{PQ} = \mathbf{p} + \mathbf{q}$ **iv** $\overrightarrow{SR} = \mathbf{p} + \mathbf{q}$

b $\overrightarrow{PQ} \parallel \overrightarrow{SR}, \quad |\overrightarrow{PQ}| = |\overrightarrow{SR}|$, so PQRS is a parallelogram.

5 a **Hint:** Let $\overrightarrow{OA} = \mathbf{a}$ and $\overrightarrow{OM} = \mathbf{m}$. **b** $1 : 2$
Find $\overrightarrow{AM}, \overrightarrow{AT}, \overrightarrow{OT}$, and $\overrightarrow{TB}$.

REVIEW SET 18A

1 a

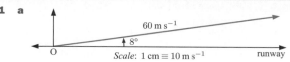

60 m s⁻¹, 8°, O, Scale: 1 cm ≡ 10 m s⁻¹, runway

b

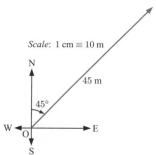

Scale: 1 cm ≡ 10 m, N, 45 m, 45°, W, O, E, S

2 a $\overrightarrow{AC}$ **b** $\overrightarrow{AD}$

3 Note: Other answers are possible.

a $\mathbf{q} = \mathbf{p} + \mathbf{r}$ **b** $\mathbf{l} = \mathbf{k} - \mathbf{j} + \mathbf{n} - \mathbf{m}$

4 a $\begin{pmatrix} 4 \\ 3 \end{pmatrix}$, $4\mathbf{i} + 3\mathbf{j}$ **b** $\begin{pmatrix} -1 \\ -5 \end{pmatrix}$, $-\mathbf{i} - 5\mathbf{j}$

5 $\begin{pmatrix} 1 \\ 4 \end{pmatrix}$ **6 a** $\mathbf{p} + \mathbf{q}$ **b** $\frac{3}{2}\mathbf{p} + \frac{1}{2}\mathbf{q}$ **7** $m = 5$

8 $\overrightarrow{WX} = \overrightarrow{YZ} = \begin{pmatrix} 1 \\ 6 \end{pmatrix}$, $\overrightarrow{WY} = \overrightarrow{XZ} = \begin{pmatrix} 6 \\ 5 \end{pmatrix}$

9 a i $p + q$ **ii** $\frac{1}{2}p + \frac{1}{2}q$

10 a $k = \pm\frac{7}{\sqrt{33}}$ **b** $k = \pm\frac{1}{\sqrt{2}}$

11 a i $q + r$ **ii** $r + q$
  b [DB] and [AC] are parallel and equal in length.

12 a $\overrightarrow{ON} = \frac{2}{3}a + \frac{1}{3}b$ **b** N is $(2, \frac{11}{3})$

13 a $\approx 11.5°$ east of due north   **b** ≈ 343 km h^{-1}

14 ≈ 41.2 km h^{-1} in the direction $\approx 232°$

15 a $(-4, 3)$ **b** $(28, 27)$ **c** $\begin{pmatrix} 8 \\ 6 \end{pmatrix}$ **d** 10 m s^{-1}

16 a $\begin{pmatrix} -3 \\ -21 \end{pmatrix}$ **b** $\begin{pmatrix} x \\ y \end{pmatrix} = \begin{pmatrix} 7 \\ 16 \end{pmatrix} + \lambda \begin{pmatrix} -3 \\ -21 \end{pmatrix}$
  c $\approx 12{:}21$ pm

17 a Hint: Let $\overrightarrow{OA} = a$ and $\overrightarrow{AB} = b$.
       Find $\overrightarrow{MB}$, $\overrightarrow{NX}$, $\overrightarrow{NC}$, and $\overrightarrow{XC}$ in terms of a and b.
  b X divides [CN] in the ratio $4 : 1$.

REVIEW SET 18B

1 a 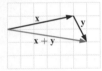   **b**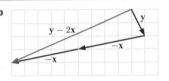

2 a $\overrightarrow{PQ}$ **b** $\overrightarrow{PR}$

3 a $\begin{pmatrix} 5 \\ 2 \end{pmatrix}$, $5i + 2j$ **b** $\begin{pmatrix} -3 \\ 3 \end{pmatrix}$, $-3i + 3j$

4 a $\begin{pmatrix} 3 \\ -3 \end{pmatrix}$ **b** $\begin{pmatrix} 7 \\ -3 \end{pmatrix}$ **c** 5 units

5 a $|\overrightarrow{AB}| = \frac{1}{2}|\overrightarrow{CD}|$, $\overrightarrow{AB} \parallel \overrightarrow{CD}$
  b C is the midpoint of [AB].

6 a $\overrightarrow{PQ} = \begin{pmatrix} -3 \\ 12 \end{pmatrix}$ **b** $\sqrt{153}$ units   **c** 5 units

7 a $r + q$ **b** $-p + r + q$ **c** $r + \frac{1}{2}q$ **d** $-\frac{1}{2}p + \frac{1}{2}r$

8 a $k = \pm\frac{12}{13}$ **b** $k = \pm\frac{1}{\sqrt{5}}$

9 a $\overrightarrow{PQ} = \begin{pmatrix} 1 \\ 3 \end{pmatrix}$ **b** $|\overrightarrow{PQ}| = \sqrt{10}$ units   **c** $(3\frac{1}{2}, \frac{1}{2})$

10 a $t = 5$ **b** C divides [AB] in the ratio $2 : 1$.

11 a

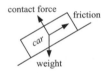

  b i isosceles triangle $\therefore$ 2 remaining angles $= 89°$ each, breeze makes angle of $180 - 89 = 91°$ to intended direction of the arrow.
    ii bisect angle $2°$ and use $\sin 1° = \dfrac{\frac{1}{2}\,\text{speed}}{|v|}$
         $\therefore$ speed $= 2|v|\sin 1°$

12 a $\approx 121°$ **b** ≈ 50.4 min

13 a i $-6i + 10j$ **ii** $-5i - 15j$
     iii $(-6 - 5t)i + (10 - 15t)j$, $t \geqslant 0$
  b after 40 minutes, $9\frac{1}{3}$ km

14 a $x_1(t) = 2 + t$, $y_1(t) = 4 - 3t$, $t \geqslant 0$
  b $x_2(t) = 13 - t$, $y_2(t) = (3 - 2a) + at$, $t \geqslant 2$
  c interception occurred at 2:22:30 pm
  d bearing $\approx 12.7°$ west of south, ≈ 4.54 km per minute

15 b $\overrightarrow{AD} = kq$ **d** It is parallel to the other two sides.

EXERCISE 19A

1 a

  c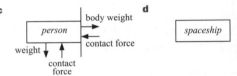

  e

  g contact force, friction, car, weight

2 The forces acting on the glider are lift, drag, and weight. The velocity will remain constant if these forces balance.

3 a $y = 100$ **b** $x = 5$, $y = 47$
  c $x = 65$, $y = 80$ **d** $x = 23$, $y = 2$

4 B because there is no other external force acting upon the spaceship.

5 a 10 N upwards. The object will accelerate upwards.
  b 0 N. The object will remain in its state of motion.

EXERCISE 19B

1 50 N   **2** $a = 2$ m s^{-2} **3** 419 400 N

4 a 30 N to the right   **b** $a = 3$ m s^{-2}

5 a 15.6 N downwards   **b** ≈ 1.59 kg

6 a 43 N   **b** horizontally in the direction of travel

7 a $\frac{1}{6}$ m s^{-2} ≈ 0.167 m s^{-2} to the right
  b $\frac{15}{17}$ m s^{-2} ≈ 0.882 m s^{-2} upwards

8 a 45 kg   **b** ≈ 4.33 kg

9 a ≈ 11.8 m s^{-2}
  b As the fuel is used up, the mass of the aircraft decreases. Assuming the forces stay the same, the acceleration will therefore increase.
  c Assuming acceleration is constant, time required $= 3.8$ seconds.

10 a ≈ 11.0 m s^{-2} **b** $\approx 20\,700$ N

EXERCISE 19C

1 a 58.8 N   **b** 147 N   **c** 235.2 N

2 a 2.5 kg   **b** 9 kg   **c** ≈ 10.3 kg

3 a 735 N   **b** 120 N

4 a $5g$ **b** $2\,\mathrm{m\,s}^{-2}$

5 a ≈ 240 kg   **b** ≈ 95.9 N

6 a 210 kg   **b** $\approx 0.714\,\mathrm{m\,s}^{-2}$ **c** $\approx 0.714\,\mathrm{m\,s}^{-2}$

7 a ≈ 3.83 seconds   **b** ≈ 71.7 m
   c $\approx 14.9m$ N upwards

8 $353\,800$ N

9 As the balloon rises, the weight of the string above the floor increases. The balloon stops moving upwards when the weight of the supporting string is equal to the buoyancy force of the balloon.

EXERCISE 19D

1 a 11.76 N upwards   **b** 3.724 N upwards
   c 49.98 N upwards

2 379.6 N upwards   **3** 1088 N upwards

4 a greater than   **b** less than   **c** same
   d same   **e** less than   **f** greater than

5 a 4753 N upwards   **b** 4830.6 N upwards
   c 4675.4 N upwards

6

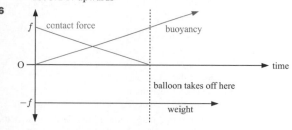

EXERCISE 19E

1 a Newton suggested that force causes *acceleration* rather than motion. Therefore motion is maintained in the *absence* of an external force.

   b The friction force between the book and the table surface is an external resistance force which changes the motion of the book. The friction force will continue to slow the book down until it comes to a complete stop.

2 From Newton's Second Law, $a = \dfrac{F}{m} = \dfrac{W}{m} = \dfrac{mg}{m} = g$ which is constant and independent of the mass of the object. Hence Newton's laws suggest that the objects fall at the same rate.

3 686 N upwards

EXERCISE 19F

1 a 137.2 N   **b** 78.4 N

2 a $\frac{1}{9}g$ **b** ≈ 87.1 N

3 a $m \approx 3.31$ **b** $m \approx 7.56$

4 ≈ 0.568 kg   **5** ≈ 2.64 kg

6 acceleration of $C = -\frac{17}{143}g \approx -0.119g$, $T = \frac{56}{143}g \approx 0.392g$

7 $m = 8$

REVIEW SET 19A

1 a

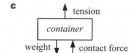

   b

   c

d

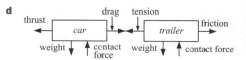

2 $x = 50$, $y = 150$ **3** 767 N   **4** $\approx 5.35\,\mathrm{m\,s}^{-2}$

5 Since the driver is travelling forward with the motion of the car, he will continue in this state unless acted on by an external force. While the accident provides an external force for the car to stop, the driver is not stopped since he is not wearing his seat belt. Therefore he continues to travel forward into the windscreen. When the driver comes into contact with the windscreen, the contact force decelerates the driver. The opposing force to the contact force (the force exerted on the windscreen by the driver) exceeds the strength of the windscreen, thereby causing it to break.

6 1.078×10^5 N

7 a $a = 0.576\,\mathrm{m\,s}^{-2}$, $T = 186$ N   **b** ≈ 2.78 seconds

REVIEW SET 19B

1 a

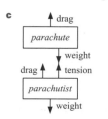

   b

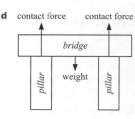

2 a $c = 98$ **b** $a = \dfrac{20}{m}\,\mathrm{m\,s}^{-2}$ **3** ≈ 41.0 kg

4 The ball will continue in its state of motion unless acted on by an external force. So, if there is nothing restraining the ball then it will roll towards the front of the train when the train decelerates, and roll towards the back of the train when the train accelerates.

5 a $a = 1.96\,\mathrm{m\,s}^{-2}$, $T = 23.5$ N
   b **i** $v \approx 4.43\,\mathrm{m\,s}^{-1}$ upwards
      ii When A suddenly stops, B continues to travel upwards and the string becomes slack. The only force on B is now its weight m g. It therefore now accelerates downwards due to gravity. It will reach a maximum, then fall back down until it comes to rest again due to the tension of the string.

6 a 813.4 N   **b** 41.5 N
   c We have assumed there is no resistance force making it more difficult for the donkey. In reality, friction would provide resistance, and the main purpose of the rolling wheels is to minimise friction.

7 a $a = \frac{1}{3}g\,\mathrm{m\,s}^{-2}$ upwards,   tension $= \frac{2}{3}g$ N
   b An extra 1 kg should be added.

EXERCISE 20A.1

1 This sample is too small to draw reliable conclusions from.

2 • The sample size is very small and may not be representative of the whole population.
   • The sample was taken in a London shopping mall. People living in the country are probably not represented.

3 **a** The sample is likely to under-represent full-time weekday working voters.

b The members of the golf club may not be representative of the whole electorate.

c Only people who catch the train in the morning such as full-time workers or students will be sampled.

d The voters in the street may not be representative of those in the whole electorate.

4 **a** The sample size is too small.

b With only 10 sheep being weighed, any errors in the measuring of weights will have more impact on the results.

5 **a** The journalist's question is worded in such a way as to lead the respondents to answer in a certain way.

b For example, "What are your views about the Government's proposed plan to move funding from education to health?".

6 **a** The whole population is being considered, not just a sample. There will be no sampling error as this is a census.

b measurement error

7 **a** Many of the workers may not return or even complete the survey.

b There may be more responses to the survey as many workers would feel that it is easier to complete a survey online rather than on paper and mailing it back. Responses would also be received more quickly however some workers may not have internet access and will therefore be unable to complete the survey.

EXERCISE 20A.2

1 **Note:** Sample answers only - many answers are possible.

a 12, 6, 23, 10, 21, 25

b 11, 2, 10, 17, 24, 14, 25, 1, 21, 7

c 14, 24, 44, 34, 27, 1

d 166, 156, 129, 200, 452

2 **a** Select 5 random numbers between 1 and 365 inclusive. For example, 65, 276, 203, 165, and 20 represent March 5, October 2, July 21, June 13, and January 20.

b Select a random number between 1 and 52 inclusive. Take the week starting on the Monday that lies in that week.

c Select a random number between 1 and 12 inclusive.

d Select 3 random numbers between 1 and 12 inclusive.

e Select a random number between 1 and 10 inclusive for the starting month.

f Select 5 random numbers between 153 and 244 inclusive. (June 1 - August 31)

g Select 4 random numbers between 1 and 52 inclusive. Choose the Wednesday that lies in that week.

3 **a** 17, 67, 117, 167, 217

b 1600 blocks of chocolate

4 **a** The people arriving first will spend more time at the game, and so are more likely to spend more than £20. Also, the sample size is relatively small.

b For example, systematic sample of every 10th person through the gate.

5 **a** systematic sampling   **b** 14 days

c Only visitors who use the library on Mondays will be counted. Mondays may not be representative of all of the days.

6 **a** 160 members

b 20 tennis members, 15 lawn bowls members, 5 croquet members

7 1 departmental manager, 3 supervisors, 9 senior sales staff, 13 junior sales staff, 4 shelf packers

8 **a** self-selected sampling

b The council will only receive the views from the public who attend the seminar. The sample may not be representative of the whole population. For example, the people who attend the seminar are likely to have strong negative opinions about the project.

9 **a** The people in the sample are particularly relevant to the study, as they are diabetic.

b 62.5%

c The volunteers must have had access to the advertisement in the medical journal, so the sample may be biased toward people who read medical journals, such as medical professionals. It may therefore exclude people who do not read such journals. The study also only looks at volunteers aged 60 and over, so the sample is biased toward people in this age group. The drug may have a different reaction for younger diabetics. If the medication is only targeted for older diabetics then this is not an issue but otherwise it may be a problem.

10 **a** All students in Years 11 and 12 were asked, not just a sample.

b 0.48

c **i** Sample too small to be representative.

ii Sample too small to be representative.

iii Valid but unnecessarily large sample size.

iv Useful and valid technique.

v Useful and valid technique.

vi Useful and valid technique.

d **v** is simple random sampling, while **iii** and **iv** are systematic sampling, and **vi** is stratified sampling.

EXERCISE 20B

1 **a** discrete   **b** continuous   **c** continuous

d discrete   **e** discrete   **f** continuous

2 *Age*: continuous, *Height*: continuous, *Wins*: discrete, *Speed*: continuous, *Ranking*: discrete, *Prize money*: discrete

3 **a** discrete

b

Number of customers	Tally	Frequency
6	I	1
7	I	1
8	IIII	4
9	III	3
10	II	2
11	II	2
12	I	1

c **i** $\approx 28.6\%$ **ii** $\approx 21.4\%$

4 **a** continuous

b

Time (t min)	Tally	Frequency
$0 \leqslant t < 5$	HHT I	6
$5 \leqslant t < 10$	HHT HHT HHT HHT HHT I	26
$10 \leqslant t < 15$	HHT HHT III	13
$15 \leqslant t < 20$	HHT IIII	9
$20 \leqslant t < 25$	HHT I	6
Total		60

c **i** 13 parents   **ii** 9 parents   **iii** 28 parents

EXERCISE 20C.1

1 **a** approximately symmetric   **b** no

2 **a**
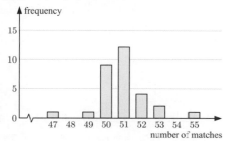

b positively skewed with outliers of 47 and 55

3 **a**

Number of guests	Frequency
0	6
1	11
2	16
3	5
4	2
Total	40

b
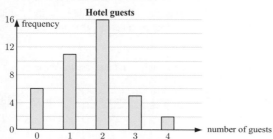

c positively skewed, no outliers

4 **a**

Number of target hits	Tally	Frequency
7	|	1
8	||||	4
9	ⅢⅡ	5
10	ⅢⅡ |	6
11	ⅢⅡ	5
12	||	2
13		0
14		0
15		0
16		0
17		0
18	|	1

b
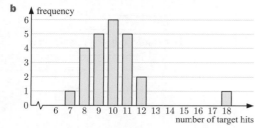

c The outlier is 18, which must be a recording error as each student took only 15 shots at the target so the maximum possible number of hits is 15.

EXERCISE 20C.2

1 **a** positively skewed, no outliers   **b** 5 units

c

Score (s)	Frequency
$5 \leqslant s < 10$	7
$10 \leqslant s < 15$	13
$15 \leqslant s < 20$	17
$20 \leqslant s < 25$	3
$25 \leqslant s < 30$	1

d **i** 30 scores
ii 21 scores

2 **a**

Height (h cm)	Frequency	Frequency density
$120 \leqslant h < 130$	1	0.1
$130 \leqslant h < 140$	2	0.2
$140 \leqslant h < 150$	7	0.7
$150 \leqslant h < 160$	14	1.4
$160 \leqslant h < 170$	1	0.1

b
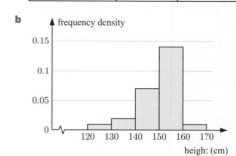

c negatively skewed

3 **a**

Time (t hours)	Frequency
$0 \leqslant t < 0.5$	1
$0.5 \leqslant t < 1$	0
$1 \leqslant t < 2$	12
$2 \leqslant t < 3$	12
$3 \leqslant t < 5$	8
$5 \leqslant t < 8$	2

b 22 customers

c
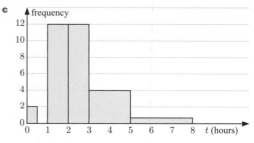

d positively skewed

4 **a** 15.32 minutes. The outlier should not be removed as the increased time could result from heavier traffic than usual, roadworks, or a traffic accident, etc.

b **i**

Time (t minutes)	Frequency
$9 \leqslant t < 10$	14
$10 \leqslant t < 11$	5
$11 \leqslant t < 12$	0
$12 \leqslant t < 13$	0
$13 \leqslant t < 14$	0
$14 \leqslant t < 15$	0
$15 \leqslant t < 16$	1

ii

Time (t minutes)	Frequency
$9.25 \leqslant t < 9.5$	1
$9.5 \leqslant t < 9.75$	3
$9.75 \leqslant t < 10$	10
$10 \leqslant t < 10.25$	3
$10.25 \leqslant t < 10.5$	2
$10.5 \leqslant t < 16$	1

c i

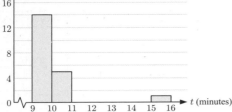

positively skewed with an outlier of 15.32

ii

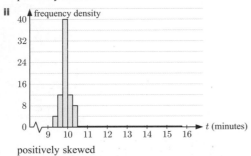

positively skewed

d c i illustrates the distribution better. It clearly shows that all the times are tightly grouped between 9 and 11 minutes, except for the outlier of 15.32.
c ii shows the distribution of times between 9 and 11 minutes in more detail, but the outlier in the interval $10.5 \leqslant t < 16$ is confusing, and we are less certain of the exact original data values.

EXERCISE 20D.1

1 a i ≈ 5.61 **ii** 6   **iii** 6
  b i ≈ 16.3 **ii** 17   **iii** 18
  c i ≈ 24.8 **ii** 24.9   **iii** 23.5

2 a mean: £29 300, median: £23 500, mode: £23 000
  b The mode is the lowest value, so does not take the higher values into account.
  c No, since the data is positively skewed, the median is not in the centre.

3 a mean: ≈ 3.19 mm, median: 0 mm, mode: 0 mm
  b The data is very positively skewed so the median is not in the centre.
  c The mode is the lowest value so does not take the higher values into account.
  d yes, 21 mm and 42 mm   **e** no

4 a i pies: ≈ 67.1, pasties: ≈ 53.6
    ii pies: 69, pasties: 52
  b Pie, as it has a higher mean and median.

5 a mean = £183 770, median = £147 200
  b mean selling price   **c** median selling price

6 £185 604   **7** 3144 km   **8** 17.25 goals per game

9 $x = 15$ **10** 37 marks   **11** ≈ 14.8 **12** 6 and 12

EXERCISE 20D.2

1 a 1 person   **b** 2 people   **c** ≈ 2.03 people

2 a i 2.96 phone calls **ii** 2 phone calls **iii** 2 phone calls
  b

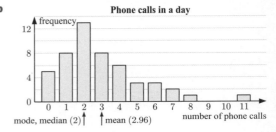

Phone calls in a day

  c positively skewed
  d The mean takes into account the larger numbers of phone calls.
  e the mean

3 a i 49 matches   **ii** 49 matches   **iii** ≈ 49.0 matches
  b no
  c The sample of only 30 is not large enough. The company could have won its case by arguing that a larger sample would have found an average of 50 matches per box.

4 a i ≈ 2.61 children   **ii** 2 children   **iii** 2 children
  b This school has more children per family than the average British family.
  c positively skewed
  d The values at the higher end increase the mean more than the median and the mode.

5 a

Pocket money (£)	Frequency
1	4
2	9
3	2
4	6
5	8

  b 29 children
  c i $\approx$ £3.17
    ii £3
    iii £2
  d the mode

6 10.1 cm   **7 a** $x = 5$ **b** 75%

8 a i £63 000 **ii** £56 000 **iii** £66 600   **b** the mean

EXERCISE 20D.3

1 a 40 phone calls   **b** ≈ 15 minutes   **2** ≈ 31.7

3 a 70 service stations   **b** $\approx 411 000$ litres (≈ 411 kL)
  c ≈ 5870 L
  d $6000 < L \leqslant 7000$ is the modal class as each class interval has the same width, and this class has the highest frequency.

4 a

Runs scored	Tally	Frequency
0 - 9	︴︴ ︴︴ ︴	11
10 - 19	︴︴ ︴︴︴	8
20 - 29	︴︴ ︴︴︴	8
30 - 39	︴︴	2
	Total	29

  b ≈ 14.8 runs
  c ≈ 14.9 runs   The estimate in **b** was very accurate.

5 a $110 \leqslant s < 120$ **b**

Score	Frequency
$80 \leqslant s < 100$	15
$100 \leqslant s < 110$	25
$110 \leqslant s < 120$	45
$120 \leqslant s < 125$	15
$125 \leqslant s < 130$	10
$130 \leqslant s < 140$	15
$140 \leqslant s < 160$	10

c 135 people   **d** $\frac{8}{27}$ **e** $\approx 18.5\%$ **f** ≈ 117

EXERCISE 20E.1

1 a *Data set A*: mean $= \dfrac{10 + 7 + 5 + 8 + 10}{5} = 8$

Data set B: mean $= \dfrac{4 + 12 + 11 + 14 + 1 + 6}{6} = 8$

b Data set B appears to have a greater spread than data set A, as data set B has more values that are a long way from the mean, such as 1 and 14.

c *Data set A*: $\sigma^2 = 3.6$, $\sigma \approx 1.90$
Data set B: $\sigma^2 \approx 21.7$, $\sigma \approx 4.65$

2 a $\sigma \approx 1.59$ **b** $\sigma^2 \approx 2.54$

3 a $\mu = 24.25$, $\sigma \approx 3.07$ **b** $\mu = 28.25$, $\sigma \approx 3.07$

c If each data value is increased or decreased by the same amount, then the mean will also be increased or decreased by that amount, however the population standard deviation will be unchanged.

4 $s \approx 2.71$ glasses

5 a *Danny*: ≈ 3.21 hours; *Jennifer*: 2 hours
b Danny
c *Danny*: $s \approx 0.726$ hours; *Jennifer*: $s \approx 0.439$ hours
d Jennifer

6 a

	Mean $\overline{x}$	Median	Standard deviation s	Range
Boys	39.1	35.5	≈ 13.6	38
Girls	49.6	49.5	≈ 7.69	26

b **i** boys   **ii** boys
c Tyson could increase his sample size.

7 a **i** *Museum*: ≈ 934 visitors; *Art gallery*: ≈ 1230 visitors
ii *Museum*: ≈ 211 visitors; *Art gallery*: ≈ 86.0 visitors
b the museum
c **i** '0' is an outlier.
ii This outlier corresponded to Christmas Day, so the museum was probably closed which meant there were no visitors on that day.
iii Yes, although the outlier is not an error, it is not a true reflection of a visitor count for a particular day.
iv *Museum*: mean ≈ 965 visitors, $s \approx 123$ visitors
v The outlier had greatly increased the sample standard deviation.

8 $p = 6$, $q = 9$ **9** $a = 8$, $b = 6$ **10 b** $\mu = \pm 8.7$

EXERCISE 20E.2

1 a $\sigma \approx 0.775$ **b** $\sigma \approx 0.775$
2 $\mu = 14.48$ years, $\sigma \approx 1.75$ years
3 a The female students' marks are in the range 16 to 20 whereas the male students' marks are in the range 12 to 19.
i the females   **ii** the males
b *Females*: $\mu \approx 17.5$, $\sigma \approx 1.02$
Males: $\mu \approx 15.5$, $\sigma \approx 1.65$

REVIEW SET 20A

1 a Students studying Italian may have an Italian background so surveying these students may produce a biased result.
b For example, Andrew could survey a randomly selected group of students as they entered the school grounds one morning.

2 a It would be too time consuming and expensive.

b

Age range	< 18	18 - 39	40 - 54	55 - 70	> 70
Sample size	50	82	123	69	26

3 a discrete   **b** positively skewed
c **i** 1 goal   **ii** 1.2 goals   **iii** 1 goal

4 a

Height (h cm)	Frequency density
$130 \leqslant h < 150$	0.05
$150 \leqslant h < 160$	1.3
$160 \leqslant h < 165$	4.4
$165 \leqslant h < 170$	3.6
$170 \leqslant h < 175$	4
$175 \leqslant h < 180$	2
$180 \leqslant h < 190$	0.3
Total	

b

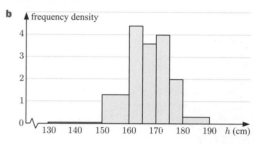

c $160 \leqslant h < 165$ cm   **d** slightly negatively skewed

5 a **i** ≈ 4.67 **ii** 5
b **i** 3.99   **ii** 3.9

6 a

	mean (seconds)	median (seconds)
Week 1	≈ 16.0	16.3
Week 2	≈ 15.1	15.1
Week 3	≈ 14.4	14.3
Week 4	14.0	14.0

b Yes, Heike's mean and median times have gradually decreased each week which indicates that her speed has improved over the 4 week period.

7 $a = 8$, $b = 6$

8 a discrete   **b** 11 - 20 points
c We do not know each individual data value, only the intervals they fall in, so we cannot calculate the mean winning margin exactly.
d ≈ 22.6 points

9 a $\sigma \approx 3.39$ **b** $\sigma \approx 3.39$

10 a Kevin: $\overline{x} = 41.2$ min; Felicity: $\overline{x} = 39.5$ min
b Kevin: $s \approx 7.81$ min; Felicity: $s \approx 9.46$ min
c Felicity   **d** Kevin

11 10

REVIEW SET 20B

1 a discrete   **b** continuous   **c** discrete
2 a systematic sampling
b A house will be visited if the last digit in its number is equal to the random number chosen by the promoter, with the random number 10 corresponding to the digit 0. Each house therefore has a 1 in 10 chance of being visited.
c Once the first house number has been chosen, the remaining houses chosen must all have the same second digit in their house number, that is, they are not randomly chosen. For example, it is impossible for two consecutively numbered houses to be selected for the sample.

3 a Petra's teacher colleagues are quite likely to ignore the emailed questionnaire as emails are easy to ignore.

b It is likely that the teachers who have responded will have strong opinions either for or against the general student behaviour. These responses may therefore not be representative of all teachers' views.

4 a

Number of tickets	Tally	Frequency
0	|	1
1	|||	3
2	卌	5
3	卌 卌	10
4	卌	5
5	|||	3
6	|	1

b

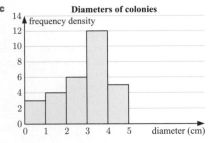

c The data is symmetric with no outliers.

5 a continuous

b

Diameter (d cm)	Tally	Frequency
$0 \leqslant d < 1$	|||	3
$1 \leqslant d < 2$	||||	4
$2 \leqslant d < 3$	卌 |	6
$3 \leqslant d < 4$	卌 卌 ||	12
$4 \leqslant d < 5$	卌	5
	Total	30

c

Diameters of colonies

frequency density / diameter (cm)

d $3 \leqslant d < 4$ **e** slightly negatively skewed

6 a 5   **b** 3.52   **c** 3.5

7 a $x = 7$ **b** 6   **8** 7 and 9

9 a $30 \leqslant x < 35$

b

Score (x)	Class interval width	Frequency	Midpoint
$10 \leqslant x < 20$	10	2	15
$20 \leqslant x < 25$	5	14	22.5
$25 \leqslant x < 30$	5	22	27.5
$30 \leqslant x < 35$	5	30	32.5
$35 \leqslant x < 50$	15	12	42.5
Total		80	

c $\overline{x} \approx 30.4$

10 a $\mu \approx 49.6$, $\sigma \approx 1.60$

b It does not justify the claim. A larger sample is needed.

EXERCISE 21A

1 a weak, positive, linear correlation, with no outliers
b strong, negative, linear correlation, with one outlier
c no correlation
d strong, negative, non-linear correlation, with one outlier
e moderate, positive, linear correlation, with no outliers
f weak, positive, non-linear correlation, with no outliers

2 a *Hours worked* is the explanatory variable.
Number of customers is the response variable.

b

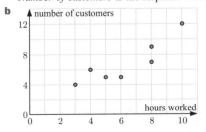

c **i** Monday and Friday   **ii** Wednesday and Sunday
d The more hours that Tiffany works, the more customers she is likely to have.

3 a

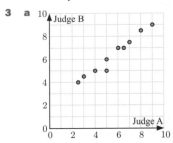

b There appears to be **strong, positive, linear** correlation between Judge A's scores and Judge B's scores. This means that as Judge A's scores increase, Judge B's scores **increase**.
c No, the scores are related to the quality of the ice-skaters' performances.

4 a **i** job G   **ii** job C

b

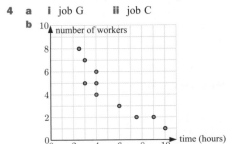

c There is a strong, negative, non-linear correlation between *number of workers* and *time*.

5 a D   **b A**   **c B**   **d C**

6 a There is a moderate, positive, linear correlation between *hours of study* and *marks obtained*.
b The test is out of 50 marks, so the outlier (> 50) appears to be an error. It should be discarded.
c Yes, this is a causal relationship as spending more time studying for the test, is likely to cause a higher mark.

7 a Not causal, dependent on genetics and/or age.
b Not causal, dependent on the size of the fire.

c Causal, an increase in advertising is likely to cause an increase in sales.

d Causal, the childrens' adult height is determined by the genetics they receive from their parents to a great extent.

e Not causal, dependent on population of town.

EXERCISE 21B.1

1 weak, positive correlation

2 a B   b A   c D   d C   e E

3 a i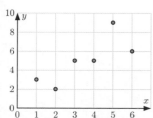

ii $r \approx 0.786$
iii moderate, positive correlation

b i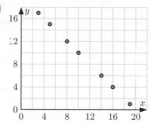

ii $r = -1$
iii perfect, negative correlation

c i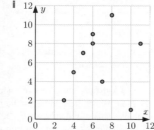

ii $r \approx 0.146$
iii very weak, positive correlation

4 a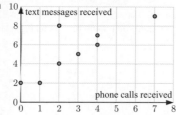

b $r \approx 0.816$
c moderate, positive correlation
d Those students who receive several phone calls are also likely to receive several text messages and vice versa.

5 a $r \approx 0.917$
b strong, positive correlation
In general, the higher the young athlete's age, the further they can throw a discus.

6 a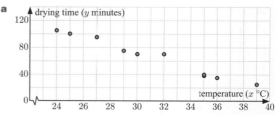

b $r \approx -0.987$ c very strong, negative correlation

7 a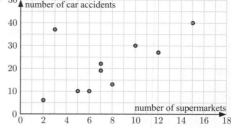

b $r \approx 0.572$
c The point $(3, 37)$, which represents 37 car accidents in a town with 3 supermarkets, is an outlier.
d i $r \approx 0.928$ ii strong, positive correlation
iii Removing the outlier had a very significant effect on the value of r.
e No, it is not a causal relationship. Both variables depend on the number of people in each town, not on each other.

8 a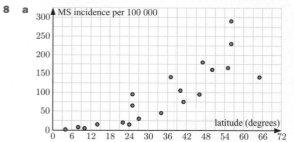

b $r \approx 0.849$ c moderate, positive correlation
d The incidence of MS is higher near the poles.

EXERCISE 21B.2

1 57.8% of the variation in the number of visitors can be explained by the variation in maximum temperature.

2 $r^2 \approx 0.598$. 59.8% of the variation in the amount of money lost can be explained by the variation in time spent gambling.

3 $r^2 \approx 0.133$. 13.3% of the variation in heart rate can be explained by the variation in age.

4 $r \approx -0.906$

5 a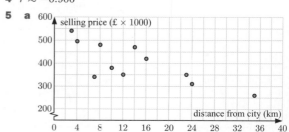

b $r^2 \approx 0.561$ c $\approx 56.1\%$

d The age of the house, the size of the land.

6 a

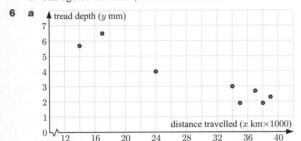

b $r^2 \approx 0.904$. 90.4% of the variation in tread depth can be explained by the variation in the distance travelled.

EXERCISE 21C

1 a, c

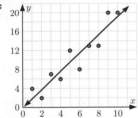

b $y \approx 1.92x - 0.0667$

2 a

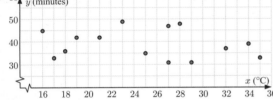

b $r \approx -0.219$

c There is a very weak, negative correlation between *temperature* and *time*.

d No, as there is almost no correlation.

3 a $r \approx -0.924$

b There is a strong, negative, linear correlation between the *petrol price* and the *number of customers*.

c $y \approx -4.27x + 489$

d ≈ -4.27; this indicates that for every cent per litre the petrol price increases by, the number of customers will decrease by approximately 4.27.

e ≈ -5.10 customers

f ≈ 105.3 cents per litre

g In **e**, it is impossible to have a negative number of customers. This extrapolation is not valid.
In **f**, this is an interpolation, so this estimate is likely to be reliable.

4 a

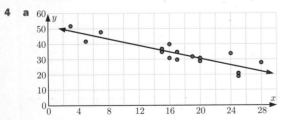

b $r \approx -0.878$

c There is a strong, negative correlation between *number of speed cameras* and *number of car accidents*.

d $y \approx -1.06x + 52.0$

e gradient: ≈ -1.06; this indicates that for every additional speed camera, the number of car accidents per week decreases by an average of 1.06.
y-intercept: ≈ 52.0; this indicates that if there were no speed cameras in a city, an average of 52.0 car accidents would occur each week.

f ≈ 41.4 car accidents

5 a, d

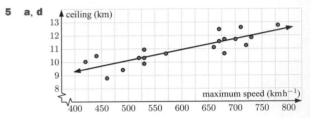

b $r \approx 0.840$

c moderate, positive, linear correlation

d $y \approx 0.008\,12x + 6.09$

e $\approx 0.008\,12$; this indicates that for each additional $\mathrm{km\,h}^{-1}$, the ceiling increases by an average of 0.008 12 km or 8.12 m.

f ≈ 11.0 km   **g** $\approx 605\ \mathrm{km\,h}^{-1}$

6 a, d

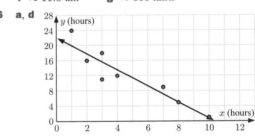

b $r \approx -0.927$

c There is a strong, negative, linear correlation between time exercising and time watching television.

d $y \approx -2.13x + 22.1$

e gradient: ≈ -2.13; this indicates that for each additional hour a child exercises each week, the number of hours they spend watching television each week decreases by 2.13.
y-intercept: ≈ 22.1; this indicates that for children who do not spend time exercising, they would watch television for an average of 22.1 hours per week.

f   **i** 9 hours per week
ii ≈ 7.22 hours per week
iii This particular child spent more time watching television than predicted.

7 a

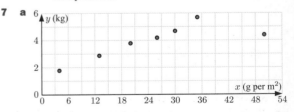

(50, 4.4) is the outlier.

b   **i** reduces the strength of the correlation
ii decreases the gradient of the regression line

c   **i** $r \approx 0.798$ **ii** $r \approx 0.993$

d   **i** $y \approx 0.0672x + 2.22$ **ii** $y \approx 0.119x + 1.32$

e The one which excludes the outlier, as this will be more accurate for an interpolation.

f Too much fertiliser often kills the plants. In this case, the outlier should be kept when analysing the data as it is a valid data value. If the outlier is a recording error caused by bad measurement or recording skills, it should be removed before analysing data.

EXERCISE 21D.1

1 a $y \approx 7.39 \times 1.82^x$ **b** $G \approx 0.607 \times 4.48^t$
 c $Q \approx 1100 \times 0.174^n$

2 a
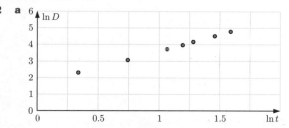

b The scatter diagram of $\ln y$ against x appears to follow a linear trend.
 c $\ln y \approx 0.0627x + 5.77$
 d $y \approx 320 \times 1.06^x$
 e **i** ≈ 529 **ii** ≈ 2874

3 a

b The scatter diagram of $\ln V$ against t appears to be linear.
 c $\ln V \approx -0.105t + 5.70$
 d $V \approx 300 \times 0.900^t$
 e ≈ 97.9 minutes

EXERCISE 21D.2

1 a $y \approx 2.72 \times x^{0.25}$ **b** $R \approx 0.135 \times p^3$
 c $T \approx 66.7 \times k^{-0.4}$

2 a
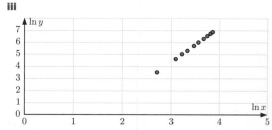

b The scatter diagram of $\ln D$ against $\ln t$ appears to be linear.
 c $\ln D \approx 1.97 \ln t + 1.62$
 d $D \approx 5.04 \times t^{1.97}$

3 a
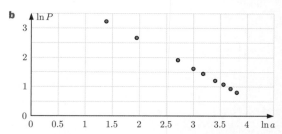

b
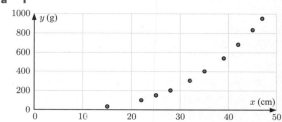

The scatter diagram of $\ln P$ against $\ln a$ appears to be linear, so a power model is appropriate.
 c $\ln P \approx -1.00 \ln a + 4.61$
 d $P \approx 100 \times a^{-1.00}$
 e $P \approx 10.0$ pascals
 The estimate is reliable as we are interpolating.

EXERCISE 21E

1 a i
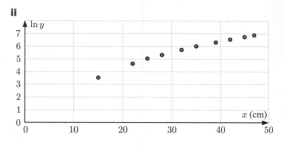

 ii

 iii

b The scatter diagram of $\ln y$ against $\ln x$ is linear.
 c $\ln y \approx 2.94 \ln x - 4.48$, $r^2 \approx 0.9998$
 d $y \approx 0.0113 \times x^{2.94}$

2　a　i

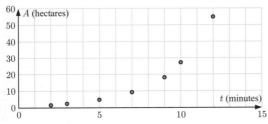

ii

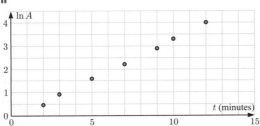

iii

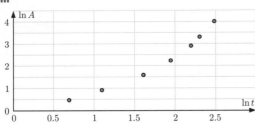

b The scatter diagram of $\ln A$ against t follows a linear trend.

c $\ln A \approx 0.347t - 0.178$,　$r^2 \approx 0.999$

d $A \approx 0.837 \times 1.42^t$

3　a　i

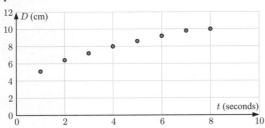

ii

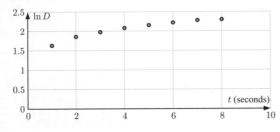

iii

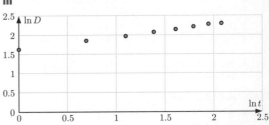

b The scatter diagram of $\ln D$ against $\ln t$ appears to be linear, so a power model is appropriate.

c $D \approx 5.08 \times t^{0.330}$

d $D \approx 7.67$ cm,　and since this is an interpolation, this estimate is likely to be reliable.

4　a　i

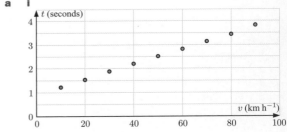

ii

iii

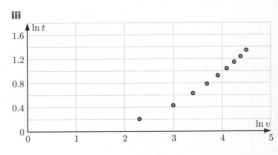

b The scatter diagram of t against v appears to be linear, so a linear model is appropriate.

c $t \approx 0.0322v + 0.906$　　**d** $t \approx 4.44$ seconds

5　a $V \approx 250 \times 1.03^t$　　**b** $V \approx £522\,000$

6　a $a \approx 0.997,\ k \approx 1.50$　　**b** appropriate, as $r \approx 1$

　　c As $a \approx 1$ and $k \approx \frac{3}{2}$,　$T \propto r^{\frac{3}{2}}$
　　　　　　　　　　　　　　　　　$\therefore\ T^2 \propto r^3$

REVIEW SET 21A

1　a strong, positive, linear correlation, with no outliers

　b weak, negative, linear correlation, with one outlier

　c strong, negative, non-linear correlation, with no outliers

2 **a** The correlation between water bills and electricity bills is likely to be positive, as a household with a high water bill is also likely to have a high electricity bill, and vice versa.

  b No, there is not a causal relationship. Both variables mainly depend on the number of occupants in each house.

3 **a**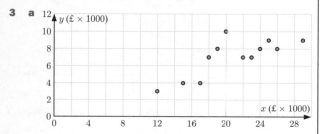

  b $r \approx 0.776$

  c moderate, positive correlation

4 **a**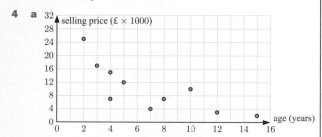

  b moderate, negative correlation

  c $r^2 \approx 0.608$

  d $\approx 60.8\%$

  e mileage, condition, and features

5 **a**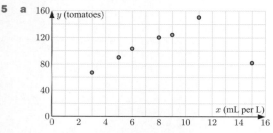

  b $r \approx 0.340$. This is a very weak, positive, linear correlation between spray concentrations and yield.

  c Yes, $(15, 82)$ is an outlier.

  d $r \approx 0.994$. Yes it is now reasonable to draw a regression line.

  e $y \approx 9.93x + 39.5$

  f gradient: ≈ 9.93; this indicates that for every additional mL per L the spray concentration increases, the yield of tomatoes per bush increases on average by 9.93.

  y-intercept: ≈ 39.5; this indicates that if the tomato bushes are not sprayed, the average yield per bush is approximately 39.5 tomatoes.

  g **i** ≈ 109 tomatoes per bush

  ii ≈ 16.2 mL per L

  h In **g i**, this is an interpolation, so this estimate is likely to be reliable.

  In **g ii**, this is an extrapolation, so this estimate may not be reliable.

6 **a**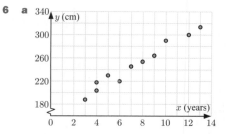

  b $y \approx 5.98x + 80.0$

  c ≈ 5.98; this indicates that each year, a child grows taller by an average of 5.98 cm.

  d ≈ 110 cm   **e** 10 years old

7 **a**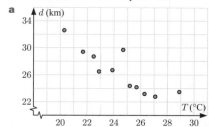

  b $r \approx -0.867$. There is a moderate, negative correlation between distance travelled and temperature.

  c $d \approx -1.11T + 53.6$ **d** ≈ 20.4 km

8 **a** $y \approx 20.1 \times 1.65^x$ **b** $P \approx 148 \times 0.435^n$

9 **a** **i**

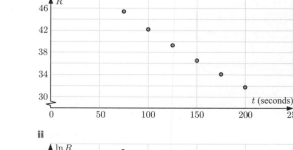

  ii

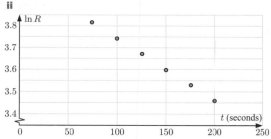

  iii

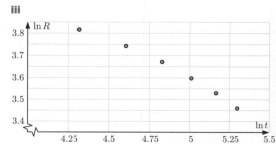

  b The scatter diagram of $\ln R$ against t appears to be linear ($r^2 \approx 0.999$), so an exponential model is most appropriate.

c $R \approx 56.1 \times 0.997^n$

d $R \approx 35.6$, and since we are interpolating, this estimate is likely to be reliable.

10 a **i**

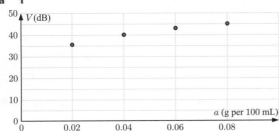

ii

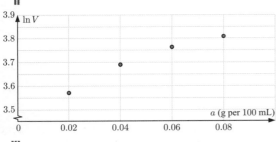

iii

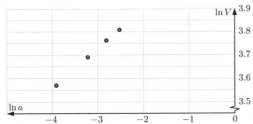

b The scatter diagram of $\ln V$ against $\ln A$ appears to be linear ($r^2 \approx 0.999$), so a power model is most appropriate.

c $V \approx 69.6 \times a^{0.172}$

d **i** $V \approx 50.2$ dB **ii** $V \approx 41.6$ dB

REVIEW SET 21B

1 a Negative correlation. As prices increase, the number of tickets sold is likely to decrease.
Causal. Less people will be able to afford tickets as the prices increase.

b Positive correlation. As ice cream sales increase, the number of shark attacks is likely to increase.
Not causal. Both of these variables are dependent on the number of people at the beach.

2 a moderate, positive correlation

b $r^2 \approx 0.619$. 61.9% of the variation in energy can be explained by the variation in fat content.

3 a

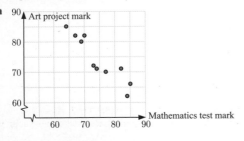

b There is a strong, negative, linear correlation between the Mathematics and Art marks.

c $r \approx -0.930$

4 a, d

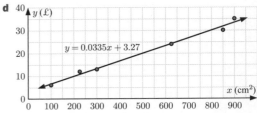

b $r \approx 0.994$

c There is a very strong, positive correlation between *area* and *price*.

e $\approx £43.42$, this is an extrapolation, so it may be unreliable.

5 a

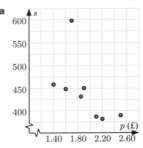

b Yes, the point $(1.7, 597)$ is an outlier. It should not be deleted as there is no evidence that it is a mistake.

c $s \approx -116p + 665$

d ≈ -116; this indicates that with every additional pound the price increases by, the number of sales decreases by 116.

e No, the prediction would not be accurate, as it is an extrapolation.

6 $y \approx 54.6 \times x^{-2}$

7 a

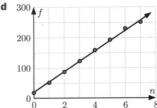

b $r \approx 0.989$, $r^2 \approx 0.978$

c There is a very strong, positive, linear correlation between cherry yield and the number of frosts.

d $y \approx 0.138x + 1.83$

e **i** ≈ 5.83 tonnes **ii** ≈ 16 frosts

8 a, d

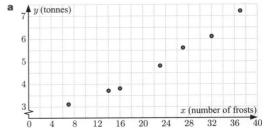

There is a very strong, positive correlation between number of waterings and flowers produced.

b $f \approx 34.0n + 19.3$

c Yes, plants need water to grow, so it is expected that an increase in watering will result in an increase in flowers.

e **i** 104 flowers $(n = 2.5)$,   359 flowers $(n = 10)$
   ii $n = 2.5$ is reliable, as it is an interpolation.
   $n = 10$ is unreliable as it is an extrapolation and over-watering could be a problem.

9 a i

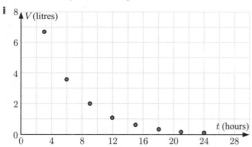

ii

iii

b $V \approx 12.1 \times (0.818)^t$
c ≈ 4.45 litres   **d** ≈ 10.5 litres

10 a $F \approx 138\,000 \times d^{-2.00}$, the graph of $\ln F$ against $\ln d$ is linear.

b **i** ≈ 162 newtons   **ii** ≈ 342 newtons
   iii $\approx 0.005\,39$ newtons

EXERCISE 22A

1 a {A, B, C, D}   **b** {BB, BG, GB, GG}
c {ABCD, ABDC, ACBD, ACDB, ADBC, ADCB, BACD, BADC, BCAD, BCDA, BDAC, BDCA, CABD, CADB, CBAD, CBDA, CDAB, CDBA, DABC, DACB, DBAC, DBCA, DCAB, DCBA}
d {GGG, GGB, GBG, BGG, GBB, BGB, BBG, BBB}

2 a

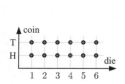

b

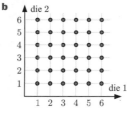

c

d

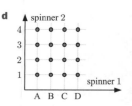

3 a

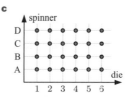

b

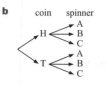

c

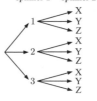

d

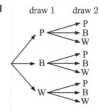

e

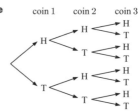

4 a **i** {(2, 1), (2, 3), (2, 5), (2, 7), (4, 1), (4, 3), (4, 5), (4, 7), (6, 1), (6, 3), (6, 5), (6, 7)}

ii

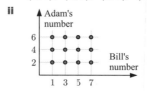

iii

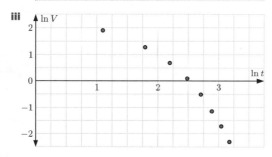

b 12 outcomes

EXERCISE 22B.1

1 a $\frac{1}{5}$ **b** $\frac{1}{3}$ **c** $\frac{7}{15}$ **d** $\frac{4}{5}$ **e** $\frac{1}{5}$ **f** $\frac{8}{15}$

2 a 4   **b** **i** $\frac{2}{3}$ **ii** $\frac{1}{3}$

3 a $\frac{1}{4}$ **b** $\frac{1}{9}$ **c** $\frac{4}{9}$ **d** $\frac{1}{36}$ **e** $\frac{1}{18}$ **f** $\frac{1}{6}$
g $\frac{1}{12}$ **h** $\frac{1}{3}$

4 a $\frac{1}{7}$ **b** $\frac{2}{7}$ **c** $\frac{124}{1461}$ **d** $\frac{237}{1461}$ {remember leap years}

5 a {AKN, ANK, KAN, KNA, NAK, NKA}

b i $\frac{1}{3}$ **ii** $\frac{1}{3}$ **iii** $\frac{2}{3}$ **iv** $\frac{2}{3}$

6 a {GGG, GGB, GBG, BGG, GBB, BGB, BBG, BBB}

b i $\frac{1}{8}$ **ii** $\frac{1}{8}$ **iii** $\frac{1}{8}$ **iv** $\frac{3}{8}$ **v** $\frac{1}{2}$ **vi** $\frac{7}{8}$

7 a {ABCD, ABDC, ACBD, ACDB, ADBC, ADCB,
BACD, BADC, BCAD, BCDA, BDAC, BDCA,
CABD, CADB, CBAD, CBDA, CDAB, CDBA,
DABC, DACB, DBAC, DBCA, DCAB, DCBA}

b i $\frac{1}{2}$ **ii** $\frac{1}{2}$ **iii** $\frac{1}{2}$ **iv** $\frac{1}{2}$

EXERCISE 22B.2

1  **a** $\frac{1}{4}$ **b** $\frac{1}{4}$

c $\frac{1}{2}$ **d** $\frac{3}{4}$

2 a 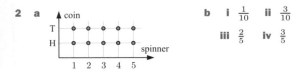 **b i** $\frac{1}{10}$ **ii** $\frac{3}{10}$

iii $\frac{2}{5}$ **iv** $\frac{3}{5}$

3 a $\frac{1}{36}$ **b** $\frac{1}{18}$ **c** $\frac{5}{9}$ **d** $\frac{11}{36}$ **e** $\frac{5}{18}$

f $\frac{25}{36}$ **g** $\frac{1}{6}$ **h** $\frac{5}{18}$ **i** $\frac{2}{9}$ **j** $\frac{13}{18}$

EXERCISE 22C

1 a $\frac{1}{24}$ **b** $\frac{1}{6}$

2 a $\frac{1}{8}$ **b** $\frac{1}{8}$

3 a 0.0096 **b** 0.8096

4 a $\frac{1}{16}$ **b** $\frac{15}{16}$

5 a 0.56 **b** 0.06 **c** 0.14 **d** 0.24

6 a $\frac{8}{125}$ **b** $\frac{12}{125}$ **c** $\frac{27}{125}$

EXERCISE 22D

1 a 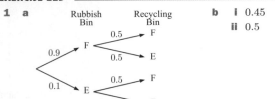 **b i** 0.45

ii 0.5

2 a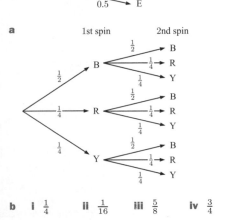

b i $\frac{1}{4}$ **ii** $\frac{1}{16}$ **iii** $\frac{5}{8}$ **iv** $\frac{3}{4}$

3 a 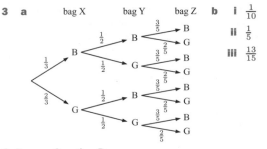 **b i** $\frac{1}{10}$

ii $\frac{1}{5}$

iii $\frac{13}{15}$

4 Penny - Quentin - Penny

To win 2 matches in a row, Kane must win the middle match, so he should play against the weaker player in this match.

EXERCISE 22E

1 a $A = \{1, 2, 3, 6\}$,
$B = \{2, 4, 6, 8, 10\}$

b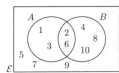

c i $n(A) = 4$

ii $A \cup B = \{1, 2, 3, 4, 6, 8, 10\}$

iii $A \cap B = \{2, 6\}$

2 a 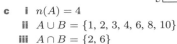 **b**

c **d**

e **f**

3 a **b**

A' is shaded. $A' \cap B$ is shaded.

c **d**

$A \cup B'$ is shaded. $A' \cap B'$ is shaded.

4 a **b**

c 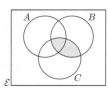   **d**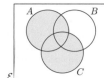

e 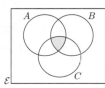   **f**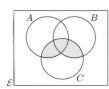

5 **a** 29   **b** 17   **c** 26   **d** 5

6 **a** $\frac{13}{62}$ **b** $\frac{49}{62}$ **7** **a** $\frac{9}{65}$ **b** $\frac{4}{65}$ **c** $\frac{52}{65}$

8 **a**

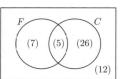

b **i** $\frac{19}{25}$

ii $\frac{13}{25}$

iii $\frac{6}{25}$

9 **a** $\frac{19}{40}$ **b** $\frac{1}{2}$ **c** $\frac{4}{5}$ **d** $\frac{5}{8}$ **e** $\frac{13}{40}$

10 **a** $\frac{7}{15}$ **b** $\frac{1}{15}$ **c** $\frac{2}{15}$

11 **a** $a = 3$, $b = 3$

b **i** $\frac{3}{10}$ **ii** $\frac{1}{10}$ **iii** $\frac{7}{40}$ **iv** $\frac{3}{8}$ **v** $\frac{5}{8}$

EXERCISE 22F

1 $P(A \cup B) = 0.55$ **2** $P(B) = 0.6$ **3** $P(X \cap Y) = 0.2$

4 **a** $P(A \cap B) = 0$ **b** A and B are mutually exclusive.

5 $P(A) = 0.35$

6 **a** yes   **b** **i** $\frac{1}{4}$ **ii** $\frac{3}{20}$ **iii** 0   **iv** $\frac{2}{5}$

7 $P(A \cup B) = 1$

Hint: Show $P(A' \cup B') = 2 - P(A \cup B)$

REVIEW SET 22A

1 **a** {ABCD, ABDC, ACBD, ACDB, ADBC, ADCB, BACD, BADC, BCAD, BCDA, BDAC, BDCA, CABD, CADB, CBAD, CBDA, CDAB, CDBA, DABC, DACB, DBAC, DBCA, DCAB, DCBA}

b **i** $\frac{1}{2}$ **ii** $\frac{1}{3}$

2 **a** $\frac{3}{8}$ **b** $\frac{1}{8}$ **c** $\frac{5}{8}$ **3** **a** $\frac{2}{5}$ **b** $\frac{13}{15}$ **c** $\frac{4}{15}$

4 **a** 0   **b** 0.45   **c** 0.8

5 **a**

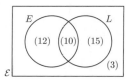

b **i** $\frac{2}{9}$

ii $\frac{5}{12}$

6 **a**

b **i** $\frac{1}{4}$

ii $\frac{37}{40}$

7 0.9975

8 **a** 0.28, $P(A \cap B) \neq 0$ **b** 0.82

REVIEW SET 22B

1 **a** $P(A') = 1 - m$ **b** $0 \leqslant m \leqslant 1$

c **i** $2m(1 - m)$ **ii** $2m - m^2$

2 **a** {BBBB, BBBG, BBGB, BGBB, GBBB, BBGG, BGBG, BGGB, GGBB, GBBG, GBGB, BGGG, GBGG, GGBG, GGGB, GGGG}

b P(2 children of each sex) $= \frac{3}{8}$

3 **a** $\frac{25}{144}$ **b** $\frac{25}{72}$ **c** $\frac{7}{16}$ **d** $\frac{4}{9}$

4 **a** $\frac{3}{25}$ **b** $\frac{24}{25}$ **5** 0.496

6 **a** 0.89   **b** 0.077   **c** 0.81

7 **a** $P(A \cup B) = 0.7$ **b** $P(A \cup B) = 0.6$

EXERCISE 23A

1 **a** continuous   **b** discrete   **c** continuous   **d** continuous

e discrete   **f** discrete   **g** continuous   **h** continuous

2 **a** **i** $X =$ the height of water in the rain gauge

ii continuous   **iii** $0 \leqslant X \leqslant 400$ mm

b **i** $X =$ stopping distance   **ii** continuous

iii $0 \leqslant X \leqslant 50$ m

c **i** number of switches until failure

ii discrete   **iii** any integer $\geqslant 1$

3 **a** X has a set of distinct possible values.

b $X = 2, 3, 4, 5, 6, 7, 8, 9,$ or 10

4 **a** $X = 4, 5, 6,$ or 7 **b** **i** $X = 5$ **ii** $X = 6$ or 7

5 **a** $X = 0, 1, 2, 3,$ or 4

b ✓✓✓✓   ✓✓✓✗   ✓✓✗✗   ✗✗✗✓   ✗✗✗✗
       ✓✓✗✓   ✓✗✓✗   ✗✗✓✗
       ✓✗✓✓   ✓✗✗✓   ✗✓✗✗
       ✗✓✓✓   ✗✗✓✓   ✓✗✗✗
                       ✗✓✗✓
                       ✗✓✓✗
 $(X = 4)$ $(X = 3)$ $(X = 2)$ $(X = 1)$ $(X = 0)$

c **i** $X = 2$ **ii** $X = 2, 3,$ or 4

6 **a** $X = 0, 1, 2,$ or 3

b HHH   HHT   TTH   TTT
              HTH   THT
              THH   HTT
 $(X = 3)$ $(X = 2)$ $(X = 1)$ $(X = 0)$

c No, for example there is probability $\frac{1}{8}$ that $X = 3$, and probability $\frac{3}{8}$ that $X = 2$.

EXERCISE 23B

1 **a** **i** yes   **ii** no   **iii** yes   **iv** no

b For **a iii**, X is a uniform random variable.

2 **a** $k = 0.2$ **b** $k = \frac{1}{7}$

3 **a** $a = 0.2$

b No, as the probabilities of each outcome are not all equal.

c 2   **d** $P(X \geqslant 2) = 0.65$

4 **a** $p(2) = 0.1088$

b $a = 0.5488$ is the probability that Jason does not hit a home run in a game.

c $p(1) + p(2) + p(3) + p(4) + p(5) = 0.4512$ and is the probability that Jason will hit one or more home runs in a game.

d

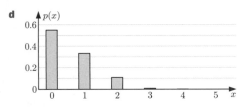

e mode = 0 home runs,   median = 0 home runs

5 **a** $k = 0.04$ **b** 0 tyres

c $P(X > 1) = 0.12$ which is the probability that more than 1 tyre will need replacing on a car being inspected.

6 **a**

x	1	2	3	4
$P(X=x)$	$\frac{3}{8}$	$\frac{2}{8}$	$\frac{1}{8}$	$\frac{2}{8}$

b

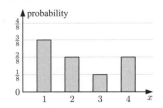

c mode = 1,   median = 2   **d** $P(X \leqslant 3) = \frac{3}{4}$

7 **a** $X = 1, 2, 3,$ or 4

b

x	1	2	3	4
$P(X=x)$	0.24	0.35	0.27	0.14

c mode = 2 bedrooms,   median = 2 bedrooms

8 **a** $X = 1, 2, 3,$ or 4

b

x	1	2	3	4
$P(X=x)$	0.48	0.28	0.08	0.16

c mode = 1 shot,   median = 2 shots

9 **a** $p(0) = \frac{1}{10}, \ p(1) = \frac{2}{10}, \ p(2) = \frac{3}{10}, \ p(3) = \frac{4}{10}$

$0 \leqslant p(x_i) \leqslant 1$ in each case, and

$$\sum_{i=1}^{n} p(x_i) = \frac{1}{10} + \frac{2}{10} + \frac{3}{10} + \frac{4}{10} = 1$$

$\therefore \ p(x)$ is a valid probability function.

b $p(1) = \frac{6}{11}, \ p(2) = \frac{6}{22}, \ p(3) = \frac{6}{33}$

$0 \leqslant p(x_i) \leqslant 1$ in each case, and

$$\sum_{i=1}^{n} p(x_i) = \frac{6}{11} + \frac{6}{22} + \frac{6}{33} = 1$$

$\therefore \ p(x)$ is a valid probability function.

10 **a** $k = \frac{1}{12}$ **b** $k = \frac{12}{25}$

11 **a** $a = 10$ **b** $P(X = 1) = \frac{3}{10}$ **c** 2

EXERCISE 23C.1

1 **a** The binomial distribution applies, as tossing a coin has two possible outcomes (H or T) and each toss is independent of every other toss.

b The binomial distribution applies, as this is equivalent to tossing one coin 100 times.

c The binomial distribution applies as we can draw out a red or a blue marble with the same chances each time.

d The binomial distribution does not apply as the result of each draw is dependent upon the results of previous draws.

e The binomial distribution does not apply, assuming that ten bolts are drawn without replacement. We do not have a repetition of independent trials. However, since there is such a large number of bolts in the bin, the trials are approximately independent, so the distribution is approximately binomial.

2 **a** $(p + q)^4 = p^4 + 4p^3 q + 6p^2 q^2 + 4pq^3 + q^4$

b $4\left(\frac{1}{2}\right)^3 \left(\frac{1}{2}\right) = \frac{1}{4}$

3 **a** $(p + q)^5 = p^5 + 5p^4 q + 10p^3 q^2 + 10p^2 q^3 + 5pq^4 + q^5$

b **i** $5\left(\frac{1}{2}\right)^4 \left(\frac{1}{2}\right) = \frac{5}{32}$ **ii** $10\left(\frac{1}{2}\right)^2 \left(\frac{1}{2}\right)^3 = \frac{5}{16}$

iii $\left(\frac{1}{2}\right)^4 \left(\frac{1}{2}\right) = \frac{1}{32}$

4 **a** $\left(\frac{2}{3} + \frac{1}{3}\right)^4 = \left(\frac{2}{3}\right)^4 + 4\left(\frac{2}{3}\right)^3 \left(\frac{1}{3}\right) + 6\left(\frac{2}{3}\right)^2 \left(\frac{1}{3}\right)^2$

$\qquad + 4\left(\frac{2}{3}\right) \left(\frac{1}{3}\right)^3 + \left(\frac{1}{3}\right)^4$

b **i** $\left(\frac{2}{3}\right)^4 = \frac{16}{81}$ **ii** $6\left(\frac{2}{3}\right)^2 \left(\frac{1}{3}\right)^2 = \frac{8}{27}$ **iii** $\frac{8}{9}$

5 **a** $\left(\frac{3}{4} + \frac{1}{4}\right)^5 = \left(\frac{3}{4}\right)^5 + 5\left(\frac{3}{4}\right)^4 \left(\frac{1}{4}\right)^1 + 10\left(\frac{3}{4}\right)^3 \left(\frac{1}{4}\right)^2$

$\qquad + 10\left(\frac{3}{4}\right)^2 \left(\frac{1}{4}\right)^3 + 5\left(\frac{3}{4}\right) \left(\frac{1}{4}\right)^4 + \left(\frac{1}{4}\right)^5$

b **i** $10\left(\frac{3}{4}\right)^3 \left(\frac{1}{4}\right)^2 = \frac{135}{512}$ **ii** $\frac{53}{512}$ **iii** $\frac{47}{128}$

EXERCISE 23C.2

1 **a** ≈ 0.0305 **b** ≈ 0.265

2 **a** ≈ 0.476 **b** ≈ 0.840 **c** ≈ 0.160 **d** ≈ 0.996

3 **a** ≈ 0.0280 **b** ≈ 0.00246 **c** ≈ 0.131 **d** ≈ 0.710

4 ≈ 0.000864 **5** **a** ≈ 0.998 **b** ≈ 0.807

6 **a** ≈ 0.0388 **b** ≈ 0.405 **c** ≈ 0.573

7 ≈ 0.0341 **8** **a** ≈ 0.863 **b** ≈ 0.475

9 **a** $\frac{1}{36}$ **b** ≈ 0.846

10 **a** ≈ 0.0905 **b** ≈ 0.622

c Yes, the probability that Shelley is on time for work each day of a 5 day week is now $\approx 87.2\%$.

11 **a** ≈ 0.0388 **b** 25 solar components

EXERCISE 23D.1

1 $p =$ the proportion of smokers in the British population

$H_0: \ p = 0.21, \quad H_1: \ p < 0.21$

2 $p =$ the proportion of cancer patients who survive more than 5 years after diagnosis on the new treatment

$H_0: \ p = 0.3, \quad H_1: \ p > 0.3$

3 $p =$ the proportion of Party A supporters

a $H_0: \ p = 0.42$ **b** $H_0: \ p = 0.42$

$\quad H_1: \ p > 0.42$ $\qquad H_1: \ p \neq 0.42$

EXERCISE 23D.2

1 **a** $p =$ the probability the magician rolls a six with a fair die

$H_0: \ p = 0.9, \quad H_1: \ p < 0.9$

b significance level ≈ 0.0159

2 **a** $p =$ the probability of rolling a four with the die

$H_0: \ p = \frac{1}{6}, \quad H_1: \ p > \frac{1}{6}$

b $\alpha = 0.05$

c Test statistic:

$X =$ the number of fours rolled in 30 rolls of the die

Null distribution: $X \sim B(30, \frac{1}{6})$

d p-value ≈ 0.114 **e** no

3 **a** $p =$ the probability of a head when the coin is flipped

$H_0: \ p = 0.5, \quad H_1: \ p \neq 0.5$

b Test statistic:
X = the number of heads in 80 tosses of the coin
Null distribution: $X \sim B(80, 0.5)$
c p-value ≈ 0.576 **d** no

4 yes   **5** yes   **6** no

EXERCISE 23D.3

1 a **i** $\mathcal{C} = \{0\}$ **ii** $\mathcal{A} = \{1, 2, 3, 4, 5\}$ **iii** $c = 0$
b **i** $\mathcal{C} = \{7, 8\}$ **ii** $\mathcal{A} = \{0, 1, 2, 3, 4, 5, 6\}$
iii $c = 7$
c **i** $\mathcal{C} = \{0, 1, 2, 3\}$ **ii** $\mathcal{A} = \{4, 5, 6, 7, 8, 9, 10\}$
iii $c = 3$

2 a **i** critical region $= \varnothing$
ii acceptance region $= \{0, 1, 2, 3, 4\}$
b no   **c** Use a larger sample size.

REVIEW SET 23A

1 a discrete   **b** continuous   **c** discrete

2 a **i** yes **ii** no **iii** no **iv** yes **v** yes **vi** yes
b the distribution in **a iv**

3 a $a = \frac{5}{9}$ **b** $\frac{4}{9}$

4 a $k = 0.05$ **b** 0.15   **c** 2

5 a $\left(\frac{4}{5} + \frac{1}{5}\right)^5 = \left(\frac{4}{5}\right)^5 + 5\left(\frac{4}{5}\right)^4 \left(\frac{1}{5}\right) + 10\left(\frac{4}{5}\right)^3 \left(\frac{1}{5}\right)^2$
$\qquad + 10\left(\frac{4}{5}\right)^2 \left(\frac{1}{5}\right)^3 + 5\left(\frac{4}{5}\right) \left(\frac{1}{5}\right)^4 + \left(\frac{1}{5}\right)^5$
b **i** $\frac{64}{3125} = 0.020\,48$ **ii** $\frac{128}{625} = 0.2048$

6 a
pentagonal   square   **b** $\frac{11}{20}$
spinner   spinner

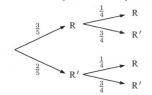

c **i** $X \sim B(10, \frac{11}{20})$
ii $P(X = 1) = \binom{10}{1} \left(\frac{11}{20}\right)^1 \left(\frac{9}{20}\right)^9$,
$P(X = 9) = \binom{10}{9} \left(\frac{11}{20}\right)^9 \left(\frac{9}{20}\right)^1$
It is more likely that exactly one red will occur 9 times.

7 yes

8 a p = the probability that the train is behind schedule
H_0: $p = 0.3$, H_1: $p < 0.3$
b Test statistic:
X = the number of times the train is late in the 10 trial runs
Null distribution: $X \sim B(10, 0.3)$
c critical region $= \{0\}$ **d** no

REVIEW SET 23B

1 a X is the number of hits that Sally has in each match.
$X = 0, 1, 2, 3, 4,$ or 5
b **i** $k = 0.23$ **ii** $P(X \geqslant 2) = 0.79$
iii $P(1 \leqslant X \leqslant 3) = 0.83$
c mode = 3 hits, median = 3 hits

3 a $X = 0, 1,$ or 2, so there are more than two possible
outcomes.
So X is not a binomial random variable.

b

x	0	1	2
$P(X = x)$	$\frac{15}{24}$	$\frac{1}{3}$	$\frac{1}{24}$

4 a $X = 0$ or 1, so there are only two possible outcomes. Also,
the probability of spinning a 3 is the same for each spin.
b ≈ 0.988

5 a ≈ 0.334 **b** ≈ 0.0931

6 a **i** ≈ 0.0751 **ii** ≈ 0.166 **b** ≈ 0.895

7 The coin is fair on a 5% level of significance.

8 a **i** acceptance region $= \{x : 13 \leqslant x \leqslant 29\}$
ii critical region $= \{x : 0 \leqslant x \leqslant 12$ and $30 \leqslant x \leqslant 100\}$
b significance level ≈ 0.0366

INDEX